W9-BKQ-448

CULTURE
and
COGNITIVE DEVELOPMENT:
Studies in Mathematical Understanding

GEOFFREY B. SAXE
University of California, Los Angeles

LEA LAWRENCE ERLBAUM ASSOCIATES, PUBLISHERS
1991   Hillsdale, New Jersey   Hove and London

370.15
Sa 97 c

Copyright © 1991 by Lawrence Erlbaum Associates, Inc.
All rights reserved. No part of this book may be reproduced in
any form, by photostat, microform, retrieval system, or any other
means, without the prior written permission of the publisher.

Lawrence Erlbaum Associates, Inc., Publishers
365 Broadway
Hillsdale, New Jersey 07642

Library of Congress Cataloging-in-Publication Data

Saxe, Geoffrey B.
  Culture and cognitive development : studies in mathematical understanding / Geoffrey B. Saxe.
    p.   cm.
  Includes bibliographical references and indexes.
  ISBN 0-8058-0273-8
  1. Mathematics—Study and teaching.   2. Cognition and culture.   I. Title.
QA11.S142   1990
370.15'651—dc20

90–40923
CIP

Contents

906515

v

Preface

This volume has taken form through the help and support I received from various teachers, colleagues, friends, and family. I am grateful to them all.

As a graduate student, I studied with Jonas Langer; his rich insights into problems of cognitive development continue to be important to me in working through the conceptual problems that I have struggled with in this volume and in my previous work. I also owe much to other individuals during my undergraduate and graduate work in these earlier years. Elliot Turiel was influential in introducing me to structural-developmental approaches to cognition, and under his supervision while I was an undergraduate, I was introduced to problems of extending structural-developmental approaches to field settings in a project on social cognition in Lower Kalskag, Alaska. His more recent work on domain distinctions in developmental analyses of social cognition has continued to influence my own thinking. Allen Black, and a community of graduate students working with Jonas at Berkeley provided a wonderful intellectual environment to pursue questions of cognitive development, and much of my own ways of conceptualizing problems of cognitive development has its roots in weekly meetings with Jonas and these friends.

I have also benefited by contact with various colleagues in my postdoctoral years. As a postdoctoral fellow under a National Institute of Mental Health training grant, I was introduced to problems of comparative research through the study of atypical cognitive development and the breakdown of cognitive functioning following brain injury at The Children's Hospital Medical Center in Boston under the guidance of Peter Wolff and at the Boston Veteran's Administration Hospital under the guidance of Howard Gardner. In the Papua New Guinea work that I summarize in the volume, I am indebted to the help and support of David Lancy, Randall Souviney, Tom Moylan, Virginia Guilford, Marshall Lawerence, and numerous other unnamed individuals. During my years on the faculty at the Graduate Center of the City University of New York, short but fruitful discussions with Michael Cole and Joseph Glick were important to me.

In accomplishing the body of the work on child candy sellers described in this volume, I benefited greatly from the supportive research environment created by Analucia Schliemann, Terezinha Carraher, and David Carraher at the Universidade de Pernambuco in Recife. Luciano Meira, a student at the Universidade de Pernambuco, assisted in many phases of the conduct of this project. Though a masters student at the time, Luciano functioned in many ways as an extraordinarily able colleague. In addition, Wilher dos Santos, Anna Ruiz, Danielle, and Marcia were students that assisted in field work and interviews throughout the project, and the high quality of data on which this volume is based collected is due to their fine efforts. Scott Lewis, a graduate student at UCLA, was very helpful in administering the interviews to the U.S. schooled sample described in Part IV.

Maryl Gearhart, Steven Guberman, Joe Becker and Marta Laupa each read and commented on some parts of or various drafts of this manuscript. In addressing their criticisms, I have been led to new insights, and I was able to make this manuscript more readable and coherent.

I am deeply grateful for the patience and support of my family—Maryl, Josh, and Ben (who was born a Brazilian)—on which this volume has taken a toll. Maryl, in particular, has played many roles in my research activities since my early work in Papua New Guinea—wife, friend, close colleague, teacher, and constructive critic. She deserves special thanks for much that is good about this work and my prior work.

Finally, the support that my parents and sister have provided over the years has been instrumental to me in forming and accomplishing goals that have led to this volume. From my first trip around the U.S. as a young teenager to a stay in a remote part of Alaska as an undergraduate to my more recent efforts in non-Western and more Western settings, I have felt warmly supported and encouraged by each of them.

ACKNOWLEDGMENTS

The research described in this volume would not have been possible without funding, and I am very grateful to several agencies that provided support. During my stay in Recife, I was supported by a Fulbright/CAPES fellowship, and the research itself and subsequent analyses were funded by a grant from the National Science Foundation (#BNS–85–09101). In addition, direct support of the research was provided by a small grant administered by UCLA through the

Spencer Foundation, and the last phases in the writing and preparation of this manuscript were conducted while I was supported by grants from the Spencer Foundation (#M890224) and the National Science Foundation (#MDR–8855643). The opinions expressed in this volume are my own and not necessarily those of the funding agencies.

CULTURE AND COGNITION: A METHOD OF STUDY

Some years ago, I visited a Papua New Guinean highlands group, the Oksapmin, for the purpose of studying the development of mathematical understandings in a non-Western culture. As a student of cognitive development, I was struck by the differences between the Oksapmins' indigenous mathematical practices and my own. In house building, arrowhead making, string bag weaving, and counting, the Oksapmins' approach to solving mathematical problems of measurement and numeration involved very different ways of thinking and very different procedures for accomplishing everyday problems (Saxe, 1982). For instance, Oksapmin often conceptualize numerical and measurement problems in terms of an indigenous, 27-body-part number system with no base structure. A number is expressed by pointing to a particular body part (like the neck) and saying the body-part name.

I had two initial reactions to the mathematical practices of the Oksapmin which were linked to my graduate training in developmental psychology, training in the structural-developmental tradition of Piaget and focusing on mathematical cognition. The first reaction was an intellectual excitement: The same mathematical operations of correspondence and measurement captured in Piagetian psychogenetic analyses that I had studied in Western children were apparent in the activities of a people from an extraordinarily foreign culture. The second was an intellectual frustration: The aspects of cognition and the texture of everyday life in Oksapmin that seemed so marvelously different from that of the West—like the Oksapmins' use of their numeration system in everyday practices—were not captured by Piagetian core constructs like conservation. While Piaget's epigenetic constructivism—the thesis that the individual generates novel intellectual structures by reorganizing prior knowledge to resolve contradictions—appeared critical to me for conceptualizing developing cognitive processes, reducing thought to a small set of Piagetian categories seemed weak as a method for the study of culture-cognition relations.

It has been 10 years since my first visit to Oksapmin. The volume that follows illustrates my efforts to synthesize a research program that provides insight into the distinctiveness of children's cognitive development across cultures but at the same time reveals universal regulative processes which transcend cultural boundaries.

In the first part of this volume, I introduce a general analytic model that targets cultural practices as important contexts for study. In subsequent parts, I apply the model to a single cultural practice—candy selling—as it has emerged in the lives of children living in northeastern Brazil. In candy selling, the relations between culture and cognitive development stand out in particularly clear relief and are particularly amenable to study.

1 Culture and Cognitive Development

Treatments of cognitive development can be understood as rooted in one of three fundamental views on the character of knowledge. Each view carries with it both problems and advantages for an adequate account.

The empiricist view is that the environment is the source of knowledge, and through experience children's knowledge comes to reflect the environment with increasing exactness. The position has its roots in philosophy (e.g., Locke) and is also formulated in modern treatments of learning (Bijou & Baer, 1961; Gagné, 1985). The promise of these treatments is to explain the way children's knowledge is shaped and organized directly by experience. But to date, the promise is far from being realized and many have argued that, in principle, rational thought structures like logical deduction cannot be accounted for solely by reference to the environment (e.g., Chomsky, 1957; Piaget, 1970).

The nativist position acknowledges the need for fundamental knowledge structures to organize experience into categories and logical systems, and its claim is that these structures are a hereditary endowment. Again, the position has ancient philosophical roots (Plato) and finds its current articulation in treatments of language (Chomsky, 1972) and cognition (Fodor, 1983). While such models explain the independence of rational cognitive structures and experience, they at the same time do not offer compelling treatments of development nor the variability of cognitive forms across cultures.

The constructivist position—in which the treatment I develop in this volume has its roots—is that fundamental aspects of knowledge neither come preformed in the genes nor in the environment, but are actively constructed by the developing individual. The aim of constructivist accounts is to show how novel cognitive structures emerge as a function of the developing subjects' commerce with a

3

social and physical environment, and the focus is on explaining cognitive development with reference to principles of self-regulated change and interaction.

The problem which is the focus of the volume is to understand the interplay between sociohistorical and cognitive developmental processes. Most fundamentally, my concern is to understand how artifacts and forms of social organization—products which have emerged over the course of social history—come to be interwoven with and are intrinsically related to the nature of children's intellectual constructions. These historical products may be conceptual as in the case of scientific concepts entailed in Newtonian mechanics, symbolic forms as in the case of numeration or writing systems, or material as in the case of tools like the lever or the computer.

In the following discussion, I consider the problems and prospects in the ways researchers in the constructivist tradition have conceptualized and studied the interplay between sociohistorical processes and cognitive developmental ones. While constructivist treatments share core assumptions, they often differ in their analytic units and in their levels of analysis. All have had difficulty in producing rich and systematic conceptual frameworks for the analysis of intrinsic relations between cognitive developmental and sociohistorical processes. After reviewing key features of these treatments in this chapter, I then turn, in Chapter 2, to my effort to work toward a more complete framework for the analysis of the interplay between cognitive developmental and sociohistorical processes.

CONSTRUCTIVIST APPROACHES

A basic assumption of constructivist treatments is that individuals create new knowledge in their goal-directed activities; in turn, new knowledge leads subjects to identify new goals. Cassirer (1957), in his philosophical treatment, expresses the constructivist dialectic between conceptual advances and goal-directed activities extraordinarily well.

> [E]ach newly acquired concept is an attempt, a beginning, a problem; its value lies not in its copying of definite objects, but in its opening up of new logical perspectives . . . one of its essential tasks is not to let the problems of knowledge come prematurely to rest, but to keep them in a steady flux, by guiding them toward new goals. . . . Here again we find that the concept is far less abstractive than prospective; it not only fixes what is already known, establishing its general outlines, but also maintains a persistent outlook for new and unknown connections. (Cassirer, 1957, p. 306)

Thus, from the constructivist perspective, goals themselves are rooted in individuals' understandings.

Empirical research on culture and cognitive development has been influenced by two constructivist treatments which differ in their description of the role of social processes in the development of the individual's self-regulative autonomous reasoning. One treatment is associated with the structural developmental approach of Piaget, and the other is associated with the sociohistorical approach of Vygotsky.

Piaget and the Structural-developmental Approach

Piaget's treatment of cognitive development is rooted in a neo-Kantian epistemology in which a principal assumption is that the world is not known directly but is assimilated by intellectual structures. Kant and Piaget shared a concern to understand how the subject comes to know the necessity of propositions about logico-mathematical and physical phenomena. The solution for both was in the properties of these cognitive structures. Piaget, however, did not share Kant's monism and took a developmental perspective. Using empirical research, he produced evidence supporting a sequence of four stages of cognitive development that extended from infancy through adolescence.

In Piaget's analysis, each successive stage constituted a new cognitive equilibrium, and for each stage Piaget's central analytic concern was to present an analysis of its structural or formal properties. In Piaget's scheme, reality for the infant at birth is no more than the extension of its hereditary reflexes, like sucking and grasping (Piaget, 1954, 1963). In the course of progressively more complex interactions with its environment, the infant transforms these hereditary reflexes into cognitive structures which make it possible, at about 18 months, for the infant to "re-present" experience, and semiotic systems (imitation, imagery, language) begin to emerge (Piaget, 1962). The representational capacity carries with it, however, new problems of coordinating representations, problems which are not solved until the next stage when concrete operational classificatory and relational structures emerge in middle childhood (Inhelder & Piaget, 1969; Piaget, 1952). Concrete operational structures provide the basis for a wide range of novel and stable concepts (e.g., quantity conservations, Euclidean and projective spatial understandings). It is not until early adolescence, however, that the individual constructs an integration of concrete operational class and relational operations into a system of formal operations which is the basis for hypothetico-deductive reasoning (Inhelder & Piaget, 1958).

To explain progress through his stages, Piaget, like Cassirer, argued that the subject is purposeful, constructing goals based on prior knowledge and creating coherent solutions to these goals in the form of novel cognitive developments. In Piaget's analysis, development proceeds by a self-regulated construction, or "equilibration," a dialectical process in which the subject resolves perturbations in the coherence of his or her structuring activities by coordinating and constructing new, more adequate cognitive structures. For Piaget, it is equilibration that guides the direction and organization of cognitive development (Piaget, 1977).

In Piaget's treatment of equilibration, the interplay between social life and cognitive developmental processes was not a core concern. Indeed for Piaget, the focus was on the formal properties of action without regard for the situatedness of actions in a sociohistorically articulated web of meanings. Nonetheless, questions of social influences on cognitive development have emerged in the work of various researchers who have attempted to extend Piaget's analyses to social processes, and Piaget himself has noted the effect of social processes on the rate of progress through his stages (Piaget, 1966, 1972). However, we find in these extensions that social life is related to cognitive development as an external process, and the way sociocultural life may be deeply interwoven with the character of intellectual functioning is unanalyzed.

Empirical Research on Culture and Cognitive Development Related to the Piagetian Framework

To study sociocultural influences on cognitive development from within the Piagetian framework, researchers have contrasted individuals' performances from different cultural groups on Piagetian tasks (for a review, see Dasen, 1972; Dasen & Heron, 1981). Typically, researchers have focused on the transition to concrete operations, using Piaget's original tasks or slight adaptations of these in varying content areas (e.g., conservation (Laurendeau–Bendavid, 1977; Opper, 1977), classification (de Lacey, 1970), motion (Za'rour & Khuri, 1977), space (de Lemos, 1974). This literature has revealed both cultural similarities and differences. Age norms from many groups suggest that children progress up through Piaget's stage of concrete operations, though there is little documentation of the emergence of formal operational structures across groups (see Neimark, 1975; Piaget, 1972). Further, the age norms for passing concrete operational tasks vary widely across cultures. Whether these cross-cultural differences reflect merely lack of appropriate accommodations of method to the different cultural contexts or actual differences in conceptual development is not entirely clear and has been the subject of considerable discussion (see Hallpike, 1979; Jahoda, 1980; Kamara & Easley, 1977; Nyiti, 1982; Piaget, 1972). Regardless, this literature sets the stage for more focused investigations of the ways that dimensions of sociocultural life may be associated with progress through Piaget's stage sequence. I will briefly consider three such dimensions.

Cultural Practices.   One sociocultural dimension isolated for study is participation in cultural practices thought to favor equilibrations. Researchers have analyzed relations between participation in such practices as pottery making and children's understanding of mass conservation in rural Mexican groups (Price–Williams, Gordon, & Ramirez, 1967; Steinberg & Dunn, 1976), practices of economic exchange and children's understanding of number conservation in West African groups (Posner & Baroody, 1979), practices of hunting and nomadic life style on spatial concepts in Canadian Eskimos (as opposed to agricultural and sedentary groups; Dasen, 1975), and schooling and various concrete operational concepts (Goodnow & Bethon, 1966; Laurendeau–Bendavid, 1977; Mermelstein & Shulman, 1967). The results of studies on practice participation and schooling are varied. Some indicate effects on concrete operational concepts; others do not. Rarely is there a detailed analysis of which aspects of practice-linked experience that were related to cognitive developmental change, and herein lies a problem with this focus. Practices are "packaged variables" (Whiting, 1976), and efforts to unpack a practice requires an analytic model that links the structure of practices with the structure of cognitive developmental processes, an analytic model that has yet to emerge in any sophisticated form within the Piagetian framework.

Social Interactions. A second sociocultural dimension isolated for analysis is social interaction (Doise & Mugny, 1984). Unlike the practice-based research, the social interaction studies are typically laboratory-based. Investigators typically draw activities from Piagetian assessment tasks and instruct dyads to work collaboratively to reach agreement on a solution. Such studies often make use of an experimental design in which children are randomly assigned to experimental (social interaction) and comparison (no social interaction) groups, and interactions in the experimental groups are often videotaped for later analysis. These studies sacrifice the naturalistic features of the cultural practice research. However, they typically provide a more detailed account of social interactional processes hypothesized to be implicated in stage change, most notably social conflict which, it is argued, sets in motion the process of equilibration. Using this kind of paradigm, researchers have studied spatial perspective taking (Bearison, Magzamen, & Filardo, 1986; Doise & Mugny, 1984; Doise, Mugny, & Perret–Clermont, 1975, 1976), proportionality in the balance (Damon, 1988), conservation (Silverman & Geiringer, 1973; Silverman & Stone, 1972), and classification (Valiant, Glachan, & Emler, 1982).

The findings from Piagetian social interaction research have often revealed effects for collaborative interactions, particularly interactions in which a modicum of social conflict is generated during joint problem solving (Bearison et al., 1986). But what we may lose access to in laboratory situations is the sociohistorical context of the interactions, a context in which elaborated conventions and activity structures give meaning to and modify the organization of interactions.

Sign-using Activities. A third sociocultural dimension isolated for study is the acquisition—or lack thereof—of particular sign forms like language or numeration and the influence of these sign forms on the emergence of cognitive structures. For Piaget, cognitive structures are not constructed through the acquisition of sign forms like language and numeration, but through the equilibration process. Thus, from the Piagetian point of view, progress through his stage sequence could not have its origins in, nor be dependent on, the acquisition or particular sign forms. To evaluate Piaget's claims, some researchers have investigated the impact of the acquisition of linguistic and numerical forms on concrete operational concepts.

In a well-known training study focusing on the acquisition of comparative terms, Sinclair (1967) taught children the meanings of such comparatives as "more" and "less" and then assessed children's understanding of Piagetian quantity concepts like conservation. Consistent with Piaget's claim about sign forms and stage progression, Sinclair found that the training had only limited effects: Only children at a transitional stage showed signs of shifting to conservation understandings. Additional language training studies in which the focus has been on training linguistic rules for conservation (rather than lexical items) have shown somewhat greater success in facilitating the development of conservation performance (see Beilin, 1976, for a review).

Comparative research has also been used to investigate sign form–cognition relations from the Piagetian perspective. Furth (1966) found that deaf children, despite their failure to develop spoken language, developed Piagetian concrete operational concepts, though at later ages than hearing children. Lancy (1983), in a study of Papua New Guinean cultural groups that used different kinds of numeration systems—from base-10 verbal systems to body systems with and without base structures—found no influence of numeration system on the ability to pass Piagetian concrete operational tasks.

As a whole, these studies indicate that while symbolic forms may affect the rate of development, they are consistent with Piaget's writings on the primacy of the endogenous process of equilibration.

Piagetian Theory and Sociocultural Processes

The Piagetian based cross-cultural research clearly lends support to the constructivist thesis of universal self-regulated processes. This body of research, however, has not led, in any rich sense, to advancing our understanding of the interplay between sociohistorical processes and cognitive developmental ones. The crux of the problem is that by reducing cognitive development to descriptions of abstract cognitive structures, we gear analytic categories to aspects of cognitive functioning that do not reflect the socially textured goals of everyday life and associated cognitive constructions.

This critique of Piagetian research on sociocultural processes is in fact applicable to a wide range of research on cognitive development. Across most research efforts, to the extent that sociocultural processes are addressed, the analytic approach is to dissect both cultural and cognitive phenomena into separate sets of elements in which the social properties of cognition are no longer recoverable. Thus, for example, within current information-processing perspectives, such elements may include speed of cognitive processing (Kail, 1986) or amount of working memory (Klahr, 1980); within the cognitive style perspective, elements consist of constructs of field dependence or field independence (Witkin & Berry, 1975; Witkin, Dyk, Faterson, Goodenough, & Karp, 1962); and within the Piagetian tradition, elements may include any of the Piagetian concrete operational concepts (Dasen, 1972; Opper, 1977). While there may be attempts to identify cultural influences on independently defined cognitions through the external connections of correlational analyses as we have seen in much of the Piagetian work, these efforts cannot lead to analyses of the intrinsic relations whereby cultural and cognitive developmental phenomena are constitutive of one another.

In turning now to Vygotsky's constructivism and related work, we find an analytic tack that differs critically in the way social processes are conceptualized in relation to cognitive developmental ones. In the Vygotskian approach, we see an analytic framework elaborated that has as its central focus intrinsic relations between cognitive developmental processes and sociohistorical ones.

Vygotsky

Vygotsky, whose psychological writings have epistemological underpinnings in the works of Marx and Hegel, outlined a specifically sociohistorical approach to cognitive development (Vygotsky, 1978, 1986). For Vygotsky, a central problem was to understand how infants who are initially impulsive, responding directly to environmental stimulation, gain control over interactions with their environments. The solution was to be found in children's appropriation of sociocultural artifacts and supports—sign forms, assistance from others, scientific concepts— to mediate their interactions with the environment. Vygotsky's view was that the appropriation of cultural artifacts liberates children from direct stimulus control and also creates an intrinsic link between cognitive development and culture.

Sign Forms

For Vygotsky, the emergence of spoken language in the children—one of various sign using activities—is at the heart of the interplay between natural and sociohistorical processes of the individual's development. Early in development, Vygotsky argued, thought and speech have separate roots: There is a preintellectual phase in speech development and a preverbal phase in the development of thought. During early childhood, these processes begin to penetrate one another; the child uses telegraphic speech first to accompany problem solving, and gradually uses speech to help solve and then to plan solutions to problems. Eventually, we see the telegraphic or "egocentric" speech of toddlerhood gradually go "underground," transforming into covert "inner speech." Thus, what was once a social artifact external to the child, is gradually transformed by the child, first into an external aid which helps organize problem solving and later into a core ingredient of conscious thought.

For Vygotsky, speech was one of a variety of cultural sign forms that displayed a complex transformation on its inward trajectory. Vygotsky's analysis of sign form use in the emergence of mediated or "voluntary" memory presents an interesting parallel. In one study, Vygotsky's purpose was to show that, as in the case of speech, the functional relation of the sign form to basic intellectual processes shifts with the inward movement. Sign forms begin as merely juxtaposed with goal-directed efforts; they are subsequently organized consciously by the child into a part of goal-directed activities as they become external solution means; finally, they become transformed into automatic and abbreviated covert mental activities. To illustrate this developmental phenomenon in the case of memory, Vygotsky presented individual children with a game-like laboratory task: Children were required to answer questions posed by the interviewer. Many of the questions required children to respond with color names, some of which they were forbidden to say. In one condition, children were also presented with a set of auxiliary materials—color chips—that could be used as a sign form. Children in the youngest group often found the chips a source of added difficulty and did not attempt to use them as a means of task solution; these children committed just as many errors on the chip and no-chip conditions. Children in the middle age groups performed better in the chip condition than in the no-chip condition; they constructed strategies to use the chips as a sign form to aid their memory. In the oldest age groups, performance was very good across chip and no-chip conditions. Vygotsky argued that adults had generated internal strategies akin to external chip manipulation to solve the task.

Social Interaction

For Vygotsky, social interactions were a critical vehicle whereby natural processes in cognitive development were redirected by social and historical influences. In social interactions, Vygotsky argued, "zones of proximal developments" are created. A zone of proximal development was defined as the difference between what a child could accomplish unassisted in problem solving and what he or she could accomplish with assistance. Vygotsky argued that socially supported activity in the zone of proximal development awakened and provided paths for intellectual development.

During the past decade, various investigators have conducted studies of adult-child interaction concerned with Vygotsky's notion of the zone of proximal development (Rogoff, 1986, 1990; Rogoff, Ellis, & Gardner, 1984; Rogoff & Gardner, 1984; Saxe, Gearhart, & Guberman, 1984; Wertsch, 1979; Wertsch, McNamee, McLane, & Budwig, 1980) or related constructs (Wood, Bruner, & Ross, 1976; Wood & Middleton, 1975; Wood, Wood, & Middleton, 1978). These studies often reveal that it is quite natural for adults to enter into children's problem solving in ways that enable children to participate with goals and means of achieving them that are more sophisticated than the children establish on their own. In one example of this work, colleagues and I (Saxe, Guberman, & Gearhart, 1987) studied 2½- and 4½-year-olds and their mothers from working and middle class families. We analyzed the children solving numerical problems unassisted and then we observed them solving the same problems with their mothers' assistance. Our analyses were consistent with Vygotsky's writings on the zone of proximal development. In social interactions with their mothers, children achieved more sophisticated goals than they did on their own. Further, an analysis of videotapes of these interactions revealed a flexibility in the ways in which the goal structure of the task emerged over the interactions. When children were having difficulties, mothers tended to simplify the numerical goals of the task, and when children were doing well, mothers tended to focus on more complex numerical goals. Such adjustments were largely independent of both age and social class. Thus, in adult-child interactions, children are accomplishing goals that are at once linked to their own constructive efforts and to sociocultural life.

Spontaneous and Scientific Concepts

Scientific concepts are interconnected and comprehensive systems of understandings which have been elaborated and refined over the course of social history. The conceptual systems entailed in Newton's mechanics or Marx's *Das Capital* are examples. Just as the child's appropriation of sign forms and assistance from others provide critical avenues for developmental processes, so too do children's learning of scientific concepts. Like sign forms and assistance from others, scientific concepts are not simply internalized, but undergo a complex transformation in their inward movement from artifacts external to the child's activity to mental processes which are interwoven with the child's intellectual functions.

Vygotsky argued that to understand the acquisition of scientific concepts requires a perspective which also includes an analysis of children's spontaneous concepts. For Vygotsky, children construct "spontaneous concepts" from the bottom–up: Children's everyday experiences are inherently local, occurring in particular contexts, and the concepts which children thus form are ones linked to situations—the bike stops more quickly when the hand brake is squeezed harder; the soccer ball goes further when it is kicked harder. Such spontaneous concepts are rich in meaning for children, but they are local and not linked with one another in general systems of interrelated understandings. Children only gradually draw connections between such isolated experiences in forming more general concepts. For Vygotsky, children construct "scientific concepts" from the top–down. In school, children are presented with scientific concepts, like those entailed in Newton's mechanics. Initially, such concepts are abstract but empty; while the child may learn the "syntax" of the relations of a network of concepts, these concepts have little apparent relation to the child's spontaneous concepts.

The development of scientific concepts proceeds downward toward the application to the situated phenomena of handbrakes and soccer balls.

For Vygotsky, it is in the interaction between the top–down movement of scientific concepts and the bottom–up movement of spontaneous concepts that we find intrinsic links between the individual and social history. In their interaction, spontaneous concepts enrich scientific concepts with meaning and scientific concepts offer generality to the development of spontaneous concepts—again, a melding of the individual with the sociohistorical.

Vygotskian Insights Applied to Cultural Practices

Though Vygotsky did not consider directly cultural practices in his writings, researchers influenced by Vygotsky have elevated practices to an important unit for analyzing culture-cognition relations. Researchers have targeted for analysis the mathematical problem solving of Kpelle rice farmers of central Liberia (Cole, Gay, Glick, & Sharp, 1971; Gay & Cole, 1965), Vai tailors' strategies for measurement (Lave, 1977), Southern California housewives' strategies for finding best buys in the supermarket (Lave, 1988), dairy workers' strategies for loading crates (Scribner, 1986), horse racing strategies for betting (Ceci & Liker, 1986), Weight Watchers dieters' mathematical strategies for solving measurement problems (de la Rocha, 1983), and schoolchildren's arithmetic from traditional societies (Brenner, 1985). In comparison with the Piagetian practice-based studies noted earlier, the Vygotskian studies often provide a more detailed analysis of the kinds of cognitive forms individuals structure to accomplish cognitive functions linked to practice participation, and the descriptions produced help us understand interdependencies between particular sociocultural and cognitive developmental processes. For instance, whether we read Scribner's descriptions of dairy workers' strategies of the use of the particular arrangement of a crate to organize a solution to a problem of retrieving a quantity of milk, or Lave's description of tailors as they make use of unique mathematical procedures to ply their trade, we find in these studies analyses of the varied mathematical forms with which adults address problems linked to their everyday activities. Nevertheless, these studies fall considerably short of addressing the core problems elaborated in the analytic writings of Vygotsky and Piaget and central to the present work.

Most centrally, these studies do not treat cognition from a developmental perspective, a perspective in which cognitive forms are understood as evolving in a complex psychogenetic process, shifting in function over the course of their evolution. For instance, we rarely observe individuals sampled at different ages or at different points in their acquisition of a trade. Even when such a sampling procedure is used, we do not find analysis of the shifting character of cognitive forms as these forms are interwoven with shifts in people's goal-directed activities (Ceci & Liker, 1986; Lave, 1977; Luria, 1976).

Further, because development is not a principal focus in the practice-based studies, we see little analysis of enculturative processes whereby children's understandings become interwoven with the cognitive achievements and practices of their social group (see Greenfield & Childs, 1977, for a noteworthy exception to this critique). Consider the situation of the child novice entering the practice of potting, weaving, or street selling. The child has little knowledge of how to participate in the practice and has not structured the sometimes sophisticated cognitive forms that are required to solve conceptual problems that emerge in the practice. In order for the child to begin to participate, there must be routes that ease the conceptual burdens. For instance, other more experienced participants may modulate the conceptual problems which novices address, and their modulation may be akin to that detailed in research on the zone of proximal development that has been reviewed. An analysis of such *in situ* processes would be critical both to a treatment of the actual goals that children of different ages or levels of expertise are addressing in a cultural practice and to understanding how cognitive forms of the individual become interwoven with those of the larger social group.

Finally, because children are not a principal focus for analysis in the practice-linked work, we find no analyses of the interplay between scientific and spontaneous cognitive forms. Perhaps the most significant question here is the way in which school learning interacts with the kinds of understandings children generate through their participation in everyday cultural practices. Despite the importance of this question from both the point of view of education and treatments of sociocultural processes in cognitive development, we have little empirical research in this area.

Cultural Practices: Toward a Developmental Perspective

In a seminal volume, *The Mind of Primitive man,* Franz Boas (1911) pointed to the critical status of cultural practices in treatments of culture and cognitive development, arguing that people generate intellectual skills in the context of the practices with which they are engaged. In his observations of native Americans, he pointed out that cultural practices vary in complexity both within and across native American groups, and the character of people's intellectual adaptations vary accordingly. We find support for Boas's conclusion in the Piagetian and Vygotsky-based research on cultural practices, though we are some distance from understanding the dynamics of the interaction that leads to these associations.

In the next chapter, I outline a research framework for gaining insight into the interplay between sociocultural and cognitive developmental processes through the analysis of practice participation. The framework shares the underlying constructivist assumptions of the Piagetian and Vygotskian formulations, and, with respect to core constructivist assumptions, the model presented here is consistent with both approaches. However, the framework presented targets a level of analysis that is not addressed by either of these formulations. Unlike the Piagetian approach, my concern is to treat cognitive development on a level of analysis in which activity-in-sociocultural context is a critical focus and cognitive developmental processes are analyzed with reference to these contexted activities. Unlike the Vygotskian writings, which do not develop core developmental and sociocultural theoretical constructs with reference to systematic analysis of core domains of knowledge, the present approach is concerned with a systematic analysis of mathematical cognition that integrates cognitive developmental and sociohistorical perspectives.

2 A Research Approach

In this chapter, I introduce a framework for the study of culture and cognitive development. Like other constructivist treatments, the framework is guided by the assumption that individuals construct new understandings in their goal-directed activities; in turn, these novel understandings influence the emergence of subsequent goals. A central aim of the current work is to understand the intrinsic relations between individuals' goals and social life that lead the individual to appropriate and specialize forms linked to their social participations.

The framework consists of three analytic components. The first is concerned with the goals that emerge during participation in cultural practices, the second with the kinds of cognitive forms and functions individuals construct to accomplish those practice-linked goals, and the third with the interplay among the various cognitive forms children structure across different cultural practices. With regard to the third component, in this volume, I am particularly concerned with the interplay between forms linked to out-of-school practices like weaving or tailoring and the forms linked to school.

To introduce this three-component analytic framework, I return to some of my research with the Oksapmin. I will show how a coordination of the three components permits particular insights into the interplay between cultural and developmental processes. The Oksapmin example focuses on a newly emerging cultural practice—economic exchange with a recently introduced currency—and the interplay between practice participation and shifts in the Oksapmin's construction of mathematical understandings. The research provides a basis to elaborate the kinds of analytic categories required for each of the three components.

THE THREE COMPONENT APPROACH:
ANOTHER LOOK AT THE OKSAPMIN

With Western contact, some traditional Oksapmin practices have given way to Western-styled ones, and the practice of economic exchange in Oksapmin trade-stores and the mathematics entailed in these exchanges are good examples. In traditional life numerical problems involved use of the body system—a system with no base structure and no distinct terms for number—to solve non-arithmetical problems in activities like counting one's pigs. To count as Oksapmin do, one begins with the thumb on one hand, and follows a trajectory around the upper periphery of the body down to the little finger on the opposite hand (see Fig. 2.1). In the new tradestore activities, Oksapmin must use the indigenous body-part counting system to solve arithmetical problems involving currency, problems that were nonexistent in traditional life.

The three-component approach applied to economic exchange in Oksapmin tradestores requires an analysis of the goals that emerge in the practice of economic exchange (component 1) and then a related analysis of the cognitive forms and their shifting functions linked to these socially textured goals (component 2). Since Oksapmin adults had no formal schooling, I could not address the interplay between cognitive forms constructed in out-of-school practices and in school (component 3); it was possible, however, to gain limited insight into this interplay through an analysis of Oksapmin schoolchildren. I will show how a coordination of these components helps to frame an analysis of the interplay between sociohistorical and cognitive developmental processes.

Component 1: Practice-linked Goals

Specifying the goals individuals form in cultural practices is an analytic endeavor of some complexity. Not only do individuals shape and reshape their goals as

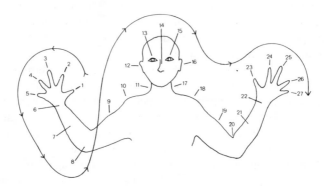

FIG. 2.1. Oksapmin body part number systems.

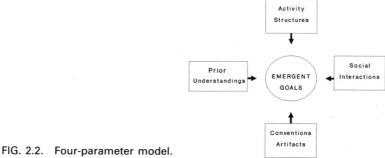

FIG. 2.2. Four-parameter model.

practices take form in everyday life, but they also construct goals that vary in character as a function of the knowledge that they bring to practices. Like Suchman's recent characterization of running rapids in a canoe (1987), while one may have a general plan of approach—goals and subgoals to accomplish in the run—when one hits the white water, goals and means of accomplishing them emerge and shift with the exigencies of the situation and one's expertise. Goals, then, are emergent phenomena, shifting and taking new form as individuals use their knowledge and skills alone and in interaction with others to organize their immediate contexts.

The discussion in Chapter 1 pointed to four parameters that are implicated in the emergence of individuals' goals, each of which is evident in the Oksapmin's tradestore-linked activities. These are the goal structure of cultural activities, the social interactions in which goals become modified and take particular forms (through assistance and negotiation), particular sign forms and cultural artifacts, and the prior understandings that individuals bring to bear on practices. Fig. 2.2 contains a portrayal of these four parameters, and I will consider the need for an analysis of each in understanding the nature of the goals which emerge in individuals' activities.

The *goal structure* of a cultural practice consists of the general tasks that must be accomplished in the practice- and task-linked motives. For instance, to participate in economic exchanges in Oksapmin tradestores, one must accomplish a purchase. In a purchase, a principal motive may be to acquire as many desired goods as possible while sacrificing as little money as possible, and mathematical goals that emerge in exchanges may be guided by this economic motive. Issues of small change in a transaction, while significant from the point of view of a normative mathematics, may be insignificant from the point of view of an individual's economics. Further, goals that emerge in one practice may be distinct from other practices in which an individual participates. For instance, in indigenous Oksapmin practices like weaving and horticulture, we do not find individuals accomplishing tasks that require arithmetical solutions.

Second, *social interactions* between participants in practices may further influence the character of the goals that individuals address. In the economic exchange in an Oksapmin tradestore, a tradestore owner may help the customer with a computation in any number of ways, thus modifying the kinds of arithmetical goals a customer addresses. Such assistance permits customers of varying degrees of competence to participate in the practice, much like mothers' assistance to their children permitted toddlers to engage in activities beyond their unassisted levels of competence in the numerical activities reviewed in the prior chapter. In the case of the tradestore, assistance may be in the form of helping a customer add coins, completing a subtraction problem in the computation of change, or helping to clarify an arithmetical problem. Regardless, problem-linked social interactions often are interwoven with the goals and subgoals that emerge and that individuals accomplish in the practice.

Third, cultural forms that have emerged over the course of social history, such as historically elaborated *sign forms* like the Oksapmin indigenous body-part counting system and *cultural artifacts* like a particular currency system, also figure into the goals that emerge in cultural practices. For instance, the body-part counting system leads Oksapmin to such goals as adding a biceps to a forearm, a representation of an addition problem which both constrains and supports the construction of particular kinds of subgoals for a computational solution. Similarly, the particular denominational structure of a currency system also influences the particular values addressed in activities and the subgoals which emerge in problem solving. For instance, in the Oksapmin case, the structure of the currency consists of a base of 20 (linked to the original currency system to penetrate the area—the base-20 system of Australian shillings and pounds) in which twenty 10-toea coins are equivalent to a 2-kina note. This system has led to particular problems when adding currency units that differ in some fundamental ways from those that emerge with a base-10 currency system. Consider, for instance, the differences in the indigenous Oksapmin system and the Western in computing 20 plus 20; in the Oksapmin system, the sum extends beyond the range of values easily represented with the system, and there is not a routine algorithm in indigenous life to accomplish the computation.

Fourth, the prior understandings that individuals bring to bear on cultural practices both constrain and enable the goals they construct in practices. In the case of the Oksapmin, we find that Oksapmin who had different levels of experience participating in the money economy bring to bear different arithmetical understandings on practice-linked problems and consequently their goals differ. Thus, an Oksapmin with little experience in the money economy typically conceptualized a purchase in terms of a multiple items-of-merchandise for multiple units of currency exchange. The goal was thus to produce an appropriate one-for-one or many-for-one correspondence. In contrast, individuals with greater expertise conceptualized problems as arithmetical ones, summing the total cost of items of merchandise.

Component 2: Form–function Shifts
in Cognitive Development

Component 2 of the approach consists of a conceptualization of cognitive developmental processes that draws on a formulation put forth by Werner and Kaplan (1962) in *Symbol Formation* and has been subsequently extended in my own work on early number development and cultural practices (Saxe, Guberman, & Gearhart, 1987). The formulation also reflects a dominant concern of Vygotsky and other Soviet writers (e.g., Leontiev, 1981; Vygotsky, 1978, 1986), to identify analytic units that preserve intrinsic relations between cognitive developmental and sociocultural processes.

The model presented here focuses on the cultural forms that are linked to practice participation and the interplay between these forms and cognitive functions which these forms come to serve. By cultural forms, I mean historically elaborated constructions like number systems, currency systems, and social conventions. In daily life, these forms become cognitive ones as they are acquired and used by individuals to accomplish various cognitive functions, functions like counting and arithmetic.

In the present treatment, a central concern is with a critical dynamic in cognitive development: the shifting relations between cultural forms and cognitive functions as they are interwoven with the socially textured goals linked to practice participation. Further observations in the Oksapmin community provide a good illustration.

With increasing participation in the new practice of economic exchange in newly introduced tradestores, Oksapmin people become engaged with novel mathematical goals that required the addition and subtraction of values, goals that do not emerge in traditional life. In this process, we witness the cultural form of body counting gradually shift in function over changing levels of economic participation. The shift is one in which the body system, a form which traditionally only serves an enumerative function for the Oksapmin, becomes a form that serves an arithmetical one. The form–function shift is a gradual and complex one, the details of which provide insight into basic processes in cognitive development and their intrinsic link to goals that emerge in cultural practices.

In traditional life, Oksapmin people use the body form to accomplish counting or enumerative functions in such activities as counting valuables. There is no context in which people use the system to accomplish arithmetical functions like the addition or subtraction of valuables. The closest activity to arithmetic in traditional life was in payment of brideprice, where members of a group would pool valuables and a person would successively tally each clan's contribution.

Interviews with Oksapmin who had different levels of participation with economic transactions showed that with increasing levels of participation, Oksapmin appropriated and specialized the indigenous cultural form—the body system—to address the emergent problems in exchange, and in this process, the function that the indigenous body-part form serves, gradually shifts. Consider four approaches to the solution of 9 + 7 coins that emerged with increasing participation in the money economy (see Saxe, 1982) depicted in Fig. 2.3 and explained herein. The approaches depicted in Fig. 2.3 are distinct cognitive forms, each linked to the indigenous cultural form of the 27-body-part counting system.

With initial participation in the money economy, Oksapmin first attempt to extend the body-counting cognitive form as it is used to serve enumerative functions in traditional activities to accomplish arithmetical tasks that emerge in economic transactions. This direct extension, however, is not adequate to accomplish arithmetical solutions, and it is not even clear that Oksapmin with little experience treat the task as one that involves the cognitive function of arithmetic. In these preliminary efforts, Oksapmin attempted to count the sum with a prior counting strategy linked to the body system. Fig. 2.3a illustrates this "global enumeration strategy." In this strategy, an individual begins with the first term (7) of the problem—thumb (1) to forearm (7)—and then continues to count the second term (9) from the elbow (8). Since the problem of nine coins plus seven coins seemed to be understood as an enumeration rather than an addition, individuals did not recognize the need to keep track of the addition of the second term onto the first term, and they typically produced an incorrect sum.

With greater economic experience, we witness a shift in function of the body system, a shift in which the body-counting form is adapted to serve a new function whose emergence has been influenced by the changing sociocultural conditions of economic exchange. This is seen in the cognitive forms Oksapmin

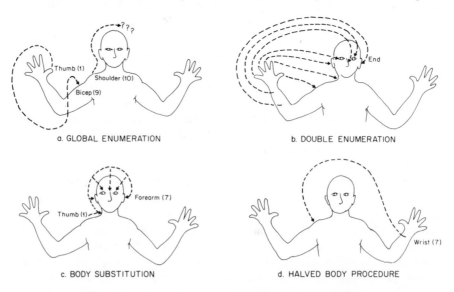

FIG. 2.3.   Oksapmin body part arithmetical strategies.

with greater participation in the money economy use to solve the problem of 9 +
7 coins: These Oksapmin make a clumsy and labored effort to restructure their
prior global counting strategy in such a way that one term is added onto the other
(the "double enumeration strategy" the depicted in Fig. 2.3b). In one example of
this strategic form (see Fig. 2.3b), individuals again enumerate the first term—
thumb (1) to forearm (7)—but now, as they enumerate the second, they make
efforts to keep track of their enumeration. Thus, the elbow (8) is paired with the
thumb (1), the biceps (9) is paired with the index finger (2), and so on, until the
ear-on-the-other-side (16) is paired with the biceps (9), yielding the answer.
Thus, in this initial extension of the body system to accomplish the arithmetical
problem, the body parts begin to take on a new function of keeping track of the
addition of one term onto another.

With higher levels in the sequence, we see the body-part-counting form progressively specialized into more sophisticated cognitive forms that serve dis-
tinctly arithmetical functions. With greater experience, individuals, rather than
establishing physical correspondences between body parts as they did previously,
efficiently use the name of one body part to refer to another in a "body substitu-
tion strategy" (Fig. 2.3c). To solve 7 + 9, the elbow (8) is called the thumb (1),
the biceps (9) is called the index finger (2), and so on, until the ear-on-the-other-
side (16) is called the biceps (9). The result is a more rapid computational
process, one in which body-part names are differentiated from the names of body
parts themselves.

Cognitive forms that are distinctively specialized to serve arithmetical and not
enumerative functions are most frequently displayed by tradestore owners who
have the most experience with problems of arithmetic that emerge in economic
transactions with currency. Here we see the incorporation of a base-10 system
(linked to the currency) as an aid in computation. To solve the same problem of
nine plus seven, tradestore owners often display a procedure termed a "halved-
body strategy" (Fig. 2.3d). With this strategic form, an individuals use the
shoulder (10) as a privileged value. In their computation, they may represent the
9 on one side of the body as biceps (9) and 7 on the other side of the body as
forearm (7). To accomplish the problem, a tradestore owner might simply "remove" the forearm from the second side (the seventh body part of 7) and transfer
it to the first side where it becomes the shoulder (the 10th). He then "reads" the
answer as 10 + 6 or 16.

The form–function shifts in the Oksapmin case reflect the Oksapmin's efforts
to accomplish socially textured goals that emerge in their everyday life of economic exchange. In attempting to accomplish these goals, Oksapmin appropriate
practice-linked cognitive forms initially specialized to serve earlier emerging
cognitive functions (enumeration) for new uses—in the case here, arithmetic. In
the process of this appropriation and specialization, the function of the body
system shifts and the original form used to accomplish enumerative functions
undergoes a progressive development. In this process, Oksapmin create, over

time, progressively more specialized and sophisticated uses of the indigenous number system, a process of specialization that is deeply interwoven with the construction of the new arithmetical function.

Component 3: The Interplay Between Learning Across Contexts

Component 3 is concerned with a longstanding problem in psychology—the problem of the transfer of learning. In addressing the problem of transfer, component 3 presupposes both of the prior ones: In order to analyze adequately the interplay between learning across practices, we must achieve some understanding of the similarities and differences in emergent goals within practices (component 1); we also must achieve some understanding of the form–function shifts that may be linked to participation in each practice (component 2). Further, when we consider the interplay between learning across practices (component 3), we find that our within-practice analysis—components 1 and 2—is more complex than the prior discussion indicates. Not only do individuals appropriate and specialize cognitive forms linked to partially distinct social histories, but in order to accomplish goals in one setting, individuals may appropriate and specialize cognitive forms linked to the other, thus creating a web of interrelations between cognitive developmental processes and sociohistorical ones.

In this volume, my use of component 3 is focused on the interplay between cognitions individuals construct in out-of-school cultural practices and in school, an area of study particularly important for treatments of culture and cognitive development and therefore meriting special attention. Both in school and out, cognitive forms individuals acquire are often linked to partially distinct social histories and activity structures. In school, for instance, children learn our standard number orthography and computational procedures that have been worked up over a complex cultural history; these are specialized forms that can be applied to any computational problem. In contrast, in everyday practices, cognitive forms are typically more restricted—they are constructed to accomplish particular goals in daily activities as we saw in the case of Oksapmin's arithmetical strategies linked to economic exchange. In Scribner's (1986) terms, such knowledge is best conceived as "practical" as distinct from "theoretical." For Scribner (following Aristotle) the crux of the difference is that "practical thinking is instrumental to the achievement of larger goals, while theoretical thinking is noninstrumental and 'complete in itself' " (p. 29).

Though new Western-styled bush schools had recently been introduced to the Oksapmin community, Oksapmin adults who participated in the tradestore economy had never attended these schools. Consequently, the study of arithmetical strategies associated with participation in the money economy could not be extended to the interplay between a comprehensive system of arithmetical relations taught in school and the practice-linked arithmetical strategies. Nonetheless, it was possible to address issues related to this interplay in an analysis of Oksapmin school children (Saxe, 1985).

In Oksapmin classrooms, the official language is English. At the time I conducted my research, mathematics instruction was based on a Western curriculum, and teachers, none of whom was Oksapmin, lacked knowledge of the Oksapmin culture, including the indigenous number system. In this Western school context, I found that Oksapmin schoolchildren, on their own, made use of their body-part system in solving mathematical problems. Further, an interview study revealed that the kinds of body strategies children used to accomplish problems shifted with grade level: While first-grade children used body strategies similar to traditional adults, children at more advanced grade levels progressively used strategies to keep track of the addition of one term on the other, strategies that resembled (but were not identical with) those of the adults with greater experience with the money economy.

The study of Oksapmin schoolchildren illustrates the way that out-of-school cognitive forms may be appropriated and specialized to address problems in school, thus leading to novel cognitive developments. It may be that Oksapmin were at the same time making use of knowledge structures acquired in school linked to the Western orthography to address problems in out-of-school practices, though this was not investigated in the Oksapmin case.

THE THREE-COMPONENT APPROACH:
A METHOD OF STUDY

The Oksapmin research illustrates the promise for the three-component method in the analysis of intrinsic relations between culture and cognition. Each component presents distinct requirements and challenges for an investigation of intrinsic relations between sociocultural and cognitive developmental phenomena.

The first component—analysis of practice-linked goals—requires an *in situ* analysis of the goals that emerge in practice participation. Here the challenge is to produce an ethnography of the practice, focusing both on its general goal structure (parameter 1) as well as the character of emergent goals linked to sociocultural processes like social interactions (parameter 2) and cultural artifacts (parameter 3). To accomplish this task, we need systematic observations of individuals as they participate in their practice; further, we need documentation of individuals with different levels of practice-expertise to determine in what way their prior understandings may be implicated in the character of these emergent goals (parameter 4).

The second component—form-function shifts in cognitive development— requires rich data on the strategies and representational forms individuals use to accomplish practice-linked goals and their changing relations to one another over the course of development. Here what is required are specialized interview methods designed to illuminate the character of practice participants' knowledge forms and their cognitive functions documented in the *in situ* analyses of component 1. Particularly important are two kinds of contrasts. First, to determine the extent to which knowledge is linked to participation in a specific practice, contrasts between same-aged individuals who are and are not practice participants are required. Second, to determine developmental transformations in practice-specific knowledge forms, contrasts among participants at different age levels (or individuals followed over time) are required.

The third component—the interplay of learning across contexts—extends the first analysis of emergent goals and the second analysis of form–function shifts. Children participate in a multiplicity of practices in which specific practice-linked cognitive problems arise, both in school and out. It may very well be that children make use of cognitive forms constructed in one context to address problems that emerge in others. Here the focus is on the way practice participants may appropriate school-linked knowledge forms to address practice-linked problems and, reciprocally, the way children in school may appropriate practice-linked cognitive forms to address school-linked problems. To determine the influence of schooling on the cognitive forms children use during practice participation, the challenge is to find same-aged children who participate in the same practice, some with schooling and some without. To determine the influence of practice participation on the cognitive forms children construct in school, the challenge is to find children in school who do and who do not participate in a common out-of-school practice.

In the three sections that comprise the body of this volume (Parts II, III, and IV) and in the concluding section (Part V), I present an analysis of intrinsic relations between sociocultural and cognitive developmental processes guided by the three-component model. My focus for study is the practice of candy selling as conducted by children in an urban center in Brazil's northeast. In applying the three-component approach, I ask a variety of interrelated research questions concerning emergent mathematical goals of the practice, the development of the mathematical forms and functions that sellers use to generate and accomplish these emergent goals, and the interplay between sellers' construction of mathematical forms and functions between their practice and the classroom. In accord with the prior discussions, to address these questions I report a range of analyses of sellers as they practice their trade as well as contrasts between distinct populations of sellers and between sellers and nonsellers. Further, the questions require a variety of methods including ethnographic techniques, structured interview procedures, and assessments of children's problem solving on a range of mathematical tasks tailored to an analysis of sellers' practice-linked mathematics.

A guide to the chapters that follow is contained in Table 2.1. The table is arranged by component and chapter, outlining (1) the principal research question asked, (2) the population groups studied or contrasted to address the question, and (3) the methods of inquiry tailored to the particular question. I will sketch the general structure of the volume following the table.

In Part II, my focus is on the mathematical goals that emerge as sellers ply their trade (component 1). In an effort to illuminate the character of these goals, each of the five chapters in this section (Chapters 3 through 7) addresses a research question linked to one or more of the four parameters of component 1. In Chapter 3, to address the question of the structure of the practice (parameter 1), I observed and interviewed sellers and various other significant groups in-

TABLE 2.1
Outline of Research Questions, Groups Studied, and Methods Used

Chapter & Question	Group(s) Studied or Contrasted	Method
PART II. COMPONENT 1: EMERGENT MATHEMATICAL GOALS		
Chapter 3. Parameter 1: What is the structure of the candy-selling practice, and how is it related to sellers' goal-directed activities?	Sellers, wholesale store clerks, wholesale store cashiers	In situ observation and interview
Chapter 4. Parameters 2 & 3: How are conventions and social interactions interwoven with emergent mathematical goals during the Sell Phase?	Sellers at three age levels: 6- to 7-year-olds vs. 8- to 11-year-olds vs. 12-to 15-year-olds	In situ observation of and interview
Chapter 5. Parameters 2 & 3: How are conventions and social interactions interwoven with emergent goals during the Purchase Phase?	Sellers and wholesale store clerks	In situ observation of and interviews
Chapter 6. Parameter 4: How are the sellers' prior understandings interwoven with their mathematical goals?	Sellers at three age levels: 6- to 7-year-olds vs. 8- to 11-year-olds vs. 12- to 15-year-olds	In situ observation and interview
Chapter 7. Parameters 1 through 4: Summary and discussion.		
PART III. COMPONENT 2: FORMS AND FUNCTIONS IN SELLERS' MATHEMATICS		
Chapter 8. Does participation with the goals of the practice influence children's mathmatical forms and functions?	Sellers vs. non-sellers	Interview using tasks linked to candy-selling practice, including number representation, bill arithmetic, ratios, and mark-up

(continued)

TABLE 2.1
(*Continued*)

Chapter & Question	Group(s) Studied or Contrasted	Method
Chapter 9. What is the nature of shifts in mathematical forms and functions in sellers' problem solving over age?	Unschooled sellers at three age levels: 5- to 7- vs. 8- to 11- vs. 12- to 15-year-olds	Same
Chapter 10. Components 1 and 2: Summary and integration.		

PART IV. COMPONENT 3: THE INTERPLAY BETWEEN LEARNING IN AND OUT OF SCHOOL

Chapter 11. What kinds of mathematical forms and functions are exclusively linked to candy selling as contrasted with schooling?	10- to 12-year-old unschooled candy sellers vs same-aged U.S. schoolchildren (non-sellers)	Interview using tasks linked to candy-selling practice, including number representation, bill arithmetic, ratios, and mark-up—interview adapted for use with U.S. children.
Chapter 12. Does schooling experience influence the nature of the mathematical forms and functions that sellers construct in the practice?	12- to 15-year-old sellers with three levels of schooling	Interview using tasks linked to candy-selling practice, including number representation, bill arithmetic, ratios, and mark-up
Chapter 13. Does candy-selling experience influence children's mathematical problem solving in school?	10- to 12-year-old second- and third-grade sellers vs. age- and grade-matched non-sellers from the same urban schools as the sellers	Interview using arithmetical problems presented in formats common in classroom settings (word and computation problems)
Chapter 14. In what way do sellers make use of forms and functions constructed in one context to solve problems in another?	Case studies of sellers	*In situ* observation and interviews of sellers solving mark-up problems

volved in the practice (e.g., wholesale store clerks). These observations revealed a four-phase structure in which primary phases were a Sell Phase (in which sellers sold their candy to customers) and a Purchase Phase (in which sellers purchased their candy from wholesale stores). In subsequent chapters (Chapters 4 through 7), I ask questions related to the way in which sociocultural artifacts and conventions of the practice (parameter 2), patterns of practice-linked social interactions (parameter 3), and sellers' prior understandings (parameter 4) are interwoven with sellers' emergent goals. To produce observations relevant to these parameters, I made use of various ethnographic and interview techniques noted in the table. These included records of seller–customer and seller–peer transactions in the streets as they sold their candy, interviews with sellers as they addressed mathematical problems that occurred in their practice, interviews with wholesale store clerks, observations of sellers' transactions with wholesale store clerks and cashiers, and an analysis of clerks' records of their own transactions with sellers. In addition to the systematic observations produced with these methods, the overall organization of methods and data-collection procedures benefited from additional informal observation and pilot interviews with sellers.

The results generated with the first component were instrumental for the analysis guided by the second, which I address in Part III: the forms and functions that sellers construct in generating and accomplishing their emergent mathematical goals (component 2). In Chapter 8, I ask whether sellers construct and specialize mathematical forms and functions specifically linked to their participation in the candy-selling practice. To answer the question, I created tasks based on the analysis of sellers' emergent goals (component 1), and I contrasted the way these tasks were approached and solved by unschooled sellers[1] and two groups of same-aged unschooled nonsellers (one group from the same urban environment and the other from a nearby rural environment). After establishing in Chapter 8 some marked differences in the forms and functions that distinguish the mathematics of sellers and nonsellers, I turn, in Chapter 9, to the developmental question. I ask whether there are regular ways young sellers' use of practice-linked forms gradually take on new mathematical functions as sellers mature. To address this question, I contrast unschooled sellers of different age levels solving the same practice-linked tasks. Finally, in Chapter 10, I present an integration of components 1 and 2, discussing the developmental interrelations between shifts with age of sellers' emergent goals (component 1) and form–function shifts in the character of their mathematics (component 2).

In Part IV, I turn to the question of the interplay between learning within and across the candy-selling practice and school (component 3), guiding my treatment by a consideration of differences in the emergent mathematical goals across the contexts (component 1) and differences in the mathematical forms and func-

---

[1]Unschooled is defined throughout as no schooling through second grade of the public school system in Brazil's Northeast.

tions children appropriate and specialize in the two contexts (component 2). In Chapter 11, I consider the extent to which mathematical forms and functions linked to the candy-selling practice are distinct from those linked to school. To this end, I compare the mathematical problem solving of unschooled candy sellers with a group of children of the same age who have no experience with the practice of candy selling nor the economic conditions in Brazil—a group of schoolchildren (fifth and sixth graders) in the United States. After establishing some marked differences in the mathematical forms and functions used by the sellers and schoolchildren, the next three chapters (Chapters 12, 13, and 14) are concerned with the interplay between learning in the practice and learning at school. In Chapter 12, I ask whether increased school experience is linked to differences in the character of sellers' mathematics. To this end, I contrast sellers of about the same age but with varying levels of school experience on the practice-linked mathematical problem-solving tasks. In Chapter 13, I again ask the question about the interplay between form–function shifts in the practice and at school, but this time the question is posed in the opposite direction: Does participation in the candy-selling practice influence the kinds of mathematical forms children use to solve arithmetical problems linked to school? To this end, I contrast same-aged sellers and nonsellers solving school-linked arithmetical tasks. Finally, in Chapter 14, I consider case studies that illuminate the interdependence between the three analytic components. Here, I illustrate the way in which sellers' emergent goals, form–function shifts, and the interplay between learning across contexts are interwoven and interdependent processes.

In Part V, I conclude the volume with an analysis of the implications of the work for a general treatment of the interplay between sociocultural and developmental processes in the cognitive development of the individual. I consider the present approach in contrast with others and the implications of the present work for future research directions.

II ▐▐ COMPONENT 1: EMERGENT MATHEMATICAL GOALS

The candy sellers who are the target of study are from Recife, an urban center in Brazil's Northeast. Relative to other Brazilian cities of comparable size, the city is poor. A substantial percentage of the population makes its living through work in the "informal sector," an unregulated, large portion of the local economy (cf. Calvacanti, 1983). Candy selling, one of many varieties of work of the informal sector, is an occupation for children from about 6 years of age.

The child candy sellers in the study typically come from poor families—many living in *favelas,* or Brazilian shantytowns.[2] Their parents and often their siblings typically work as well in the informal sector in such occupations as maids, car washers, and street vendors of a wide range of merchandise as diverse as plastic buckets, razor blades, tools, and postage stamps. The sellers work their trade for long hours, and many of the sellers never attend school or drop out early in order to deal with their own and their families' strained economic predicaments.

Recife's informal sector has emerged in the context of Brazil's rapidly inflating economy, and inflation is interwoven with the business transactions of the informal sector at every level, including the transactions of the candy sellers. For instance, the 250% annual inflation rate at the time of the study meant that the price

---

[2]Information on sellers' backgrounds and general characteristics of the selling activities was collected in an interview study reported in Appendix B.

FIG. II.1.   Some currency units in circulation during the period of study.

which candy sellers paid for candy boxes at wholesale stores had increased to very large values.[3] A box of candy purchased when the study began (July, 1985) cost from 3,600 to 12,000 cruzeiros (depending on the type of box) and 4 months later cost 6,500 to 20,000 cruzeiros. The high inflation rate also meant considerable variability in the wholesale price of boxes, since stores do not all raise their prices at the same time, making comparative shopping worthwhile.

Inflation has also impacted on the currency system, which in turn influences the mathematics of sales transactions. Due to the inflation rate, the Brazilian government has repeatedly shifted and modified its unit of currency to keep the ever upward-moving numerical values manageable. Consider Brazil's recent

---

[3]This figure is the rate reported by the federal government. The actual rate is generally considered to be substantially greater.

history: In the 1940s, the *rei*—a former Brazilian unit of currency—was inflated to such an extent that Brazil shifted its unit of currency, creating the cruzeiro (1,000 reis were made equivalent to 1 cruzeiro). In the late 1960s, cruzeiros were devaluated into a new currency (the *cruzeiro novo*), again by a factor of 1,000, and centavos (1/100 of a *cruzeiro novo*) were issued; the new coins had the values of 10 centavos to 50 cruzeiros, and bills ranged from 1 to 1,000 cruzeiros. However, as inflation persisted, the government issued the 5,000 cruzeiro bill, then the 10,000 bill and, in 1984, the 50,000 bill (along with a request by the government that prices no longer mention centavos). During the period in which the study was conducted, the 100,000 cruzeiro bill was issued, together with coins of 100, 200, and 500 cruzeiros. Just after the study was completed, the government issued a new currency system, based on the *cruzado* (1 cruzado = 1,000 cruzeiros). Thus, the recent history of currency presents both changing material for exchange (as in the issue of new bills) and radical shifts in pricing (as in the recent shift from the cruzeiro to the cruzado). Figure II.1 contains a photograph of some of the principal currency units in circulation during the period of the study.

In the following four chapters, my concern is to understand candy sellers' mathematical goals, which emerge as they work their trade to achieve the larger objective of economic survival. I guided my analysis of sellers' emergent mathematical goals by the four parameters of the first analytic component: I proceed, in Chapter 3, by laying out the general structure of the practice (parameter 1), providing an overview of its four-phase cyclical organization and the specific sociocultural processes that are interwoven with this four-phase structure. In Chapters 4 and 5, I consider specific phases of the larger structure, and I present empirical studies that show the way particular kinds of social interactions (parameter 2) and cultural artifacts and practice-linked conventions (parameter 3) are interwoven with sellers' emergent mathematical goals across the phases of the practice. In Chapter 6, I turn to an analysis of the way differences in the understandings that sellers bring to the practice influence their emergent mathematical goals (parameter 4). I conclude, in Chapter 7, with a summary description of the principal mathematical goals of the practice and their intrinsic links to the four parameters of component 1.

3

Parameter 1: The Structure of the Candy-selling Practice

Child candy sellers are entrepreneurs, and their principal motive linked to their selling activities is economic: They are concerned with making money. Rarely is the candy-selling occupation the exclusive year-round practice of a child seller. Rather, depending on children's perceptions of market conditions, children shift their selling practices to such merchandise as fruit (especially for seasonal crops of specific fruit types), popsicles (especially during the hot summer months), puffed wheat (especially when wholesale prices are favorable relative to other merchandise), or plastic shopping bags (especially at Christmas time).

It is useful to conceptualize the candy sellers' practice as consisting of a four-phase cyclical structure, though the structure is not consciously represented in the minds of the sellers; rather, this structure emerges as sellers and related actors work toward accomplishing their economic goals under particular social, cultural, and economic conditions (e.g., a high inflation, a wholesale candy industry, social attitudes toward children and work, a history of the practice). This structure both promotes and constrains the particular kinds of mathematical goals children generate in the activity.

The four-phase cyclical structure is depicted in the inner rectangle of Fig. 3.1. The structure consists of a Purchase Phase, a Prepare-to-Sell Phase, a Sell Phase, and a Prepare-to-Purchase Phase. As indicated in the figure, during each phase of the cyclical structure, various sociocultural processes like inflation, practice-linked conventions and artifacts, and social interactions with peers and customers, are interwoven with sellers' activities and, in important ways, these sociocultural processes figure into the mathematical goals that emerge in the practice.

During the Sell Phase, sellers ply their trade, searching for customers. They

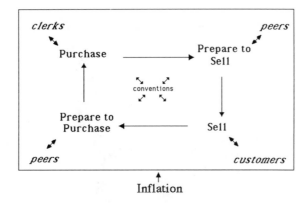

FIG. 3.1.   Four-phase structure of the candy-selling practice.

sell units of candy to customers (candy bars, lifesavers, gum, etc.) from boxes purchased wholesale. In their search for customers, sellers often walk the downtown streets, yelling their retail price and their particular variety of candy. Some sellers board buses and sell to a captive audience, others approach potential customers who wait in lines at movie theaters or bus stops, and still others stand in the street selling to customers through the bus windows when buses are stopped (see Fig. 3.2). In their transactions, arithmetical problems emerge as sellers make sales transactions and negotiate with customers.

Once a seller exhausts his (all were boys) merchandise, he begins a Prepare-to-Purchase Phase. He must decide both the type of candy to sell next and where to purchase the candy. Candy of a wide variety of types (chocolate bars, lollipops, gum) is sold in over 30 different wholesale stores scattered in the downtown area. The candy is packaged typically in 30 to 100 units per box (sometimes plastic bags). A seller's deliberation about the next type of candy to purchase and the specific store where he will accomplish the purchase is often based on his perception of local market conditions (what type of candy sells well), the cost of a box at a specific store, and his available cash. In this phase, mathematical problems emerge as sellers sum their available cash, compare different prices, and often discuss with other sellers where they might find the best buys.

During the Purchase Phase of the practice, sellers typically buy one of a wide variety of boxes. During a full day, sellers may return to the stores several times. In the stores, candy boxes (often labeled with prices) are stacked on open shelves behind a long counter. A clerk stands between the counter and the shelves, retrieving merchandise for customers and writing bills which customers take to pay at a small cashier's booth. During this Purchase Phase, arithmetical problems emerge in transactions with cashiers and clerks as sellers compute and negotiate what they must pay for their purchase; further, as is often the case in other phases, these arithmetical problems are interwoven with particular cultural ar-

FIG. 3.2.   A seller offering hard candy at the price of 3 for Cr$1000.

tifacts like the denominational units of currency, the large numerical values entailed in candy purchases caused by inflation, and standard orthography used to represent box prices on the shelves and on the bills issued for purchases.

During the Prepare-to-Sell Phase, sellers price their wholesale box purchases of candy for retail sale. Such wholesale-to-retail translations present some complex arithmetical problems linked to artifacts of the practice: The seller pays a large value for a multi-unit box in the wholesale store and now must compute the retail price for units of candy so that he will make a profit. Sometimes this pricing is accomplished in the streets alone or with other sellers (see Fig. 3.3); other times it is accomplished in wholesale stores with the aid of store clerks.

FIG. 3.3.   Sellers pricing candy while sitting at a bus station plaza.

In sum, as sellers ply their trade, a four-phase cyclical structure emerges in which mathematical goals of the practice take form. The cyclical structure is interwoven with various sociocultural processes, including an inflating economy, practice-linked artifacts and conventions, and social interactions. Further, sellers' mathematical goals are not consciously planned by the sellers nor are they determined by the conventions and artifacts of the practice. Rather the goals emerge in the practice, as sellers attempt to address their larger economic objectives of making money. When mathematical goals do emerge they take varying forms, often interwoven with sellers' economic motives, sociocultural processes, and the mathematical understandings children bring to the practice.

4

Parameters 2 and 3: Social Interactions and Practice-linked Artifacts and Conventions—A Focus on the Sell Phase

The purpose of this chapter is to gain an understanding of the way social interactions and practice-linked conventions are interwoven with the sellers' mathematical goals during the Sell Phase of the practice. To this end, child sellers who varied in age and years of schooling were observed practicing their trade in the streets. Though the focus is on the Sell Phase, neighboring phases are documented as well, since these phases were in part linked to street activities: While they are in the streets, children sometimes share information on pricing merchandise (Prepare-to-Sell Phase) and on finding stores with the "best buys" (Prepare-to-Purchase Phase).

METHOD

Subjects

Twenty-eight candy sellers were observed. Four were 6- to 7-year-olds (mean age = 6.8, sd = .50 years), seven 8- to 11-year-olds (mean age = 10.3, sd = 1.10), and seventeen 12- to 15-year-olds (mean = 13.2, sd = 1.1). Sellers ranged in schooling from none to the completion of the sixth grade (median grade level completed = second). In the sample, the correlation between grade level and age was not statistically significant ($r = .13$). All were males, since the total population of sellers is virtually all males.

Procedures

Subject Recruitment. Sellers were recruited on the streets while they sold their merchandise. Twenty-two children were asked to participate while selling candy.

An additional 6 children (during one of the periodic lulls in the candy-selling practice) were approached as they were selling other merchandise (generally tangerines), questioned as to their experience at candy selling as described in Appendix A, and then, if their experience was appropriate, offered a contribution toward the purchase of a box of candy if they would let an observer watch them sell. Since the observations of both groups of candy sellers yielded similar results, these groups were pooled in the reported analyses.

Observational Record.   Observers followed candy sellers and recorded each child–customer transaction involving a sale; this record included the sale price and the number of units purchased, as well as any bargaining that occurred. In addition, any peer interactions and mathematics children used were also recorded. During lulls in a child's practice (e.g., while waiting for the arrival of a bus carrying potential customers), the observer asked the child how he priced the candy for retail sale, how much he paid for the box, and how many units were in the box at the time of purchase. (Sellers' solutions to these pricing problems are reported in Chapter 6.) In general, sellers appreciated the interest in their activity by adults and were often very willing informants.[4]

RESULTS

The record for each seller was partitioned into observations of three types: (1) sellers' *social interactions with customers* (generally occurring in the Sell Phase as children made sales and produced change), (2) sellers' *interactions with peers* related to the selling practice (generally occurring in the Prepare-to-Sell and Prepare-to-Purchase Phases as sellers discussed issues of pricing and territoriality), and (3) sellers' mathematical efforts at translating wholesale-box prices to retail-unit prices (generally occurring in the *Prepare-to-Sell* Phase as sellers priced their candy for retail sale but also elicited from sellers during lulls in the Sell Phase). For each observation type, my concern was to understand the nature of the mathematical environments that emerged in the practice with particular attention to the way children's mathematical goals were interwoven with cultural artifacts and practice-linked conventions. In this chapter, I present analyses of sellers' interactions with customers and with peers—the first two observation types. I present the analysis of sellers' mathematical efforts—the third observation type—in Chapter 6 where I address issues concerning the way sellers prior understandings are interwoven with the emergence of their mathematical goals.

---

[4]Prior to data collection for the studies, considerable groundwork was laid by pilot observations and interviews. Such preliminary work was instrumental for gaining entry into the candy-selling community as well as for framing empirical questions about the mathematical environments that emerge during the candy-selling practice.

Social Interactions with Customers

Sellers' transactions with customers varied in their frequency from one seller to another. These transactions included simple exchanges of a bill for units of candy as well as more complex bargaining transactions. Regardless of the frequency and the complexity of the interactions, the conventions and artifacts of the practice entered into the mathematical goals that emerged in principal ways. I will first consider the frequency of sellers' transactions with customers and then the content and complexity of the mathematical goals that emerged in the transactions.

Frequency of Sales Transactions.   The rate of sales transaction varied markedly over the period of observation for individual sellers. When a line of people formed to wait for a bus or when commuters boarded a bus and were waiting for it to depart, sellers generally capitalized on the idle audiences; it was in such periods that children's sales peaked. In selling at such gatherings, the seller typically walked up and down the line of potential customers with the box of his merchandise in the crook of his arm and bills in the other hand and called out the price he was asking for his candy (and perhaps some special reason for a customer to purchase his candy such as a reduced cost relative to other sellers). This aggressive selling style is stereotypical of the practice, and when a seller gives advice to another or when a bus arrives with a load of potential customers, a seller may indicate that it is time to *bota mola*—an expression that is unique to the practice. One seller (No. 12) described this style as follows: "*Bota mola* means to sell well—to shout loudly, go inside the bus [not just sell from windows], to show your candy to everyone!".

The frequency of sale transactions was computed for each seller by dividing the total number of minutes of the observation by the number of completed sales, yielding an average interval (in minutes) between sales. The mean interval was 19 minutes (sd = 10 minutes). A significant correlation between interval and age (tau$_B$ = .24, $p < .05$) reveals that the younger children tended to complete transactions more frequently than older children. This finding is in accord with a general consensus among sellers: Some customers buy candy not only for its value as merchandise but also as a sympathetic gesture, and younger children seem to elicit more sympathy than their older peers. For instance, an 8-year-old and his older brother were observed selling the same kind of candy in the same bus line (an uncommon practice, as noted later). Later, the 8-year-old was asked, "Why are you selling the same type of candy in the same place as your [older] brother?" He responded that he follows his brother and still sells candy—"sometimes he [my brother] tries to sell to people and no one buys, but then I pass, and sometimes they buy." Some sellers clearly attempt to capitalize on such human responses even when they may no longer be able to elicit such sympathy by their young age:

OBS No. 3 (11 years) was selling at the bus terminal to people waiting in line to board a bus for some minutes without a sale. After several unsuccessful attempts at informing customers that his candy was a "good deal" since other sellers sell lifesavers for four packages for Cr$1000 whereas he was selling for five for Cr$1000, the seller called out "BUY MOTHER MARY TO HELP ME!" and shortly thereafter made two sales. To sell his last five, the boy pleaded with a man in line to buy his candy, and the man said he didn't want to because the candy was sticky (a frequent problem for sellers in the heat of the Northeast). The boy said they were not and told the man to examine the packages one by one to see. The man eventually bought the lifesavers and told the boy that he bought them only to help him out.

Emergent Goals During Seller–customer Transactions.   In the sellers' transactions with customers, the potential for complex arithmetical problems is great, especially when sellers are dealing with numbers of such great magnitude. For instance, if a seller was selling candy for Cr$379 per unit, each transaction would generate a complex arithmetical problem if the customer did not provide exact change. Regardless, the speed of a transaction would be slow. Pricing conventions have evolved that markedly reduce the complexity of problems that would arise if candy were sold for unrounded values.

1. The Influence of Pricing Conventions on Emergent Mathematical Problems.   The most notable pricing convention involves selling candies in sets for 1000 cruzeiros as in the foregoing observation. Fig. 4.1 contains a frequency distribution of each candy seller's *most common transaction price* during the observation period. The table indicates that virtually all of the sellers used the "x units per Cr$1000" pricing convention, regardless of candy type and wholesale price. The use of such pricing conventions was unrelated to sellers' age levels.

Though units-per-Cr$1000 was the most common convention, children did offer other prices for their candy; each of these less common alternative conventions displayed similar properties to selling by the Cr$1000 bill. Every price recorded made reference to a specified number of units for a single bill of currency and every price was a multiple of 1000 cruzeiros. Thus a child might sell the same merchandise for five units/Cr$1000 and two units/Cr$500. In fact, selling fewer units for a greater profit was a common means of compensation for the difference in speed of sale.

OBS No. 8 (14 years). The seller was yelling "ONE IS Cr$500 AND THREE IS Cr$1000." During a lull, the observer asked, "Why are you using those prices?" and the seller responded "BECAUSE THE CUSTOMER WILL SEE THAT IF ONE IS Cr$500 THEN TWO SHOULD BE Cr$1000, AND SINCE I OFFER ONE FOR Cr$500 AND THREE FOR Cr$1000, HE IS GOING TO SEE THAT HE GETS A GOOD DEAL BY BUYING THREE FOR Cr$1000, BECAUSE HE THINKS THAT HE IS GETTING ONE FOR FREE AND THAT WAY I SELL FASTER."

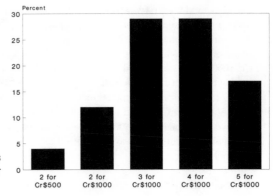

FIG. 4.1. Percentage of sellers
using 1 of 5 price ratios as their
most common.

Some children—particularly younger ones—resisted selling their candy for
more than one price even when faced with the opportunity to bargain, since using
multiple selling prices complicates the mathematics of sales.

> OBS No. 5 (10 years). The child was selling his candy at five for Cr$1000 when a
> customer asked the child to sell one for Cr$200. The seller refused, despite some
> effort on the part of the customer. Later, the observer asked the child why he did not
> complete the sale for the alternative price, and the seller replied, "IF I SELL ONLY
> ONE, MY BOX WILL BE INCOMPLETE," suggesting that he would not know
> how to adjust the pricing on his remaining candies.

Some children clearly used a greater number of alternative prices during the
observation periods than others (e.g., 6/Cr$1000, 2/Cr$500, 1/Cr$200). In
using multiple price ratios, sellers attempt to increase the likelihood of a sale;
however, the multiple prices also lead to additional mathematical problems (e.g.,
reasoning about ratios and/or proportions). Figure 4.2 contains the number of
different prices for which children retailed their candy as a function of age group.
Younger children tended to use fewer different selling prices than their older
peers ($tau_B = .28$, $p < .05$).

The use of the pricing convention of units/Cr$1000 has evolved over the
history of the practice. Several reports from children indicated that in days when
wholesale prices were lower, the number of units in retail prices were referenced
to the Cr$500 bill, and before that, the Cr$200 bill. Such a grounding of unit
prices in a single bill serves multiple functions in sellers' activities. The convention reduces the need for on-the-spot computations for change in transactions, it
facilitates adjustments for inflation since one may merely manipulate the number
of units sold for Cr$1000, and it facilitates communications among peers by
providing a stable and relatively small set of price options for discussion. Use of
the convention also gives rise to mathematical goals with particular properties.
For instance, in comparing prices, sellers do not compare the retail price of a
single unit; they compare pricing ratios.

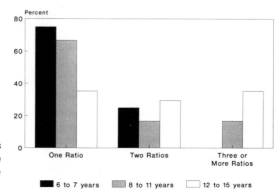

FIG. 4.2. Percentage of sellers using 1, 2, or more than 2 price ratios as a function of age group.

2. The Influence of Customer Bargaining on Emergent Mathematical Goals. Customers' efforts to bargain with children occurred in 17% of the observational episodes. Most efforts at bargaining on the part of customers were intended to increase the number of units per Cr$1000. Here is one example:

> OBS No. 8. (14 years). The child was selling two boxes of different types of candy, "Gram Prix" at two for Cr$1000 and "Zorro" at five for Cr$1000. A customer requested five Zorros and presented a Cr$5000 bill. Before giving change, the boy offered the Gram Prix at three for Cr$1000 (discounted from the seller's original price). The customer asked if the child would sell four Gram Prix for Cr$1000. The boy said that he couldn't because one Gram Prix in the store was more. The customer insisted, but the boy said no. Then, the boy said that he would sell three Gram Prix and two Zorros for Cr$1000. The customer did not agree, still asking for four Gram Prix for Cr$1000. The boy would not agree and returned Cr$4000 as change for the customer's original purchase of five Zorro for Cr$1000.

We see in such instances of bargaining that new mathematical goals emerge that are interwoven with the artifacts of the practice. In the instance described, the interaction leads to a consideration and reconsideration of price ratios in relation to one another and in relation to the wholesale price of the two boxes. Further, in such transactions, the blend between the economics and the mathematics of the activity is particularly striking. The sellers' shifting price structure arises from his money-making motive. The sellers' economic concerns are clearly driving his mathematical computations.

3. The Influence of Reduced Sales on Price Setting. Sellers displayed concern to price their candy for speedy sale, and this concern led some to modify their retail unit prices prior to exhausting all the units in a boxy.

> OBS No. 10. (14 years). The child was offering "Chocolate Danny" at two for Cr$1000 for 35 minutes until he made his first sale inside a bus. Another 20

minutes passed, and he changed his price to three for Cr$1000. He explained to the observer that it was just too hard to sell two for Cr$1000.

In such readjustments of selling price as a function of sellers' perception of market conditions, we see again the emergence of mathematical problems and solutions that are interwoven with the price ratio convention and, in this case, anticipated social interactions with customers. In the case of the seller described, the increase of the number of units per Cr$1000 requires a reconsideration of his retail price per units to the wholesale price he paid for the box.

Peer Interactions

A second form of social interaction that led to the emergence of mathematical goals was interaction between peers. Both collaborative and agonistic interactions were observed. These peer interactions were related largely either to issues of territoriality or retail pricing.

Territoriality.   One threat to profits is competition with other sellers. In the selling practice, conventions have emerged that allow sellers and/or groups of sellers to lay claim to different locations in the downtown area for selling; those who violate the informal rules—generally new sellers in the area—are identified as "crabs" (*siri*). Crabs often create special problems, not only because they may sell the same merchandise as the seller who works the location, but also because they frequently sell their merchandise at a lower price.

OBS No. 16. (14 years). [The seller was asked why he only sells at this bus stop and not other places.] "I LIKE TO SELL IN THIS STOP AND ANY PLACE ON AVENUE GUARARAPES—THIS AREA IS BETTER THAN OTHER PLACES. IN OTHER PLACES THERE ARE MANY CRABS." [What happens if a crab comes?] "IF A CRAB ARRIVES IN MY AREA, I GO WITH MY FRIENDS TO THROW HIM OUT, BECAUSE CRABS LIKE TO SELL CHEAPER, AND THAT ANGERS PEOPLE THAT SELL IN THIS AREA. IF HE SELLS FOR THE SAME PRICE, WE ALSO TELL HIM TO LEAVE, BECAUSE THE CRAB BRINGS HIS FRIENDS, AND THE AREA BECOMES FULL OF SELLERS AND THERE IS MUCH CONFUSION."

OBS NO. 14. (12 years). [The observer asked, Why do you sell on Avenue Guararapes?] "BECAUSE IT'S MY PLACE, AND IF I GO TO ANOTHER PLACE AND IT'S AN AREA OF SOMEONE ELSE, THEY'LL HIT ME." [And if another comes to this area?] "I'LL HIT HIM AND ORDER HIM TO LEAVE."

OBS NO. 4. [So, what happens if a crab approaches?] "WE ALL GET RIGHT IN FRONT OF THE CRAB AND SELL FOR LESS THAN THE CRAB IS SELLING FOR. IN THAT WAY, WE DRIVE THE CRAB AWAY. ONCE HE LEAVES, WE SELL FOR OUR REGULAR PRICES."

Issues of territoriality enter into sellers' mathematics when they evaluate their competitors' prices relative to their own. For instance, consider the problem when two children are selling the same type of candy for two different prices— one for three for Cr$1000 and the other for two for Cr$500. In order to determine who is undercutting whom, a seller must compare ratios (units/currency denomination) as well as the wholesale prices paid for the candy.

Retail Pricing.   There were two types of social interactions observed related to price setting: apprenticeship, where one individual sets the price for another, and negotiations or clashes between sellers related to pricing issues.

Apprenticeship was only observed in 4 of our 30 sellers and, in each case, the seller was 6 or 7 years of age. In each case, the seller's parent or older peer bought the box for the child and instructed him to sell the candy at a specified price.

Negotiations and clashes among sellers over price were observed in children older than 7. Sellers typically compared their own pricing ratios with those of others. Some sellers clashed.

OBS No. 32. There are five children (all sellers) at a bus stop. Two children are discussing pricing, Joao who is selling lifesavers for 3/Cr$1000 and Paulo who is selling the same kind of lifesavers for 4/Cr$1000. João felt that he was disadvantaged because of Paulo's cheaper price (4/Cr$1000). João tells Paulo that he should lower the number of packages he sells. Joao says, "IT'S BETTER TO SELL 3/Cr$1000." Paulo says, "THAT'S ROBBERY!" João replies, "THAT'S YOUR PROBLEM." A fight begins to break out, and the other boys separate Paulo and João. Paulo and João go separate ways without any resolution.

Other sellers negotiated, justifying their price ratios with price ratios used by other sellers, or with respect to differences in the cost and effort of different ways of packaging their merchandise.

OBS No. 33. Four boys (ranging in age from 12 to 14 years) were selling packages of a new brand of chiclets, Goma de Mascar Nechar. Prior to selling chiclets, all were selling a popular type of chocolate bar (Dizioli), but all local wholesale stores had run out of Dizioli, so they turned to chiclets. Three of the four were selling the gum, 5/Cr$1000; for those three, a box of 100 cost Cr$10500 (wholesale price per unit = Cr$105); the remaining seller was selling the gum, 6/Cr$1000; for this one, a box of 100 cost Cr$10000 (wholesale price per unit = Cr$100).

A to B: "B, YOU'RE SELLING 6/Cr$1000!" (retail price per unit = Cr$167).

B: "I'M SELLING 6/Cr$1000 BECAUSE I WASN'T DOING MUCH BUSINESS."

A: "What?!"

B: "I BOUGHT THE BOX FOR Cr$10000, AND THAT'S WHY I'M SELLING 6/Cr$1000."

C then interjected, "THERE's A LITTLE BOY AROUND HERE WHO'S SELLING 8/Cr$1000." (retail price per unit = Cr$125). . . .

A: "YOU WANT TO FINISH FIRST AND THAT'S THE REASON YOU'RE SELLING 6/Cr$1000. "

B: "I'M SELLING FOR THE PRICE I WANT, AND YOU SELL 5/Cr$1000 BECAUSE YOU'RE SELLING YOURS IN LITTLE BAGS. (Little plastic bags were a newly emerging packaging strategy of some sellers; sellers inserted the number of units in a set to be sold into each bag. The bags cost the sellers a small amount of money and some time in packaging.)

In this interaction, we find the mathematical content of the interchange interwoven with conventions of the practice in a fundamental way. We see that price ratio comparisons are the basis for evaluating one another's retail prices. Further, we find equations between practice-linked labor (like putting candy into the newly emerging use of plastic bags for packaging candy) and money (the higher retail price for candy) are used as a basis for reconciling disputes between different price ratios.

Whether in apprenticeship relations or in interactions between equals, we find occasions in which, in the course of the interactions, mathematical goals emerge as interwoven with practice-linked conventions and artifacts that give form to these goals. In the case of apprenticeship, the novice is given a price ratio for which to sell his goods, a ratio that defines the form of exchanges that are legitimate with customers. In the case of interaction between equals, we find that in the course of discussions and arguments, children consider and reconsider relations between their own price ratios, other children's price ratios, and the relations between both and wholesale box prices.

Goals that Emerge in the Sell Phase and Neighboring Phases: Their Relation to Practice-linked Artifacts/Conventions and Social Interactions

The mathematical goals that emerge during the Sell Phase are interwoven with practice-linked artifacts, conventions, and social interactions in principal ways. These emergent goals are varied and they include the identification of the numerical values of currency, arithmetical operations on units of currency and candy, comparisons of ratios, and mark-up of wholesale box prices into retail unit prices.

Artifacts like the inflating currency system and social conventions like price ratios are interrelated with sellers' mathematical goals throughout the Sell Phase. In computations with currency—a common activity as sellers count their money—a seller must identify the numerical value of the bills. Further, the large numerical values of currency used in the sale of candy lead sellers to attempt computations with large numbers, computations that may differ markedly from other practices where currency does not take on such great values. Further, in selling with the conventional price ratio, the ratio leads sellers to conceptualize the value of his candy in the street in a mathematical form that has some consequence for emergent mathematical goals of the practice. While the young seller may limit his use of this ratio to guiding his transactions with customers, the price ratio convention contributes to older sellers' ratio comparison goals and thus to mathematical problems of some complexity.

Social interactions in the Sell Phase included two principal types: one between sellers and customers and the other between sellers and their peers. Both types were principal contexts in which mathematical goals emerged.

In sellers' transactions with customers, sellers pose their prices to customers in the ratio form—most typically multiple units for a single bill denomination (typically, 1000 cruzeiros). The use of the ratio is itself often the product of a seller's goal-directed efforts to translate his wholesale box price into a retail unit price, and the use of the ratio in transactions with customers sets the stage for further negotiations (bargaining) with customers in which the seller may need to reconsider the relation between his wholesale box price and retail ratio price or comparisons between different ratios. Further, in these interactions, sellers form goals of identifying bill values offered to them for their candy and, on occasion, arithmetical goals of producing additions and subtractions of currency.

In interactions between a seller and his peers, a seller may construct ratio comparison goals as in their transactions with customers. In peer interactions and negotiations, the comparisons are linked to competitive selling as when one seller eyes another seller's price. Further, these goals may take on elaborated forms as when sellers compare different price ratios and justify one ratio as more appropriate than another in arguments with peers. Sellers' interactions with peers may also take on more collaborative forms. Not only did we observe and hear reports by sellers of collaborative interactions of price setting in groups, but sellers typically cite that in their initiation into the practice of selling they received help from peers and relatives (see Appendix B), and it is likely that this help entailed some discussion about pricing.

In addition to these more or less direct ways in which social interactions are interwoven with emergent mathematical goals, in social interactions sellers' emergent goals may also be influenced by the interpersonal dynamics that are linked to the economics of the activity. For instance, in seller–customer transactions, the customer is ultimately in the position of evaluating the adequacy of the seller's mathematical solution in an exchange. Thus, if the seller advertises for one ratio and uses another (e.g., by giving the wrong number of candies, or requesting the wrong amount of money), the seller learns that he must reckon with the customer (if caught). Further, not only is the customer a person to whom the calculation may need to be justified, but the customer may attempt to influence the sellers' pricing in choosing to bargain and, in bargaining, a seller may be faced with new problems in which he generates new mathematical goals involving the recomputation of wholesale box price to retail unit price.

While artifacts, social conventions, and social interactions are interwoven with the emergent goals of the practice, we have also seen that the nature of the problems with which sellers were engaged varied as a function of sellers' ages. For instance, the younger sellers tended to circumvent ratio comparison problems by selling their goods for only a single pricing ratio; they also typically did not participate in bargaining negotiations. I will return to the issue of the way that sellers' prior understandings are interrelated with the goals that emerge in the practice in Chapter 6. In the next chapter, I turn to the Purchase Phase of the practice, showing further ways in which social interactions and practice-linked artifacts and conventions are interwoven with the emergent goals of the practice.

5 Parameters 2 and 3: Social Interactions and Practice-linked Artifacts and Conventions—A Focus on the Purchase Phase

The purpose of this chapter is to characterize the kinds of mathematical goals that emerge in children's activities during the Purchase Phase of the practice as they select and buy a box of candy in wholesale stores. Though the focus in this chapter is on the seller's purchase of boxes in the stores, store clerks may provide assistance in pricing for retail sale (Prepare-to-Sell Phase) and sometimes may direct children to other shops that contain other types of candy for which children are looking (Prepare-to-Purchase Phase). As a consequence, analyses of these transitional phases are also reported.

From preliminary observation of children's activity between the completion of the sale of a box and their purchase of a new box, there appeared to be a prototypical script for children's purchases: Prior to entering a store, a seller determines what type of candy he wants, based either on direct knowledge or recent recommendation by others about current cost and sellability (Prepare-to-Purchase Phase); a seller then seeks his targeted type at a favored store(s) or at a store where he or friends have noted that prices are low for the targeted type. If the store does not have his first choice (or, perhaps his second choice), he will leave for another known store.

The script has important implications for the kind of mathematics problems that emerged during the Purchase Phase. First, rather than reading numerals to determine and/or compare wholesale prices, sellers would often rely on oral communications for wholesale price information either while the seller was in the store or prior to store entry. Second, sellers would usually not "shop" for boxes by contrasting different stores' prices nor the price per unit of boxes that contain different quantities. Comparative shopping would usually be circumvented by the prepurchase information exchange among sellers or by a seller's prepurchase decision to buy a particular type of box.

In order to provide more detailed information on the sellers' Purchase Phase activities, a three-part study was conducted. In part 1, sellers were observed as they made wholesale purchases in stores. In part 2, wholesale clerks were interviewed about their assistance to children, and a subset of these clerks kept written records of their commercial transactions with the sellers. In part 3, a follow-up interview was conducted with clerks to explore possible shifts in clerks' assistance to sellers as a function of inflationary shifts in wholesale candy prices.

METHOD

Subjects

The subjects for this study were child candy sellers and wholesale store clerks. The sellers were all boys between 7 and 15 years of age who entered wholesale stores and appeared interested in making a purchase ($n = 50$ boys, mean age = 12.6 years, sd = 1.8 years, grade level from no schooling to seventh grade [median = third grade]). Included in this sample were the five children who were paid to allow us to observe them sell during a slow period of candy selling. The profiles of the paid sellers were similar to the 45 others that were observed during the normal course of their day's practice.

The wholesale store clerks were recruited from 14 wholesale stores in the downtown Recife area. Stores were all within an area of about one square mile; clerks ranged in age from about 18 to 40 and included males and females. In general, clerks had a sympathetic view of the child sellers and seemed to enjoy participation in the study; nearly all store clerks contacted did participate. Clerks were offered payment for their participation; most accepted.

Procedures

Part 1. Observations in Wholesale Stores.   On the basis of pilot observations and interviews, an observation form for sellers' in-store behavior was developed to provide information on the ways mathematical problems arose in the store context. Observers were trained to use the form to produce semistandard notes on sellers' in-store activities.

The form was devised on the basis of pilot observations and, in the end, it was divided into five sections: (1) *General activity.* Observers noted the sequence of one or more of the following actions of sellers related to selecting a box for purchase: Child scans shelves for boxes of candy, child asks clerk for a specific type of candy, child asks clerk for the price of a specific candy type, child asks clerk for prices of various specific types of candy, child asks clerk if any boxes are on sale, child tries to bargain with clerk, child purchases box(es). (2) *Reading numerals.* Observers noted whether child asked the clerk the price of a specific box. Each child was also asked upon his departure how he knew the price of the box he had purchased. (3) *Calculations during the purchase.* Observers noted the cash value of the child's purchase and whether the child paid with the exact currency. (4) *Retail pricing.* Observers noted whether a clerk gave any assistance to the child with retail pricing, such as a calculation of how much profit the child would make if he sold units for a particular price. (5) *Postpurchase questions.* Upon each seller's departure, he was asked his name, age, and level of schooling.

Part 2. Clerk Interview on Assistance and Clerks' Records. (1) *Assistance.* Clerks were interviewed about the kinds of assistance they offered, if any, to children who purchased boxes of candy. We recorded the types of assistance cited spontaneously by the clerk and, for each type, the clerk's example of an instance when he or she gave that type of assistance. If clerks did not mention all of the assistance types listed in Fig. 5.1, they were asked if they had ever given the unmentioned types of assistance. (2) *Clerks' records.* Nine of the 14 clerks who participated in the interviews agreed to keep records of their assistance. Clerks were given forms to record aspects of each transaction with a child seller: the child's characteristics (age, amount of schooling), the child's purchase (the cost of the child's purchase, the number of bills and the amount the child gave to the cashier, whether the child received change), and the clerk's assistance, if any. The coding form contained a place for each type of information, and all clerks were trained and rehearsed the record-keeping task with us. As a check on the adequacy of clerks' records, a member of the research team interviewed clerks about their record keeping and examined clerks' records during the data collection phase. Each participating clerk recorded transactions for 2 or 3 days.

Part 3. Clerk Interview—The Effects of Inflationary Shifts in Wholesale Candy Prices on Assistance Offered to Sellers. Within a week following their

Reading Numbers

1. Clerk tells seller price of box
2. Clerk tells seller number of units in box

Pricing

1. Clerk tells seller what he should sell box for
2. Clerk calculates the wholesale price per unit in box
3. Clerk suggests retail price in units/Cr$1000
4. Clerk tells how much profit at a specified retail price

Saving Money

1. Clerk tells seller what candy types are on sale
2. Clerk lowers the purchase price for seller
3. Clerk responds to seller's efforts to bargain
4. Clerk suggests a less expensive box
5. Clerk tells the child what candy type is selling well

FIG. 5.1.   Assistance types probed in clerk interviews.

record keeping, each of the nine clerks was interviewed individually regarding the assistance clerks provided to candy sellers and whether this assistance shifted as a function of inflationary shifts in wholesale candy prices: (1) When the price of candy goes up in your store (due to inflation), what do you think happens to the amount of assistance you give to children? (2) Do you think that there is a difference in the amount of assistance you give in the first days after prices go up compared to some weeks after prices go up? (3) What are the types of assistance you give most often just after prices go up? (4) What are the types of assistance you give most often a couple of weeks after prices go up?

RESULTS

Observations in Wholesale Stores

General Activity Analyses.   Many sellers did not engage in comparative shopping after entering a store. Our observations indicated that when sellers entered a store, they generally knew what type of box they wanted to purchase and they generally completed their purchase in that store. Of the 50 observations, 78% terminated in a purchase, and in 85% of these purchases, children asked for or about only one box type. Only 4% of the children asked whether there were special sales (a common promotional ploy for wholesale stores) and only 4% tried to bargain.

Reading Numerals.   There was suggestive evidence that many children did not (perhaps could not) read numbers in the course of their purchase. Of those children whose activity terminated with a purchase but never asked the clerk the price of a box (45%), two-thirds did not look at the shelves to find the price. From queries to the children as they departed, of the 39 sellers who terminated their shopping with a purchase, 41% said that they already knew the purchase price (from friends or a previous purchase at the same shop), 54% asked the clerk, and 5% stated that they already knew but they asked the clerk anyway. None stated that they had read the posted prices.

OBS No. 50. 7 years. The child asked for "Drops Santa Fe." The clerk gave him the box, and the child paid at the cashier. After the purchase, the child was asked if he knew the price of the candy, and if so, how he knew. He said, "I ALWAYS BUY HERE, AND YESTERDAY MY FATHER BOUGHT HERE."

OBS No. 48. 10 years. The child asked the clerk whether he had "CHICLETE NECTAR," and the clerk said he did not. The child then asked if the clerk had "DROPS SANTA FE," and the child made the purchase. After the purchase, the observer asked the child whether the child knew the price of "DROPS SANTA FE" before he purchased the box. The seller responded "YES, I BUY HERE EVERY-

DAY, AND WHEN THE PRICE RISES, THE CLERK TELLS ME [before I buy]."

In sum, many children seemed not to "shop" for candy, but rather knew from which store they wanted to purchase, what they wanted to purchase, and how much their purchase would cost.

Calculations at the Purchase. Children's purchases ranged from Cr$1000 (for two boxes of sticky candy on sale) to Cr$54000 (for multiple boxes) with a median of Cr$8500. Sixty-four percent of children who purchased candy paid with exact change, indicating that they had added up their bills (a number of these children had the cash presummed prior to entry into the store). Other children made on-the-spot computations.

Retail Pricing. The clerks helped some children price candy for retail sale. Of those children whose entry into the store ended with a purchase, 21% received some assistance from a clerk with retail pricing (e.g., how much to sell units for, the wholesale price by unit).

OBS No. 51. 14 years. The child asked whether the clerk had a box of "CHICLETE NECTAR," and the clerk indicated that he did not. As the seller turned to leave, the clerk said that he was selling "DROPS SANTA FE" and that it was selling well on the streets. The seller then asked how many should be sold for Cr$1000. The clerk said four for Cr$1000. The child asked, "HOW MUCH FOR ONE?" The clerk responded, "ONE FOR Cr$250 AND TWO FOR Cr$500."

OBS No. 47. 9 years. The child asked the price of "DROPS SANTA FE," and the clerk said Cr$7500. The child then stood thinking and apparently waiting while looking at the clerk. The clerk told the child to sell four for Cr$1000 and that would be a good profit and that all the boys are selling at that price. The child then requested two boxes.

Most children, however, did not receive specific assistance with retail pricing during our observations.

OBS No. 49. 14 years. The seller asked if the clerk had "CHOCOLATE DI-ZIOLI." The clerk said no but that if the child bought "DROPS SANTA FE" he would make a good profit. The child asked, "HOW MUCH IS A BOX?" and the clerk responded, "Cr$7500." The child asked, "HOW MANY COME IN A BOX," and the clerk responded, "50." The child thought for a few minutes and then bought the box.

Our observations within the wholesale stores points again to the way in which sellers' mathematical goals and means of accomplishing them are interwoven with properties of the candy-selling practice. We observed that sellers, on occasion, use store clerks as resources to accomplish pricing problems linked to the practice—whether it be reading prices or translations of wholesale to retail prices. Further, we find that selecting a box to purchase, sellers rely on advice of peers and do limited comparative shopping.

Clerk Interview on Assistance and Clerk's Records

The prior analyses offer some insight into sellers' activities in wholesale stores. Such observations were limited by the amount of time we had available for observation. In this section, I report findings from the interviews with clerks, findings that corroborate and supplement the prior analyses.

Interview.   The results of the clerks' interviews on types of assistance they had ever offered sellers are contained in Fig. 5.2. The majority of clerks reported spontaneously that they provided assistance in reading numerals (telling the child the prices), pricing for retail sale (telling the child how many to sell for Cr$1000), and saving money (directing the child to sale items). After further questioning about categories not mentioned spontaneously, the majority of the clerks gave an example of each category of reading numeral assistance and retail pricing assistance. These results suggest that, though assistance with retail pricing may not occur with great frequency, it is nonetheless a common form of assistance used across wholesale stores.

Clerks' Records.   Clerks recorded a total of 123 transactions (median = 10) with sellers who ranged between 5 and 15 years of age (mean = 12.4 years, sd = 2 years) and ranged in grade level between no school to eighth grade (median =

FIG. 5.2.   Percentage of store clerks ever offering assistance for specified assistance type (from interviews with clerks).

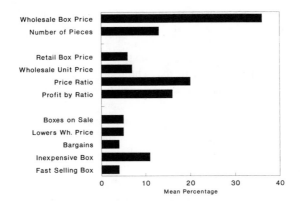

FIG. 5.3.   Mean percentage of assistance types used by clerks in transactions with sellers (from clerks' diaries).

third grade). Fig. 5.3 contains the mean proportions of the nine clerks' assistance types over all of their transactions. The figure is consistent with the results from the observational study. Clerks reported that they tended to give more help with reading prices than with retail pricing, though there is a consistent pattern of help with retail pricing. The range of assistance offered to sellers across clerks was wide; some clerks offered no assistance of any kind and some offered a good deal of assistance in each category. One contributing cause of this wide range was the variation of wholesale prices across shops. One clerk recorded no help on any of his 18 transactions. His store had been having a sale for a favored type of candy, and he reported that children came, asked for the box, paid, and left to sell for a price peers had agreed upon. Other stores had prices that had recently increased, and these increases may have contributed to more requests for assistance on the part of sellers.

To obtain some index of the kinds of computational problems sellers faced in their purchases, clerks recorded the number of bills the child gave the cashier, and the price of the seller's purchase. The purchases ranged from Cr$1500 to Cr$90000, and the median price of purchase was Cr$9000. These figures are comparable to the figures cited in the observational study. For the majority of the transactions (68%), children paid with the exact amount of currency, and the number of bills sellers used to pay ranged from 1 to 67 with a median of 5 bills (mean = 6.9, sd = 9.7).

In summary, the observational records of clerks corroborates and amplifies the observational study of the prior section. In their transactions with sellers, we not only see the principal artifacts and conventions interwoven with the mathematical goals, but the interactions themselves become important resources for sellers in accomplishing the Purchase Phase and neighboring phases of the practice.

The Effects of Inflationary Shifts in Wholesale Candy
Prices on Assistance Clerks Offered to Sellers

Fig. 5.4 contains clerks' judgments about shifts in amount of assistance as a function of inflationary changes in the wholesale prices of boxes. Clerks' responses to each of the questions were assigned to one of three categories. *More* assistance included those answers in which a clerk said that the amount of his or her assistance increased. *Mixed* assistance included those answers in which a clerk indicated that some aspects of their assistance would increase and other aspects would decrease. *Less* assistance included answers in which a clerk said that the amount of his or her assistance would decrease.

Most clerks judged that, just after prices increase, the amount of assistance they give to sellers increases (Kolmogorov–Smirnov Goodness of Fit Test, $z = 2.12$, $p < .001$) and that 2 weeks after prices increase, the amount of assistance they give decreases (Kolmogorov–Smirnov Goodness of Fit Test, $z = 2.48$, $p < .001$).

> COBS No. 1. My help goes up because they understood the previous pricing—how much they were paying and how much they should sell it for. With the new price, it's different, and they must know how to calculate it. They go to other stores looking for the same candy-type at a lower price.

Another clerk responded similarly:

> COBS No. 2. My help is more than when they are already accustomed to the price. When prices increase I tell them so they are not confused when they have to pay [the cashier]. They then want to know how much to sell it [the box] for in the streets, because they're lost with the new pricing.

Even when clerks gave "mixed" responses—responses that indicate that clerks' assistance increases for some sellers and decreases for other sellers—the de-

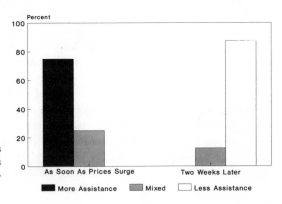

FIG. 5.4. Percentage of clerks reporting shifts in assistance as a function of surges in wholesale prices.

creased help is due to the fact that some sellers then choose to make their purchases elsewhere.

> COBS No. 3. I give less help, because when prices rise children go to other places and few ask for information. For those who want to sell the same kind of candy, I give more help because I have to tell everything again—how much to sell for Cr$1000, and the profit they will make.

Clerks' responses to the questions concerning type of help as a function of the timing of an inflationary shift revealed that the most common type of help just after an inflationary shift was a translation from wholesale to retail price (50%), whereas the most common type 2 weeks after a shift was no help at all (50%).

Goals that Emerge in the Purchase Phase and Neighboring Phases: Their Relation to Practice-linked Artifacts, Conventions, and Social Interactions

Like the Sell Phase, sellers' goals that emerge in the Purchase and neighboring phases are interwoven with the artifacts, conventions, and social interactions of the practice. These emergent goals included the determination of the wholesale price of a box of candy, arithmetical computations with currency in preparing to purchase or in making a purchase, and the translation of wholesale box prices into retail unit prices after a purchase.

Some of the principal artifacts and conventions partially constitutive of these emergent goals of the Purchase Phase were also ones noted in the Sell Phase. For instance, like the Sell Phase, in the Purchase Phase, we observed evidence that sellers formed goals of producing arithmetical computations with currency (when they determined the amount of ready cash they had or in determining change); we also observed that sellers formed goals of translating wholesale box to retail unit prices in terms of the ratio convention (in discussions with clerks). Other artifacts, however, differed from those of the Sell Phase. For instance, the wholesale stores often used the number orthography to denote candy box prices— numbers that showed values in the thousands of cruzeiros.

The principal patterns of social interactions with which the emergent goals were interwoven in the Purchase Phase were between sellers and clerks and sellers and cashiers. Like the Sell Phase's collaborative and helpful interactions between sellers and customers and sellers and their peers, seller–clerk interactions often facilitated sellers' participation in the practice. In seller–clerk interactions, we found that clerks often acted as important buffers for the mathematical problems of the practice. Their assistance allowed sellers of varying levels of competence to participate, reducing the complexity of the mathematical goals sellers had to construct and address. When sellers requested assistance in determining wholesale box prices (because of lack of ability to read the printed orthography), clerks provided it. When sellers had difficulty translating whole-sale box prices into adequate retail unit prices (or chose not to try), clerks again provided assistance of varying sorts—from telling a seller for what price the box should be sold for to telling the child the price ratio to use to make an adequate profit.

Clerks differed in the amount of help they provided, and we found some evidence that these differences were measured ones that emerged (at least in part) due to shifts in economic conditions. We found that when there were inflationary surges in wholesale box prices in stores, clerks reported that they provided greater assistance, and, when prices leveled off, they provided less assistance. Thus, sellers' mathematical goals were interwoven with their interactions with the store clerks, and the nature of these interactions were linked to broad socioeconomic processes.

While clerks' assistance is likely a critical buffer for children's participation in the practice, both reducing the complexity of mathematics and guiding children to new appropriate goals for accomplishing the mathematics of the practice, clerks themselves often were busy people and were not entirely dependable as resources. Further, it was not unknown for clerks to make mistakes. Thus, in addition to their own concerns to control their activity, there was some press for sellers themselves to accomplish the problems of the Purchase Phase without an explicit dependence on the clerks.

6

Parameter 4: Sellers' Emergent Mathematical Goals and Their Prior Understandings

In the prior chapters, we have seen that the selling practice can be described with reference to an emergent structure in which various sociocultural processes become blended in sellers' mathematical goals. What remains to be examined is the role of sellers' own sense-making activities in constructing mathematical goals. The purpose of this chapter is to address this issue.

The role of the understandings that children bring to bear on novel problems is particularly well explicated in Piaget's writings (Piaget, 1963, 1970) and receives somewhat similar treatment in related constructivist accounts (e.g., Case, 1985; Greeno, Riley, & Gelman, 1984). For Piaget, goals are an outward manifestation of children's cognitive activities, and as such, goals are both enabled and constrained by the cognitive structures children use to construe and understand problems. From the Piagetian perspective, then, goals are not contained in artifacts, conventions, nor forms of social organization. Rather, they are constructed by individuals with their prior understandings. Indeed, from the Piagetian perspective, developmental shifts in children's understandings provide opportunities for children to elaborate new and more complex goals.

We have already reviewed some evidence that sellers' understandings are implicated in ratio comparison goals, and that, with age, children may generate different goals involving ratios. Recall that younger sellers tended only to price their candy for a single ratio; in contrast, older sellers often used two or more ratios. In the present chapter, I turn to a different mathematical problem that is also central to the practice—children's translation of wholesale box prices to retail unit prices—and differences in the mathematical goals and subgoals children structure as they draw on different resources to accomplish the problem.

To show the way sellers' understandings are implicated in the mathematical goals that they structured, I use two related analyses. In the first, I analyze the character of sellers' solution strategies, showing that different strategies entail different structures of subgoals. For instance, when faced with a problem of translating a new box of candy containing 30 chocolate bars that was bought for Cr$4500 into a retail unit price, some sellers may consult an adult or another authority for a solution. Clearly, the subgoals constructed in such a solution approach differ in significant ways from those constructed in a solution in which a seller computes the wholesale price per unit and multiplies that price by a mark-up percentage. In the second analysis, I correlate the different solution strategies with a rough measure of children's prior understandings—age of sellers.

METHOD

In the course of the observational study described in Chapter 4, all but two of the 6- to 15-year-old sellers were asked during a lull in their selling to show how they priced their candy for retail sale. Sellers' answers and/or computations were coded as one of four general strategies differing in the way children used other people and conventions to structure subgoals and solutions to their price transla-tion task. The strategies consisted of (a) reliance upon other people, (b) prog-ressive count of candy based on the price ratio convention, (c) division of count based on price ratio convention, (d) computation of wholesale unit cost. These solution strategies, which, as will be explained, differ markedly in the subgoals they entail, were analyzed as a function of sellers' prior understandings—in-dexed here by sellers' age and level of schooling.

RESULTS

Fig. 6.1 contains the distribution of children's wholesale to retail pricing strat-egies. Each strategic form entails a different mathematical goal structure, and these strategic forms varied markedly as a function of age. I will consider each strategy type.

Reliance upon Others in Retail Price Setting.   Some children explained that they did not know how to price candy and that they set their price on the recommendations of others (including wholesale store clerks, parents, and older peers). The mathematical subgoals entailed in the price translation computations therefore did not emerge in these children's activities. The strong correlation between this response category and age and level of schooling ($tau\ C_{age,code} = -.83$, $p < .0001$; $tau\ C_{grade,code} = -0.68$, $p < .001$) supports the thesis that children's prior understandings influences whether they form computational

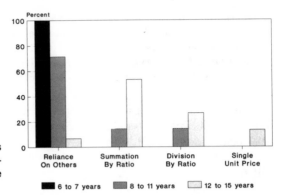

FIG. 6.1. Percentage of sellers using 1 of 4 translation strategies as a function of age group.

goals for price translations in the practice. Each of the four 6- and 7-year-olds cited advice from another person in setting prices, whereas only one of the fifteen 12- to 15-year-olds referred to the advice of another for his translation.

Summation by Price Ratio Convention.   Many of the sellers did produce computations to solve the translation problems, and the most common strategy was the use of the price ratio convention (selling x units for a particular bill denomination) to determine the potential gross yield of a box. In this strategy, a seller would select a possible retail sale price of x units per Cr$1000 and then count out the entire box by equivalent groups of x units, each group summed by an additional Cr$1000. In this strategic form, the principal arithmetical goal is to produce a progressive summation of two linked series—one a progressive addition in the value of the box with each new sale, and the other the iteration of the successive sets of units defined by the price ratio. The seller then compares the wholesale price of the box with his possible retail price to determine the possible profit (and repeats the procedure with another value for x if necessary until he was satisfied). The following example illustrates use of this procedure.

OBS No. 10. 14 years. 30-unit box paid Cr$8000. (How did you decide on your prices?) "IT DEPENDS ON THE PERSON I'M SELLING TO. IF SOMEBODY DOESN'T WANT TWO FOR Cr$1000. THEN I MAKE IT THREE FOR Cr$1000." (If you sell the chocolates at two for Cr$1000, how much will the box sell for?) THE BOX WILL SELL FOR Cr$15000." (And how much profit will you make?) Cr$7000. (How do you know this?) "LOOK, THERE ARE 30 CHOCO-LATES IN THE FULL BOX [the boy empties the chocolates from the box and then places them carefully back in, two at a time; as he places each group he counts, "ONE THOUSAND, TWO THOUSAND, THREE THOUSAND, etc." until he counts the last set of two as, "FIFTEEN THOUSAND"] "SEE, THIS IS THE WAY!" (And if you sell the chocolates at three for Cr$1000, how much will you profit?) "I'LL SELL THE BOX FOR Cr$10000 AND I'LL PROFIT Cr$2000."

(And how do you know that the full box will be sold for Cr$10000?) [The boy again took all the 30 chocolates out of the box, repeating the procedure counting by groups of three, ending with a total of Cr$10000.] "SINCE I"LL SELL THE CHOCOLATE AT TWO FOR Cr$1000 OR THREE FOR Cr$1000, I'LL ONLY KNOW HOW MUCH I'M GOING TO PROFIT AT THE END."

While this seller does not cite a specific norm for determining an adequate profit, a number of sellers did cite a convention which they referred to as "meio-pelo-meio" or "half-half." The convention prescribes that the gross sales of a box should double the wholesale price, half for the purchase of the next box and half for profit.

The correlation between use of the price ratio strategy and age (*tau* $C_{age,code}$ = .36, $p < .05$) supports the argument that sellers' prior knowledge is implicated in the computational goals that they generate. This strategic form was the most common strategy of the 12- to 15-year-olds (53% of whom used this strategy).

Computation of Retail Price by Division Based on Units per Cr$1000. A third, more abbreviated, approach to retail pricing was also based upon the use of a sale price of x units per Cr$1000. In this procedure, a seller divided the total number of units in a full box by the value of x in a possible price of x units per Cr$1000 and then added the suffix "thousands." Thus, a box of 30 units sold at three per Cr$1000 would gross $(30/3) \times 1000 = $ Cr$10000. The procedure thus eliminates the successive count of the candy by the price ratio. While the procedure requires less time, the mathematical procedure is a less transparent one.

OBS No. 08. 14 years. 50-unit box paid Cr$6000. This 14-year-old seller was in the fifth grade. (How much will you sell the full box of Zorro for?) "FOR Cr$10000." (How do you know you'll sell the full box for Cr$10000?) "I COUNT HOW MANY UNITS THERE ARE IN THE BOX, WHICH IS 50, AND I DIVIDED IT BY FIVE BECAUSE I'LL SELL FIVE FOR Cr$1000, THEN IT GIVES Cr$10000." (How much will you profit?) "I'LL PROFIT Cr$4000." (Do you think this is a good profit?) "IT'S NOT SO GOOD, BUT I CAN EARN A LITTLE." (Why don't you sell some other way to earn more?) "BECAUSE EVERYBODY SELLS LIKE THIS. IF I SELL FOR MORE THE PEOPLE WON'T BUY THE ZORROS. SO, WE HAVE TO SELL ALL THE SAME." (Who taught you to sell like this?) "THE WAY TO SELL I LEARNED BY MYSELF. IN THE BEGINNING I WAS SHY, SO I SOLD LITTLE, BUT NOW I'M SELLING WELL." (And, who taught you how to calculate it all the way you do: you take the units and divide them by what you will sell?) AH!! THAT I LEARNED IN SCHOOL!"

By the sellers' own report, this pricing approach was linked to arithmetical knowledge gained in school. In addition, the correlation between this strategy and age level was also significant (*tau* $C_{age,code}$ = .31, $p < .05$).

Computation Based on Wholesale Single Unit Price.   Perhaps the strategy most closely related to algorithms taught in school contexts is one in which the wholesale value of a single unit of candy is determined and then a mark-up of that absolute worth of the unit is made in the determination of a retail price: [wholesale price / number of units in box] × [100% + % markup] = retail price per unit. Only two children used such an approach that approximated this one; both of these sellers had completed the fifth grade and were in the 12- to 15-year-old age group. An example follows.

> OBS No. 07. 13 years. 50-unit box paid Cr\$7000. Like the prior seller, this seller was also in the fifth grade. The seller was offering his candy to customers at four bars for Cr\$1000 (see Fig. 6.2). (How much are you going to sell the full box for?) "I'M GOING TO SELL THE BOX FOR Cr\$12500." (How much will you profit after selling the full box?) "I'LL MAKE Cr\$5500." (The seller was asked to explain his calculations. He used a paper and pencil and performed a variety of calculations by standard algorithmic methods (see Fig. 6.2*a–f*): First, to determine (or confirm) the wholesale cost of each unit of his candy bars, he multiplied, using the standard school algorithm 50 bars (the number in the full box) by Cr\$120 (a value he believes is the wholesale price per unit he paid [Fig. 6a]). His computation was correct (Cr\$6000), but he explains: THAT'S WRONG (referring to the fact that he wanted to obtain a product of Cr\$7000—his wholesale purchase price). He then proceeded to again use the standard algorithm, multiplying 50 (candy bars in the box) by Cr\$140 (a revised value he believes is the wholesale price per unit he paid for the box) and he obtains Cr\$7000 (Fig. 6b). He appears pleased by his result and explains: "EACH CANDY COSTS ME Cr\$140 (Fig. 6c). SINCE I SELL ONE CANDY FOR Cr\$250, I PROFIT Cr\$110 PER UNIT (Cr\$250 − Cr\$140 = Cr\$110; Fig. 6d). IF I SELL FOUR FOR Cr\$1000, I PROFIT Cr\$440 (Fig. 6e)." In order to calculate his net profit, the boy then multiplied Cr\$440 (his profit after each time he sold 4 bars) by 12 (the number of potential sales in his 50-bar box using the selling convention 4 bars for Cr\$1000), using the standard algorithmic approach, and achieved the appropriate product, Cr\$5280 (Fig. 6f). The interviewer then asked Luciano about the remaining two bars in his box that would be left after 12 sales. The last 2, he responded, "I'LL SELL FOR Cr\$500 OR LESS."

Unlike the prior sellers, this seller uses a derived value—the wholesale unit price—as a critical step in his calculation. He achieves this value through the use of algorithmic procedures, procedures that are linked to schooling.

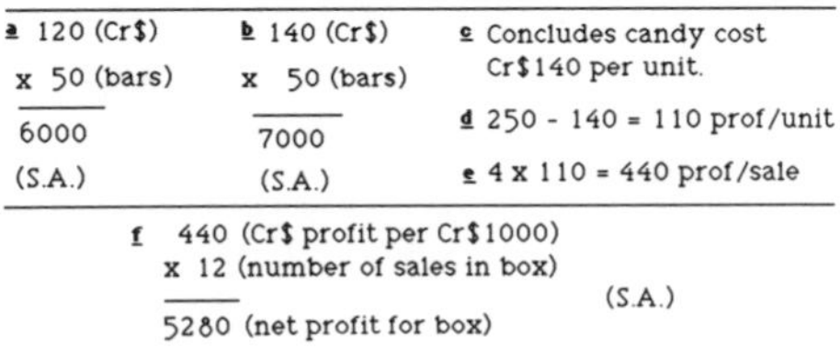

a 120 (Cr\$)	b 140 (Cr\$)	c Concludes candy cost
x 50 (bars)	x 50 (bars)	Cr\$140 per unit.
6000	7000	d 250 - 140 = 110 prof/unit
(S.A.)	(S.A.)	e 4 x 110 = 440 prof/sale

f   440 (Cr\$ profit per Cr\$1000)
x 12 (number of sales in box)   (S.A.)
5280 (net profit for box)

FIG. 6.2. Schematic of a 5th-grade seller's solution to his price translation problem.

SELLERS' PRIOR UNDERSTANDINGS AND
EMERGENT MATHEMATICAL GOALS

In Chapters 3 through 5, I documented the kinds of mathematical goals that emerge over the course of the practice and the way specific sociocultural processes are interwoven in children's goal-directed activities. In the present chapter, we come back to points that are at the heart of constructivist formulations of cognitive development: Children's goals are rooted in their understandings, understandings which both constrain and enable their goal-directed efforts. The analysis of sellers' price strategies shows that while all sellers have as resources access to other people as well as practice-linked artifacts and conventions, sellers deploy these various resources in different ways in constructing goals and subgoals.

7 Emergent Mathematical Goals of the Practice: A Summary and Discussion of the First Analytic Component Applied to the Candy-selling Practice

The prior four chapters show the way sellers' mathematical goals are interwoven with the four parameters of the first analytic component: the structure of the practice (parameter 1), principal artifacts and conventions of the practice that become transformed into practice-linked sign forms (parameter 2), patterns of social interactions (parameter 3), and sellers' prior understandings (parameter 4). In this chapter, I highlight the principal mathematical goals and their intrinsic links to the four parameters.

Table 7.1 contains, in outline form, a description of three of the four parameters of the practice and the principal goals that often emerge in this four-phase structure. The omitted parameter is sellers' prior understandings, a dimension that is interwoven with each of the other parameters and one that I include in the subsequent discussion.

We have seen in Chapter 3 that the structure of candy sellers' practice is organized principally with respect to economic motives and consists of four phases shown in the table and previously illustrated in Fig. 4.1. In the Sell Phase, sellers try to sell their boxes quickly while making a profit; in the Prepare-to-Purchase Phase, sellers try to identify a fast-selling box for purchase; in the Purchase Phase, sellers accomplish their purchase; and, in the Prepare-to-Sell Phase, sellers mark up their wholesale candy box into a retail price for units. While the motives for participation are principally economic, throughout the practice sellers generate mathematical goals and subgoals to achieve their economic ends. To understand the character of these mathematical goals required a further inquiry into their intrinsic relations with artifacts and conventions, social interactions, and sellers' prior understandings.

Chapters 4 and 5 were concerned with the way the artifacts (like currency),

TABLE 7.1

Interrelations between 3 of the 4 Parameters of Component 1
and Sellers' Principal Emergent Mathematical Goals

3 of 4 Parameters			
Structure of Practice	Artifacts and Conventions	Social Interactions	Emergent Mathematical Goals
SELL PHASE. Principal objective: To sell quickly and make a profit	Inflating currency; issue of new currency units; price ratio use	With peers: collaborative and competitive pricing. With customers: sales transactions, bargaining	Identification/comparison of currency units in transactions with customers; arithmetical operations with currency; ratio comparisons; reconsideration of wholesale to retail mark-up in terms of price ratio convention
PREPARE-TO-PURCHASE PHASE. Principal objective: To identify a fast-selling box for purchase	Number orthography indicating box prices in wholesale stores: currency to sum in determining available cash	With peers: sellers advise one another about best buys. With clerks: clerks tell box prices, clerk indicates sale items	Identifying numerical prices of wholesale boxes; comparing cost and value of changing prices of wholesale boxes; arithmetical operations on currency
PURCHASE PHASE. Principal objective: To purchase a box	Currency to purchase, number orthography indicating box prices on box and on bill of sale	With clerks: Clerks aid computations. Wih cashiers: cashiers require payment, read values on bills of sale	Determining currency values; arithmetical operations with currency; determining orthographic values on bill of sale
PREPARE-TO-SELL PHASE. Principal objective: Determine retail price for units	Box of candy; price ratio convention, half-half convention	With clerks and relatives: clerks and relatives provide information about retail pricing. With peers: Price setting interactions	Mark-up of wholesale box to retail unit prices in terms of price ratio convention and half-half convention; arithmetical operations entailed in price translations

Note: The fourth parameter and its relation to the three parameters in the table and to sellers' emergent goals is discussed in the text.

conventions (like the price ratio), and patterns of social interaction (like those between seller and seller or seller and customer) were interwoven with the organization of sellers' mathematical goals across the four-phase structure. These sociocultural constructions are rooted in the social history of the practice, and the forms they currently assume contributed to the character of sellers' goals in significant ways.

We have seen that in the Sell and the Purchase phases, the inflating currency values leads sellers to address problems of number representation and calculation involving large values in everyday transactions. Indeed, the numerical values typically used by sellers are in the triple- to quintuple-digit range. In the Sell Phase, sellers had to identify these large bill values in exchanges with customers, and in the Purchase Phase, sellers had to identify values in interactions with clerks and cashiers. Further, in the Prepare-to-Purchase Phase, sellers produced arithmetical computations with these currency values when they determined how much available cash they had to spend for a box, and in the Purchase and Sell phases they, on occasion, produced computations with clerks, cashiers, and customers. Further, the government's issue of new currency units (and its subsequent shift to the cruzado system) has meant that sellers must repeatedly shift their basic units of computation, shifts that create new computational challenges.

Chapters 4 and 5 also revealed that the price ratio selling convention (selling multiple units of candy for a single bill denomination) was linked to the emergence of additional mathematical goals. The use of the convention contributed to sellers' ratio comparison goals of the Sell Phase when a child either considered selling his units for different prices and weighed the advantages of different pricing ratios (e.g., two for Cr$500 vs. five for Cr$1000) or in various practice-linked social interactions such as peer price setting, crab confrontations, or customer bargaining. The use of the price ratio convention also contributed to sellers' goals of translating wholesale box prices into retail unit prices in terms of this convention.

Chapters 4 and 5 also revealed that the various sociocultural artifacts, conventions, and patterns of social interactions interact with one another in complex ways in sellers' activities, interactions that further modify the character of sellers' mathematical goals. For instance, sellers' ratio comparison goals shift as a function of the decreasing buying power of currency. During the study, Cr$1000 was the chief denomination for pricing and entered into all price ratios; however, the history of the practice is such that there was an evolution of this base denomination with the inflating economy—during prior periods, the base ratio figures were Cr$500, Cr$200, and Cr$100. In wholesale–retail translation goals, the frequent and irregular surges in the wholesale prices due to inflation create new problems for wholesale–retail price translation.

While sometimes conventions, artifacts, and social interactions may complicate the mathematical goals in seller–customer transactions, as when ratio pricing leads to ratio comparison goals or when customer–seller interactions result in bargaining, other times interaction patterns lead to simplification of goals. For instance, sometimes sellers used other people as resources to modify the mathematical subgoals, and such interactions were particularly evident between sellers and wholesale store clerks in the Purchase Phase when clerks modulated their assistance to sellers as a function of wholesale price surges. Additional forms of helping interactions were documented in the Prepare-to-Purchase Phase when sellers relied on peers and adults for price referrals as well as in the Prepare-to-Sell Phase when sellers may collaborate and obtain help in price setting interactions from other peers or rely on relatives for retail prices.

The parameter of prior understandings was addressed directly in Chapter 6 though an analysis of the goals and subgoals that emerged in sellers' price translation strategies as a function of age and schooling experience; however, throughout Chapters 4 and 5 as well I noted instances of the way that sellers' prior understandings, as indexed by age and prior schooling, interacted with sellers' emergent mathematical goals. In sales transactions, younger children typically were the ones that only used a single pricing ratio, simplifying the number representation/comparison and arithmetical problems and reducing the possibility for the emergence of ratio comparison problems. There was also evidence that the younger children aroused more customer sympathy as evidenced by their greater sales as well as informal reports by other sellers and informants. Through this sympathy, younger sellers were more likely to find customers' offering assistance in facilitating transactions when there were problems in making change. Finally, as the analyses of Chapter 6 revealed, the young sellers were not engaged with problems involving the translation of wholesale box prices into retail unit prices. Rather, this translation was accomplished for them by an older relative. Sellers' levels of schooling also were associated with the way they apprehended the problem of translating wholesale box prices into retail unit prices. Sellers with more schooling demonstrated strategies that were more closely linked to algorithms children would learn in school whereas sellers with less schooling generally relied on the less formal strategies linked to the selling convention.

In sum, the mathematical problems identified in the practice—though shifting in character for sellers of different age levels and levels of schooling—include the representation and comparison of large numerical values (generally not in terms of the standard number orthography), additions and subtractions of large numerical values with currency, ratio comparisons of retail unit prices, and translations of wholesale box prices into retail unit prices (adjustments for inflation in this pricing). Part II will deal, in some depth, with the mathematical forms and functions sellers' specialize to accomplish their emergent goals and form—function shifts in sellers' developing mathematical understandings.

III

COMPONENT 2: FORM–FUNCTION SHIFTS IN CANDY SELLERS' MATHEMATICS

In Part III, my concern is to extend the second analytic component—form–function shifts in cognitive development—to an analysis of candy sellers' mathematics. Guided by an analysis of the emergent mathematical goals of the practice presented in Part II, I focus now on the kinds of cognitive forms sellers use to accomplish mathematical problems and the cognitive functions these forms serve.

The sellers targeted for study had little or no formal schooling, and the analyses of their solutions are guided by the assumption that unschooled sellers would use representational and computational forms for number that differ from the orthography-based computational forms taught in school. On the basis of the ethnographic studies reported in Part II, I expected to find that sellers would have low levels of competence in reading numerical values expressed in the standard orthography. Indeed, in observations in the wholesale stores, we did not observe any sellers reading prices, and wholesale store clerks noted that reading prices was one of the principal forms of assistance they offered to the sellers. Further, we found little evidence of sellers using paper-and-pencil calculations during the course of their practice.

Instead of representing number with standard orthographic symbols in their calculations, I considered it a strong possibility that sellers would make use of currency to serve a representational function. Further, in solving such problems involving arithmetic with large values, ratio comparisons, and translations from wholesale to retail prices, I expected that sellers would not rely on standard algorithmic forms taught in school, but would generate procedures for computation linked both to currency and to the practice-linked conventions described in the preceding chapters.

Preliminary evidence that the currency system is a principal form in sellers' mathematics was reported in the observational studies in Part II: Children did not make use of paper-and-pencil computations in the conduct of their practice despite the large numerical values on which they performed their computations, and children typically circumvented reading numerals in their wholesale purchases. Evidence that children generated convention- and currency-linked computational strategies was reported in Chapter 6. To solve problems involving the translation of wholesale to retail prices in the Prepare-to-Sell Phase; many sellers made use of the convention of selling candy for a set of units, x, for Cr$1000, incrementing their count of x by Cr$1000 until they arrived at the price they would gross for the box.

To probe the nature and development of candy sellers' mathematics, two sets of contrasts are reported. In Chapter 8, I compare candy sellers' mathematics with that of their nonselling peers. In Chapter 9, I compare the mathematics of child candy sellers at three different age levels.

8 The Influence of Practice Participation on Sellers' Mathematics[5]

The purpose of this chapter is to determine whether participation in the candy-selling practice leads children to distinct forms of mathematical representation and problem solving. To this end, tasks were administered involving four kinds of practice-linked mathematical problems. Problems included number representation of large values, arithmetic problem solving with large values, ratio comparisons, and translations of wholesale-box to retail-unit prices.

To analyze whether sellers utilize distinct forms for specialized mathematical functions in addressing these problems, sellers' solution strategies were contrasted with those of children with less experience in addressing problems that arise in the selling practice—an urban and a rural group of nonsellers. Urban nonsellers are engaged as buyers with generally the same commercial environment as the sellers, but not as venders. Rural nonsellers use the same currency system, but their level of exposure to commercial transactions is considerably more limited than their urban counterparts. Thus, contrasts across groups should reveal the distinctiveness of children's mathematics linked to participation in the candy-selling practice. In particular, sellers should display more adequate understandings than nonsellers in solving problems more uniquely linked to the candy-selling practice, problems like arithmetic with large values, ratio comparisons, and wholesale-to-retail translations. Urban nonsellers in contrast to rural nonsellers, insofar as they participate in the same economic community as the candy sellers, should demonstrate more sophisticated levels of understanding than the rural nonsellers.

---

[5]Some of the data presented in this chapter were previously published in Saxe (1988).

OVERVIEW OF METHODS

The Population of Children in the Study

The recruitment of children differed by population group. The candy sellers were recruited by Brazilian university students in the streets as the sellers sold candy, tangerines, or puffed wheat. Children who were vending in the streets were administered a preliminary screening interview to determine their candy-selling experience, an interview procedure described in Appendix A. The urban non-sellers included in the study were recruited from first- and second-grade classes at public schools in Recife, the same or similar schools that sellers attended, had attended, or would have attended if they had enrolled in school. Potential subjects were administered an interview to determine whether they had any vending experience, and only children who did not were selected to participate in the study. Like the sellers, all urban nonsellers were between 10 and 12 years of age. Unlike the sellers, all urban nonsellers were enrolled in school during the time the study was conducted. The rural nonsellers were recruited in small, remote towns about 100 miles from Recife, which were the sites for a separate study on straw weaving (Saxe, 1989; Saxe & Gearhart, in press).[6] Like the urban children, the rural children were between 10 and 12 years of age and were only included if they had not progressed beyond the second grade.

The complete sample for the present study included 23 sellers (mean age = 10.8 years, sd = 1.0 year; mean grade level = 1.6, sd = 0.6), 20 urban nonsellers (mean age = 10.8 years, sd = 0.8 years; mean grade level = 1.8, sd = 0.4), and 17 rural nonsellers (mean age = 10.6 years, sd = 0.8 years; mean grade level = 1.3, sd = 0.5).

Overview of Procedures

In the following sections, only an abbreviated description of the procedures is presented—a complete description of task procedures is contained in Appendix C. Even though children did not sell candy in the rural community, a couple of children in the community did occasionally sell popsicles, and the rural children were therefore familiar with the idea of child venders. (Rural sellers were not included in this sample.) Many rural children also made occasional trips to towns, where they had an opportunity to observe street venders. Thus, despite the relative lack of experience with vending practices, rural children had some exposure to such practices with which to interpret our description of selling candy.

In the administration of the procedures to the nonsellers, children were presented with a description of the selling practice during the initial phase of the

---

[6]Contrasts between same-aged candy sellers and rural straw weavers on topological spatial tasks revealed that weavers had generated more complex topological understandings than the sellers.

interview and were asked to pretend that they were a candy seller during the interview. To facilitate further children's understanding of the tasks, the non-sellers were told the function of each task in the selling practice. Because there was less cash in the economic environment of the rural nonsellers, it was felt that the presentation of large amounts of currency would jeopardize rapport with children. To deal with this issue, the rural nonsellers were not administered certain task conditions that contained unusually large sums of currency; these conditions will be noted in the appropriate sections.

REPRESENTATION OF LARGE NUMERICAL VALUES

There are two ways that sellers could represent large numerical values in the practice. One way is though our *standard orthography*. As a part of practice participation, sellers must produce arithmetical computations with large values, and the standard number orthography would be useful in solving such problems. Further, the prices of candy are often posted in the wholesale stores, and the ability to read these values would be useful to sellers. An *alternative system* to represent large numbers in problem solving would be to use currency units (bills and coins) as tokens for number by identifying the numerical values of currency on the basis of the figurative characteristics of currency units (e.g., colors, pictures) and manipulating these units in problem solving. Utilizing currency in this way, coupled with the assistance of store clerks and peers to help read prices, could also serve as a representational vehicle in solving practice-linked problems.

Procedures

To determine children's ability to use the standard orthography, we asked children to *read* and to *compare* 10 pairs of multidigit numerical values, values that were within the range that they addressed in their practice (e.g., 2,000 vs. 1,500; 3,456 vs. 4,000). For five pairs of numbers, children were told that they were comparing the amount of candy in large bags and, in the other five, they were told they were comparing cruzeiros.

To determine children's ability to use currency as an alternative system for large number representation, I constructed three types of additional tasks. In *Bill Identification Tasks*, sellers were asked to identify the values of 12 bills or printed bill values in each of three conditions (see Fig. 8.1): (a) standard bills, (b) bills with their numbers occluded by tape, (c) photocopies of cutouts of the numbers. In the *Currency Comparison Tasks,* sellers were presented with 14 pairs of currency units and asked to tell which was the larger of the two (e.g., bills of Cr$200 vs. Cr$1000) as well as the multiplicative relations between units—how many of the smaller units were equivalent to the larger unit (five Cr$200 are equivalent to 1 Cr$1000). In *Exchange Tasks*, children were present-

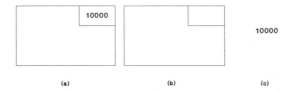

FIG. 8.1. Schematic of the 3 conditions used in the bill identification task: (a) standard bills, (b) bills with numbers occluded, and (c) photocopy of numbers from bills.

ed with a large bill denomination (e.g., Cr$5000) and told that a customer wanted to purchase goods that were worth a particular value (e.g., Cr$2300). To document children's knowledge of currency equivalence relations in problem solving, children were told that they could request change for their large bill from the interviewer who had a bank of smaller bills, but that they had to specify the bills needed for a fair exchange.

RESULTS

Children's Knowledge of the Standard Orthography

Children's recognitions of each of the 20 numbers were coded with respect to one of three categories: *correct recognition, partitioning errors* (partitioning number strings into smaller segments—e.g., 129 read as 1, 2, and 9), and *misplaced zero errors* (e.g., 129 read as 1,029). Children who produce partitioning errors do not use the conventional rules for incorporating a series of digits into a single numerical expression. Misplaced zero errors suggest a different problem: Children attempt to integrate digits into a single numerical expression yet do not fully understand place value rules. With this scheme, it was possible to code 67% of all responses. The predominant response types uncoded were those in which the child stated that he did not know the answer or responded with a number that had no apparent relation to the targeted number.

   The number of responses of each of the three response types was summed for each child, and the mean percentage of each response type as a function of population group (sellers, urban nonsellers, rural nonsellers) is presented in Fig. 8.2. The figure shows that none of the population groups displayed a high level of competence reading numbers. Indeed, the urban nonsellers, the group that achieved the highest level of performance, achieved only 50% mean correct. A 3 (population group) $\times$ 2 (problem condition, repeated) ANOVA on the number of correct identifications revealed an effect for population group ($F(2,59) = 13.43$, $p < .0001$). Duncan's Multiple Range Test revealed that both the urban nonsellers and the sellers achieved more correct responses than the rural nonsellers and that there was not a statistically significant difference between the sellers and urban nonsellers.

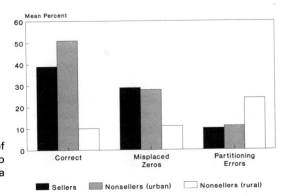

FIG. 8.2. Mean percentage of each of 3 response types to reading number problems as a function of population group.

Two additional 3 (population group) × 2 (problem condition, repeated) ANOVAs were performed on the number of misplaced zero and partitioning errors. The analyses revealed effects only for population group in each analysis: number of partitioning errors, $F(2,59) = 9.17$, $p < .005$, and number of misplaced zero errors, $(F(2,59) = 6.33$, $p < .005)$. Duncan Multiple Range tests revealed that the rural nonsellers committed the less sophisticated error type—partitioning errors—to a greater extent than both the sellers and urban nonsellers, and that the sellers and urban nonsellers committed the more sophisticated error type—place value errors—to a greater extent than the rural nonsellers.

Children's ability to produce ordinal comparisons between the numbers was analyzed by assigning one point for each of the 10 comparisons. Fig. 8.3 contains the percentage of correct comparisons as a function of population group. Though the sellers and nonsellers achieved a large proportion of comparisons correct, the likelihood of achieving any single item correct on these tasks was 50% (unlike the number identification problems). A oneway ANOVA using total number of comparisons correct as a dependent variable revealed a main effect for population group, $F(2,59) = 16,61$, $p < .001$, and Duncan comparisons re-

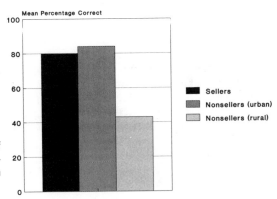

FIG. 8.3. Mean percentage of correct responses to orthography comparison problems as a function of population group.

vealed that both the urban sellers and nonsellers achieved higher scores than the rural nonsellers.

In sum, as expected, children's knowledge of the standard orthography is quite limited. All groups performed poorly at identifying values, and while the urban children achieved significantly better scores in comparing numerical values than the rural group, by itself the utility of such an ability for producing everyday calculations and price evaluations is quite limited. An unexpected finding in identifying numerical values was the superior performance of the urban nonsellers to the sellers (although this difference was not statistically significant). In retrospect, it is likely that the source of the trend is a greater recency of the nonsellers' school experience. As previously noted, all of the nonsellers were enrolled in first or second grade at the time of the study. In contrast, many of the sellers were not currently enrolled in school (or were never enrolled).

Currency as an Alternate Representational System for Large Numerical Values

Identifying Numerical Values on the Basis of the Orthography vs. Figurative Characteristics of Bills: Bill Identification Task.   The protocols herein provide an indication of the character of children's efforts on the currency identification tasks. As is evident, the children have well-developed abilities to identity currency with or without the identifying numbers visible, but poor ability to identify the same numerical values on the basis of the standard orthography.

S No. 28. 10-year-old seller, no school. S No. 28 is presented with the conditions in the following order: Standard Bills, Numbers Occluded, Numbers Only. On the Standard Bills and Numbers Occluded, S No. 28 identifies each of the 24 presented bills with its correct numerical value. In contrast, on the Numbers Only condition, he identifies only 2 of the 12 numbers correctly, and these correct identifications appear to be by chance. He identifies the presentations of "100," "1,000," "5,000" and "10,000" all as five thousand, and he identifies the presentations of "200" and "500" as ten thousand.

S No. 21. 11-year-old seller, first grade. S No. 21 is presented with the conditions in the following order: Numbers Occluded, Numbers Only, Standard Bills. On the Numbers Occluded and Standard Bills conditions. S No. 21 identifies each of the 24 presented bills correctly. However, on the Numbers Only condition, he identifies only 3 of the 12 numbers correctly (the 2 "200" presentations and 1 of the 100 presentations). He identifies 1 presentation of "100" as ten, the two "500" presentations as five, the two 1,000 presentations as ten, the two 5,000 presentations as five, and the two "10,000" presentations as ten.

S No. 32. 11-year-old seller, second grade. S No. 32 is presented with the conditions in the following order: Numbers Only, Standard Bills, Numbers Occluded. S

No. 32's performance on the Standard Bills condition is apparently influenced by the order in which the conditions were presented—the Numbers Only condition was presented first, on which he performed poorly, identifying only 1 of 12 correctly. When then presented with the Standard Bills condition, he tried to read the numbers and did not identify a single bill correctly. Finally, however, when presented with the Numbers Occluded condition—the condition in which he could not attempt to read the numbers—he identified all 12 bills correctly.

These cases provide some clear evidence that some of the children sampled have difficulty relying on the numbers printed on the bills yet are still able to identify the bills without using the standard orthography. S No. 32's protocol is perhaps the most striking in this regard. Not only does he achieve all correct identifications in the Number Occluded condition, but in the Standard Bill condition, he appears to be confused when focusing on the numbers. S No. 28 and S No. 21 also show that their ability to identify the numerical values of bills outstrips their ability to identify these same values with the number orthography—indeed, both identify all bills correctly in the occluded and standard conditions, whereas they only identify a small fraction of the same values when they are represented in orthographic form.

To analyze children's performance on the currency conditions as a function of their selling experience, the percentage correct of each child's identifications of the 12 values in each condition was determined. Fig. 8.4 contains the percentage of correct identifications as a function of condition (Standard Bills, Numbers Occluded, and Numbers Only) and population group. A 3 (condition, repeated) × 3 (population group) ANOVA revealed main effects for both condition ($F(2,120) = 80.83$, $p < .0001$) and population group ($F(2,60) = 9.37$, $p < .0005$) and a group by condition interaction ($F(4,120) = 9.72$, $p < .0001$). Duncan Multiple Range tests showed that for the Standard Bills condition, there were no group differences (virtually all children from each group achieved all correct); however, for the Numbers Occluded condition, sellers and urban non-

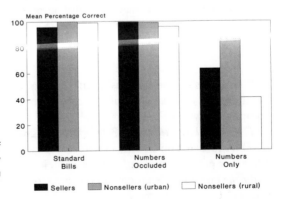

FIG. 8.4. Mean percentage of correct responses to currency identification problems as a function of population group.

sellers correctly identified more bills than the rural nonsellers, and for the Numbers Only condition, urban nonsellers correctly identified more number values than sellers, and sellers identified more than rural nonsellers. Duncan Multiple Range Tests also revealed a consistent pattern in performance across conditions for each group: There were no groups that differed in their performance on the Standard Bill and Numbers Occluded conditions. However, all groups performed better on the Standard Bills and Numbers Occluded conditions as contrasted with the Numbers Only condition. These results then do indicate that children across population groups had developed an ability to use bills themselves as signifies for large values and did not need to rely on their imperfect knowledge of the standard number orthography to read these values.

Children's Knowledge of Numerical Relations Between Currency Values. The prior analyses of children's ability to identify the numerical values of currency do not indicate whether children treat these values as terms in a numerically ordered system. In the Currency Comparison tasks, two aspects of children's ability to identify numerical relations between currency values were analyzed: knowledge of ordinal relations between currency units and knowledge of multiplicative relations between currency units. In each case, children received one point for each correct ordinal or multiplicative comparison for each problem within the Cr$1 to Cr$100 range (seven ordinal and seven multiplicative comparisons) and the Cr$100 to Cr$10000 range (seven ordinal and seven multiplicative comparisons).

The following protocol illustrates a child's ability to identify ordinal and multiplicative relations between currency denominations as well as this child's greater proficiency in dealing with the larger values.

S No. 22. 10-year-old seller, first grade. S No. 22 is presented with the currency comparisons in a haphazard order. For the comparisons that involve Cr$100 up through Cr$10000, he identifies each of the seven ordinal relations and each of the seven multiplicative relations correctly; in contrast, he identifies only a few of the relations between currency units that involve comparisons between Cr$1 and Cr$100. For instance, he states that 20 Cr$5 coins are equivalent to 1 Cr$10 coin, that 50 Cr$10 coins are equivalent to one Cr$50 coin, that 2 Cr$1 coins are equivalent to 1 Cr$20 coin, that 4 Cr$10 coins are equivalent to 1 Cr$20 coin.

S No. 22's performance is a fairly typical one. The mean percentage correct for children's ordinal and multiplicative comparisons as a function of population group is shown in Fig. 8.5.

1. Ordinal relations. A 3 (population group) × 2 (value range, repeated) ANOVA revealed no significant effects for either value range (1 to 100 vs. 100 to 10000) or population group. The large majority of all groups achieved at least six of the seven comparisons correct on comparisons involving values of Cr$100 and less and Cr$100 and more.

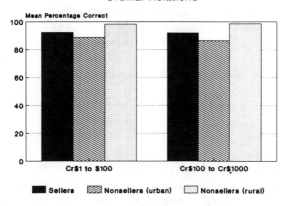

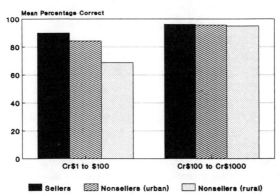

FIG. 8.5. Mean percentage of correct responses to currency comparison problems as a function of value size and population group.

2. Multiplicative relations. A 3 (population group) × 2 (currency value, repeated) ANOVA revealed a significant interaction between currency value and population group ($F(2,57) = 3.88$, $p < .05$), and a main effect for currency value condition ($F(1,57) = 24.42$, $p < .001$). Duncan comparisons revealed that both the urban and rural nonsellers achieved more correct answers to the problems involving the larger as contrasted to the smaller values, whereas there was no difference in the sellers' performance across the problems. Duncan comparisons also revealed that the sellers achieved more correct identifications on the smaller value problems than the rural nonsellers.

Children's Facility with the Denominational Structure of the Currency System: Making Change.   In order to determine children's flexible use of the currency system in problem solving, children were presented with two problems that required them to exchange a large denomination for smaller currency denominations so that the appropriate change could be returned to a customer. The problems differed in the size of the customer's currency to be exchanged (Cr$5000 or Cr$10000) and the price of the merchandise requested by the customer (Cr$2300 or Cr$6630). In each task, the interviewer displayed in clear view a bank of bills and coins of all denominations ranging from Cr$1 to Cr$10,000. The child had to specify the change he wanted for the bill, and the child was told that the interviewer would only make the transactions if the child specified a fair exchange. The child could make up to six requests for change, and after the sixth request, the task was terminated.

The goal of the analysis was to determine group differences in children's facility in manipulating the denominational structure of the currency system in making change. Children whose pattern of exchanges led them to the appropriate set of denominations to produce change prior to their sixth exchange were coded as "successful" and those who did not were coded as "unsuccessful." The number of requests during the task was also recorded for successful children.

The 12-year-old seller's performance excerpted herein provides some indication of sellers' facility with the structure of the currency system evident on our exchange tasks. The seller accomplishes the Cr$5000 problem with a single request and the Cr$10000 problem with two requests.

S No. 6075. 12-year-old seller, second grade. S No. 6075, on his first attempt for problem 1, offers the following accurate exchange for the Cr$5000 bill: 4 × Cr$1000, 1 Cr$500, 2 Cr$200, and 1 Cr$100. From this exchange, he takes 1 × Cr$100, 1 Cr$200, and 2 Cr$1000 bills and gives the appropriate remainder to the customer. For the Cr$10000 problem, the child requests the following bills on his first exchange for the Cr$10000: 1 × Cr$5000, 4 Cr$1000, 2 Cr$500, 2 Cr$200, and 1 Cr$100. He then makes a second request for 1 Cr$50 and 5 Cr$10 coins for his Cr$100 bill. The child then gives the customer the correct change.

Many children were not as proficient as S No. 6075. The nonseller described in the following case, while having demonstrated considerable knowledge of the many-to-one relations between currency units on the prior task, had some difficulty with both exchanges. Consider his difficulties in producing the appropriate denominations in problem 1.

S No. 801. 12-year-old, second grade, urban nonseller. S No. 801 requires four exchanges for a successful solution to problem 1. He first inappropriately requests 6 × Cr$500 bills, and he is told that the request cannot be made. His subsequent three requests are each for a fair exchange and are interwoven with his problem solution. For his Cr$5000 bill, he requests five bills of Cr$1000; he then attempted to give change, offering two bills of Cr$1000, finding that he did not have the proper denominations, he requested two bills of Cr$500 for a third bill of Cr$1000;

he then added one of his Cr$500 bills to his two Cr$1000 bills, and, again finding that he did not have the appropriate denominations, he requested five Cr$100 bills for one of his additional Cr$500 bills. He then collected two Cr$1000 bills and three Cr$100 bills. He exclaims, AH! NO! IT'S Cr$2600, NO, Cr$2700, and then gives 2 × Cr$1000, 1 Cr$500, and 2 Cr$100 in change.

Fig. 8.6 contains both the percentage of children who successfully accomplished each exchange task and, of these children who successfully completed the tasks, the number of exchanges required for successful completion (rural nonsellers were not administered this task).

Whether children succeeded in accomplishing the exchange tasks differed across population groups only for the more complex problem (Cr$10000). On the Cr$5000 condition, all of the children in both population groups successfully

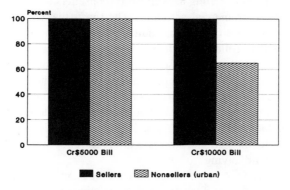

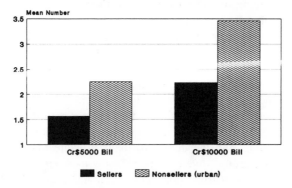

FIG. 8.6.   Children's solutions to exchange problems as a function of population group.

completed the task. In contrast, on the Cr$10000 bill task, while all of the sellers successfully completed the task, only 65% of the urban nonsellers did (chi-square $= [1, N = 42] = 6.89, p < .01$, though two of the four cells had expected values less than 5).

To determine differences in number of exchanges required to achieve success, separate, oneway ANOVAs were performed on the number of exchanges to solution for each problem for the successful children. The analyses revealed that of the children who successfully completed the task, sellers required fewer exchanges for both problem 1 ($F(1,41) = 5.81, p < .05$) and problem 2 ($F(1,33) = 10.0, p < .005$).

SUMMARY

The representation of large numerical values is a critical cognitive function for the mathematics of candy selling as well as for nonsellers to the extent to which they are engaged in commercial activities. The forms that children appropriate and specialize to serve this function are quite distinct from those that are taught in school. Indeed, candy sellers and their nonselling peers develop the ability to identify large units of bills on the basis of their figurative properties as evidenced by children's high levels of performance on the number occlusion tasks. Further, all children showed knowledge of ordinal relations between units as well as the multiplicative relations between units, though the urban children showed greater knowledge than the rural children. Finally, the sellers demonstrated greater knowledge of the denominational structure of the currency system than the urban nonsellers in problem solving.

These findings are very much in accord with the analyses of the first analytic component: Differences in children's engagement with goals involving the identification of and computation with large currency values predict differences in children's specialization of currency as a sign form for number representation. All of the unschooled Brazilian children studied have some level of familiarity with the Brazilian currency system, though sellers, by virtue of their trade, have greater involvement with such goals than the urban nonsellers, and the urban nonsellers, by virtue of their greater participation in a commercial economy, have greater involvement than the rural nonsellers. It follows, then, that all children show facility in identifying bill values with numbers occluded and identifying ordinal relations between bill values, and, that as tasks require more specialized knowledge of currency as a representational system—like knowledge involving multiplicative relations and the denominational structure of the currency system—the population groups diverge. Sellers show more specialized knowledge than urban nonsellers and urban nonsellers show more specialized knowledge than rural nonsellers.

ARITHMETICAL COMPUTATIONS

Like currency-linked representational problems, arithmetical problems often emerge in the selling practice. In sales transactions with customers, in buying boxes at wholesale stores, and in determining available cash, the seller is engaged with arithmetical problem solving involving large values.

To investigate children's arithmetical strategies, children were asked to sum a set of bills and then to subtract the amount of a purchase from their total. There were two addition problems which differed in the number of bills to be added and the sum of those bills. In the first problem, the child was presented with a stack of 12 bills (totaling Cr$8600) and in the second problem, the child was presented with a stack of 17 bills (totaling Cr$17300). There were two subtraction problems which differed in the price of a box to be purchased, and the amount of money available to purchase the box. In each case, the child was presented with a box of candy immediately after each addition problem and told the price (Cr$3800 after the first and Cr$7600 after the second). In each case, the child was asked to pay the appropriate amount for the candy, and then to tell how much change he should receive (the child did not have the exact change in either case). For problem 1, the values were arranged such that the only appropriate value that could be offered was the Cr$5000 bill, and for problem 2, the only appropriate value was the Cr$10000 bill. Rural nonsellers were only administered the first addition and the first subtraction task.

Currency Addition Problems

The protocols to be presented provide some indication of the kinds of problems the addition of a large set of bills presents to children as well as some of the strategies nonsellers and sellers use to accomplish the addition.

S No. 805. 10-year-old urban nonseller, second grade. For the first problem, the addition of 12 bills totaling Cr$8600, S No. 805 does not change the order of the bills and makes a number of addition errors leading him to the incorrect result of Cr$6800. For the second problem, S No. 805 again begins with the haphazard order, but stops adding on the 13th bill after he has made a number of computational errors. He reorders the bills into one which is somewhat more regular, and on the 16th bill (the next to the last bill) he has reached the value of Cr$6800, a value which is in error by Cr$500. The last remaining bill is the Cr$10000, and he states that he has Cr$6800 and Cr$10000 and that he does not know how to total them.

S No. 39. 11-year-old seller, first grade. For the first problem, S No. 39 does not change the order of the 12 bills and adds them correctly to Cr$8600. For the second problem, S No. 39 reorganizes the bills into groups that sum to convenient values of Cr$1000. He first takes the Cr$10000 bill, then adds to that three Cr$1000 bills, and five Cr$200 bills; to that he adds three couplets of Cr$500 bills, and he finally adds the remaining Cr$200 and Cr$100 bills; he terminates with the correct answer, Cr$17300.

The percentage of children achieving correct solutions to each addition problem as a function of population group is presented in Fig. 8.7. To assess differences in accuracy as a function of population group, each child was assigned a score consisting of the absolute difference between his summation and the actual value of the bills (Cr$8600 in problem 1 and Cr$17300 in problem 2). Kruskal–Wallis oneway ANOVAs on these difference scores revealed an effect for population group only for problem 1 (chi-square $(2, N = 58) = 11.14, p < .005$); sellers achieved more accurate sums than both urban nonsellers (Mann–Whitney U Test, $U = 141, z = -2.18, p < .05$) and rural nonsellers (Mann–Whitney U test, $U = 83, z = -3.35, p < .001$). On problem 2, though a larger percentage of sellers achieved correct summations than did nonsellers, this difference did not attain statistical significance.

An analysis of children's strategies across problems 1 and 2 suggests children differed in the way they approached the two problems: Some of the children shifted the order of arrangement of bills in order to create subgroups that could be summed to convenient values—multiples of Cr$500 or Cr$1000. Shifts tended to occur more frequently for problem 2, the more complex problem than for problem 1 for both the sellers (65% vs. 30%) and the urban nonsellers (65% vs. 40%), though this difference was only significant for the sellers (chi-square $(1, N = 46) = 4.27, p < .05$). Thus, while both sellers and urban nonsellers showed some evidence that they differentiated between the complexity of these two problems in their strategic approaches, the urban nonsellers showed greater tendency to treat the problems of equivalent complexity than the sellers. Consistent with the prior findings of children's poor performance on the standard orthography tasks, none of the children used the number orthography in paper-and-pencil solution strategies for either problem.

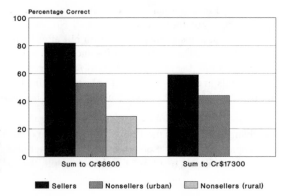

FIG. 8.7. Percentage of children with correct answers to currency addition problems as a function of problem and population group.

Subtraction Tasks

Children's performance on the subtraction tasks was analyzed in two parts. The first was children's response to the request for the appropriate amount for the purchase of the item specified in the problem from their 12 or 17 bills in problems 1 and 2 respectively. The second was their computation of the appropriate change to be received. The following protocols illustrate some typical solutions to the subtraction problem.

> S No. 806. 10-year-old, second grade, urban nonseller. For problem 1, S No. 806 counts his bills in order to pay the correct amount for the candy box. After finding that he does not have enough to pay for the box with exact change, he presents the Cr$5000 bill. He is asked whether he should receive change, he thinks and says that he should receive Cr$2200 (incorrect). (How did you figure that out?) He replies, "WHEN MY MOTHER TELLS ME TO BUY THINGS THAT ARE Cr$3800, I GET Cr$2200." For problem 2, S No. 806 produces a similar solution, again erring by Cr$1000. He first counts his bills in order to pay with the exact amount, but again finds that he does not have enough. He offers the Cr$10000 bill, and he is asked whether he should receive change. He responds that he should, he thinks and says that he should receive Cr$3400. He is asked how he figured, and he responds, "Cr$7600 FOR THAT (BOX), GIVING Cr$10000, BRINGS BACK Cr$3400."

> S No. 33. 10-year-old, second grade, seller. For problem 1, S No. 33, after adding and finding that he cannot pay with exact change, presents the Cr$5000 bill. He claims that he should receive Cr$1200 in change (correct). He is asked to explain, and he says, referring to the box price of Cr$3800, "Cr$200 MAKES 4 (meaning Cr$4000), AND Cr$1000 MORE MAKES Cr$5000." For problem 2, S No. 33 quickly gives the Cr$10000 bill, explaining that he does not have the appropriate change. He says that he should receive Cr$2400 (correct) in change, and explains, referring to the Cr$7600 box price, "PUT Cr$400 AND IT BECOMES 8 (Cr$8000); PUT Cr$2000 MORE AND IT BECOMES 10 (Cr$10000)."

Though virtually all sellers and urban nonsellers offered the appropriate amount in the initial purchase requests in problem 1—the Cr$5000 bill (86% and 100%, respectively), significantly fewer rural nonsellers offered the appropriate amount (only 53% did) (chi-square (2, $N = 58$) = 13.58, $p < .01$). Virtually all sellers and urban nonsellers offered the appropriate denomination, Cr$10000, for problem 2 (91% and 95%, respectively). Some sellers who did not offer the appropriate amount in the problem produced a value that anticipated the change question—they offered Cr$5800 in problem 1 and Cr$10600 in problem 2 in order to minimize the number of bills required for change.

The percentage of children's correct answers to the calculation phase of the subtraction tasks as a function of population group is presented in Fig. 8.8. Like the addition problems, to assess differences in accuracy as a function of population group, each child was assigned a score consisting of the absolute difference between his answer and the correct answer. A Kruskal–Wallis ANOVA per-

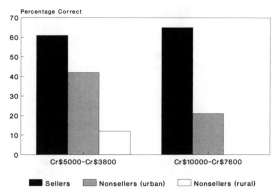

FIG. 8.8. Percentage of children with correct answers to currency subtraction problems as a function of problem and population group.

formed on children's difference scores as a function of population group revealed a significant effect for problem 1 (chi-square $(2, N = 59) = 8.39, p < .05$), and Mann–Whitney U tests revealed that rural nonsellers achieved significantly less accurate scores than both sellers ($U = 104, z = 2.89, p < .05$) and urban nonsellers ($U = 118, z = 1.72, p < .05$). On problem 2, sellers achieved more accurate scores than urban nonsellers (Kruskal–Wallis, chi-square $(1, N = 41) = 6.5, p < .05$). As in the addition problems, none of the sellers used paper-and-pencil strategies, though a few of the second-grade nonsellers did.

SUMMARY

Like the findings for large number representation, all groups sampled showed some abilities to compute with large numerical values and, on the more complex problems, many children demonstrated specialized strategies to manipulate arithmetical relations with large values (e.g., bill regrouping strategies). Further, with both the addition and subtraction problems, as problem difficulty increased, sellers show more sophisticated solutions than both groups of nonsellers. Thus, for addition on the easier problem, all groups demonstrated moderate to high levels of performance, whereas for the more difficult problem, sellers showed more accurate performance than the nonsellers. For subtraction, on the less complex problem, sellers' performance did not differ significantly from urban nonsellers' (though both groups achieved a greater number of correct scores than rural nonsellers); on the more complex subtraction problem, sellers again did achieve more accurate solutions than urban nonsellers.

COMPARING RATIOS

The analyses of Part II revealed that problems involving ratio comparisons are linked closely to the selling practice. Ratio comparison problems emerge in the selling practice as a child independently considers possible prices for retail sale (e.g., three units for Cr$1000, two units for Cr$500), when peers agree not to compete and negotiate an agreed price (e.g., three vs. four for Cr$1000), when a child encounters a competitive "crab" and evaluates the crab's prices relative to his own, and in bargaining transactions when a customer may offer a different price. The tasks described herein were used to assess differences in children's ability to produce ratio comparisons as a function of population group. The tasks are set in the context of retail pricing conventions: Children were presented with three problems in which they were asked to evaluate which of two retail sale prices would yield the greater relative profit.

To introduce the ratio comparison problems, the interviewer presented a bag of *Pirulitos* (a type of candy) and told the child the following: "Suppose that you bought this bag of *Pirulitos,* and you must decide the price you will sell the pieces for in the street." The interviewer then administered the three ratio comparison problems, one by one that varied in pricing ratios to be compared: one Pirulito for Cr$200 vs. three Pirulitos for Cr$500, one Pirulito for Cr$200 vs. seven Pirulitos for Cr$1000, three Pirulitos for Cr$500 vs. seven Pirulitos for Cr$1000. In each case, the child was asked to identify the pricing ratio that would yield the greater profit.

The following protocol provides an example of a common difficulty children experience in conceptualizing ratio comparisons. S No. 910 focuses solely on the value of the bill in the pricing ratios, ignoring the differences in numbers of units sold for the bill denominations.

S No. 910. 10-year-old rural nonseller, first grade. S No. 910 is presented with each of the three ratio comparison problems, and for each he gives an evaluation based on a direct comparison of the currency denomination in each ratio. In comparing one for Cr$200 to three for Cr$500, he states that three for Cr$500 will bring the most profit "BECAUSE YOU WILL MAKE MORE MONEY. SELLING IT FOR Cr$200 YOU WILL MAKE LITTLE AND SELLING IT FOR Cr$500 YOU WILL MAKE MORE." In comparing one for Cr$200 to seven for Cr$1000, he chooses the seven for Cr$1000 because "THIS WILL BRING MORE MONEY." Finally, in comparing three for Cr$500 to seven for Cr$1000, he again selects seven for Cr$1000, justifying his choice by arguing "BECAUSE THIS (seven for Cr$1000) WILL BRING MORE MONEY AND THE OTHER (three for Cr$500) WILL BRING LESS."

The child in the following protocol shows an initial attempt at ratio comparison that resembles that of S No. 910. However, after being challenged with the countersuggestion on the second ratio comparison problem, he sees a need to coordinate the number of units offered with the price requested (a countersuggestion expressing the opposite choice of the child's was presented after each problem for each child; see Appendix C). The countersuggestion appears to prompt the child to a reconsideration of his solution strategy, leading the child to a correct judgment and adequate justification for the third comparison.

S No. 801. 12-year-old urban nonseller, second grade. S No. 801 is presented with each of the three ratio comparison problems, and appears to arrive at a relative conception of ratio over the course of the three problems. For the first problem— comparing one for Cr$200 to three for Cr$500—he bases his choice on the bill denominations, choosing three for Cr$500: "BECAUSE IT'S MORE THAN THIS (one for Cr$200)." (How do you know that you'll make a greater profit here—three for Cr$500)? "BECAUSE THIS IS Cr$200 AND THIS IS Cr$500. WITH THIS (Cr$500) YOU'LL MAKE Cr$300 MORE. (The interviewer then presents the countersuggestion: Another boy that I talked with chose one for Cr$200 as the one that brought more profit. I want you to explain to me how you would show this child that he was wrong.) S No. 801 repeats his argument, "BECAUSE HERE (one for Cr$200) YOU MAKE Cr$200 AND HERE (three for Cr$500) YOU MAKE Cr$500." For the comparison between one for Cr$200 and seven for Cr$1000, S No. 801 follows the same argument and chooses seven for Cr$1000 "BECAUSE HERE YOU WILL MAKE Cr$1000 AND HERE YOU WILL MAKE Cr$200." (How do you know you will make more money here?) BECAUSE THIS IS Cr$200 AND THIS IS Cr$1000. (Show me what you did to discover that you have a bigger profit this way.) Now, S No. 801 introduces a new line of reasoning, but does not change his choice: "THIS (one for Cr$200) SELLS EACH FOR Cr$200 AND THIS (seven for Cr$1000) GOES ONE FOR Cr$150" (apparently making an approximate division of Cr$1000 by seven). (The interviewer then presents the countersuggestion: Another boy that I talked with chose one for Cr$200 as the one that brought more profit. I want you to show me how you would show to this child that he was wrong.) HE IS RIGHT! BECAUSE FOR Cr$1000 AT ONE FOR Cr$200 YOU SELL FIVE. HERE (seven for Cr$1000), NO." This apparently new insight is sustained in the last problem in which he contrasts three for Cr$500 with seven for Cr$1000: S No. 801 correctly chooses three for Cr$500 "BECAUSE IT'S LESS CANDY." (How do you know you make more profit there?) "HERE, THERE ARE SIX CANDIES (three for Cr$500) AND HERE THERE ARE SEVEN, SO YOU LOSE ONE CANDY."

We see in S No. 801's protocol a gradual shift in structuration of the problem. While he begins, like S No. 910, with a direct comparison between the cash involved in the two ratios, through repeated presentation and countersuggestion, he constructs an adequate basis for comparing two ratios.

Finally, the following two sellers demonstrate conceptualizations of ratios as involving terms that need to be coordinated with one another, and they demonstrate solution forms that are well structured from the start, ones linked to the practice of selling. In each case, we see two different approaches to achieving the coordination, sometimes by equating candy units and comparing currency and other times by equating currency and comparing candy units. In both cases, the comparison strategies are linked to iterating sales transactions of the practice.

S No. 26 11-year-old seller, second grade. S No. 26 is presented with each of the three ratio comparison problems, and for each he chooses the correct pricing ratio.

In comparing one for Cr$200 to three for Cr$500, he chooses one for Cr$200 "BECAUSE HERE (ONE FOR Cr$200) I'D SELL THREE TIMES THREE OF THESE CANDIES AND I'D MAKE Cr$600, AND IN THE OTHER ITS THREE FOR Cr$500. SO, I WOULD MAKE MORE SELLING ONE FOR Cr$200." In comparing one for Cr$200 with seven for Cr$1000, S No. 26 uses a similar argument for selecting one for Cr$200. "BECAUSE (selling one for Cr$200) FIVE I SELL FOR Cr$1000 AND THE OTHER I SELL SEVEN FOR Cr$1000." Finally, in contrasting three for Cr$500 with seven for Cr$1000, S No. 26 chooses three for Cr$500 "BECAUSE SIX I WOULD SELL FOR Cr$1000 AND THE OTHER WAY I WOULD SELL SEVEN FOR Cr$1000."

S No. 60. 12-year-old seller, second grade. S No. 60 is presented with each of the three ratio comparison problems, and, like S No. 26, for each he chooses the correct pricing ratio. In comparing one for Cr$200 with three for Cr$500, S No. 60 says, "ONE FOR Cr$200 BRINGS MORE PROFIT AND THREE FOR Cr$500 YOU SELL FASTER." (How do you know?) "BECAUSE AT THREE FOR Cr$500 I LOSE Cr$100 FOR EACH SALE." (How do you know you make more profit with one for Cr$200?) "BECAUSE THREE AT ONE FOR Cr$200 WILL BRING Cr$600, AND I WOULD LOSE Cr$100 IF I SELL IT THE OTHER WAY, THREE FOR Cr$500." For problem 2, in comparing one for Cr$200 with seven for Cr$1,000, S No. 60 says, "ONE FOR Cr$200 BECAUSE HERE (one for Cr$200) FOR EACH SALE I EARN Cr$400 AND IN THE OTHER (seven for Cr$1000) I LOSE Cr$400 FOR EACH SALE." (How do you know?) "BECAUSE ONE FOR Cr$200 SELLS FOR FIVE FOR Cr$100 AND THE OTHER (seven for Cr$1000), I LOSE TWO CANDIES THAT COST Cr$400" (implying that the child is considering the candy as having a "real" worth of Cr$200 per unit).

Both S No. 26 and S No. 60 justify their ratio choices with common term solutions. S No. 26, in his solution of the first problem, equates the number of units of candy and compares the resulting cash produced by the two retail prices (three for Cr$600 vs. three for Cr$500); in his solutions for both the second and third problems, he equates the cash and then compares the number of units (five for Cr$1000 vs. seven for Cr$1000 and six for Cr$1000 vs. seven for Cr$1000, respectively). S No. 60, in his solutions to the first two ratio problems, distinguishes between amount of profit per transaction and speed of sale. When focusing on amount of profit, he produces common term solutions: like S No. 26, in the first problem. S No. 60 equates the units, comparing the cash (three for Cr$600 vs. three for Cr$500), and in the second problem, he equates the cash and compares the units (five for Cr$1000 vs. seven for Cr$1000). In both cases, he presents his answer in terms of what he sees is the cash lost or gained as a result of selling for one or the other of the two ratios.

To determine whether there were differences in children's ability to solve the ratio problems, each child's response to each problem was coded with regard to whether a common term approach was used. *Common term* approaches were those in which children justified their ratio choice be reference to a comparison of number of units for a common selling price or by reference to a comparison of selling prices for an equivalent number of units. There were two additional (but rare) variants of the common term approach (included as instances of it). In the first variant, a child attempted to find a common term through an approximate division operation, dividing each currency value by the number of units in the ratio and then comparing the resulting unit prices (less than 5% of the total number of justifications were of this type). In the second variant, the child found a common term but either because of an oversight or due to a conceptual confusion reported that the larger number of units sold at the common price yielded a larger profit (less than 3% of the total number of justifications were of this type).

The large majority of responses that were not common term approaches consisted of responses in which children made an absolute comparison of the money in the two pricing ratios without equating the ratios for number of units. S No. 910's protocol presented examples of this approach. Most children who did not make explicit justifications seemed to base their judgments on absolute approaches. Virtually all children who did not justify their judgment selected the ratio with the greater bill value as the one which would yield the greater profit.

Figure 8.9 contains the mean percentage of problems for which children used common term approaches as a function of population group. Of those children who used common term approaches, a large percentage also spontaneously indicated the amount of additional profit (in candy, cruzeiros, or both) that they would make with their appropriate choice. Such appropriate analyses of profit accompanied 47% of the common term justifications.

A oneway ANOVA performed on the number of common term approaches children used over the three problems revealed a significant effect for population group ($F(2,57) = 10.05, p < .0005$). Duncan Multiple Range tests revealed that sellers used a greater number of common term approaches than both groups of nonsellers and that there were no significant differences between urban and rural nonsellers' performances. Just as in the analyses for number representation and arithmetical operations, we find that over the course of sellers' use of price ratio

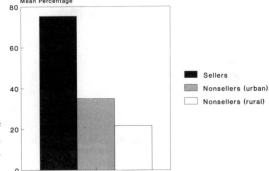

FIG. 8.9. Mean percentage of common term solutions to ratio problems as a function of population group.

convention forms in their selling activities, sellers are specializing cognitive functions for ratio comparison that are distinct from their nonselling peers.

TRANSLATING WHOLESALE BOX PRICES INTO RETAIL UNIT PRICES IN AN INFLATING ECONOMY

In Chapter 6, I presented an analysis of sellers' efforts to translate the wholesale box price of their candy into retail prices for units. In the analyses to follow, I contrast the solution forms used by sellers with those of the urban and rural nonsellers.

Recall a seller's predicament with regard to price translation. He has paid from Cr$2500 to Cr$12000 for a box of 30, 50, or 100 units. He must translate this bulk rate into a retail price such that he not only makes a reasonable profit per sale but also sells candy at a reasonable pace. Further, this translation must be accomplished in an inflating economy in which the wholesale price for a particular box type on one day may be higher the next time the same box is purchased.

In order to determine the effects of practice participation on children's price translations, two sets of tasks were devised. For one set, children were asked to translate wholesale box prices into retail unit prices without any mention of inflation; for the other set, children were queried about how they adjusted their pricing to accommodate inflationary surges in box prices.

Translating Wholesale Box to Retail Unit Prices Without Inflation

Two retail pricing tasks were presented to children. These tasks were modeled directly on the analyses of sellers' price translation problems described in Chapter 6. The tasks varied in the number of units in a box, the wholesale price of a box, and the type of candy in the box. In the first problem, the child was presented with a 50-unit box of *Chupetim* costing Cr$3500; in the second, the child was presented with a 30-unit box of *Chocolate Leila* costing Cr$8500. In each case, the child was asked for how much he would sell the box in the street.

We have already seen in Chapter 6 some of the solution strategies of sellers. The most common strategy that led to an adequate translation involved a count of the candy by different price ratios, counts which yielded gross retail values for the box. I have excerpted some examples of nonsellers' solution strategies that may be contrasted with those of the sellers presented in Chapter 6. The excerpts show the difficulties that children experience in approaching the problem; for many children, the focus is simply on selling the candy rather than producing a mathematical coordination between the wholesale price, the gross retail value of the box, the retail unit price, and the net profit.

S No. 913. 10-year-old rural nonseller, first grade. S No. 913 is presented with the problem of producing a retail unit price for a 50-unit box that cost Cr$3500 (wholesale price). He says he would sell the whole box for the same price, Cr$3500, and that he would sell each unit for Cr$500 to customers (at one for Cr$500, the whole box would actually sell for Cr$25000). He is asked if he sold the whole box at one for Cr$500, how much profit he would make. He said "Cr$3000," then "Cr$2000." He was asked to explain, and he said he didn't know. He was asked again how much he would want to sell the whole box of candy for and he again affirmed the wholesale price, Cr$3500.

S No. 807. 11-year-old urban nonseller, second grade. S No. 807 is presented with the problem of producing a retail unit price for a 30-unit box for Cr$8500. S No. 807 states that he will sell the whole box for Cr$10000 and that he will charge customers one for Cr$4000. (How do you know that price is good for you?) "BECAUSE I BOUGHT ONE FOR Cr$3000" (referring to a prior transaction). (Show me what you did to find out.) "BECAUSE I'LL MAKE MORE (than the wholesale price.)."

S No. 910. 10-year-old rural nonseller, first grade. S No. 910 is presented with the problem of producing a retail unit price for a 50-unit box that cost Cr$3500 (wholesale price). In response to the interviewer's questions, S No. 910 says he would sell each unit for Cr$100 and that the whole box should be sold for Cr$10000 (at one for Cr$100, the box would actually sell for Cr$5000). He is asked how he knew that one for Cr$100 is a good price. "BECAUSE IF IT'S EXPENSIVE NO ONE WILL WANT TO BUY. SO I WOULD SELL IT FOR THAT PRICE." In addressing follow-up questions, S No. 910 did not make a more explicit link between the wholesale box price and the retail unit price.

S No. 912. 12-year-old rural nonseller, first grade. S No. 912 is presented with the problem of producing a retail unit price for a 50-unit box that sold for Cr$3500 (wholesale price). He says he would sell the whole box for Cr$12000, and that he would sell each unit for Cr$300 to customers (at one for Cr$300, the whole box would actually sell for Cr$15000). He is asked how he knew that one for Cr$300 is a good price. He states: "BECAUSE I SELL ONE FOR Cr$300 AND I MAKE MONEY AND THE CUSTOMER WILL BUY FROM ME." As with S No. 910, follow-up questions did not yield a more explicit link between the wholesale box price and retail unit price.

The difficulty that these children have in producing an adequate retail price appears to involve two interrelated factors. One difficulty is related to children's economic understandings and the other is related to their mathematical understandings.

With respect to their economic conceptions, S No. 913 seems to have difficulty in understanding that the price for which one sells a box must be coordinated with the price that one for pays for the box plus compensation for work produced in selling (profit). Indeed, S No. 913 argues that the wholesale box price and retail box price should be equivalent. Other children appear to compensate work entailed in selling by creating a profit margin; however, they do not appear to understand that the effect of setting the price too high is the risk of reduced sales which, in turn, affects profit. We find such an approach in S No. 807's protocol; the seller sets his retail price at one for Cr$4000 for a 30-unit box that cost Cr$8500. These kinds of economic reasonings are in fact widespread in children and, as Berti and Bombi (1988) have documented, occur across cultures (see also Becker & Saxe, in press).

With respect to the mathematical solutions to the problem, none of the sellers cited produce an adequate coordination between a retail unit price and a retail box price (e.g., a retail unit price of two for Cr$1000 for a 30-unit box would yield a retail box price of Cr$15000). While S No. 910 and S No. 912 both produce retail prices in which there is a reasonable profit margin, both appear to guess or estimate at prices, and do not use a strategy that would lead to a coordinated solution.

To analyze group differences in children's translations as a function of selling experience, two aspects of children's solutions were coded: First, some children offered the retail unit price in terms of the price ratio convention (selling multiple units for a single bill denomination); other children offered the retail unit price in simply a single unit price. Since use of the price ratio convention may complicate the problem for some in that when the convention is used children must solve for multi-unit retail as opposed to single-unit retail prices, whether children used the price ratio convention in their retail price answer was coded; second, children's coordination between their retail price for units and the retail price for the entire box was used to define an adequate solution (e.g., as above, a retail unit price of two for Cr$1000 for a 30-unit box should yield a retail box price of Cr$15000).

Price Ratio Convention Use

Children's retail prices were coded as one of two categories: *Standard convention pricing*—selling multiple units for a specified bill denomination (usually Cr$1000) and *single units pricing*—selling only a unit of candy per currency value.

Fig. 8.10 shows the distribution of children's convention use as a function of population group for both problems. Virtually all of the sellers priced their goods with respect to the standard convention. In contrast, virtually all of the nonsellers priced their candy by single units (problem 1, chi-square (2, $N = 60$) = 44.81, $p < .0001$; problem 2, chi-square (1, $N = 43$) = 29.11, $p < .0001$).

Solutions to Price Translation Problems

Children's solutions to the pricing problems were regarded as "appropriate" if they achieved a coordination between their stated retail price for units and their stated gross price for the box, and "inappropriate" if they did not. For instance,

Box Cost: 50 Units @ Cr$3500

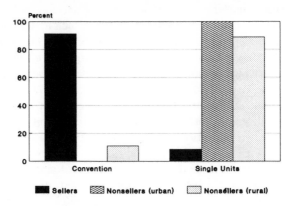

Box Cost: 30 Units @ Cr$8500

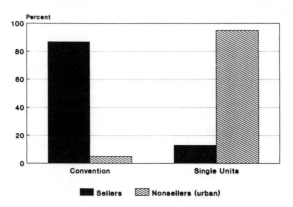

FIG. 8.10.   Percentage of children using the price ratio convention as a function of problem and population group.

an appropriate coordination for problem 1 would be a determination of a gross price of Cr$10000 for the 30-unit box and retail unit price of three units for Cr$1000. (None of the children who produced no or negative profit achieved adequate coordinations.)

Two types of appropriate solutions were coded. These consisted of *Count by Price* solutions as detailed in Chapter 6 (as *Count by Cr$1000* solutions) and *covert* solutions. Recall that *Count by Cr$1000* solutions were those in which a child would tally candy in terms of the price ratio convention; in a prototypical solution, the child would tally the cash value of each potential sale as he moved subgroups of candy aside (e.g., three at a time if the price ratio was three for Cr$1000) until he achieved a gross price for the box; the child would then compare the potential gross price achieved through this tally with the wholesale price to determine the profit margin. *Covert* solutions consisted of an appropriate coordination between wholesale and retail prices, but one in which the procedure that the child used to accomplish this coordination was not made public (despite probing). In covert strategies, some children probably used more specialized versions of the *Count by Cr$1000* strategies documented in Chapter 6, strategic forms that would be carried out without actual counting of the candy. Recall that in one such strategy, children divided the total number of units in a box (e.g., 30) by the number of units to be sold for Cr$1000 (e.g., in the price ratio two for Cr$1000, the number would be two); children then added the suffix "thousand" (i.e., multiplied the result by Cr$1000) to obtain the gross earnings from the box: $(30/2 \times 1000 = Cr\$15000)$. It is also possible that some children achieved an appropriate coordination by guessing.

Inappropriate solutions consisted of all those in which the child did not achieve a coordination between his gross price and retail unit price.

Fig. 8.11 contains a distribution of children's solution types on the retail pricing problem as a function of population group. Chi-square comparisons revealed no differences in children's tendency to use successful *Count by Price* strategies and successful covert strategies. To determine group differences in children's adequate solutions, these two strategy types were pooled. Contrasts across population groups revealed that while the majority of sellers used appropriate solutions for both problems, only a minority of nonsellers did so. While for problem 1, these differences were only significant between sellers and rural nonsellers (chi-square $(1, N = 40) = 5.81$), $p < .02$), for problem 2, these differences were significant between sellers and urban nonsellers (chi-square $(1, N = 43) = 4.97$, $p < .05$). It is important to note that on both problems, the sellers use of the price ratio convention (selling multiple units for Cr$1000) meant that the arithmetical complexity of the problems that they addressed was more complex than the nonsellers who virtually all priced their candy as single units.

The findings for children's mark-up strategies show that the use of the price ratio convention is not only interwoven with and contributes to children's specialization of functions involving ratio comparison, but also leads children to specialize new mathematical functions for wholesale to retail mark-up. In the *Count by Cr$1000* strategy and its related forms, sellers have specialized a mathematical means of coordinating their wholesale cost of a box with their retail sales prices. It is a specialization of this mathematical form that their nonselling peers do not achieve and clearly linked to practice participation.

Adjusting for Inflation

With Brazil's inflating economy, sellers are often faced with the problem of whether or in what way they should make corresponding adjustments in their

Box Cost: 50 Units @ Cr$3500

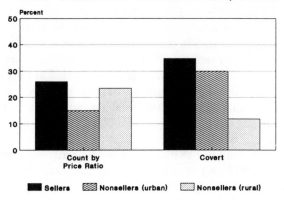

Box Cost: 30 Units @ Cr$8500

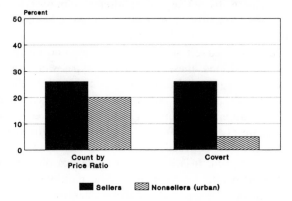

FIG. 8.11. Percentage of children using 1 of 2 appropriate strategy types to mark-up problems as a function of problem and population group.

retail prices for inflationary surges in the wholesale cost of candy boxes. One solution is a proportional one: The proportional relation between wholesale price and retail price before an inflationary surge should be matched with that after an inflationary surge. Clearly, such a proportional approach would be a useful guide for sellers in making retail pricing adjustments—proportional increases would preserve the buying power of the profit as well as maintain a "reasonable" retail price for candy relative to the state of the economy. In Part I, we found evidence that sellers used a pricing convention that compensated for inflation, the convention of "meio-pelo-meio," or "half-half." To sellers, the convention means that a good retail price was one that enabled the purchase of another box with half the gross yield, allowing the seller to keep the other half as a net profit. In this way, rises in wholesale prices are proportionally compensated by retail price adjustments, and sellers using this convention would maintain a profit margin of 100% (providing that the cost of their next box had not increased).

To assess the influence of practice participation on children's mathematical reasoning about price adjustments, children were presented with two problems which varied in format. For the first problem, children were told the initial wholesale price of a box of candy (Cr$4000) and were asked to generate an appropriate retail price for the *entire* box. They were then asked to reproduce this mark-up after inflation led to a specified rise in the wholesale price of the same box type (to Cr$7000). Thus, the child was presented with the following proportionality problem: Cr$4000 : Cr$??? :: Cr$7000 :: Cr$???. In the second problem, children were told both the wholesale price (Cr$3000) and the gross retail price (Cr$6000) a seller used during one time period; the child was asked to reproduce the mark-up after an inflationary rise in wholesale prices (to Cr$9000). Thus, the child was presented with this proportionality problem: Cr$3000 : Cr$6000 :: Cr$9000 : Cr$???. At the outset of each problem, children were asked if they expected wholesale prices to rise over the time interval used in each problem; all sellers and nonsellers responded that they expected prices to rise.

Children's Retail Price Adjustments for Inflationary Shifts in Wholesale Prices

Children's price adjustments for inflation differed as a function of population group, ranging from ones in which children made no profit at all to ones in which children made proportional adjustments.[7] The nonseller's protocol below shows no awareness that the *relation* between the wholesale and retail price at time 2 should match the one at time 1.

S No. 915. 11-year-old rural nonseller, first grade. S No. 915 is presented with the second inflation task (Cr$3000 : Cr$6000 :: Cr$9000 : Cr$???). He responds, "Cr$11000" and is asked the reason for his decision. He responds "BECAUSE I'LL MAKE MORE MONEY THAN Cr$9000. THIS PRICE OF Cr$11000 IS BETTER THAN I SET AT CHRISTMAS BECAUSE IT WAS ONLY Cr$6000 THEN." (But at Christmas your profit was Cr$3000 and now you want a profit of Cr$2000. Why?) "BECAUSE AT CHRISTMAS IT WAS LESS EXPENSIVE AND TODAY IT'S MORE EXPENSIVE. IF I SOLD IT FOR Cr$12000 IT WOULD ALSO BE BETTER THAN CHRISTMAS."

While the following child is concerned with referencing his current increase to the prior increase, the adjustment is not sensitive to the relative increase of the

---

[7]In phrasing the proportionality tasks, we were careful to emphasize that the relation between wholesale and retail price between one time period was the targeted relation to reproduce at the second time period.

inflationary surge; he merely applies the additive difference between wholesale and retail price at time 1 to produce the difference at time 2.

S No. 804 10-year-old urban nonseller. S No. 804 was introduced to the first inflation problem Cr$4000:XXX :: Cr$7000 : YYY. For the wholesale price of Cr$4000, S No. 804 responded with a retail price of Cr$5000, and for the whole-sale price rise to Cr$7000, the child responded with a corresponding rise in retail price to Cr$8000. He was asked how he knew that was a good price, and he responded, "BECAUSE IT'S A LOT MORE. THE SELLER HAS TO MAKE A PROFIT TOO." S No. 804 was presented with the second inflation (Cr$3000 : Cr$6000 :: Cr$9000 : Cr$???). He responded Cr$12000 and is asked the reason for his decision. He responded, "BECAUSE I'LL MAKE Cr$3000 IN PROFIT (LIKE BEFORE)."

The following sellers do make adjustments that are sensitive to inflation. First, consider one seller who offered a proportional response and used the "half-half" convention as a determinant of his proportional solution:

S No. 51 12-year-old seller, second grade. S No. 51 was introduced to the first inflation problem Cr$4000 : XXX :: Cr$7000 : YYY. For the wholesale price of Cr$4000, the child responded with a retail price of Cr$8000, and for the wholesale price rise to Cr$7000, the child responded with a corresponding rise in retail price to Cr$14000. The child was probed about his rationale for these answers, and he responded that he did "half-half" in both cases. For the retail price adjustment he said, "I DID Cr$7000 PLUS Cr$7000 WHICH GIVES Cr$14000. IT'S 'HALF-HALF.' I TAKE Cr$7000 OF THE Cr$14000 FOR THE PURCHASE (of another box) AND Cr$7000 FOR ME." (But today you want a profit of Cr$4000, and when Christmas comes you said that you will want a profit of Cr$7000. Why?) "BE-CAUSE THE PRICE WENT UP IN THE WHOLESALE STORE." (How do you know how much to increase your price?) "I JUST DO 'HALF-HALF' ".

Now consider a seller who used the same convention as a basis for a *partial adjustment* for inflation, a partial adjustment dictated by other material features of the problem.

S No. 60. 12-year-old seller, second grade. S No. 60 was introduced to the second inflation problem and responded, "I BUY THE BOX FOR Cr$9000 AND IT COMES WITH 30 UNITS (pointing to the 30-unit box) SO I SHOULD SELL TWO FOR Cr$1000 AND THEN THE WHOLE BOX WILL GO FOR Cr$15,000 (correct calculation). WHEN I DO THESE CALCULATIONS, I DO 'HALF-HALF,' OR MORE THAN HALF [of gross earnings] IS GOOD TO GO FOR MY PROFIT." . . ."IT'S RIGHT TO MAKE MORE THAN HALF SO I SHOULD SELL ONE FOR Cr$1000 AND MAKE Cr$30000 (correct calculation).

In S No. 60's solution, the problem is conceptualized in terms of the price ratio convention of selling multiple units for Cr$1000. This price ratio convention use sets constraints on the extent to which S No. 60 can satisfy the half-half convention. While Cr$18000 is the half-half solution to the problem (of which he appears to be aware), the price ratio convention of selling multiple units per Cr$1000 allows for only two possible solutions to the problem that are close to Cr$18000: Cr$15000 (at three for Cr$1000) or Cr$30000 (at two for Cr$1000).

To analyze group differences, children's price adjustments for inflation were coded as one of five categories that are represented in the examples given: In *No Profit* responses, one or both of children's retail prices would yield no net profit or a loss (as in the case when a child states that the retail price at time 2 should equal the retail price at time 1). In *No Adjustment* responses, children's net profit at time 2 was less than the child's net profit at time 1 but greater than 0 (see S No. 915). In *Absolute* responses, the child's net profit at time 2 was exactly equiv-

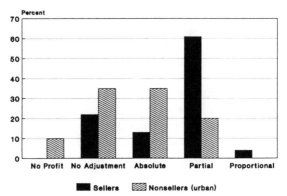

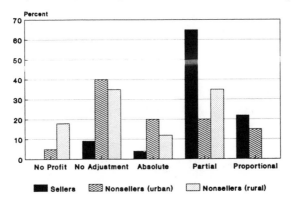

FIG. 8.12.   Percentage of children using 1 of 5 adjustment types to inflation problems as a function of problem and population group.

alent to that at time 1 (see S No. 804). In *Partial Adjustment* responses, the child's net profit at time 2 was greater than the absolute profit at time 1, yet the relation between the wholesale and retail price at time 2 was not proportional to that at time 1 (see S No. 60). Finally, in *Proportional Adjustment* responses, the relation between the wholesale price and the retail price at time 2 was proportional to that at time 1 (see S No. 51).

Fig. 8.12 contains a distribution of children's assigned adjustment categories as a function of population group for both problems 1 and 2. There were relatively few proportional responses for either problem type in any population group, though for problem 2, slightly less than one-fourth of the sellers offered proportional responses. To determine group differences, the two most sophisticated response categories—partial and proportional—were pooled for each problem and contrasted with all other categories that were also pooled. Chi-square analyses revealed that sellers more frequently provided partial and proportional adjustment responses (combined) than the urban nonsellers for problem 1 (chi-square $(1, N = 43) = 7.13, p < .01$) and that sellers more frequently provided more partial and proportional adjustment responses (combined) for problem 2 than both the urban nonsellers (chi-square $(1, N = 40) = 13.85, p < .001$) and rural nonsellers (chi-square $(1, N = 40) = 9.31, p < .005$).

The low frequency of proportional responses and high frequency of partial adjustment responses in the sellers' solutions highlights the pragmatics of children's pricing. Indeed, while by "school" standards these nonproportional adjustments might be viewed as errors, by practice standards they can be viewed as intelligent accommodations to the predicament of operating in an inflating economy under the constraints of a particular number of units contained in boxes and particular selling conventions.

SUMMARY

The problem of price translation is one that emerges regularly in the candy-selling practice. The findings of this section indicate that sellers appropriate and specialize conventions of the practice (like the price ratio and half-half conventions) in both translating their wholesale box purchases into retail unit pries and in adjusting for inflation. In sellers' specialization of these sociocultural forms, new functions emerge, functions that are instrumental in achieving independence from others in the practice and different from those of their nonselling peers.

Similarities and Differences Between Sellers' and Nonsellers Mathematics at 10-to-12 Years of Age

We have seen in this chapter evidence that, as a function of population group, children acquire and specialize various cognitive forms in their daily activities and that they have elaborated cognitive functions in different ways and to different extents. Consider the forms and functions in each of the domains sampled in this chapter.

With respect to the representation of large numerical values, we saw that the standard orthography is not the privileged form for the function of representing number, despite its widespread use. Indeed, on the orthography tasks, both sellers and nonsellers alike performed poorly. In contrast, on the alternative representation tasks, both sellers and nonsellers showed a differentiated knowledge of the currency system and were able to use currency to represent large values. Sellers, however, had more specialized knowledge of this cultural form than their nonselling peers. Sellers showed broader knowledge of bill relations on the multiplicative relations task and sellers as contrasted with nonsellers were better able to use their knowledge of the denominational structure of currency in solving problems of equivalence exchanges on the denominational exchange tasks.

As the tasks used in the study became mathematically more complex and more exclusively linked to the practice of candy selling, we saw further evidence of differences between the knowledge of sellers and nonsellers. On the Bill Addition and Subtraction tasks, both sellers and nonsellers showed that they had specialized currency-based computational strategies to serve arithmetical functions, like reordering bills into convenient values of Cr$500 or Cr$1000. Sellers, again, however, showed more sophisticated performances than the nonsellers, particularly on the more complex addition and subtraction tasks.

Finally, on the ratio and price translation tasks, we found marked differences between sellers' and nonsellers' performance. On the ratio tasks, the large majority of sellers showed a well-articulated understanding of the relative value of numbers in price ratios. In contrast, the nonsellers tended to treat the numbers in the price ratio as absolute values. On the pricing tasks, most of the sellers organized their calculations in terms of the price ratio of the practice and produced coordinated wholesale box and retail unit prices. In contrast, nonsellers did not structure their solution with reference to the price ratio convention and their solutions less frequently contained coordinated wholesale box and retail unit prices.

The findings and interpretive analysis presented here support two conclusions: First, with practice participation, sellers develop mathematical understandings distinct from nonpractice participants; and second, these developments are ones that are interwoven with the mathematical and economic problems linked to the practice. Before turning to issues of development, I would like to point to the specificity of the cognitive constructions documented here.

Recall that the rural nonsellers were straw weavers (footnote 6). In a separate study on weaving in collaboration with Maryl Gearhart, we documented the spatial problems with which these children are engaged in the course of weaving (Saxe & Gearhart, in press). In order to determine the specificity of mathematical form–function shifts across practices, I administered spatial (topological) tasks to both the weavers and to the candy sellers (Saxe, 1989). Consistent with the thesis that children structure and specialize cognitive forms and functions in constructing and accomplishing emergent goals in practices, the findings on the topological tasks show that the straw weavers' knowledge (alias rural nonsellers) outstrips that of the candy sellers (alias urban nonweavers). Thus, candy sellers develop mathematical forms and functions that are interwoven with their economic practice, and straw weavers develop forms and functions that are specific to the spatial problems that emerge in their weaving practice. Later in this volume (Part IV), I will argue that such differences in specialization of knowledge forms across different domains have important consequences in understanding the interplay between learning across cultural practices—problems traditionally defined as learning transfer.

In sum, the findings in this chapter show that children in this study appropriate cultural forms in conceptualizing, addressing, and solving mathematical problems that emerge in their daily activities. In the case of both sellers and nonsellers, we saw that this form consisted principally of currency. In the course of their activities, sellers, in addition, used such forms as price ratios and pricing conventions (like half-half) in constructing and accomplishing mathematical problems. While these forms are culturally rooted, they become cognitive and shift in function as children come to know, use, and specialize them in addressing problems that emerge in their daily activities.

As a whole, these findings show similarities and differences in the mathematics of sellers and nonsellers by 10 to 12 years of age—the age range sampled in this study. The differences in forms and functions between the mathematics of sellers and nonsellers prompt the question of the developmental course whereby sellers' mathematics is taking on the properties revealed in this chapter. In Chapter 9, I address this developmental question in analyzing age-related shifts in sellers' solutions to the battery of tasks, sampling both younger and older sellers and focusing on relations between form and function in sellers' cognitive development.

9 The Development of Sellers' Mathematics

In this chapter, my focus is on the development with age of sellers' mathematics. My concern is to trace the way cultural forms like currency and price ratios are increasingly specialized as they come to serve new mathematical functions over the course of sellers' development. To this end, the same tasks described in Chapter 8 were administered to sellers of different age levels, each of whom had little or no schooling.

In the recruitment of candy sellers to participate in the study, my concern was to find sellers who had not progressed beyond the second grade and who could be assigned in approximately equal numbers to one of three age groups: 5- to 7-year-olds, 8- to 11-year-olds, and 12- to 15-year-olds. As indicated by clerks' records in the ethnographic data reported in Part II, sellers between 5 and 7 were rare, and we were only able to recruit five of them who satisfied our recruitment criteria (specified in Appendix A). As a consequence, "seller-initiates" were included in the 5- to 7-year-old group—5- to 7-year-olds who were not candy-selling entrepreneurs, but children who helped their parents sell in the informal sector (e.g., vegetables, candy). Since many of the older sellers in the study were themselves initiated into entrepreneurial selling by first aiding their parents in the informal sector, our inclusion of seller initiates seemed appropriate.

In the study, the 5- to 7-year-old group included 15 children (mean age = 6.7 years, sd = 0.5 years; mean grade level = 0.5, sd = 0.5; grade level range = no school to first grade), the 8- to 11-year-old group included 20 children (mean age = 10.0 years, sd = 1.1 years; mean grade level = 1.6, sd = 0.6 years; grade level range = no school to second grade), and the 12- to 15-year-old group included 22 children (mean age = 12.6 years, sd = 1.0 years; mean grade level = 1.7, sd = 0.5; grade level range = no school to second grade). The entire sample was boys (as were virtually the entire population of candy sellers). The protocols of the 10- to 12-year-old sellers who participated in the analyses of Chapter 8 are also used as data in the analyses presented in this chapter.

REPRESENTATION OF LARGE NUMERICAL VALUES

Part II contained little evidence that sellers at any age used the standard orthography in their everyday practice; instead, there was some indication that sellers made use of the currency system for large number representation. The findings from Chapter 8 were consistent with the observational study, showing that by 10 to 12, sellers had developed only limited competence in decoding numbers represented in terms of our standard orthography, and that they had developed considerable competence in using currency for large number representation.

The purpose of the analyses reported in the present chapter is to extend the treatment of sellers' use of currency as a specialized cognitive form for number representation to an analysis of the shifting relations between form and function linked to currency use over sellers' development. To this end, sellers were administered all three types of currency representation tasks described in Chapter 8: Bill Identification problems in which sellers were required to identify bill values in three conditions (Standard Bills, Numbers Occluded, and Numbers Only); currency comparison problems in which sellers had to identify both multiplicative and ordinal relations between bill values; and exchange problems in which sellers had to make use of their knowledge of the denominational structure of the currency system in problem solving. In addition to these currency tasks, sellers were also administered the orthography-based representation tasks to determine whether there was a significant development in sellers' ability to decode the orthography by 12 to 15 years of age.

RESULTS

Currency as an Alternate Representational System for Large Numerical Values

Though sellers at each age level had specialized knowledge of currency such that they could use it in the selling practice, the particular representational function differed between sellers and over age levels. These differences became increasingly apparent on the tasks involving the more complex representational functions involving multiplicative relations and the exchange tasks requiring specialized knowledge of the denominational structure of the currency system.

Bill Identification Problems.   Some illustrative protocols of the youngest age group on the bill identification problems are now presented. These protocols illustrate well both sellers' competence at identifying bill values as well as their problems in identifying numbers based on the standard orthography.

> S No. 10. 7-year-old seller, first grade. S No. 10 is presented with the conditions in the following order: Standard Bills, Numbers Occluded, Numbers Only. On the Standard Bills and Numbers Occluded, S No. 10 identifies each of the 24 presented bills with its correct numerical value. In contrast, on the Numbers Only condition, he does not identify any correctly. He reads the two presentations of "100" as "six" and later as "eight," the two presentations of "200" both as "ten," the two presentations of "500" as "ten" and later "eight," the two presentations of "1,000" as "six" and later "eight," the two presentations of "5,000" as "eight," and the presentations of "10,000" as "6" and later "7."

> S No. 09. 7-year-old seller, first grade. S No. 09 is presented with the conditions in the following order: Numbers Only, Standard Bills, Numbers Occluded. On the Standard Bills and Numbers Occluded, S No. 09 identifies each of the 24 presented bills with its correct numerical value. In contrast, on the Numbers Only condition, he identifies only one presentation of "1,000" correctly. He reads the presentations of "100" as "one thousand" and later as "ten thousand," the presentations of "200" as "one thousand" and later "four thousand," the presentations of "500" as "seven thousand" and later "five thousand," the second presentation of "1,000" as "four," the presentations of "5,000" as "two thousand" and later as "two," both presentations of "10,000" as "five thousand."

The disparity between these sellers' ability to identify numerical values in terms of currency units and the number orthography is quite striking. Indeed, although both sellers identify each presentation of the 24 bills correctly, they identify few of the number only presentations correctly.

The number of correct identifications of the 12 values in each of the three conditions was summed for each seller. Fig. 9.1 contains the mean percentage of correct identifications as a function of condition and age group.

A 3 (condition, repeated) $\times$ 3 (age group) ANOVA on sellers' scores revealed main effects for condition ($F(2,108) = 77.90$, $p < .0001$) and age group ($F(2,54) = 10.33$, $p < .0005$) but no interaction. Duncan Multiple Range tests showed that sellers achieved fewer correct identifications on the Numbers Only condition than either the Standard Bills or the Numbers Occluded condition and that there were no differences between the Numbers Occluded and the Standard Bills condition. Duncan tests for the main effect for age group revealed that both the 8- to 11- and 12- to 15-year-olds achieved higher scores than the 5- to 7-year-olds, indicating that the older groups had generated more specialized abilities to identify the numerical values of bills than the younger group.

Despite the effect for age on the Number Occlusion and Standard Bill conditions, Fig. 9.1 shows that the 5- to 7-year-olds performed at high levels, identifying most of the bills accurately. Indeed, an inspection of error profiles of the 5- to 7-year-olds revealed that on the Number Occluded condition, 73% of the 5- to 7-

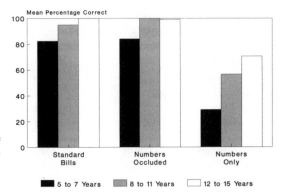

FIG. 9.1. Mean percentage of correct responses to currency identification problems as a function of age group.

year-olds (and all of the 8- to 11-year-olds and 12- to 15-year-olds) identified each of the 12 bill values correctly. These findings indicate that at a very young age, most sellers and seller initiates display a competence for identifying large currency values on the basis of the figurative characteristics of bills, a competence that would allow them to identify effectively currency values in everyday economic transactions.

Currency Comparison Task: Sellers' Knowledge of Numerical Relations Between Currency Values. To probe further age-related shifts in sellers' specialization of currency as a form that could serve the function of large-number representation, sellers at each of the three age levels were administered the currency relations tasks. Recall that in these tasks, a subject had to indicate which of two currency units was the greater (the ordinal relations question), and how many of the smaller was equivalent to the greater (the multiplicative relations question). Each subject received seven ordinal and seven multiplicative problems for values ranging from Cr$1 to Cr$100, and the same number of problems for ordinal and multiplicative relations for values ranging from C$100 to Cr$10000. Specialized knowledge of currency relations would be essential for a seller to use the currency system numerically—that is, beyond merely identifying denominations in transactions like seller–customer exchanges.

Fig. 9.2 contains the mean percentage of correct answers to questions about the ordinal and multiplicative relations between currency units as a function of currency values and age group. For the ordinal comparison questions, a 3 (age group) × 2 (currency value, repeated) ANOVA revealed no significant differences, and an inspection of the figure shows that the performance of each age group was nearly perfect.

For the multiplicative relations, a 3 (age group) × 2 (currency value, repeated) ANOVA revealed main effects for age group ($F(2,54) = 14.50$, $p < .0001$) and currency condition ($F(1,54) = 24.19$, $p < .0001$) and a significant interaction ($F(2,54) = 4.11$, $p < .05$). Duncan Multiple Range tests to determine the source of the currency value × age group interaction revealed that the 5- to 7-year-olds and the 8- to 11-year-olds, but not the 12- to 15-year-olds, more frequently identified relations accurately for the large values (Cr$100 to Cr$10000) than for the small values (Cr$1 to Cr$100). Duncan tests for the age effect revealed that the 8- to 11-year-olds and 12- to 15-year-olds did not differ from one another but that both achieved more correct solutions than the 5- to 7-year-olds.

These findings together with those on sellers' bill identifications show further age differences in the extent to which sellers have specialized currency as a form that can serve the function of large number representation. While all groups achieved a mean of greater than 80% of the ordinal relations comparisons correct, this was not the case for multiplicative relations. In contrast to ordinal

Ordinal Relations

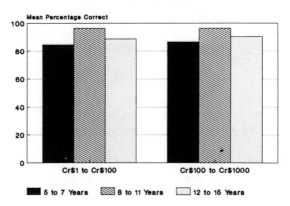

Multiplicative Relations

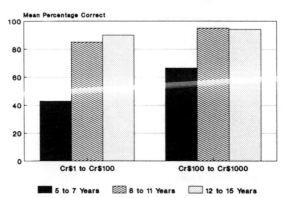

FIG. 9.2. Mean percentage of correct responses to currency comparison problems as a function of value size and age group.

relations, the 5- to 7-year-olds' knowledge of multiplicative relations with large values outstrips their knowledge of multiplicative relations with smaller values. The lack of this value effect on the ordinal comparisons problems may be accounted for by the regular increase of size of currency units as a function of numerical value in the denominations which range between Cr$1 to Cr$100 (all of which are coins); thus, for the small value tasks, this size support for appropriate comparisons may have facilitated the near-ceiling level of performance on small value comparisons by sellers and thus washing out the possible effect for value size.

While the value size effect for multiplicative relations is perhaps surprising from the point of view of models of number development which point to sellers' facility with small values prior to large values (see Fuson, Richards, & Briars, 1982; Siegler & Shrager, 1984), this finding makes sense when we consider the value ranges that sellers are engaged with in their practice—typically those above Cr$100. With age, sellers specialize further knowledge of both small and large multiplicative relations with currency, and by 12 to 15, the asymmetrical performance for value size no longer occurs.

Sellers' Facility with the Denominational Structure of the Currency System: Exchange Tasks.   Sellers were presented with both exchange problems that required making change for a large denomination (Cr$5000 or Cr$10000) for smaller currency denominations in order to complete a purchase of an item that cost one of two values (Cr$2300 or Cr$6630) so that the appropriate change could be returned to a customer (either Cr$2700 or Cr$3370). Like the analysis presented in Chapter 8, sellers whose pattern of exchanges led them to the appropriate set of denominations to produce change prior to their sixth exchange were coded as "successful" and those who required more than six exchanges (counting requests for incorrect exchanges) or who provided an incorrect amount of change were coded as "unsuccessful."

The following examples illustrate some of younger sellers difficulties in accomplishing a correct solution to the problem.

S No. 14 7-year-old seller, first grade. S No. 14 seemed reluctant to differentiate the denominations beyond a breakdown of the Cr$5000 and Cr$10000 bills into 1000-cruzeiro bills. For the Cr$5000 problem, the child requested 5 × Cr$1000 bills in exchange for the Cr$5000 bill (correct exchange). The child did not ask for further exchanges and instead offered Cr$3000 in change to the "customer." For the Cr$10000 problem, the child asked for 10 × Cr$1000 bills in exchange for the Cr$10000, and again, did not ask for further breakdown of the currency, offering Cr$6000 for the customer's change.

S No. 27 8-year-old seller, second grade. S No. 27 successfully completed both problems, but required a series of requests. For the Cr$5000 problem, the child requested 10 × Cr$500 bills in exchange for the Cr$5000 bill. Then, counting these

10 bills three times (and finding each time that he could not give the customer appropriate change), he requested an exchange of 5 × Cr$100 bills for 1 × Cr$500 bill. The child then separated Cr$2300 from the total and gave the rest for change. For the Cr$10000 problem, the child again requested 10 × Cr$500 bills and an additional 5 × Cr$1000 bills in exchange for the 1 × Cr$10000 bill. The child then made five successive incorrect requests to exchange on of his Cr$500 bills: 10 × Cr$100 bills; 4 × Cr$100 bills, 5 × Cr$10 coins, a request repeated three times; the final request was to exchange the Cr$500 for 10 × Cr$10 coins and 4 × Cr$100 bills. The exchange was made and the child put aside Cr$6630 and gave the rest for change.

S No. 14 and S No. 27 show characteristic problems the young sellers experience with the exchange task. S No. 14 has difficulty with translating the larger denomination into appropriate smaller denominations via knowledge of multiplicative relations. S No. 27, while demonstrating knowledge of multiplicative relations, accomplishes the transaction through multiple trades.

Fig. 9.3 contains both the percentage of sellers who successfully completed the exchange problems, and of those sellers who were successful, the mean number of exchanges required for a successful solution. Sellers' success in accomplishing the task differed as a function of age group for both problems. For the Cr$5000 problem, all of the 8- to 11-year-olds and 12- to 15-year-olds successfully accomplished the task; in contrast, only 47% of the 5- to 7-year-olds successfully accomplished this problem (pooling 8- to 11-year-olds with 12- to 15-year-olds to obtain greater expected values, chi-square $(1, N = 57) = 21.08$, $p < .0001$). For the Cr$10000 condition, virtually all of the 8- to 11- and 12- to 15-year-olds achieved successful solutions (95% and 100%, respectively), whereas only 33% of the 5- to 6-year-olds did (pooling 8- to 11-year-olds with 12- to 15-year-olds to obtain greater expected values, chi-square $(1, N = 57) = 25.3, p < .0001$). Fig. 9.3 also shows that of those sellers who successfully completed exchanges, the number of exchanges required was similar, though sellers required more exchanges for the Cr$10000 as contrasted with the Cr$5000 task. A 2 (problem type, repeated) by 3 (age group) ANOVA was performed on sellers' number of requests for an exchange. The analysis showed no difference over age in number of exchanges, but an effect for problem type: Sellers required a greater number of exchanges for the Cr$10000 problem $(F(1, 41) = 19.08, p < .0001)$.

In summary, sellers' solutions to the exchange problems reveals a marked shift over age. Only a minority of the 5- to 7-year-olds were able to accomplish the exchange problems successfully, whereas in the oldest groups, sellers' performances were at or near ceiling. The older groups' success with the problems reveals that the currency has taken on properties as both the object of calculation and itself is the symbolic vehicle for calculation. In applying and orchestrating what has become a well-differentiated knowledge of ordinal and multiplicative relations between large values, the older groups of sellers are able to construct solutions to mathematical tasks of making change involving very large sums.

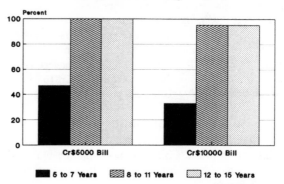

Percentage of Sellers Who Successfully Completed Exchange Tasks

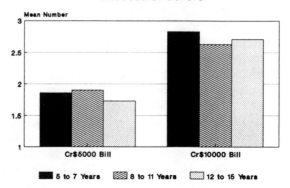

Mean Number of Exchanges Required for Successful Sellers

FIG. 9.3.   Sellers' solutions to exchange problems as a function of age group.

Sellers' Knowledge of the Standard Orthography

Sellers' performance on the numbers-only condition of the currency task showed that by 12 to 15 years, sellers display some competence reading numbers, though the competence still does not equal that of their bill identification abilities. Their performance on the number orthography tasks (Reading Numbers, Number Comparisons), presents more information on their ability to read and compare values expressed in the standard orthography. An analysis of sellers' performances revealed that while on the number comparisons problems, 12- to 15-year-old sellers identified the appropriate ordinal relations between two values on an average of 80% of the problems, they identified these values correctly on less than 50% of the problems. Thus, even the oldest sellers' abilities to decode the standard orthography are poor, and markedly so in contrast with their ability to identify the numerical values of currency units.

Form–function Shifts in Currency-based Number Representations

Sellers' performance on the prior tasks suggests a progressive interplay between the specialization of knowledge of the currency system (a cultural form) and the construction of mathematical functions for number representation over the course of their development. The specialized knowledge of currency documented in the prior pages includes knowledge of the numerical names of different bill values (nominal forms), knowledge of the ordering of named pairs (ordinal forms), and knowledge of multiplicative relations between named pairs (multiplicative forms). The representative functions are analogously varied. These include a nominal one involving the use of names (or tokens) to refer to numerical values, an ordinal one involving the transformation of names or tokens into order relations, and a multiplicative one involving the transformation of ordered names into many-to-one equivalences, equivalences that define the denominational structure of the currency system.

The interplay between form and function in sellers' developing number representational abilities is an important process guiding and setting constraints on development. We have seen that many 5- to 7-year-old sellers have constructed considerable knowledge of the names of bill values (nominal forms): Almost three-fourths of the youngest sellers achieved all correct identifications on the number occluded condition of the bill identification task. These specialized cognitive forms not only allow sellers to communicate about and refer to particular bills by value in the street. Such specialized knowledge also sets the stage for forming knowledge about numerical relations—both ordinal and multiplicative—between values.

As in the case of sellers' specialization of nominal forms for currency identification, we found that by 5 to 7 years, sellers had developed knowledge of order relations between currency units. Ordering relations between bill values is a function distinct from the nominal one entailed in the identification of currency units. We found no age differences in sellers' abilities to identify appropriate ordinal relations, and all sellers performed at high levels on the ordinal relations tasks. Specialized knowledge of ordinal relations between currency pairs contributes further to sellers' ability to engage in activities of the practice in communicating about relative values of bills. This knowledge may also lead young sellers to consider whether different-valued currency units can be equated, and such considerations give rise to the emergence of a new cognitive function— multiplicative relations.

In sellers' performances on the multiplicative relations problems, we found age differences, though even the youngest age group of sellers showed some competence. Specialized knowledge of multiplicative relations provides a basis for sellers to consider multiple bill sums in transactions with customers and peers, knowledge which, in turn, would facilitate children's creation of a more comprehensive understanding of the general structure of the currency system.

Sellers' solutions to the exchange tasks provides an opportunity to consider further the extent to which sellers have specialized knowledge of currency as an articulated system that can be used to represent number. Indeed, the problem of making change for a value like Cr$10000 in order to satisfy the constraints of returning change for a Cr$6630 purchase requires that sellers cognize currency as having a hierarchical denominational structure of some complexity, and apply this knowledge in structuring a solution. While many young sellers could not complete the tasks successfully, all of the sellers in the two older groups did. Further, some showed more specialized solution strategies than others in their knowledge of equivalence relations: Some sellers accomplished a complex exchange problem with a single complex request as in the case of S No. 6075 from Chapter 8, whereas others requested repeated (and labored) smaller exchanges to accomplish the same problem as in the case of S No. 27.

While there has appeared an implicit argument that the various functions reviewed are ordered in their mathematical complexity, the psychological realization of these functions in development is clearly not strictly sequential. Indeed, the findings suggest a multilineal development in which the various lines of specializing knowledge of currency (nominal, ordinal, multiplicative) are occurring more or less concurrently. Indeed, in the case of nominal identifications and multiplicative relations, we observed concurrent age-related shifts in each of these cognitive forms rather than a sequential emergence. The multilinearity of the specialization of forms and functions thus creates the possibility of an interplay between them such that the child's specialization of one form of currency-linked knowledge may be appropriated and used in constructing another. Thus, a seller's efforts to determine different combinations of bills equivalent to a new currency denomination he heard had been issued (e.g., the Cr$100000 note) might provoke him to seek to identify the issue. Or, a seller's identification of the new issue may lead him to ask questions about multiplicative relations with respect to other currency units.

ARITHMETICAL COMPUTATIONS

To determine age-related shifts in sellers' specialization of currency-linked forms to accomplish arithmetical functions, the arithmetical tasks described in Chapter 8 were administered to the three age groups of sellers. In these tasks, sellers were asked to sum a set of bills and then to subtract the amount of a purchase from their total. There were two addition problems, one requiring sellers to add 12 bills (totaling Cr$8600) and the other requiring sellers to add 17 bills (totaling

Cr$17300). There were two subtraction problems. In each case, the seller was presented with a box of candy immediately after each addition problem and told the price (Cr$3800 after the first and Cr$7600 after the second). In each case, the seller was asked to pay the appropriate amount for the candy (the seller did not have the exact change in either case), and then to tell how much change he should receive. For problem 1, the values were arranged such that the only appropriate value that could be offered was the Cr$5000 bill, and for problem 2, the only appropriate value was the Cr$10000 bill.

Currency Addition Problems

Some of the younger sellers' performances on the currency addition problems differed markedly from those of the older sellers. Consider the young seller's use of his bill identification knowledge in producing a nonarithmetical solution to both addition tasks.

> S No. 10. 7-year-old seller, first grade. For the first problem, S No. 10 does not change the order of the 12 bills and merely identifies their value, one by one. For the second problem, S No. 10 again uses the haphazard order, merely identifying the value of the individual bills. When he finishes with the last bill, the one of Cr$10000, he states, "THERE ARE Cr$10000."

In S No. 10's solution, currency identification has become a way of coping with a problem of currency addition.

An inspection of the younger sellers' protocols shows that S No. 10's approach is not unique in solving the currency addition problems. Five of the fifteen 5- to 7-year-olds appeared as if they were engaged with a counting or bill identification task rather than an arithmetical computation. These children either merely counted the bills as equivalent nonmonetary units (e.g., 1,2,3, etc.) or merely enumerated individual bill values (e.g., Cr$500, Cr$200, Cr$500, etc.) as did S No. 10. These strategies suggest that for the younger children, arithmetic with large bill values may be a function only just beginning to emerge.

A second difference in the way sellers approached the currency addition problems was with regard to their manipulation of the bills in performing their addition. In each age group, some sellers showed a solution form in which they reordered our haphazard order of the bills (e.g., as largest to smallest or into convenient values summing to Cr$500 or Cr$1000); the distribution of sellers who reordered as a function of age group is presented in Fig. 9.4. The tendency of sellers to reorder the bills increased as a function of age group, though this tendency was only significant for problem 1 (chi-square $(2, n = 56) = 11.55, p < .005$).

Fig. 9.5 contains the percentage of sellers who achieved accurate solutions to the Currency Addition tasks as a function of age group. To assess group dif-

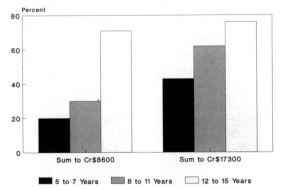

FIG. 9.4. Percentage of sellers who changed order of bills on summation problems as a function of problem and age group.

ferences in accuracy, each seller was assigned a score consisting of the absolute difference between his summation of the value of bills and the actual value of the bills. Sellers' performance improved as a function of age group (Kruskal–Wallis one-way ANOVAs: Problem 1: chi-square $= 18.98$, $p < .0001$; Problem 2: chi-square $= 15.47$, $p < .001$). Mann–Whitney U-tests revealed that, for both problems, both the 8- to 11-year-olds and the 12- to 15-year-olds achieved more accurate performances than the 5- to 7-year-olds, and that the performances of the 8- to 11-year-olds and 12- to 15-year-olds did not differ.

Subtraction Tasks

Sellers' solutions to the subtraction problems varied markedly over age group. In the following protocol, the 6-year-old seller is either not aware of the need to produce the subtraction, solving the subtraction problem as merely one of an exchange of cash for merchandise, or he is overwhelmed by the complexity of the problem, and radically simplifies it.

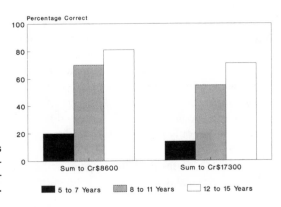

FIG. 9.5. Percentage of sellers with correct answers to currency addition problems as a function of problem and age group.

S No. 05. 6-year-old, first grade. For problem 1, S No. 05 counts his money by simply naming the bill values. He then offers Cr$7400 to pay for the box which he believes is Cr$5500. When asked whether he should receive change for his Cr$3800 purchase, he replies that he should not. For problem 2, S No. 05 produces another count of his money in order to produce payment for the box. In his count, however, he proceeds by identifying bill values; he concludes with the surprising ("guesstimate") that he has Cr$200500. He then offers the Cr$10000 bill for the purchase. When asked whether he should receive change, he responds that he should not.

S No. 05's solution of no change for the subtraction problem was not uncommon in the youngest age group. Fig. 9.6 contains the percentage of sellers in three subtraction response categories as a function of age group: correct answer,

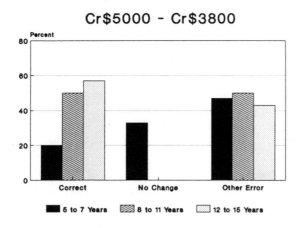

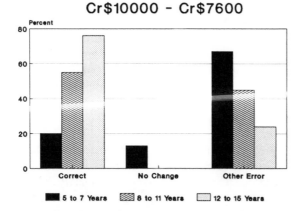

FIG. 9.6. Percentage of sellers producing correct, no change, or other responses to currency subtraction problems as a function of problem and age group.

no change, and computation error. An inspection of Fig. 9.6 reveals that the only age group that contained sellers who responded that no change should be returned were the 5- to 7-year-olds, indicating that these sellers, as in the case of their solutions to the addition tasks, may not have conceptualized the problem as one involving an arithmetical operation.

To determine age shifts in sellers' accuracy in solving the subtraction problems, the difference between the seller's answer to the subtraction problem and the correct answer was calculated. Kruskal–Wallis ANOVA performed on these difference scores as a function of age group revealed differences in sellers' accuracy on both problems (problem 1, chi-square $(N = 56) = 11.2$, $p < .005$; problem 2, chi-square $(N = 56) = 13.33$, $p < .005$). Follow-up tests revealed that for both problem types, the two older age groups achieved more correct scores than the younger groups and that the two older groups did not differ from one another.

Form–function Shifts in Currency-based Addition and Subtraction

Sellers' solutions to the arithmetical problems showed a pronounced shift over age level, particularly between the 5- to 7-year-olds and the two older age groups. Like the currency representation tasks, these shifts display shifting relations between form and function in sellers' solutions over age. Some of the 5- to 7-year-olds appeared to conceptualize the arithmetical problems in terms of earlier emerging functions of counting, bill recognition, and exchange. To accomplish these tasks, these young sellers appropriated and deployed forms of which they had specialized knowledge, sometimes counting and sometimes labeling the bills in the currency addition tasks and requesting merely an exchange of goods for currency in the currency subtraction tasks.

Sellers' identification of bill value denominations and count of those denominational values may be an important route to their construction of arithmetical functions linked to currency. In summing three bills, each Cr$1000, a seller produces a counting operation of 3 strokes, but one that results in a very large sum, Cr$3000. Indeed, in coordinating counting with a burgeoning understanding of the denominational structure of the currency system, the young seller begins to create a new arithmetical function, a function interwoven with the structure of currency.

While some 5- to 7-year-olds radically transformed the arithmetical problems into nonarithmetical ones, others showed evidence of structuring and deploying an arithmetical function. These 5- to 7-year-olds clearly identified the arithmetical problems in these tasks, and they used their knowledge of the cultural forms to attempt a summation of bills by progressively incrementing their sum by successive bill values, though their solution forms were often not well adapted to the characteristics of the problems. For instance, on the addition tasks, the younger sellers often did not reorder the bills, and they typically achieved inaccurate solutions. In contrast, the older sellers much more typically used specialized strategies of bill reordering, appropriating their knowledge of multiplicative relations to create convenient values (e.g., Cr$1000, Cr$500). When these older sellers did not reorder bill values, they nonetheless typically achieved accurate solutions. Such accuracy without the aid of bill-reordering strategies suggests that these older sellers had specialized covert means of keeping track of bill values.

In sum, just as we observe an interplay between form and function in sellers' currency-based representations, we observe an analogous process in sellers' emerging arithmetical knowledge.

COMPARING RATIOS

Recall that in Chapter 8, children were presented with three ratio comparison problems and, for each problem, they were asked which ratio would yield the greater profit (problem 1: one for Cr$200 vs. three for Cr$500; problem 2: three for Cr$500 vs. seven for Cr$1000; and, problem 3: one for Cr$200 vs. seven for Cr$1000). Now, we consider age-related differences in sellers' solutions of these problems.

To document differences, sellers' responses were coded with respect to whether they used a common term approach (e.g., equating the number of units of candy across the two ratios in order to compare the cash worth of the candy). Similar to the findings presented in Chapter 8, the large majority of children who did not use a common term approach based their judgments on a direct comparison between the value of the bills in the price ratios. The 7-year-old seller described here illustrates such a justification as well as a variation on this justification type.

> S No. 10. 7-year-old seller, first grade. S No. 10 is presented with each of the three ratio comparison problems. In comparing one for Cr$200 to three for Cr$500, he chooses three for Cr$500, stating that, "I'LL MAKE A LOT OF MONEY." (countersuggestion) "I'M STILL SAYING THAT I'LL SELL THREE FOR Cr$500—IT'LL GO FAST." In comparing one for Cr$200 to seven for Cr$1000, he chooses the seven for Cr$1000 because "YOU'LL MAKE A LOT OF MONEY." Finally, in comparing three for Cr$500 to seven for Cr$1000, he selects seven for Cr$1000 "BECAUSE YOU'LL MAKE A LOT MONEY.' (How do you know you'll make more money here seven for Cr$1000)? "BECAUSE HERE (seven for Cr$1000) THERE'S MORE MONEY" (countersuggestion) "SEVEN FOR Cr$1000 BRINGS MORE MONEY.'

In S No. 10's comparisons, sometimes he is concerned with making more money by selling for the greater bill denomination (as when he contrasts Cr$200 with

Cr$500 in his first comparison). At other times, he appears to assert that selling more units will make money. While this could be true, S No. 10 does not reference this assertion of greater number of units to the amount of money requested for each. In no comparison does he produce a coordination between the number of units across the ratios that would allow for an adequate comparison.

S No. 05, like S No. 10, did not use a common term approach, though S No. 05 introduces somewhat different considerations as a basis for his judgment.

> S No. 05. 6-year-old seller, no school. S No. 05 is presented with each of the three ratio comparison problems, and for these comparisons his notion of profit seems to be undifferentiated with the speed of finishing his box. In comparing one for Cr$200 to three for Cr$500, he chooses one for Cr$200 stating that, "IT'S CHEAP AND YOU'LL SELL MORE.' In comparing one for Cr$200 to seven for Cr$1000, he chooses the seven for Cr$1000 because "YOU'LL FINISH FAST; THEY'LL BUY FOR Cr$1000 AND YOU'LL FINISH FAST.' (countersuggestion) "I STILL THINK THAT Cr$1000 IS BETTER THAN Cr$200 . . . ."

Here, finishing fast may be equated with making more profit. S No. 05 sometimes cites speed of sale as a basis for his judgment of profit and sometimes cites the amount of units sold as a basis for his judgment. While such economic considerations are relevant to a determination of which ratio would yield the greater profit, S No. 05 appears merely to equate selling fast and making money without constraining this judgment by the amount he invested in the box or relative profit per ratio.

The percentage of common term approaches across the three ratio problems was calculated for each seller in the sample. Fig. 9.7 contains the mean percentage of common term approaches as a function of age group. A oneway ANOVA on sellers' common term scores revealed group differences ($F(2, 52) = 7.82$, $p < .005$). Duncan Multiple Range tests revealed that the 8- to 11-year-olds and the 12- to 15-year-olds achieved significantly higher scores than the 5- to 7-year-olds. Though the 12- to 15-year-olds' scores were higher than the 8- to 11-year-

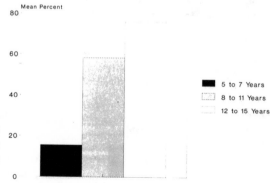

FIG. 9.7. Mean percentage of common term solutions to ratio problems as a function of age group.

olds, these differences were not statistically significant. There was also an age-linked trend in sellers' spontaneous assertions of the amount (in cruzeiros or candy) lost or gained by a given ratio (e.g., a seller might argue that one makes more profit in selling one for Cr$200 in contrast to three for Cr$500 because, in the second ratio, one loses Cr$100; see the excerpt from S No. 60 under Comparing Ratios in Chapter 8). Of the 12- to 15-year-olds who used a common term approach, between 71% and 89% spontaneously offered the cost/gain analysis on the three problems; of those 8- to 11-year-olds who used a common term approach, between 18% and 45% on the three problems spontaneously cited the cost/gain analysis.

Form–function Shifts in Sellers' Ratio Comparisons

Sellers' solutions to the ratio problems showed a pronounced shift over age level, a shift marked by an interplay between the use of price ratio forms in the selling practice and the emergence of cognitive functions involving ratio comparison. Recall that young sellers use ratios in their transaction with customers from a young age in the Sell Phase. The function that it served was to mediate transactions with customers—candies were exchanged for a particular bill denomination. We have seen that when young sellers were queried about ratio comparison problems, they seem unaware of adequate ways to compare ratios. We saw that most of the 5- to 7-year-olds and many of the 8- to 11-year-olds did not conceptualize the ratio comparison problems as ones which required the intermediate step—to reference the cash price across ratios to the number of units for sale, or to reference the number of units for sale across ratios to a common cash price.

We observed clear illustrations of such direct contrasts in the protocols of the young sellers cited. In these excerpts, while both numbers of units and amount of cash are critical elements in sellers' deliberations, these two elements are not related to one another—even when they are considered by the same seller in the same protocol for the same problem. S No. 10, for instance, chooses three for Cr$500 over one for Cr$200, saying that he will "MAKE A LOT OF MONEY," apparently contrasting directly Cr$200 with Cr$500; later, he contrasts these ratios but focuses solely on units, arguing that he will sell more quickly by selling three as contrasted with one unit, losing sight of the differences in cash to which these units must be referenced. Similarly, S No. 05 argues that selling one for Cr$200 yields a greater profit than three for Cr$500, not by referencing units to price, but by contrasting Cr$200 with Cr$500, arguing "IT'S CHEAP AND YOU'LL SELL MORE."

The use of the price ratio form in the street provides some clear opportunities for sellers to generate a new cognitive function in which price ratios can take on new mathematical properties that allow for adequate ratio comparisons. One path to the emergence of this cognitive function involving ratio comparisons is revealed in S No. 26's solution cited in Chapter 8 under Comparing Ratios. In S

No. 26's protocol, he conceptualizes the ratio comparison problem directly with reference to the activity of selling. In contrasting one for Cr$200 with three for Cr$500, S No. 26 justifies his judgment by noting the consequence of repeated sales: "HERE (ONE FOR Cr$200) I'D SELL THREE TIMES THREE OF THESE CANDIES AND I'D MAKE Cr$600, AND IN THE OTHER IT'S THREE FOR Cr$500. SO, I WOULD MAKE MORE SELLING ONE FOR Cr$200." In S No. 26's justification as well as that of many others, we see an appropriation and repeated application of sales transactions in terms of the price ratio form; in so doing, S No. 26 structures a basis for understanding the relative value of the terms in the ratio. It may be that as sellers repeatedly encounter problems of ratio comparison in the practice, such ratio comparison strategies become more distant from the act of selling, a point I return to in a consideration of transfer in Chapter 14.

TRANSLATING WHOLESALE BOX PRICES INTO RETAIL UNIT PRICES IN AN INFLATING ECONOMY

To document age-related shifts in sellers' translation of wholesale box prices into retail unit prices, the two retail pricing problems and inflation problems were used. For the pricing tasks, sellers were asked to translate wholesale box prices into retail unit prices without any mention of inflation; for the inflation tasks, sellers were queried about how they adjusted their pricing to accommodate inflationary surges in box prices.

Translating Wholesale Box to Retail Unit Prices

As in Chapter 8, the retail pricing tasks varied in the number of units in a box, the wholesale price of a box, and the type of candy in the box. In the first problem, the seller was presented with a 50-unit box of *Chupetim* costing Cr$3500; in the second, the seller was presented with a 30-unit box of *Chocolate Leila* costing Cr$8500. The following protocols present some illustrations of the youngest sellers' solutions to these problems. Note, particularly, that while we see various cultural forms of the practice emerging in sellers' solutions, we see little, if any, evidence that sellers attempt to use these forms to achieve a coordination between retail box and retail street prices.

> S No. 05. 6-year-old seller, no school. S No. 05 is presented with the problem of producing a retail price for a 50-unit box that cost Cr$3500 (wholesale price). He states that he will sell the whole box for Cr$1000 and that he will sell the candy one for Cr$100 to customers in the street (this unit price would actually lead him to a gross profit of Cr$5000). (How do you know that's a good price for you?) "IT'S GOOD BECAUSE MY GRANDMOTHER TAUGHT ME." For the second prob-

lem of producing a retail unit price for a 30-unit box for Cr$8500, S No. 05 states that he will sell the whole box for Cr$2000 and that he will charge customers one for Cr$500 (at one for Cr$500, the box would sell for Cr$15000). (How do you know that price is good for you?) "BECAUSE I KNOW." (Show me what you did to find out.) "BECAUSE Cr$500 IS NOT CHEAP AND IT'S NOT EXPEN-SIVE." Clearly, S No. 05, on his own, does not regard the importance of consider-ing the wholesale price in this computation.

S No. 10. 7-year-old seller, first grade. S No. 10 is presented with the problem of producing a retail price for a 50-unit box that cost Cr$3500. He states that he will sell the whole box for Cr$15000 and that he will sell the candy one for Cr$500 to customers in the street (this unit price would actually lead him to a gross of Cr$25000). (How do you know that's a good price for you?) "BECAUSE IT'LL BRING A LOT OF MONEY." (Show me what you did to find out.) "I DON'T KNOW." For the second problem of producing a retail unit price for a 30-unit box for Cr$8500, S No. 10 states that he will sell the whole box for Cr$8700 and that he will again charge customers one for Cr$500 (at one for Cr$500, the box would sell for Cr$15000). (How do you know that price is good for you?) "BECAUSE I'LL MAKE LOTS OF MONEY." (Show me what you did to find out.) "I DON'T KNOW."

S No. 06. 6-year-old seller, no schooling. For both pricing problems, S No. 06 shows little awareness of the need to coordinate wholesale price with the retail price, though he shows some partial knowledge of the pricing conventions. S No. 06 is presented with the problem of producing a retail unit price for a 50-unit box that cost Cr$3500. He states that he will sell the whole box for Cr$3500 and that he will sell the candy one for Cr$300 to customers in the street (this unit price would actually lead him to a gross sale of Cr$15000). (How do you know that's a good price for you?) "BECAUSE I'LL MAKE MORE." (Show me what you did to find out.) "ONE IS Cr$300 AND TWO IS Cr$500. IF A CUSTOMER WANTS FOUR HE'LL PAY Cr$1000. I'LL MAKE Cr$5000 FOR THE BOX." For the second problem of producing a retail unit price for a 30-unit box for Cr$8500, S No. 06 states that he will sell the whole box for Cr$10000 and that he will charge custom-ers one for Cr$500 (at one for Cr$500, the box would sell for Cr$15000). (How do you know that price is good for you?) "BECAUSE I'LL MAKE MORE." (Show me what you did to find out.) "TWO IS Cr$1000, FOUR IS Cr$4000."

In these solutions, we find the various cultural forms of the practice—the use of varying price ratio conventions (e.g., S No. 06's one for Cr$300, two for Cr$500, or four for Cr$1000), the appeal to more knowledgeable others in pricing (e.g., S No. 05's appeal to his grandmother), and the large currency denominations. For the most part, however, we find little if any evidence that sellers even attempt to coordinate retail box and retail street prices with one another. Indeed, S No. 05 produces retail box prices that are below his wholesale cost while his retail unit prices are considerably above his cost. S No. 10 produces retail box prices that are either way above cost (a retail box price of Cr$15000 for a wholesale box at Cr$3500) or only very slightly above cost (a retail box price of Cr$8700 for a wholesale box at Cr$8500) and, in both cases, produces unit prices that are widely discrepant from his box prices. Finally, S No. 06 again offers retail box prices that are either identical with wholesale prices or somewhat above (Cr$8500 to Cr$10000). For both problems, his coordination of his stated retail box price again differs markedly from his wholesale box price.

While these various forms of the practice as they appear in the young sellers' solutions do not lead to coordinated adjustments, at the end of S No. 06's protocol we see some indication of a path that would ultimately lead to the adequate coordination described in sellers' solutions of Chapters 6 and 8. S No. 06 asserts that he will sell his box for the single unit price of one for Cr$500, and in justifying this price, he begins a count, presumably indicating that "one would sell for Cr$500, two is Cr$1000, four is Cr$4000." While the third term of this double enumeration is in error, S No. 06 appears to have a budding insight into ways of translating his price per units with a retail box price. However, this young seller is only beginning to appreciate the coordinations required for an adequate solution, for left unaddressed in his approach is the relation between his wholesale box prices and his retail box prices. Clearly, in S No. 06's solution, we are far from the adequate orchestration of these forms to serve the pricing function which characterize the *count by ratio* and related strategies detailed in Chapters 6 and 8 (and subsequently in 15).

Use of Price Ratio Convention

Fig. 9.8 contains the distribution of sellers' retail prices for the mark-up problems—sellers' use of the standard convention (selling multiple units for a bill denomination, usually Cr$1000) and sellers' single unit pricing as a function of problem and age group. For both problems, only a minority of the 5- to 7-year-olds used the price convention. In contrast, the large majority of the 8- to 11-year-olds and 12- to 15-year-olds used the convention (problem 1, chi-square (2, $n = 56$) = 19.16, $p < .0001$; problem 2, chi-square (2, $n = 56$) = 14.02, $p < .001$). As noted, an important consequence for pricing in terms of the ratio convention in single units is that the structure of the pricing problem differs— when a seller prices in terms of the convention, he must translate his wholesale box price into a multi-unit price, a problem with a somewhat different structure than the same translation into a single unit price.

Solution Strategies.   Fig. 9.9 contains a distribution of the two strategy types that yielded coordinated box and unit prices as a function of age for each problem. The figure reveals that only rarely do 5- to 7-year-olds produce coordinated solutions, and that these sellers' solutions were covert and might well have been guesses. With age, sellers increasingly produced adequate solution strat-

Box Cost: 50 Units @ Cr$3500

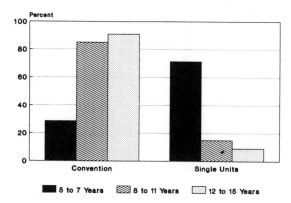

Box Cost: 30 Units @ Cr$8500

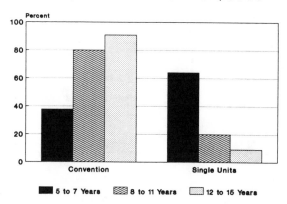

FIG. 9.8. Percentage of sellers using the price ratio convention as a function of problem and age group.

egies for both problem 1 (chi-square (2, N = 57) = 12.23, p < .005) and problem 2 (chi-square (2, N = 57) = 17.16, p < .001). Additional chi-square tests revealed that for both problems we see a shift over age groups toward more adequate coordinations in sellers' solutions to the pricing problems. For problem 1, two contrasts were statistically significant: between the 5- to 7- and 8- to 11-year-olds (chi-square (1, N = 35) = 5.59, p < .05) and that between the 5- to 7- and 12- to 15-year-olds (chi-square (1, N = 37) = 9.76, p < .01). For problem 2, again, two contrasts were significant: between the 8- to 11- and 12- to 15-year-olds (chi-square (1, N = 4.68, p < .05) and between the 5- to 7- and 12- to 15-year-olds (chi-square (1, N = 37) = 14.20, p < .001).

Box Cost: 50 Units @ Cr$3500

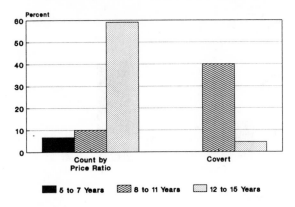

Box Cost: 30 Units @ Cr$8500

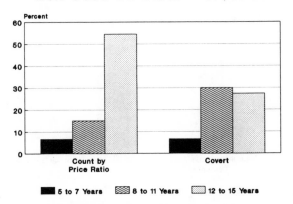

FIG. 9.9. Percentage of sellers using 1 of 2 appropriate strategy types to mark-up problems as a function of problem and age group.

Adjusting for Inflation

As in Chapter 8, the two inflation problems presented to sellers varied in problem format. For the first problem, sellers were told the initial wholesale price of a box of candy (Cr$4000) and were asked to generate an appropriate retail price for the *entire* box. They were then asked to reproduce this mark-up after inflation led to a specified rise in the wholesale price of the same box type (to Cr$7000). Thus, the seller was presented with the following proportionality problem: Cr$4000 : Cr$??? :: Cr$7000 :: Cr$???. For the second problem, sellers were told both the wholesale price (Cr$3000) and the gross retail price (Cr$6000) a seller used during one time period; the seller was asked to reproduce the mark-up after an inflationary rise in wholesale prices (to Cr$9000). Thus, the seller was presented with this proportionality problem: Cr$3000 : Cr$6000 :: Cr$9000 : Cr$???. Like Chapter 8, sellers' adjustments for inflation were analyzed with respect to their awareness of the existence of inflation and their pricing adjustments to compensate for inflation.

The examples will provide some illustrations of the youngest sellers' efforts. Though most young sellers showed little awareness of the concept of profit and that prices need to be adjusted due to inflationary surges, they nonetheless expected wholesale prices of the specified boxes to rise over time. (For problem 1, only one 5- to 7-year-old responded that he did not expect wholesale prices to rise, and for problem 2, only three members of the 5- to 7-year-old group did not expect prices to rise.) Despite sellers' general awareness of inflation, in the following protocols we see no awareness of the need to adjust prices to make a profit, and there is no evidence whatsoever of the need to produce proportional adjustments.

S No. 05. 6-year-old seller, no school. S No. 05 was introduced to the first inflation problem Cr$4000 : XXX :: Cr$7000 : YYY. For the wholesale price of Cr$4000, S No. 05 responded with a retail price of Cr$2200, and for the wholesale price rise to Cr$7000, the child responded with the retail price of Cr$1500. He was asked how he knew that was a good price and he responded, "BECAUSE IN AN INSTANT PEOPLE WILL BUY IT." (Show me how you figure this out.) "FOR THAT PRICE THE CANDY WON'T BECOME OLD—IT'LL SELL QUICKLY." S No. 05 is then presented with the second inflation (Cr$3000 : Cr$6000 :: Cr$9000 : Cr$???). He responds, "Cr$1000" and is asked the reason for his decision. He responds, "BECAUSE IT'S CHEAP AND YOU'D FINISH SOON SO THE CANDY DOESN'T BECOME OLD." (As noted in Part I, during the summer months, the intense heat tends to melt chocolate bars and to render sugary candy sticky.)

S No. 03. 7-year-old seller, no school. For the first inflation problem, Cr$4000 : XXX :: Cr$7000 : YYY, S No. 03 gave identical retail prices as were given for wholesale prices, Cr$4000 and Cr$7000. (How do you know [you marked prices in the same way as before]?) "BECAUSE I GET THE SAME MONEY." For the second problem, Cr$3000 : Cr$6000 :: Cr$9000 : ???, the child again responded with an adjusted retail price that was equivalent to the new wholesale price, Cr$9000. (How do you know [you marked prices in the same way as before?]) "BECAUSE IT'S ENOUGH TO BUY ANOTHER BOX."

Two features of S No. 05 and S No. 03's protocols are particularly noteworthy. One concerns the wholesale-to-retail price relation at time 2 as contrasted with time 1. The other concerns their awareness of the need to make a profit.

Neither show a concern to reference the relation between their wholesale and retail price at time 2 to that at time 1. Instead, both focus on the prices at time 2, S No. 05 apparently focuses only on the retail price at time 2, arguing "FOR THAT PRICE, THE CANDY WON'T BECOME OLD—IT'LL SELL QUICK-

LY . . . BECAUSE IN ONE INSTANT PEOPLE WILL BUY IT." S No. 03 is concerned with both the wholesale and retail price at time 2, noting that in selling his box at cost that "I GET THE SAME MONEY."

Neither S No. 05 nor S No. 03 show an awareness of the need to make a profit. They offer retail prices that are below or equal to the wholesale prices. In the case of S No. 05, his concern is to sell his box at an inexpensive price (which happens to be below wholesale cost) so that he will have a high volume of sale, apparently unaware of the constraint his wholesale price sets on his retail price. S No. 03 also neglects a consideration of profit in his decision to make his retail price the same as his wholesale prices "BECAUSE IT'S ENOUGH TO BUY ANOTHER BOX."

In the case of S No. 10, we find an emerging concern to make money. However, this concern does not appear to be referenced to the constraint of speed of sale, and S No. 10 proposes some extraordinarily high prices that, like S No. 05, do not appear to be referenced to his wholesale price. In the following case, we see an initial concern for profit, but still no awareness of the need to reference the wholesale-to-retail price relation at time 2 to that at time 1.

S No. 10. 7-year-old seller, first grade. S No. 10 was introduced to the first inflation problem Cr$4000 : XXX :: Cr$7000 : YYY. For the wholesale price of Cr$4000, S No. 10 responded with a retail price of Cr$7000 and for the wholesale price rise to Cr$7000, he responded with the retail price of Cr$80000. He was asked how he knew that was a good price and he responded, "BECAUSE YOU'D MAKE A LOT OF MONEY." S No. 10 is then presented with the second inflation (Cr$3000 : Cr$6000 :: Cr$9000 : Cr$???). He responded Cr$80000 again and he was again asked the reason for his decision. He responded, "BECAUSE YOU'D MAKE A LOT OF MONEY." He was then given the countersuggestions and follow-up questions to which he responded that he did not know.

The focus on only the price relation at time 2 in solving the mark-up problems that have been presented is characteristic of the solution of the younger sellers. In S No. 06's solution to the following problem, we see a shift toward a concern with the relation between the mark-up at time 1 with that of time 2. However, his solution to the second problem suggests that this first solution may be merely a perseverative response and that S No. 06 is merely focusing on increasing his retail price by his favored value of Cr$1000.

S No. 06. 6-year-old seller, no schooling. S No. 06 was introduced to the first inflation problem Cr$4000 : XXX :: Cr$7000 : YYY. For the wholesale price of Cr$4000, S No. 06 responded with a retail price of Cr$5000 and for the wholesale price rise to Cr$7000, the child responded with the retail price of Cr$8000. He was asked how he knew that was a good price and he responded, "BECAUSE IT'LL DO." S No. 06 was then presented with the second inflation (Cr$3000 : Cr$6000 :: Cr$9000 : Cr$???). He responded, "Cr$10000" and he was asked the reason for his decision. He responded, "BECAUSE I KNOW." (He was then given the countersuggestion: But at Christmas your profit was Cr$3000 and now you want a profit of Cr$1000. Why?) "BECAUSE THE PRICES ROSE." (How do you know how much to increase the prices?) "IT'S MORE EXPENSIVE. YOU HAVE TO SELL FOR MORE." (Show me how you figure this out.) "I DON'T KNOW."

S No. 06 appears to have a sense that one needs to make a profit in selling, offering answers in which retail prices at time 2 are higher (but not markedly higher) than wholesale prices. Thus, in the first problem, he offers a selling price at time 1 and time 2 of Cr$1000 above the respective wholesale prices. While these prices suggest he may be concerned with an additive equivalence across the two sale periods, and thus considers one price relation with reference to the other, his price for the second problem (Cr$10000) suggests that he merely adds Cr$1000 to any wholesale price to a retail price and is unconcerned with replicating the relation across time periods in either an additive or proportional sense (indeed, selling at Cr$10000 at time 2 for the second problem leads to a loss of Cr$2000).

Fig. 9.10 contains the distribution of sellers' assigned categories (using the same coding scheme as that presented in Chapter 8) as a function of age group for problems 1 and 2. In the figure, I have excluded from analysis two 5- to 7-year-olds from problem 1 and one 5- to 7-year-old from problem 2: these sellers offered responses in which, like those of S No. 10, the profit margin was at least sevenfold.

Fig. 9.10 reveals that the nature of sellers' adjustments for inflation differed dramatically over age. For both problems, the majority of the youngest sellers offered *No Profit* adjustments, whereas none of the 8- to 11-year-olds or 12- to 15-year-olds offered such responses (contrasting *No Profit* with all other response types, and pooling 8- to 11-year-olds with 12- to 15-year-olds, problem 1: chi-square $(1, N = 55) = 20.86, p < .001$; for problem 2: chi-square $(1, N = 57) = 25.58, p < .001$). Further analyses revealed that with age, sellers increasingly offered partial and proportional adjustments for both problem 1 (chi-square $(2, N = 55) = 8.19, p < .05$) and problem 2 (chi-square $(2, N = 56) = 34.26 \, p < .0001$). Follow-up chi-square tests revealed that for problem 1, the only significant contrast was between the 5- to 7-year-olds and the 12- to 15-year-olds (chi-square $(1, N = 35) = 5.55, p < .05$); for problem 2, contrasts were significant between both the 5- to 7-year-olds and 8- to 11-year-olds (chi-square $(1, N = 34) = 13.95, p < .001$) and between the 5- to 7-year-olds and the 12- to 15-year-olds (chi-square $(1, N = 36) = 24.56, p < .0001$).

On problem 2, we noted in the case of S No. 60 presented in Chapter 8, some sellers opted not to use a proportional solution because of the constraint of the price ratio convention. Selling candy for 18000 cruzeiros for a 30-unit box would not allow a solution (in selling multiple units for Cr$1000). As a result, S No. 60 vacillated between Cr$15000 and Cr$30000, two solutions to the problem that

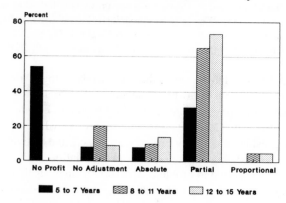

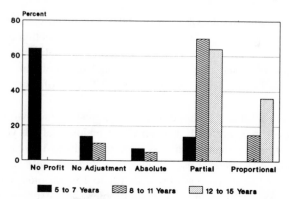

FIG. 9.10.   Percentage of sellers using 1 of 5 adjustment types
to inflation problems as a function of problem and age group.

would allow him to sell his candy for three for Cr$1000 or two for Cr$1000,
respectively. An inspection of sellers' responses that were coded as "partial" for
problem 2 suggests that quite a few sellers underwent similar deliberations, and
that these deliberations were more characteristic of the older two age groups.
Neither of the two 5- to 7-year-olds who offered partial adjustment responses
offered Cr$15000 or Cr$30000 as their retail price. In contrast, five of the
fourteen 8- to 11-year-olds and five of the fourteen 12- to 15-year-olds who
offered partial adjustment responses offered either Cr$15000 or Cr$30000 as
their partial adjustment prices.

Sellers' explicit reference to the "half-half" convention increased over age
group but only for the second inflation problem did the increase approach statis-

tical significance. In problem 1, 7% of the 5- to 7-year-olds, 15% of the 8- to 11-year-olds and 14% of the 12- to 15-year-olds referred to this convention (chi-square $(2, n = 57) = 2.42, p = $ n.s.) and in problem 2, none of the 5- to 7-year-olds, 15% of the 8- to 11-year-olds, and 32% of the 12- to 15-year-olds referred to the convention (chi square $(2, n = 57) = 5.72, p = .057$).

In summary, many of the 5- to 7-year-olds demonstrate little awareness of the need to make adjustments in markups after inflationary price rises; these sellers appear to focus on either simply the retail price at time 2 or the relation between their wholesale and retail price at time 2. In contrast, the older sellers increasingly raise their absolute profit margin after an inflationary shift, and an increasing number explicitly use the selling convention of "half-half" to achieve this pricing adjustment. These absolute, partial, and proportional adjustments imply that sellers are considering the relation between wholesale and retail prices at both selling periods in achieving their solutions.

Form–function Shifts in Sellers' Wholesale to Retail Price Translations

The mathematical problems that sellers address in translating wholesale prices into retail prices are framed by their developing economic understandings—particularly their understanding of profit and the various economic processes in which this concept is interrelated (e.g., concepts of labor, of merchandise). In an effort to accomplish their translations with differing conceptualizations of profit, sellers of different ages show that they appropriate and specialize in different kinds of practice-linked forms to accomplish different kinds of mathematical functions.

For the younger sellers, we found little evidence that they referenced their retail prices to their wholesale prices either in the mark-up or in the inflation problems. In both problem types, many young sellers either produced lower retail prices than wholesale prices or exorbitantly high retail prices. Further, in solving mark-up problems, many young sellers did not appear to understand that one must balance an interest in pricing a box to make an unlimited amount of money with an interest in producing a large volume of sales. We saw, for instance, in the case of S No. 10 that he sets his retail box price of a Cr$3500 box at Cr$80000, "BECAUSE YOU'D MAKE A LOT OF MONEY," apparently quite unaware of the consequences of such a price for retail unit price and its probable effect upon sales. In the case of S No. 05, he sets his retail box price at a lower price than his wholesale price "BECAUSE IN AN INSTANT PEOPLE WILL BUY IT . . . FOR THAT PRICE THE CANDY WON'T BECOME OLD—IT'LL SELL QUICKLY", apparently unaware of the effect of such a price on profit.

For the older seller, the concept of profit and the way it is handled in wholesale to retail translations is constrained by two aspects of the practice's structure.

A seller must price his box greater than what he paid for it so that he will make money and, generally, the more money the better. This constraint is modified by a second one—speed of sale: The seller must price his box low enough so that he will be able to find customers who are willing to pay for his candy. We saw this tradeoff between unlimited monetary gain and speed of sale expressed well in the protocol of older sellers in Chapter 6. In OBS No. 08, the 14-year-old seller explained that his profit of Cr$4000 (wholesale cost Cr$6000, Retail box price: Cr$10000) was "NOT SO GOOD, BUT I CAN EARN A LITTLE." When asked, "Why don't you sell some other way to earn more?", he responded, ". . . IF I SELL FOR MORE THE PEOPLE WON'T BUY THE ZORROS."

Older sellers were much more likely to show evidence of a tension between balancing speed of sale with maximizing the intake of cash per sale. Some older sellers resolve this tension by specializing practice-linked forms to serve functions that differ markedly from those of the younger sellers, functions that are often mathematical in character. For instance, the price ratio itself becomes a means of coordinating wholesale box with retail prices, through the *count by ratio* strategies. In these instances, the price ratio takes on a mathematical function in solutions of the mark-up problems. In the inflation problems, the half-half convention is appropriated and used by the older sellers to guide appropriate price setting, a form that takes on new mathematical meaning with the emergence of a concern to consider the mathematical relation between wholesale to retail prices at time 2 with that of time 1.

FORM–FUNCTION SHIFTS
IN SELLERS' MATHEMATICS

The analyses presented in this chapter show that sellers are appropriating and specializing practice-linked forms to serve their own ends in constructing and accomplishing emergent mathematical goals, and further, that new and varied mathematical functions develop through this process; these novel functions, in turn, create conditions for the appropriation and specialization of new forms. Thus, we have seen the process of shifting relations between form and function in various mathematical domains of the practice sampled in the study including number representation, currency arithmetic, ratio comparisons, and mark-up. While the preceding analyses have focused on form–function shifts within domains, these shifts may occur more or less concurrently with one another across domains, and it is likely that relations across domains are instrumental to the developmental process. Consider ways in which shifts in one domain may provide important conditions for specialization of forms in another.

In their specialization of knowledge of currency as a means to accomplish representational functions (nominal, ordinal, multiplicative), sellers may draw on the emerging cognitive function of arithmetic, though the way in which such arithmetical knowledge may be used probably differs with the age of the seller. For the young seller, an emerging arithmetical function may be essential for beginning to structure multiplicative relations between values, like two Cr$100 bills is equivalent to one Cr$200 bill. For the older seller, arithmetic may be critical for determining relations between new issues of currency and values already known. For instance, with the issue of the Cr$100000 bill, a seller could compute arithmetically the number of Cr$5000 bills equivalent to the Cr$10000 bill.

In sellers' specialization of strategies to accomplish arithmetical functions like the arithmetical composition of bill values in problem solving, sellers must draw on their knowledge of bill values. For younger sellers, the use of such knowledge may be limited to calculating simple sums between large values like Cr$500 plus Cr$100. For older sellers, they may draw on their knowledge of multiplicative relations between currency units in structuring complex bill ordering and re-grouping strategies.

In their construction of ratios and means of comparing ratios, sellers may draw on both their developing representational knowledge of currency as well as arithmetical knowledge. For the young seller, in constructing and accomplishing ratio-regulated exchanges with customers, young sellers may use their knowl-edge of currency to identify appropriate bill values and they may draw on their knowledge of arithmetic to produce computations in such exchanges. With age, sellers may increasingly incorporate their specialized representational forms for representing large values in generating contrasts across ratios; and, in construct-ing these contrasts, they may draw on their knowledge of arithmetic in construct-ing equivalence relations between ratios.

In sellers' construction of wholesale to retail price translations, we see their use of the various specialized knowledge forms interwoven with one another in their solutions. For the young seller, wholesale to retail price translations are not common in the practice. With age, sellers increasingly draw on their representa-tion of large values, their arithmetical problem solving, and their knowledge of ratios in structuring coordinations between wholesale and retail prices. For in-stance, in the *count by price ratio* strategy, we see a specialized use of the price ratio as a means to translate wholesale to retail prices, and arithmetical opera-tions with currency to produce appropriate mark-ups.

A final word on sellers' use of currency in mathematical problem solving: In the early structuration of the multiplicative and ordinal relations between curren-cy units, I have suggested that for the young seller, knowledge of ordinal and multiplicative relations between bills is not a symptom of children's concep-tualization of bills as a numerical series. Rather, bills themselves may be simply contrasted as different nominal values that may be compared and contrasted and knowledge of ordinal and multiplicative relations may be "local" to specific comparisons. As such, currency is merely the functional equivalent of a number system in dealings with customers.

As sellers become involved in addressing numerical and arithmetical goals, they may increasingly specialize the early emerging knowledge of these ordinal and multiplicative relations such that they are increasingly deployed numerically. In this process, the seller must create intermediate values between currency denominations, and as such, a numerical series is progressively constructed that is increasingly independent of the denominational structure of the currency system. While no longer depending directly on currency for the representation of values, the older seller may nonetheless invoke currency in new ways as a symbolic vehicle in computation. For instance, we have seen that many of the older sellers reordered the bills as a means to facilitate their bill additions, organizing subgroups of currency units into convenient values.

So far, we have not yet compared nor discussed the relation between the knowledge forms of the young seller and the older nonseller. Such a contrast is relevant to discussions of the relation between cognitive development and expertise (see Chi, Glaser, & Rees, 1982; Glaser, 1986). If one examines their performances across the various mathematical tasks, one finds that in general, the older (10- to 12-year-old) nonsellers tend to show similar (though somewhat more advanced) levels of performance than the 5- to 7-year-old sellers across the tasks.

The relation between young sellers' and older nonsellers' performances is complex, and must be addressed at two levels of analysis. First, we can ask the specific question, are there fundamental differences in understandings of the young sellers and the older nonsellers in their mathematical problem solving despite similar performances on the mathematical tasks presented in the prior chapters? Second, to the extent to which we conclude that there are no fundamental differences in problem solving within a specific domain, we can ask are these similarities indicative of similarities in the understandings of young sellers and older nonsellers across other knowledge domains?

With regard to specific comparisons in the performances of young sellers and older nonsellers on the mathematics tasks, the prior discussions provide some reasonable possibilities. First, it may be that some young sellers are able to make use of conventions of the practice in ways that allow them to achieve adequate solutions to problems based on conceptual knowledge that is less differentiated than a child who does not have intimate knowledge of the practice. Thus we find that some sellers may be able to draw on the price ratio convention in addressing mark-up problems where the older rural nonseller may have no knowledge of such conventions and, to solve the problem adequately, may define the problem in quite different terms that require more complex cognitive coordinations. Such an explanation points to the interwoven nature of strategic approaches and conceptual understandings. Second, in other cases, it may be that young sellers have structured sophisticated understandings that are on a par with the older nonsellers. Neither explanation precludes the other, and it is likely that one explanation is appropriate in one circumstance and the other in another.

With regard to the more general issue of the relation between the cognitions in other domains of the young sellers and the older nonsellers, I have already noted that the nonsellers (rural) who are straw weavers develop more sophisticated topological concepts than their candy-selling age-mates. Such findings suggest that children who participate in different practices develop more sophisticated cognitive forms and functions linked to those specific practices. While these developments may not be obvious to the examiner studying children's knowledge in one particular knowledge domain, they may nonetheless be important aspects of cognitive organization and problem solving. Such aspects may be revealed with participation in a new practice; with repeated encounters with problems of a new sort, such prior knowledge may be appropriated, and be a basis for both organizing particular kinds of goals and specializing forms in unique ways—a process that we have already seen illustrated in the newly emerging practices of economic exchange in the Oksapmin community. This line of interpretation then, bears directly on the interplay between learning across practices, an issue that we turn to in Part IV.

10 Form–function Shifts in Sellers' Mathematics: Links between Components 1 and 2

To understand more fully the interdependence between sociocultural and cognitive developmental processes in sellers' developing mathematics requires an integration of the two sets of analyses presented in prior chapters. Analyses of the enculturation process—the social organization of the practice and its emergent goals that allows sellers of different ages and ability levels to participate (component 1 presented in Chapters 3 to 7) must be integrated with the analysis of form and function in sellers' mathematics (component 2 presented in Chapters 8 and 9). While I have pointed to this integration in the prior chapter, in the present chapter I sketch a further integration, one that I return to in the concluding chapter.

The analysis of the social organization of the candy-selling practice revealed that to participate, mathematical goals of some complexity had to be accomplished involving the representation of large values (as when sellers sold to customers in the street), complex addition and subtraction (as when sellers counted their money in preparation for a purchase), ratio comparisons (as when sellers considered their own price relative to a crab), and adjusting for an inflationary economy in pricing (as when sellers translated their wholesale box prices to retail prices). Despite the complexity of the mathematical problems generated in the practice, the organization enabled sellers of varying age levels to participate. Indeed, the mathematical goals which emerged for sellers differed in complexity as a function of age, but, regardless of age, sellers were able to function effectively in the practice.

For the 5- to 7-year-olds, participation in the practice necessarily entailed the use of various cultural forms. Indeed, the principal mathematical goals involved exchanges of currency for merchandise in transactions with customers mediated by sellers' use of the price ratio: Sellers sought exchanges between multiple units of candies and a single bill denomination or bills summing to that denomination. The additional culturally rooted forms sellers organized to accomplish these exchanges were themselves interwoven with the emergent problems; to accomplish exchanges, sellers had to identify bills by their numerical value and, upon occasion, sellers tallied their currency. Thus, the culturally evolving forms of currency and price ratios become the young sellers' cognitive forms as they are appropriated and used. As these forms are used, sellers may both structure more differentiated knowledge of the arithmetical structure of the currency system, and they learn to sell at different ratios.

Noteworthy as well in the activities of the young seller are the mathematical goals that did not emerge. Five- to 7-year-old sellers did not engage in the more complex mathematical problems of the practice, such as complex bill additions, wholesale–retail price translations, adjustments for inflation, and ratio comparisons. For these sellers, the solution of these problems was largely accomplished by relatives, peers, and store clerks, or were simply avoided by sellers (e.g., refusing to negotiate prices, selling for only a single ratio). Such social support, combined with the affective appeal of young sellers to customers, appeared to give rise to a particular ecology that led sellers to generate a mathematical competence that served them well in the practice, a competence that is quite distinct from that of the older sellers.

Through 8 and 11 years, the emergent mathematical goals of the practice gradually shifted in complexity. Sellers became engaged with phases of the practice in which arithmetical problems typically arose involving addition and subtraction of bill values, and some became involved with translation of wholesale box to retail unit prices. In more or less concert with these newly emerging problems, the 8- to 11-year-olds structured and specialized culturally rooted cognitive forms to accomplish new problems. They used their knowledge of bill values in specializing computational procedures to solve addition and subtraction problems; they began to use their knowledge of price ratio conventions to produce retail prices for candy, and they demonstrated an emerging ability to compare price ratios. Despite their increasing independence in accomplishing practice-related goals, when needed, sellers drew on the assistance of store clerks and peers.

At 12 to 15 years, sellers showed additional shifts in the mathematics of the practice. Sellers were increasingly engaged in producing their own mark-ups and they showed increasing ability to coordinate wholesale box and retail unit prices in their mark-up solutions. In ratio comparisons, sellers more frequently used common term approaches, more specialized strategies for the summation of currency, and more sophisticated price translation strategies. While some sellers still drew on the assistance of store clerks and peers as they accomplished practice-linked problems, many structured a mathematics which allowed them considerable mathematical independence, yet one that reflects an orchestration and specialization of the practice-linked forms of price ratio conventions, currency, and means of negotiating social interactions.

Despite sellers' mathematical competence displayed in the given analyses, if mastery of "school mathematics" were taken as the measure of sellers' competence—where "school mathematics" is defined as knowledge of the standard number orthography and computational procedures—12- to 15-year-old sellers' mathematical competence would be assessed as deficient. Recall, for instance, that a majority of the 12- to 15-year-old sellers failed to identify more than half of the written values correctly on the reading numbers task, a level of performance that alone would result in errors if these sellers attempted arithmetical algorithms on orthographic representations. Sellers' performances on the tasks linked to the selling practice, however, revealed a mathematics that differs in its organization from the mathematics taught at school, a mathematics well adapted to solving the practice-related problems involving the representation of large values, arithmetical transformations on large values, multiplication and division of values in pricing translations, ratio comparisons, and retail price adjustments to wholesale markups. Indeed, even the youngest sellers performed competently in the practice, their mathematical activities interwoven with the various sociocultural supports.

In subsequent chapters, I move on to address directly the links between the mathematics of the school classroom and the mathematics of out-of-school activities of which candy sellers' mathematics is an instance: Does the mathematics of the practice influence how sellers appropriate and specialize forms taught at school? Do forms children learn at school influence the way sellers construct and address problems of the practice?

IV

COMPONENT 3: THE INTERPLAY BETWEEN LEARNING IN AND OUT OF SCHOOL

My concern in the following chapters is to extend the first two components of the research model—emergent goals (component 1) and form–function shifts (component 2)—to an analysis of the interplay between learning across the practice of candy selling and school mathematics lessons. To accomplish this extension, we need to consider first the way that emergent mathematical goals in school may be distinct from those that take form in the candy-selling practice and then consider the way cognitive forms linked to one context may be used to accomplish problems in another.

In Parts I and II, I showed that the emergent mathematical goals of the candy-selling practice could be understood with reference to four parameters: activity structures, cultural artifacts, social interactions, and children's prior understandings. Let us now contrast the mathematical goals that emerge in the selling practice and in school with reference to these parameters.

I argued in Part II that the activity structure of the candy-selling practice is economic, and the seller's principal motive (especially for the older seller) is to make money. We have already seen that this money-making motive colors candy sellers' mathematical goals in some fundamental ways. The economic orientation of sellers means that the norms for solving practice-linked problems may not be principally mathematical ones. Indeed, what constitutes an adequate solution to a mark-up problem is ultimately evaluated with respect to economic considerations and mathematical operations may only be invoked as a heuristic in achieving this end. Further, in cognizing the relevant terms in a mark-up problem, children are guided by their economic understandings. Thus, sellers are engaged with such questions as "For what price should I sell this box for in units?" or "How much profit should I make?" While sellers may make reference to deductive necessity within a mathematical structure in performing arithmetical operations, a principal motive of the activity is to make an income and economical considerations may, and often do, take precedence over mathematical ones in problem solving. Consider, for instance, the seller (S No. 60 from Chapter 8, under Inflation) who appeared to be aware of and acknowledge the proportional solution to the pricing problem, Cr$3000 : Cr$6000 :: Cr$9000 : ???. He argued, however, that this value is inappropriate since the use of the price ratio convention allows only two reasonable prices for a 30-unit box which had a wholesale price of Cr$9000 using the half-half convention—two for Cr$1000, a price that would yield a gross value of Cr$15000, and one for Cr$1000, a price that would yield a gross of Cr$30000.

In school mathematics lessons, children's principal motives differ from those of selling candy. In school, mathematics is an object of study without a pragmatic end. Rather than being motivated by economic concerns, the child in school may be striving to do well on a test, to achieve teacher approval, or (as one would hope) to understand properties of mathematics itself—as a deductive system that can be used flexibly in problem solving. The pedagogical objective in many mathematics classes is for children, when doing mathematics, to appeal to mathematical norms of correctness without worldly constraints.

These differences in motives associated with the selling practice and with school mean that mathematical error takes on different meaning across the two contexts. In solving problems in the selling practice, candy sellers are often not concerned with achieving mathematically exact solutions to problems when the value of the cruzeiro is worth so little—in fact, it would be unwise to do so. Sellers even use an expression coined for the Cr$100 bill, the "skin of a mouse," at best, a valueless denomination. Sellers' principal concern lies in the loss of significant income. In contrast, in the school classroom error is evaluated with reference to mathematical norms. An error, regardless of its numerical size or the other extramathematical constraints bearing on problem solving, is an error.

Marked contrasts between social interactions and principal artifacts also highlight differences between the emergent mathematical goals in candy selling and in school. In candy selling, the interactions are often between equals, whether in price setting with peers, or dealing with crabs selling for different ratios. While sellers do rely on more knowledgeable others like store clerks, the reliance is generally to accomplish specific practice-linked tasks and often is not specifically to teach problem-solving approaches or impart understandings through extended explanations. These are interactions which enable sellers to continue with their business. Further, unlike school, for the most part the seller has the ultimate say on what determines the appropriate way to sell; it is the seller himself who bears the loss or gain of his selling efforts and it is a loss intrinsically linked to his mathematics.

In school, children participate principally in asymmetrically organized interactions in which the teacher attempts to transmit a structured curriculum, the parameters of which are often unknown to the child. These interactions are typically not organized to lead to some successful pragmatic goal, but are organized expressly to teach or to provide children with opportunities for learning for its own sake, opportunities for which children may see little intrinsic purpose. The school curriculum is rooted in specialized mathematical forms (Hindu-Arabic number orthography, place value, arithmetical algorithms) that are often a direct target of instructional interactions. These specialized mathematical forms have emerged over an extended and complex cultural history (for noteworthy accounts of this history, see Damerow, 1986; Menninger, 1969; Nickerson, 1988; Schmandt–Besserat, 1984; Swetz, 1987). While the Hindu–Arabic system (first introduced to Europe in the 11th century) is remarkably efficient compared with prior ones, it is also more opaque conceptually; the mathematical meaning of the procedures used for addition with carrying and subtraction with borrowing are not obvious to the uninitiated. In school, children construct mathematical goals that are interwoven with these orthographic forms, and they are expected to develop specialized knowledge of arithmetic using these forms.

SCHOOL MATHEMATICS: CHILDREN'S DIFFICULTIES AND SOME PRELIMINARY NOTES ON THE INTERPLAY BETWEEN MATH LEARNING IN SCHOOL AND OUT

We have a considerable research literature on elementary children's school-linked mathematics (for reviews see, for example, Baroody, 1987; Hiebert & Behr, 1988; Resnick & Ford, 1981). This literature documents elementary schoolchildren's difficulty in acquiring an understanding of arithmetical algorithms (Brown & Burton, 1978; Resnick & Omanson, 1987), fractions (Behr, Lesh, Post, & Silver, 1983; Ohlsson, 1988), and ratios and proportions (Hart, 1988; Inhelder & Piaget, 1958; Karplus, Pulos, & Stage, 1983; Lesh, Post, & Behr, 1988). Even when children do demonstrate facility with these representational and algorithmic forms, the conceptual meaning of these forms is often not clear. Long after children acquire the ability to identify multidigit numbers like 235, children will argue that the 2 in the numerical expression is equivalent to the value of two units rather than two units of 100 or 200 (Fuson, 1989; Kamii, 1986; Miura & Okamoto, in press). Or, after mastering algorithms for subtraction, when queried, children are often perplexed when asked about the reason for changing values of 0s to 9s even when they solve the problems correctly (Cauley, 1988; Hiebert, 1984). In solving ratio and proportion problems, many children have difficulty comparing relations across numerical pairs, as we have seen illustrated in young sellers and nonsellers reasoning on the inflation problems in Chapters 8 and 9.

Out-of-School Mathematics Learning. The opaqueness of orthography-linked mathematical operations leads some school children to try to make sense of classroom mathematics by applying what they know—sometimes knowledge generated in out-of-school activities—to problems in school. In a series of studies, Miura and her associates (Miura, 1987; Miura, Kim, Chang, & Okamoto, 1988; Miura & Okamoto, in press) as well as others (Fuson, 1988; Miller & Stigler, 1987; and Song & Ginsburg, 1987) have produced some relevant documentation. They have argued that Asian children—children who outperform their non-Asian peers on tests of mathematics achievement—have the advantage of the regular morphological structure of number words in their language (a language that is clearly acquired out of school) that matches the orthographic structure of written number. Miura and others have pointed out that children who speak an Asian language have the advantage of being able to use this linguistic structure in making sense out of orthography-linked arithmetical concepts and operations.

Other evidence of children's use of out-of-school knowledge for solving mathematics problems that emerge in school comes from analyses of arithmetical problem solving. Children in the early primary grades use strategies that they have not been taught in school—ones that they have invented (or reconstructed) on their own. Typically, these out-of-school strategies involve counting procedures or regrouping of values of the sort documented in candy sellers' arithmetic with bills (Brenner, 1985; Carraher, Carraher, & Schliemann, 1985; Carraher, Carraher, & Schliemann, 1987; Carraher, Schliemann, & Carraher, 1988; Fuson, 1988; Pettito, 1979; Posner, 1982).

A study with Oksapmin schoolchildren noted previously provides an interesting display both of the use of out-of-school learning to accomplish problems in school as well as children's specialization of these out-of-school forms in the process of their application. In an *in situ* analysis of children taking an arithmetic test in class, I documented that Oksapmin children were using their indigenous body-part system to solve Western arithmetical problems (teachers had no knowledge of the Oksapmin system and did not realize that use of the system was occurring). To determine children's arithmetical strategies, I interviewed Oksapmin schoolchildren at different grade levels as well as their nonschooled peers. I found that third graders used their body-part system in such a way that they kept track of the addition—much like those Oksapmin adults with some experience with the money economy described in Chapter 2. Further, when presented with problems beyond the range of the Oksapmin system, problems like 34 + 12, I found that Oksapmin sixth graders, but not third graders, had specialized solutions to these problems that combined aspects of Western and Oksapmin numeration. Children would begin with the English number word, 34, and simply count up while pointing to the first 12 body parts of the indigenous system to get the answer, 46 [pointing to the ear]. In contrast, I found that unschooled Oksapmin teen-agers (the "controls"), when attempting to solve a problem like 9 + 16, would deploy ineffective body-part-counting strategies to add, strategies resembling those of the traditional adults described in Chapter 2. The adolescents did not keep track of the addition of one term on to the other. Thus, in bringing to bear their indigenous number system to solve mathematical problems that emerge in school, Oksapmin children develop new computational procedures that are well adapted to the school context, specialized knowledge forms that are unknown to their teachers.

Transfer of Learning. The problem of the interplay between knowledge forms across practices is, in traditional terms, a problem of learning transfer— children's application of learning in one context to solve a problem in another. While there is an extensive research literature on learning transfer, this literature does not provide much insight into basic processes that may be implicated in learning across contexts like school and an out-of-school practice like candy selling. In the transfer literature, one which builds on traditional learning (Thorndike, 1922) as well as more recent cognitive theories (Collins & Gentner, 1987; Gentner, 1983; Gick & Holyoak, 1980), transfer has largely been studied in the laboratory. While constructs that have emerged may be suited to understanding the constrained phenomenon of the laboratory, they are of limited value when we move to the field (see Neisser, 1976). Children are typically trained to some criterion on a short-term basis and then on a single occasion administered tasks that vary in their "similarity" to training. Perhaps, given this paradigm, it is not surprising that transfer effects are notoriously limited. In considering the interplay between learning across contexts like candy selling and school mathematics, we can point to the specific problems with laboratory-based studies for understanding processes of transfer in everyday life.

In problem solving linked to daily activities like schooling or candy selling, unlike problem solving in the lab, children are engaged with the same or similar problems on a repeated basis rather than on a single occasion (e.g., repeatedly translating wholesale box into retail unit prices as in the selling practice, or repeatedly solving arithmetic problems on work sheets as in school). When we compare these recurrent problems across practices, we find often that the correspondence between problems is only partial. Similar problems typically differ somewhat in their structure; further, individuals' motivations in addressing similar problems in context, like school and candy selling (e.g., learning motives, economic motives) may lead them to quite different ways of conceptualizing the ostensively similar problems. In order for transfer to be adequate, an individual must transform and specialize prior learning to the new problem context. Such a process would suggest that transfer itself may not occur in an instant, but may be best conceptualized as a constructive process that occurs over time with repeated encounters, false starts, and efforts to come to terms with problems encountered over and over again.

Additional differences between the laboratory and daily activities point to further reasons for rethinking the study of transfer when we consider the interplay between learning across practices. In practices, unlike the lab, social supports may provide important opportunities for accomplishing transfer, helping the child draw connections across contexts (see Laboratory of Comparative Human Cognition, 1986; Lave, 1988). For instance, in the selling practice, the store clerk may help the seller by reading the orthography on the candy box or by producing a calculation to help the seller determine a retail price. Similarly, the adept teacher may make use of currency as a lesson plan. Thus, transfer—as it occurs in daily life—may be socially supported. Further, in practices, unlike the lab, knowledge forms involved in solving practice-linked problems are often well known to children, and some depth of knowledge may be important in appropriating and transforming prior knowledge to new contexts (Brown, 1989).

The form–function model may provide unique insights into the transfer of learning across cultural practices. Just as we may understand cognitive development as a protracted process of appropriation and specialization of cognitive forms to serve emerging cognitive functions, transfer can be conceptualized as a similarly protracted process of appropriation and specialization of cognitive forms to serve functions that are interwoven with particular contexts. For instance, in the practice of candy selling, we have seen that sellers structure an arithmetic involving very large values linked to the currency system. It may be that sellers who go to school make use of their currency-based arithmetic in making sense of the school-linked orthography-based arithmetic. Further, as we saw in the case of Oksapmin schoolchildren, such sellers, through participation in the classroom, may adapt and organize their currency-linked arithmetic schemas in new ways that allow them to solve the orthography-based arithmetical problems of the classroom. Similarly, it may be that the schooled child, when first introduced to the candy-selling practice, makes use of his orthography-based arithmetical knowledge in structuring solutions to these problems. As in the case of the seller attending school, the schooled child selling candy may, over time, increasingly specialize and structure school-linked computational strategies to solve problems that emerge in the practice. Indeed, we have already seen some evidence of such specialized school-based strategies in Chapter 6 in the fifth-grade sellers' solutions to the mark-up problems. Recall, for instance, OBS No. 07, in which the seller orchestrated a variety of school-linked algorithmic procedures to arrive at a retail price for his candy, an orchestration which was clearly not taught in school but one which is adapted to the recurrent problems of the practice.

EXTENDING THE MODEL TO THE STUDY
OF THE INTERPLAY BETWEEN LEARNING
ACROSS PRACTICES

In the next four chapters, my concern is with the interplay between mathematics learning in school and in the candy-selling practice. The analysis is motivated by a concern to understand the way that forms constructed in and out of school become interwoven and specialized across social contexts.

In Chapter 11, I document differences between the mathematical forms used by schooled nonsellers and nonschooled sellers as they approach the candy-selling tasks detailed in prior chapters. The schooled nonsellers have no experience with the Brazilian currency system or the candy-selling practice; they are children schooled in the United States: In contrast, the nonschooled sellers, while matched for age, have little or no experience with the mathematics of the classroom. The chapter then provides a means for contrasting a mathematics of the classroom with a mathematics of the selling practice.

In Chapters 12 and 13, I focus on the interplay between the mathematical forms and functions children structure in school and in the candy-selling practice. In Chapter 12, I focus on the way increasing school experience affects sellers' specialization of forms to approach mathematical problems linked to the candy-selling practice. In Chapter 13, I focus on the way candy-selling experience may influence the kinds of mathematical forms sellers use to address arithmetical problems linked to the classroom context. Here, I contrast two groups of school children, sellers and nonsellers, as they approach and solve arithmetical problems linked to school.

Chapter 14, the concluding chapter of Part IV, contains a more focused treatment of issues of appropriation and specialization of cognitive forms in the candy-selling practice. Unlike Chapters 12 and 13, which rely principally on group comparisons of problem solving, my concern in this chapter is to consider some particular cases and analyze the way in which transfer in sociocultural practices may be understood in terms of the form–function model.

11 Some Contrasts between Mathematics of the School and of the Candy-selling Practice

The purpose of this chapter is to compare the specialized mathematical forms and functions of children who have largely school-based as contrasted with largely candy-selling practice-based experience. The chapter, then, sets the stage for an analysis of the remaining chapters of Part IV: The interplay between forms linked to school and to the selling practice as sellers may appropriate and progressively specialize strategies for addressing problems across these two contexts for mathematical activities.

To compare mathematical problem solving linked to school and to the candy-selling practice, I contrast two groups of same-aged children as they approach and solve the candy-selling tasks used in Part II. One group consisted of schoolchildren in the fifth and sixth grades from the United States who attend a high-quality university elementary school and have no knowledge of the candy-selling practice; this group has no prior knowledge of the candy-selling practice nor the Brazilian currency system. The other group consisted of age-matched candy sellers with little or no schooling. The data for this group were previously reported in Chapter 8, and are cited here for comparison purposes.

METHODS

Subjects

The U. S. children were all about 11 years of age ($N = 18$, mean age = 11.1 years, sd = .54) and were in the equivalent of the fifth or sixth grade at a university laboratory elementary school. The child candy sellers, in comparison,

142

had not progressed beyond the second grade, but like the schooled children, were also about 11 years of age ($N = 23$, mean $= 10.8$ years, sd $= 1.0$).

Since some of the candy sellers had a little schooling (up through the second grade), it is important to note the character of this limited experience in relation to that of the U. S. children. The U. S. children attend a highly regarded private university laboratory school—the school accepts applicants on a quota basis (determined by an effort to match the demographic distribution of the United States), and the ratio between applicants and acceptances is one which makes gaining admission very difficult. The math curriculum at the school emphasizes a guided discovery approach to mathematics education; teachers typically try to integrate mathematics into various parts of the curriculum and math is regarded as an important curricular goal.

Those child candy sellers who completed and then dropped out of school at grades 1 or 2 attended public elementary schools in Brazil's Northeast, schools that most would evaluate as being of poor quality. In these schools, teachers do not have comparable educational background to those in the university laboratory school, and attendance rates for both teachers and students is low in the Brazilian schools. The curriculum at these public schools stress drill-and-practice. A further difference is that the children come from very poor communities; the public school system is not used by parents with sufficient funds to send their children to private schools.

Tasks and Procedures

All tasks described in Appendix C were administered to the U. S. schoolchildren with the exception of the currency-based representation tasks (the Bill Identification tasks, the Currency Relations tasks, and the Exchange tasks). To orient the U. S. children to the battery of tasks, the interviewer explained to children the origin of the problems. Children were told the following:

> I'm going to be telling you some stories that involve math problems. The stories are about children who sell candy in the street in a country that's far away from here. It's a country called Brazil. Have you ever heard of that country? It's in South America, and many children who live there sell things to make money—things like candy. They go to big stores where they buy boxes of candy like lots of packages of chocolate bars, and then they take the bars out of the packages and sell them to people as the people wait for buses or walk to and from work.
>
> Now, when children sell their candy, sometimes they have to solve math problems. For instance, sometimes they have to read numbers as when they're in a store buying their boxes of candy. Other times they have to add up how much money they made or give change to a customer. Sometimes these are hard problems, because in Brazil, the kind of money they use is money that has large numbers. I want to show you some of the Brazilian money.

All children were then introduced to the Brazilian currency. They were shown six bills, and each denomination was given. The bills were then shuffled and each child was asked to recall the value of each bill. In order to proceed with the tasks, a child had to name each bill's denomination correctly two times. If the child missed a bill, the child was required to repeat the task until two passes through the denominations were accomplished successfully. In addition to this general introduction, prior to each task type, children were told about how problems like the ones they were to solve emerged in the selling practice. Every child passed the introductory screening.

RESULTS

Fig. 11.1 contains a summary presentation of the schooled nonsellers' as compared with the unschooled candy sellers' correct solutions to the tasks. On some tasks, sellers and schooled children show marked differences in the percentage correct across population groups, differences indicating differential competence with particular mathematical forms (orthographic representations) or using mathematical knowledge to solve complex arithmetical problems (mark-up); on other tasks, while there are no differences revealed by percentage correct, there are often nonetheless differences in the strategic forms children used to accomplish the tasks (e.g., bill arithmetic and ratio comparisons). I will focus on similarities and differences across the groups' performances.

Representation of Large Numerical Values

Fig. 11.1 shows that children's performances on the orthography-based number representation tasks revealed quite different profiles of competence as a function of population group. The schoolchildren's scores reflect high level of competence in decoding our standard orthography for representing large values. All identified all 20 values correctly, and, on the Orthography comparison tasks (not contained in Fig. 11.1), again, all children achieved perfect performance. Since the U. S. schooled children had no experience with the Brazilian currency system, they were not administered the alternate representation tasks (the Brazilian currency system), and they could not be expected to use the system to represent large values. In contrast to the schooled nonsellers' high scores on the number orthography tasks and their inability to use the Brazilian currency system as a means of representation, the unschooled sellers show low levels of competence in using the orthography as a computational system; further, recall from Chapter 9 that the unschooled sellers had highly specialized knowledge of the Brazilian currency system.

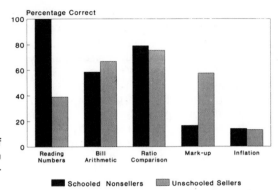

FIG. 11.1. Mean percentage of correct responses to 5 problem types as a function of population group.

Arithmetical Computations

Regardless of population group, most of the children achieved correct answers to the arithmetical problems. An ANOVA performed on the total number correct on the four arithmetical problems—the two bill addition and two bill subtraction tasks—revealed no difference as a function of population group. Further, both the schooled and unschooled children ordered the bills into convenient values on the addition problems at about the same frequency (about 50%).

What did differentiate the groups was again linked to competence with the number orthography. While none of the sellers used paper-and-pencil strategies on either the addition or subtraction tasks, some of the schooled children did and differences in usage were statistically significant for each of the four problems (chi-squares $(1, N = 41)$ were between 4.9 and 6.5 $p < .05$).

Comparing Ratios

Like the arithmetical computations, children's performances on the ratio tasks were at high levels regardless of population group. Most children were able to choose which of two ratios (e.g., three for Cr$500 or seven for Cr$1000) would yield the larger profit and justify their judgments with common term approaches.

Despite the high levels of justification across populations, an additional analysis of children's justifications revealed differences in the use of school-linked orthographic forms in justifications as a function of population group. While none of the candy sellers used paper-and-pencil approaches to solve the ratio problems, some of the schooled children did. Consider the following application of school-linked arithmetical procedures to solve the ratio problems.

S No. 706. 12 years old, schooled nonseller. In order to solve the problem of comparing 1 for Cr$200 vs. 3 for Cr$500, S No. 706 creates an imaginary box of candy containing 21 units, and he then, by means of multiplication and division algorithms, proceeds to determine the money one for Cr$200 would be generated by each ratio if those 21 candies were sold. He responds that $\frac{1}{200}$ will make the most profit. He writes as he speaks: "IF I HAD A BAG OF 21 AND SOLD BY 3 I MAKE 3,500; BUT, IF I HAD 21 AND SOLD BY 2S . . . WAIT . . ." he writes, "21 DIVIDED INTO 200 IS 10 . . . .I DON'T KNOW, HOW DID I DO THE OTHER PROBLEM. OH YEAH, 21 × 200 (writes 21 × 200 = 4200, 7 × 500 = 3500). OH, I SEE WHAT I DID, THIS WAY I WOULD MAKE 4200, I WOULD HAVE BEEN $700 RICHER."

In S No. 706's solution, he does not compare ratios directly. Rather, he creates an imaginary value for his box, 21 candies, and he uses this value as a common term. S No. 706 then computes, using division procedures and school-linked multiplication algorithms, how much in cash each ratio would yield after a sale of 21 candies had been completed.

S No. 713 presents a different use of the school procedure to arrive at a common term to compare ratios. Unlike S No. 706, S No. 713 first uses a school algorithmic approach to find the price per unit of candy sold at one ratio (three for Cr$500). In S No. 713's solution, he adapts the school-based division and multiplication algorithms in order to create a common term in units of seven in order to compare three for Cr$500 with seven for Cr$1000, a comparison (like that of S No. 706), unobserved in sellers.

S No. 713. 11 years old, schooled nonseller. In order to solve the problem of comparing 3 for Cr$500 vs. 7 for Cr$1000, S No. 713 uses a paper-and-pencil strategy. He first uses long division to divide 3 into 500, and he obtains the correct result, 166, remainder 2. He then multiplies 7 × 166 on paper, obtaining the correct product: 1,162. He concludes that three for 500 is the better deal because "IF YOU BUY SEVEN OF THIS (3 for Cr$500) IT WOULD BE 1,162 WHICH IS MORE THAN SEVEN FOR 1,000."

Like the sellers whose protocols were cited in Chapter 8, S No. 706 and S No. 713 produce common term solutions to the ratio comparison problems, yet the character of their solutions differ markedly from the unschooled sellers. These children structure their solutions in terms of school-linked algorithms, and in the course of their solutions they elaborate subgoals that are interwoven with these orthographic-based forms.

Translating Wholesale Box Prices Into Retail Unit Prices in an Inflating Economy

The schooled children's solution to both of the price translation tasks differed markedly from those of the unschooled sellers. Fig. 11.1 shows that only a small minority of the schooled children achieved adequate coordinations between wholesale box prices and retail prices, whereas a majority of the unschooled children achieved adequate coordinations (problem 1, chi-square (1), $N = 43) = 9.77$, $p < .005$; problem 2, chi-square (1, $N = 45) = 4.28$, $p < .05$). The solution strategies of those sellers and schooled nonsellers who produced appropriate coordinations also differed markedly as indicated in Fig. 11.2. All of the schooled children who did achieve an adequate coordination used a school-linked strategic form; moreover, about half of the schoolchildren on each problem type—regardless of the adequacy of the solution—attempted an approach that made use of a school algorithm. In contrast, most of the unschooled sellers used forms involving a count by the ratio convention or a covert procedure, one presumably linked to a convention-based computation as detailed in Chapters 6 and 8.

The following example illustrates well a schoolchild's efforts to structure a coherent school-based strategy to solve the problem of mark-up. The approach

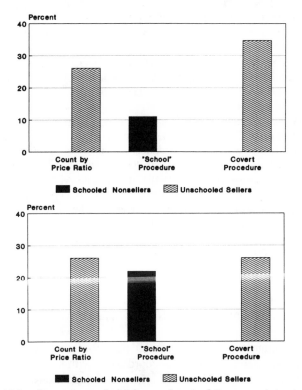

FIG. 11.2. Percentage of children using 1 of 3 appropriate strategy types to mark-up problems as a function of problem and population group.

begins as one in which the child deploys school-linked algorithms by trial and error to determine a retail box price. In his final solution to the second problem, the child has created an economical solution to the mark-up problem.

S No. 713. 11-year-old, schooled nonseller. S No. 713 is presented with the problem of producing a retail unit price for a 50-unit box that sold for Cr$3500 (wholesale price). He says that he will sell the whole box for Cr$4000. He is asked for how much he will sell the pieces to the customers, and he produces the following calculations with paper and pencil, each time using school-linked algorithmic procedures. First he divides 50 into 3500, achieving the correct answer, 70. He says "WHAT I THINK I SHOULD SELL IT FOR IS MORE THAN 70. I CAN MAKE A PROFIT." He then, in succession, multiplies the following numbers, apparently in an effort to find the appropriate retail unit price to achieve the gross value of 4000. He multiplies 50 times 70, achieving the correct answer, 3500, though unsatisfied since he does not achieve his targeted value of Cr$4000; he multiplies 50 times 100, achieving 5000—again correct, but still off his mark; he multiplies 87 times 50, achieving the correct answer, 4350, but still, he is dissatisfied. He says, "SINCE THE WHOLE BOX IS 4000, YOU GOT TO MAKE IT AROUND, YOU HAVE TO DIVIDE 50 INTO 4000, SO YOU HAVE TO GET IT, BECAUSE OTHERWISE THEY WOULD HAVE IT CHEAPER TO BUY THE WHOLE BOX." He does not follow this well-reasoned strategy, but instead multiplies 50 times 83, exclaiming, "IT'S STILL NO GOOD." S No. 713 finally multiplies 50 times 80, achieving his targeted product, Cr$4000, and exclaims, "EIGHTY EXACTLY!". For the next problem, producing a retail unit price for a 30-unit box that sold for Cr$8500, S No. 713 produces a more direct approach, an approach that is again linked to school algorithmic procedures. He says that he will sell the whole box for Cr$9000. He is asked how much he will sell the pieces for, and he produces the following computations, again using the school-linked algorithmic procedures. He divides 30 into 8500, and achieves the answer 283, remainder 10. He then says, "OH, I DID IT WRONG AGAIN" (he erases his computation) and now divides 30 into 9000, achieving the correct result, 300, and exclaims, "300 A PIECE." He is asked to explain, and he says, "YOU HAVE TO MAKE IT SO SELLING EACH PIECE IS THE SAME AS SELLING THE WHOLE BOX. IF IT WAS MORE THAN EACH PIECE IT WOULD BE A BETTER DEAL TO BUY THE WHOLE BOX."

S No. 713 presents a coordinated solution in both mark-up problems, though the strategy he uses to accomplish this solution shifts. Across S No. 713's solution efforts, he formulates subgoals of his solution with reference to school-linked algorithms; in both problems, he solves first for wholesale price per unit, and sets what he regards as an adequate retail price for the entire box. In his effort to produce a retail price per unit value coordinated with his stated box value, S No. 713 experiments with different algorithm-based solutions, and in the end, deduces the most economical one of dividing his targeted retail box price by the number of units in the box.

Adjusting for Inflation

Fig. 11.1 shows the percentage of children who offered values that were consistent with a proportional solution to the pricing tasks. While the difference between groups is not statistically significant, schooled and unschooled children's non-proportional adjustments to the inflation problems did differ markedly, and such nonproportional adjustments are revealing about differences in the groups' mathematics. Fig. 11.3 contains the mean percentages of the two types of nonproportional adjustment categories, absolute and partial. As in Chapters 9 and 10, for absolute adjustments, the difference between the wholesale and retail price at time 2 was the same as that at 1. For instance, in the problem in which at time 1 the wholesale and retail prices are Cr$3000 and Cr$6000, respectively, and at time 2 the wholesale price is Cr$9000, the absolute solution would be Cr$12000, a difference in each case of Cr$3000. For partial adjustments, the difference between the wholesale and retail prices at time 2 had to be greater than the absolute difference between the wholesale and retail price at time 1. Thus, for the same problem, the solution had to be greater than Cr$12000, but not Cr$18000 (the proportional solution). In addition, responses that were considered unreasonable—those that were 400% greater than the proportional responses—were not included as partial adjustments (there was only one such response, and, as was the case in Chapters 9 and 10, such answers were excluded from the analyses).

An analysis of group differences in children's nonproportional adjustments revealed that schooled children more often offered absolute adjustments ($U = 83.5$, $W = 501.5$, $z = -3.69$, $p < .001$), whereas sellers more typically offered partial adjustments ($U = 97$, $W = 268$, $z = -3.08$, $p < .005$). The differences in these response types may well indicate quite different conceptualizations of the problem. The sellers more typically treat the problem as an economic one, one in

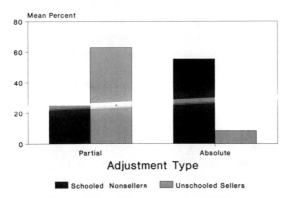

FIG. 11.3. Mean percentages of children's partial and absolute adjust-ment responses to inflation problems as a function of population group.

which error means not making a sufficient profit. The schooled children more typically approach the problem as one in which there is a single mathematical solution, computing the wholesale and retail prices at time 2 to match the value at time 1, and in so doing, they do not adjust for the relative shift in the value of the currency.

Summary of Differences in Schooled Nonsellers and Unschooled Sellers Specialization of Mathematical Forms and Functions

This chapter illustrates differences in schooled nonsellers' and unschooled sellers' specialization of mathematical forms to accomplish cognitive functions that are linked to their different activity settings.

Children's performance on the orthography-based representation tasks revealed that schooled children acquire facility with the representational orthography, whereas unschooled sellers do not. However, as we have seen in prior chapters, the sellers' lack of a differentiated knowledge of the number orthography is compensated by a well-specialized knowledge of the numerical structure of the Brazilian currency system. Indeed, the analyses of Chapter 8 revealed that sellers performed at very high levels on the Currency Identification, Currency Relations, and Currency Exchange tasks.

Children's performances on the currency arithmetic tasks showed that schooled nonsellers, more than unschooled sellers, rely on orthography-based calculation and algorithmic forms. In contrast, sellers make use of forms linked to the currency system.

Children's performances on the mark-up tasks showed that schooled nonsellers have greater difficulty in producing adequate coordinations between wholesale box and retail prices. Further, unlike the sellers, they do not price the candy in terms of multiple units (the sellers' convention) and they frequently cast the mark-up problems in terms of arithmetical algorithms. These differences lead the schooled nonsellers to specialize strategic forms that are quite different from those specialized by the unschooled sellers.

Finally, schooled nonsellers, unlike the unschooled sellers, most typically offered prices that reflected an absolute adjustment for inflation; while this shift appropriately reflects an effort to reproduce the relation between periods of sale, the relation that is reproduced is inappropriately an additive one and does not take into account the decreasing value of the cruzeiro. In contrast, while sellers do not offer any more proportional answers than nonsellers, they nonetheless offer a greater number of partial adjustments, adjustments in which the buying power of the cruzeiro is more or less preserved across time periods.

The foregoing findings illustrate that it would be inappropriate to conceptualize differences between the mathematical competence of schooled nonsellers and unschooled sellers merely along some metric of mathematics achievement.

Indeed, the findings show that in structuring solution forms to serve functions linked to their different activity contexts, the children construct different kinds of mathematical knowledge. The schooled child makes use of a specialized knowledge of the number orthography as a central feature of mathematical problem solving, whereas the unschooled child does not, relying instead on specialized knowledge of numerical representations linked to the currency system. Further, in structuring solutions to each of the problem-solving tasks—arithmetic, ratio comparison, and mark-up—we saw that children across groups differed in the way they accomplished these problems. These differences were linked to the specialization of practice-linked conventions or school-linked algorithms, cognitive forms which differed markedly across groups and were interwoven with the way in which the mathematical problems presented to the two groups were conceptualized and accomplished.

12   The Influence of Schooling on Sellers' Mathematics

We have seen in Chapter 11 that schooled nonsellers who have no involvement with the Brazilian economy acquire a mathematics that is distinct from that of sellers' mathematics in various ways. In contrast to nonschooled sellers, schooled nonsellers acquire a well-differentiated knowledge of our number orthography, and they use orthographic-based procedures to address arithmetical problems linked to the candy-selling practice. In the next three chapters, I probe the possible interplay between the mathematical forms that children use and specialize in school and the practice-linked forms that children use and specialize in candy selling.

I noted in Part II that while some candy sellers have little or no school experience, others have been to school for many years. In the present chapter, by studying same-aged sellers with differing levels of schooling, I analyze the effect of schooling experience on the mathematical forms and functions which sellers have specialized to accomplish practice-linked problems.

METHODS

Subjects

Sellers were recruited for study using the same procedures as those detailed in Part II and in Appendix B, and they were assigned to one of three groups, based upon their schooling experience. An unschooled group included twenty-two 12- to 15-year-old sellers with schooling experience that ranged from no school at all up through and including second grade (mean grade = 1.73, sd = 0.46; mean age = 12.64, sd = 0.95). These children were the same as the 12- to 15-year-olds in Chapter 8, and they are included here for comparison purposes. The sellers with moderate schooling included 23 sellers who had school experience up through the third or fourth grade (mean grade = 3.48, sd = 0.59; mean age = 13.57, sd = 1.12). The sellers with greatest schooling included 19 sellers who had school experience up through the fifth, sixth, or seventh grade (mean grade = 5.47, sd = 0.70; mean age = 14.11, sd = 0.66). As in the studies reported in Parts I and II, all children were boys.

Tasks and Design

All sellers were administered the candy-selling tasks detailed in Appendix C and described in prior chapters. The forms of data analysis and statistical techniques also parallel the prior analyses with one exception. Despite the narrow age range of the sellers sampled (all sellers were between 12 and 15 years of age), an ANOVA revealed that sellers' age varied with group assignment ($F(2,61) = 12.81$, $p < .0001$). When possible, I used a statistical technique—analysis of covariance (ANCOVA)—to control for the confound between age and school experience (when the distribution on the dependent variables does not rule out a parametric test). The ANCOVA provides a means to eliminate statistically the variation in sellers' task performance associated with age prior to testing for the association between schooling and task performance.

RESULTS: REPRESENTATION OF LARGE NUMERICAL VALUES

The analyses of Chapter 11 showed that schooled nonsellers, in contrast with unschooled sellers, show a remarkable competence with the standard number orthography in both reading and comparing values as well as using this representational form in computations. To determine whether such orthographic competence emerges as a function of school experience in the candy sellers and whether access to the alternate currency-based system persists with increasing school experience, contrasts were made between sellers at varying levels of schooling on the orthography and alternate representation tasks.

Fig. 12.1 contains the means of the percentage correct for the orthographic representation tasks (identification and comparison) as a function of schooling. By fifth to seventh grade, most sellers achieved a perfect or near-perfect performance on both task types. Analyses of covariance (using sellers' age as a covariate) revealed that performance improved as a function of school experience (identifying numerical values, $F(2,60) = 20.74$, $p < .0001$; comparing numer-

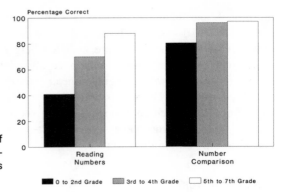

FIG. 12.1. Mean percentage of correct responses to orthography representation problems as a function of schooling.

ical values, $F(2,60) = 7.84$, $p < .001$). Thus, schooled Brazilian child candy sellers, like their U. S. nonseller counterparts, acquire considerable competence with the number orthography, and this competence improves with schooling.

When we turn to currency tasks, we find that regardless of schooling, children develop competence to use currency as a basis to represent large numerical values. Figs. 12.2, 12.3, and 12.4 contain children's performance on the Currency Identification tasks, Currency Comparison tasks, and Exchange tasks, respectively. The figures show that for virtually all tasks and all conditions, children's performance was at or near ceiling regardless of schooling. The only exception was children's performance on the Numbers Only condition on the Currency Identification task in which, as expected, children's ability to read numbers printed on bills increased with school experience ($F(2,60) = 11.77$, $p < .0001$). On the exchange tasks, the mean number of trades required did not differ as a function of school experience.

In sum, schooling offers sellers a new, historically linked form to represent large values, a form that may not only be used in identifying box prices in wholesale stores, but may also be appropriated in structuring more specialized

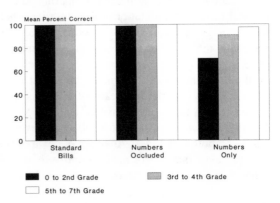

FIG. 12.2. Mean percentage of correct responses to currency identification problems as a function of schooling.

Ordinal Relations

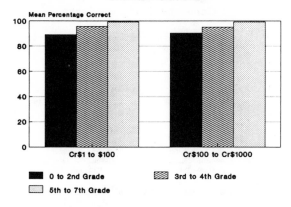

Multiplicative Relations

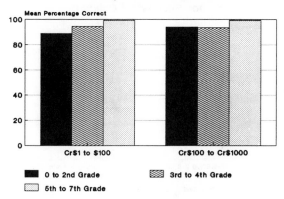

FIG. 12.3.   Mean percentage of correct responses to currency comparison problems as a function of value size and population group.

computational forms to address more complex mathematical problems of the practice.

ARITHMETIC, RATIO COMPARISONS, MARK-UP, AND PROPORTIONS

Fig. 12.5 contains the mean percentage correct for children's performances on the Currency Arithmetic, Ratio Comparisons, and Pricing tasks (Mark-up and Adjusting for Inflation) as a function of schooling. In the figure, for each task type the mean percentage correct was computed across problems. For the Currency Arithmetic, mean percentage correct consisted of the percentage correct of the

Percentage of Children Who Successfully Completed Exchange Tasks

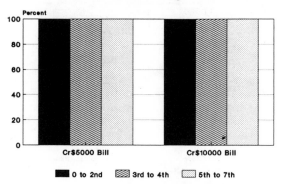

Mean Number of Exchanges Required for Successful Children

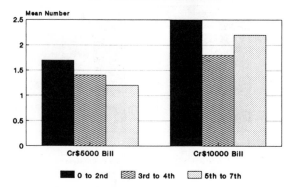

FIG. 12.4.   Sellers' solutions to exchange problems as a function of schooling.

Currency Addition and Subtraction tasks combined. For the ratio comparisons, mean percentage correct consisted of the mean number of common term answers. For the Mark-up task, mean percentage correct was defined with reference to whether children produced a coordinated solution on the two problems, and for the inflation task, mean percentage correct was defined as a proportional adjustment for the two problems. An ANCOVA was performed for each task type as a function of school experience and the ANCOVAs yielded no significant effects. However, an analysis of children's solution strategies provides some insight into shifts in some of the strategic forms children brought to bear on practice-linked problems as a function of school experience.

For the Currency Arithmetic problems, some children employed paper-and-pencil strategies and increased use of these strategies was associated with school

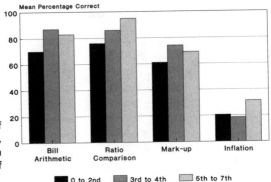

FIG. 12.5. Mean percentage of correct responses to arithmetic, ratio, mark-up, and inflation problems as a function of schooling.

experience. While none of the unschooled or third to fourth graders used paper-and-pencil procedures to solve either of the subtraction problems, on problem 1, 21% of the fifth to seventh graders did so at least once and on problem 2, 26% of the fifth to seventh graders did so at least once (collapsing unschooled and third to fourth grades to achieve greater expected values, problem 1: chi-square $(1, N = 64 = 6.83, p < .01)$; problem 2: chi-square $(1, N = 64 = 9.45, p < .005)$.

For the ratio comparison problems, all sellers, regardless of level of schooling, performed at high levels; while the figure shows a trend that with increased school experience sellers achieved a greater number of common term approaches, differences in common term approaches across levels of schooling were not statistically significant. Further, unlike the algorithm-based strategies reported in the schooled nonsellers' solutions of Chapter 10, none of the schooled sellers attempted such approaches.

For the Mark-up problems, we find again differences as a function of school experience. Figure 12.6 contains the distribution of the sellers' solution strategies that led to adequate box price and unit price coordinations as a function of population group. In the figure, we see that there is an inverse relation between price ratio summation strategies and school-linked computational strategies. With school experience, price ratio summation strategies tended to decline whereas school-linked (single-unit) computational strategies tended to increase. As illustrated in the following fifth-grade seller's solution, with the increasing frequency of school-linked computational solutions, we also see a shift away from the pricing convention (of multiple units for a bill denomination) to single-unit pricing. The trend is revealed in Fig. 12.7 and was significant for both problem types (problem 1, collapsing the two groups with least schooling to obtain greater expected values, chi-square $(1, N = 64) = 4.24, p < .05$; problem 2, uncollapsed across groups, chi-square $(2, N = 63) = 6.15, p < .01$. Follow-up analyses on problem 2 revealed that only significant contrast was between the group with the least and the group with the most schooling (chi-square $(1, N = 41) = 4.36, p < .05$).

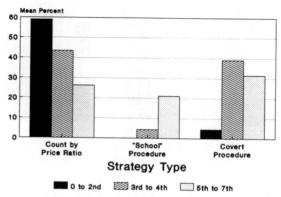

Box Cost: 50 Units @ Cr$3500

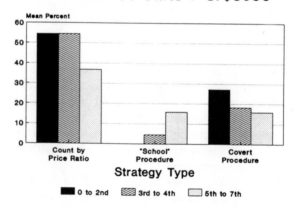

Box Cost: 30 Units @ Cr$8500

FIG. 12.6. Percentage of sellers using 1 or 3 appropriate strategy types to mark-up problems as a function of schooling.

S No. 92. 14-year-old seller, fifth grade. S No. 92 is presented with the problem of producing a retail unit price for a 50-unit box that sold for Cr$3500 (wholesale price). He says that he will sell the box for Cr$10000 and sell the units to customers at one for Cr$200 (coordinated solution). (How do you know that this is a good price for you?) "BECAUSE BY SELLING ONE FOR Cr$200 I'LL MAKE Cr$10000." S No. 92 uses the long form of the school-linked multiplication algorithm, solving the problem 50 units × Cr$200 = Cr$10000. For the second problem of producing a retail unit price for a 30-unit box for Cr$8500, S No. 92 says that he will sell the box for Cr$15000 and sell the units for one for Cr$500 (coordinated solution). Again, he demonstrates his solution by the long form of the school-linked multiplication algorithm, solving the problem 30 units × Cr$500 = Cr$15000.

Box Cost: 50 Units @ Cr$3500

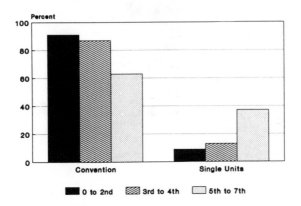

Box Cost: 30 Units @ Cr$8500

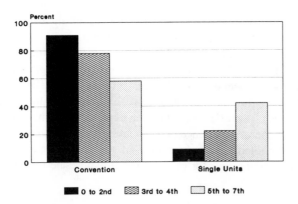

FIG. 12.7.   Percentage of sellers using the price ratio convention as a function of problem and schooling.

We can see in S No. 92's solution a possible explanation for the decline of the pricing convention used in mark-up. S No. 92's use of single-unit prices allows for a direct application of the multiplication algorithm. It is likely that this procedure is a translation of the summation by price ratio strategy into school-linked forms, a solution form that stands midway between nonschooled approaches and schooled approaches outlined in Chapter 11. Rather than counting sales transactions one by one and progressively summing the gain in cash with each transaction enumerated, the schooled seller appropriates the school-linked multiplication algorithm. With the algorithm, the seller accomplishes the complete iteration in a single mathematical operation, an operation in which the

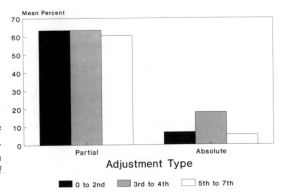

FIG. 12.8. Mean percentage of sellers' partial and absolute adjustment responses to inflation problems as a function of schooling.

number of sales transactions as represented by the number of units in the box is multiplied by the posited price per unit. Of the schooled sellers who used overt school-linked computational strategies, all multiplied the number of units in the box by a retail sale price per unit.

For the inflation problems, children did not differ in mean percentage of proportional adjustments as a function of school experience, though the mean percentage ranged from 18.5 to 31.5 over levels of schooling (see Fig. 12.5). Fig. 12.8 contains a breakdown of children's absolute and partial adjustments. Unlike the schooled nonsellers' preponderance of absolute adjustments analyzed in the prior chapter, the majority of sellers' solutions that showed adjustments showed partial ones, regardless of schooling experience. It may be that practice participation (or general experience in living in Brazil's inflating economy) led to an increase in schoolchildren's awareness of the need to go beyond absolute adjustments in compensating for price surges in wholesale boxes.

SUMMARY

Sellers' performance on the number representation tasks revealed that with increasing school experience, sellers acquire the ability to decode the standard orthography; further, their performance on the currency arithmetic and mark-up tasks reveal that with schooling they also acquire school-linked algorithmic forms to solve arithmetical problems.

In sellers' solutions to these candy selling tasks, we see an interweaving of practice-linked and school-linked forms in sellers' specialized solution strategies. This blending of forms in sellers' specialization of school- and practice-linked strategies was most pronounced on the mark-up tasks. On these tasks, we found that while unschooled sellers made use of count by price ratio strategies using the standard price ratio convention of multiple units for a single bill denomination, with increasing school experience, sellers' strategies increasingly incorporated the use of a multiplication algorithm and shifted to the use of single-unit pricing. The use of the multiplication algorithm appears to reflect a more or less direct increase in the economy of the price by ratio strategy. Rather than summing sales transactions one by one in achieving the potential street price for a box, sellers use the multiplication algorithm to determine, in a single operation, the potential street price for sales that exhaust the entire box of candy.

13

The Influence of Selling Experience on Learning Mathematics at School

In this chapter, the question posed in Chapter 12 is reversed. Now, instead of asking whether schooling experience influences candy sellers' mathematics, the question addressed is whether candy-selling experience influences the child's mathematics of the classroom.

The findings presented in Chapter 9 showed that while sellers with little or no schooling in mathematics used different procedures than schooled nonsellers, these procedures were often adequate ones. Indeed, unschooled sellers showed a well-differentiated knowledge of the Brazilian currency system, they showed that they could organize the currency into convenient values in solving arithmetical problems, and they demonstrated interesting and adequate strategies for solving ratio and pricing problems, in some cases, more adequate than their U. S. schooled peers.

To determine whether sellers used mathematical forms linked to the selling practice to address problems in school, I presented both second- and third-grade sellers and nonsellers with arithmetical problems of the types typically encountered in school. Some of the problems contained high values whereas others did not, and some of the problems were in word (story) format whereas others were in computation format. The focus of analysis was the similarities and differences in children's solution strategies.

METHODS

Subjects

The sellers and nonsellers were from similar (poor) social class backgrounds and all attended or had attended Recife public schools. The sellers included 12 second-grade children (mean age = 11.6 years; sd = .79 years) and 12 third-grade children (mean age = 12.5 years; sd = .70 years). The nonsellers included 9 second-grade children (mean age = 11.1 years; sd = .3 years) and 10 third-grade children (mean age = 12.3 years; sd = .5 years). ANOVAs did not reveal significant age differences between these groups at second-grade or third-grade level.

The Problems and Procedures

The specific problems used in this study are presented in Fig. 13.1. The battery of problems sampled the typical types of computation problems presented in school and included addition, subtraction, multiplication, and division operations in word problem and computation problem format. The battery included eight word problems and four computation problems, and the word problems included four problems containing low numerical values and four problems containing high numerical values. For each value type, each basic arithmetical operation (addition, subtraction, multiplication and division) was represented once. The computation problems included four high value problems with each of the four arithmetical operations represented. Each of the problems presented in computation format was identical to one of the problems presented in word format so that direct comparisons could be made between solution strategies for word and computation problems.

The order of presentation of these problems was counterbalanced within grade level and population group. Half of the children within each grade level and population group received the word problems and then the computation problems, and the other half received these problems in the opposite order. Further, within the word problems, half received the "high" number problems first and the other half received the "low" number problems first.

Coding Children's Solutions

Children's efforts to solve the problems were often characterized by false starts, or by reattempts after an interviewer inquired about how the child came to a particular solution. What was taken as the answer and solution to be coded was the child's best effort for each problem over the course of the child's efforts. If in

Operation	Word Problem	Computation Problem
Addition		
Low Values	28+26=?	...
High Values	790+470=?	790+470=?
Subtraction		
Low Values	46-18=?	...
High Values	1320-480=?	1320-480=?
Multiplication		
Low Values	20x6=?	...
High Values	15x200=?	15x200=?
Division		
Low Values	63-3=?	...
High Values	4200-3=?	4200-3=?

FIG. 13.1. Problems used for school arithmetic study as a function of operation, problem type, and problem values.

the course of using a strategy a child made a computation error involving the addition of one digit to another or the subtraction of one digit from another (e.g., added 8 + 5 and obtained 14), the child was given credit for a "successful" strategic form, providing it would have led to an accurate solution had the computation error not been committed; however, he was not given credit for an accurate answer. If the child achieved an accurate answer but by a covert method, the child was given credit for an accurate answer but the strategy was left uncoded. As a result of these scoring procedures, the number of successful strategic forms and the number of correct answers do not always sum to the same value in the figures presented herein.

Children's Accuracy

Fig. 13.2 contains the mean number of computations for which children achieved an accurate solution as a function of grade level and selling experience. The figure reveals a marked difference between the performance of sellers and non-sellers. A 2 (grade level) × 2 (selling experience) ANOVA showed that sellers obtained more correct answers than nonsellers ($F(1,39) = 6.48, p < .05$). While the difference between sellers' and nonsellers' scores at grade 2 as contrasted with grade 3 appears quite marked, the interaction only approached statistical significance $F(1,39) = 3.91, p = .055$.

To determine whether some problem types were contributing to the effect more than others (word as opposed to computation problems or problems containing high as opposed to low values), two additional ANOVAs were performed—one for problem format and the other for problem numbers.

Fig. 13.3 contains the mean percentage correct of the four problems presented in word format as contrasted with the four matching problems presented in computation format. A 2 (problem type, repeated) × 2 (grade level) × 2 (selling experience) ANOVA revealed no interaction between population group and problem format. However, the analysis did reveal a two-way interaction between

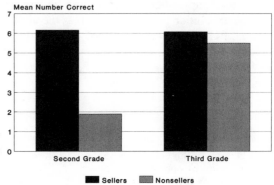

FIG. 13.2. Mean number of correct responses to arithmetic problems as a function of grade level and population group.

Second Grade

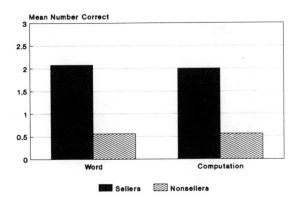

Third Grade

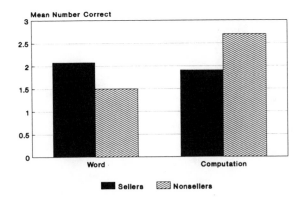

FIG. 13.3.   Mean number of correct responses to word and computation problems as a function of grade level and selling experience.

grade level and selling experience ($F(1,39) = 5.26$, $p < .05$) and a main effect for grade level ($F(1,39) = 4.72$, $p < .05$). Duncan post hoc comparisons revealed that at grade 2, sellers achieved more correct solutions than the nonsellers, whereas at grade 3, there were no significant differences in sellers' and nonsellers' performances. Thus, like the analysis performed on all 12 problems reported on the combined word and computation problems (presented in Fig. 13.2), there was a tendency for sellers to achieve more correct answers than nonsellers at grade 2 but not at grade 3. In the present analysis, however, this tendency achieved statistical significance.

Figure 13.4 contains the mean number correct for all of the word problems partitioned into those four containing "low" values and those four problems containing "high" values. A 2 (problem type, repeated) × 2 (grade level) × 2

Second Grade

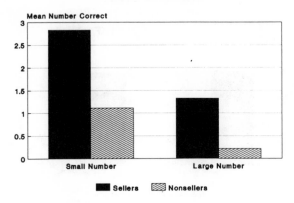

Third Grade

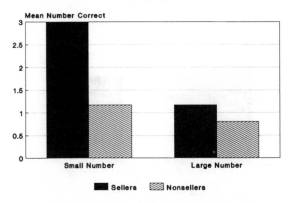

FIG. 13.4. Mean number of correct responses to small- and large-number word problems as a function of grade level and selling experience.

(selling experience) ANOVA revealed two main effects, one for selling experience ($F(1,39) = 13.30$, $p < .001$) and the other for problem type ($F(1,39) = 70.33$, $p < .0001$) and no interactions. Sellers achieved more correct solutions than the nonsellers, regardless of problem size and grade level, and both sellers and nonsellers achieved more correct solutions on the problems involving lower values.

Children's Strategies

The prior analyses show that selling experience contributes to children's ability to solve school mathematics problems accurately at grade 2. However, the analyses did not provide insight into whether sellers and nonsellers were structuring solutions involving practice-linked vs. school-linked solution forms. In the present analysis, I focus on the strategies that children used to address the arithmetical problems and the ways these forms may shift as a function of grade level and selling experience.

Children's adequate strategies to the problems were classified into two types: *Regrouping strategies* consisted of approaches in which children manipulated the terms of the problem by either the recomposition of values or by a combination of recomposition operations and counting operations. These strategies are similar to the ones documented in sellers' additions on the bill arithmetic tasks, strategies in which children grouped values into convenient ones (e.g., Cr$200 + Cr$200 + Cr$100 + Cr$500 = Cr$1000). Such strategies also have been documented by others studying children engaged in vending practices (e.g., Carraher, Carraher, & Schliemann, 1985). *Algorithmic strategies* consisted of those that followed standard algorithmic forms for addition and subtraction with carrying or borrowing or standard algorithmic forms for multiplication or division—forms typically linked with schooling.

Consider the variety of regrouping and counting approaches to solving addition and multiplication problems displayed by the following seller who is in the second grade:

S No. V205. Seller, second grade. S No. V205 is presented with the problem 28 + 26 = ? in word problem format. S No. V205 thinks for a while and responds "53." While he produces an incorrect answer, he does demonstrate an adequate strategy. After being asked to show how he figured the answer and he responds, "TWENTY WITH TWENTY MAKES FORTY. AND, WITH EIGHT AND THEN SIX MORE IT MAKES FIFTY-THREE." He does not use paper and pencil. For the problem 790 + 470 = ?, again presented in word problem format, S No. V205 demonstrates a similar regrouping strategy, this time achieving the correct answer. First he thinks and says, "FOUR HUNDRED PLUS SEVEN HUNDRED IS ONE THOUSAND, ONE HUNDRED. NOW I HAVE NINETY AND SEVENTY . . . I TAKE AWAY TEN FROM THE SEVENTY AND PUT IT ON THE NINETY, AND IT'S ONE HUNDRED. SO, I HAVE ONE THOUSAND TWO HUNDRED AND SIXTY ENVELOPS." For the problem, 20 × 6 in word problem format, S No. V205 first counts again with his fingers, "2, 4, 8, 10, 12." Then S no. V205 counts again with his fingers, "20, 40, 40 + 40 IS 80. THOSE ARE FOUR BOXES, NOW I DON'T KNOW WHAT TO DO MORE." (He then spontaneously takes the paper and pencil and writes down a column of six twenties—"20". He then points as he counts to the column of numbers, "20, 40, 40 AND 40 MAKE 80, 80 WITH 20 MAKE 100, 100 WITH 20 MAKE 120." S No. V205 is then presented with the problem 15 × 200 = ?, again in word problem format. He responds, "FOR THIS I HAVE TO ALSO USE PAPER." He then writes the number "200" five times in a column. "HERE I HAVE 5 BOXES [he counts the number while he performs the addition] 200, 400, 600, 800, 1,000. I HAVE TO WRITE MORE ON THE PAPER. [He then writes the number "200" an additional 10 times, and continues counting by 200s to 3,000.] THERE ARE 3,000 ORANGES."

S No. V205 demonstrates three distinct strategic forms in his solution to the school-based problems. First, in solving $28 + 26 = ?$, he recomposes terms into "convenient" values to restructure the problem into the following form: $\{\{\{20 + 20\} + 8\} + 6\}$. In his solution to $790 + 470 = ?$, S No. V204 uses a similar but modified procedure in which he uses an intermediate value, 10, to create a convenient value of 1,000. Thus, S No. V204 restructures the problem as follows, $\{(400 + 700) + (70 - 10) + (90 + 10)\}$. In solving both $20 \times 6 = ?$ and $15 \times 200 = ?$, S No. V204 uses paper and pencil to write down each iteration in the multiplication problems, and then, by serial addition, he achieves the correct answers.

The following seller, who is in the third grade, displays a variety of regrouping approaches to solving subtraction problems.

S No. V304. Seller, third grade. S No. V304 is presented with the problem $46 - 18 = ?$ in word problem format. He thinks and responds, "28." He is questioned about how he arrived at the answer and responds, "I FIRST TOOK AWAY 6 FROM THIS NUMBER (46) AND THEN TOOK AWAY 12 MORE MARBLES, SO I TOOK AWAY 18 MARBLES IN ALL. THE ANSWER IS 28." ($(46 - 6 = 40)$ [$18 - 6 = 12$] $(40 - 12 = 28)$ [$12 - 12 = 0$]). S No. V304 is then presented with the problem $1320 - 480$ again in word problem format. He responds, "960, NO, 940." He is asked how he arrived at that answer and he responds, "I FIRST I TOOK AWAY 320 AND THEN I TOOK AWAY 160 MORE. SO I WAS LEFT WITH 940." ($1320 - 320 - 160 = 940$ [$480 - 320 = 160$] [$160 - 160 = 0$]).

Like S No. V205, S No. V304 restructures the terms in each of the two problems into convenient values. In solving $46 - 18 = ?$, the seller produces a convenient value of 40, restructuring the problem as follows: $46 - 6 = 40$, decrementing 18 by 6 $\{18 - 6 = 12\}$; $40 - 12 = 28$, decrementing 12 by 12 $\{12 - 12 = 0\}$. In solving $1,320 - 480 = ?$, S No. V304 uses a similar approach, first producing a convenient value of 1,000 $\{1,320 - 320 = 1000\}$ $\{480 - 320 = 160\}$, and then subtracting the remainder from 1,000 $\{1,000 - 160 = 840\}$.

Some children used hybrid strategies—strategies that combine regrouping approaches with elements of algorithmic procedures—to solve the problems. The following is a somewhat extreme instance:

S No. V309. Seller, third grade. S No. V309 is presented with the problem $790 + 470 = ?$ in computation form, and solves it correctly (see Fig. 13.5). When questioned about his solution strategy, he explains, referring first to the units column, "0 PLUS 0 EQUALS 0"; then referring to the tens column and using a regrouping strategy, "NINE (of 790) MINUS THREE IS SIX, AND THREE PLUS SEVEN IS 10 AND 10 PLUS SIX IS 16." He writes down the six and carries one to the hundreds column. Again he uses a regrouping strategy to add the numbers in the hundreds column: "FOUR MINUS THREE IS ONE, AND THREE PLUS SEVEN IS 10. TEN PLUS ONE PLUS ONE IS 12," and he writes down the number 12.

Description of Procedures:

c. b. a.

1

790

+ 470

d. 1260

a. 0+0=0; writes 0.

b. 9-3=6, 3+7=10; 6+10=16; writes 6, carries 1.

c. 4-3=1, 3+7=10; 10+1+1=12, writes 12.

d. Reads 10,260.

FIG. 13.5. A seller's hybrid strategy to a multidigit addition problem in computation format.

While his final answer is correct, he reads the value as 10,260, making a place value error described in the analysis of children's identifications of numbers represented with the standard orthography.

S No. V309 shows the orchestration of forms linked to school and to out-of-school learning in his solution to the school problems. His approach reflects his effort to achieve a coherent solution in which he draws on knowledge generated across contexts.

Analysis of Strategy Types as a Function of Selling Experience and Grade Level

In the following analyses, children's strategies were classified as algorithmic when they made use of a column format to solve the problems—whether or not they used some regrouping of terms.

Fig. 13.6 contains the mean number of the problems for which children used appropriate regrouping or algorithmic strategies. A 2 (strategy type, repeated) $\times$ 2 (grade level) $\times$ 2 (selling experience) ANOVA revealed one 2-way interaction—strategy type by selling experience ($F(1,39) = 24.77$, $p < .0001$). The ANOVA also revealed main effects for strategy type ($F(1,39) = 24.19$, $p < .0001$) and selling experience ($F(1,39) = 10.30$, $p < .01$). Duncan post hoc comparisons to determine the source of the interaction between selling experience and strategy revealed that there were no differences between the nonsellers' successful use of regrouping strategies and algorithmic strategies, whereas the sellers used a greater number of successful regrouping strategies than algorithmic strategies (in a ratio of about 5 to 1 at grade 2).

It may be that problem format was a contributor to children's strategy choices. For instance, computational format may favor school-algorithmic approaches and word format may favor the out-of-school regrouping approaches. To address this question, two additional 2 (problem type, repeated) $\times$ 2 (grade level $\times$ 2 (selling experience) ANOVAs were conducted on the eight matched word and computation problems. In the first case, an analysis was performed on children's use of successful algorithmic strategies. In the second case, the analysis was performed on children's use of successful regrouping strategies. The mean percentage of

Second Grade

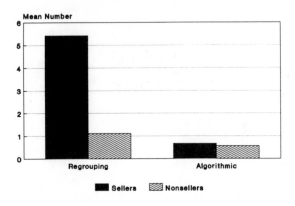

Third Grade

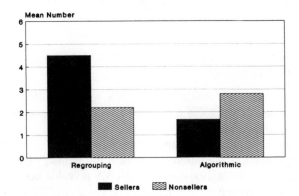

FIG. 13.6. Mean number of successful school algorithmic and regrouping strategies as a function of grade level and selling experience.

children's successful algorithmic and regrouping strategies as a function of problem type and selling experience is contained in Figs. 13.7 and 13.8.

The analysis of successful algorithmic strategy usage revealed main effects for
problem type ($F(1,39) = 8.62, p < .001$) and grade level ($F(1,39) = 9.61, p <
.005$) but no effects for selling experience. Children, regardless of selling experi-
ence, were more likely to use successful algorithmic strategies on the computation problems than the word problems, and third graders used more successful
algorithmic strategies than second graders.

The analysis of successful regrouping strategy usage revealed main effects for
problem type ($F(1,39) = 11.33, p < .005$) and selling experience ($F(1,39) =
22.37, p < .0001$). Children were more likely to use regrouping strategies on the

Second Grade

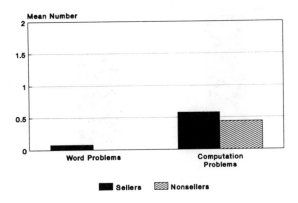

Third Grade

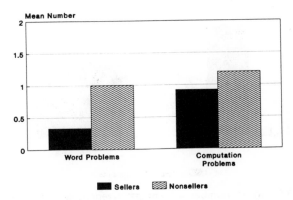

FIG. 13.7.   Mean number of successful algorithmic strategies as a function of problem, grade level, and selling experience.

word format as contrasted with the computation format, and sellers as contrasted with nonsellers were more likely to use regrouping strategies regardless of problem format.

These findings, then, indicate while sellers used more appropriate regrouping strategies across both computational and word problems than the sellers, their use of regrouping strategies was more frequent on word problems, and their use of school-linked algorithmic strategies was more frequent on computational problems. Similarly, while nonsellers used more algorithmic than regrouping strategies, nonsellers' use of regrouping strategies was more frequent on word, as contrasted with computational, problems.

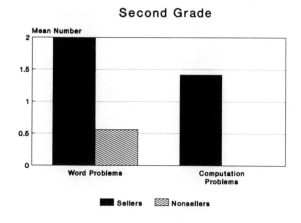

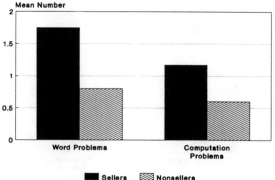

FIG. 13.8.   Mean number of successful regrouping strategies as a function of problem, grade level, and selling experience.

SUMMARY

The evidence from this chapter shows that sellers as contrasted with nonsellers are more adept at solving school-linked arithmetical problems. Further, the analysis of children's strategies revealed that a source of sellers' success was their specialized knowledge of regrouping, specialized strategic forms that we have seen some evidence of in Chapters 8 and 9 in sellers' bill reordering to solve the currency addition tasks. In their solutions to the school-linked problems, we see the appropriation of these out-of-school cognitive forms and further specialization of these forms to accomplish school-linked arithmetical problems. Perhaps the most revealing case of this cited in the chapter was S No. V309's hybrid strategy, in which he orchestrated knowledge of regrouping with the carrying algorithm in achieving a solution to a multidigit addition problem.

Differences between sellers' and nonsellers' number correct and types of strategies used were most pronounced at grade 2. Indeed, at grade 2, there was more than a threefold difference in the number correct, and sellers used five times more adequate regrouping strategies than nonsellers. Further, while sellers used more adequate regrouping strategies than adequate algorithmic strategies, the distribution of adequate strategy types in the nonsellers did not differ. By grade 3, nonsellers showed that they made considerable progress in specializing adequate strategies, and these developments consisted of increased usage of both adequate regrouping and algorithmic forms.

14 Appropriation and Specialization in the Practice

In the prior chapters, we have seen some evidence that children make use of cognitive forms linked to one practice (either school or candy selling) to accomplish problems in the other. We have not addressed in any detail, however, the constructive process entailed in children's across-context "transfer." To this end, in this chapter, I consider two instances of transfer involving price translation procedures of the Prepare to Purchase Phase. In one case, I consider sellers' specialization of knowledge generated in the Sell Phase of the practice to accomplish the price translation problem; in the other case, I consider sellers' specialization of school-linked procedures to accomplish the same problem of price translation.

The case material excerpted for analysis is taken from Chapters 6 and 9. In the excerpted material, we find that, whether we consider cases of transfer within the candy-selling practice as sellers' goals shift or from school to the practice of candy selling, transfer may be best understood in developmental terms—as a process of transforming prior cognitive forms into means of accomplishing new functions through a process of progressive specialization.

TRANSFER OF KNOWLEDGE WITHIN THE PRACTICE: A SHIFT IN PRICE RATIO USE

In the ethnographic treatment of Part II, we found that price ratios were only used by young sellers in the Sell Phase (in transactions with customers). In contrast, these ratios were used by older sellers in the Prepare-to-Sell Phase as a principal feature of strategies to translate wholesale box prices into retail unit prices. The use of the price ratio in the Prepare-to-Sell Phase could be understood in terms of traditional models of transfer; from the learning perspective, ratio use increases in its field of application; from a cognitive perspective, knowledge constructed in the Sell Phase is aligned with a problem in the Prepare-to-Purchase Phase. We find, however, in the following examples, that such traditional analytic approaches do not capture a profound shift in the semiotics of sellers' activities. The shift is one in which the seller reorients his early emerging form of price ratio use to take on a new, anticipatory function. Let us first review the character of ratio use for the young seller in the Sell Phase and then the older seller in the Prepare-to-Purchase Phase.

Young sellers were often told for what price ratio to sell a box by their mother or older sibling, and, in turn, they guided their transactions with customers accordingly in the Sell Phase. In selling, the young seller's use of the price ratio conventions is directed toward the customer—the price ratio implicitly defines, by authority of the relative or more knowledgeable peer, what constitutes a fair exchange of goods for money between customer and seller. For the young seller, the ratio is constitutive of the transaction itself and does not refer beyond it. We found no evidence in Part II that in the young seller's use of the ratio, each sale is treated as anything but an independent action. These actions are not progressively registered, but are treated successively, culminating in an empty candy box and a wad of bills. Indeed, no cognizing of what should be a gross value for the box is entailed in the activity of seller–customer transactions.

We found in Part II that by 12 to 15 years most children produced their own Prepare-to-Sell Phase calculations. In many of these calculations, we found that sellers increasingly appropriated a representation of seller-to-customer sales transactions—signified by the Sell Phase price ratio—to a Prepare-to-sell Phase computation. In the following excerpt, note the elevation of the price ratio to serve this referential function in the computation of a gross value for the box: The ratio is now used to refer to potential discrete customer-to-seller transactions unlike the Sell Phase use, while the seller produces a progressive summation of a potential gross value of the box for the selected price ratio.

S No. 26. 11-year-old seller, second grade. S No. 26 is presented with the problem of producing a retail unit price for a 50-unit box that sold for Cr$3500 (wholesale price). He takes the candy out of the box and arranges the units in groups of six, counting each group by 1000 (Cr$1000, Cr$2000, Cr$3000 . . .). He then rearranges the entire 50-unit box of candy into groups of seven and proceeds counting each group again by 1,000 cruzeiros. He then states, "I'LL SELL THE WHOLE BOX FOR Cr$7000, MAKING Cr$3500 FOR THE (NEXT) BOX AND Cr$3500 FOR ME" (the half-half convention). (What will you charge the customers in the street?) "SEVEN FOR Cr$1000." For the second problem of producing a retail unit price for a 30-unit box for Cr$8500, S No. 26 again takes the candy out of the box, this time arranging the candy in groups of two. He again counts the groups by units of 1,000 cruzeiros, ending with Cr$15000. He states, "IT WAS Cr$8500 AND

I'LL MAKE Cr$6500. IT'S BETTER TO SELL THIS WAY BECAUSE IT'LL GO QUICKLY" (referring to the fact that the will not make as much net profit as the box cost, as the half-half convention would dictate).

In the case of S No. 26, we see the child uprooting the ratio from its transactional status in the Sell Phase and restructuring its use to serve an anticipatory function. Rather than mediating between customer and seller, the ratio is used referentially—to refer to such potential transactions. It is this symbolic use that allows the seller to recalibrate potential gross prices. Further, this symbolic environment provides the seller with greater opportunities for constructing mathematical relations that emerge in the act of selling. For instance, a seller may discover the relation between increases in ratio size and decreases in the gross value of his box. In the excerpt, we see that S No. 26 already understands this mathematical relation—as the number of units per bill denomination increases, the gross value of the box decreases.

In the following two excerpts, we see further specializations of price ratio use in Prepare-to-Sell Phase computations. In the first example, the seller condenses two sales into one, and produces a more efficient calculation than did S No. 26. These computations are abbreviated ones in which price ratio use is condensed and more distantly related to the act of Sell Phase transactions. Consider first, the following sellers' abbreviated use of the price ratio in his translation.

OBS No. 11 (12 years, completed first grade). The seller begins his day with a full box of candy bars. The box contains 30 units, and he paid Cr$8000 for the box. He's selling the bars at three for Cr$1000. (Observer: "How much will you sell the full box for?") . . . . "I COUNT LIKE THIS" (illustrating a count of the bars in groups of three by a value of Cr$1000—See Fig. 14.1). "THESE TWO (two groups of three) BRING Cr$2000, THESE TWO (two groups of three) Cr$4000, THESE TWO Cr$6000 . . . THESE TWO Cr$10000. I COUNT LIKE THIS 'CAUSE I'M GOING TO SELL THE CHOCOLATE AT THREE FOR Cr$1000, AND THIS WAY THE FULL BOX WILL BRING Cr$10000." (How much will you profit after selling the full box?) "SINCE THE BOX COST ME Cr$8000 AND I'LL SELL THE FULL BOX FOR Cr$10000, MY PROFIT WILL BE Cr$2000." (Do you think your profit will be good?) "IT'S NOT GOING TO BE VERY GOOD. BUT, IF I SELL TWO FOR Cr$1000, IT'S GOING TO BE HARD TO SELL, AND IF A SOLD FOUR FOR Cr$1000, I'D LOSE TOO MUCH." (Who taught you to sell chocolate like this?) "NOBODY. I TAUGHT MYSELF."

S No. 39. 11-year-old seller, first grade. S No. 39 is presented with the problem of producing a retail unit price for a 50-unit box that sold for Cr$3500 (wholesale

FIG. 14.1. Schematic of a 12-year-old unschooled seller's specialized solution strategy to his price translation problem.

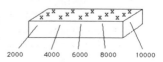

2000   4000   6000   8000   10000

price). He justifies a price of five for Cr$1000 in the following way: ". . . BE-CAUSE FIVE OR SIX FOR Cr$1000 IS GOOD. SELLING AT FIVE FOR Cr$1000 WILL BRING MORE PROFIT." (Show me what you did to find out.) He said ". . . 10 OF THESE WILL BRING 2000, 20 WILL BRING 4000, 40 WILL BRING 8000, AND 50 WILL BRING 10000." He accomplishes this calculation without removing the candy from the box.

What were separate potential sales transactions in the Sell Phase for these two sellers are now collapsed into abbreviated additions. In their production of potential gross values for the boxes, sellers produce a progressive summation, two by two, in which they coordinate subsets of candy (e.g., 10 to 50) with the price the candies will bring (e.g., Cr$2000 to Cr$10000). In the greater economy of effort in this highly specialized use of the price ratio, the price ratio itself becomes more distantly related to the actual process of selling. Indeed, in the cases of the two sellers, there is no longer a direct correspondence between a sales transaction and a count in the mark-up calculation. Instead, each count entails two transactions. Further, the representation of these transactions is now no longer so transparent. While in the case of OBS No. 11, the seller extracts groups of candy to keep track of his progressive summation of cash, in the case of S No. 39, he leaves all candy in his box, performing a rapid tally of the retail value of the box.

In sum, in the foregoing protocols, we see instances of transfer from the act of commerce in the Sell Phase to the act of pricing of the Prepare-to-Purchase Phase. The process is one of reorganizing Sell Phase activity into a schematic form—one in which only a trace of the seller–customer exchanges are preserved and represented by the price ratio. The two components of the ratio are then used as a vehicle for computation, a vehicle which is progressively specialized into more abbreviated cognitive forms.

TRANSFER OF SCHOOL-LINKED KNOWLEDGE
TO THE PROBLEM OF PRICING

Some sellers made use of school-linked knowledge to solve the translation problems. Like the cases of transfer which we have cited, the appropriation of school-linked knowledge forms to address adequately the problems of the Prepare-to-Purchase Phase requires a conceptualization of the pricing problem in terms of the Sell Phase of the practice.

In the following case, a schooled seller shows his spontaneous efforts to use school-linked procedures to address the price translation problem, a strategy that we have already noted in reviewing schooled children's solutions to the candy tasks in Chapter 11.

S No. 92. 14-year-old seller, fifth grade. S No. 92 is presented with the problem of producing a retail unit price for a 50-unit box that cost Cr$3500 (wholesale price).

He says that he will sell the box for Cr$10000 and sell the units to customers at one for Cr$200. (How do you know that this is a good price for you?) "BECAUSE BY SELLING ONE FOR Cr$200 I'LL MAKE Cr$10000." (Show me what you did to know.) S No. 92 uses the long form of the school-linked multiplication algorithm, solving the problem 50 units × Cr$200 = Cr$10000. For the second problem of producing a retail unit price for a 30-unit box for Cr$8500, S No. 92 says that he would sell the box for Cr$15000 and sell the units for one for Cr$500. Again, he demonstrates his solution by the long form of the school-linked multiplication algorithm, solving the problem 30 units × Cr$500 = Cr$15000.

S No. 92's solution shows similarities and differences to less schooled sellers who have been cited (OBS No. 11, S No. 39). Like S No. 26, S No. 92 conceptualizes the problem as one that requires a computation of a potential gross value for the box. Rather than using the price ratio to organize his computation in a repeated addition operation of subsets of candy, S No. 92 uses the school-linked multiplication algorithm. In using this algorithm, S No. 92 structures the problem without regard to the selling convention. S No. 92 restricts his retail sale price to single units of candy, a restriction that allows him to apply the multiplication algorithm directly to a selected retail unit price to determine the potential the gross value of a box (see Chapter 10).

We have already seen in Chapter 6 that the application of school-linked procedures may be further specialized to address the price translations. Recall that seller S No. 07 (Chapter 6) made use of school-linked algorithmic multiplication procedures to determine the amount he paid per unit for a particular wholesale box, in this instance a box of 50 candy bars selling at Cr$7000. To determine the wholesale price per unit, S No. 07 estimated a unit wholesale price, multiplied the estimated wholesale price by the number of units in his box (50) using the school algorithmic procedure, found that the product did not equal the wholesale price, and then readjusted his estimate appropriately, and again performed the school-linked multiplication algorithm, this time achieving a match. Once satisfied with the wholesale price per unit of Cr$140, he proceeded, in turn, to show how he arrived at his particular retail price per unit, again with school-linked computational procedures. In the end, he showed his translation of a wholesale price per unit in terms of the price ratio convention.

In the case of S No. 07, we see the school-linked multiplication procedure adapted and specialized as a series of guided multiplications and adjustments to determine an intermediary wholesale unit price, which in turn is converted into a retail price in terms of the price ratio convention. The procedure is one which was not taught in school, but emerges as the seller specializes his school-linked knowledge to bear on the problems of the practice. We might imagine a further specialization and abbreviation of these procedures involving a division operation as the seller generates greater insights into the structure of the problem through his repeated efforts.

The analyses presented point to some of the developmental processes that may be entailed in the act of transfer linked to cultural practices. We see that in recurring activities like practices of candy selling and schooling—contexts in which knowledge is well learned and in which similar problems emerge on a repeated basis—transfer is a protracted process. In their repeated efforts to solve practice-linked problems, individuals attempt to structure problem contexts in coherent and more adequate ways: Over the repeated structuring of problems and problem solutions, sellers specialize novel cognitive forms and functions that are suited to the practice with which they are engaged. In sellers' extended efforts, the processes of development and transfer (or, in terms more closely linked to Vygotsky's writings, learning and development) merge into a single process in which both are intrinsically linked to one another and both have intrinsic links to sociocultural life.

CONCLUDING REMARK

In the analyses given, I have used individuals sampled at particular points in time to point to processes that may be involved in transfer of knowledge linked to practices. The systematic analysis of transfer of the form sketched here would require not only analyses of practices with reference to the parameters in which emergent goals are understood, but also longitudinal analyses of the process of appropriation and specialization—an analytic and empirical task that extends beyond the scope of this volume.

V CULTURE AND COGNITIVE DEVELOPMENT

15 Epilogue

I began this volume with a concern to probe the relations between cognitive development and culture. The problem is one of the most complex in the social and behavioral sciences and one that cuts across a range of academic disciplines, including psychology, anthropology, and education. In its complexity, one discovers a labyrinth of choices in structuring methods of approach and interpretive directions. So often, researchers have defined the constructs of cognition and culture as entirely independent of one another, one located in the individual and the other in the environment. We see this clearly both in approaches that focus primarily on cognitive processes like information-processing approaches (Greeno, Riley, & Gelman, 1984; Klahr & Wallace, 1975) as well as approaches that are concerned with relations between sociocultural and cognitive developmental ones, including Piaget-based accounts (Dasen, 1977, 1985; Hallpike, 1979), ecocultural accounts (Berry, 1966, 1974, 1984), and socialization accounts (Hess & Shipman, 1965). In these approaches, analytic categories are cast in acultural terms and then processes of "social transmission" are often examined to determine the effects of culture on the measurement of cognitive constructs. I have argued, in Part I, that such an analytic tack ends in limited treatments of relations between the two constructs. In Vygotsky's terms, we end with analysis of "external connections" where, from the psychological point of view, the problem is to understand intrinsic relations. Indeed, consider what the results might have been from the present study of candy sellers had the investigation use solely measures linked to Piagetian or more eclectic treatments of cognitive development.

Had the investigation used only Piagetian measures of operational development, perhaps analyses would have shown that candy sellers are more advanced

183

than their nonselling peers on measures of conservation, classification, and seriation, but perhaps not; perhaps we would have found age-related shifts in the sellers in these cognitive domains from preoperational structures to concrete operational structures. Regardless of the outcomes, the analyses would provide little information about the interdependent relations between evolving artifacts like currency and conventions like price ratios and sellers' elaboration of cognitive forms and functions linked to these sociocultural processes. Further, we would have no sense of the interdependence of the social interactional processes that are interwoven with children's cognitive ones that would permit practice participation. Indeed, we would have no analyses of the candy sellers' shifting understandings and their intrinsic links to their distinctive social history.

In the body of this volume, I have taken as a core proposition that at an important level of analysis culture and cognition are constitutive of one another, a proposition contained also in recent discussions of the problem (Cole, 1988; Lave, 1988; Minick, in press). Social conventions, artifacts, and social interactions are cognitive constructions and cannot be understood adequately without reference to cognizing individuals. At the same time, individuals' cognizing activities are interwoven with conventions, artifacts, and other people in accomplishing problems of daily life. This interdependence between cognition and cultural processes has led me to pursue a tack that elevates the analysis of intrinsic relations to central focus.

To reveal core properties of intrinsic relations, I targeted in Part I the practice of candy selling, treating this practice as a microcosm in which general properties of the interdependence between culture and cognitive development would be revealed. As a means of further constraining my field of inquiry, I focused principally on mathematical cognition.

The candy-selling practice was well-suited for my purposes. The complex web of cultural artifacts and social processes linked to the practice was extraordinarily accessible for analysis; further, it was also a practice in which I had the opportunity to make comparisons between children that more clearly illuminated the way in which sociocultural processes were blended with cognitive developmental ones—comparisons between sellers and nonsellers, sellers of different ages, and same-aged sellers and nonsellers solving problems linked to school and to the candy-selling practice.

To focus squarely on intrinsic relations between cultural and cognitive developmental processes throughout the volume, I have taken as core constructs the mathematical goals that emerge during practice participation and the cognitive forms and functions children construct which both influence these emergent goals and result from sellers' constructive efforts to accomplish these goals. From my perspective, the focus on emergent goals and form–function relations has been critical. It has provided a level of analysis in which it is possible to preserve the culturally textured properties of individuals' conceptual activities while gaining insight into fundamental processes central to developmental change. In emergent goals, we find the constructive efforts of the child as they emerge in sociocultural artifacts like currency and as they are negotiated in social interactions like those with store clerks or customers; in form–function relations, we find dynamic processes of developmental change as children transform artifacts and prior understandings into increasingly specialized cognitive instruments and, in the process, create new cognitive functions.

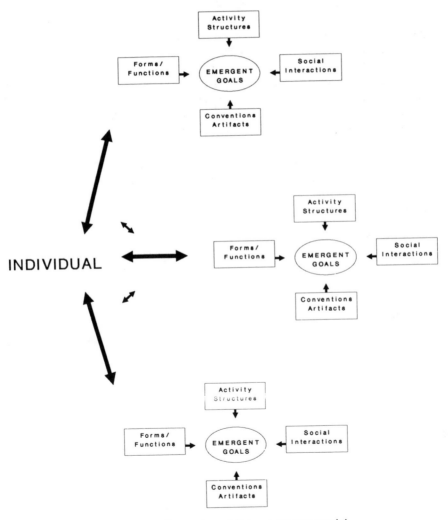

FIG. 15.1. Expansion of four-parameter model.

CONCLUDING REMARK

Whether we consider cognitive development in remote regions of Papua New Guinea, in middle- and working-class communities in Brooklyn, or in an urban center in Brazil, we find cognitive developmental and sociocultural processes interwoven with one another in complex ways. Indeed, in a fundamental sense, we are all like the candy sellers. Fig. 15.1 presents a generalized portrayal.

As the figure shows, in our daily lives, we are engaged with multiple practices. Within practices, goals emerge that must be accomplished, avoided, or reckoned within the achieving of larger objectives. Across practices, the understandings we generate in one may be appropriated and transformed to structure and restructure goals in another. Further, the practices in which we participate often tolerate our incompetence. Sometimes tolerance is consciously designed, as in the case of school curricula that gradually up the ante to present a flow of new but measured challenges. In other cases, the tolerance has emerged through a particular set of sociocultural conditions like candy selling in which young children participate who have very limited mathematical skills. In the tolerance that both permits and emerges through participation in practices, practices are enculturating. In participation, we work to approach and accomplish emergent problems that have taken form over a social and cultural history. In our participation in these practices, we construct understandings and novel symbolic forms that are intrinsically linked to sociocultural life and to our own constructive efforts.

Appendix Recruitment of Sellers
A

Virtually all sellers were recruited by female Brazilian university students in the streets as the boys sold candy, tangerines, or puffed wheat. Children were informed about the study and then, with their consent, were administered a preliminary screening interview to determine whether they had at least 3 months of candy-selling experience. In the interview, children were questioned about whether they had sold candy between intervals of major Brazilian holidays including (Christmas, Carnival, Sao Joao, Festa do Carmo), and sellers answers were used as a basis to determine whether they had sold candy for at least a 3-month period. Sellers who met the criteria were asked if they would participate in the study and told that they would be paid (about) Cr$5000 for their participation (the exact amount changed with inflation—the selection of a payment price was based on a decision to pay sellers somewhat more than they would make in the equivalent amount of time selling candy).

Appendix B

Background Information on Sellers and Their Practice

To produce information on sellers' backgrounds and everyday activities, child sellers were interviewed individually after their consent was obtained for participation but prior to participation on the interview on mathematical concepts. Sellers were questioned about their parents' occupations, their own schooling, their introduction to the selling practice, the amount of time they currently devote to the practice, and the amount for which they paid and sold their last box of candy (to gain systematic information on pricing practices).

Subjects

The final population of children selected consisted of boys ranging from 6 to 15 years of age; these children varied in amount of schooling (from no school through the completion of seventh grade).

Setting

The interviews were conducted in a large, bright room leased for the study. The room was located in an office building in downtown Recife, close to areas in which children conducted their candy-selling practice.

Procedures

Interview. Aside from questions regarding demographic information important for the management of the study (the location of stores most commonly frequented, and general background information on sellers such as other merchandise that they have sold, the seasonal shifts in their own selling activities, etc.), children were interviewed about their own backgrounds and the conduct of their practice. *a. Parents' occupations.* What do your parents do? Do they work? (If yes) What are their occupations? *b. Schooling.* Do you go to school? (If yes) What grade are you in? (If no) Did you ever go to school? (If yes) When did you leave school? Why? *c. Initiation into the practice.* How did you begin selling candy? Explain. Who taught you how to sell candy? When you first started selling candy, how did you know what price to sell for? Did anyone help you to set prices? Who? *d. Time intensity of practice.* How many times a week do you sell (or did you sell) candy? How many hours a day do you do this? *e. Pricing.* The last time you bought a box of candy, how much did you pay? How much did you sell the box for?

Who taught you how to sell?

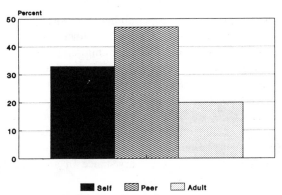

Did anyone help with initial pricing?

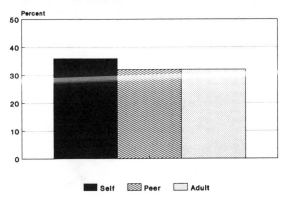

FIG. B.1. Percentage of sellers' self, peer, and adult responses to questions about initial assistance in selling candy.

RESULTS

Children's responses to questions about parents' occupations revealed that virtually all children came from families in which the father and/or mother were either unemployed, or worked in the informal sector (e.g., jobs such as brick layers, vegetable sellers, drivers, or laundry maids). Questions about school attendance revealed that 36% of the population sample were not enrolled during the time of the study, and 60% of those who were not enrolled in school either left school or never enrolled because of the need to make money. The remaining 40% cited reasons such as moving residence or parents not paying the normal school fee as reasons for not being enrolled.

Children spend long hours at work. Children's reports indicated that they sell between 1 and 7 days per week (median = 6 days) and for 3 to 14 hours per day (median = 9 hours). The median number of hours per week devoted to sales was 50.

The analysis of the questions pertaining to assistance with the practice (whether anyone initially taught the child and whether anyone initially helped the child with pricing) were coded as to whether children reported that they received any help at all, were aided by peers (e.g., siblings, friends), or were aided by adults (e.g., mother, store clerk). The distribution of children's answers is contained in Fig. B.1. The majority of children reported being introduced to the practice and initially being aided in the practice by either peers (47% taught, 32% initial aid in pricing) or adults (20% taught, 32% initial aid in pricing). Evidence presented in Part II suggests that well after children become veteran sellers, they maintain a dependence on others for assistance in solving various problems generated in the course of the activity.

In order to gain insight into the percent mark-up from wholesale to retail prices, children were asked the price they paid for the last box they purchased and the amount they sold the box for. The median purchase price for the last box was Cr$6500 and the median price was Cr$12500. The median mark-up was 75% (the mean was 89%, sd = 53%).

Appendix C

Extended Description of Tasks

NUMBER REPRESENTATION: STANDARD ORTHOGRAPHY

Identifying and Comparing Numerical Values Using the Standard Orthography

Children were presented with 10 pairs of numbers, pair by pair, and asked to compare them; if children did not read the numbers aloud in their comparison (most did), they were asked to read the values as well. Each number of the pair was printed on a card (about 10 cm by 10 cm). Five number pairs were embedded in a question about cruzeiros (the Brazilian unit of currency), and 5 pairs were embedded in a question about the number of candies in a sack (a familiar means of packaging a certain type of candy). The order of question type for each block of 5 pairs was counterbalanced, and one half of the subjects within each age group were administered *set A* number pairs (2,000 vs. 1,500; 3,456 vs. 4,000; 935 vs. 1,000; 150 vs. 146; 168 vs. 321) for the cruzeiro questions and *set B* (3,000 vs. 2,500; 4,567 vs. 5,000; 847 vs. 1,000; 160 vs. 152; 489 vs. 932) for the candy questions and the other half *set B* for the cruzeiro questions and *set A* for the candy questions.

1. Cruzeiro Question. The child was told, "Let's say that we have two wallets containing money, one with this much [the interviewer presents a card containing the first of two numerals of the numeral pair] and the other with this much money [the interviewer presents a card containing the second of two numerals of the numeral pair]. Which wallet contains more money? Why?"

191

2. Candy Question. The child was told, "Let's say that we have two bags of candy, one has this amount [the interviewer presents a card containing the first of two numerals of the numeral pair] and the other has this amount [the interviewer presents a card containing the second of two numerals of the numeral pair]. Which bag contains more candy?"

NUMBER REPRESENTATION: USE OF CURRENCY

Identifying Numerical Values on the Basis of the Orthography vs. Figurative Characteristics of Bills

Children were presented with 12 trials in each of the three conditions. In the *bill condition,* children were presented with 12 bills individually (2 of each of the following six values: Cr\$100, Cr\$200, Cr\$500, Cr\$1000, Cr\$5000, Cr\$10000). Prior to the presentation, the interviewer said: "Now I'm going to show you some bills and you tell me how much each is worth." In the *Numeral Occluded Condition,* children were presented with 12 identical bills and instructions as in the bill condition, except that all numerals on the bills were occluded with opaque tape. In the *Numeral Only Condition,* children were presented with 12 cut-out black-and-white photocopies of the numerals from the bills in the *Bills Condition.* The interviewer told the child, "Now I'm going to show you some numbers from bills and you tell me how much each is worth." The trials were randomized for each subject and the conditions were counterbalanced within each population group.

Identifying Numerical Relations Between Currency Values

The child was presented with 14 pairs of bills and/or coins (the order was of presentation was randomized for each subject) and asked to compare them to determine which was the greater value and how many of the lesser value was equivalent to the greater value. The pairs consisted of the following: Cr\$5 (coin) vs. Cr\$10 (coin); Cr\$10 (coin) vs. Cr\$50; Cr\$10 (coin) vs. Cr\$100 (bill); Cr\$500 (bill) vs. Cr\$1000 (bill); Cr\$100 (bill) vs. Cr\$500 (bill); Cr\$100 (bill) vs. Cr\$1000 (bill); Cr\$5000 (bill) vs. Cr\$10000 (bill); Cr\$1000 (bill) vs. Cr\$5000 (bill); Cr\$1000 (bill) vs. Cr\$10000 (bill); Cr\$1 (coin) vs. Cr\$20 (coin); Cr\$5 (coin) vs. Cr\$20 (coin); Cr\$10 (coin) vs. Cr\$20 (coin); Cr\$20 (coin) vs. Cr\$100 (bill); Cr\$100 (bill) vs. Cr\$200 (bill).

With the presentation of each pair, the interviewer said the following: "Which of these is more money?" [Child responds] "Let's say that you have this money (*the greater value*) and you go to a store to get change. How many coins (or bills) of (*the lesser value*) do you need to get for change?".

Children's Facility with the Denominational Structure of the Currency System: Exchange Tasks

Children were presented with two problems that required them to exchange a large denomination for smaller currency denominations so that the appropriate change could be returned to a customer. The problems differed in the size of the customer's currency to be exchanged (Cr$5000 or Cr$10000) and the price of the merchandise requested by the customer (Cr$2300 or Cr$6630). *1. Exchanging a Cr$5000 bill to accommodate a Cr$2300 purchase.* The interviewer said the following: "Let's say that you just bought a box of candy and began selling. You don't have any money left because you spent it all to buy your box. You are beginning to sell and you find your first customer. He's a tourist who has never seen this kind of candy and decides to buy a lot to take home. He wants to buy Cr$2300 worth of candy. But you have a problem because he doesn't have change—he only has a Cr$5000 bill. And there's another problem: You don't have change and the customer said that he wants to receive exact change or else he won't buy any. But, you remember that you know a man that has a store very close by and he always has change." "Now, pretend that I'm the store owner and that you come to ask me for change for the Cr$5000 bill. But you have to tell me what kind of change you want. You need to tell me what types of bills you want and how many bills and coins of each type. Do you understand? I will change your money in any way you want and as many times as you want, you just have to ask." In clear view in front of the interviewer is a separate stack of each denomination of money from Cr$1 to Cr$10000." "Ready? The customer gives you Cr$5000 but he only wants to buy Cr$2300 of candy and to get exact change. Now you arrive with your money at my store and are going to ask me for the type of change you want. Understand? Let's begin." The interviewer terminated the process of exchanging bills either when a child believed that he had achieved the appropriate units of currency to make change for the customer or when the child made six requests (correct or incorrect) *2. Exchanging a Cr$10000 bill to accommodate a Cr$6630 purchase.* The identical task as in problem No. 1, but with a change as indicated in the currency values. The interviewer terminated the problem either when a child believed that he had achieved the appropriate units of currency to make change for the customer or when the child made seven requests (correct or incorrect).

ARITHMETICAL COMPUTATIONS: ADDITION AND SUBTRACTION

Adding and Subtracting Values

1. Addition Tasks. There were two addition problems which differed in the number of bills to be added and the sum of those bills. In the first problem, the child was presented with a stack of 12 bills (totaling Cr$8600) and told, "Suppose you started the day with this amount of money [the interviewer hands the child the stack]. Would you count the money for me?" The child was provided with paper and pencil and told that he could use the paper and pencil, talk aloud, or anything else he liked, to help him find out how much was in the stack. The stack was arranged in a standard order: Cr$500, Cr$500, Cr$200, Cr$500, Cr$500, Cr$200, Cr$200, Cr$200, Cr$100, Cr$500, Cr$200, Cr$5000. In the other addition problem, a stack of 17 bills totaling Cr$17300 was used. The order was: Cr$1000, Cr$500, Cr$100, Cr$200, Cr$500, Cr$500, Cr$200, Cr$200, Cr$1000, Cr$500, Cr$200, Cr$500, Cr$1000, Cr$200, Cr$200, Cr$500, Cr$10000. *2. Subtraction tasks*. There were two subtraction problems which differed in the price of a box to be purchased, and the amount of money available to purchase the box. In one problem, children were told "Suppose you decided to buy this box of *Chupetim* (a box of *Chupetim* was presented) that costs Cr$3800 in the store. Show me how much you would give to the clerk." This task followed the addition problem totaling Cr$8600, and the child had the stack of Cr$8600 from which he could offer payment. If the child did not offer the Cr$5000 bill from the stack, the child's value was noted, and the child was presented with the Cr$5000 bill and told that he should give the clerk that amount. The child was then asked, "should you receive change?" If the child responded yes, the following additional questions were asked: "How much change? How do you know? Show me". In the second subtraction problem, children were told, "Suppose you decided to buy this box of *Danubio* that costs Cr$7600 in the store. Show me how much you would give to the clerk." This task followed the addition problem totaling Cr$17300, and the child had the stack of Cr$17300 from which he could offer payment. If the child did not offer the Cr$10000 bill, the child's value was noted, and was presented with the Cr$10000 bill and told that he should give the clerk that amount. The remainder of this task was identical to the first subtraction task.

COMPARING RATIOS

Comparing Retail Price Ratios

To introduce the ratio comparison problems, the interviewer presented a bag of *Pirulitos* (a type of candy) and told the child the following: "Suppose that you bought this bag of *Pirulitos* [bag of candy presented], and you must decide the price you will sell the pieces for in the street." The child was then administered three problems successively that varied in pricing ratios to be compared: one Pirulito for Cr$200 vs. three Pirulitos for Cr$500, one Pirulito for Cr$200 vs. seven Pirulitos for Cr$1000, three Pirulitos for Cr$500 vs. seven Pirulitos for Cr$1000. For each of the three problems, the following problem format was used: "Let's say that you have to choose between two ways of selling: (for the first problem, one for Cr$200 or three for Cr$500, one *Pirulito* was then placed on top of a Cr$200 bill and three were placed on top of a Cr$500 bill; the analogous presentation of materials was used for each successive problem). Which way do you think that you would make the most profit? Why? How do you know you would make a bigger profit this way? Show me what you did to discover that you have a bigger profit this way." If the child did not demonstrate his strategy for solving the problem, he was presented the following countersuggestion: "Another boy that I talked with chose [the opposite of the subject's choice] as the one that brought more profit. I want you to show me how you would prove to this child that he was wrong."

TRANSLATING WHOLESALE BOX PRICES INTO RETAIL UNIT PRICES

Two forms of the retail pricing task were presented which varied in the number of units in a box, the wholesale price of a box, and the type of candy in the box. For each task, the interviewer said: "[Child's name], I discovered something very important about children that sell candy. I think that boys that sell in the streets must mark their prices well, right? I think that a good price marker must know how much he should make—not a profit too big because then no one will buy, and not a profit too small because then he won't make money, right? Let's say that you bought a box of 50 *Chupetim* for Cr$3500 (or 30 *Chocolate Leila* for Cr$8500). To mark the price well, how much should you sell the box for? How much should you sell the individual pieces for to the customers in the street? How do you know that this price [child's stated price for units] is good for you? Show me how you know."

ADJUSTING FOR INFLATION

Inflation Problems

There were two problems which varied in format: In the first problem, children were told the initial wholesale price of a box of candy (Cr$4000) and were asked to generate an appropriate retail price for the entire box. They were then asked to reproduce this mark-up after inflation led to a specified rise in the wholesale price (to Cr$7000). Thus, the child was required to solve the following proportionality problem: Cr$4000 : Cr$??? :: Cr$7000 :: Cr$???. In the second problem, children were told both the wholesale price (Cr$3000) and the gross retail price (Cr$6000) a seller used during one time period; the child was asked to reproduce the mark-up after an inflationary rise in wholesale prices (to Cr$9000). Thus, the child was required to solve the following proportionality problem:

Cr\$3000 : Cr\$6000 :: Cr\$9000 : Cr\$???. To aid comprehension of the inflation tasks, several props were used: four identical boxes of candy, two full and two empty, and a drawing of a Christmas tree. (Prior to the start of the first task, the child was presented with the tree and asked if he knew what it was; virtually all children knew, and the few that did not recognized it as soon as the interviewer identified it.)

Problem 1: Cr\$4000 : Cr\$ x :: Cr\$7000 : Cr\$ y. The interviewer told the child: "Let's say that today you bought a box of this candy for Cr\$4000 [a complete box of candy presented, and Cr\$4000 in currency placed next to it]. How much do you think you should sell the box for to be a good price marker? [An empty box of candy was placed below the full box, and the amount that the child cited was placed next to it in currency.] Now, [Name of child], listen carefully to this story. Do you think there's still much time before Christmas? [The picture of the Christmas tree was presented to the right of the boxes and currency.] Do you think that when Christmas arrives this box will still cost Cr\$4000? [If the child responded, "no," the interviewer said, "You're right, prices will rise between now and Christmas." If the child responded, "yes," the interviewer said, "No, with time, the price of things goes up. Isn't that right?".]

Now, I have a problem for you. I heard that by Christmas time [present picture of tree], a box of this type will cost Cr\$7000 [a new full box placed with Cr\$7000 next to the box]. Now, I want you to tell me how much you should sell this box for in the streets at Christmas time, but mark the price in the same way you've done today. So look, today you buy the box for Cr\$4000 and decide to sell for [price that child cited]. At Christmas time you will buy the same type of candy for Cr\$7000. How much do you think you must sell the box for at Christmas time to continue to price in the same way—just as well as you've done today? How do you know? Show me how you figure that.

[If the child responded with an answer that was not identical to "today's" profit (i.e., $[x - \text{Cr\$4000}] + \text{Cr\$7000}$), the child was asked the following additional questions: "But today you want a profit of $[x - \text{Cr\$4000}]$, and when Christmas comes you said that you will want a profit of $[y - \text{Cr\$7000}]$. Why? How do you know how much to increase the prices because of inflation (or rising prices)? Show me what you do to find out how much you should increase your prices."]

Problem 2: Cr\$3000 : Cr\$6000 :: Cr\$9000 y. Do you remember when last Christmas was? Was it a long time ago? Last Christmas, let's say you bought this box of *Chocolate Danny* for Cr\$3000. You knew how to price well. So, you decided to sell the box for Cr\$6000. Now, [name of child], listen to this story. Time has passed since Christmas; do you think that today *Danny* still costs Cr\$3000?" [If the child said "no," the interviewer said: "You're right, prices have increased," and if the child said "yes," the interviewer said: "No, when time passes prices of things rise, right?".]

Now, I have a problem for you. Today you bought a box of this same chocolate in the store for Cr$9000. I want you to price it for sale in the streets in the same way you priced it last Christmas—price it just as well—so that you're still a good marker of prices.

So look, last Christmas you bought the box for Cr$3000 and decided to sell it for $6000. Today, you bought the same box for Cr$9000. How much do you think you should sell the box for today to continue to be a good pricer and to mark prices in the same way you did last Christmas? How did you do it? Show me.

[If the child responded with an answer that was not identical with last Christmas's profit (i.e., [[Cr$6000 − Cr$3000] + Cr$9000 = Cr$12000]) the child was asked the following additional questions.] But last Christmas your profit was Cr$3000, and now you want a profit of (child's desired profit). Why? How do you know how much you should increase your prices due to inflation? Show me how you know how much to raise your prices.

References

Baroody, A. J. (1987). *Children's mathematical thinking: A developmental framework for pre-school, primary, and special education teachers.* New York: Teachers College, Columbia University Press.

Bearison, D. J., Magzamen, S., & Filardo, E. K. (1986). Socio-cognitive conflict and cognitive growth in young children. *Merrill–Palmer Quarterly, 32*(1), 51–72.

Becker, J., & Saxe, G. B., (in press). Review of A. E. Berti & A. S. Bombi, *The child's construction of economics.* In *Developmental Review.*

Behr, M. J., Lesh, R., Post, T. R., & Silver, E. A. (1983). Rational number concepts. In R. Lest & M. Landau (Eds.), *Acquisition of mathematics concepts and processes* (pp. 91–126). New York: Academic Press.

Beilin, H. (1976). Constructing cognitive operations linguistically. *Advances in child development and behavior* (pp. 67–106). New York: Academic Press.

Berry, J. W. (1966). Temne and Eskimo perceptual skills. *International Journal of Psychology, 1,* 207–229.

Berry, J. W. (1974). Radical cultural relativism and the concept of intelligence. In J. W. Berry & P. R. Dasen (Eds.), *Culture and cognition: Readings in cross-cultural psychology* (pp. 225–230). London: Methuen.

Berry, J. W. (1984). Towards a universal psychology of cognitive competence. *International Journal of Psychology, 19,* 335–361.

Berti, A. E., & Bombi, A. S. (1988). *The child's construction of economics.* New York: Cambridge University Press.

Bijou, S. W., & Baer, D. M. (1961). *Child development: Vol. 1. A systematic and empirical theory.* New York: Appleton–Century–Crofts.

Boas, F. (1911). *The mind of primitive man.* New York: Macmillan.

Brenner, M. E. (1985). The practice of arithmetic in Liberian schools. *Anthropology and Education Quarterly, 16,* 177–186.

Brown, A. (1989). Discussion of Symposium Papers: Children's Constructs and Educational Processes. *1989 Meetings of the American Educational Research Association.* San Francisco.

Brown, J. S., & Burton, R. B. (1978). Diagnostic models for procedural bugs in basic mathematical skills. *Cognitive Science, 2,* 155–192.

Carraher, T. N., Carraher, D. W., & Schliemann, A. D. (1985). Mathematics in the streets and in schools. *British Journal of Developmental Psychology, 3,* 21–29.

Carraher, T. N., Carraher, D. W., & Schliemann, A. D. (1987). Written and oral mathematics. *Journal for Research in Mathematics Education, 18,* 83–97.

Carraher, T. N., Schliemann, A. D., & Carraher, D. W. (1988). Mathematical concepts in everyday life. In G. B. Saxe & M. Gearhart (Eds.), *Children's Mathematics* (pp. 71–88). San Francisco, CA: Jossey Bass.

Case, R. (1985). *Intellectual development: Birth to adulthood.* Orlando, FL: Academic Press.

Cassirer, E. (1957). *Philosophy of symbolic forms: Vol. 3. Phenomenology of knowledge.* New Haven, CT: Yale University Press.

Cauley, K. M. (1988, April). *Children's misconceptions about the multidigit subtraction algorithm.* Paper presented at 1988 American Educational Research Association meetings, New Orleans.

Cavalcanti, C. (1983). *Viabilidade do setor informal: A demanda de pequenos serviços no grande Recife.* Recife, Brasil: Fundacaco Joaquim Nabuco.

Ceci, S. J., & Liker, J. K. (1986). A day at the races: A study of IQ, expertise, and cognitive complexity. *Journal of experimental psychology: General, 115*(3).

Chi, M. T. H., Glaser, R., & Rees, E. (1982). Expertise in problem solving. In R. J. Sternberg (Ed.), *Advances in the psychology of human intelligence.* (Vol. 1). Hillsdale, NJ: Lawrence Erlbaum Associates.

Chomsky, N. (1957). A review of B. F. Skinner's *Verbal Behavior. Language, 35,* 26–58.

Chomsky, N. (1972). *Language and mind.* New York: Harcourt Brace Jovanovich.

Cole, M. (1988). Cross-cultural research in the socio-historical tradition. *Human Development, 31,* 137–157.

Cole, M., Gay, J., Glick, J. A., & Sharp, D. W. (1971). *The cultural context of learning and thinking: An exploration in experimental anthropology.* New York: Basic Books.

Collins, A., & Gentner, D. (1987). How people construct mental models. In D. Holland & N. Quinn (Eds.), *Cultural models in language and thought* (pp. 243–265). New York: Cambridge University Press.

Damerow, P. (1986). Individual development and cultural evolution of arithmetical thinking. In S. Strauss (Ed.), *Ontogeny and Historical Development.* Norwood.

Damon, W. V. B. (1988). *Peer collaboration as a context for cognitive growth.* Colloquium delivered to the Graduate School of Education, University of California at Los Angeles.

Dasen, P. R. (1972). Cross-cultural Piagetian research: A summary. *Journal of Cross-cultural Psychology, 3*(1), 23–39.

Dasen, P. R. (1975). Concrete operational development in three cultures. *Journal of Cross-cultural Psychology, 6,* 156–172.

Dasen, P.R. (1977). Are cognitive processes universal? A contribution to cross-cultural Piagetian psychology. In N. Warren (Ed.), *Studies in cross-cultural psychology* (Vol. 1). London: Academic Press.

Dasen. P. R., & Heron, A. (1981). Cross-cultural tests of Piaget's theory. In H. C. Triandis & A. Heron (Eds.), *Handbook of cross-cultural psychology: Developmental psychology* (Vol. 4, pp. 295–341). Boston: Allyn & Bacon.

de Lacey, P. R. (1970). A cross-cultural study of classificatory ability in Australia. *Journal of cross-cultural psychology. 1*(4), 293–304.

de la Rocha, O. (1983, November). *The reorganization of arithmetic practice in the kitchen.* Paper presented at the 82nd annual meeting of the American Anthropological Association, Chicago.

de Lemos, M. M. (1974). The development of spatial concepts in Zulu children. In J. W. Berry & P. R. Dasen (Eds.), *Culture and cognition: Readings in cross-cultural psychology.* London: Methuen & Co.

Doise, W., & Mugny, G. (1984). *The social development of the intellect.* Oxford, England: Pergamon.

Doise, W., Mugny, G., & Perret–Clermont, A. N. (1975). Social interaction and the development of cognitive operations. *European Journal of Social Psychology, 5*(3), 367–383.

Doise, W., Mugny, G., & Perret–Clermont, A. N. (1976). Social interaction and cognitive development: Further evidence. *European Journal of Social Psychology, 6,* 245–247.

Fodor, J. A. (1983). *Modularity of mind: An essay on faculty psychology.* Cambridge, MA: MIT Press.

Furth, H. G. (1966). *Thinking without language.* New York: Free Press.

Fuson, K. C. (1988). *Children's counting and concepts of number.* New York: Springer–Verlag.

Fuson, K. C., Richards, J., & Briars, D. J. (1982). The acquisition and elaboration of the number word sequence. In C. Brainerd (Ed.), *Children's logical and mathematical cognition: Progress in cognitive development* (pp. 33–92). New York: Springer–Verlag.

Gagne, R. M. (1985). *The conditions of learning and theory of instruction.* New York: Holt, Rinehart and Winston.

Gay, J., & Cole, M. (1965). *The new mathematics and an old culture: A study of learning among the Kpelle of Liberia.* New York: Holt, Rinehart, & Winston.

Gentner, D. (1983). Structure-mapping: A theoretical framework for analogy. *Cognitive Science, 7,* 155–170.

Gick, M. L., & Holyoak, K. J. (1980). Analogical problem solving. *Cognitive Psychology, 12,* 306–355.

Glaser, R. (1986). On the nature of expertise. In F. Klix & H. Hagendorf (Eds.), *Human memory and cognitive capabilities: Mechanisms and performances.* Amsterdam: Elsevier Science Publishers B. V.

Goodnow, J. J., & Bethon, G. (1966). Piaget's tasks: The effects of schooling and intelligence. *Child Development, 37,* 573–582.

Greenfield, P. M., & Childs, C. P. (1977). Weaving, color terms, and pattern representation: Cultural influences and cognitive development among the Zinacantecos of Southern Mexico. *Interamerican Journal of Psychology, 11,* 23–48.

Greeno, J. G., Riley, M. S., & Gelman, R. (1984). Conceptual competence and children's counting. *Cognitive Psychology, 16,* 94–134.

Hallpike, C. R. (1979). *The foundations of primitive thought.* New York: Oxford University Press.

Hart, K. (1988). Ratio and proportion. In J. Hiebert, & M. Behr (Eds.), *Number operations in the middle grades* (pp. 198–219). Reston, VA: The National Council of Teachers of Mathematics and Lawrence Erlbaum Associates.

Hess, R. D., & Shipman, V. C. (1965). Early experience and the socialization of cognitive modes in children. *Child Development, 36,* 869–888.

Hiebert, J. (1984). Children's mathematics learning: The struggle to link form and understanding. *Elementary School Journal, 84,* 497–513.

Hiebert, J., & Behr, M. (1988). *Number operations in the middle grades.* Reston, VA: National Council of Teachers of Mathematics and Lawrence Erlbaum Associates.

Inhelder, B., & Piaget, J. (1958). *The growth of logical thinking from childhood to adolescence.* New York: Basic Books.

Inhelder, B., & Piaget, J. (1969). *The early growth of logic in the child.* New York: Norton.

Jahoda, G. (1980). Theoretical and systematic approaches in cross-cultural psychology. In H. C. Triandis & W. W. Lambert (Eds.), *Handbook of cross-cultural psychology* (Vol. 1). Boston: Allyn & Bacon.

Kail, R. (1986). Sources of age differences in speed of processing. *Child Development, 57,* 969–987.

Kamara, A. I., & Easley, J. A. (1977). Is the rate of cognitive development uniform across cultures?—A methodological critique with new evidence from Themne children. In P. R. Dasen (Ed.), *Piagetian psychology: Cross-cultural contributions* (pp. 26–63). New York: Gardner Press.

Kamii, C. (1986). Place value: An explanation of its difficulty and educational implications for the primary grades. *Journal of Research in Childhood Education, 1*(2), 75–86.

Karplus, R., Pulos, S., & Stage, E. K. (1983). Early adolescents' proportional reasoning on "rate" problems. *Educational Studies in Mathematics, 14*, 219–234.

Klahr, D., & Wallace, J.G. (1976). *Cognitive development: An Information-processing view.* Hillsdale, NJ: Lawrence Erlbaum Associates.

Klahr, D. (1980). Information-processing models of intellectual development. In R. H. Kluwe & H. Spada (Eds.), *Developmental models of thinking.* New York: Academic Press.

Laboratory of Comparative Human Cognition (1979). Cross-cultural psychology's challenges to our ideas of children and development. *American Psychologist, 34*(10), 827–833.

Laboratory of Comparative Human Cognition (1986). Culture and cognitive development (pp. 295–356). In W. Kessen (Ed.), *Manual of child psychology: History, theory and methods.* New York: Wiley.

Lancy, D. F. (1983). *Cross-cultural studies in cognition and mathematics.* New York: Academic Press.

Laurendeau–Bendavid, M. (1977). Culture, schooling and cognitive development: A comparative study of children in French Canada and Rwanda. In P. R. Dasen (Ed.), *Piagetian psychology: Cross-cultural contributions* (pp. 123–168). New York: Gardner Press.

Lave, J. (1977). Tailor-made experiments and evaluating the intellectual consequences of apprenticeship training. *Quarterly Newsletter of the Institute for Comparative Human Development, 1*(2), 1–3.

Lave, J. (1988). *Cognition in practice: Mind, mathematics, and culture in everyday life.* New York: Cambridge University Press.

Leontiev, A. N. (1981). *Problems in the development of the mind.* Moscow: Progress Publishers.

Lesh, R., Post, T., & Behr, M. (1988). Proportional reasoning. In J. Hiebert, & M. Behr (Eds.), *Number operations in the middle grades* (pp. 93–118). Reston, VA: National Council of Teachers of Mathematics and Lawrence Erlbaum Associates.

Luria, A. R. (1976). *Cognitive development: Its cultural and social foundations.* Cambridge, MA: Harvard University Press.

Menninger, K. (1969). *Number words and number symbols.* Cambridge, MA: MIT Press.

Mermelstein, E., & Shulman, L. S. (1967). Lack of formal schooling and the acquisition of conservation. *Child Development, 38*, 39–51.

Miller, K. F., & Stigler, J.W. (1987). Computing in Chinese: Cultural variation in a basic cognitive skill. *Cognitive Development, 2*, 279–305.

Minick, N. (in press). Mind and activity in Vygotsky's work: An expanded frame of reference. *Cultural Dynamics.*

Miura, I. T. (1987). Mathematics achievement as a function of language. *Journal of Educational Psychology, 79*, 79–82.

Miura, I. T., Kim, C. C., Chang, C-M., & Okamoto, Y. (1988). Effects of language characteristics on children's cognitive representation of number: Cross-national comparisons. *Child Development, 59*, 1445–1450.

Miura, I. T., & Okamoto, Y. (in press). Comparisons of U. S. and Japanese first graders' cognitive representation of number and understanding of place value. *Journal of Educational Psychology, 31*(1).

Neimark, E. (1975). Intellectual development during adolescence. *Review of Child Development Research, 4*, 541–594.

Neisser, U. (1976). General, academic, and artificial intelligence. In L. B. Resnick (Ed.), *The nature of intelligence* (pp. 135–144). Hillsdale, NJ: Lawrence Erlbaum Associates.

Nickerson, R. S. (1988). Counting, computing, and the representation of numbers. *Human Factors, 30*(2), 181–199.

Nyiti, R. (1982). The validity of "cultural difference explanations" for cross-cultural variation in the rate of Piagetian cognitive development. In D. Wagner & H. Stevenson (Eds.), *Cultural perspectives on child development*. New York: W. H. Freeman.

Ohlsson, S. (1988). Mathematical meaning and applicational meaning in the semantics of fractions and related concepts. In J. Hiebert, & M. Behr (Eds.), *Number operations in the middle grades* (pp. 53–92). Reston, VA: National Council of Teachers of Mathematics and Lawrence Erlbaum Associates.

Opper, S. (1977). Concept development in Thai urban and rural children. In P. R. Dasen (Ed.), *Piagetian psychology: Cross-cultural contributions* (pp. 89–122). New York: Gardner Press.

Pettito, A. (1979). *Knowledge of arithmetic among schooled and unschooled African tailors and cloth-merchants*. Unpublished doctoral dissertation, Cornell University, Ithaca, NY.

Piaget, J. (1952). *The child's conception of number*. New York: Norton.

Piaget, J. (1954). *The child's construction of reality*. New York: Basic Books.

Piaget, J. (1962). *Play, dreams, and imitation in childhood*. New York: Norton.

Piaget, J. (1963). *The origins of intelligence in children*. New York: Norton.

Piaget, J. (1966). Need and significance of cross-cultural studies in genetic psychology. *International Journal of Psychology, 1,* 3–13.

Piaget, J. (1970). *Genetic epistemology*. New York: Columbia University Press.

Piaget, J. (1972). *The child's conception of the world*. Totowa, NJ: Littlefield, Adams.

Piaget, J. (1977). *The development of thought: Equilibration of cognitive structures*. New York: Viking.

Posner, J. (1982). The development of mathematical knowledge in two West African societies. *Child Development, 53,* 200–208.

Posner, J. K., & Baroody, A. J. (1979). Number conservation in two West African societies. *Journal of Cross-Cultural Psychology, 10,* 479–496.

Price–Williams, D., Gordon, W., & Ramirez, M. (1967). Manipulation and conservation: A study of children from pottery-making families in Mexico. *Memorias del XI Congreso Interamericano de la psicologia,* Mexico City, 106–121.

Resnick, L. B., & Ford, W. W. (1981).*The psychology of mathematics for instruction*. Hillsdale, NJ: Lawrence Erlbaum Associates.

Resnick, L. B., & Omanson, S. F. (1987). Learning to understand arithmetic. In R. Glaser (Ed.), *Advances in instructional psychology* (Vol. 3, pp. 41–96). Hillsdale, NJ: Lawrence Erlbaum Associates.

Rogoff, B. (1986). Adult assistance of children's learning. In T. E. Raphael (Ed.), *The contexts of school based literacy* (pp. 27–42). New York: Random House.

Rogoff, B. (1990). *Apprenticeship in thinking*. New York: Oxford University Press.

Rogoff, B. & Gardner, W. (1984). Adult guidance of cognitive development. In B. Rogoff, & J. Lave (Eds.), *Everyday cognition* (pp. 95–116). Cambridge, MA: Harvard University Press.

Rogoff, B., Ellis, S., & Gardner, W. (1984). The adjustment of adult-child instruction according to child's age and task. *Developmental Psychology, 20*(2), 193–199.

Saxe, G. B. (1982). Developing forms of arithmetic operations among the Oksapmin of Papua New Guinea. *Developmental Psychology, 18*(4), 583–594.

Saxe, G. B. (1985). The effects of schooling on arithmetical understandings: Studies with Oksapmin children in Papua New Guinea. *Journal of Educational Psychology, 77*(5), 503–513.

Saxe, G. B. (1988). The mathematics of child street vendors. *Child Development, 59,* 1415–1425.

Saxe, G. B. (1989). *Transfer of learning across cultural practices*. Paper presented at the 1989 biennial meetings of the Society for Research in Child Development, Kansas City.

Saxe, G. B., & Gearhart, M. (in press). The development of topological understandings in unschooled straw weavers. *British Journal of Developmental Psychology*.

Saxe, G. B., Gearhart, M., & Guberman, S. R. (1984). The social organization of early number development. In B. Rogoff & J. V. Wertsch (Eds.), *Children's learning in the zone of proximal development. New directions in child development* (Vol. 23, pp. 19–30) San Francisco: Jossey–Bass.

Saxe, G. B., Guberman, S. R., & Gearhart, M. (1987). Social processes in early number development. *Monographs of the Society for Research in Child Development,* No. 216, *52*(2).

Schmandt–Besserat, D. (1984). Before numerals. *Visible language, 18,* 48–60.

Scribner, S. (1986). Thinking in action: Some characteristics of practical thought. In R. J. Sternberg & R. K. Wagner (Eds.), *Practical intelligence: Nature and origins of competence in the everyday world* (pp. 13–30). Cambridge, England: Cambridge University Press.

Siegler, R. S., & Shrager, J. (1984). Strategy choices in addition and subtraction: How do children know what to do? In C. Sophian (Ed.), *Origins of cognitive skills* (pp. 229–293). Hillsdale, NJ: Lawrence Erlbaum Associates.

Silverman, I., & Geiringer, E. (1973). Dyadic interaction and conservation induction: A test of Piaget's equilibration model. *Child Development, 44,* 815–820.

Silverman, I., & Stone, J. (1972). Modifying cognitive functioning through participation in a problem-solving group. *Journal of Educational Psychology, 63,* 603–608.

Sinclair, H. (1967). *Langage et operations.* Paris: Dunod.

Song, M. J., & Ginsburg, H. P. (1987). The development of informal and formal mathematics thinking in Korean and U. S. children. *Child Development, 58,* 1286–1296.

Steinberg, B. M., & Dunn, L. A. (1976). Conservation competence and performance in Chiapas. *Human Development, 19,* 14–25.

Suchman, L. (1987). *Plans and situated actions: The problem of human-machine communication.* New York: Cambridge University Press.

Swetz, F. J. (1987). *Capitalism and arithmetic: The new math of the 15th century, including the full text of the Treviso arithmetic of 1478* (trans. D. E. Smith). La Salle, IL: Open Court.

Thorndike, E. L. (1922). *The psychology of arithmetic.* New York: Macmillan.

Valiant, G., Glachan, M., & Emler, N. (1982). The stimulation of cognitive development through co-operative task performance. *British Journal of Educational Psychology, 52,* 281–288.

Vygotsky, L. S. (1978). *Mind in society.* Cambridge, MA: Harvard University Press.

Vygotsky, L. (1986). In A. Kozulin (Ed.), *Thought and language.* Cambridge, MA: MIT Press.

Werner, H., & Kaplan, B. (1962). *Symbol formation.* New York: Wiley.

Wertsch, J. V. (1979). From social interaction to higher psychological processes. A clarification and application of Vygotsky's theory. *Human Development, 22,* 1–22.

Wertsch, J. V., McNamee, G. D., McLane, J. B., & Budwig, N. A. (1980). The adult-child dyad as a problem solving system. *Child Development, 51,* 1215–1221.

Whiting, B. B. (1976). The problem of the packaged variable. In K. F. Riegel & J. A. Meacham (Eds.), *The developing individual in a changing world.* Chicago: Aldine.

Witkin, H. A., & Berry, J. W. (1975). Psychological differentiation in cross-cultural perspective. *Journal of cross-cultural psychology. 6,* 4–87.

Witkin, H. A., Dyk, R. B., Faterson, H. F., Goodenough, D. R., & Karp, S. A. (1962). *Psychological differentiation.* New York: Wiley.

Wood, D., Bruner, J. S., & Ross, G. (1976). The role of tutoring in problem solving. *Journal of Child Psychology and Psychiatry, 17,* 89–100.

Wood, D., & Middleton, D. (1975). A study of assisted problem-solving. *British Journal of Psychology, 66,* 181–191.

Wood, D., Wood, H., & Middleton, D. (1978). An experimental evaluation of four face-to-face teaching strategies. *International Journal of Behavioral Development, 1,* 131–147.

Za'rour, G. I., & Khuri, G. A. (1977). The development of the concept of speed by Jordanian school children in Amman. In P. R. Dasen (Ed.), *Piagetian psychology: Cross-cultural contributions* (pp. 216–226). New York: Gardner Press.

Author Index

Subject Index

VERMONT STATE COLLEGES

0 0003 0497429   8

DISCARD

DATE DUE

SEP 30 1991			
GAYLORD			PRINTED IN U.S.A.

GIVING THE LOVE THAT HEALS

Also by Harville Hendrix, Ph.D., and Helen Hunt, M.A.

The Couples Companion: Meditations and Exercises for Getting
    the Love You Want
The Personal Companion: Meditations and Exercises for Keeping
    the Love You Find

Also by Harville Hendrix, Ph.D.

Getting the Love You Want: A Guide for Couples
Keeping the Love You Find: A Personal Guide

GIVING THE LOVE THAT HEALS

A Guide for Parents

HARVILLE HENDRIX, Ph.D.,
AND
HELEN HUNT, M.A.

POCKET BOOKS

New York   London   Toronto   Sydney   Tokyo   Singapore

POCKET BOOKS, a division of Simon & Schuster Inc.
1230 Avenue of the Americas, New York, NY 10020

Copyright © 1997 by Harville Hendrix

All rights reserved, including the right to reproduce
this book or portions thereof in any form whatsoever.
For information address Pocket Books, 1230 Avenue
of the Americas, New York, NY 10020

ISBN: 0-671-79398-5

First Pocket Books hardcover printing November 1997

10 9 8 7 6 5 4 3

POCKET and colophon are registered trademarks
of Simon & Schuster Inc.

Text design by Stanley S. Drate/Folio Graphics Co. Inc.

Printed in the U.S.A.

SPECIAL APPRECIATION

for

Jean Coppock Staeheli

We want to dedicate this page to our writer, Jean Coppock Staeheli, who took two incomplete manuscripts, pages of inchoate notes, and dozens of oral interviews and transformed them into a manuscript that is clear, well organized, and compassionate. Because of her keen intelligence, her deep insight into what we were trying to express, her superior writing skills, and her patience and steadfastness with our many changes, she has helped us bring a five-year project to an excellent conclusion. Thank you, Jean.

We dedicate this book to our six children, each of whom, in her or his unique way, has been our teacher.

Hunter
Leah
Kimberly
Kathryn
Mara
Josh

Acknowledgments

No one is an island unto himself, and no book is created solely by its authors. We are indebted to many sources directly and indirectly. Harry Stack Sullivan's theory of the interpersonal; Heinz Kohut's view of empathy and connection; Eric Berne's insights into transaction patterns; Margaret Mahler's developmental theory; Martin Buber's concept of the "between," the I-Thou relationship, and the power of dialogue; Robert Coles's focus on the moral development of children and the illumination of children's spirituality; Daniel Stern's interpersonal theory of the infant and the "nascent self"; John Bowlby's view of the secure child; Martin Hoffman's view of infantile empathy; Jerry Lewis's and Robert Beavers's research on the family; Benjamin Spock's understanding of the value of kindness and nurturing on demand; Berry Brazelton's gifted insights into infants and children; Sigmund Freud's theory of the unconscious; Carl Jung's theory of the collective unconscious; Martha Welch's view of "holding time"; Paul McLean's view of the tripartite brain; Lloyd deMause's history of childhood; Paul Davies's concept of "animated star dust"; Danah Zohar's view of the conscious universe; and many others who have become so integrated into our thinking that we cannot sort them out. We are also debtors to the western spiritual tradition for our metaphysical views and for a faith perspective for conscious parenting.

We have been inspired by the example of three sets of parents: R. J. and Edwina Patterson, David and Susan Bagwell, Jack and Janie McNairy, whom we feel intuitively live out the principles of this book.

We also want to thank many people who have made special contributions, among them are Laura Torbet, Meg Blackstone, and Elizabeth Neustader for their work on the early drafts of the manuscript, Sanam Hoon for help with research articles, Kathy Borrego for helping with technical details and managing our office so we could write, Teresa Setchell for her companionship with Leah and Hunter when we were unavailable, Bernadette Gallegos for handling our phone calls, and Delma Fernandez and her staff for seeing that we had lunch when we were under pressure during the final stages of the writing, and all the other members of our staff who contributed to this task in countless and subtle ways.

Our deepest appreciation goes to our children, Hunter, Leah, Kimberly, Kathryn, Mara, and Josh, who have been our teachers about conscious parenting, our cheerleaders as this project came to its conclusion, and who were patient with our neglect of them as parents while writing a book on parenting.

About the Authors

Harville Hendrix, Ph.D., and Helen Hunt, M.A., are husband and wife. They are cofounders of the Institute for Imago Relationship Therapy, for which Dr. Hendrix serves as president. For the past fifteen years they have worked together to cocreate Imago Relationship Therapy and the concepts of the "conscious marriage" and "conscious parenting." The results of their collaboration led to the publication of the best-sellers, *Getting the Love You Want: A Guide for Couples,* and *Keeping the Love You Find: A Personal Guide,* both authored by Hendrix. They are coauthors of *The Couples Companion, The Personal Companion, Giving the Love that Heals: A Guide for Parents,* and *The Parents' Companion,* due to be published in 1998. They are also responsible for a seven-hour videotape on couples, which has been seen on over three hundred public television stations, and the workshop Intimate Partnership as a Spiritual Path.

Harville Hendrix is a pastoral counselor who has spent more than thirty-five years as a therapist, educator, workshop leader, and public lecturer. He was on the faculty of Perkins School of Theology, Southern Methodist University, for nine years prior to his transition to private practice and specialization in intimate partnerships. He is a graduate of Mercer University, which has awarded him an honorary Doctorate of Humane Letters. He holds a theology degree from Union Theological Seminary and earned an M.A. and a Ph.D. in Religion and Psychology from the Divinity School, University of Chicago, where he was a University Fellow. His denomination has honored him with the 1995 Outstanding Pastoral Counselor of the Year award. The American Association of Pastoral Counselors, in which he is a Diplomate, has given him their 1995 Distinguished Contribution Award. He is a clinical member of the International Transactional Analysis Association and a member of the American Group Psychotherapy Association and the Association for Imago Relationship Therapy.

Helen Hunt, M.A., M.L.A., graduated from Southern Methodist University, from which she received one master's degree in Psychology and another in the Liberal Arts. She has been involved nationally as an activist in several women's organizations. She founded the Sister Fund, which supports the empowerment of women and girls, and she co-founded the Dallas Women's Foundation and the New York Women's Foundation, where she served as head of the board for five years. She has served on boards of other women's organizations and on several foundations. For her contributions to women's empowerment she has received awards including installation in the Women's Hall of Fame. Currently, she is involved in the interface between activism and spirituality and offers seminars internationally on this subject. In addition to being a cocreator with Harville of the Imago Process and its application to couples and parents, she copresents lectures and workshops with him on relationship and spirituality.

Their books are published in over twenty-five languages. Dr. Hendrix has appeared on all major talk shows, including nine appearances on *Oprah Winfrey,* one of which won her an award for the "most socially redemptive" daily talk show. He speaks regularly on radio shows locally and nationally and has been written up in numerous magazines and newspapers internationally. His Institute for Imago Relationship Therapy has certified over one thousand clinicians as Imago therapists and has a faculty of twenty-one clinical instructors who teach Imago Relationship Therapy worldwide. More than one hundred certified workshop presenters present more than four hundred workshops yearly in several countries.

He and Helen have six children and live on a ranch in northern New Mexico.

Contents

IV

Discover Your Child

V

Creation of a New Legacy

VI

Tools for Conscious Parenting

Introduction

I have been privileged over the course of my career as a psychotherapist and teacher to sit with people while they explored their most important personal relationships. For years my practice focused on marriage and how people could build an enduring relationship of love and companionship based on the first spark of romantic attraction. This was a question that interested me, personally as well as professionally, and I devoted several years to developing a framework for helping marriage partners become passionate friends.

When I felt that I had learned enough to be helpful in print, I wrote *Getting the Love You Want: A Guide for Couples*. I did this with the support and inspiration of my wife, Helen Hunt. Since then Helen and I have begun to work and write together, as indicated by the fact that both our names are on the cover of this book.

We are now turning our attention as writers to the most challenging and important relationship of all: parenting. It would have been artificial and dishonest for either Helen or me to attempt to write this book alone. So from now on the voice of this book will be the "we" voice. When one of us is recounting a particular experience of his or her own, we will let you know which of us is speaking.

A source of great happiness for us is the opportunity we have to present these ideas together to public and professional groups. And we are pleased to find that a new interest is developing out of these experiences. We are beginning to see the great potential that exists for spiritual growth in intimate and committed relationships, and we look forward to exploring these possibilities further in the future.

OUR FAMILY

It is obvious that our interest in parenting begins on a personal level with our own experience as parents. For that reason, let's start by saying something about us and our children. After all, if we are to connect with you on something as personal as parenting, it makes sense to know something about us on a personal level.

We are a blended family with six children. Each of us brought two children to our new marriage fifteen years ago, and we have two children from our marriage together. Both of us have graduate degrees in psychology. Harville is a pastoral counselor with thirty-seven years of experience as a psychotherapist, eighteen of which have been focused on couples. For fifteen years Helen has been a community activist, interested in empowering the disadvantaged, with a special emphasis on the lives of women and girls.

The experiences we had trying to make a blended family out of a group of persons with very different personalities gave immediacy as well as urgency to our search for insight into parenting. We wanted to discover what makes families work. We had six very good reasons for wanting to learn how to do it right. Really, we had eight very good reasons, if we count ourselves. One of the greatest gifts we've received from our years of parenting is the knowledge that every bit of effort on our children's behalf has been returned to us as a double blessing. The first blessing is that we had the satisfaction of watching our children flower. The second is that we ourselves grew more centered and more authentic every time we recovered from a setback, resolved a conflict, or intentionally negotiated a difficulty. We learned that what we give to our children we give to ourselves.

That is not to say it was easy or that we were always aware of the blessings. Most often parenting was hard day-in-and-day-out work, especially since our parenting styles were not always congruent. Instead of being one harmonious tapestry, we were more like separate shreds of cloth trying to hold ourselves together.

All of our children have been our teachers, and the two children we still have at home continue to show us the way. For example, we worked out conscious parenting's primary tool, intentional dialogue, in their presence. We didn't think up these ideas and tell our children how to do it. They were our partners as we learned how to make these ideas function in a real family with real children and real parents. All of our own frailties, misapprehensions, and mistakes are woven into the text of the book, although we hope they are invisible. There have been times when we felt overwhelmed by our frustrations and our exhaustion, and we had to console ourselves with the conviction that what counts is to continue working at becoming more self-reflective and more centered in the changes we wanted to make.

OUR WORK

As we have said, our marriage has been a laboratory and a collaboration that has led to the cocreation of a theory of intimate relationships that we call Imago Relationship Therapy. While the core of this theory is about marriage, we have found that what we learned about marriage has deep relevance for parenting.

We have learned that our work on our personal transformation affects our children, who are then free to grow up retaining most of their innate spirituality. They will be healthier and happier—and less likely to spend their adulthood trying to get over their childhood. The clues for healing our deepest wounds come from information we receive from our children, especially during those moments when we find ourselves most reactive to them. It is then that as parents we can turn to each other and, with the awareness gained from our children, work to cocreate a conscious marriage. In essence, this is the work of personally recovering a state of emotional wholeness and of enabling our children to do so as well. Parenting becomes a spiritual practice as a result of this process.

When we look at what has interested us over the years, it's easy to see how an interest in marriage and intimate love led to an interest in parenting. In 1988, we published *Getting the Love You Want: A Guide for Couples.* In 1992, we brought out another book called *Keeping the Love You Find: A Personal Guide,* which was written for people who wanted to create an intimate partnership. And then we coauthored two meditation books, *The Couples Companion* and *The Personal Companion,* as daily guides for implementing the insights of the original two books. As an additional way of making these ideas widely available, we developed professional training for therapists and workshops for couples and singles. These programs are now offered internationally, and thousands of couples who have had experience using them have reported dramatic transformations in their marriages.

Because of our emphasis on the impact of childhood on marriage, people began asking whether we would consider writing a book for parents. We were hesitant at first. We were struggling with our own attempts to blend our families, and because we hadn't yet discovered conscious parenting, our older children were having some difficulty. We had so much to learn that we felt that we didn't have much to say. We knew we needed to become students before we could teach others.

So that's what we did. And while we are now ready to share our views, we still consider ourselves students. We have come to the conclusion that there are no experts in parenting—only children and parents who are works in progress. Our relationships with our older children are going better as a result of what we've learned, and those with our younger children are going exceptionally well. But we still prefer to think of ourselves as resources rather than models.

MARRIAGE AND PARENTING

When *Getting the Love You Want* was published, a lot of material on the subject was already in print. This is also the case for parenting. Many books, newsletters, and workshops give good advice to parents who want to do a better job with their children and enjoy them more. And still, it seems to us that there are new and centrally important things to be said about being a good parent that haven't been said yet.

Over the years researchers, child psychologists, and educators have learned a lot about the child. But there has been less investigation into the parenting relationship itself. We know more about the child as an individual entity than we do about how parents and children function together in the circle of connection that contains and shapes them both. We have ample information about how to safeguard a child's survival, but we know less about how to safeguard the child's *connection*, something that is accomplished within the unique environment of the parenting relationship.[1]

As we became more and more interested in the relationship between parents and children, we came to a conclusion that amazed us: the people who were most successful in marriage relationships were the same ones who were most successful in parenting relationships. Why? Partly because marriage and parenting have some important things in common. For one thing, they share a fundamental progression through stages. Both begin with romantic attachment, move into the power struggle, and then (if you're smart and lucky!) on into healthy interdependence. And the imago, which is the internalized image of one's parents, shapes both relationships in fundamentally important ways. *Our choice of marriage partners is affected by the unconscious internal picture we carry around inside ourselves of our own parents. And the way we parent our children is also powerfully influenced by the internalized experiences we had with our parents during childhood.*

At the same time, there are obvious differences between marriage and parenting. You never expect your children to meet your needs in the same way that you hope your life partner will. And your obligations and responsibilities to your children are significantly different from your obligations and responsibilities to your mate.

THE AWARENESS AT THE CENTER

But at the center of both relationships, if they are successful, is the commitment to become more *aware*—of yourself, the other person, and the ways in which your imago influences your choices and behavior. The people who did well at both marriage and parenting made a commitment to become conscious about the process. They were willing to see what was hidden in themselves and, without prejudice, to understand the connection between past wounding and present functioning. They were able to override their self-protective impulses in favor of responses that were less me-centered and more relationship-centered.

Learning to live in this way takes effort. It is unfamiliar to most people and often difficult. But the rewards give meaning to life. They include all the benefits that come from good interpersonal relationships, including a growing sense of harmony within yourself and an experience of living that connects you deeply to everything around you. To live in conscious awareness is to live as if you and the universe were in tune, vibrating to the same musical chord.

When you allow yourself to recognize the contours of your own emotional history and the shape of your current family interactions, you become empowered. You see yourself for who you really are and see your children for who they really are. Just this increased awareness alone, without any other help, means that you are more likely to avoid mistakes and are better able to act effectively to get what you want for yourself and the children you love.

So how do you become more conscious?[2] That, of course, is what we hope you'll learn by reading this book. We were not interested in making this book an instructional "how to" book for parents, although it does contain many concrete parenting suggestions. To answer the need for practical guidance based on the concept of conscious parenting, we have written the *Parents' Manual* for people who want to understand in greater detail (1) how they were parented, (2) how they themselves are now parenting, (3) their marriage or other intimate partnership and how it affects their parenting, and (4) a growth plan for making changes. The *Parents' Manual* may be ordered by following the instructions on the order page at the back of this book.

In addition, *The Parents' Companion: Meditations and Exercises for Giving the Love that Heals* will be published in 1998. This is a book of thoughts, meditations, and practical suggestions that will help parents make use of the ideas in this book in very practical, concrete ways. Organized as a "book of days," it will contain 365 pages with a distinct parenting focus for each day of the year.

But our emphasis here is on reenergizing parenting by presenting a new vision of what is possible between parents and children. We wanted people to see that conscious parenting is a healing activity in which ordinary tasks and conversations become the medium for spiritual and emotional growth. When a parent provides the child with what she needs, the parent returns to himself the tender care he needs to heal his own wounds, thus completing a circle of love that reaches far beyond the two of them.

THE PATH

Every parent is unique, every child is unique, and the relationship between them is deeper and more complex than any we could invent. We don't want to trivialize the richness of human experience by misleading you into thinking that interactions with your child are simple and predictable. Rather, our goal is to help you understand who you are, find out who your child is, and develop your parenting skills within the context of an informed awareness of how children usually grow.

If this sounds beyond your reach, let us reassure you that it requires no special talents or skills on your part. All parents can become more conscious, if they choose to do so. Consciousness is a natural state, available to everyone. There are only two requirements: an awareness that you are not as conscious as you want to be, and a willingness to engage in the process of deep self-reflection.

To begin the process, you simply start with the inclination to trust we're right when we say that conscious parenting is better than unconscious parenting.[3] As you read through the book, allow yourself to reflect on what we are saying and think about how it applies to you. And then practice the techniques we're recommending with your own children and see what happens. If they work, you make a commitment to conscious parenting and close this book knowing that you will be able to continue the process on your own.

We believe that every parent can learn how to be a better one. And that is the spirit in which we offer you our observations and suggestions. If you have read *Getting the Love You Want* and are already committed to a conscious marriage, then some of these ideas will be familiar to you and perhaps easier for you. But prior familiarity with the concept of conscious marriage is not necessary.

This book is written for the single parent, as well as the married parent; for the parent in the blended family; for the parent who has had the benefit of therapy, as well as the one who has not; for the parent who already does pretty well; and for those who feel there is a long way to go. Our intention is most definitely not to blame parents for the difficulties their children may be having, but to show how, in our imperfect world and in our incomplete state of evolution, all of us have been parented imperfectly and parent our children imperfectly but in ways that can be understood and changed. Blame has no place in this worldview. We are interested in seeing things as they are and accepting what is true. When we have the information we need, let's see what we can do to change that which can be changed.

We know that you want to learn how to be a better parent *right now* at the same time you are continuing to learn other important things in your life. We invite you to join us now as we explore this new vision for a kind of parenting that preserves your wholeness and the wholeness of your child.

Harville Hendrix and Helen Hunt
May, 1997

1

CONNECTION

1

A World of Connections

You must be the change you wish to see in the world.
—MAHATMA GANDHI

THE CHILD AT THE CENTER

*I*n anticipation and wonder humankind approaches the new millennium and begins to look at our old world with new eyes. Everywhere there is evidence that we are seeing our lives differently. We are now thinking in terms of what *connects* one thing to another rather than what *separates* them.[1] We talk excitedly about the "in-between,"[2] the interactive energy between different things that helps define and shape each element. Our experience is described in interconnecting circles and the long lines of continuum, rather than in distinct and separate dots. We find our understanding deepened when we are drawn, by imagination and observation, to patterns of interaction and connection.

This way of reviewing the world has been gathering force throughout this century. As physicists became more knowledgeable about the behavior of atomic and subatomic particles, their language of connection[3] has helped those of us who are not physicists see the dynamic connections among all things.

This relational perspective has been instrumental in shaping our personal view of parenting as a dynamic relationship and of the parent and child as changeable, evolving beings who constantly influence each

3

other. And this same predisposition to think in terms of connections helps explain our enduring interest in children.

Children are very much part of everything we do. Whenever we think through a social problem or help people re-create their relationships or simply live our own lives deeply, we always come back to the center and encounter again our concern for children. When we read about violent crime, we imagine the child who fires the gun. When we visit the local health clinic, we worry about the child whose parents can't afford professional care. When we hear about the destruction of old-growth forests, we wonder what happens to a child who grows up without trees. Our work as therapists led us to the subject of marriage, and marriage leads us to parenting, and parenting leads us back again to children.

At home the pattern is the same. Our lives center on our six children, two at home and four now off on their own. They are with us even when we shut the door and resolve firmly to work. We talk with friends and end up trading news of which child is doing what. We travel, and our internal clocks are still tuned to the children we left. We talk together about our plans for the future, and our attention is drawn to where our children will be in this unfamiliar landscape.

THE CONNECTION BETWEEN CHILDHOOD AND PARENTHOOD

Over the years our in-depth investigation of marriage kept leading us to observations about parenting. We found we couldn't decipher the behavior of marriage partners without understanding something of their childhood experiences.

These observations helped establish the conceptual framework for the book. They gave us insight into the complexities of family relationships and eventually led to the development of the concept of *conscious* parenting. They help us see that, indeed, everything is connected to everything else. We will explore these observations briefly here and discuss them further throughout the book.

We observed that wounding gets passed on as a legacy. When we asked people about their early experiences, we began to understand how poor parenting is passed down from one generation to the next in patterns that repeat.[4] If a father has received either too much parental attention or not enough during a particular stage of his own development, he will have trouble knowing how to facilitate his own child's growth through that stage. His parents didn't handle him well when he was thirteen, let's say, so he doesn't know what to do to meet his child's particular needs at that stage. It follows that his son will also be stymied by the challenge of helping *his* children at that point in their development. And so it goes. The observation that parents wound their children in the same stage of development in which they were wounded told us a lot about the problems that parents themselves had a hard time understanding.

We observed that people have innate impulses to get married and become parents, but there is no built-in program for how to do either. We learned that people get married for survival reasons, in the hope that their partners will be able to meet their unmet childhood needs. But they have no innate knowledge of how to get their needs met. People become parents to meet the survival needs of their children and to have the joy of raising them. But they have no innate knowledge of how to meet their children's needs. We found that both partners and parents welcomed guidance on how to achieve their goals.

We observed that where people get stuck in parenting is an indication of where they are stunted psychologically. People exhibit the same patterns of difficulty in both marriage and parenting, because these difficulties arise from the same initial psychological problem. If a woman cannot meet a particular need in her husband, she will most likely not be able to meet it in her child. What she can't give to her partner, she can't give to her child. It was important for us to understand why. We learned that the reason she can't meet the need has more to do with *her* and her childhood history than it has to do with her husband or child or what they are asking for. She can't give what she didn't get. In order for her to be able to see and meet the legitimate needs of her child (or partner), she must understand what she didn't get from her own parents and must find a way to make up the deficit. When she begins this process of self-healing, she will be freed from the constraints of always having to defend herself. This in turn frees her to really see and respond to the people around her.

We observed that the process of becoming a conscious marriage partner is similar to the process of becoming a conscious parent. We were immediately struck by the carryover of skills. For example, a woman who wants to become a conscious marriage partner must change certain things about herself: her tendency to react negatively, to criticize, to judge, and to become defensive. She will need to learn to use intentional dialogue, to stretch to meet her partner's needs even when it feels uncomfortable, to create an environment of physical and emotional safety, and to maintain boundaries that allow for connection but also separation. These same changes must be made by a parent who wants to become a conscious parent. In both relationships, the parent/partner learns how to participate in creating the safety, support, and structure that maintain the emotional and spiritual health of the connection between herself and the people she loves.

We also observed that there is one important difference between parenting and marriage. In a conscious marriage, partners *grow* when they stretch to meet the needs of the other, and they *heal* when their needs are met by their partner. The process is mutual. In marriage it is appropriate for a partner to grow by meeting the needs of the other partner, but it is *not* appropriate for a parent to try to heal by having the child meet his needs. The process for parents and children is not mutual. The parent must heal his childhood wounds in an adult relationship and not in his relationship with his child.

We observed that parenting offers another path for personal healing. The sense in which marriage can be healing is that partners restore their own wholeness when they stretch to meet each other's needs, giving to the other what is often hardest to give. The sense in which parenting can be healing is that parents restore their own wholeness when they stretch to meet the needs of their children at precisely those stages at which their own development has been incomplete. Through marriage and parenting, partners and parents can recover parts of themselves that have been lost. Both marriage and parenting give people the chance to receive for themselves what they give to their partner or child. They get what they give. In this way, both marriage and parenting can be transformational, because the healing experiences these relationships can provide will change the very character of the people involved.

We are distressed by how much grief people experience in trying to repair the damage of childhood. During the thinking and planning for this book our interest has developed into a concern for our whole society. What would life be like for adults who did not have to spend so much time getting over childhood? What would our society be like if it were not filled with wounded adults? In fact, we wonder whether our society can repair itself and solve its problems without the fundamental changes in marriage and parenting that embrace greater consciousness.[5]

OUR POINT OF VIEW

We integrated these observations into a theory of conscious parenting against a particular philosophical background. This is the spiritual context for our understanding of how parents and children interact in relationship with each other.

When we look at parents and children, we see a vision that can be expressed only in poetic, metaphorical terms. We use metaphor to describe the vision because it is a way of pointing to a truth that lies beneath the surface and deals with the essence of things. This does not mean that our vision is useless in the practical world. On the contrary, the vision becomes the center of our thoughts and intentions about parenting. We want to parent from this center. We seek to do things that are consistent with our vision.

This is one metaphor we use: The parent and child are held in the same orbit together. Sometimes the space of the orbit is very big, reaching all across the world; sometimes the space of the orbit is as small as the space between two people who hug. But the power of the attraction, the bond that holds them in relationship to each other, is powerful regardless of the physical distance or the age of the child.

Another way we express this same understanding is to speak of the tapestry of life. We say that the parent and the child are woven together into a tapestry of living experience by the countless threads and stitches of their interactions with each other. Each of them is part of the design. You can't tell the exact point where the thread that weaves through one becomes the thread that weaves through the other. This does not mean that they don't have boundaries. They do. Respecting boundaries is one of the important ways parents remind themselves that they and their children do not have the same identities. But still there are similar threads that weave through both. And this is true whether we are talking about biological families with newborns or families in which children and parents meet later.

Regardless of which metaphor we use, we are expressing our deep conviction that one of the things we know about the nature of life is that parents and children are profoundly connected. The systems, techniques, and suggestions in this book flow from this conviction. You and your child are bound together in one of the most sacred and intimate relationships it is possible to experience. Be mindful of it, be careful, be reverential. It is possible to tear it.

A TEAR IN THE TAPESTRY

The metaphor of a tapestry is useful partly because the metaphor of tearing is useful. It helps you to be more careful of your child when you interact with him. You recognize tearing when you see other parents do it, and sooner or later you recognize it when you have done it yourself. The mom on the soccer field screams at her son when he misses a kick; the father discounts his daughter's achievement in school; you blame your child for your own loneliness. Some of these tears are small and can be repaired. Some of them are gaping holes that will be passed on again when your children raise their own children.

When do these tears happen? You realize that they are more likely to happen when you're not paying attention to the moment or when you yourself are experiencing emotional pain. In other words, they happen when you are self-absorbed, unaware that you are tired or upset over something else, or simply ignorant of the effects of your words. In that encounter, you are unconscious. It happens even to good parents.

We want to help you do more stitching together and less tearing apart. We want you to strengthen the connections you already have, even when your child is pulling and tugging in another direction. We want you to become more conscious about the way you interact with your child and intentional about what you can do to help your child grow into successful adulthood. The whole process is simple to understand, although we know it is not easy to do.

PARENTS

Another manifestation of the connection between parents and children is our conclusion that *if we want to take better care of children, we have to take better care of ourselves.* We have come to realize that looking after the welfare of children means looking after the welfare of their parents. Parents need permission for introspection and self-reflection and help in sorting out what they find. They need to know that their own mental, emotional, and spiritual health is important.

This book will give you important information about the care of parents. Our goal in the pages ahead is to guide you into behavior that is better for you and for your children. But knowing what to *do* comes from knowing how to *be*, and knowing how to be comes from a better *understanding* of the patterns of interaction between parent and child.

We recently had a conversation with a mother that illustrates what we mean. The mother has a four-year-old daughter who pitches a fit every morning about getting dressed. The little girl insists on picking out her clothes herself but is never satisfied with her choices. Whatever comments the mother makes seem to make matters worse. The mother is concerned because she loses her temper with her daughter every time. This is how she recounts their interaction:

Mother: (*observing the sour expression on her daughter's face and bracing herself for the inevitable*) What's wrong? You look very pretty today.
Daughter: No I don't. I don't like this dress.
Mother: Well, I like it. But if you don't, why don't you change into something else?
Daughter: You don't like this dress. You think I look bad.
Mother: (*frustration barely controlled*) No, I don't. What makes you think that?
Daughter: (*in tears*) Because you want me to change my clothes.

This mother wants to know how to *do* this interchange better. And it's true that doing something different might help. For example, if the mother had known about intentional dialogue, a primary technique that we will discuss in detail in this book, she would have focused her attention on reflecting her daughter's feelings back to her. But, in addition, the mother would benefit from having a better understanding of what was happening under the surface.

It is normal for a four-year-old to be testing her own identity, separate from her mother's. It is useful to know that such "battles" over seemingly trivial matters are a healthy way for her daughter to be discovering her own separateness. A mother who knows that this behavior is normal and is not surprised when she sees it can relax and respond to the drama without fearing that there is something wrong with her child or with her. In addition, it would be constructive for her to dig into her own past experience to see what she can find out about why her daughter's behavior angers her so much.

This simple story captures the essence of our message. Conscious parents are aware of the developmental needs of their children and are attentive to opportunities for meeting them. And conscious parents know themselves well enough to know why they react the way they do and to change if they need to. Knowing what to do comes from knowing what is happening underneath the surface of the interaction.

Our goal in this book is to present an understanding of parenting so complete that parents will be able to act intentionally, grounded in the center of this knowledge. What they *do* then becomes a unique expression of who they are, but who they *are* is influenced and shaped by their greater understanding of themselves as parents and as people.

Perhaps our ultimate goal is to help people heal *before* they have children, either through conscious marriage or other conscious relationships. Imagine what it would be like if husbands and wives, within the crucible of marriage, became whole before they undertook to nurture and guide the next generation! Successful parenting would depend not on having the right child or the right circumstances, but on having the drive to uncover their own pain and remedy it. Parents would understand that the wholeness of a child depends on the wholeness of those who care for her.

We know that this is not yet the way of the world. People don't yet know that the power of transformation lies in the people they live with. Our hope is that parents who haven't finished their healing work before their children are born (and that's most of us) are able to begin it soon afterward. In this way adult healing and parenting flow together, sometimes merging into a single process enriched and strengthened by the power and energy of each.

THE CHILD

Parents tell us they are awestruck by the birth of their babies. They welcome their children into the world with a profound sense of mystery and wonder. Somehow, parents intuitively know that their children emerge from the universe as a natural part of it. They arrive as physical beings with needs that must be attended to, but it seems as if that is only part of who they are. A child represents more than can be directly experienced through the senses. She comes from our bodies and from our lovemaking, but she also comes from the universe that made her.

And through his child the parent will participate in the evolutionary processes of life in the universe. When astronomers describe the universe, they use the words of the human life cycle: "The *birth* of a star." "The *stillborn* planet." "The *young* stars." "The *aging* universe." "The *death* of the comets." We describe the cosmos in terms of what we already know, and what we know, our everyday human experience, is a reflection of cosmic processes.

The child's parents also participate, through him, in the evolutionary consciousness of our species. The course his life will take can be understood as another metaphor: the journey that human beings have traveled for the past three million years. We were born into a profound oneness with nature; we differentiated and began exploring our world; we formed an identity as humans distinct from other forms of life; we developed the competence of mastery over our environment; we grew in compassion for the fragile beauty of life different from our own; and then last (and we are not there yet) we attempt to form an intimate relationship with the rest of our environment that is mutually protective and reverential. A child grows through phases on the way to maturity that are like this journey of his forefathers, and the parent who helps this natural plan unfold participates in another fundamental process.

With the birth of their babies parents experience what it is like to love unreservedly and without conditions, often for the first time. It's no accident that parents respond this way. Nature's first imperative is to do whatever she can to ensure the survival of the young. Babies come packaged in a way that invites protection and nurture so that it will be possible for them to progress from childhood to adulthood. Nature is not interested in having babies remain babies, because they are too fragile in that state. She does whatever she can to help them finish childhood so that they can then ensure the survival of others who come after them.

When we think of our own babies, two moments come to mind. We remember when our daughter Leah was just a few days old and would lie in bed beside us on her tummy. For hours we would watch her, stroking her soft skin, hopelessly overcome by the physical reality of her. With Hunter it was the same. We remember taking him as a newborn to an especially inviting park on a sunny afternoon. We were indifferent to the sensational beauty of the landscape while we gazed into his basket, fully captured by the perfection we found there.

Every parent has such experiences. That's the way it is. When babies come into the world whole and perfect, we feel intuitively their place in the natural order. They come with messages for us about what is beautiful and what is important. In their presence we are more open to Martin Buber's[6] thoughts about the sacredness of everyday life and more likely to feel the connection between ourselves and the rest of creation. And we remember Buber's sadness at the thought that babies are born forgetting their cosmic connection. We want to parent them so that they remember.

PARENTS AND CHILDREN TOGETHER: THE PARADOX OF SEPARATENESS WITHIN CONNECTION

Within the circle of parent and child there is room for the child to begin his lifelong journey toward increasing independence, the metaphorical journey through evolution. As one father told us, "I knew from the very beginning that my primary task as a parent was to help my children leave me. My wife and I have done a pretty good job of that. The great thing is that my son and daughter are both in their late twenties now, and we couldn't be more attached to each other. We're separated, and we're attached."

This is one of the recurring themes of the book. As we shall see, unconscious parenting comes from an inability on the part of a parent to distinguish between himself and his child. We call this inability *symbiosis*,[7] and we explore it in detail in later chapters. One of the most challenging life-tasks of any parent is to experience oneness with a newborn and then to gradually help this infant grow into a person who is *not* the parent—to see the ways the child is different and to honor them, not only by allowing differences but by genuinely appreciating them.

THE BRAIN

In order to understand why it is often so difficult for the parent to distinguish between herself and her child, we have to know something about our biological evolution. Our brains have evolved in a very particular way, and the story of that evolution has important implications for the problems of unconscious parenting. We are alerted to the nature of the problems by our use of the word "unconscious."

Using Paul McLean's[8] model, we can understand the brain as having developed in three concentric layers. The first is the inner layer of the brain stem, which controls automatic biological functions, such as the circulation of blood, breathing, sleeping, and the contraction of muscles. The second layer is the limbic system, which controls emotions. And the third layer is the large cerebral cortex, which controls the cognitive functions of conscious thought—observing, planning, organizing, responding, and the creation of new ideas. This is the part of your mind that you think of as being "you."

The first two layers of the brain we call the "old brain." The third we call the "new brain" or the "cognitive brain." The old brain functions mostly outside of our awareness; its primary concern is self-preservation. It acts for survival. It gets its information, not from the incoming data of direct perception, but from the images, symbols, and thoughts produced by the new brain. That means that it doesn't make distinctions between what happened then and what is happening now or between *him* and *me*. Its ability to categorize things is very crude. "Is it safe?" "Should I attack or run away?" "Should I have sex?" "Should I nurture?" "Should I allow myself to be nurtured?"

The new brain, on the other hand, processes information and impressions directly from cognitive experience. It is looking for the logic behind experience, the cause-and-effect relationships that help make sense of the bewildering array of sensory stimulation we receive every day. It registers important subtleties that distinguish this person from that person. It helps us know that this person is not me, that now is different from then. And to some extent the analytical capacity of the new brain can moderate the instinctual reactions of the old brain.

It is important to understand that the conscious part of us can influence the unconscious part of us. It is possible to reduce the number of times we react to our children and our partners as though they were enemies we need to defend ourselves against. Parents can learn to probe their past experiences, understand more clearly the defenses that have helped protect them from pain, think through whether these defenses are appropriate and effective *now*, and decide to act with conscious intention in ways that may be counterinstinctive but are more conducive to preserving healthy intimate relationships.

THE CHILD'S ENVIRONMENT

Every child comes into the world with a unique combination of potential and limitation that form his temperament. His parents interact with him and influence how his personality develops. Other environmental factors are also very important. Factors such as the socioeconomic status of the family, the birth order, and the character of the neighborhood all shape his personality. We are not going to explore them here because these issues are well discussed in other places.[9] Our contribution is to emphasize the role of the parent in determining whether the child is able to maximize the benefits from positive environmental factors and recover from the effects of the negative ones.

THE NEEDS OF THE CHILD

Throughout history children have not been considered to be "real" people in the sense we mean it today. In ancient Rome, for example, the father of the family had life-and-death jurisdiction over all the members of his family and household. If he didn't want a child for any reason, the child was taken to the Forum and left to die. During the Middle Ages in Europe the lives of children were precarious. Children were expected to become adults almost as soon as it was clear that they were not going to die as infants, which most did. A child was valued to the extent that she filled a need for her parents. As late as Victorian England it was difficult for families to see a child as a person: some children were sentimentalized as innocent ideals, while others where cruelly treated as slave labor. Until recently, in fact, parenting has been extravagantly parent-centered. The child was expected to meet the parent's needs—even if the parent needed the child to die.[10]

Child abuse and neglect are not unheard-of today in our country either. It is ironic that against a background of increasing child abuse, there are now parts of our society where the balance has tipped way over in the other direction. In these families parenting is excessively child-centered, and parents make extraordinary, sometimes damaging financial, emotional, and time sacrifices for the sake of what they hope will be the happiness and future success of their children.

We are interested in an approach that is neither parent-centered nor child-centered, one that balances the needs and wishes of both parents and children in order to create personal wholeness for both. This kind of parenting is relationship-centered: it focuses on what happens between parents and children, or as we refer to it, the "in-between."

To strike a healthy balance, it's important to know what it is that children need from their parents. We think of it this way: *Every child has the need to survive, to feel alive and express his aliveness, and to experience his connection to others and to that which is greater than himself.* Let's explore briefly what these ideas mean.

The need to survive: This is the child's basic need, and it can be met only through contact with parents or other caring adults. His connection with them is the practical vehicle through which he learns that he can get the food, water, and shelter he needs. And it is the emotional vehicle through which he learns that he can have the loving interaction he needs, that he will be able to take care of himself when he gets older, and that he will be able to connect meaningfully with other people. This first experience of survival through parental connection teaches him how to form other survival connections later and to be confident about their success.

The need to feel alive and express his aliveness: The child is born with an awareness of wholeness, connection, and life energy. He is born into a state of relaxed joyfulness, and throughout his life he yearns to reexperience that state. He feels his aliveness when he discovers his power to affect his environment and when he learns that what he does makes a difference. He feels it in his appreciation for the ways that he is similar to the people around him and the ways he is different. He feels it in the fleeting nature of his emotional states and his ability to enjoy them without grasping or hanging on too long. He feels it when he is aware that he lives in a connectional universe in which he has a part to play.

Children naturally express themselves in the world, unless they are constrained by the repressive influence of a parent or some other powerful person. The child will use his voice to sing and shout, his muscles to run and dance. He will cry and laugh and frown. He will touch and smell and talk and hear and see. And he will exercise his right to voice his own thoughts so that he can be understood by others, confident that what he has to say is important.

The need to experience his connection to others and to that which is greater than himself: This entire book can be understood as an explanation and exploration of this need. The child is born into connection with his parents and, through his parents, to the cosmos. His developmental journey through the rest of childhood can be understood as a series of ever more sophisticated impulses to connect to the physical and existential realities of his life. First to his physical environment, then to a widening circle of other people, and on to the mental, emotional, and spiritual contexts in which he lives. The parent, by teaching him to be in healthy connection in the first place, gives him the tools to form the other connections that will allow him to reach his potential as a human being.

These are the basic needs of the child, and it is the parent's job to create the conditions under which these needs can be met. The parent does this by being attuned to the child and by developing an instinct for what the child needs. This includes setting appropriate boundaries. The parent wants the child to develop an awareness that his self-expression must become part of a tapestry that includes the self-expression of all other living things. In order to accomplish this and all the other tasks involved in raising children, the conscious parent acts from the center of self-knowledge within a context of information about the child and with the conscious intention to achieve certain outcomes.

WHEREVER YOU ARE, YOU CAN BEGIN FROM HERE

We've designed this book to be helpful to you no matter where you are in your parenting cycle. Whether your child is an innocent infant or a troubled teenager, the system of conscious parenting described in this book will help you understand yourself and your child better. You will know what to do to help your child meet the challenges inherent in her development as she continues to become more fully herself.

As we shall discuss, all of us participate in moments of unconscious parenting, and problems arise no matter who we are. It's never too late for your children, even if they are grown and out of the house, and it is never too late for you as a parent.

Jon Kabat-Zinn, in his book, *Wherever You Go, There You Are,*[11] examines the importance of learning to live in the present, without habitual regret for the past or pie-in-the-sky longing for the future. He says very plainly, "Whatever has happened to you, it has already happened. The important question is, how are you going to handle it? In other words, 'Now what?' "

This is our frame of reference also. Wherever you are in the parenting process, whatever has already happened—this is where you are now. So now what?

LET'S START WITH WHAT YOU'RE DOING RIGHT

We'll make a bold statement: *If you are reading this book, you are already doing a lot right as a parent.* How do we know? You've picked up this book. You care enough to be curious about what we're saying. So, already we can predict that:

1. You care about your children.
2. You think parenting is important.
3. You recognize that parenting, to some degree at least, is a skill.
4. You know that you are capable of learning new things.
5. You believe that you can take action to make things better.

Even if only one of these statements is true, there is good reason for believing that you will end up being a good parent. We suggest that you reread each of the above statements and ask yourself how strongly you agree that it applies to you. Take your time to think about them.

What you are doing is beginning to formulate for yourself a set of beliefs or values that will guide you in the process of becoming a better parent. These statements can become the foundation for your belief that you will be able to incorporate the principles of conscious parenting into your life. It is important to know from the very beginning that a positive orientation toward learning can make a tremendous difference. Whenever you bring a positive set of convictions to the learning process, you have taken the first step.

We know that our readers come from a variety of life circumstances. Some of you are from traditional two-parent families. But many of you are single parents who either have various child-sharing arrangements or are parenting alone. We are clear about our bias that it is better for children if they have two parents devoted to their progress, but in no way do we intend to imply that single parents cannot be conscious parents who raise wonderful, healthy children.[12]

We have tried throughout the book to speak of the parent as both mother and father equally.[13] It is true that the mother is often the primary caregiver in the early months or years, but not always. And whatever we say about the mother in that role is equally true for the father who has that same early, intense involvement. We want to emphasize that fathers too are wounded; they must also learn to grow and heal, and whenever possible they must become equal participants with mothers in their children's lives.

We also do not want to neglect the importance of grandparents. For simplicity's sake, we most often talk about "parents," but by this we mean any caring adult who has primary responsibility for the child. Increasingly, grandparents are functioning in the role of parents. But even when they aren't doing so, they can have profound positive effects on the self-esteem and the competence of their grandchildren.

THIS BOOK

This is a book about the transformational process of conscious parenting. It is a book with an idea, a view of parenting that can change how people think. We believe that helping people reach a new understanding of the parenting relationship is more important than teaching a new set of rules or guidelines for coping with children.

This is a book about what the child *is*. Not a book about what the child ought to be or how parents can get their child to do what they think is best. It's a book about the child as a human being who is born whole and about how parents can preserve the child's wholeness while she is under their care.

The book makes a statement about how important it is for a parent to become self-reflective and to make changes in his or her personality as part of the process of becoming conscious. Learning about parenting skills and about children's needs is necessary, but not sufficient. The parent must undertake the task of self-change.

This is a book about how the parent can recognize what changes she needs to make by noticing when she has repeated negative reactions to her child's natural developmental behavior. The parent learns to see her child as a mirror reflecting back her own unfinished childhood and the parts of herself that have been lost. It is a book about how parents can grow through the process of parenting their children well.

There is tough information here. We pull no punches about how the cycle of wounding will continue until parents undertake to become more conscious in their relationship with each other and their children. One of the reasons we felt compelled to write the book was our concern that broken marital and parental relationships have become endemic in this society. It is a fact that nearly sixty percent of all marriages end in divorce.[14] More than half of those divorces involve children still living at home. In a population of about seventy-nine million couples, the implications are staggering. There is no doubt that the problems of unconscious parenting are felt deeply on both a personal and social level, but we believe that the solution must start on the personal level. Today's parents must decide that the wounding stops with them and the healing starts with them. Only then can we begin to address the social problems that are worsening around us.

How we parent our children reveals a great deal about how we were parented. When a particular parent-child interaction reveals how strongly we parents resemble our own mothers or fathers, that insight can be extremely disheartening. But in the end, we have written this book to show how this insight can also be a catalyst for exploring unresolved issues originating in our own childhoods. *Giving the Love that Heals* offers a unique opportunity for personal transformation that will lead us to a conscious, and thus healthier, relationship with our children.

2

The Imago Family

The Prince rushed up and lifted her out of the casket.
He told her all that had happened and begged her to be
his bride. Snow White consented with sparkling eyes,
so they rode away to the Prince's home where they
prepared for a gay and gala wedding . . . and they all
lived happily ever after.[1]

*A*s a young child in nineteenth-century Europe, you might have heard, from your mother or nurse, the story of Snow White and of how your life can be transformed by falling in love. In some magical and unexpected moment, a virile and handsome Prince Charming leans gently over the raven hair of a beautiful maiden, tilts her face up to his, and kisses her tenderly on the lips. That one gesture awakens them to a life more wonderful than any they have ever seen or known before. *The message: Fall in love with the right person and you will live happily ever after.*

A century and a half later, in 1981, other young women (and men, too, one supposes) had an opportunity to thrill to another fairy-tale romance. But this story begins where the earlier one left off—with the wedding. First, the exquisitely beautiful young bride and her prince. She was devoted to him and eager to please. Then came the birth of their first perfect son, and then the second son. . . . And then, surprisingly, a breath of discontent—an expression of unhappiness—and finally, to our dismay, a growing stream of pain that overflows the banks of marriage and floods into public awareness. Eleven years later they part. The romance is over. The perfect family—Prince Charles, Princess

Di, and their children—has feet of clay just like the rest of us. *The message: It isn't that easy.*

ROMANCE

One of these stories is a fairy tale; the other is biography. Obviously, they are not the same. Fairy tales are not journalism, and we don't expect them to chronicle real life. But these two stories are interesting for what they have in common: both of them give shape to our deep longing for the magical transformation of love. With a single kiss we are relieved forever from the tragic and tedious problems of real life and transported into a state that echoes the spiritual harmony and wholeness we possessed when we came into the world.

Ordinary people, too, know what it's like to fall in love and feel as if they're holding court in a world of great beauty and promise. We are delighted when these private desires can be played out on a royal stage. Yes, kings and queens act in their own private dramas, but they are also playing our song.

At some point, though, real life begins to intrude. Things get complicated. We start disappointing each other. Sooner or later, we sit across the breakfast table from each other and realize that we are not living the dream. Our lives have more in common with celebrity biography than romantic fiction. We start worrying about what will happen with the children.

It would be going too far to say that what happened to Charles and Diana is what happens to everybody. Only a little more than *half* of all marriages in this country end in divorce,[2] and approximately half of all children grow up in households where a divorce has occurred. But we might think of Charles and Diana's story as a cautionary tale. It's what you do *after* the romance has faded that counts.

THE WHOLE STORY

As an exposition on human behavior a tale from the Brothers Grimm clearly has its limits. The story ends before it gets too messy. It doesn't say a word about the inevitability of marital discord or how the unsophisticated Snow White (used to the company of rough-hewn dwarves) was going to be able to satisfy the sophisticated requirements of the rich

and worldly Prince or how they will manage to raise their children together when she smothers them with attention and he's never home.

To a storyteller, these complications aren't a problem. They don't
even exist. But these are exactly the real-world realities that interest us.
We may not care so much about Snow White's difficulties, but we do
have some interest in sorting through our own. In the spirit of self-
discovery, we speculate endlessly about what happened to Charles and
Diana. And we wonder what's happening to the rest of us who, despite
our high hopes and our best efforts, can't seem to stay the course long
enough to raise our children together.

A MODEL

At some point we realized that understanding the dynamics of marital
and parenting relationships requires more than speculation and story-
telling. We needed a model to help us see what happens underneath
the surface. Without one, we can't know which past experiences get
woven into the fabric of family relationships only to weaken them in
the present and which imperfections are likely to grow into problems
that ultimately undermine commitment. Without a model we can't
know how to repair a crack before it gets bigger. We're left crossing our
fingers, hoping it will turn out all right.

Twenty years ago, we started tracing the cracks in our own relationships, and then in others. As the years went by, we began to understand
the patterns, and the patterns began to form themselves into a model
that made sense of the high emotion of new love and everything that
follows after that. This model, Imago Relationship Therapy, explains
why people behave the way they do beginning from the time they fall
in love with each other and continuing through the stages of getting
married, falling out of love with each other, having children, and spending all those years engaged in the most difficult job of all—parenting
their children. In other words, the model covers the questions we have
about Snow White and Prince Charming, and the questions we have
about Princess Diana and Prince Charles.

As you read what we've learned, picture what we are saying in three
dimensions. Think of computer models that now show us how language
is processed in the human brain or the way a thunderstorm develops or
the swirling patterns of atmosphere above Jupiter's core. We see these
interactive systems in the round, all the different parts at once, as a

hologram.[3] We see how the system as a whole is influenced and changed by the subtle interactions that occur at specific points.

Families, too, can best be seen as multidimensional interactive systems. The kinds of connections mothers and fathers make with each other and with their children serve to mold them as individuals and shape the identity of the family as a whole.[4] The "family" we see at any given moment is the result of all the connective interactions that have gone on before. Think back to just one of the conversations you and your family members have had around the dinner table. A single family conversation has all the subtlety and complexity of any "living" organic process. And it is subject to some of the same observations we make about such processes in the natural world.

NATURAL PATTERNS

Scientists today feel that they are on the verge of significant breakthroughs in understanding the subtleties and complexities of living organic processes and the nature of the universe. Every day they uncover patterns or pieces of patterns that advance our understanding of everything from the way pine seeds whorl on the surface of a cone to the way stars give birth to galaxies. When we uncover a pattern in the natural world, we get insight into what is "true" and learn what we need to make the next discovery.

One well-known mathematician, for example, now defines mathematics as "the science of patterns."[5] In a similar way, we think of Imago Theory as "the science of patterns in marriage and parenting." Like all good and true patterns, those in Imago Theory explain "what is," suggest what causes deviations, and propose what can be done about them.

TWO UNIVERSAL LAWS

As is true for life in general, Imago Theory understands human behavior in families to be subject to two universal laws. The first is that *within entities, general patterns get passed on.* If that were not true, there would be no animal species, and therefore no kind of animal we could call "lion" or "mouse" or "tadpole." Of course, within these patterns there are individual variations. Very few patterns get passed on exactly. Let's take zebras. All zebras are recognizable as zebras, distinct from every other animal. We recognize them by the pattern of stripes in their coats. But every single zebra that has ever lived has had a slightly different pattern from every other. That's why the mother circles the baby zebra until she imprints her pattern on his mind. Then he can recognize her and know where to go for lunch. In humans the general patterning gets passed on, but the way each child manifests the pattern is different.

Our second universal law is that *things change*. Given what we've just said about the sameness of inherited patterns, this sounds contradictory. Many times in the course of our discussion about parenting we will encounter paradoxes in which two contradictory things seem to be true at once. When we encounter a paradox, we know we have gotten beneath the surface of the subject and are beginning to approach one of the many mysteries that lie at the heart of being human. This is one of them: Things tend to stay the same, *and* they can change.[6] Sometimes these changes can happen within a generation—the baby is different in some significant way from the parents. But many of the changes are so slow that our human time frame doesn't allow us to chart their evolution.

These two great processes are examples of how patterns in the universe are reflected in us and in all of life. And they are fundamental to Imago Theory. Shifting for a moment from the language of natural science to the language of behavioral science, we can say that parents pass on to their children all kinds of patterns that they, in turn, will pass on to *their* children in an unbroken line, unless something is done on purpose to disrupt the family legacy.[7] This is true for marriage, and it is particularly true for parenting. *The most accurate predictor of how you will parent is how you were parented.* Human beings have a very strong preference for the familiar. Unless we consciously think to do otherwise, we will do "what comes naturally" and repeat what we are used to, the way things have *always* been done. In order to do something different, we need to become self-conscious about our functioning and take definite steps to replace the familiar with something else.

BECOMING CONSCIOUS

When we say we need to become conscious, we mean something more than the mere awareness that is common to all life-forms.[8] We are referring to something for which only humans seem to have the capacity—

self-awareness or self-consciousness. We are alluding to the effort that is necessary for humans to become more self-reflective than they are now. We humans are constructed so that our level of self-awareness is powerful but not perfect. And becoming conscious is hard work.

It's not easy to see the complex psychological patterns that form our unique identities. They are embedded deep inside us and are formed by the transitory interactions we have with others that leave no visible trace. We don't wear them on our backs, as zebras wear their stripes. And because we are human and our brains have evolved in a particular way, these patterns are not only hidden from others, but hidden from ourselves as well.

The people closest to us have a better chance of seeing them than we do. If a family member says, "You *always* do that," or, "Whenever I do *this*, you do *that*," we sometimes recognize ourselves in the pattern and the pattern in us. Often we don't. It can take a while to recognize our own habitual responses and the hidden emotional fires that fuel them. We have no problem seeing what other people are doing, but to see ourselves—that takes a little more time.

By uncovering psychological patterns, Imago Theory helps people become more understandable to themselves. When they hear the story that Imago Theory tells, they try it on to see if it makes sense of *their* motivations and behaviors. Does it enlarge their self-understanding and allow them to predict their own behavior? If so, they end up saying to themselves, "*That* must be why I do such and such. I never realized it before, but it makes sense."

Some people feel resistant to the idea that their most personal behavior is subject to general rules. We all have a natural tendency to see ourselves as unique in all respects. After all, each of us is born with a body and a brain like no one else's, into a particular family in a particular time and place. Our lives feel very private, and very personal. We don't like hearing that we fall in love, marry, and parent our children according to patterns that are true for everybody. But we also benefit from knowing that there is a coherent system that describes the way we interact with each other. Once the system is understood, it brings us closer to the truth of family relationships. It helps us create a path out of the common muddle of pain and confusion that characterizes so much of family life.

THE STORY

We have been talking about the behavior patterns that Imago Theory has uncovered in marriage and parenting. Now it's time to see what they are. These are the patterns that lie beneath the surface of our awareness and strongly influence how we think and feel about our spouses and our children. The story is more complex than the one we will tell here. Here it will be presented briefly to convey the scope of our subject. We will elaborate on it later in this chapter, and explore it in depth for the remainder of the book.

ROMANCE: *ON THE SURFACE* . . . Two people fall madly in love. They've never felt this way before. They delight in their differences and feel complete in each other's company in a way they never have with anyone else. They have a sense that the happiness will last forever.

UNDERNEATH . . . They have chosen each other for very specific reasons, even though they are not aware of them. Each of them has been attracted to a partner who exhibits the strongest traits of one or both of their own parents. While they are drawn to a match of both positive and negative traits, the negative traits seem to have extra power. This means that people are drawn to partners that closely resemble the parent they had the most difficulty with in childhood. This is part of the euphoria: Their parentlike partner can meet their needs in a way their parents never did.

MARRIAGE: *ON THE SURFACE* . . . The romance lasts for some time, and then it begins to fade, usually after about three years, if they are lucky. For some couples it fades on the wedding day. Conflicts begin to surface, and marriage partners end up wondering if they made a mistake. Their partner doesn't seem to be the same person they thought they were marrying. This isn't what they bargained for.

UNDERNEATH . . . The same difficulties they had with their parents start surfacing with their partners. Each of them expects the other to continue to meet his or her needs completely and is disappointed when this doesn't happen. Both of them feel as if they are giving more than they are getting. Whether they get past this power struggle or not depends on whether they can reinvest the relationship with an empathic understanding for the way each of them was injured in the relationship with his or her parents. In order to realize their potential for becoming passionate friends, they will need to create a conscious marriage in which they learn how to be healing partners for each other. Then they will be able to revisit and dress each of the wounds that continue to keep them from being complete and whole human beings. For more information about how to create a conscious marriage, you may want to read *Getting the Love You Want: A Guide for Couples.*

THE BIRTH OF A CHILD: *ON THE SURFACE* . . . Into this greater or lesser marital power struggle, their first baby is born. They are ecstatic. They are committed to doing everything they can to be good parents.

UNDERNEATH . . . The child is born whole—physically, emotionally, and spiritually. To the extent that his parents are attuned to his evolving needs, they maintain the baby's connection to himself, to his immediate environment, and to the greater world into which he was born and from which he came. If they can see him for *who* and *what* he is and continue to meet his evolving needs as he develops, they will be able to facilitate his unfolding into a unique and complete human being. Their ability to be attuned to him will depend to a large extent on where they are in their marriage. Have the childhood wounds they each brought to the marriage—and that cause problems there—been addressed? If not, these unresolved personal and marital issues will adversely affect their ability to parent. Even if they are both emotionally mature and their relationship is solid, they will make mistakes in their interactions with their child. No parent, no matter how devoted, is perfectly attuned and able to meet the baby's needs every waking moment.

PARENTING DIFFICULTIES: *ON THE SURFACE* . . . One parent or the other starts having trouble with his or her new role as parent. For now, let's identify that parent as the mother. She realizes that she isn't maintaining a wholesome connection with her son, and that she is behaving in ways that surprise and appall her. She may blame superficial things, like aspects of her son's character that come and go or the stress she's under at work or something her husband is doing. It doesn't feel to her that there is a consistent way of understanding the difficulties. She's at a loss.

UNDERNEATH . . . Often a parent has no clue about why she is having problems with her child. But the perspective of Imago Theory[9] is that there are reasons that explain what kind of problem she is having . . . and why . . . and why now. These reasons are directly linked to the problems her parents had with her when she was a child and the consequent damage that resulted to her psyche during their clumsy or hurtful interactions with her. Whether they intended to or not, her parents wounded her.[10] They may have ignored her or criticized her or smothered her with unwanted attention or undercut her efforts to be independent or didn't allow her to be angry. The list is a long one, as we will see in later chapters. At those places where her own growth and wholeness were damaged, she responded by scarring over the wound.

These "scarrings" serve the purpose of protecting her from further pain. They can take many forms, including the kind of defensive behavior we are all familiar with: denying parts of ourselves and exaggerating others. The net result is that her natural self has been distorted into something that is not natural to her, but which through the years has become an established part of her character. The scarrings are what are causing the trouble now. They impair her ability to respond well to her own child. In particular, she will have trouble with her son at exactly the point her parents had trouble with her. Her woundedness contaminates her ability to parent him because her own unmet needs keep getting confused with *his*. The healthy psychological distance so necessary to conscious parenting is very difficult to achieve when you confuse yourself with your child.

COMMENTS BY OTHERS: *ON THE SURFACE* . . . The mother may not know what the trouble is, but her husband makes a critical remark that suggests *he* knows what's going on. She isn't doing it right! She is not receptive to his observations. She's defensive. Some days later he is again critical, and she is again defensive. "If he thinks it's so easy, he should try doing more of the parenting."

UNDERNEATH . . . Parenting partners often don't have a language for conveying information about the parenting process, especially if what they want to convey is critical of the other parent. The mother, who is responding poorly in the first place because she has been wounded, is supersensitive to criticism that gets close to her injury. Her defenses get activated now when it feels as if the old pain might come to the surface.

INSIGHT: *ON THE SURFACE* . . . Whether she rejects her husband's criticism or not, she will begin to realize that she is reacting to her child in ways that hurt the child and disturb her partner and that feel out of her conscious control. She ends up asking herself, "Why am I doing this?"

UNDERNEATH . . . Some parents, of course, are never able to engage in even *this* much self-assessment. They can't ask this question because they never make the link between what they are doing and what the child is doing that disturbs them. They tend to blame the child himself or someone else, or they tend to blame themselves globally and unhelpfully for being "bad," "inadequate," or "unlucky." We have a name for this kind of blind, egocentric parenting that never sees the child and his needs as requiring separate consideration. We call this *unconscious* parenting. Unfortunately, this is the way most of us parent and the way most parents in history have always parented until they were jarred into some sort of self-reflection.

Fortunately, the mother in our example is open to hearing that there is a systematic way of understanding and addressing her parenting problems. It is comforting to her to realize that while she is not directly responsible for the generation of her problems, she is responsible for doing what she can to heal them. She is particularly interested to hear that wounded parents tend to react to their children in one of two exaggerated and harmful ways: either they withdraw and hide behind barriers and are underinvolved, or they have vague or lax barriers and become overinvolved. One of these styles may explain her "hair-trigger" anger over things that don't even seem to bother her husband.

THE OPPORTUNITY: All people have trouble parenting their children some of the time. Some have more trouble than others, just as some marriages have more grief and struggle than others. But not everybody knows that the inevitable challenges of parenthood offer a once-in-a-lifetime opportunity. There is no better way for an adult to heal childhood wounds and become a whole person than through the self-revelation that can occur during the parenting process.

Specifically, the problems you have with your children offer you invaluable information about what parts of you are unfinished or incomplete as a result of your childhood. You can use this information to become a whole person who can learn how to be a conscious parent and marriage partner. Your efforts to become a more conscious person will have a profound effect on your child. He will pick up this way of being in the world and will pass it on to his children. Being engaged in the process of completing your own growth and development will be good for you, good for your marriage or other intimate relationships, and most important, good for your child.

We have now brought our story to the point where our mother is ready to do something to become a more conscious parent. Instead of being disheartened by the connections she sees between her own emotional difficulties and the difficulties she's having with her son, she can be energized by them. She doesn't have to feel that she is being blamed, because she isn't. For one thing, in one major way, she's off the hook. The Imago perspective is that parenting problems stem from incidents and events that happened during the childhood of the parent and were outside her control. This way of seeing things can help the mother avoid sinking into feeling guilty or bad because she's having trouble. She has an obligation to do what she can to make herself strong now, but she doesn't have to feel as if her character is fatally flawed. As we have said, things can change.

HERE IS WHAT A PARENT CAN DO:

1. DISCOVER HER CHILD. She can learn more about her child by educating herself about the stages of growth that children naturally go through as they mature into adults. Although most parents are unaware or are only vaguely aware of these stages, they are well documented and well understood. The conscious parent knows that a central part of her role is to support her child's changing needs as he evolves into adulthood. She does this by providing emotional and physical safety, support for all his developmental impulses, and the structure and boundaries he needs every step of the way.

2. IDENTIFY HER PARENTING STYLE. She can identify which style she exhibits in her unconscious parenting, because this will offer clues about what to change in herself at each stage of her child's development. Her parenting style is not a rigid category that exactly describes her behavior, but a description of an overall tendency that she has to respond one way or the other. Every parent has elements of both styles and may manifest characteristics of either style in any given situation. But, still, it will be helpful to her to know that most often she exhibits one style over another. If she tends to explode her emotions outward (as a maximizer), her partner will tend to hold his emotions inside (as a minimizer), and *vice versa*. Parents are opposites of each other because of the unconscious selection process that brought them together in the first place and because they tend to become polarized on many issues over the years.

3. DISTINGUISH HER CHILD FROM HERSELF. She can be especially alert when she finds that she's having trouble seeing and treating her child as a separate person. We call this unhealthy confusion of identities *cognitive symbiosis*. If she can't feel this truth in her bones—*my child is not me*—then she needs to be very careful. She will likely not

have good judgment about what safety, support, or structure she can provide that will meet his needs in the present situation, in the present moment. Her own unmet needs will keep intruding, and she will parent him as she herself would like some magical parent to love, guide, and protect her. This may or may not meet his needs. Most likely, it won't.

4. GATHER INFORMATION ABOUT HER PARENTING. She can recognize that the people around her and the parenting process itself offer a gold mine of information that will help her do things better. There are several sources available to her: her own emotional and intense reactions to her child; her memories of what her own parents were like when they parented her; her memories of how she felt about herself and her life at each age; the thoughts and feelings expressed by her own child; opinions and observations from her spouse and from other people; information from reading and from observing others; and observations she herself makes about her relationship with her child.

5. IDENTIFY HER GROWTH POINTS. She can put together a picture of what her parenting looks like and identify her "growth points," those places of conflict or discomfort with her child that indicate that she needs to do some healing of her own incompleteness. Most people have some idea of when and how their own mental and emotional growth was interrupted, and they will resonate to some possibilities of wounding more than others. This sense of having had trouble accomplishing a particular childhood task at a particular stage is useful for pointing the way toward whatever healing work needs to be done. It is essential for her to know that without doing some work on herself she cannot help her child successfully pass through the developmental stages that she herself did not pass through successfully. She will have to work on completing her own unfinished childhood in order to consciously parent her child.

6. IDENTIFY HER CHILDHOOD WOUND. She can gather information about herself and the damage that has been done to her. The more information she has, the more she can bring to the healing process. If she has either diagnostic information about what the wound was or a *sense* of what it was, she can begin to heal. But *no matter what level of self-knowledge she has*, she can begin to repair the damage—if she has an adult partner to do the work with.

7. BECOME AWARE OF HER BELIEFS ABOUT PARENTING. Whether she is aware of it or not, she has a view of who parents are, how children have to be treated, and how they should behave. Consciously or unconsciously, she knows what parents have to do for their

children. And she wants to do it well, even when her core beliefs are not in any child's best interest. These beliefs come from her parents, what they said, how they treated her, and what she internalized from them when she was little. When she is not aware of her beliefs, she will act them out, no matter the consequences for the child.

8. COMMIT TO THE HEALING PROCESS. If she is married, she and her husband can make a commitment to become conscious parents and work together as healing partners. If she is unmarried, she can work with an adult friend or romantic partner who is committed to her and who really wants to help.

9. LEARN INTENTIONAL DIALOGUE. She can establish roots for the healing partnership through three fundamental processes: mirroring, validating, and empathizing. These processes come together in a way of talking with partners and children that we call *intentional dialogue*. Intentional dialogue allows people to reestablish broken connections. People learn to relax their defenses, understand each other's point of view, and then feel empathy for the other's subjective experience. The processes heal wounds, even when people don't know exactly where and how they have been wounded, or exactly which parts of them are damaged.

10. MAKE INTENTIONAL DIALOGUE HER WAY OF BEING IN THE WORLD WITH OTHERS. She can make intentional dialogue a habit—not just as a way of talking, but as a way of life. When she does, other people, including her child, become both more real and more accessible to her. By mirroring, validating, and empathizing with her child, she knows what to do to help him grow up well. And she is able to clarify her own needs and get them met appropriately so that they don't intrude into her relationship with her child.

This is the basic story that Imago Theory tells. When we read it, we see another paradox emerge, one with great significance for understanding why we do the things we do. It is this: *Many of our conscious actions have unconscious beginnings.* We do many of the things we do for reasons we are not aware of. Many of our visible actions have invisible roots. Our logical, reasoning mind is a crucial part of who we are, but it is not the only mind we have.

THE POWER OF WHAT WE DON'T REMEMBER

The most profound mysteries of being human center in what we don't yet know about the human brain. We all know what we mean when we refer to the "mind" in ordinary conversation, and we have no trouble making ourselves understood when we talk about "consciousness." And yet scientists furiously debate what these concepts mean and cannot agree on the physical manifestations of mind and consciousness. Is mind to be found in the structures of our gray matter, the chemical processes that are activated within these structures, or the electrical signals that fire the chemistry? Or is the brain a transmitter of a consciousness outside itself?[11]

And what about memory? Memory may be the most important function of the brain and the one that is most difficult to understand. How do our brains store experience? How does this past experience stay inside us and, without being consciously remembered, continue to influence what we do and think now, today? How can we account for the distortions in memory that inevitably occur during the process in which past experience is perilously reconstructed into scenes that we swear actually took place?

THE IMAGO

We don't yet know the physical mechanisms by which unconscious memories continue to influence present functioning, but we know that they do. This has great relevance for Imago Theory. In marriage, as we have seen, the unconscious brain is influential in whom we choose to marry. What happens is this: Each person stores in his brain a picture of all the traits, interactions, and experiences he has had with his parents. This inner picture is called the "imago." He is not aware of the existence of the imago, but it is there, and it is powerful. In infancy the imago functions to help the child distinguish his parents from other adults as a matter of survival, just as it does for the baby zebra. In adulthood, as we have seen, the imago functions unconsciously to connect the person with a partner who in many ways replicates the character structure of the parents, in this way offering the opportunity to heal earlier wounds, a more sophisticated manifestation of survival. As far as we know, this doesn't apply to zebras. The person you marry is an imago match, and your imago match becomes your parenting partner.

THE "PARENTING PRINT"

The unconscious brain is a powerful force in another aspect of family life as well. We have already said that we know that children internalize[12] the experiences they have with their parents. They copy on the inside, in their minds, their interpretation of what they have encountered on the outside during interactions with parents and other important caregivers. Significantly, they absorb the emotional maturity or immaturity of the parent, and they absorb the parent's moral character. How the parent handles conflict or deals with disappointment or sorts out moral dilemmas makes an indelible impression on and in the child. Who the parent is (and not just what the parent says) becomes part of the child's self. This inner picture of the parents influences the choice of marriage partners. It also influences what kind of parent they become and what kind of people they end up becoming.

We are led, then, to an important conclusion: *the single most important predictor of how you will parent is how you were parented as a child.* Your parents' actions and inactions have formed the person you are today, even if you can't remember all of them. It's as if we had "parenting prints" in our brains in the same way that we have fingerprints on our fingers. Each parenting print is unique and identifying. We can't ink them on paper, but we can come to know them by observing how they manifest themselves in the way we respond to others in close personal relationships, especially parenting.

With zebras general patterns get passed on, but each baby zebra shows the patterning a little differently. It's the same with people. We can describe with assurance the process, or pattern, you will follow in choosing a mate or in passing on a mental and emotional legacy to your children, but exactly how these details will manifest themselves in your life depends upon your personal history. Our aim in this book is to give you as much information as possible to help you recognize your own unique pattern for yourself.

THERE'S MORE TO THE STORY

Often someone who wants to understand a complex, dynamic system wants to understand it all at once. Since that usually isn't possible, the most practical method is to get a feel for the system as a whole and then fill in some details. We have just told "the story" to give you a chance to see the general patterns we see when we look at parents and children. We want these patterns to start becoming familiar to you. But we realize that you will also benefit from knowing a little more detail right now about certain important concepts.

Each of the sections that follow is a very brief explanation of some aspect of how Imago Theory works. In succeeding chapters we will expand these sections into separate chapters so that we can discuss them in depth. We are proceeding this way because we want to give you the opportunity to become comfortable with some of the general ideas of Imago Theory before you involve yourself in the personal stories and details that will make them real and vivid for you. In this way, you will start getting a clearer picture of what has brought you to where you are in your parenting and what you can do to make things better.

UNCONSCIOUS PARENTING

We once heard a father say to his son, "The only reason I had you was so you could do things for me!" That's an example of unconscious parenting—a particularly naked one. But often unconscious parenting can be harder to see than that. We can detect it in the response of the mother who is deliriously happy when her daughter scores a goal, as though it were happening to her. The unconscious parent, or any parent in an unconscious moment, is not able to see her child as separate from herself and interacts with her as though *she were her child and her child were her.*

In the next chapter we will come to understand why all of us participate in unconscious parenting to some degree and how the particular form of unconsciousness we manifest is influenced by the experiences we had with our own parents growing up. Parents who were wounded in particular ways will be prone to wounding their children in exactly these same ways. A father who was undervalued by his own father is likely to underestimate his son's worth. A mother whose athletic talents were frustrated is more likely to be overly invested in her daughter's athleticism. Patterns of unconscious parenting are passed from parent to child until one parent in the line decides to interrupt the legacy and to undertake her own healing. In the next chapter, we explore the many faces of unconscious parenting and its implications for our children and our society.

THE WOUNDED CHILD AS TEACHER

A mother and father were distressed because their twelve-year-old son was so lackadaisical. He didn't have any ambition; he was so slow; he didn't want to play soccer. Every evening was one long nag session. "Did you do your homework yet?" At the same time, these two parents were seriously stressed-out by the unremitting demands of two careers, two children, church and community obligations, nurturing their own relationship, and their desire to find time for private artistic and musical pursuits. Here in the middle of this admittedly overscheduled family was a son who wasn't buying it.

Over time, these parents came to see their son as their teacher. The mother said, "I'm beginning to think that maybe our son isn't the problem. Maybe he's here with us, the way he is, to teach us something about what's important. Maybe all this running around, hurry-hurry, isn't what we're supposed to be doing."

From problem child to teacher—that's a stunning turnaround! These parents were able to use their unhappiness with their child as an opportunity to see their lives differently. Think of it this way: You are the wounded child who has grown up to have children of your own. Your wounds are still inside of you, although you may not be aware of them. They come out in your relationship with your spouse, and they come out in your relationship with your children. Because you are wounded, you wound your own child by not valuing and accepting him for who he is, just as you were not accepted by your parents for who you are. You may not wound him seriously or often perhaps, but you wound him nonetheless. This is the pattern that will continue until you recognize what you are doing and take conscious steps to do something different.

You can learn to recognize when you are reacting out of your own woundedness. It is happening when you repeatedly react with intensity, usually negatively, to your child's normal behavior. Your overreaction is a clue that you have encountered what we call a "growth point." A growth point is a place in the parenting process that is difficult for you. It directs you to some incompleteness or injury in yourself that is a place of potential healing for you.

Your child will teach you about your own healing and about many other things. Most important, of course, she will teach you what you need to do to parent her well. First, you treat her with the same respect with which you would treat someone you thought you could learn from, and then you watch and listen for the message she is sending.

THE HEALING OF THE PARENT

The wholeness and health of the children depend upon the wholeness and health of the parents as individuals and of their partnership as a unit.[13] As we have said, children absorb their parents' level of emotional and moral maturity. More than what the parents say, the child stores how the parents *are* in the world. This does not mean that parents have to be perfect to raise healthy, well-adjusted children. But it does mean they need to be engaged in the process of becoming conscious—of their children's needs and their own unmet needs. The fact that they are wrestling with important emotional issues and sharing the process with their children, when it's appropriate, is more important than how wounded or unwounded they are.

Parents who engage in the process of becoming conscious for the sake of the child will be able to finish their own psychological development and restore their own wholeness. It won't be easy. There are few models to guide us, because conscious parenting has never been done before. As a species, we are engaged in a new phase in our personal and cultural evolution. A child who sees his parent in the process of becoming a conscious person will be equipped to do the same in his own life and will contribute to the increasing consciousness of our species.

While the child and the parenting process itself supply clues to the parent about what she needs to heal in herself, the healing is done in a healing partnership that she forms with her spouse or other committed adult. She may do her own healing work *for* her child, but she doesn't do it *with* her child.

THE TOOL OF INTENTIONAL DIALOGUE

A mother and her fifteen-year-old daughter are talking in the school principal's office. The mother has had to leave work and come straight to the school because her daughter has just been caught smoking marijuana on school grounds. The mother is furious and the daughter is tight-lipped. There will be a hearing.

> **Mother:** What in the hell do you think you're doing? I had to leave work in the middle of my staff meeting to get here. I don't need this. Why are you doing this? Answer me!
> **Daughter:** What do you want me to say?
> **Mother:** Explain yourself. This is humiliating.

This, of course, is a tirade masquerading as a conversation. And the mother's being upset is understandable. Maybe she and her daughter will be able to talk later, once the mother is finished reacting. But even in this difficult situation, it would have been possible for the mother and daughter to interact in such a way that their connection is maintained and they each learn something from the other about an issue that divides them. It could have gone like this:

Mother: I have to tell you that I'm surprised to be sitting here with you now. I didn't expect to hear that you were using drugs on the school grounds or anywhere else. I need for us to talk so I can understand why you did this and how you feel about it.

Daughter: I know you're upset and I'm sorry for that.

Mother: Yes, I'm upset, but more than that, I'm puzzled. I need to understand what is happening with you.

Daughter: You don't understand.

Mother: You're right. I don't understand now. I need you to help me by talking to me about what is happening inside of you. I want to know and help.

Daughter: It's a way of being accepted. These are the only kids who like me.

Mother: Let me make sure I'm getting this. Smoking marijuana is a way of making friends?

Daughter: Yes.

Mother: Is there more about that?

Daughter: Well, yes. I feel alone and different. When I smoke, I feel a part of the group.

Mother: Let me see if I am getting this. You feel alone and different, but when you smoke you feel a part of the group. Did I get it?

Daughter: Yes. That's it.

Mother: Well, that makes sense. I can see how you are feeling and thinking. If I got it right, you think you have to smoke to have friends. I can imagine your loneliness. It's hard when you feel you have to do something like this to feel part of the group. (*She reaches out and takes her daughter's hand.*) If you think it's either smoke or be out in the cold, I can see why you might smoke. I think we need to explore that idea a little further. There must be other ways to get to know people and make friends that don't involve smoking pot.

This is an example of intentional dialogue. Intentional dialogue is a way of structuring the communication between two people so that it contains *mirroring* (checking with the other person to make sure you are understanding correctly), *validating* (letting the other person know that it's all right for her to have the thoughts and feelings she is having, even if you don't agree with them), and *empathizing* (entering into the state of mind of the other person in order to feel what the other is feeling).

We have talked about how important it is for the parent to be engaged in the process of becoming conscious. Intentional dialogue is the way to do that. It is the principal tool of conscious parenting. Intentional dialogue between partners, and between parents and their children, is the most powerful way to maintain connection or restore it if it has been ruptured.

THE CONSCIOUS PARENT AND THE HEALING OF THE CHILD

The conscious parent meets the needs of the child by providing safety, support, and structure for the child as she moves through each developmental stage. He is attuned to the unique personality and temperament of his child and able to see what his child needs as she grows and changes. He is educated about the developmental stages of children and is able to stay alert and flexible in interactions with her.

He is intentional in his interactions with his child, rather than reactive. And this intentionality can be seen in his use of intentional dialogue in conversations, especially when the conversations are difficult. He takes the processes of intentional dialogue—mirroring, validating, and empathizing—and finds ways to make these responses part of his daily interactions with his child.

He has tools for dealing with his child's frustrations, anger, and regressions that turn these potentially disruptive emotional responses into occasions for strengthening the child's wholeness and maintaining her connection to her parents, her immediate environment, and the larger world. And he has ways of promoting laughter, creative expression, spiritual depth, and moral character as his child begins to express the journey through life.

THE STAGES OF GROWTH

We remember a visit from a mother and her six daughters, all of the children under the age of eight. It was at Christmastime. The mother arrived carrying her three-year-old, with her five older sisters walking behind like ducklings. We met the brood at the door and handed the three-year-old a plate of Christmas cookies. "Would you like to hand these out to your sisters for us?" we asked. "NO!" came the reply. "All mine! They're all mine!"

Children mature in stages. At the age of three, they haven't done all the emotional and social maturing we hope they will have achieved by the age of, say, thirty. They do the work in stages, according to an innate evolutionary agenda that unfolds in about the same way for every child, unless something terrible happens to stunt the child's normal development.

Each stage is characterized by an impulse that is an expression of the child's desire for connection and her impulse to experience that connection in the real world. In the attachment stage, the impulse is the desire to remain connected to the parent or caretaker. In the exploration stage, the impulse is the desire to connect to the environment. In the identity stage, the impulse is the desire to connect with others in order to learn who he is. When they reach middle childhood, which we call stage of concern, the impulse is to connect with others outside the family, especially same-sex peers. In the intimacy stage, which occurs in adolescence, the impulse is expressed in the desire to experience intimacy, sometimes sexual intimacy, with others of the opposite sex.[14]

The problems the child has later in life are the result of not evolving through these stages of development successfully. The conscious parent knows it is her job to help her child do that. She also knows that her child's growth and development looks like a spiral staircase. Each developmental impulse has its origin around a particular age but is visited over and over again as the child walks up the stairs of her life and as her experiences become more sophisticated and more complex. The same tasks reappear as the child gets older, each time at a higher level of development. This means that opportunities for healing occur over and over again, in childhood, in marriage, and in parenting. Our hope is that this book will help you prevent or repair the wounds of your children while they are directly in your care.

POSSIBILITIES FOR A CONSCIOUS FUTURE

Perhaps there is no greater contribution we can make in our lifetimes than helping our children become people who are mentally, emotionally, and morally strong. In the process of learning to parent in this way, we ourselves are healed from our personal pain and released into the larger world to do what we can to raise the dignity and value of all of life. In this sense, conscious parenting is a spiritual discipline.

Now that we have introduced you to the Imago Theory basics, we are ready to open the next door and start exploring these ideas in more depth. As you will recognize from our discussion in the next chapter, unconscious parenting is the norm. What form did it take when you were a child and what form might it be taking now as you parent your own children? Having a good, clear picture of the problem is the first step in resolving it.

11

RUPTURE OF CONNECTION

3

The Unconscious Parent

I've never felt so alone. I don't think I'm a worse mother
than my mother was, but raising kids is so much
harder today. I suppose you could say that my mother
neglected us kids. I can't afford to shut my eyes for one
minute, or my two boys will get in trouble. I don't feel
like I have what I need to do a good job.
—MOTHER OF TWO TEENAGE BOYS

A lot of very good people are having trouble feeling like good parents. There are decent, hardworking, law-abiding, churchgoing, school-supporting, child-loving people who feel overwhelmed by the magnitude of the job. They are distressed to find that what they always thought would be "natural" doesn't come so easily. Not only is rearing children hard, but many parents are less successful at it than they thought they would be. And national statistics reflect this. Some members of the population are doing well, but others are having significant problems.

In order to understand what is happening, we have to reexamine some fundamental patterns. It is time to take a new look at the relationship between parent and child and to reconsider how to maximize the healing potential that is inherent within it. We can establish parenting relationships that are good for *both* parents and children without sacrificing one to the other. We can parent our children in ways that meet their needs even when social circumstances are difficult, as they are for so many people. Whether a child is disadvantaged by being born into an overabundant or an underabundant environment, parents can nurture the qualities of compassion, creativity, productivity, moral intelligence, and spiritual awareness that our world needs now more than ever.

The inspiration for our new vision of parenting grows out of our understanding of what is not working now. In this book our focus is very fine. We are looking at the problems that come up in the *relationship* between parent and child on a personal level. We are well aware that there are other ways to examine the problems our children are having. For example, it is important to try to understand the complexities and implications of the declining quality of public education, increasing juvenile crime, the high level of teenage drug use, and the difficult realities of economic life, to name just a few.[1] These are important matters of great interest to us.

But there is a matter we think is even more important: the everyday interaction between parents and children. We believe that most problems in the public arena will be resolved only to the extent that radical changes are made in the home. Private moments have great social significance, as they reverberate outward from the home. When the same personal difficulties are repeated in household after household, whole generations grow up unable to contribute fully to their own happiness or their community's well-being.[2]

In this chapter and the one that follows, we will take a long, hard look at the problems that most of us have in the way we parent. We will examine private acts of unconsciousness between parent and child and see what effect these patterns have. We will form a clear model of what unconscious parenting sounds like, what it looks like, and how it hurts. In the next section we will start talking about how to change it.

WE ARE ALL UNCONSCIOUS

Our use of the term "unconscious" may sound negative, but we don't mean it to be. We contrast "unconscious" with "conscious," and it sounds as though we may be opposing "bad" with "good." But our intention is to use the term "unconscious" as a description rather than a judgment. The term refers to the beliefs we hold, the actions we take, and the behaviors and feelings we experience that are "out of awareness" and therefore out of our control.[3] So universal is unconsciousness and so common are the difficulties that arise from it that we might as well call human parenting unconscious parenting.

Unconsciousness and consciousness occur along a continuum for all of us. None of us are openly aware all the time, or closed and unaware all the time. Our intention here is to help people move to a place where they act and speak with greater conscious awareness most of the time. It is important for us to underscore that unconscious parents are not bad people. They are wounded people who have not had a chance to heal into greater self-awareness and self-acceptance. We are talking, in other words, about most of us.

In fact, many unconscious parents also have wonderful qualities. They are good people who are kind, caring, and committed. Our purpose is to see the unconsciousness in ourselves and in everyone around us with a compassionate heart. A colleague of ours talks about his experience in understanding how these two seemingly opposed realities can occur in one person. "When I start feeling judgmental, I always think of my grandmother. She is a saint and has been the true mother of our family. There isn't anything she wouldn't do for us. But . . . she doesn't listen. She asks me something about myself and then is silent, waiting for me to stop talking. Then she says something to either approve or disapprove, or says something about herself. She is the center of her universe. I love her, everyone does, and she would do anything for anyone as long as she thought it was what they needed. But she has yet to know the inner world of anyone around her."

LISTENING FOR REACTIONS

Let's start by learning more about what unconscious parenting is. Perhaps we can get a better sense of what the concept means by familiarizing ourselves with how it *sounds*. The following are verbal reactions to the upsetting things kids do or want to do and are examples of what unconscious parenting sounds like:

- *"Don't do that. I told you not to tip your chair back. You never listen. See what happens!"* This from a mother whose six-year-old daughter has just leaned her chair back and tipped it over, hurting herself in the process.
- *"Get out of the street. If I ever see you do that again, that bicycle is gone. Now, put it away. You obviously don't know what you are doing. You are so careless."* This from a father whose son was just learning to ride a bicycle and who had lost control and ridden into the street.

- *"You can't be tired. You must just be hungry. Here, eat this apple."* This from a mother whose preschooler wanted to rest at the shopping mall.
- *"No way are you staying out until midnight. You know what happens. Girls get pregnant."* This from a father whose fifteen-year-old daughter was going on her first date.

These are simple examples of understandable but potentially wounding parental reactions to everyday events. They may be hurtful, but whether or not they are really damaging depends on whether they are part of an overall pattern that violates the essential self of the child. When we refer to unconscious parenting, we mean more than a single overreaction. In its mild form unconscious parenting is everyday experience in which we think we know what our children want or feel, or what they should want or feel. In its extreme form, unconscious parenting is a pervasive pattern of cruelty and neglect that permeates every aspect of a person's life.

LISTENING FOR LIFE STORIES

Unconscious parenting may be the defining pattern of interaction in the family. This example comes from a twenty-nine-year-old woman executive of a national hotel chain, whom we'll call Susan. She sought help regarding her boyfriend's distress about her "unapproachable and emotionally cold nature." She came to therapy carefully groomed and well dressed and had a decidedly successful presence. During the second session the therapist felt that a bond of trust was beginning to build and asked her to talk about herself as a child:

Susan: You're the only other person I've ever told this to besides my boyfriend. My father killed himself when I was ten, hung himself. I wasn't home when it happened, and I never saw the body. For the longest time, I didn't believe he was dead. I thought maybe he just decided to walk out on us. He was a handyman, and I remember that he and my mother used to argue about some woman who always needed help with painting or the tile on her floor or some repair. But the worst was the dinner table. There were six of us: my mom, my two sisters, my brother, me, and him. I always had to sit beside him on his right. He wanted me near him so he could pick on me. I was the oldest. He never actually hit me. But he would slam down his hand near my plate or sweep my dinner onto the floor or yell at me for no reason. There were about three years there when this happened every night. "What are you lookin' at? You got a problem? Damn right you got a problem. You gonna have one you don't quit lookin' like that." It got so I couldn't eat. Neither could anyone else. I don't know why he picked me out from the rest.

When Susan was asked what effect her father had had on her life, she said she didn't think she carried too many scars. Her denial is not uncommon, because pain of this kind is often repressed. And after she talked for a while, she did concede that she is a perfectionist in her professional and personal life and that she has trouble with the closeness of an intimate relationship. We feel her pain, and the fact that she cannot shows how deeply and completely she has defended herself against her terrible wounding.

REMEMBERING

But unconscious parenting doesn't have to involve neglect, abuse, or abandonment, though it's easier to see it in a story like Susan's. It can be a lot less terrifying and still have a profound effect on the developing child. Here is a story from Harville's childhood that illustrates another way that automatic, unexamined reactions on the part of a parent (or in this case, a surrogate parent) can assume great significance for a child.

When I was about seven years old, I recall coming into the house one day singing loudly. I washed my hands and went to the dinner table to eat, still singing my song. I stopped long enough to join in a prayer of thanks with my sister and brother-in-law, who were in reality my "parents," since my mother and father had died when I was younger. As soon as the food was served, I started up my song again. Suddenly my brother-in-law looked at me sternly and said, "No singing at the dinner table. It's bad." "Why?" I asked. He lost his temper and said, "Just stop or leave the table!" I was stung.

Later, when I visited my brother-in-law as an adult, I asked him about it. He couldn't remember the incident, but he did say that his own mother had told him the same thing. He assumed that singing was "disrespectful to her and sinful." He was taught to eat in quiet reverence, fearing God and the disapproval of his parents.

When I became a parent, I was blessed with children who could sing and loved to sing, and I've always encouraged them to sing anytime, anywhere. But it took years of personal work and a change in my theology to undermine the power of that instruction. Sometimes I still have an uneasy feeling, especially when I join my children's singing at dinner. I hear inside my own head, "Don't sing at the table."

THE COMMON THREADS

What do these examples of unconscious parenting have in common? In each of them, the parent has no awareness of the consequences of his actions and makes no reference to the feelings of the child while he is taking action. The parent acts from his perception of what the child is doing but with *no understanding of how the child feels* or why he is doing what he is doing. The parent is not being consciously intentional, even when he is well-intentioned.

What else characterizes unconscious parenting?

It cuts. First, whether we are talking about a one-liner a parent delivers in a moment of fear for the child's safety or a pervasive pattern of abuse that ignores the essence of the child, *unconscious parenting is a knife*. It slices through the connection the parent has with her child, severing the invisible bond between them. It slices through the connection the child has with the universe, severing the cosmic bond. And it slices into the child himself, severing the bond he has with parts of himself that he now learns are not acceptable and must die.

Because his relationship with his parents is the medium through which a child experiences the qualities of the universe, a disruption between parent and child is an important matter. Will the child learn that the universe encourages wholeness, health, balance, consciousness, and love? Or will he experience the universe as cold, blind, and unfeeling? However he experiences it, his life will be shaped by this awareness.

By the overt but unconscious reaction of a parent, the little girl who tipped her chair over is cut off from a universe that cares whether she has hurt herself. The little boy who accidentally strays into the street while trying to learn to ride his bike is cut off from a universe that is tolerant of mistakes. The preschooler who is told to eat instead of rest is cut off from a universe that honors his bodily needs. The teenager who is made to feel guilty because she wants to stay out a little later with her date is cut off from a universe that allows her to have new experiences. Susan has been cut off from a universe where intimate contact is safe.

We know we are enumerating these losses as though they were permanent and irredeemable, but they are not. Though there are single incidents of incredible violence that are so damaging to children that they do not heal, these are not common, and we are not talking about them here. If it were not possible to heal from moments such as the ones we have described, or even from patterns of unconscious parenting such as the one Susan faced, we would all be doomed. Very few of us were raised by conscious parents. Very few of us are conscious parents ourselves. It's not a question of *whether;* it's a question of *how often and in what ways* we are unconscious in our closest relationships.

It is an inheritance. And this brings us to the second characteristic that all forms of unconscious parenting share. *Unconscious parenting is an inheritance.* Its roots reach back to parenting in ancient civilizations; its branches include parenting in all modern cultures.[4] All unconscious parents in all ages have parented from the deepest center of their wounded selves, perpetuating the pain of their past and repeating it in the future. It is the incomplete, unacknowledged, fearful, and shamed part of the parent that speaks and passes the legacy on to his children.

From a short story by Tobias Wolff, titled "*Nightingale,*"[5] here is one father's moment of recognition. He has just realized how big a role his own past has played in the dreadful mistake he just made with his son:

> Dr. Booth had wanted Owen out of the house. That was the truth, and it made no sense to him now. The impatience he felt, coming upon his son reading or playing with his dog, doing nothing, dreaming—why? What was the crime? As a boy, he himself had wanted nothing more than the chance to dream. It had come seldom in that crowded, industrious house, and never lasted long. Why should he begrudge his son what he had most desired? Why should he begrudge his son his childhood?

He is beginning to have regrets. For many years, he thought he saw his son for who he was, and he didn't like what he saw. He has allowed his disapproval and dislike of his own child to build up until he has impulsively enrolled him in a military school to teach him some discipline. He realizes, after it's too late, that his initial vision had been distorted by leftover resentments from his own cold and demanding childhood.

Like many parents, he has been living in a world of self-created paradox. He has begrudged his son what he himself most desired. Unconsciously, he has acted from some internal blueprint that influences his actions in ways that are contrary to his child's best interests. He misreads clues, misinterprets behavior, and gets the answers all wrong, seeing difficulties where none exist and never understanding the real problems at all.

We see this pattern often. A father or a mother carry a lot of anger at being cheated out of what they so badly wanted and needed when they were young. In a nightmare of unconscious retribution, they deprive their own children of the same things. They don't plan to become the same kind of cold, high-expectation parents they experienced as children, but they do.

It is unaware. These parents who feel cheated don't realize what they are doing to their children. This is the third characteristic that defines unconscious parenting. *It is unconscious.* Freud has given us the language we need to talk about why so much of who we are is hidden from our awareness. And only a small part of our conscious mind is available to us at any moment. It's easy to see why this has to be the case. What if we had to be consciously aware of all the rules of grammar, vocabulary, and syntax in order to speak intelligible sentences? What if we had to be aware of how to move our muscles in order to walk? What if we had to be aware of the mechanics of driving every time we turned on the ignition?

In the same way, the complexities and nuances of our ordinary, everyday mental and emotional experience is available to us a little out of our conscious awareness. It's there. We rely on the accumulated wisdom of our past experiences to shape the present moment for us. But we cannot be aware of all of our entire experiential legacy at any one time. If we were, we would be crushed by the weight of our own experience.

The wisdom of our unconscious also helps us know what to do to survive. It alerts us to danger and helps us move fast to counteract whatever is threatening us. Without it we might not live very long, because we would have to remember and process more information than is possible in a few critical moments. But as we will see, this survival function is a double-edged sword. Without mitigating counsel from the rational part of our brain, the unconscious can give us bad information—sometimes incomplete, sometimes inappropriate, and sometimes inaccurate. Something can *seem* threatening, and cause us to attack or react as if our lives were in danger, when the appearance is in fact deceptive. In this case we are not under threat and to react as though we were is counterproductive.

The aim here is for selective consciousness. We don't want to be swamped by our perceptions, but it is possible and desirable to open ourselves to more of what and who we are. When we stop denying parts of ourselves and protecting and hiding ourselves from ourselves, we come to know who we really are and accept ourselves. That means that more of our real self is available in our relationship with our children. We no longer need to parent them from a constricted, judged self but can respond to them from an open, accepting, loving self that is freer to accept and love them. It is possible to recognize our unconscious self and, in so doing, meet our own pain. When we meet our pain, we can begin to love our hurt parts back to health.

It causes exaggerated reactions. This brings us to our fourth characteristic of unconscious parenting. *Unconscious parenting is reactive.*[6] Parents know they have touched a sore spot in themselves when they find themselves over- or underreacting to something their child says or does. The hot buttons children push or the words they say that make parents pull back into their own safe space—these say more about *the parent* than they do about the child. Emotionally intense reactions that occur repeatedly and seem excessive to the parent, the child, or another adult are indications of a potential growth point for the parent. She has just identified an issue or a pattern that touches something important and painful in her own life. This is a gift. Parents need to know what their growth points are in order to move beyond them.

It is ignorance. Finally, unconscious parents don't realize that they are often overreacting to their child's normal behavior. This is because *unconscious parenting is ignorant of the specific needs of the child at each developmental stage.* There is no doubt that a child's perfectly healthy behavior can sometimes be annoying. If annoying behavior gets misidentified as problematic behavior, the parent's lack of conscious support can freeze the child's development at that stage. In another of parenthood's many ironies, *parents will have the most trouble guiding their* children through the stage that they themselves had trouble with when they were children.

A mother's fear may cause her to impose her worldview onto her child. She will impute her own fears and worries to her child, and will not fully recognize and honor that the inner world of her child is different from her own. If the mother found it difficult to pass through the exploration stage, for example, then she may be afraid when her daughter begins to explore the world.

To summarize, the unconscious parent behaves in ways that show little or no awareness of the unique or developmental needs of her child. She has no awareness of why she reacts the way she does or what effect she intends her reaction to have on her child. Whether these responses are negative or positive, intense or mild, what they all have in common is that they do not include sensitivity to the child's inner world. The unconscious parent doesn't participate in the child's worldview, but operates out of her own view of how the world works and what she thinks is best. In this sense the child becomes an object in the subjective drama created by the parent instead of being encountered as another, separate, sacred person.

SYMBIOTIC FUSION

Now that we have some idea of what unconscious parenting looks like, it's appropriate to ask where it comes from. What is the underlying problem that spawns all these different ways of rupturing connection? A parent who cannot see herself as separate from her child has developed a *symbiotic* relationship with the child. All forms of unconscious parenting come from *symbiosis*.

In Imago Relationship Theory we define *symbiosis*[7] as someone constructing an image of another person to which he relates as if it *were* the person. It is, moreover, the inclusion of this image within his own subjectivity that erases the boundary between himself and the other person. Symbiosis is present when a parent acts as though his child necessarily feels and thinks as he himself does, with no recognition of or respect for the otherness of the child. A parent who is symbiotic with his children is unsure about where he ends and they begin. He gets frustrated and angry when they don't read his mind and act accordingly.

Symbiosis both causes and results from the self-absorption that comes from the parent's own childhood wounding. The parent's own fundamental needs have not been met, so he projects his own constraints and wishes onto his children, who offer him another chance to live life the way he wished he had. Symbiosis is an expression of incomplete development on his part. He had children before he finished his own growing up. Problems such as blaming, distancing, inconsistent responses, and emotional incest occur when the parent reacts to his child in a way that attempts to take care of *his own* needs instead of interacting with his child to meet the *child's* needs.

The Old Brain

All parents have the tendency to be symbiotic. For some it is an occasional temptation, and for others it becomes a way of life. As you will recall, our old brain, even when we are not wounded severely, has trouble distinguishing between what has happened to *me* and what is happening to my children, who are *not me*. It has trouble distinguishing between what happened *then* and what is happening *now*. In heated moments, our wounds click in and we have only a "centric" consciousness. *My* feelings, *my* questions, *my* desires take over, and I lose the capacity to operate from a reality that includes the fact that *your* feelings, *your* questions, and *your* desires figure equally in the picture. The capacity to discern the finer distinctions between you and me, between then and now, are functions of the more sophisticated new brain, the cerebral cortex. Becoming conscious requires overriding the gut-level, me-centered survival instincts of the old brain. That's why we often say that conscious parenting is counterinstinctual.

Examples Are Everywhere

We all come to parenting with ideas about how we want ourselves to be and how we want our children to be. Sometimes our preconceptions are so overpowering that they prevent us from seeing and enjoying the child we have in front of us. Sometimes our children don't seem good enough. When that happens, we have a hard time helping them build on their real strengths and allowing them to be who they are.

Disappointed parents are all around us in popular culture and in real life. In fact, the theme of a father who is unable to accept the choices of his young-adult son is so common as to be a cliché. A recent example comes to mind. In the Hallmark Hall of Fame movie *Calm at Sunset*, a family conflict revolves around whether the younger son in the family is going to be able to do what he wants with his life. He has dropped out of college and returned home so he can work as a deckhand on a fishing boat. He wants to make fishing his life, saving enough money to have his own boat someday. His father, a struggling fisherman himself, is disappointed and cannot accept his son's rejection of college and a professional or white-collar career.

At one point his loving but worried mother asks her son, "But what about going back to college in the fall? What about getting your degree and going on to law school? You always wanted to be a lawyer." Her son answers, "No, Mom, *you* always talked about law school. *You* always wanted me to be a lawyer."

In television drama the lines are so clearly drawn! And sometimes in real life symbiosis is also overt and unmistakable. A woman recently related to us how her domineering father had a habit of calling her up, whenever he had had too much to drink, to tell her that she was a loser just like him. He was disappointed in her. He wanted her to achieve the success that had eluded him. He felt he never got a lucky break, he was too much of a pushover, he never figured out how to work the system— and that was why he couldn't hold a job or keep his marriage together. He told her *she* was just like him; she was a loser, too.

Even if this father had *never* said these words and had just acted as though they were true, the result would have been the same. She and her father were locked in a power struggle for her soul, and for many years her father won. Throughout her growing up years, she had trouble developing a self that she felt free to express.

In the next chapter, "The Child as Teacher," we will discuss how the self of a child fragments and becomes inaccessible to her as she develops defensive reactions to the intrusions of unconscious parenting. And we will see how this leads to self-hatred as the child unconsciously turns her back on some of her traits and exaggerates others in an attempt to present a self that is acceptable to her parents.

Parental Projection

Children who have had trouble expressing a full self grow up into adults who have the same problem. When symbiotic interactions originate from parents, it means that these parents have not become fully differentiated selves. In their own self-absorption, they have not completed the developmental task of becoming whole. They do not really know who they are. They cannot distinguish between themselves and their children, and they cannot respect clear boundaries between themselves and their children. And what they do not know about themselves, they unconsciously project onto their child.[8]

Parents in the symbiotic state don't know that the traits they experience in their children that bother them so much are aspects of themselves that they have rejected. They project unacknowledged aspects of themselves onto their children as restrictions, attributes, or wishes. In reality, what they are rejecting in their children, they have previously imprisoned or buried in themselves. At some point their own parents said to them, "You cannot be like that," or "I don't want to believe you are like that." Now they say to their own children, "You cannot be like that and be accepted in this home."

It's important to note that not all projected traits are undesirable. Some projected traits represent undeveloped positive potential in the parent. When a mother is awed by the "child prodigy" living under her roof, she may be admiring her own undeveloped intellectual potential. When she talks about her infant's extraordinary athletic ability, she may be reflecting her own unfulfilled dreams of becoming a sports superhero.

In yet another pattern of symbiotic projection, she may interact with her child as though *he* were the parent. She uses the child as a resource for herself. She interacts with him in a way that meets *her* needs for a nurturing parent. Since she requires this of him if he is to keep his mother's attention and love and thus survive, the child surrenders his childhood and becomes a premature adult who attempts unsuccessfully to become a parent to his parent.

Finally, a parent who is full of rules and child-rearing wisdom received from external sources—the way things are "supposed" to be done, without regard for the needs of the particular child—is exhibiting symbiotic behavior. All the information in this exchange goes one way, from parent to child. In conscious parenting the arrow points both ways, and parent and child learn wisdom from each other.

HOW DO YOU KNOW IF YOU'RE BEING SYMBIOTIC?

One of the basic tenets of this book is that language has the power to transform relationships. Intentional dialogue, as we will see in Chapter 5, is the most powerful tool parents have in their efforts to overcome symbiosis. Everything a conscious parent does, as we will see in Chapter

6, is done in the spirit of intentional dialogue. But even before we get to these in-depth discussions, let's begin our exploration of language right now by listening to the way parents can betray their unconscious assumption of fusion with their children by the words and sentences they use in everyday speech.

The Power of Language

Spoken language is the primary medium of interaction between parents and their children. It is a gift that enables a speaker to make the past or the future an experience of the present. When a father says, "Remember the time we went to the beach?" or "You can have that for your birthday," he is giving his child a gift in the present moment.

Language makes what is invisible visible. In describing the way a white horned owl looks against the snow, a father calls forth a vivid picture for his young son. When a mother talks about the way a prism disperses light into a spectrum, her daughter sees rainbows.

Language also makes us *feel*; for example, joy, as in "I love you," or pain, as in "Wait until your father gets home; he'll give you what for!" Children learn to speak as they are spoken to, whether in the language of their culture or in the symbiotic language of their parents. Language is the medium by which parents can imprison their children or free them to be themselves.

Recognizing Our Symbiotic Phrases

Unfortunately, unconscious parents often imprison their children by the words they use. Learning to talk differently is a path to conscious parenting. Below is a collection of sentences that reflect symbiotic consciousness. Each is paired with its opposite to indicate a parental consciousness that is not symbiotic and that can distinguish between oneself and others.

1. We often hear symbiotic language when parents are frustrated.

SYMBIOTIC:

"I am so tired of having to tell you that." OR "You didn't feed your pet again. You are so lazy; I wonder if you'll ever learn."

NONSYMBIOTIC:

"I know that I have told you several times about taking care of your pets. Have I been unclear?" OR "Do I need to say it in a different way? I get the feeling that I have not made myself clear." OR "I am aware that you did not feed your pet again. Tell me what you plan to do about it."

2. **We often hear symbiotic language when parents make assumptions that their children know what to do in a given situation.**

SYMBIOTIC:

"I can't believe you did not know what to say to your teacher. You sound like you have never been in this situation before."

NONSYMBIOTIC:

"I am confused about your response to your teacher. Can you tell me what you were feeling?"

3. **We often hear symbiotic language when parents are frustrated because their children don't immediately comprehend what they mean.**

SYMBIOTIC:

"You know what I mean." OR "What do you mean, you don't understand!"

NONSYMBIOTIC:

"Am I being clear?" OR "Do you have any questions?" OR "Is there any part of this that does not make sense to you?"

4. **We often hear symbiotic language when parents judge their children to be wrong because their views or feelings are different from those of the parents.**

SYMBIOTIC:

"You can't mean that!" OR "That's a stupid thing to say." OR "I can't believe that you believe that!" OR "You will make a mistake if you continue to believe that."

NONSYMBIOTIC:

"So you are saying, if I understand it, that . . ." OR "I want to hear all you have to say about that. I am interested in your thinking." OR "If

I understand you, you believe that . . . Is that right? Well, I can see your point of view. Will you listen to what I believe?"

5. **We often hear symbiotic language when parents fear losing control because their children are not behaving in ways the parents expect.**

SYMBIOTIC:

"I don't know what I am going to do with you." OR "I have tried everything and nothing works. You are incorrigible."

NONSYMBIOTIC:

"I realize you are upset right now, and I am sure we can work things out." OR "I can see that you have strong feelings about that and you want to be heard."

6. **We often hear symbiotic language when parents use "we" when referring to what their children feel and think, before clearing it first with the children.**

SYMBIOTIC:

"We had a great time at the zoo." OR "We are all feeling great today, aren't we?" OR "We loved our vacation, didn't we kids?"

NONSYMBIOTIC:

"I had a great time at the zoo. What was it like for you?" OR "I feel great today. How do you feel?" OR "I loved our vacation. How did you feel about it?"

7. **We often hear symbiotic language when parents are intense about attributing negative traits to their children.**

SYMBIOTIC:

"You have no heart." OR "You are untrustworthy." OR "You are selfish."

NONSYMBIOTIC:

"If I get it right, you are feeling hurt and angry, and you want to do something to get even. Is that right?" OR "I am aware you did not do what you said you would do. Will you tell me why you changed your mind?" OR "I know you are angry about what happened, but I want you to find another way to deal with the situation. I would like to talk with you about what you can do next time." OR "I am not sure exactly what you are feeling, but I know that sometimes when I feel angry, I want to hurt people. Are you feeling something like that?"

8. **We often hear symbiotic language when parents are overly involved and overly committed to their children's goals and activities.**

SYMBIOTIC:

"You must be a lawyer [or doctor, teacher, etc.]." OR "You have to learn competition skiing. You will be good at it and love it." OR "You didn't play hard enough today; you will never succeed if you don't try harder."

NONSYMBIOTIC:

"What would you like to be when you grow up?" OR "I understand you just love skiing, but that you don't really want to ski competitively. I will support you as far as you want to go." OR "I wish I could have skied competitively. Sometimes I wish you would do it so I could at least brag that one of my kids did it. But I am more interested in your doing what you want to do." OR "I am aware that you played differently today, not quite as hard as usual. Would you like to talk about how you were feeling or what was going on in your mind?"

9. **We often hear symbiotic language when parents state that what their children are experiencing isn't real.**

SYMBIOTIC:

"You don't think that." OR "You are not sick." OR "How could you feel cold? It is hot in here." OR "That is not what happened, and you know it." OR "I don't care what you think; that is not the way it is."

NONSYMBIOTIC:

"Sounds like we had different experiences; tell me about yours, and then I want to tell you about mine." OR "From what I hear you say, you are feeling sick today. Tell me about it." OR "I don't understand how two people can feel hot and cold in the same room. But that is what seems to be happening. Would you like me to get you a sweater or turn up the heat a bit?" OR "We seem to have different memories of what happened. Let's tell each other what we each experienced in the situation. Then we can understand each other better." OR "I am very interested in what you think about it. We may have different thoughts, and that is okay, but we must understand each other's point of view."

10. **We often hear symbiotic language when parents talk as though there were an absolute truth and they have access to it. This is often accompanied by frustration at the fact that the child's behavior indicates he does not know the "truth."**

SYMBIOTIC:

"You know what is right." OR "I can't believe you don't know that." OR "Any smart person would know that." OR "You know I am right."

NONSYMBIOTIC:

"I have a point of view about what do in this situation, and I want you to know what I think. Since I don't know what you think, let's talk about it so we can make it happen differently." OR "I don't know what is right about that, but I do know what I think about it, and I want you to know my thoughts. I may have to make the decision, and you may not like it, but I am the parent and I am responsible for your welfare." OR "It makes sense to me that you did not know about that since you have not had any experience with it." OR "I know you are very smart and you can figure it out. If you need help, just let me know."

11. **We often hear symbiotic language when parents suggest that they know how their children are feeling or ought to feel in a situation.**

SYMBIOTIC:

"I know how you are feeling." OR "You should be feeling that, given what you did." OR "Any decent person would feel that way." OR "Don't you know how you should feel about that?"

NONSYMBIOTIC:

"Tell me how you are feeling. I don't know, but I want to." OR "If I were in your shoes, and that happened to me, I would be feeling . . . , but you may have a different feeling [or I hear you are having a different feeling]." OR "I can imagine how a person who cares would feel about that, but I may be wrong." OR "Sounds like you don't know quite how you ought to feel about that. How *do* you feel?"

The symbiotic statements above are united in their lack of awareness that we live in a relative universe with multiple intelligences and that different people see things differently. None of us have a monopoly on the truth. None of us can stand in one place and see the whole truth. Like everything else in the universe, our relation to one another is constantly changing. All things are in motion, and that influences the state of every other thing. Everything modulates in response to changing contexts, and everything looks different if viewed from another angle. There is no center from which we can see the whole, no absolute position that makes all other positions peripheral. We ourselves are peripheral to the position of another.[9]

An unconscious parent believes he stands in the center of the truth with regard to his children. But to relate to his child, or anyone else for that matter, a parent must change his perception of himself as the center of the universe and risk the indeterminate possibilities of a relative universe. A conscious parent knows this, and he approaches other people and who they are with a spirit of inquiry and with respect for experiences different from his own.

As you read through this list of symbiotic sentences above, you may have recognized yourself, or you may have remembered other symbiotic sentences you've used, or you may have remembered things other people have said. We find it useful to encourage people to write these sentences down on paper and also to write down nonsymbiotic alternatives. We have suggested a way to do that in Chapter 15. These alternatives are sentences that will allow you to express yourself accurately in the same problem situation, but which will also explicitly acknowledge that *your child is not you and you are not your child.* These alternative sentences come from a consciousness in which you have differentiated yourself from your child. Learning to speak nonsymbiotic sentences not only will free your child from your projections, but will increase your sense of your own boundaries. Your words will show an enhanced understanding of your child's experience and a desire to respect and help maintain his wholeness.

UNCONSCIOUS PARENTING STYLES

In the previous chapter we defined Imago Relationship Theory as the science of patterns in marriage and parenting. One of the most important is the pattern of interaction parents demonstrate as they go about the daily business of raising their children. Some parents are naturally attuned to their children and intuitively respond with accuracy to their children's frustration and joy. But most of us did not learn conscious attunement from our own parents, and we manifest one of two unconscious parenting patterns: we are underinvolved, or we are overinvolved.

In order to make these two styles comprehensible and memorable for the reader, we will often talk about them in their more extreme forms. But these descriptions should be read with certain things kept in mind. For one, the characteristics we describe occur along a continuum. They fall along a line that progresses from subtle to obvious. Depending on the severity of the childhood wound the parent sustained and his stage of development at the time, he will exhibit either strong characteristics or more subtle characteristics of one parenting style. For this and other reasons, it can be difficult for him to recognize himself. Besides it always seems to be easier for us to identify the behavior of other people. And this provides us with a clue to understanding ourselves better. If a husband can't identify his own parenting style but can clearly see that his wife is underinvolved, for example, he can be reasonably certain that he is overly involved. In all families, the tendency is for one parent to have the overinvolved style and the other parent to have the underinvolved style.

Although it is not intentional on the part of the parents, there is a lot of wisdom in raising children with exposure to both styles. The two approaches provide a balance within the system of the family, so that the children are not always subjected to one way of responding to the world, to the exclusion of the other. There is a positive value in the balance this provides. Simply put, the parent who holds in her energy provides necessary stability, and the parent who expresses his energy provides necessary creativity and emotional facility. The problem is that these positive characteristics become negative when parents become rigid and not flexible. Ideally, each parent would freely and easily move from one style to the other as appropriate, depending on the requirements of the particular parenting situation. And some parents can do that. Most of us, however, tend to be bound to one kind of response and have difficulty with the other, and loosening those bonds requires conscious attention.

Potentially, every child has the capacity to respond to her environment with the whole range of survival strategies that is possible for human beings. But each child grows up in a family that selects some over others. And every child identifies with the strategies of the parent who is dominant for him or her. In the same family, different children can identify with different parents, and therefore with different defensive strategies. So each child grows up with a style that has been selected and integrated to the point where it feels completely natural.

So, as you read the descriptions that follow, keep in mind that you will see characteristics of both styles in yourself and in your spouse. As the book progresses, you will be able to see more clearly which style you tend toward and how this tendency affects the way you parent your children.

Parents who are underinvolved most likely had a dominant parent (a parent who influenced them more strongly or with whom they had more trouble) with the same underinvolved style. A parent with an underinvolved style is called a minimizer. Conversely, overinvolved parents probably had a dominant parent with the same overinvolved style. A parent with an overinvolved style is called a maximizer.[10] As we have said, we are all mixtures of both. There is no black and white, although most people recognize pretty quickly that they are more one than the other.

The maximizer expresses her behavioral and emotional energy more intensely than the minimizer. Neither style is attuned to the child's needs; instead, they are expressions of the needs and defenses of the parent. The parent's unconscious style is an adaptation[11] she has made to her own wounds rather than an in-the-moment response she makes to the needs of her children. Her habitual reactions are like paw prints in the snow. They say something about who she is and where she's been. Fortunately, habitual reactions can be changed.

The Minimizer Parent. Let's talk about the minimizer first. When the minimizer was a child, the parent with whom she had the most difficulty was emotionally and often physically unavailable to meet her needs. When she approached her parent with a need, her parent's response was to push her away with rejection or lack of response. Sometimes her parent shamed her or responded in a way that made her feel guilty or incompetent. He offered her no guidance about relating to her friends or to the opposite sex. Those responses were so painful that the child eventually withdrew, shutting down her own energy, feeling helpless and depressed, and sometimes worthless and alone. She learned not to ask, and later, in order to feel safe, she learned not to express need. Without contact with her own needs, she became insensitive to the needs of others, thus copying the parent who was the source of her greatest pain and becoming in adulthood a minimizer parent herself.

The minimizer parent, preoccupied with her own life as an adult, has little time for her children. She's not warm and seems to be incapable of empathy. Whatever feelings she has, she keeps to herself. Having no contact with her own needs, she is impatient with the needs of her child. She shares little of her thoughts or experiences with her children, and she doesn't ask about theirs. She is a loner who usually does not share her space with her children. Her boundaries are rigid. Having had no support as a child, she tends to take direction only from herself and offers little direction to her children. When she is crowded, she may react impulsively, handing out punishment or making demands. She exerts control and then withdraws into her shell. Insensitive to the needs of her children, she leaves their care to others, usually her spouse, and takes little part in seeing to the child's welfare. When she is involved with her children, it is usually to engage them in competition or to talk to them on an intellectual or abstract level. She is quiet at the dinner table, disturbing herself only to correct or discipline. She does not know how to share her feelings and become intimate. Her children do not feel close to her. They often fear her, and they learn very early not to bother her. The child of a minimizer parent grows up emotionally alone.

The Maximizer Parent. When the maximizer was little, the parent with whom he had the most difficulty tended to be ambivalent, sometimes warmly available and sometimes emotionally or physically absent. When this parent was available, she tended to project her own needs onto her child and to parent him as she wished she had been parented. She showered him with so much attention that she smothered him. But when he became demanding, she often withdrew or pushed him away. When he was curious, she overprotected him. Having no clear sense of herself, she could not validate her child's emerging identity or teach him how to become competent. She overstructured her child's relationship to peers, teaching him to meet *their* needs instead of his own.

The maximizer parent has identified with *his* maximizer parent and now carries on the same tradition. He is so full of unmet needs that he smothers his child with affection as a way of vicariously meeting his own needs. He is full of feelings and fears, often sharing them with his child in the form of warnings about the dangers of the world. When he is frustrated at his child, he will explode with anger or rage and then collapse with remorse and apology. He invades every part of his child's life, giving advice she hasn't asked for. He likes his children to keep their doors open so he can hear if they are sleeping well or doing something wrong. He talks incessantly at the dinner table, inquiring into the private lives of his children, interfering with their relationship to their peers. He likes to have lots of people around to increase his security, so he encourages his children to have friends over often. He feels children have no ability to know what they want and offers them what they haven't asked for and often do not need.

When he feels tragic or joyful about something, he expresses intense emotion and hopes others will share in it. He acts impulsively, expressing his feelings as if they were unimportant, and tends to overvalue other people's point of view. Having little sense of self, he takes direction from others about how to raise his children, keeping himself and his children dependent.

Since his boundaries are lax, he does not know how to protect his space from his children or how to honor their space, in turn. When he cannot get his way with a child, he will manipulate or bribe and claim that what he is doing is in the child's best interest. When he cannot have his way, he collapses into passivity and depression, coercing his child to take care of him. His life is unfocused, self-abnegating, and martyred. He presents himself as a self-sacrificing person who meets other's needs before his own, but those who benefit from his generosity end up feeling guilty after he repeatedly points out what he has done for them. The child of a maximizer parent grows up without being able to clearly separate from his parent and become an independent adult.

Identifying Your Style. The chart on page 67 summarizes the essential features of the maximizer and minimizer parent. At this point, you may be wondering to what degree you are an unconscious parent and whether you are over- or underinvolved with your children. You may recognize some aspects of yourself and your parenting style in both columns of the chart. This may make it difficult to put yourself in either category. Be assured that the labels we are using are only for the purpose of helping us make some useful distinctions for the sake of discussion and clarity. They aren't meant to make you feel pigeonholed. As you read this and later chapters, don't be alarmed if you find some descriptions that fit you but are unattractive. Nearly all of us are wounded to some degree, and our parenting is affected by it. Our courage to recognize the wound and own it is our source of hope.

It can be difficult for people to come to terms with the reality that each of us identifies most strongly with the parent we had the most trouble with, although we certainly internalize traits from both. Thus, the child who had a dominant minimizer parent becomes like his minimizer parent, and as a parent himself he becomes underinvolved. The child who had a dominant maximizer parent becomes like his maximizer parent, and as an adult he becomes by turns overinvolved and neglectful. The good news is that this legacy is not written in stone. Minimizing and maximizing are only defenses; they are not the essence of the person. They can be changed. Underneath the armor of every parent is the original person, with the potential for full aliveness and empathic relating that has been there since birth.[12]

In the chart on page 67 you may find some characteristics in both columns that apply to you. This is to be expected, since all of us have the capacity for all of the defenses used by minimizers and maximizers. Each of us tends to select one or the other as a means of protection because it is more adaptive for us. But there are at least two kinds of situations in which we might switch. First, we might change tactics when the dominant or selected defense does not work. If a minimizer, for example, fails to get the safety he needs by withdrawal, he might become aggressive. Or a maximizer who fails to get the attention he needs by exaggeration and self-sacrifice might start withdrawing and containing his energy. The second situation occurs when we are in the presence of another person whose similar defense is more exaggerated than our own. For example, if we, as maximizers, are relating to another maximizer who exaggerates more than we do, we might downplay our energy in order to maintain a balance of energy in the exchange, and therefore avoid a collision. On the other hand, if we, as minimizers, are relating to a minimizer who withdraws more than we do, we will be more expressive in order to maintain a balance and keep the interaction alive.

It sometimes happens that a parent will switch styles. When this happens, the other will switch in response. A minimizer might switch to being a maximizer in response to a child who retreats from contact. A maximizer might switch to being a minimizer in response to a child who is having a tantrum. In other words, these are not fixed categories for us, however much one tends to predominate over the other in an individual. When the context changes, we can change in response.

As you review the chart on page 67, assess on a scale of one to five the degree to which you exhibit each characteristic. A 1 would indicate that you always do this, 2 indicates that you almost always do it, 3 indicates that you sometimes do it, 4 indicates that you occasionally do

THE BEHAVIORS OF MAXIMIZER AND MINIMIZER PARENTS

MAXIMIZER	MINIMIZER
Tends to explode feelings outward.	Tends to implode feelings inward.
Tends to exaggerate emotions and smother children with attention.	Tends to diminish emotions and withhold them from the child.
Tends to be dependent on others for guidance about rearing children.	Tends to deny dependency and ignore advice of others about children.
Tends to exaggerate his own needs and needs of children.	Tends to deny his own needs and devalue child's needs.
Tends to act compulsively. Appears open and subjective, but is secretly defensive.	Tends to obsess but shares little of his or her inner world.
Tends to be overly inclusive of others in his personal space and invasive of children's space.	Tends to exclude others from his personal space and avoid children's space.
Tends to cling to his children while claiming excessive generosity.	Tends to neglect children's feelings, thoughts, and behaviors and withhold his own.
Tends to have unclear self-boundaries and to be unaware of his children's boundaries.	Tends to have rigid self-boundaries but includes children in his boundaries.
Tends to be outer-directed; generally asks for direction from others.	Tends to be inner-directed; takes direction mainly from himself.
Tends to focus self-sacrificingly on the needs of others.	Tends to think mainly about himself.
Tends to act impulsively.	Tends to obsess compulsively about what to do.
Tends to act submissively and manipulatively.	Tends to try to dominate others.
Tends to alternate between aggressiveness and passivity.	Tends to be passive-aggressive.

it, and 5 indicates that you never do it. It might help to write the numbers down on the page. This will help you see, not only which parenting style you have, but to what degree. And it will remind you of the fluidity of these descriptions (see chart, page 67).

In the next chapter, as we look at life from the point of view of the child, we will continue exploring these concepts. You will be able to continue sorting out how you were parented and how your childhood experiences now influence your perceptions and your behavior as you shepherd your own children toward adulthood.

A PERSONAL EXAMPLE

Almost all of us can see ourselves in the patterns of unconscious parenting described above. We want you to know that both of us have walked this road. Both of us have come face-to-face with our own inabilities and our own inadequacies. We have had to humble ourselves before the evidence that we were wounding the children we so deeply loved. We have had to change.

Here is how one father now understands his own struggle to break out of the pattern of symbiotic fusion with his firstborn son:

> As a young man and a father, I was unable to separate my son's childhood from my own. I was raised by sharecroppers in the south, and we worked hard just to survive. This is what I brought to my role as a parent. I exacted from him what had been exacted from me as a boy. I had transcended my origins, and I expected him to be just as driven to achieve. In essence, I was forcing his experience to be my experience, even though I knew that the times and the circumstances had changed. And I was full of anger and envy when he didn't see things the way I saw them. For many years, instead of facing my own conflicting feelings about my childhood, I attacked and criticized him, withdrawing my love and making my son feel bad about himself.
>
> The realization of what I was doing was the beginning of my work on parenting. I began to see the pattern of my behavior and recognized my inability to differentiate my son's childhood from my own childhood. With the help of serious reading and therapy, I realized that I would have to carefully focus my awareness on cultivating an understanding of my unconscious motiva-

tion. Specifically, I needed to recognize where I was incomplete and see how those areas interfered with my ability to give my son what he needed from me. As my own personal struggle in my marriage revealed to me the imago that I held inside, so my journey as a father revealed to me what I called the symbiotic fusion that many of us have with our children. We are unable to recognize on a deep level that we are not our children. This fusion inhibits us from being the parents our children need. The work I did took years, but the results have benefited my entire family and myself. Now I take genuine pleasure in my son's artistic endeavors, and in turn, I give him encouragement to follow his true path.

We tell you this story to underscore once again that we are all more or less in the same boat and that transformation is possible, even with a child who is grown and gone. As we said in the beginning of this chapter, the first step in this transformation is understanding. In order to clarify our discussion of unconscious parenting, we now present a summary of how an unconscious parent *thinks*. If you recognize your own ideas in any of these statements, rejoice that you have begun your own parenting transformation.

WHAT AN UNCONSCIOUS PARENT THINKS

1. An unconscious parent sees his child as an extension of himself and thus privy to all that the parent thinks and feels.
2. An unconscious parent believes that his reality is the only true reality, thus confusing parental authority and responsibility with godlikeness.
3. An unconscious parent believes he is responding to the child's behavior, when in actuality he is usually responding to something that happened to himself in the past.
4. An unconscious parent believes that the child's experience is not valid unless it is congruent with his own.
5. An unconscious parent believes that the child has the same information he has.
6. An unconscious parent believes it is her job to shape her child and that the child's behavior reflects directly on her.
7. An unconscious parent believes that all children are alike and is unaware that children develop in stages.

8. An unconscious parent believes that conflicts between parent and child arise because of something the child is doing wrong and does not see her own part in the difficulties.

9. An unconscious parent sees the parental role as fixed and the child's as pliable, so there is nothing the parent thinks she can learn from her child.

THE NEXT STEP

It can be comforting to remind ourselves that children give parents a lot of latitude. Children become attached to their parents and love them even though the parents are flawed and their parenting isn't perfect. In fact, a child can learn a lot from a parent who makes visible his attempts to grow and to learn and to do things better. Children are flexible, and parents too have a greater capacity to stretch and change than they sometimes realize. In the next chapter we will continue our discussion of symbiosis and unconscious parenting styles as we focus on how parents can learn from their own children how to be better parents and more complete human beings.

4

The Child as Teacher

In life, the issue is not control, but dynamic
connectedness.
—ERICH JANTSCH, *The Self-Organizing Universe*

DYNAMIC CONNECTION

Science is just beginning to help us realize a new synthesis—between the mind and the body, between the material and the spiritual, and among all things that exist within the universe. We now know that we are held equally close by insects and by stars. The last molecule of the beetle's wing was born when the universe began, as were the particles of life that allow our human lungs to breathe and our brains to know.

All the things that occupy our world, whether made by us or not, are created from a few handfuls of elements. And the stuff of life is in all the things of life. Humans are not made from finer materials than worms, and the chemistry that creates us both is substantially the same.

We are born connected, the circumstances of our birth being a reflection of the mechanics of the universe. The modern study of physics[1] is giving substance to our inborn yearning for connection. Now when we look around us we are beginning to see things differently. Where we used to see categories, we now see a continuum. The line between you and me and the line between ant and leaf are not so sharp. We know the differences between us, but we are better able to see what connects us to each other and are more sensitive to the processes that include us in the same system. We are sensitive to the energy flow *between* different forms of life and the interaction that includes them both.[2]

One unexpected result of this new view is the curious way in which physicists begin to sound like poets. To the poet, other living organisms announce our place in the family of nature. To the physicist, mathematically predictable processes do the same. But they both end in the same place, in the experience of dynamic connectedness and the unity of all things.

Our work with couples and with families has always focused on connectedness. Our concern is not primarily man's union with the ant and the leaf, but with the way people are connected to each other in their intimate relationships. You can think of this chapter as being about the dynamic connectedness of parents and children. We are going to focus on how much children can teach their parents about children, about parents, and about the creative energy that unites all of life.

REVISIONING THE CHILD

Throughout history the child has been many things to the parent: appendage, clone, laborer, surrogate parent, burden.[3] As part of our revisioning of the parenting relationship, we are advocating that parents adopt a new way of seeing a child, not as one of the above, but as *an emissary from the conscious universe and as a teacher.* A child is born from the cosmos itself into wholeness, experiencing fully the reality of her wholeness. She is born with an innate developmental plan for her completion, which is consonant with the processes of the universe and which includes self-expansion, self-completion, self-repair, and self-reflection. She and we also are a point where the universe becomes conscious of itself.[4]

The job of the parent is to maintain connection to the child so that she can maintain her connection to her parent and so that she can maintain her awareness of connection to the cosmos. She will then be able to expand her connection in an ever-widening circle of relationships through all the developmental stages of attachment, exploration, identification, concern, and intimacy. The parent's responsibility is to meet the needs of his child through these developmental stages and to support the expression of her inborn self.

The conscious parent is able to do this, because he has undertaken his own journey toward consciousness. As he progresses, he takes in feedback from himself, from others, and, most important, from his child. Feedback from himself comes in the form of *emotional reactions* to the child. Feedback from spouses, partners, and other adults comes in the form of their *approval* of what he is doing or their *discomfort* with his parenting, expressed as criticism, advice, or suggestions. Feedback from the child comes in the form of *resistance* to his parenting, *passive compliance* to his parenting, or *positive response* to his parenting.

In this chapter we will talk about the importance of all these different kinds of feedback. But, because our underlying goal is to help parents revision their children as teachers, we will emphasize what parents can learn from their children. In order to see your child as teacher, you must first see her for who she is. When you truly see her, you have taken a critical first step in being able to give her what she needs and in releasing yourself from the bondage of your own past.

THE CHILD YOU HAVE

Parents can start by making every effort to see the child they have instead of the one they *think* they have. This is easy to say, but as we have seen, it is hard for many parents to do. Walk into any supermarket, and it's likely you'll hear yourself or some other parent say things like the following: From a mother, gesturing to her teenage daughter: "Why do you want to go to nursing school? You just *think* you want to go. You won't like it." Or a father to his seven-year-old son: "You don't want to take ballet. You're strong and athletic. Soccer will be better." Or from the exasperated mother of a tired two-year-old: "Don't tell me you're tired! Do what I tell you to do."

By now we are alert to this kind of language as an indication of symbiosis. In such moments at least, these parents are unable to form an accurate picture of who their children are or to respond to them in a way that respects their individuality. The feeling you get from overhearing these interchanges is that the parent has decided what's best, and it's no use for the child to argue.

A parent who wants to start seeing the child she *has* must look beneath the surface for the patterns that govern their relationship. A child will respond to his parent's actions and words in certain predictable ways. In her role as parent, his mother will interact with her child according to certain patterns that either interfere with or allow her full comprehension of him as a unique and beautiful person. The parent can become aware of her blind spots, which result not from a cognitive inability to see or understand but from unaddressed needs that belong to her. She can learn how her own wounds are diverting her attention from her child.

Even if the parent grew up in a safe, nurturing environment, she still carries invisible wounds. From the very moment she was born, she has been a complex, dependent creature with a never-ending cycle of needs, and her parents, no matter how devoted, responded to her imperfectly. Her wounds may be small and manageable, but they are still there.

Knowing this can help explain the misfires we all experience in parenting our children—our withdrawals and overreactions that seem to come out of nowhere. If our wounding has been minimal, we are puzzled by these blips on the screen; if our wounding has been deeper, we are thrown into confusion by our exaggerated reactions.

THE EFFECTS OF SYMBIOSIS

Before we look at the kinds of information a parent can receive directly from her child, let's deepen our understanding of the patterns that cause the problems. Just what happens to a child on the receiving end of such remarks as those we overheard in the supermarket? How and in what way does the child get wounded? As we said in the preceding chapter, a child in a symbiotic relationship with a parent is in pain and, as a result, becomes self-absorbed. Pain is self-centered. It closes in on itself and blocks the reception of information from the outside. When the child isn't able to receive and use information from his environment, he loses his ability to create his world in concert with his real-world experience. As a consequence his brain begins to *make up* a "real" world in its place, and the child relates to the world of his own creation as though it were real, without inquiry or consultation. Other people become constructs of his imagination and are created according to his emotional state and his needs. In this state of emotional symbiosis, there is no distinction between the inside and the outside, between the self and another person. There is no awareness of two realities, no I and Thou.[5] Everything is related to as an IT and treated as an object. The child, and later the adult, has no awareness that what he is perceiving is not real.

One indicator of symbiosis is irritability and frustration when other people do not demonstrate a perfect congruence with the child's ego-centered world. The unique experience of other people is devalued and replaced by his own. As he gets older, if his own self continues to be overlooked or overruled, he will exert pressure on others to be more like him by threatening, devaluing, or criticizing their experience. In his unconscious insistence that other people share his subjective states, his thoughts, and his feelings, he will become more like his symbiotic parent until he functions with the same code of behavior. He will treat others in the same way he has been treated and follow the same maxim: *We are one, and I am the one.*

Paying the Price. A child who has been parented by a symbiotic parent pays a price. Every time she has an encounter with a parent who does not see and respect her for the person she is, a part of her is wounded in the encounter. This is what we mean by *wounding: stunting a child's impulse toward wholeness in order to make him more acceptable to his parent.* The parent, of course, does not intend to stunt the impulse. But he does intend to regulate or control the behavior. It is important to understand that wounding can be in the form of giving a child too much, as well as not giving enough. A child who is overprotected is as wounded as one who is underprotected. A "spoiled" child has not been given the boundaries and limits he needs in order to thrive.

In these unconscious interactions, the child feels that her survival is threatened, and she will respond by unconsciously hating the part of herself the parent has injured. She will repress or reject that part, and it will become part of her "fragmented self." Her fragmented self contains those aspects of her character that are natural to her but that have become denied, disowned, or lost through hurtful encounters with the parent. One of the observable effects of wounding is that the child tends to retreat into herself, becoming more self-absorbed and less able to identify with others.

But her fragmented self never really goes away. As we have seen, it has its own will to survive. Those parts of her missing self that are not permitted to come into conscious awareness will surface as traits or characteristics that she attributes to other people. In other words, as the wounded child grows up, she will *project* the same missing traits or characteristics onto other people as her parents did onto her. Because she is unconsciously compelled to maintain her wholeness—even if it is an artificial wholeness—she will relate to the traits she projects onto other people, either critically or adoringly, depending upon the trait. And she will not know she is doing it.

Relating in such a way maintains a relationship to her missing self. This is one of the many ways that a child who has been wounded by unconscious parenting will deal with her wounds. Unless she takes steps to heal them, they will break to the surface to cause grief in the relationships she has with intimate partners and with her own children.

THE FRAGMENTED SELF

A child who is wounded by symbiotic parenting will feel under attack. His impulse to act for survival directs him to get rid of whatever behavior of his unleashed the fury of the all-powerful parent. He will put up defenses around the parts of himself his parents don't approve of and begin to protect his soft, vulnerable inner self with a tough, impenetrable outer self. This action serves the very real purpose of keeping him safe, but at a terrible cost. Repression prevents the growth and development of the whole person. He starts building walls between himself and the outside world, brick by brick.

Let's take a closer look at how repression serves to protect the child from aspects of his character that, at some level below awareness, he perceives to be dangerous to his survival because they are threatening to his parent. Below the surface the core self splits into four different "selves" as a defense against the wounding that results from symbiotic parenting. These are the *presentational self*, the *lost self*, the *disowned self*, and the *denied self*.

The Presentational Self: Some qualities and characteristics in a child may become exaggerated or manufactured. The child may turn himself into an actor in order to disguise the parts of himself he needs to hide, presenting other traits that serve his purpose better. He puts together a persona that seems to serve him well, even though it is not natural to him.

One person who came to understand the magnitude of his presentational self in shaping his life choices is a man we'll call James, a middle-aged general manager whose marriage was in shambles. Here he describes the collapse that had begun over two years before: "I crashed. I broke down, and my life just fell apart. Nothing I did worked anymore. I was a lousy father and a lousy husband. I was failing at my job. My life felt like one big lie. There was my outside life that everyone thought was great, and there was my inside life—which I don't share with anyone, can't share in fact. It's like I had two different lives."

When James talks about being broken, he is profoundly accurate. His wholeness *had* been broken. He had spent his life till then living out a part in someone else's drama. In order to recover his lost wholeness, he had to reconstruct for himself and his wife the kind of wounding he had experienced as a child. As he thought about his relationship with his mother, he began to see some connections between the "lie" he felt he was living and his childhood experience: "My mother had had a hard time growing up, especially because of her father. She had me late in her life. I was her only son. She wanted me—no, she *needed* me—to be a certain way. I had to have certain thoughts, ones she could handle. There were choices I needed to make in order to make her feel better about the choices she had made. She didn't want to be hurt. Now I can see that it didn't have much to do with me. Going into business, holding the same good job forever, was what was okay with her. Not what I wanted. I don't like managing people. Whenever I did or said something that wasn't in her program, she accused me of being just like her father—irresponsible, unpredictable, selfish. So I did everything I could to be the opposite—responsible, predictable, and unselfish, at least as she defined it."

If the child's real self is not accepted, then he will create a presentational self that runs interference for him. Often, as in James's case, this presentational self is socially acceptable, charming, outwardly successful, and positive—a source of parental pride. Sometimes, however, the presentational self is tough, uncooperative, and a source of parental embarrassment. In either case the child may have the sense of something artificial in the beginning; but if the persona works for him, this awareness will gradually diminish, and he will actually believe that he is the Poor Soul or John Wayne or the Long-Suffering Martyr—or whichever character he has adopted.

The Lost Self: In this form of repression, the child seems to lose the four functions of the self: thinking, feeling, moving, and sensing disappear from the child's awareness and from view of parents and others. The parent still sees parts of her child, but the parts that are not supported become fugitive, even to the child himself. These parts are different from the presentational self that the child shows to the world and to himself. The lost self simply seems to be missing. It's not hard to see how this can happen. The parent devalues her child's thoughts, and he loses confidence in his ability to think; the parent ignores his feelings, and he loses the part that is empathic; the parent yells at him to stop running or making noise, and he freezes some or all of his muscles. The parent may also shame him for touching his body, and he loses contact with his sensuality. There are many figures of speech to describe this hidden psychological process. We can say the lost self has *camouflaged* itself and *forgotten* itself, thereby escaping from view in order not to encourage parental rejection.

Continued disapproval from a parent not only forces the child's real self underground but creates a sense of loss that the child may recognize only later in life. As one of our clients, whom we'll call Leanne, recalls, "The most intense times I had with my father were when he was being critical. I remember one time I couldn't compete in a track meet because I was having cramps, and he accused me of taking a 'woman's way out.' I remember another time when I won a home-economics award when I was fourteen. I had to make a speech about my project in front of the judges. When I asked my dad afterwards how he liked it, he told me that starting out by correcting the pronunciation of my name was arrogant and insulting to the person who introduced me. That's all he said." Leanne smiles ironically when she says she grew up "not having a brain." Her wall of defense was built on the fiction that she could not think clearly.

Leanne's older sister manifests the pain of parental criticism in a slightly different way. Not only does she "stuff" her feelings, but, as she says, "I stuff my face." In one of the great ironies of obesity, the more she weighs, the more invisible she becomes as a person to the people around her. Who can be critical of someone who isn't there?

The Disowned Self: In this form of repression, the child doesn't just hide or act. She disowns the existence of certain traits or characteristics in herself, even when they are obvious to others. Ironically, these parts of the self are disowned as *not me*, even though *others see them as positive*. Perhaps the most common example is sexuality. Many children learn to feel that sexual impulses are unacceptable. Through interaction with parents and other adults, they come to see the sexual part of themselves as naughty, ugly, unmentionable, and even dangerous. We now realize how many adult sexual dysfunctions in our society can be traced to the disowned self.

But other traits can be disowned, as well. One woman we worked with grew up on a ranch with four brothers and had trouble accepting the soft, vulnerable part of herself. "I spent my whole childhood proving myself. I could ride as well as my brothers. I could go without food all day. I could hoist lumber. I could shoot injured calves. I would have been left in the dust if I'd been soft." It was only after childhood, as she experienced what it was like to be loved for herself alone, that she realized she could cry when she felt something deeply.

The Denied Self: When the child perceives a trait to be negative, he will deny it. Often these "negative" traits are really manifestations of the child's drive to survive and are, in and of themselves, neither negative nor positive. The child is expressing a legitimate developmental impulse that the parent, because of her own wounding, has trouble dealing with. The trait gets labeled as negative by a critical parent, and therefore becomes assimilated as negative by the child, because of the parent's reaction.

Let's take Hal's experience as an example. His mother reacted negatively whenever he appeared to be angry. In another family his emotional intensity might have been ignored or channeled into healthy ambition. But in Hal's family such emotions were considered frightening. Hal was an only child whose parents were older. His father retired when Hal was nine years old and spent most of his time in the greenhouse and in the garden. His mother was a kind and gentle woman who only felt safe in an atmosphere of soft-spoken cooperation. When Hal was little and he wanted to argue a point in conversation or when he talked about "killing" the other guy in spelling competitions, his parents were appalled. He soon learned to fear and hate the part of him that wanted to compete and win. For many years, he believed that he simply didn't have much drive. He developed the part of his personality that was nurturing and kind, avoiding situations in which he would have to compete against other people.

There are many ways a child may deny a part of herself and never know it. She replaces the denied trait with a more acceptable one, and becomes oblivious to the denial. For example, it has been common for young girls to deny the competitive part of their natures. A girl may develop a rationale to "explain" this to herself by calling herself a "good sport"—someone who would rather make everyone happy through cooperation than disrupt social harmony through "self-aggrandizing" competition. In this case, the denied self (her competitive self) is not mourned as a loss; instead, its replacement (her cooperative self) is exalted as a virtue.

In other cases the denied self may not even be recognized by the child. How often have we heard an angry teenager (or adult, for that matter) insist, "I am *not* angry!" She may admit to having a strong sense of justice, but not to being angry. Or as one young woman of our acquaintance puts it, "I don't *do* anger."

Beth, a young professional with two teenage daughters, described to us a moment of revelation when one of her children named out loud one of *her* denied traits. "My oldest daughter just called me a control freak. I was hurt and insulted. At first I didn't believe it, but when I thought about it, I realized that she wasn't the kind of kid who mouthed off disrespectfully. I asked my husband about it and I went back and asked her about it again, and the answers I got were, 'Well . . . you do seem to have a *powerful* need to organize people and make sure that things come out right.' I'm still trying to sort out how much of that is good and how much is overboard. After all, I've built my business on my ability to keep things under control, and I think that a lot of my kids' successes have come because I was paying attention."

Very few character traits are all bad or all good. Most are two-edged swords. Beth was shocked to get feedback that she was a high-control person. She disliked this trait in others (her mother, for example) and would have found it unacceptable in herself. For years the members of her household were experiencing what they perceived as excessive control, while Beth saw herself being a dedicated, concerned mother who paid more attention than most. Self-discovery is not always comfortable. But now Beth has the opportunity to consciously create for herself the guidelines that will help her stay "dedicated and concerned" without crossing the line into patterns of unhealthy symbiosis and overcontrol.

LOST WHOLENESS

These four different kinds of fragmented selves can be collectively referred to as the missing self. You can see how they constitute the lost wholeness of the child. To reformulate what we have already learned about the missing self: The child manifests these behaviors and traits as part of his will to survive, but the parent experiences them as negative. Unconsciously, the child gets the message that he might not survive if he knows he has these traits and if he exhibits them, so they stay unconscious and projected. The negative valuation placed on the missing self by parents or other powerful people (and eventually by the child himself) results in unconscious self-hatred.

The drive toward wholeness is so great that the child will connect with these missing parts of himself by projecting them onto other people and then relating to them. Even when he relates to them negatively, his drive toward wholeness has been fulfilled. The child is in a double-bind: Not to be whole imperils survival, but to be whole risks disconnection from parents on whom he is dependent for survival. To be whole is to risk death; not to be whole is to risk death. So the child opts for disguising, losing, disowning, or denying those parts of himself that risk disconnection from his parents. At the same time he maintains wholeness by projecting these same traits onto other people. He can then relate to the traits.

Projection: We have looked at projection before with regard to the child. Now let's look in more detail at the way projection works in parenting. The part of our brain that is the oldest and least evolved has trouble distinguishing between self and others. It also has no sense of time, so everything in its environment is eternal and everywhere. This characteristic serves us well in some ways and makes life difficult in others.

In the case of projection, the parent assigns to the child unacceptable traits or behaviors that are actually part of the parent's missing self.[6] Without realizing what she is doing, she accuses her child of being lazy or irresponsible or selfish, unconsciously enumerating those parts of herself that have caused her grief. It never occurs to her that it's a case of her own mistaken identity. Without realizing it, she expects her children to own up to these traits by both admitting to them and assimilating them. Parents who project usually get their wish. Tell a child often enough that he is "irresponsible," and you're likely to end up with a child who is irresponsible or who has created an elaborate defense against what he considers to be his "irresponsibility."

Common examples are everywhere. We recently heard a caring mother say to her teenage daughter that she thought her dress and manner were too sexually provocative. We had worked with her daughter for several months and had not had the same reaction. It made us wonder about the *mother's* sexuality. What ghost was rising up from the denied self of this parent?

In another example, a father who happens to be a minister told us about his sixteen-year-old son, who started being vocal at school about "overly liberal" political opinions. The father explained to us that the political content didn't bother him as much as his son's "intensity and his insistence that everyone—whether they're interested or not—engage him in debate." The boy's political science teacher praised his ability to formulate and defend arguments, but his father was distressed. Another father might have found this behavior positive, or at least harmless. But to this father such loquaciousness was a matter of great discomfort. The question we ask is, why? Why is the father so quick to label his son as an out-of-control talker, and why does it matter so much?

Stereotypes can make it easy to see psychological patterns very clearly. Consider the "stage mother," who keeps alive her own thwarted ambitions by working tirelessly for the success of her child.[7] There are many examples of famous people who have had stage mothers, or stage fathers—Mozart, Milton Berle, Judy Garland, and Yehudi Menuhin come to mind. In each case, single-minded parents seem to have brought their own talents to successful fruition through the lives of their offspring. Of course, it helps to have supremely gifted children.

Surely it isn't a bad thing to have ambitions for a child. What matters is how hard the parent pushes and whether her plans have anything at all to do with the temperament and needs of her child. Because a stage mother or a sports mother or a music mother often intrudes too much on the innate integrity of her child, even professionally successful children of stage parents often exhibit serious wounding. For children who fail to meet their parents' expectations, the wounding can be even greater.

Lisa describes her mother as a stage mother. At the age of forty-three, she is still trying to piece together the complexities of their relationship: "I don't know why my mother did this to me. She was always pushing me—music lessons, debate teams, camp, running for class office. I was shy. I was scared. I just wanted to be safe. She didn't do this to my other two sisters, only me. The worst was making me be a model. I was in the finals of a Gerber baby contest, and ever after that she entered me in child beauty contests and took me over to model for a big department store here. I did it, but I resented it, and I felt like a fake. I felt like I succeeded at those things because she did it for me. I was a big fake."

Lisa has clues about her mother's motivations. She understands that her mother considered herself plain-looking and suffered because of it. She also knows that there had been intense sibling competition in her mother's family. Her mother had worked hard at playing the piano and dancing as paths toward self-fulfillment and recognition but had abandoned them when she was overshadowed by her four sisters, all of whom she thought were more beautiful and talented than she was. Lisa finds that it helps her to remember this about her mother. When she allows herself to imagine what her mother's childhood was like, she can feel her mother's hurt at being ignored by a work-obsessed father and a too-busy mother. Empathy with her mother's childhood difficulties helps her understand her mother better, and she is able to feel, recognize, and let go of some of her anger.

All of these examples tell the story of parents who project aspects of their own natures onto their children. Sometimes projection is a single act with minor consequences, and sometimes it's a lifelong pattern that drastically affects the child's life for good or ill.

Self-hatred: We have talked about the unconscious self-hatred that is triggered in the child when a parent or other authority figure disapproves of part of the child's self. The wounding that results is even easier to see when an adult actually *abuses or damages* part of the child's self. Childhood sexual abuse is an extreme example of how the wounding of the child leads to the child's hatred of herself. One family we worked with came to us when the parents discovered that their beloved teenage daughter, a star athlete with many friends, had been sexually molested as a young child over a period of two or three years by a close family friend. As her distraught father told us, he is now able to understand a lot of his daughter's behavior in light of these terrible events: "Once she told her mother and it was out in the open, so many things made sense. She's erratic. She doesn't focus. She's scattered and unable to follow a single course of action. I know she could do better in school. One minute she lashes out cruelly at me, and the next she's all lovey-dovey. She's a beautiful, talented girl who attracts good-quality boys, but her relationships are self-destructive. She keeps the high-quality boys at arm's length and then gets involved with guys that have been beaten by their fathers or been passed around from relative to relative. She has no idea who she is. She slices off parts of herself and shows different parts to different people. It hurts me to say this, but I don't think she really has a 'self.'"

The violation of this young woman's sense of self has been so great that she has become increasingly unable to construct an adequate defense. Her missing self is united primarily in its self-hatred. It will take years of work to help her finish the job of growing up that was so cruelly disrupted at the age of seven. And it will take patient work to help her reintegrate the parts of her that she has despised and split off during the ten years since.

Fortunately, not all stories of self-hatred are so extreme. We find it in the lives of many children whose wounds are less traumatic. Let's explore the concept further, starting with an important premise: *Children are just trying to be themselves as whole persons.* If there is any doubt about what we mean, consider a little boy in a sandbox who, within the space of five minutes displays, quite naturally, a whole array of selves. He grabs his friend's toy truck because he wants it, he picks his nose, he touches his genitals, he cries when sand gets in his eye, he becomes Superman, and he kisses his baby sister. This is human life unfettered. Good parents will want to guide the child in adopting the positive social norms of the culture. But many parents won't know where to draw the line between limits that serve a child well and limits that stunt the child unnecessarily. A parent who moves to restrict, prohibit, or disapprove of child behaviors solely because she is uncomfortable with them runs the risk of wounding her child. Almost certainly she is uncomfortable because her own parents disapproved of that behavior or some version of it.

When the parent rejects or tries to stifle a natural impulse or a natural function in the child, we can see the birth of self-hatred. The child will do anything he can to protect himself from parental rejection. He will even hate the parts of himself that imperil his parents' love and cause them to reject him. To the child, rejection equals abandonment and abandonment equals death. He must do what he can to survive.

It is useful to describe this as a sequence: the child manifests some perfectly natural impulse in his actions, the parent reacts with disapproval, the child registers the impulse as bad and dangerous, and he hates himself for having it. In real interactions between children and parents, of course, such patterns are far from linear and straightforward. The child doesn't make a rational decision to hate himself; such self-rejection is the result of scattered events of whose impact neither parent nor child is fully aware. With or without the parents' or child's awareness, the consequences can be devastating.

The ability to receive love: There is a correlation between self-hatred and the inability to receive love. Our unconscious cannot accept avowals of love for parts of us we hate or don't know we have, even when those parts reflect positive traits. In order for us to receive the love of others, we have to work through our self-hatred in concert with a marriage partner or another intimate partner committed to consciousness. In a relationship of this kind we can learn to love in another what we have rejected in ourselves.

This is how it works: As long as there is self-hatred, we not only cannot accept love from others but cannot love ourselves. The path to self-love is to love in other people what we reject in ourselves. How can we do this? First, by seeing that the part of another person that we dislike is a projection of a part of ourselves that we dislike. Second, by seeing that this trait or behavior helps the other person survive (just as it has helped us survive). We have to see that the "negative" trait serves a positive function. Third, we must then accept that the trait is functional in the other person, and we must come to value it for the purpose it serves. When we understand, accept, and eventually love it in the other person, we come to understand, accept, and love it in ourselves.[8] This is the path of self-acceptance and self-love: *what I do for others is done also for me.*

THE PARENT AS STUDENT

It is not too strong to say that a great many of the ills that beset our society and infect our collective history can be attributed to the legacy of individual self-hatred that we have been discussing. To free our children from the impact of our own self-hatred, we must learn to recognize the qualities we unconsciously hate in ourselves, admit that we have them, and do the work of loving ourselves back to a state of wholeness and acceptance.

Although our children are not our healers, they have a role to play in that healing process. It can be a revelation and a relief to understand that what a parent dislikes in her child can exist as a potential for her own further growth. Remember the mother who accused her teenage daughter of "sexually provocative" behavior? That same quality of sexual freedom and sensual enjoyment that she projects onto her daughter could become a guide for what she needs to develop in her own life. When she recognizes and accepts it in her daughter, she can get in touch with it in herself.

It's the same for the father with the politically assertive son. He has an opportunity to ask himself whether his role as a clergyman cuts off his need to express his convictions on socially unpopular issues. Maybe he is unconsciously expressing his own need to be a whole person who has a safe avenue of self-expression. Regardless of what he does with this insight, he will have made an important internal reconnection by understanding why he has overreacted to a natural impulse in his son. If he can learn to appreciate in his son what he isn't allowing in himself, he can take a first significant step toward healing a wound. In this sense, when parents promote the wholeness of their children, their actions are healing for them as well.

In order for us to make use of the information our children give us about our own sore spots, we must see our children differently. We must think of them as illuminators of our darkness. We must train our ears to listen for the message they bring us about our own pain and our own capacity for wholeness. We must look for the diagnostic potential in our failed interactions with them. And the whole time we are learning from them, we must not forget our primary obligation to them: we are guardians of their unique spirits, and we are responsible for helping them unfold into emotionally and spiritually mature human beings.

THE CHILD AS TEACHER

No one knows more about the way we parent than our own children. They are on the front lines with us every day. We form a continuous information feedback loop with them. They let us know whether our actions and reactions are in balance or are weighted too much in one direction or the other.

In order to interpret the signals accurately, we must rely on the cognitive, rational parts of ourselves. If we react to our children only from primitive survival instincts, we will make many mistakes. After all, parenting tears open our own wounds. Having children leaves us vulnerable to frightening emotions. The sharp pain in the gut, the catch in the throat, and the pounding headache are all signs of seismic emotional events triggered by our lives with our children. In the face of such emotive onslaughts, we might mistake our children for the enemy, or just as dangerous, we might not be able to distinguish them from ourselves.

Observing the child: Without doing anything else, parents can use their eyes and ears to observe and make note of their child's behavior, interests, ways of relating to others, degree of self-motivation, and emotional patterns. The prime directive here is for parents to practice impartiality, to check what they are seeing against what they might have expected to see, and to let go of preconceived notions. Often children's actions speak very clearly to an impartial observer, but are barely comprehensible to their parents. But sometimes, parents are able to be very clear about what they observe.

A mother we know reminisced about eavesdropping on her daughter at play with her friends at an early age: "So here we are with eight second-grade girls in our basement, and I hear my daughter yelling, 'You're not doing it right. We have to have a plan. I'll be president of the club, and you will . . . and you will . . .' And then she was giving them all orders. Of course, it was a disaster. Some of them ignored her, and one friend, Shandy, really took exception to being told what to do. They got into a royal fight over it. Suzy has always wanted to be the boss. She was the kid who asked for an elaborate calendar system—you know, the kind that business executives use—as a graduation present from eighth grade."

This mother, if she had been acting unconsciously, might have felt compelled to intervene, either through a sense of personal embarrassment at her daughter's bossiness or from a sense of responsibility to her daughter to "save" her key friendships. But she had realized that it was more important for her daughter to explore the consequences of her temperament—as long as the consequences were not dangerous or long-lasting—than it was to straighten out a short-term problem for her. How many times do parents fail to observe an important element of their child's nature while attempting to "rectify" a situation that the parent, not the child, finds uncomfortable? The purpose of observation is to gain information, not control.

There is, however, an additional step this mother might have taken. Given what we know about how children mirror their parents, this mother might profitably ask herself, "From whom has my daughter picked up these traits?"

Noting the child's reaction to the parent: Parents can train themselves to sharpen their hearing, to listen for what a child thinks or feels about encounters with his parents, instead of listening *only* for signs of obedience or disobedience. Children who live in a safe environment of mutual respect with their parents are free to give them feedback about what effect their parenting is having.

The fourteen-year-old son of a friend of ours told us that he hoped we would emphasize this point: "When children can't talk to their parents about something without fear of being punished, children won't talk. If you can't trust your parents, you won't tell them about the small things, much less the big things. I hope you are putting that in the parenting book." This young man had good reason to find this important. He told us that while he and his friends had recently played softball at a friend's house, his friend had accidentally thrown the ball through a bedroom's glass window. The friend had been terrified to tell his parents, so our storyteller decided to tell them *he* had done it. Sure enough, the parents hit the ceiling and responded by telling the boys to go home.

Asking questions helps parents become more aware of how their children see them. All children communicate through their actions and reactions. Is this child open to his parent's thoughts, guidance, and limits, or does he rebel or resist? Consistently negative reactions give a parent clues about how to identify issues that need attention.

When a parent accepts the limited nature of her own perceptions and becomes more receptive to the truth of her child's perceptions, her world expands. Children's views are a source of information; they don't have to be a trigger for conflict. An especially good source of information is the criticism children express, whether it is spoken or unspoken.

Small children have perfected a whole range of physical and emotional reactions that parents can read loud and clear. The stiff body of defiance, the wilted look of defeat, the eruption of laughter—this is feedback of the most eloquent kind. Older children can be asked directly about their feelings through the safe mechanism of intentional dialogue. If a parent has been modeling the capacity to admit errors and learn from mistakes, the child will be familiar with the kind of give-and-take that keeps relationships healthy.

One Mother's Education

A young mother, whom we'll call Julie, illustrates how important it is for parents to make the effort to see, hear, and understand the messages their children are trying to send them about who they are. Julie began therapy after embarking on a second marriage following a difficult period of divorce and single motherhood. As a result she spent a good deal of time thinking about her own childhood, which, although generally happy, had existed in a world of strong parental ambition. She wanted to send a different message to her own children: "I think I grew up in a family in which there were very high expectations for achieving. Those expectations were expressed rather subtly, actually; not 'We expect you to make A's.' And it wasn't just, 'Well, of course you'll . . . etc. What do you mean you're not running for student body president? Of course you . . .' It was subtler than that. Including my three brothers, all of us are absurd overachievers, and we've paid big prices for that in many different ways. As a reaction against that kind of atmosphere, I think I tried to tell my kids that there were lots of things in life other than being popular in class or having the lead in the play. I wanted to emphasize the joy of simply doing what you're doing and being one of the group."

As she explored the relationships in her own family, she paid close attention to her own two children, their personalities and preferences. She wanted to construct an approach to achievement that would embody expectations that are appropriate but not too high. Three examples illustrate points of reference she used for discovering her sons.

Recognizing how the child feels: Her first story comes from a point when her marriage was beginning to break up. This is an important story because it reminds parents that children don't always communicate in words. The parent must be alert to a whole array of signals that convey information about the child's frame of mind. "I remember being at the beach in Florida on a family vacation and turning around and seeing Billy standing there literally wringing his hands. And I had the sense of, oh, my goodness, this is a little guy who's worried about something. And that was a shock, because I hadn't seen him in that light before. This is an image that sticks with me as a parent. Here's a little boy who should have been utterly engaged in building a sand castle. Instead, he's working on something internally. That was not a happy realization for me, because I didn't want him to feel worried. But it told me that he was sensitive to some of the hard things in my marriage that I thought my husband and I were hiding from the kids."

Recognizing what the child needs: During times of personal crisis, such as divorce, parents can easily become so self-absorbed that they don't see their children. Myopic self-involvement can easily distort perceptions, making us blind to the children in front of us. Sometimes, however, the problem is not situational myopia, but everyday preoccupation with worries and concerns that have nothing to do with the child.

While she was working hard to make ends meet as a single mother, Julie took her other son, Jeff, shopping. "Again, this was during those very difficult years of divorce. The kids had changed schools, and we were going to buy new school clothes. I was very conscious of money and a tight budget. So I was deliberately trying to scale down the purchases. Jeff was going into sixth grade and needed a new jacket. There were two available: one had a designer label, and the other one was a less expensive, generic version without the label which was three, four, or five dollars less. And so I said, 'Let's go for the one without the label.' Jeff looked me straight in the eye, and he said, 'Mom, I need the other one.' I'm so glad I was paying attention. I said, 'Okay, I understand.' And I didn't regret it."

Julie could have debated whether her son actually "needed" the more expensive jacket, but she was able to see that, within the context of his life at that moment, the "cooler" jacket satisfied a real need for social acceptance. At that moment, she was wide awake and receptive to the signals. There were other times, though, when she felt as if she were sleepwalking through her interactions with her children, stumbling over obstacles and mumbling half-remembered lines. What always woke her up was the "realness" of her two boys. They laughed; they grabbed her tight in bear hugs; they smelled like oiled baseball mitts. Most of the time, they themselves brought her back to paying attention, and then she could make sense out of what she was hearing and seeing.

Recognizing what children want: Julie's third story illustrates how important it is to be attuned to what the child wants rather than only to what the parent wants. She remembered a time when one of her sons sent a clear message, and she was able to step in and give him the support he needed to go after what he wanted. "It wasn't so much an intervention on my part with Billy as it was clear support of a path he wanted to take, but was hesitant to take. He had tried playing football as a freshman in high school because his father, the divorced father, held football as an extremely high value. Billy hated it. That last summer, before football practice started, he had a job at the community pool. Some of the older high-school guys were on the water polo team and were encouraging Billy to join them. He realized he liked them and he liked the sport. But he agonized about disappointing his dad." Julie told us, "My support was in the form of, 'Do what's best for you. Do not do what's best for your parents. Do what your heart tells you is the best thing for you to do.' He chose water polo."

In each of these moments, Julie was able to recognize that her children were separate from her, feeling their own feelings and expressing their own needs, even if subtly. A more symbiotic parent might have been irritated at her little boy wringing his hands in the sand, might have insisted that her teenager have some respect for her money worries and choose the less expensive jacket, and might have implored her older son to placate his father by playing football instead of water polo. But Julie did not confuse her own needs for more peace of mind and more money with the needs of her children, as they found ways to let her know what she could do to ease their anxiety in each of these situations.

Accepting the feedback: Julie knows full well that she will learn more from her children if they are free to be themselves in front of her. If they are already wounded and hiding, her task of knowing them will be more difficult. She says she has always tried to give her kids the message that she was curious about them. And then when they revealed something to her, she reminded herself to be accepting. To help her remember the "accepting" part, she often thought of an incident that had happened when Jeff was a little boy, maybe five or six. He came into the house with his fist closed around something. "What is it?" she asked. "Won't you show it to me? I'd really like to see it." He didn't want to show her, saying that he didn't think she'd like it. Finally, she got worried and insisted. Slowly, he opened his fingers to reveal a huge, black, hairy spider. She freaked. And he started to cry. She had said she wanted to see it; in fact, she had forced him to show it to her, and then she had been terribly upset. She considers the incident an object lesson. If we want our kids to reveal things to us, we can't allow ourselves to become upset when they do.

There are many ways parents can intentionally gather information about their parenting. As we have said, the primary source is the child himself. If a parent wants to know what her child thinks of her, she doesn't have to look very far for the information. He will tell her in words, and show her in body language. He will reflect back the information she needs to keep her on the right track, if she is willing to receive it. And if he knows it is safe, he will grace her with full expressions of his wild and unpredictable personality.

Dialogue as a Vehicle for Discovery

The most important way for a parent to get to know a child, or anyone else for that matter, is to use intentional dialogue. Dialogue provides both the vehicle and the energy for maintaining their connection, especially when it is conducted in the spirit of inquiry. Dialogue is a two-way conversation whose central characteristic is listening in such a way that the child will be encouraged to keep letting you know how she feels, what she thinks, and what she needs. In Chapter 5, "Intentional Dialogue," we explain in detail how to absorb the spirit of dialogue into interactions with a child, as a way of maintaining connection, and how to use it as a practical tool to help parents and children know and appreciate each other on a deeper level. For now, let's just say that what we want is a calm, *safe* environment in which parents and children can exchange information about who they really are. When we talk with our children and we listen, they teach us a great deal.

David, a colleague, has a story from his family life that shows how dialogue works. He and his wife Judy are two of the most conscious parents we know. He told us about an experience they had had talking with their son and daughter, Peter and Jill, about a baby-sitter the children didn't like: "We liked the baby-sitter. She was a sweet girl, a daughter of friends. We couldn't see the problem, but we wanted to honor the kids' wishes. They were probably ten and nine years old. We said, 'Okay. How about you guys get your next baby-sitter? Let's talk about how we go about getting a baby-sitter and why we happened to get this person this time and how we can choose a different person next time.' So we talked about it, and they decided to call the university. Jill did the calling and made arrangements with a college freshman. She was a culinary-arts student who came over and made ladyfingers with them. She worked out fine."

As this story shows, David and Judy did several things that are important in dialogue. They listened to what their children had to say. They validated their children's point of view, even though they didn't share it. They couldn't see what was wrong with the current young woman who was sitting for them, but they took at face value the fact that their children found her boring and overly authoritarian, even though replacing her was an inconvenience for them. When the kids found someone they liked, their parents had supported their decision.

Dialogue teaches us how to listen to our children. And it teaches them how to listen to us. When the spirit of dialogue infuses their conversation, children and parents trust each other. They form an information feedback loop that is continuous, balanced, and participatory. The parent gets an additional source of information by asking for feedback and then listening to and accepting it. "Was I too fast to react to what you were telling me? Do you want me to think about it longer next time?" "I think you are letting me know that you think I'm being unfair. Am I right?" We must be able to hear the answers then and accept them with gratitude. This doesn't mean that we assume our children are always right; but knowing what they are thinking gives us more options when considering what to do next. And it opens up the possibility of gaining insight where we had none before.

Exploring New Worlds

Parents also make discoveries about their children when they provide opportunities for them to have new experiences and to explore a little. There is more to David's baby-sitting story that illustrates this point. After Jill and Peter had developed their selection process for a new baby-sitter, they had to use it again, with their parents' permission, because their new baby-sitter joined the swim team and had to spend long hours in the pool. "The kids called the university again. Somehow they got connected to a young woman who was blind. She wanted to talk to my wife to make sure we knew she was not sighted. And so Judy went to the phone and talked for a while—it was a long conversation. Finally, Judy said, 'Okay, that's fine.' So this blind student came to our house. She was well prepared. She said, 'I need to know where this is and this is and what phone numbers to use,' and so forth. Peter and Jill spent the evening with this girl. And when we came home that night, of course the house was dark. We thought, 'Oh, my god! Something terrible has happened!' We had forgotten. But she was sitting calmly in the dark reading braille. And so we had her back many more times. She had demonstrated to us that she could be trusted to do the job—and the kids liked her—so we saw no problem with continuing."

It's not difficult to imagine most parents vetoing this idea from the start. It makes sense to have some reservations. David and Judy also wrestled with it, but they trusted in the end that their children had gone through a responsible process for the selection, and they wanted to support the creative initiative that such a choice demonstrated. David summed it up this way: "I can't imagine that we would have made this choice, but they did it for themselves. It taught us a lot about Jill and Peter—that they were willing to say, 'Let's do it.' "

Parent and child both learn when a child has the chance to "try things out." If there are choices, the child enters into an adventure of self-discovery by finding out what she is interested in, what she has an aptitude for, and what she wants to continue.

Shedding Preconceptions

Parents can discover things they don't already know about their children, if they keep their eyes open. One father we know found out that his daughter had more maturity and more talent than he thought. "Elizabeth was very shy when she was little—you know, one of those little girls who's always hiding behind her mother, wanting to be invisible. She was scared to get up in front of the class and do show-and-tell. We had to rescue her one time from the haunted house at her school's Halloween party. But she surprised us. When she was in the fourth grade, her music teacher asked her to play something on the flute for the winter program. I thought to myself, 'No way!' But she got up in front of five hundred parents and kids and played 'We Three Kings.' Cool as a cucumber. No problem. It made my wife and me ask ourselves what happened. Never would we have predicted she would do that."

This father got to face a new aspect of his daughter that he had never seen—or had never been willing to see. Without the opportunity provided by the Christmas concert, he might have classed Elizabeth as a scared little kid indefinitely. Maybe he would even have sheltered her from new experiences he "knew" she wouldn't have been comfortable with. It's interesting to think about what would have happened if Elizabeth had not been able to play well in front of the school. Would that have confirmed her father's opinion that she was not able to handle challenging situations? Would it have embarrassed him to have a daughter who "failed" in public? Would he have discouraged her from experimenting with performance again?

These questions bring up another important point, as a corollary to the idea of exploration: it's not wise to be too invested in a child's interests or performance. Elizabeth's father got to learn early that children move through a variety of experiences as they get older. They change. Some interests become lifelong passions, and others are only short-term dalliances. This has to be a natural process, not something twisted into what fits an organized adult's requirement for neatness.

We will see in Section IV that children progress naturally through a series of normal stages, each of which is characterized by its own impulse and its own set of developmental tasks. An important part of the parent's role is to be aware of these stages and to create opportunities for the child to explore new ways to test his newfound interests and skills.

USING FEEDBACK FROM OTHER ADULTS

The kinds of information we receive from other adults, sometimes solicited and often unexpected, can be a gold mine for parents. Sources of information, books, teachers, friends, professionals, are everywhere—if we are able to use them. The problem is that people are sometimes resistant to observations about their children or their parenting. When a parent fears the criticisms of other people, he does not understand that they may be putting their finger on exactly what was wounded in him. That's why he is having trouble with criticism in the first place. Their criticism stirs up his unconscious defense against these traits in himself and therefore stirs up his self-hatred. No wonder he resists input. No wonder he sometimes counterattacks—or, at the very least, ignores feedback that feels dangerous.

Sometimes, however, the people around the parent have their own agendas. Their relationship with the parent is subject to the same kinds of complexities that parents' relationships with their children have. A grandparent might not be an unbiased, disinterested observer. Some intelligent evaluation needs to be exercised in determining whether a particular adult who knows the child has an opinion worth listening to. Positive opinions are usually easy to hear, but even these can be screened out by a defensive parent. Negative ones can be harder to hear but are even more important to listen to.

The importance of schoolteachers: A teacher can offer unique and important information about the children in her classroom. She sees them in situations their parents never do, and her observations can provide valuable insights about behavior that is puzzling or troubling. A teacher's interest in a child is a gift to the parents. One young mother, Jane, received just such a gift from her son's teacher, although at the time it felt more like a blow.

For some time Jane had been concerned that her son Ryan wasn't doing well in school. He attended an exclusive private school that emphasized not only academics but also personal growth and responsibility. Jane was able to use the resources of the school to zero in on some of the problem: "I had known that Ryan wasn't, well . . . Everybody felt that here's a kid that had tremendous aptitude and abilities and he's not really engaging them. The metaphor was, he was a fire that just wouldn't light. Everybody was trying to rub sticks, and it wasn't going anywhere. So I was used to hearing that, but what stunned me was when one of the teachers said, 'You know, I don't think he really feels all that good about himself.' It struck me like a ton of bricks. But when I thought about it, I knew it was true and very perceptive. It was like, 'How could this kid not feel good about himself?' I thought he was wonderful; he had all of these attributes, and I felt we had been very positive with him. One of the most revealing things was the marks on self-esteem on this test he took. He thought really poorly of himself. It was extremely difficult for me to accept."

Usually when a teacher talks with a parent about a child, the parent's antennae are already up. What does this teacher think about my child and about me as a parent? An unconscious parent wants to hear that there is no problem, especially not one he has to deal with or that could be laid at the door of "poor parenting." Jane felt rocked in her own preconceptions about who her son ought to be, the level at which he should be achieving, and her identity as a mother. How could she be the mother of a son with low self-esteem? Because the teacher's assessment didn't fit with her preconceptions, there was a danger that she might reject the evaluation. As it turned out, Jane was able to use the idea that perhaps her son didn't feel very good about himself to continue exploring his lackadaisical attitude toward schoolwork. She and Ryan's father began looking for ways to help him gain a sense of competence and effectiveness in his daily life.

LEARNING FROM THE PARENT'S OWN REACTIONS

The most important source of information for the parent is his own emotional reactions to his child's behavior. While some behaviors would arouse any parent to respond, those parental responses that are negative, intense, and repetitive are an almost certain clue that a parent has found a point of potential growth for himself. Think of it this way: *You know you are face-to-face with the unfinished business of your own childhood when you respond with strong negative feelings to your child's behavior.*

Intense emotional reactions don't have to be obvious to be valuable as a source of self-knowledge, and the parent doesn't need to act on his observations immediately. He can discover a great deal about himself by reflecting on actions and responses he *might* have made. He can think *before* he acts or, at least, *while* he is acting. He can learn to pause and do nothing rather than plunge blindly ahead and risk the possibility of wounding his child.

When a parent does experience intense, nonrational, mystifying reactions to certain encounters or experiences with his children, that's a signal that he needs to ask himself some questions. He has just uncovered a *growth point* in himself, an issue or a feeling that has the potential for yielding information that can help him continue his own personal development. "Why did I react that way? Am I afraid of something?" Inappropriate levels of fear, sadness, anger, or conversely, elation and relief are signals to the parent that he has just activated an old wound and might do well to investigate further.

We have learned that it is precisely at those points where parents feel most uncomfortable in their interactions with their children that there is work for the parent to do. Conflicts are a rich vein of information, almost always leading back to places in the parent that are incomplete or unhealed.

Do parents always like what they see in their children? The answer, of course, is no. Many of the things our children do make us uncomfortable. That's why it's important to understand that many of these embarrassing or dead-end behaviors can be appropriately understood as faulty experiments. Over the course of time children end up rejecting many of them on their own. Other behaviors start as clumsy attempts to solve problems and become more refined and appropriate as the child matures. As we have said, in Section IV we will explore in depth the particular skills that children need to acquire at different stages of growth. This information can help parents interpret child behaviors that would otherwise be puzzling or distressing. It's important to know that maturing is an organic process littered with failed experiments.

But when a parent turns away from the child she has discovered, it's time to do some soul-searching. Let's say the child seems lazy, distant, shy, quick to anger, bossy, unmotivated, or socially inept. The parent might ask herself whether she is seeing something that isn't there or whether she is disliking something that really *is* there. Is she assigning him one of her own disowned traits, even though he doesn't really have it? Or, if he really does have the quality she blames him for, why does it bother her so much? What makes it hard for her to accept her child as he is?

One of the hardest behaviors for parents to accept in their children is anger. But anger is a signal, a message. It provides an excellent opportunity to learn about hidden parts of both the child and the parent. Learning to express anger is a normal part of a child's development, but repressing it can cause some real damage. In the case of the next example, the repressed anger of a father made it very difficult for him to handle his adolescent son's expressions of anger and contempt.

Paul, the father, recounted his son's eruptions: "I think the thing that is hardest for me is when I have to acknowledge the ways Jeremy is that I don't want him to be. I can't take it when he flies off the handle. And it's very hard for me to deal with the way he belittles his friends, criticizing them. I hate it. He'll get into this put-down mode with his friends. It's like, 'I'll rank on you; you rank on me.' They say they're not serious, but I find it hard to take."

At a later point Paul remembered the way his anger had been treated by his parents when he was growing up: "When I think about it, in my family you didn't show negative emotions. You didn't show any of the depression or anxiety, fear, anger—you just didn't. I had accepted that you needed to conceal it. When I was a kid, I remember being punished any time I was angry. When I look back on it, I realize I stifled my anger so much that I had to be suffocating to show it. And then it was usually ignored, punished, or ridiculed. I remember once I was so mad at my sister—I was desperate—that I threw water in her face. And I got in trouble for it. You know, it's really difficult for me to be pleasant and smiling all the time, and not to be angry or depressed. When you asked just now, 'Why do you feel you have to be pleasant and smiling all the time?' it was like a total shock to me that it was okay to show negative emotions to my kid. You mean I have that option?"

The unconscious parenting that Paul experienced resulted in the repression of his feelings. His parents were not comfortable with his emotional intensity. Whether he was aware of it before he had his own children or not, he now knows from his reaction to his son that he was probably wounded in this way.

Reevaluating the parent's childhood: Outbursts of anger may or may not indicate a problem in a child. But how the parent reacts does tell the parent something about himself. The message for Paul was that he could use his discomfort at his son's anger to explore his own experiences and beliefs about an emotion he had disowned in himself. He now has permission to work at accepting his son's anger as a way of getting in touch with it in himself. He has the chance to rewrite the vague but powerful childhood rule, "If you get mad, bad things will happen."

Every day, children illuminate the childhoods of their parents, both by calling attention to problems and by inviting grown-ups to participate with them in the sensations and experiences of being young. Parents can accept this invitation to discover the world as a new source of delight. Not only do children teach parents important lessons about their younger selves, but they evoke forgotten memories that parents can reexperience with pleasure.

THE OBSERVATIONS OF A SPOUSE OR PARTNER

A final source of information for the parent is a spouse or longtime partner, although it can often be hard to hear what this person has to say. As we said in our discussion of the fragmented self, feedback from people close to the parent is often threatening, because it pinpoints exactly what the parent prefers to keep from consciousness.

But a parent who wishes to become more conscious must open herself to input from those close to her. Partners can provide information to each other that no one else can. Partners watch each other parent; they do a lot of it together. They hear complaints, they share anguish, and they observe patterns. The instinct for emotional survival may tempt fathers and mothers to tune each other out, but their observations can illuminate behaviors and attitudes that may not be obvious any other way. Parents need to look for the grain of truth that is at the heart of a critical comment.

The way a critical remark is delivered is telling. Comments that are sensitive to the feelings and prior wounds of the partner and that are delivered in the spirit of inquiry can be invaluable. Repetitive, emotional criticisms, on the other hand, need to be considered with caution. Often they are disguised statements of the unmet needs of the critical partner. They say as much about the critical partner's dissatisfactions as they do about the parenting techniques of the spouse. When a husband says, "My wife is too strict," for example, that may express as much about his unmet need for tolerant acceptance as it says about his children's needs. He may be projecting his need for more freedom onto his children. A wife who constantly nags her husband about not spending enough time with the children may really want him to spend more time with *her*. This perspective can help complaining partners develop a way of addressing the issues of their relationship along with rethinking their parenting skills.

As we have seen, the path to consciousness leads beneath the obvious. The overreactive father is protecting something vulnerable in himself. The mother who shrinks from involvement is doing the only thing she knows how to do to survive. When parents understand that and begin to uncover and heal their wounds with compassionate hearts, they change those things they are doing that hurt their children. In this sense their children have led the way toward a type of togetherness that can change and honor them both.

PARENTING AS HEALING RELATIONSHIP

No matter how old your children are now or what wounds you carry from your childhood, the possibility of healing is open to you. As a parent, you can learn to open your mind to what is present around you and let go of your identification with the constrictions and judgments of the past. Your children offer you a chance for self-discovery while you are discovering who they are. Your relationship with them can be a way to pinpoint the divisions, the opinions, the conflicts, you carry within yourself. They can help you discover what lies beneath your fractured perceptions and enjoy the peace and tranquillity of your original nature, the relaxed joyfulness that is yours to reclaim.

III

RESTORATION OF
CONNECTION

5

Intentional Dialogue

My stepfather's style almost never varied. First a slow
and elaborate introduction to the subject at large, and
finally, at the right moment, a sudden reduction to the
essential. It was simple and remarkably
successful—after the bewildering opening verbiage, he
would turn eagerly, his eyes sparkling and his head
thrown forward in a parody of anticipation to see the
effect of his logic. It was always a difficult moment. He
wanted more than a sign of recognition, a sign you had
understood; he wanted you to become him, to discard
immediately all ideas of your own and totally accept
the closed frame of reference in which he saw whatever
problem it was you were discussing.
—FRANK CONROY, *Stop-Time*

*T*hat is what it was like for young Frank Conroy to have a conversation with his stepfather. Understanding what his stepfather is saying
isn't enough. Frank has to act, think, talk, and feel just like him. He is
there to be an actor in his stepfather's drama, to meet his stepfather's
needs for affirmation and even affection.[1]

In our discussion of the unconscious parent in Chapter 3, we explored the concept of symbiosis. It is obvious that Frank and his stepfather have a symbiotic relationship. We know enough about the legacy
of symbiosis to be able to gather that Frank's stepfather probably had
had a symbiotic relationship with his own father, who almost certainly
told him what to do and how to think. Without realizing it, he treats
Frank the same way. He has forgotten how it feels to be interrupted,

103

discounted, and overlooked. He simply does what comes naturally to him and either assumes that Frank is his double or insists that he be.

Symbiotic relationships look hopeless. There appears to be no way for Frank and his stepfather to undo years of damage or to find a respectful way to separate without rupturing the connection between them. Acting like carbon copies of each other isn't the same as being truly connected, at least not in the sense we've been talking about it. But here we encounter another paradox. The truth is that the same process that disentangles them can also strengthen the bond between them. They don't have to break apart in order to separate into two distinct people.

A father with no reverence for the life of his son cannot be said to have a healthy connection with him. It would be more accurate to say that the father in the situation described here has a distorted connection with himself. Only when he can recognize his son as a different person from himself and come to know him as such, can he form a connection based on caring for another person. Only then will he start on a spiritual path that leads to a balanced view of his own self in relation to other living things, each of which has a self with as much worth as his does.

There is a way out of symbiotic relationships and a way to improve *every* relationship, including those that are already solid. It is available to everyone. And it's never too late to use it. Even if Frank were old enough to leave home, his stepfather could have learned to talk and listen to him in a new way. He could have learned to interact with his son so that the focus stayed on Frank's development and needs, rather than on his own. He could have learned to *sound* and *act* like a conscious parent, even before he became one. He could have improved his parenting many times over. He could have stopped using the negative patterns he inherited by learning how to communicate with his son through intentional dialogue.

Intentional dialogue can be understood and practiced by reading and following the suggestions in this chapter. It takes time to make it completely natural and automatic, as it does when you learn to do anything new. It is too late for the real Frank, but it's not too late for you. You can start right now, today, even if your children are in their twenties, to make your encounters with them more pleasant, more respectful, and more profound. Intentional dialogue teaches you how to be a consistent, purposeful parent who nurtures the connection with her children while helping them achieve the independence that is the goal of childhood. Dialogue works because it creates safety, allowing those who participate in it to relax emotionally and then physically.

In this chapter we will discuss how intentional dialogue works and the importance of the core message you want to send your child in *all* your interactions. There will be examples to learn from, special considerations for young children, and general considerations that affect the quality of communication between parents and children.[2]

THE CORE MESSAGE

Regardless of anything else the parent wants to accomplish in a particular communication with her child, there is one purpose that transcends all others. The parent wants to deliver and to have her child hear this core message: *You're okay. You have permission to be who you are, to be fully alive and express your aliveness, and to experience connection with others and to that which is greater than yourself.* Everything the conscious parent does in words, through body language, and in action backs up this central message of okay-ness.

If these words sound familiar, it's because we've already used them to talk about the basic needs of every child. The natural, inborn imperative for every child is to survive, to be fully alive, and to experience connection. Parents meet their children's needs when they facilitate this essential mandate. This core message lets the child know in many different ways that she is honored and valued as a separate person and that her basic needs will be met. This is the ulterior motive the parent has every time she talks with her child.

THE PROCESSES OF INTENTIONAL DIALOGUE[3]

When couples are working to understand each other in marriage, they must be able to communicate well with each other. Through effective communication they are able to experience themselves in relation to each other and, therefore, to maintain the dynamic connection between them. They experience the empathy that allows each of them to participate in the joy and the pain of the other by transcending the boundaries that can so easily divide them.

When we speak of communicating, we are talking about the verbal and nonverbal exchange of information, meaning, and feelings between two people. While we often say that we cannot *not* communicate,[4] we have learned that good communication skills alone may not solve problems or resolve issues. But no problems can be solved or issues resolved without these skills.

Effective communication is especially important between parents and children because the way we talk and listen to our children has a profound effect on who they become.[5] Words shape a child's identity. Facial expressions become part of his experience. Your behavior is part of what he carries with him into the world. What you do counts.

The problem is that what a parent does in the present moment is partly determined by events that are not occurring in the present moment. He is being cued offstage by people who aren't even in the room now. The cue card may be held by his father, who barked at him when he tried to show him his art work, or his mother, who finished his sentences for him. The parent reads the lines as though they were coming from him, the present adult, but they are really coming from someone else, from a different time and a different place.

Our work with couples and families has always emphasized the importance of a dialogic framework that both promotes conscious relationships and contains the essence of conscious relationships. At its heart, it delivers the core message of permission and acceptance to children and parents alike. When we teach this way of communicating to partners in marriage, we call it *couples' dialogue*. When we teach the same skill to parents, we call it *intentional dialogue*.

In both forms of dialogue three different processes are evident: mirroring, validating, and empathizing.[6] In any given exchange, any or all of these processes might be present. Mirroring is the one present most often. But even if the particular words that signal mirroring, validating, and empathizing are not spoken, any interaction can still be *in the spirit of* intentional dialogue. When the issues are the most intense and the emotions are running the highest, that's when a parent wants to be especially conscious of communicating in this way.

Mirroring is the process of accurately reflecting back the content of a message. Repeating back the content accurately is called *flat mirroring*. Flat mirroring can be more difficult than it sounds. One can very easily, without realizing it, mirror back just a little more than was sent or just a little less. A person who gives back a little more is doing *convex mirroring*. A person who gives back less, by zeroing in on one point that interests him and ignoring the rest, is doing *concave mirroring*. Maximizers often "repeat" the message through convex mirroring by adding something of their own for the purpose, conscious or not, of shaping the other person's thoughts and feelings. An example of convex mirroring is the mother who mirrors back to her teenager "So you're feeling guilty that you came home late for dinner" when what the child actually said was that she was sorry she didn't start for home sooner because the traffic was so bad. Minimizers often "repeat" a message through concave mirroring by highlighting the one thing they think is important. An example of concave mirroring is the father who responds to his son's loss of a baseball game by saying "You're telling me you lost" when what his son actually said was how excited he was that they almost won the game. Mirroring done with integrity can help us stop ourselves from repeating or paraphrasing for the (perhaps sinister) purpose of influencing another's thinking.

Repeating another person's words back to him is one form of mirroring. But the most common form of mirroring is paraphrasing. When we paraphrase, we state in our own words what we think another person is saying. So often we assume that we know what the other person is saying when we really don't. We are just guessing. We may be good guessers, and we may be right most of the time, but unless we mirror and check whether we've got it right, the danger exists that we will misunderstand. It can also be tempting during the process of mirroring to interpret before we fully understand. But if our interpretation is based on errors of understanding, then our interpretation will also be in error. Besides ensuring accuracy, mirroring lets a child know that her parent is willing to put aside his own thoughts and feelings for the moment in order to understand her point of view. For most parents this is a rare moment of self-transcendence.

Validating is the process of indicating to another person that what he or she says is making sense. You are setting aside your own frame of reference and appreciating the logic, the reality, and the worth of another person within his own frame of reference. Your words send the message to your child that her way of looking at things is valid. To validate her experience *does not* mean that you necessarily agree with her or that her thoughts and feelings reflect your own. It means that you surrender your place at the center of and source of "truth" and allow space for *her* interpretation of reality. When you mirror and validate your child, you are setting up the conditions that allow her to meet her basic need to express herself. The trust and closeness between you will grow, making it easier for her to trust and be close to others.

Empathizing is the process of recognizing the feelings of another person while he or she is expressing a point of view or telling a story. There are two levels of empathy. On the first level we reflect and imagine the feelings another person is expressing. On a deeper level we experience emotionally—actually feel—what he is experiencing. Such empathic experiences are healing and transforming in themselves to the participants, *independent of what is being communicated.* During these moments, both participants transcend their separateness and experience a genuine meeting of minds and hearts. When you engage in dialogue with your child, you understand your child, and at least for a moment, you see the world through her eyes.

WHEN TO USE INTENTIONAL DIALOGUE

Intentional dialogue is especially valuable when emotions are running high. Although you want all your interactions with your children to be infused with the spirit of mirroring, validating, and empathy, you will want to be especially purposeful in using intentional dialogue during those times when

1. You and/or your child want to be listened to and understood.
2. You and/or your child are upset about something and want to discuss it.
3. You and/or your child want to discuss a topic that might be touchy.

One of the most important things we have learned from the experience of parenting six children is to accept intense emotions as normal, as part of the give-and-take of all close relationships. Feeling frustrated or worried or disappointed or angry is not bad. If you over- or underreact to your child's normal emotions, that's a signal to you that you have something to reflect on and perhaps work on in yourself.

When your child expresses negative emotions during your conversations with her, you can learn to be a container for her intensity. Simply hold it without doing anything with it: You don't have to fix anything; you don't have to change her mind; you don't have to "educate" her into another point of view. And you don't have to explode, or run away and hide. Intentional dialogue teaches people to hang in there, find out what's happening, and reach beyond themselves into the world of the other person and become part of her experience for a while.

Intentional dialogue holds you to the center. If you tend to be a minimizer or a maximizer, intentional dialogue will help you overcome both of these inclinations and simply be in the conversation with your child, freed from the preconceptions and constraints that might normally cause you to overreact or to withdraw.

INITIATING INTENTIONAL DIALOGUE

In dialogue one person is the *sender* (the person who initiates the discussion) and the other person is the *receiver* (whose job it is to understand what the sender is saying). In couples' dialogue, either marriage partner can play either role. In intentional dialogue with children, the parent may have to switch back and forth between roles in order to help the child learn how to play his part. Obviously, a younger child or a child of any age who is just being introduced to this tool will need a good deal of support while learning.

At first, you will be the one who initiates intentional dialogue with your child, and you will need to be somewhat formal about it. He will learn from you how to participate, so keep in mind that you are both a participant and a teacher at the same time. Your goal is to teach your child how to engage in this kind of communication and to become comfortable enough with the process to be able to initiate such conversations with you in the future.

As we said, when two adults are involved, either one can initiate intentional dialogue. Typically, the sender issues the invitation to the receiver, because the sender is the one who has the message and who needs to be understood. In the case of a parent and his child, the parent will sometimes have to initiate intentional dialogue on behalf of the child when he knows that she has a message for him but is unwilling or unable to begin the dialogue process on her own. The father, who will be the receiver, temporarily adopts the sender's role in order to help his daughter get started. Once intentional dialogue has begun, he goes back to the role of receiver. A child who has been taught intentional dialogue and is comfortable with it will be able to initiate the interaction as sender herself.

What follows is the simplest model for initiating intentional dialogue. Here, the father is beginning the discussion on his own behalf. He has a message he wants his daughter to understand.

INITIATING INTENTIONAL DIALOGUE: EXAMPLE 1

Sender/Parent: *(initiating the dialogue)* I would like to talk with you about something. Is this a good time?

Receiver/Child: This is a good time. [OR] I can't right now. How about later? *(Note: It is important for the conversation to take place as soon as possible after the invitation and for both the parent and the child to indicate that they are ready for such a conversation.)*

Sender/Parent: *(if now is a good time)* I've been thinking about [the subject] and I wanted to let you know how I feel about it. [Delivers the message.] Did I make it clear?

In the next example, the child is visibly upset and obviously has a message to send to the parent but is either unwilling or unable to begin. The parent helps by suggesting that they talk.

INITIATING INTENTIONAL DIALOGUE: EXAMPLE 2

Receiver/Parent: It looks to me as if you have something you want to say to me. Maybe it would be a good idea for us to talk about this. Am I right?

Sender/Child: Yes.

Receiver/Parent: Can you tell what is on your mind? I want to understand what's going on with you.

Sender/Child: I feel that [sends the message].

Receiver/Parent: Let me make sure I've got it right. You feel that [mirrors the child].

Now that you have the basic idea of how to start, let's go on to model and give specific examples of how to mirror, validate, and empathize. We want to give you plenty of examples so that the sound of dialogue will become familiar to you. To learn a new way of talking takes some rehearsing, a lot of listening (especially to yourself), and a lot of trying it out live. You have to practice many, many times before it becomes part of your natural speech.

When you and your children are learning, they may complain that intentional dialogue is stilted and artificial. It is unfamiliar to them, too. Don't be put off by this reaction. Remember: You are the parent, and it is your responsibility to teach your child what you think is important for him to learn; you know that intentional dialogue will benefit your child in every way; and you know that changing anything takes time. It's up to you to stick with it.

THE MODEL FOR MIRRORING

Once the sender and receiver have agreed to talk and the sender has delivered most of his message, the receiver mirrors, checking to see that she has understood. If she has, the sender continues to express himself until he has said what he wanted to say. If the receiver has not understood, the sender tries repeating that part of the process, using different words, and the receiver mirrors again until the message is clear.

Here is a model for how mirroring works. Real life, of course, is not a schematic diagram and has a tendency to flow outside the lines, but when you are learning something new, it's helpful to have a model. In this example the parent is the sender, who initiates the interaction. He then becomes the receiver as he listens to his daughter express her point of view.

> **Sender/Parent:** I want to talk to you about [states subject in neutral, descriptive terms]. Do you understand what I'm referring to?
>
> **Receiver/Child:** Yes. You want to talk to me about [paraphrases or repeats what her father has just said].
>
> **Sender/Parent:** In the first part of this conversation, I want to make sure that you understand how I'm feeling about this. And then, when we can both tell that I am being clear and you are understanding, I want to listen while you tell me how you feel. Is that okay?
>
> **Receiver/Child:** Okay.
>
> **Sender/Parent:** I [delivers the message by describing how "I" feel—or think, or want, or see—and using words that are neutral and nonthreatening]. I want to make sure I'm being clear. Can you let me know that you've understood?
>
> **Receiver/Child:** I understand. You feel [OR think, want, see; mirrors her father].
>
> **Sender/Parent:** Yes. [If the child got it right; OR] Almost. [OR] Not quite. (*Note: If the child hasn't understood, then the parent sends the message again and asks the child to mirror back to him what the child thinks she has heard.*)
>
> **Receiver/Child:** You said [and mirrors what the parent has said].

Notice that the parent keeps repeating the message, using different terms until the child can mirror accurately.

Sender/Parent: It's important to me that you understand my point of view, and I want to understand yours. I want to listen now while you tell me what you are thinking and feeling.

The child becomes the sender and the parent becomes the receiver.

Sender/Child: I think [sends the message].
Receiver/Parent: I want to make sure I'm understanding you. If I got it right, you think that I [mirrors the child's message]. Did I get it?
Sender/Child: Yes. [OR] No. [OR] Sort of.

The child sends and the parent mirrors until the parent gets it correctly.

This may look complicated on the printed page, but the idea is very simple: you listen; you check to see that you've understood correctly; when you know that you have understood, you listen some more until the other person is finished. Then you can switch roles.

EXAMPLES OF MIRRORING

In order to make mirroring, validating, and empathizing as clear as possible, we will be giving examples of how these processes work in real conversations in the dialogues of three different families. The first dialogue is between Mrs. Grimes and her three-year-old daughter, Rebecca. The second is between Mr. Sands and his eleven-year-old son, Jason. The third is from Mrs. Robinson and her seventeen-year-old daughter, Sarah.

Let's begin with Mrs. Grimes. In our first example she is interacting with Rebecca the way she did before she learned about intentional dialogue. This is an example of how an *unconscious* parent might talk to her young daughter. We will give her a chance to start over again later.

Scenario #1: Mrs. Grimes has just hung up the phone from a conversation with Rebecca's best friend's mother. The other mother had called to ask if Rebecca could spend the night at their house as a birthday surprise for her daughter. Mrs. Grimes regretfully declines because Rebecca is not completely recovered from a respiratory infection and is still taking antibiotics. Rebecca, who has overheard the conversation, has plunked herself down on the floor and thrown her teddy bear across the kitchen.

Mrs. Grimes: *(to three-year-old Rebecca)* Don't throw your teddy bear on the floor! I'm not going to buy you any more toys if you can't treat them better than that! This just proves to me that you're still sick. It's a good thing you're not going over to Andrea's tonight. I'm glad I made that decision.

Rebecca: *(wailing)* I want to go. I'm not even sick. You don't know anything.

Mrs. Grimes: Don't talk to me like that. You're not going, and that's that. You're not well enough. Come on now, get up off the floor so I can set the table. And stop crying!

Rebecca: No!

Mrs. Grimes: Go to your room!

Comment: We're saying, not that this is terrible, just that Mrs. Grimes is not intentional during this exchange. Mrs. Grimes seems to be *reacting* to Rebecca, rather than *acting* from an awareness of what she wants to achieve. She is not being *intentional* during this exchange. Maybe she learned from her own mother that a child's disappointment and anger are to be ignored and that a child who says no needs to be reprimanded. Or maybe Mrs. Grimes is tired or in a hurry. Whatever the reason, she has not sent her daughter the core message that it's okay to feel whatever she feels and to express it. In fact, the message she's sending is quite the opposite.

In the next sample dialogue, Mrs. Grimes will have another chance. This is how the conversation might go if Mrs. Grimes was conducting it in a more conscious way, after having had some experience with intentional dialogue. Here she is initiating the dialogue and mirroring her daughter's feelings.

Receiver/Mrs. Grimes: Rebecca, I would like to sit down next to you on the floor. Is that all right?

Sender/Rebecca: No, I don't want you here.

Receiver/Mrs. Grimes: Okay, if you don't want me next to you, I'll sit over here out of your way. [She sits on the kitchen floor a few feet away from her daughter.] You must be mad at me.

Sender/Rebecca: No, I'm not mad!

Receiver/Mrs. Grimes: So, you are not mad. I thought you were, because you just threw Teddy across the floor.

Sender/Rebecca: You're making me miss the overnight. I'm *not* sick. I want to go.

Receiver/Mrs. Grimes: So, you are not really sick, and you really want to go. Is that right? And you are upset that I told Andrea's mother I didn't think you were well enough. Did I get it right?
Sender/Rebecca: Yes.

Comment: So far, Mrs. Grimes has initiated dialogue with her daughter, encouraged her to express her anger, and then mirrored Rebecca's feelings back to her to make sure that she, the mother, is understanding correctly. The next step will be for Mrs. Grimes to validate Rebecca's anger and disappointment.

But before we get to validating, let's drop in on another conversation, this time with Mr. Sands and eleven-year-old Jason. Again, let's first see how the conversation might go if Mr. Sands was acting as an unconscious parent who had never heard of intentional dialogue.

Scenario #2: Mr. Sands has just gotten a phone call from Jason's sixth-grade teacher in which the teacher explained that Jason was caught openly cheating on an English test. The teacher wanted Jason's father to know what had happened and to make sure that his son attends detention at school next Saturday morning.

Mr. Sands: (*puts down the phone and yells into the other room, where Jason is watching TV*) Jason, get in here right now! Turn off that noise and get yourself in here on the double!
Jason: You don't have to yell at me. What'd I do now?
Mr. Sands: I'll tell you what you did. I just got off the phone with your teacher. He says you cheated on your English test. How could you do that? How could you do that to your mother and me? Now you have to go to detention. That's humiliating. What's the matter—you're not smart enough to pass the test without cheating? Answer me.
Jason: I guess not.

Comment: We understand why Mr. Sands is upset. It's terribly distressing to find out that your son is cheating in school. But, clearly Mr. Sands is being reactive here rather than intentional. In order to become intentional he might need to pause for a few moments after the phone call before interacting with Jason. During the pause he can think about what he wants to accomplish in that conversation. It might be a good idea to find out why Jason cheated on this test, since he has not cheated before.

So let's transform Mr. Sands into a more conscious father. This Mr. Sands wants to send a message to his son about what has happened, and he wants to receive a message from his son about what has happened. In this scene Jason and his father are somewhat familiar with the concept of mirroring, because although they have never used that word or been formal about dialogue, Mr. Sands does have fairly good listening skills, and Jason has had the experience of being listened to.

Sender/Mr. Sands: Jason, I want to talk with you about something important. Ordinarily I would ask if this is a good time for you, but this is a matter I feel we have to talk about now. Would you please turn off the TV and come sit beside me in the family room?

Receiver/Jason: Oh, no. What'd I do now?

Sender/Mr. Sands: You sound worried. Please come sit with me, and I'll tell you what's on my mind. [Jason sits down.] I just got a call from your teacher. He tells me that you and he had a conversation today where you admitted cheating on your English test. I guess I need to know whether that's true, and if it is, then we need to talk about it. I have some definite feelings about cheating, and I'm sure you do, too. Did you cheat?

Receiver/Jason: (*looks scared and his eyes fill with tears*) Yeah, I cheated.

Sender/Mr. Sands: You cheated. Is there more about that?

Receiver/Jason: I was scared about the test. I didn't do so well on the last one, and I didn't want to get another D. Are you mad at me?

Sender/Mr. Sands: Let me make sure I understand: if I got it right, you cheated because you were afraid that unless you copied someone else's paper you wouldn't know the right answers. And after not doing so well on the last test, it would be hard on you if you didn't do well on this test. Have I got that right?

Receiver/Jason: Yes. Are you mad?

Sender/Mr. Sands: You are wondering whether I am mad. Well, I'm not sure what I'm feeling yet. I do know that I'm upset. Cheating is a very important matter to me. So is the fact that you were worried that you wouldn't do well on your English test without cheating. We need to talk about these issues until we really understand each other. And then we need to figure out what to do next. But first, I want to know that you understand where I'm coming from. Am I being clear so far?

Receiver/Jason: You're upset and you think cheating is a big deal, and we need to talk more.

Sender/Mr. Sands: That's right.

Comments: Mr. Sands initiated dialogue with Jason right on the spot. He presented his message in simple, factual terms with no jumping to conclusions and no blaming. Mr. Sands is mirroring Jason, and he is also encouraging Jason to mirror him. Although Mr. Sands initiates the dialogue as sender, he does a lot of listening. He needs to understand what is motivating Jason to engage in this behavior. That means Jason will have to do a lot of sending, and Mr. Sands will have to do a lot of mirroring before he knows what is pushing his good boy to do this. When we pick up on this dialogue again later, we will see what part validating plays in this drama.

Our third example is an illustration of symbiotic fusion, a concept we introduced at the beginning of this chapter. You may remember that symbiosis occurs when the parent acts as if her child were an extension of herself, as if her child thinks as she thinks, feels as she feels, wants what she wants, knows what she knows. This is a problem Mrs. Robinson has in her relationship with her seventeen-year-old daughter, Sarah. Conducting the conversation as an unconscious parent, Mrs. Robinson demonstrates her difficulty in treating her daughter as an independent person.

Scenario #3: Sarah met with her high-school guidance counselor today to talk about applying to college, and she brought home some brochures and other printed information. She's not sure where she wants to go to school, but she's thinking that the nearby community college might provide about the right amount of challenge. Mrs. Robinson wants her daughter to be more ambitious and to apply to a number of private colleges. At the very least she wants her to apply to the state university she herself had attended. Their attempts to communicate ended in a fight, with Sarah shouting on her way out of the room, "You don't listen to me. You only want me to do what *you* want me to do."

Some time has passed and Mrs. Robinson has gone upstairs and knocked on Sarah's bedroom door. Here is Mrs. Robinson's conversation with Sarah:

Mrs. Robinson: Sarah, I want to talk to you.

Sarah: About what?

Mrs. Robinson: You stomped off before I had a chance to say what I wanted to say. I just don't want you to do something you'll regret. If you go to a community college, you'll be doing yourself a disservice. You won't like it. And all your life, you'll wish you had reached for more.

Sarah: What you mean is *you* don't think it's good enough. *You* wouldn't like it. How do you know what I'd like and what I wouldn't like?

Mrs. Robinson: You're my daughter.

Comment: Poor Mrs. Robinson and poor Sarah. Mrs. Robinson is talking as though her job is to persuade her daughter to do what *she* wants her to do, instead of understanding what Sarah would be comfortable with. Let's give this mother another chance. Let's say that some version of the earlier blowup did happen, but that Mrs. Robinson has had a chance to collect her thoughts and remind herself of the underlying goals of intentional dialogue. She is now ready to have a conversation with Sarah in which she listens and mirrors until she understands Sarah's point of view.

Receiver/Mrs. Robinson: Sarah, I'm not happy with my part in the misunderstanding we just had. I'd like to talk about it a little more. Is this a good time?

Sender/Sarah: I suppose.

Receiver/Mrs. Robinson: I'm guessing that you're feeling like I'm not listening very well to you. I think I kind of jumped in too soon with my own opinions without waiting to hear your thinking about why the community college would be a good place for you next year. Right?

Sender/Sarah: *(sarcastically)* Just a little.

Receiver/Mrs. Robinson: Okay, I'm ready to listen now. I want to hear what you're thinking about school and where you want to go.

Sender/Sarah: Whenever I try to tell you how I feel, you don't listen. So what's the point?

Receiver/Mrs. Robinson: So I don't listen when you try to talk to me.

Sender/Sarah: That's right.

Receiver/Mrs. Robinson: I hear that, and it is true that I didn't

just now. I'm ready to listen now. I would like to interrupt you every so often—just to check with you that I'm understanding what you're saying. Is that okay?
Sender/Sarah: Okay.

Comment: In this dialogue Mrs. Robinson has to provide evidence to Sarah that Sarah can trust her. Sarah will probably not unburden herself to her mother unless she can see that her mother is putting aside her own preconceptions and making an effort to understand the issue through Sarah's eyes.

Mirroring occurs throughout all parts of intentional dialogue. We have found in our own experience that if the parents do it enough, the kids will pick it up too, until it becomes second nature for everyone.

THE MODEL FOR VALIDATING

By validating a child often, the parent helps the child learn how to validate. When the parent models the behavior he wants his child to exhibit, the child will begin doing it. As the child is validated, he will validate others. Here is a model for how a parent can validate his child:

Sender/Child: [Expresses thoughts.]
Receiver/Parent: What you are saying makes sense. Given your experience, it makes sense that [paraphrases the message]. Right?
Sender/Child: Yeah, [expands on the message a little more].
Receiver/Parent: Well, I can see that, too. You're making sense, because [fills in the reasoning of the child].
Sender/Child: It sounds so stupid to say it.
Receiver/Parent: So you think that sounds stupid. I can see why this is bothering you.
Sender/Child: You can?

Comment: The parent is sending a powerful message back to his child here. The message is "You're okay; what you're thinking is understandable; you're not crazy or off-base." Even if the parent feels that his child is being overly sensitive or is misinterpreting the situation or not seeing clearly, the parent starts by validating what his child is thinking. The child's view may not be the same as the parent's individual and adult perspective on the situation, but it is reasonable that someone else, especially someone who is a child, might see it this way. Validating does not mean that you agree. It does *not* mean that you wouldn't like your child to have a different point of view. It simply means that the child has a right to his own thoughts and feelings and that you, the parent, recognize and honor that right.

EXAMPLES OF VALIDATING

Let's return to Mrs. Grimes and her three-year-old daughter, Rebecca, who is disappointed at not being able to spend the night at Andrea's house. Here Mrs. Grimes is already doing some validating by putting into words what she thinks her daughter may be thinking.

> **Receiver/Mrs. Grimes:** So you really want to go over for the night?
>
> **Sender/Rebecca:** Yes, I do. Andrea's my best friend.
>
> **Receiver/Mrs. Grimes:** Well, it makes sense to me that you would want to go, because you don't feel sick and Andrea is your best friend. I can understand that.
>
> **Sender/Rebecca:** You can?

Comment: A less conscious parent might say and do other things in this exchange. For example, she might try to justify her decision to keep Rebecca home, or she might give her a lecture on the importance of taking care of her health. But all Mrs. Grimes is doing here is saying, "I know you wanted to go and you're disappointed, and I understand why." It's that simple.

When we left Mr. Sands, he was saying that he and Jason need to talk together about the cheating so that they understand each other's point of view. Let's see now how Mr. Sands validates his son, even in the midst of his anger with him.

> **Sender/Mr. Sands:** I can tell that you're feeling kind of bad about this. It's embarrassing to be caught doing something you're not proud of, isn't it?
>
> **Receiver/Jason:** (*mumbles*) Yeah.
>
> **Sender/Mr. Sands:** I can understand that. And I can see the sense in your thinking that you could not afford *not* to do well on another test.
>
> **Receiver/Jason:** Yeah.

Comment: By validating Jason's fear of being shamed by another failure on his exams, Mr. Sands is not saying that he approves of cheating or that Jason's actions are acceptable to him or that cheating is no big deal. He is simply saying, "I can see how you're thinking; I understand it; I respect it." Mr. Sands has a much better chance of influencing his son because he is able to deliver this message. It's much easier for a child to learn and change when the parent is respectful than when the parent is hostile.

In our third example Mrs. Robinson has just promised Sarah that she will listen to her daughter in an attempt to understand what she is saying as an independent person who has her own opinions and feelings.

> **Sender/Sarah:** I don't want to go to a big, fancy college. I'm afraid I won't be able to do well.
>
> **Receiver/Mrs. Robinson:** Going to state university feels like a big step—one that feels too big for right now?
>
> **Sender/Sarah:** Yes, it scares me. It's not like high school was a piece of cake, you know?
>
> **Receiver/Mrs. Robinson:** You are making sense. I can see you're thinking that high school was difficult and going to a big university seems even more challenging.
>
> **Sender/Sarah:** So you understand? I don't sound crazy?
>
> **Receiver/Mrs. Robinson:** Well, I do understand what you are saying, and you don't sound crazy.

Comment: As was the case for Mr. Sands, Mrs. Robinson is concentrating on understanding her daughter's thoughts and validating them. She isn't telling her that everybody thinks like that or that she is wrong. She isn't saying that meeting and overcoming fears builds strong character. She is providing her daughter with the emotional safety that will allow this young woman to look at her thoughts and explore them a little, without having to submerge them or cover them up. Thinking that is devalued, unacknowledged, denied, or covered-up tends to create confusion and indecision. It interferes with the ability to consider other alternatives.

THE MODEL FOR EMPATHY

The final process of intentional dialogue is empathizing. Empathy is an essential quality of civilized life. If we weren't able to hear other people's feelings or, on a deeper level, to put ourselves in the shoes of people different from us, we wouldn't be able to pass just and humane laws. We wouldn't be able to work for the preservation of national parks we'll never visit or even be able to help older people onto the bus. Raising empathic children should be one of our most primary personal and social concerns.[7]

Empathy is something children learn at home from parents who practice it. A child learns the words to express his empathic feelings when he hears them from you. The message of validation is "I understand that you think this way." The message of empathy is "I am feeling that with you right now." This is powerful. It lets the child know that he is not alone, that the two of you are connected even when you differ.

Here is the model for empathizing with your child:

Sender/Child: [Expresses feelings.]

Receiver/Parent: When I let myself be you for a moment, I feel [whatever the child has just said]. [OR] I can imagine that you must be feeling [places a label on what she imagines the child's feeling to be]. [OR] It makes sense to me that you would feel that way. [OR] I feel like crying myself when I hear you talk about this. [OR] I can feel how frustrated you must be. [OR] I feel so happy inside when I look at your face and see you smiling. [OR] Just now, I feel so disappointed that you [interprets the child's feelings].

EXAMPLES OF EMPATHY

Let's see how Mrs. Grimes would empathize with Rebecca:

Receiver/Mrs. Grimes: I'm hearing your disappointment, and I can imagine you also feel sad about that. Is that your feeling?

Sender/Daughter: Yes, I am disappointed and sad.

Receiver/Mrs. Grimes: I can feel your sadness.

How would Mr. Sands empathize with Jason?

Sender/Mr. Sands: I hear your fear of failing, and I can imagine you may have been afraid of feeling ashamed if you had flunked. And that made you feel kind of desperate.

How would Mrs. Robinson empathize with Sarah?

Receiver/Mrs. Robinson: I am hearing that you feel afraid about going to a big college, and you were afraid that I wasn't going to listen to you—that I would push my own wishes on to you. I can understand why you would be afraid of that. I have done that to you in the past. Given that I have done that in the past, your feelings make sense.

As you can tell from the way these three different parents dialogue with their children, the words vary, but the spirit is the same. Each parent has found his or her own language for letting the child know that "We are connected," "I recognize you as a person independent from me within our connection," and "You are okay." As you begin to dialogue with your child, you too will find your own words.

WHAT HAPPENS WHEN INTERACTIONS ARE UNCONSCIOUS?

As we've seen from our three examples, intentional dialogue is *consistent:* you listen, work to understand, and remain respectful of your child's point of view in every encounter you have with her. Intentional dialogue is *purposeful:* you know which specific outcomes you want, and overall, you know that you want your child to get the message that she's okay. Intentional dialogue is *intentional:* you have a way of structuring dialogue that furthers your aims as a conscious parent, even if at a particular moment you are not feeling very intentional yourself.

In contrast, unconscious interactions are *inconsistent:* you don't listen, you don't understand, and you are not respectful of your child's point of view. Unconscious interactions are *nonpurposeful:* you lose sight of what is best for your child, and you act out of your own needs, sending your child the message that she is not okay. Unconscious interactions are *reactive:* you respond to your child as though she were the cause of your negative feelings of disappointment, rage, or low self-worth, rather than correctly assessing that the cause is from some other place and time.

We began each of our sample dialogues by reporting the unconscious conversations each of our three parents had with their children, because it can be helpful to see how to do it wrong. To help you become even more adept at recognizing your own unconscious ways of talking with your children, here are a few more examples that are very common. Do you recognize yourself in any of these responses?

UNCONSCIOUS	CONSCIOUS
You don't like shrimp. You never eat shrimp!	I'm surprised you're eating the shrimp. I didn't realize you liked it.
I don't care what you want. You're not going.	I realize that you really want to go, but in this instance, I'm saying no.
You can't go out looking like that! You look like a sexpot.	Wait a minute. We need to talk. I'm not comfortable with what you're wearing.
You always do that. You act like you don't care about anybody but yourself.	Let's talk about what just happened here. I feel like you didn't hear what I just said.
It's for your own good. I only want what's best for you.	I know we feel differently, but I want you to understand what my thoughts are. I also want to know what's on your mind.

There are several things to note about this brief list of examples. First, the conscious statements are in the "I" form. The parent makes his point by saying what he thinks, feels, wants, observes, etc. In the unconscious examples the parent presumes he knows what his child thinks, feels, wants, or observes. Even the last example, "It's for your own good," doesn't take the child into account, but relies instead on reference to global "truth" for its authority.

The second feature is that the unconscious examples are filled with words like "always" and "never," rather than making reference to the specific incident in the specific moment. It's easy to feel labeled and judged by such statements.

But, even more important than the specific words of unconscious talk is the message that such interchanges send to your child. They say, "I know more than you. Don't think, feel, act, and sense on your own, because that's not okay."

In this context it is helpful to remember Frank Conroy and his stepfather, and Sarah and Mrs. Robinson in her unconscious mode. In both cases the parents are symbiotically fused with their children. Their connection doesn't allow room for seeing and appreciating the unique differences that exist between people, whether they are related or not. This kind of connection is really no connection at all in the sense that we mean it here, because the parent doesn't truly know the child. He only knows an image or projection of the child as it relates to his needs. He uses the child to meet his needs. And there is no meeting between two people who are unknown to each other and unappreciated by each other.

COMMUNICATION WITH PRESCHOOL CHILDREN

If you have children under the age of six, there are some special considerations for communicating with them effectively. Even though very young children do not have the vocabulary of the rest of us nor the experience to accurately pinpoint abstract ideas, you will want to talk to them with the same respect and intelligence that you show when you talk to everyone else. Whether you use all the words of intentional dialogue or not, you will want to preserve the spirit of mirroring, validating, and empathizing. And sometimes these processes happen best when they are carried out without words.

For example, it's easy to see how to mirror with an infant. The baby smiles, you smile; the baby frowns, you frown; the baby coos, you coo. You let him know you're with him by your synchronous body language and the tone of your voice.

With toddlers and children under six, you will want to physically get down to their level when important communication is going on. Imagine the difference between talking to someone eighteen feet tall and someone your own height.

When your child is scared or worried or angry, you will want to initiate physical contact with her to help her feel safe and connected to you. A gentle touch or a hug does more than words to validate and empathize with a young child. If you are too close, or if the child doesn't want physical contact at that moment, she will let you know by pulling away.

Your body language is at least as important as what you say. The expression on your face and your relaxed and listening stance let the child know you are interested and ready to hear what he has to say. For the child, it is an unforgettable moment when a powerful adult stops what she is doing, turns her receptive face to him, gets down on his level, and invites him to tell her what's on his mind.

If you are puzzled or troubled by a child's behavior at any particular moment, ask the child about it. Treat your child as a person and see if you can find out how he is feeling. "Is something wrong?" "Are you hurting?" "Are you mad about something?" "Is something bothering you?" "Can I help you with something?"

One mother we worked with told us about an encounter she had with her four-year-old son. One afternoon, her easygoing child seemed uncharacteristically out of sorts. Finally, after a couple of hours of nothing going right, she asked him what was wrong. "You're a bad mother," he informed her. "You don't put me to bed when I'm tired."

Another mother we know told a similar story about her five-year-old daughter. A couple of years earlier, her husband, the child's father, had had a heart attack and ended up spending a week in the hospital. He did well, but during the time he was in the hospital, around the fourth day or so, this mother began to notice that her daughter was not doing so well, not eating, appearing very listless. Before this the mother had been preoccupied with her husband's medical emergency and hadn't noticed what was happening with her child. When she asked, this is what her daughter said, "I'm sad. My daddy has died, and I won't see him anymore." Once she asked, it was easy for the mother to clear up the misunderstanding by taking her child to see her father in the hospital.

It is validating to a young child when you can verbalize what he is thinking. Always encourage him to tell you first so that you don't have to guess. But if the words don't come easily to your child and you think you know what's going on, you can ask a question that may help him identify and explore what's troubling him.

As an example, let's assume that this is the first day that you have left your three-year-old off at day care. You pick him up after he's had a rough day. Now you want to talk with your child about the experience, following the guidelines for intentional dialogue adjusted as appropriate for a three-year-old. This is how the dialogue might go:

> **Receiver/Mother:** Sometimes the day is hard. How was it for you?
> **Sender/Child:** I don't like that school.
> **Receiver/Mother:** So you don't like that school. Is there more about that?
> **Sender/Child:** Nobody likes me.
> **Receiver/Mother:** You don't think you have a friend there?
> **Sender/Child:** No.

Receiver/Mother: You don't like school because you don't have a friend there. That makes sense. And I can imagine that makes you sad. Is that your feeling?

Sender/Child: Yes, I am sad, and I don't want to go back.

Receiver/Mother: I see. So you don't want to go back. Well, let's talk about what we can do about that. Some other children may be feeling the same way. Maybe we can find one and invite him over for a play date. How does that sound to you?

Sender/Child: Okay. I guess so.

Comment: This mother is verbalizing on behalf of her child, mirroring, and validating. She is able to put into words what is worrying him and to do so in a matter-of-fact way. She is careful not to use words that are full of misery or terror. She wants to convey that she understands how he is feeling and that such feelings are normal. Other people feel that way, too.

OTHER WAYS TO ENCOURAGE GOOD COMMUNICATION

Pay Attention to the Physical Setting: Sometimes with kids the right topic comes up at the wrong time, and you know you have to pursue it anyway. Your twelve-year-old may be ready to tell you about his pot smoking while you are driving in heavy traffic. Your sixteen-year-old may tell you she needs birth control in the middle of Aisle 8 while you're shopping for canned tuna. Even when you're caught by surprise, you want to keep your wits about you and remember to mirror, validate, and empathize—no matter what else you're doing at the time.

But if you have some choice in the matter, it's a good idea to pay attention to the physical setting of your dialogue. With older children, either you or they can initiate dialogue by asking "Is this a good time?" A reasonable answer is "Yes. In five minutes. After I finish paying this bill [or whatever]."

You will both want to be sitting down. We know one mother and her two sons who always sat down for important conversations—on top of their kitchen counter. That was the signal that it was safe to go ahead and talk about intimate matters.

You will want to have as few distractions as possible. Ringing telephones, blaring television sitcoms, and loud music do not encourage successful dialogues. You want the setting to be as peaceful and quiet as possible.

Show That You're Listening: *You will want your body language to be open and receptive.* You may want to close your eyes for a moment and remember a time when you knew that someone was really listening to you. Can you picture how that person looked? Eyes on you, body slightly forward, muscles relaxed, facial expression open. This is how to show your child that you are ready to listen.

You will want to keep quiet while your child is talking. If you've ever been well-listened to, you know how satisfying the experience is. The other person lets you speak until you have no more to say, without interrupting or talking over you—even if you spiral off the subject or temporarily run aground. It's hard for some people to tolerate silences, but an experienced listener knows that sometimes silence is the precursor to very productive talk.

Show That You Care: *Be nonjudgmental.* Your stance will be encouraging, courteous, tolerant, and respectful. That shows that you are *caring.* In addition, because you are being *intentional,* you will keep in mind the core message you want to send your child (that it's okay for her to have these feelings and express them) and you will be nonreactive. You also want your part in the dialogue to be *nonjudgmental,* and last, you will be as *nonintrusive* as possible. You want to find out what's in your child's heart and mind, not to try to control her thoughts and feelings with your own opinions and comments.

YOU TRY IT

The easiest way is to begin by doing whichever part is most natural for you. Of these three processes—mirroring, validating, and empathizing—which feels the most comfortable? For many people, it's mirroring. They find they can repeat back something someone has said or paraphrase it without too much trouble. If you find paraphrasing difficult, you can start by repeating their words verbatim and then progress to paraphrasing.

Our suggestion is that you find at least one opportunity to mirror with your child today. In order to do that, you will have to pay more attention to the way you and your child interact. You will find yourself listening more closely to the conversations you have together.

After you've intentionally engaged in whichever process is easiest for you, begin to experiment with the other two. Use them in conversation whenever you can, and see what happens. Make note of how your child responds when you say, "Let me make sure I'm understanding you right," or "I can see how you would feel . . ." We predict that your child will become more trusting, more able to express his feelings, and more open to hearing what you have to say.

Your goal is to learn to dialogue and to stay with it until you reach empathic connection with each other. Once you do that, you will not be defending yourself in interchanges with your child, and your child will not have to defend herself against you, either. In an atmosphere of mutual understanding you will begin to undo whatever damage has been done by previously unconscious interaction, and you will begin to build solidly on the new empathic connection you have formed.

To build this connection, you have to do more than dialogue with your child. You have to teach your child to dialogue with you. At some point, you will want to be explicit about the purpose and the language of intentional dialogue and to explain why you say and do the things you do. Then teach her how to communicate this way by cueing her and expressing appreciation for her efforts.

Intentional dialogue can become a ritual, a habit that your family does regularly. It is a way of being in the world. It's a stance that you take that expresses respect for the otherness of all people and a willingness to learn about points of view different from your own.

In some ways, practicing intentional dialogue is analogous to praying. Prayer is also a way of being in the world. You don't always stop to pray. Your whole life is prayer. In the same way, you don't always stop to dialogue. Intentional dialogue can become a ritual, a habit that your family does regularly. Your own life can become a dialogue.

We want to send you into the next chapter dialoguing with your child. Talk in a way that evokes listening. Practice relating to your children in a nondefensive way. Instead of reacting, mirror. Every time you want to react, mirror instead. Sprinkle your conversations with the phrases of intentional dialogue:

I'm not sure; what do you think?
Let me repeat that so I'm sure I'm understanding.
Do you want me to say that again, just to make sure I'm being
   clear?
It sure sounds like you're mad.
I'm disappointed for you.

I'm so glad you can tell me how you are feeling.
It feels good to me that I can tell you how I'm feeling.
That makes sense to me.
That doesn't sound silly to me. But I can imagine that you might
   be feeling that way.

Learning the new language of intentional dialogue will help you grow as a parent and as a person. It interrupts any tendency you may have to be symbiotic with your child and allows you to become a more distinct self, while achieving greater clarity of thought and feeling. As you are learning this language, and experiencing what it's like to be more intentional, the next chapter will help you take action to become a more conscious parent. You have some direction about how to talk with your children. Now it is time to learn what else to *do*.

6

The Conscious Parent

We must learn to imagine what we already know.
—PERCY BYSSHE SHELLEY

A NEW VISION

We need to give birth to a new vision of parenting. This vision would be based on what we know about the special bond between parent and child, through which even ordinary communication is a sacrament. It would be based on reverence for what our children can bring to us, as well as what we can bring to them. By their light, we see what is hurt and hidden in ourselves, and we open creatively to new ways of responding to problems. Through them, we understand that parenting is a spiritual process in which we get back tenfold the love we give.

There are very few models for this kind of parenting. All of us are pioneers. We must chart this new vision step by step in a spirit of humility, guided by our own commitment to look within ourselves at our flawed perceptions, our ill will, and our pain. We know this is different from old models of parenting, which have been parent-centered and based on the idea that the parent is a static figure, all-seeing and all-knowing. It is also different from newer models of parenting that are excessively child-centered and equally out of balance.

We are reaching toward a new model in which the parent-child relationship itself is in the center. The emphasis is on maintaining the qual-

130

ity of the relationship rather than on serving the needs of one person at the expense of the other. It may not be obvious, but this is a profoundly sacred process. A parent who teaches her child to be in such a relationship is teaching him to respect and honor all of life. She is teaching him that the high virtues of loving kindness and moral behavior are not separate from ordinary life. They are to be found within it in the intimate relationships and everyday connections that give it substance.

THE QUESTION

In his book *The Moral Intelligence of Children,* Robert Coles asks this question, "How ought we, you and I, as parents or as teachers (parents are, again, always teachers), do the best possible job of handing on our principles and convictions and values to this next generation?"[1]

This is a pressing question—coming as it does from a teacher and writer who has distinguished himself with a lifetime of important work on behalf of children and young people. Every generation has a right and an obligation to pass on its values to the children of the next generation. But we would like to enlarge the scope of Dr. Coles's question by acknowledging what *a child* can pass back to her parent: the essential information about herself that allows the parent to respond to *her* instead of to something inside himself. With this broader dynamic in mind, our question then becomes, *"How can we, as parents, do the best possible job of meeting the individual needs of each of our children, while at the same time passing on the values we consider to be important for all of them?"* And how can we be intentional about these goals?

This is a suitable focus for this chapter, keeping in mind that we have found many answers already. Specifically, in Chapter 4, "The Child as Teacher," we talked about how a parent can learn about himself and his child by thinking of his child as his teacher. In the chapter preceding this one, "Intentional Dialogue," we introduced the concept that everyday conversation can become an instrument for preserving the bond between parent and child without the distortion of symbiotic fusion. Now it's time to see what else a parent can do, *in the spirit of dialogue,* to teach the child what he needs to know in a way that respects his integrity. This is the essence of conscious parenting.

BEING INTENTIONAL WHEN IT'S NOT EASY

There are times when conscious parenting is difficult. The bond with our children can seem more like a yoke. In such moments of acute self-involvement, a parent doesn't have time to gather his wits before he speaks. He must rely on the habits of mind he's already established. In these moments, either he has already developed the habit of intentionality[2] that will carry him through or he hasn't. If he hasn't, he won't be able to reach for habit under stress. The example that follows shows how it is possible to be intentional even in stressful situations. This is conscious parenting distilled to its essence. The father in this story could have become angry, but instead he acted with calmness and dignity to preserve the self-esteem of his children and the positive boundaries appropriate for him and his wife.

> Patti and I were making love one evening in bed. We forgot to lock the door. All of a sudden it came open. So we stopped and I looked around. Both kids are standing there.
>
> Lindsay was about seven or eight and Jim was nine or ten. They said, "What are you doing?" I said, "We're making love and we'd like some privacy." Jim immediately got red in the face and said, "Oh," and got out of there fast. But Lindsay just stood there. I said "Lindsay?" and she said, "What?" I said, "We'd like to be alone." And Lindsay said, "I want to watch. I'll be quiet."
>
> Her reaction was, "*Hmmm*, this is interesting." I said to her in an even but firm voice, "No, we don't want you to. We'd like to have some privacy. So close the door and go back to bed." "Okay," she said. And she did.
>
> The thing is, we didn't treat her any different than we would have treated an adult friend who might have stepped into the room. We didn't try to hide anything or disguise anything. We didn't get mad and we didn't say, "Knock before you come in," or anything like that. It was just a matter of: This is what's happening and this is the way we deal with it.

An atmosphere of trust is obviously part of the ecosystem of this household, which, as is true for every family, is made up of numberless everyday elements and events that are interconnected. No single incident between parents and children can be fully understood without having a sense of the entire system. These children know that they are loved, that they can trust their parents, and that when their parents say no, they mean it. For them a potentially difficult situation became just one more experience of mutual respect in an atmosphere that contains both bounty and boundaries.

In every family there are moments like this one. There are always unexpected intrusions that are potentially embarrassing or even anger producing. In these situations unconscious parents speak and act "without thinking" to protect themselves, regardless of whether their reactions will embarrass or shame their children. Conscious parents are able to countermand these unconscious survival messages of the old brain with the more rational responses of the new brain. Their words are kinder and gentler. They are spoken from an awareness of the big picture and not from defensive reactions to perceived injuries in the present moment.

In order to become intentional, parents must be willing to look at what is hidden in themselves. Wounds that go unexamined have power. They influence what we say and do, and years later, when we can no longer remember exactly what happened or why we feel this way, these hurtful moments still hang over us like black clouds. We may not be able to trace exactly the line of pain that goes from our mothers and fathers down to us and through us into the alchemy of marriage and on to our own children. But the line is there, mixed in of course with the kindness and caring and humor that also get passed along.

CONSCIOUS PARENTING: THE COMMITMENT

We are born out of a conscious universe into consciousness.[3] It is our natural state to be open to ourselves and the world in an accepting way, without censoring or disapproving. A young child greets his experiences as they are: he is curious and ready to learn from the sounds and sights and feelings that flow through him moment by moment. It is only later that he learns to protect himself, to hide what is unacceptable, and to fool himself and others about who he really is. This loss of awareness is a way of coping with experiences that have caused him grief in the past by breaking his connection to his true nature, to other people, and to the cosmos.

All of us have been that child. We have grown up with blank spots where conscious awareness could have been manifest. Fortunately, we can recover. Parents can make the decision to understand themselves and their children more deeply. And when they do, they choose the path of consciousness. They commit themselves to an *intentional* course of action. To intend an outcome and cause it to happen requires a decision to engage in behaviors that will achieve the desired result. In order to do that, the parent must have an awareness of the condition she wants to change, the impediments that have to be overcome, and the actions that must be taken.

If symbiosis is the human problem, then differentiation and empathic connection are the human solution. The intentionality of the conscious parent replaces the reactivity of the unconscious parent. The capacity to differentiate from the child replaces the tendency to fuse with him. Empathic connection replaces defensive projection.

A parent knows he is intentional when, in a moment of stress, he says and does the things that support the outcomes he has chosen while sending his child the core message that she is okay. He is not at the mercy of his own emotions or his own history. He is able to put aside his preconceived formulations and old assumptions about who his child is, and he can focus on responding to her real needs, free from any outdated, unrecognized agenda of his own. The child's innate wholeness is his guide and inspiration. The child who experiences this kind of connection with a parent learns how to make this kind of connection with others.

The goal for us is to lay the groundwork that will make it possible for our children to become adults who are whole and fully alive, naturally expressing their life energy without inhibition. With six children of our own, we know that it is difficult to keep this goal in mind in the middle of the daily grind.

We have already framed unconscious parenting as a continuum, and it makes sense to think of consciousness as occurring along a continuum also. There are degrees of consciousness in parenting. One point along the continuum is achieved by having and using *cognitive information* about children and about good parenting strategies. This stimulates consciousness. Another point along the continuum is *awareness* of our oneness, our own inner unity, and our connection to a larger whole. Another point further along the continuum is *experiencing oneness* with ourselves and with everything in the universe. Our deepest yearnings are to be wholly connected, as we were when we were very young. That is why any connectional act feels good and right to us, from the simplest—touching another person or sharing a story—to the most sublime mystical experience.[4]

Our intention in this chapter is to help you take the next step toward conscious awareness for yourself, whatever that might be. Certainly, we will provide you with cognitive information. But we also hope to stimulate your awareness by deepening your understanding of yourself, your partner if you have one, and your children.

Although we have already talked a lot about intentional dialogue, we want to begin with it again. In the last chapter we focused on how to do it; here we want to help you see how it is both the change agent for and the manifestation of conscious parenting. It is both cause and effect. And there are additional tools that can be used with intentional dialogue that will allow parents to handle common parenting situations. In a way, these tools can be considered *extensions* of intentional dialogue, because they deepen and expand its spirit.

DIALOGUE AS THE CATALYZING AGENT OF CONSCIOUS PARENTING

Dialogue is a growth process for a parent as he learns to suspend his own subjectivity temporarily and stretch to include the subjectivity of another person. This opens him up to new information, which is essential for his continuing growth. Dialogue is also the catalyst for dissolving symbiosis and facilitating differentiation, so that a parent can move from seeing the child as an extension of himself to seeing his child as a distinct other. As his pattern of symbiotic relating begins to dissolve and his capacity to differentiate grows, he restarts his own growth through developmental stages that he was unable to complete earlier in his life. He can proceed to adulthood without having to detour at spots where his own development was arrested. In this way dialogue helps parents complete their childhoods and finally achieve adult consciousness.

DIALOGUE AS A LIFESTYLE

To be an agent of transformation, dialogue needs to become a lifestyle. It begins as a mechanism for verbal communication, but if practiced daily, it can become an *orientation* or an *attitude* toward life. It is an attitude characterized by real understanding and empathy for life experiences or points of view different from one's own. It is characterized by patience, nonjudgment, and moderation. It is a way of being in which we make the intentional response instead of the instinctive one.

The hard work of practice eventually makes dialogue a habit. Over time, as control over reactivity improves, dialogue becomes less mechanical and more natural. Then, even though some transactions might not include all three steps of mirroring, validation, and empathy, the parent's relationship to his children becomes dialogic in spirit. The counterinstinctual response replaces unconscious reaction because it better serves the goal of survival. Dialogue is inherently compatible with the human yearning for safety and support, because it provides a structure within which all hearts can be known and within which ruptures in connection can be repaired.

BY APPOINTMENT ONLY

We recommend dialogue whenever tensions appear in transactions or conversations. This will contain any negative energy and create a safe emotional space in which to communicate whatever a child or his parent is feeling. We recommend that parents use the "appointment only" process when they want to initiate a conversation about a specific concern, whether it is positive or negative, and that they teach their children to do the same. This prevents the spontaneous expression of thoughts or the dumping of feelings when the other person in the dialogue is not prepared. It is unwise to bring negative energy to a child who hasn't been prepared for it. The child may become defensive or at best inattentive. She may make a negative or reactive response and may be unable to do anything but give her sullen or guilty compliance.

The appointment process consists simply of making a statement: "I would like to make an appointment with you to talk about a [something]." The "something" may be a frustration or a hurt, an appreciation or a simple request. The responsibility of the other person is to say yes and set a time, either right now or later, and if later, to keep the appointment without having to be reminded. This communicates to the other person that his or her feelings are being valued. Setting an appointment should become automatic, and when it does, it replaces reactivity with conscious intentionality.

HANDLING FRUSTRATIONS:
THE BEHAVIOR-CHANGE REQUEST

The behavior-change request[5] is often used in conjunction with intentional dialogue. It is especially useful in dealing with specific frustrations but can only be used with children whose language skills are developed enough to put their feelings and frustrations into words. The process can go both ways. The frustration may be one the parent has with her child or one the child has with her. For instance, a parent might be frustrated that his child has not done her chores. Or the child has a dog that he tends to neglect, for example, thinking that since he has to get off to school, Mom will fill in. Or he may be frustrated that Mom was not there to pick him up after school on time.

After making an appointment, when the receiver is ready, the person with the frustration simply describes the behavior that frustrated him. It should be stated in a matter-of-fact way, with minimal intensity and no anger. (There is another tool for expressing anger, which we will discuss in a moment.) The receiver should mirror the frustration until the sender is finished, asking "Is there more?" whenever there is a long pause. The receiver should then validate the frustration and communicate empathy about what the sender might be feeling. When the parent teaches her child this process, she will have to be patient until he understands the steps. Again, the best way for him to understand is to let him be the sender first and practice until everyone has it down pat. Then the parent can ask him to be a receiver of *her* frustrations.

This is how a behavior-change request works: Begin with an intentional dialogue—all three steps. After the expression of empathy, the receiver asks the sender to name three specific behavior changes that the receiver might make, any one of which will render the frustration obsolete. Three is important, because it gives the receiver some options. The sender should be encouraged to make them specific and time-limited. For example:

Sender: For the next month, I want you to pick me up exactly on time. [OR] I don't want you to be more than five minutes late for the next month. [OR] For the next month, if you are more than five minutes late, I want you to take me out for a milk shake.

The receiver mirrors the three requests back, picks only one, and states exactly what she will do. Of course, common sense is important here. If the child makes three requests that are inappropriate, the parent needs to let the child know her requests are too demanding or too broad or not possible for some other reason. Then the parent can help the child express requests that are more reasonable. After the exchange, it is important to make physical contact, a hug or handshake, in order to reinforce the restoration of connection.

CONTAINING ANGER

Anger is a positive emotion. It protects us from actual or anticipated danger. It is also the other side of hurt, shame, and humiliation— emotions and experiences that also stir the survival instinct. If anger were always suppressed, passion would atrophy, and our children could become victims of many dangerous circumstances.

Although in nonintimate situations, anger has protective elements, in intimate situations, between parent and child or between spouses, anger is sometimes a protest against separation or the deprivation of one's needs. "Why are you gone so much?" or "Why don't you talk to me?" are common complaints of many children. They are attempts to satisfy a need as well as to restore connection. *When uncontained, anger sabotages a desired outcome.* It achieves the opposite result from that desired. When anger is contained and expressed appropriately, it achieves its goal. We teach a process for dealing with anger called the *container.*

Most frustrations stir up mild irritations rather than the passion of anger. Usually they can be resolved by using the three-step dialogue process, sometimes with the addition of the behavior-change request. When these are used regularly and successfully, children seldom become angry, because their needs are met and they feel safe and connected. But on occasion the frustration is intense and anger flares up. When a child is angry or her parents are angry at her, emotional injury is a real possibility. Most of us are tempted to suppress our children's anger and express our own—something parents seem to feel they have a right to do and their children don't! (This is especially true if the anger is directed at the parent.) But anger doesn't have to be prohibited or suppressed. Parents and children, both, can learn to express it inside the dialogue process. When it is allowed to evolve within the container process, it quickly dissolves and, in fact, deepens the bond between parent and child.

The Container Exercise:[6] Since anger is usually a response to a frustration of some sort (a disappointment, a feeling of being shamed, or a hurt), the procedure is essentially the same as the behavior-change request process, with one variation. When the sender/child is describing the frustrating behavior, the receiver/parent encourages him to amplify his feelings as much as he wants to. Using "I" language, he is encouraged to scream things like, "I hate it when you are late. I feel so mad about it. I don't want to be left at school alone again!" Sometimes it is important to encourage the use of "you" in order for the full intensity of the child's fury to be discharged: "You are never on time. You don't love me if you can't get to school on time." When the child's anger reaches its apex, the parent should then ask, "And how does it hurt you when I am late?" It is not unusual for the child to respond, having spent his anger, by breaking into tears and sobbing out the pain behind the anger. At which point the parent should take the child in her arms and hold him until the sobbing ceases. When the crying is over and the tears are dry, then the parent should mirror all that she has heard, and then move into the behavior-change request process, asking the child to describe three different ways the parent might change that would "make a difference," or "help." To complete this interaction, it is important to engage the child in a fun activity that evokes a belly laugh. Laughter transforms the emotional tone of the interaction, permits the event to be stored in memory with positive associations, and triggers internal neurochemical changes that support the emotional reconnection of the child to the parent.

When the child uses the container process with a parent, we recommend that the intensity be moderated, that the dissolving into tears be omitted, and that the parent not ask the child to hold her. We find that all the other steps work well in this process for helping the child deal with anger.

ALLOWING REGRESSIONS

A father at a soccer game squints his eyes closed and shakes his head at his son, who has just been hit hard by the largest player on the other team. The boy clenches his teeth, holds back his tears, and lies there. But he cannot get up. When they remove him from the field by stretcher and examine him, he is found to have a broken leg. How does the father react to this? Sometimes parents want their children to act like grown-ups and have no patience with sobbing or crying. Their discomfort with their own tears is transferred to the child as a prohibition. "Don't be a crybaby," in a form of gender discrimination, is often verbalized to boys—whereas girls are often expected to be tender and tearful. Some parents are uncomfortable with the tears of even small children and infants and are constantly "shushing" them into silence. "You will wake up the neighbors" or "What's the matter?" are designed to suppress the emotions of the child and comfort the parents; so is rocking, shaking, or hitting them.

Sometimes children, no matter what their age, just can't hold it in. They are hurt, tired, or frustrated. Their playmate hit them, their best friend rejects them, their first love abandons them, the other team trounces them, their pet dies on them, their favorite CD hides from them. They collapse into tears, they sob, and they need comfort. And when they do, parents need to be their solace. Our children's tears, like our own, are expressions of the human capacity to care and to feel deeply. They should be honored as expressions of our helplessness and as expressions of deep joy. Without the capacity to cry for ourselves and for the fate of others, we lose our connection with both ourselves *and* others at an empathic level.

Sometimes when people cry they regress, or go back, into feelings and states they experienced earlier in their lives. Parents need to nurture children who regress in ways that *enhance* the regression rather than limit it. When children are allowed to hit bottom and become infantile, they reintegrate at a higher, more secure level of development. If a parent is available in a supportive way, the child internalizes him as a tender, loving person, and this model becomes available as part of his or her own future parenting.

The Holding Exercise: We teach parents to meet their children's needs for safety and reassurance through what we call the holding exercise.[7] This helps parents respond appropriately to their child's immediate need for safe reassurance, especially when there is no time to set up an appointment or to discuss things rationally. It also allows the child to regress when they need to.

In the holding exercise the parent finds a comfortable place to sit and asks the child to sit in his lap with her face over the parent's heart or nestled into the cradle of his neck. Holding her conveys all the safety in the world at that moment. Any words that the parent uses in addition should convey the message that "You can share with me all that you are feeling; I love you always and no matter what, and I will always be here for you; you can cry as much as you want to."

The parent replaces any "shushing" with encouraging murmurs and gentle stroking. He is validating the child's state of mind, not telling her that she has nothing to worry about and not telling her that she will soon be over it. The child feels safe and supported, soon stops crying, and is then likely to be ready to discuss the problem. If there is anything to be done, they can work out a plan together.

Sometimes all the child needs is time to cry and be supported. Safe within the bond of connection and calm after the release of emotion, the child is infused with a sense of peace. There is no substitute at any age for frequent loving and supportive physical contact. It may be helpful for a parent to remember such moments of safety when she was a child or to remember what she would have liked to have had from her parents at such times.

The following story from a friend of ours is a testament to the power of the internalized parent. This father finds himself doing just what his own father would have done:

> We lived on a farm when the kids were little. I remember one day when Peter ran across a field and ran belly height into a barbed wire fence. He was scared; he was sure that he had been torn apart. It looked pretty bad, blood was coming right through his shirt and everything. But I picked him up and saw that it wasn't serious. I held him and I was stroking him on the back, and I was saying, "Darn it, anyway. Darn it, anyway." At that moment, I realized that those were the exact words that my dad would have said to me in the same situation. I think that was the first time I had one of those illuminations that I was being my dad. It taught me an awful lot about parenting and about people in general. I realized that in certain circumstances, those things just pop right out. I hadn't ever used that expression "darn it, anyway" in my recollection. It was my dad's voice coming out of me.

CONSCIOUS PARENTING PROVIDES SAFETY, SUPPORT, AND STRUCTURE

Our true authority as parents derives from the skill we have in helping our children navigate the passage of childhood toward adulthood. The essence of our children is entrusted to our care. When we keep them safe, help them flourish, and guide them through rough waters, we preserve the connection with the cosmos that is the birthright of every child.

We do that by creating an environment that serves three purposes: (1) it is physically safe, (2) it is emotionally supportive of the child's growth into a unique human being, and (3) it is structured to include limits or boundaries. Although we talk about them separately, these purposes overlap and are interactive. For example, when we provide structure, we are also taking care that the environment is physically and emotionally safe. What follows are some general guidelines for conscious parents to follow in order to provide safety, support, and structure for their children. In addition to these general guidelines, we will make specific suggestions in later chapters for use with children at successive stages of development.

PROVIDING SAFETY

Physical safety is the primary requirement of every living thing. It includes having shelter and enough to eat and freedom from fear of physical harm. For an infant or a small child every step away from her parents contains an element of fear. A baby wants to be reassured and held almost all its waking hours. As the baby grows older and more adventuresome, she gradually learns that it's all right to leave the enfolding arms of her parents and start exploring. But the least shock or unpleasant surprise brings her back for comfort. Her parents are there to *keep* her safe and to let her *know* that she is safe.

A baby who is always held and protected when she needs to feel safe, a child who is always sure her parents will be there when she is afraid, will grow into a curious and adventuresome child. But a child whose needs are met unevenly, who is sometimes smothered with affection and sometimes left to her own devices, will cling to the parent in the fear that he will not be there for her when she needs him. Her curiosity is limited to the world within "safe" reach of her parents. If her parents don't make her feel safe when she needs it, she will probably feel generally insecure and have trouble being comfortably alone.

The conscious parent not only provides the basics of food, shelter, and clothing, but is also aware that children have safety requirements that must be met, whether it is convenient to meet them or not. And she knows that the safety requirements of each child may vary somewhat. Johnny may be very bold and need only occasional reassurance; his brother may be a fearful child who requires much more attention. A conscious parent knows that it's important to be there for each of these sons.

The conscious parent responds to her child's needs whether she can understand them or not. In any given moment, it may be difficult for

her to feel what her children are feeling. To her, the Halloween costumes are amusing and shouldn't be scary to anybody. She can't understand why her thirteen-year-old is afraid to go to school with his new
haircut. She is impatient with her eight-year-old's reluctance to shake
hands with a stranger.

But whether she shares his feelings or not, whether she understands
them or not, she recognizes how he feels and does what she can to
make his physical and emotional world as safe as possible. Often she
physically reassures him with hugs or a hand on the arm; often she
verbally reassures him. As one of our friends sometimes says to his
children, "You are as safe as if you were in God's pocket."

PROVIDING SUPPORT

*The conscious parent uses "I" instead of "you" to express his own point of
view.* The most important way he can support his child is by validating
how she feels and who she is. When he uses "you" to express *his*
thoughts and feelings, he is really attempting to transplant his views
into his child.

Consider this example. Here, a youth soccer coach is talking to one
of his nine-year-old players, who has just twisted his ankle: "That isn't
so bad. You have to understand that you can't expect to play soccer
without getting hurt. When you give it your 'all,' that sometimes means
that you have to experience a little pain. You have to throw your body
on the line."

What this coach is really saying is: "I don't want to hear how you're
feeling. I don't want you to make a fuss. Be like me. I am tough, and I
can take it. If you can't, you're going to be a disappointment to me." A
more conscious response would have been: "I can tell that really hurts.
I know that sometimes when I play, I run the risk of getting hurt, too.
As long as I don't really injure myself, I figure that it's worth it. I could
see that you gave it a big effort out there. I like that, because I can see
how committed you are to doing a good job for the team. Now take it
easy for a while, and then you can go back into the game when you feel
better." It's true that the coach is still trying to influence how his player
feels, but he is not doing it by putting words in his mouth. He is clear
about the boundary between them and is letting the child have his own
feelings.

The conscious parent allows her child to express himself. As we have said, this is one of the primary needs of every child. As much as possible, the parent must own up to her own opinions and feelings and let her child have his.

More than *allowing* her child to express himself, she will want to find ways to *encourage* him to express himself. "What do you think?" "How did you feel when the teacher said that?" "I know what Cindy said, but I'm interested in what you thought about it." "How do you feel now?" When she encourages her child to tell his story, express his version of reality, or finish his own thoughts without editorial comment, she is validating him as a person who has the right to see the world from his own perspective.

In our discussion of intentional dialogue in the previous chapter, we pointed out that there will be times when a child will have trouble giving voice to his feelings. He might be too angry or upset to express things clearly, or he might be so young that he doesn't quite have the vocabulary. At those times, it is appropriate for a parent to voice what she thinks he is feeling but is unable to say, as long as she does so in the spirit of inquiry rather than inquisition: "Are you feeling . . . ?" "Maybe you feel . . ." "I'm guessing that you feel . . ." "This could make a person feel kind of . . ." These words are spoken in the spirit of intentional dialogue, for the purpose of encouraging a child to explore his own feelings and learn how to express them.

Also in the spirit of intentional dialogue, it helps if a parent can do most of her listening from the perspective of someone who is *disinterested*.[8] This is different from *uninterested*. Disinterested means "unbiased by personal interest or motive; not influenced by personal motives." It means that she hears her child; she validates and empathizes with his point of view without taking a stand or becoming overly involved emotionally. This gives him permission to really explore how he feels without fear that she will disapprove or try to change him.

Being disinterested does not mean that a parent doesn't care about expanding her child's point of view or even on occasion influencing him to think differently. She does care. But she does that *after* she has validated his feelings. Then she is very direct about how she thinks and how she feels. She might say something like, "I understand how you could feel that way. I wonder if you would be up for hearing a slightly different point of view?" Or "You are letting me know that you are upset. I can see that and I understand it. May I tell you how I feel about it—not as a way of saying that you shouldn't feel what you're feeling, but as a way of seeing it a little differently?"

The conscious parent allows his child to question authority and values. This is difficult for most parents. We want our children to be independent thinkers who can make wise decisions that must sometimes go against prevailing opinion. And at the same time, we want our children to show appropriate respect and to learn how to live in a world of authority and standards. It's a fine line.

Unconscious parents tend to become either too rigid or too indifferent. If they are rigid, they set up lots of rules and draw lots of lines, demanding adherence to authoritarian pronouncements. One of the problems with this approach is that the child of such a parent assumes there are rules for every situation and looks to people in authority to provide them. At some point later on she may rebel against this self-obliterating way of living, having decided that all rules are bad and all people in authority are evil.

If the unconscious parent is indifferent, then the child is left to fend for herself in a world of conflicting and bewildering choices. She doesn't get the guidance and support she needs in order to sort through the array of behaviors that are in evidence around her. She isn't sure whether it's okay to cheat as long as she is not caught, or whether it's okay to say she won't tell a secret and then tell it, or whether it's okay to shoplift a lipstick at the supermarket. After all, there are plenty of people who do all these things. What's wrong with them? This is a question that requires the input of an involved, conscious parent.

Clearly what's needed is a balance of healthy skepticism about prevailing opinions and values along with healthy respect for those same values and the people who stand for them. Conscious parents look for opportunities to explore these issues with their children by encouraging questions and providing examples. Opportunities are everywhere. For example, a parent might recount human-interest stories from the daily newspaper and invite his children to say what they would do in similar circumstances. He might bring home vignettes from his workplace and discuss them with his children. He might tell stories about his parents, their grandparents, and other relatives that illustrate the value of behaving according to a code of ethics. And he will definitely talk about his own daily experiences with an eye toward teaching his children which values he wants them to incorporate into their lives.

Most important perhaps is for him to listen to the stories his children tell *him* and help them discover the lessons that are already illustrated by their own experience. Whatever else he does, he lets his children maintain their own opinions and test them out in the real world. He offers himself as guide and supporter for exploring alternatives. Through intentional dialogue he models his values and gives his children the information they need to function well in the world.

The conscious parent learns to observe and question himself. Before he reacts with automatic assumptions about what his child should believe and say, he asks himself where his automatic reaction is coming from. What are his assumptions based on? Do they need to be reexamined? Is this really a good time and a good way to teach his child about this value?

PROVIDING SUPPORT
. . . by teaching appropriate behavior.

Most teachers learn their craft through training and experience. A new parent with a firstborn child has the benefit of neither. There is no training manual. Parents must learn what they can from the experience itself. Every time a father interacts with his son, he is given opportunities to learn who he is, who his child is, and how he can best meet his child's needs. As his child gets older, the father learns through trial and error when to press a point, when to express a personal opinion, and when to let his child come to his own conclusions and learn from his own mistakes.

Parents also learn by watching other parents. Perhaps there is a mother or father in his circle of friends who is particularly effective as a parent. He watches and he imitates. Parents can also learn a lot from their children's teachers. Good teachers have the advantage of emotional distance and of knowing a whole range of children. They are less concerned about hammering home a point or controlling behavior than parents are, and they are trained to watch for cues that help two-way communication, responding to signs that they are being heard and understood. A good teacher knows that a healthy share of communication depends on body language, a relaxed atmosphere, and an assumption of mutual trust.

What needs to be underscored is that teaching a child appropriate behavior is one of the major ways a parent loves and supports her children. Sometimes parents are confused about whether they should set standards. The confusion seems to come from uncertainty about whether a parent who insists on standards is in some way stifling her child's self-expression or squelching his spirit. Our view is that one of the rights and duties of a parent is to teach her child values and appropriate behavior. Once the child knows what his parent thinks is important and what she expects, he can modify these views to suit himself as he becomes more mature. Again, following the guidelines for intentional dialogue will keep a parent from going wrong. She will be neither too authoritarian, nor indifferent or lax.

The conscious parent uses his child's behavior as an opportunity to teach rather than punish. Honestly speaking, we cannot think of any time that a conscious parent would need to punish a child. Aside from the question of whether punishment is a useful technique for helping children learn, it is clear that punishment of a child by a parent is an expression of parental exasperation and anger at least as often as it is an attempt to teach. A parent needs to understand that misbehavior is *almost certainly not* the child's attempt to personally destroy or thwart him. It is a signal that something needs attention, and it is an opportunity for the child to learn. It can also be seen as an opportunity for the parent to learn.

The word "discipline" derives from the Latin word *disciplina*, meaning "instruction" or "method." Disciplining children should therefore teach them something. The purpose of punishing is to make someone suffer. Making children suffer punishment may teach them humiliation, rebellion, or vengefulness, but it rarely teaches them anything about correcting behavior. Parents can be effective in helping children change their behavior by being firm and clear about what is expected, allowing them to discover the natural consequences of misbehavior, and setting up circumstances in which they can make amends or redress wrongs.

Often what looks like misbehavior in young children may be something else. A child may be tired or hungry or unwell or even thirsty. (Or, she may be going through a perfectly natural stage of development that happens to be difficult for parents, which is an important subject we discuss throughout Section IV, "Discover Your Child.") Sometimes the best thing to do is to call a time-out, make sure that basic needs are met, and give the child a chance to rest and regroup.

The conscious parent provides clear instruction when teaching new behaviors. An unconscious parent assumes that the child knows what the parent knows and that his child can connect a lot more of the dots than is possible. Spoken or unspoken, the message to the child is "This is obvious; you should have known how I wanted it done." While it makes sense to hold a child responsible for listening to what is being communicated, it makes no sense to expect unspoken instructions to be understood or followed. That's why mirroring is so important. When a conscious parent requests that her child do something, she gives clear and specific instructions and then asks her child to rephrase them for her so she'll know she's been understood.

The conscious parent focuses on his child's behavior rather than her character and motivation. Remember that the overall goal of all communication with the child is to convey the core message: "You are okay." This is the message even when the child messes up. She has to understand that the parent is unhappy with what she has done but is not questioning her value as a person. In order to send the message that it is the *behavior* of his child that needs correcting and not her personhood, the conscious parent uses expressions like "It upsets me when you act this way," rather than "You are a bad girl." You don't want to say or imply that she is not a good enough person.

A conscious parent does not make demeaning assumptions about his child's ulterior motives or about her character. He is able to distinguish the difference between this untruthful, irresponsible, disappointing thing his child has done and the basic nature of the child. Negative assumptions create a predisposition on the part of the parent to punish the child.

The conscious parent honors her child's cooperation with more energy than she used to call attention to a particular problem. The parent has a choice about what she sees and what she considers to be important. She can see all the ways her children disappoint her, or she can see all the ways they delight her. If she wants to encourage the positive qualities of her children, she is generous with appreciation and praise. Children are by nature eager to please their parents, and parents can capitalize on this impulse by celebrating with enthusiasm whatever they see that pleases them. By accentuating the positive, they are parenting within a context of pleasure and positive expectations. When the conscious parent treats any cooperation on the part of a child with more energy than she treats the mistakes, she is letting the child know that what he does right means more to his parent than what he does wrong.

The conscious parent helps her child understand that decisions have consequences. Almost every one of our actions results from a *decision* to act, even if the decision comes so close to the action that they seem simultaneous. Conscious parents know how important it is to pause and reflect before they make decisions, and they can teach their children the same approach. Their children learn by watching how their parents respond in situations in which difficult decisions must be made. And they learn even more when their parents talk about the process with them, including mentioning consequences that have befallen the parent when the parent acted either too fast or out of anger.

One of the most important ways children learn about consequences is to experience them firsthand. It is so tempting for parents to shield their children from the consequences of their actions, to protect them from the outcomes of their decisions. It's natural to do what can be done to make life easy and pleasant for children. It takes intentionality for the parent to say to himself, "My son has just made a poor decision. I know it, but I'm going to let him discover it for himself. He will learn it better from this experience than from my warnings." And it takes even more intentionality to have the self-discipline to let the lesson unfold.

The conscious parent never withdraws when things get difficult. Withdrawal out of frustration or in anger is a sign that a parent has given up on his child in a difficult situation. This ruptures, at least for the moment, the parent's connection with his child. At the same time it sends the child the message that it is okay for *her* to walk away whenever things get tough. Obviously this is not a message the parent wants to send. Instead, the conscious parent wants to let his child know that she is still okay and that he will be available to her to work this problem out for as long as it takes. Most important, she needs to know that he will not abandon her.

Whenever emotions run too high, it's a good idea to take some time out. This is not the same as withdrawing. A time-out is a breather during which both parents and children can regain some perspective, so that when they get together again to resume the dialogue, they can do so with more composure. Taking time out is diffusing and restoring; withdrawing is devastating.

PROVIDING SUPPORT
. . . by maintaining the child's self-esteem.

The conscious parent offers love and support without conditions. This is the essence of the cosmic connection between parents and children. The child knows that her mother and father are not placing restrictions on how much they love her and support her. They will not love her more or less because she performs in a particular way. The child knows that they love and support her, not for how she acts, but for who she is. This is basic. It means that they don't overpraise for jobs well done and don't punish for jobs poorly done. They focus on her and not her performance, and their attention is held by the process she is engaged in and not the outcome.

Let's give an example. Let's say that a six-year-old hands her mother a drawing of a horse. Instead of saying, "That's a very good horse; I'm so proud of you," the mother could say, "I'm so happy to see you doing some art work. I love it when you sit down and draw. I know it makes you happy. And you make me happy." She might then invite her child to talk about it with her. The difference is that there is no confusion in the child's mind about whether her mother's positive reaction might be tied to skill in executing the drawing. The mother reacts positively to her daughter's involvement in doing something she enjoys and to her as a person.

The conscious parent stays in the present, avoiding negative references to the past. Sometimes it pays to have a short memory. What if we were all judged by our mistakes in the past? We would all be condemned to disappoint ourselves and everybody else. The conscious parent interacts with her child from the perspective that her child is growing and learning and that mistakes are valuable as teaching opportunities. Every day is a new day; the future is open.

The conscious parent always preserves a child's sense of her own worth by avoiding the practice of shaming and devaluation. A conscious parent does not call attention to her child's "faults" in a public way. If she were to do that, the child would feel condemned because of who he is, not just what he has done. And if he's condemned as a person, what's the use of trying to learn to do things differently or trying to please a parent who has given up on him? Condemning the child ruptures the connection between them and ruptures his connection with a part of himself. If he is bad, then the bad part has to be ostracized, hidden, or punished, and he becomes less than whole, less than himself, as a result. How much better to approach mistakes in a neutral way and describe the behavior that needs changing and then the desired, expected behavior. This offers hope and conveys the expectation that the child will learn from this experience and live to triumph another day.

The conscious parent avoids manipulating his child's behavior by making comparisons to others. All parents sometimes wish their kids were different. But the conscious parent pauses to ask himself, "Why am I feeling this way? Is this what is best for my son, or is this what I want?" When, in the parent's considered judgment, it would be best for the child to change, the parent engages him in intentional dialogue, including a behavior-change request, and lets him know what changes he would like to see. He refrains from using any of his power in negative ways for the purpose of manipulation.

Making comparisons is one of many weapons the unconscious parent uses to manipulate his child. "If only you practiced the violin the way Eric does, you wouldn't be making all those mistakes," says an unconscious parent. What is also being silently conveyed here is, "I want you to stop irritating me with all those wrong notes. I pay good money for those lessons. Eric might be a better son to me than you are, so if you want my love, you will act the way he does." It doesn't take much imagination to see how the son could feel both devalued and discouraged and, we might add, unlikely to love the violin.

The conscious parent avoids criticisms. A professional critic is someone who judges performance. A professional teacher is someone who works to help a student reach his performance potential. We have already established that a conscious parent can take delight in her child's high performance, but she is not overly invested in it. She is at bottom neither a critic nor a professional teacher. More important to her is her child's growth and self-esteem. When she has something critical to say to her child, she follows the guidelines of intentional dialogue, so that the context of the discussion is supportive and mutual.

PROVIDING SUPPORT
. . . by helping the child experience joy.

The conscious parent creates opportunities for fun. Never underestimate the value of having fun together. Having fun maintains and enhances a sense of well-being. Family outings are a time-honored way of doing this. Trips to the zoo, picnics, and movies are obvious examples. The best occasions are those that parents and children can *both* enjoy together, because nothing helps children have fun as much as Dad's or Mom's pleasure in their presence. A friend of ours used to take her kids swimming at the YMCA on Friday evenings and then out to dinner afterward. Another family we know decided to go on Sunday walks with the object of walking across all the bridges in their city. Board games are good fun for those who enjoy them. The object is *mutual* fun.

The Positive-Flooding Exercise:[9] Many times it's the simple moments of enjoying each other's company that count most. Here is a positive exercise that parents can do with their children to increase good feelings all around. The parent makes an appointment with her child for a time to be alone together. When the time comes, she asks him to sit down. She then walks around the child's chair and says out loud all the wonderful things she can think of about him. Helen has done this often with Leah, our youngest daughter. As she moves around the room, sometimes stopping to dance or throw her arms around Leah, she says things like, "You are simply gorgeous. Your heart is so big, and I love your laugh. When you smile, I can't help but laugh back. You are so intelligent, and I'm so pleased with the drawing you did yesterday of the mountain lion. You are a wonderful dancer. You are the best, and the brightest, and I'm so happy to be your mom!"

We call this the positive-flooding exercise. The first time a parent does it, her child may be suspicious or uncomfortable. Being appreciated takes some getting used to. But after a few times the child will start internalizing all those wonderful things about herself. She will also find that her father or mother is wonderful and loving and also funny.

It's important when doing the exercise that the child feels loved and honored, not made fun of. When the child decides that, as silly as he is, Dad is loving her seriously, she begins to let the praise in. That's when the joyful smiles and laughter begin. The child can also do the same exercise for him. It feels good for both of them.

This kind of exercise has a boomerang effect on parents. Feeling this good and this loving reconnects us with our innate spirituality. These moments remind us why we are doing the work of parenting. The next time we forget, the positive-flooding exercise can remind us that joy exists just waiting for us to seize it.

Laugh deeply and often. It's very important for parents not to take themselves too seriously. Conscious parents have broad shoulders and are good sports. They aren't easily offended by their children. And they don't tease their children often, especially when the teasing is really sarcasm dressed up as fun. They don't have fun at their child's expense.

The Jump-Start Belly Laugh:[10] Laughter is part of the attraction that holds children and parents together. Be on the lookout for opportunities to laugh together. An exercise we use that helps people get started is called the jump-start belly laugh. The parent begins by dropping his arms, bending his knees, and bouncing up and down with his whole body. Watching this, his child will probably begin to giggle, since the parent looks so silly. He then encourages her to do the same ungainly waddle-bounce. While bouncing, parent and child repeat "Ha!" with each bounce. In a few seconds, everyone will be roaring with laughter. It sounds silly, but then that's the point.

Some adults find this difficult at first, because to them *silly* means *vulnerable*. But once they try it, they put aside their dignity and bounce along with the best of them, enjoying the contagious good feelings.

The conscious parent creates opportunities for his child's creative self-expression. Pablo Picasso once said, "Every child is an artist. The problem is how to remain an artist once he grows up." The first step a parent can take is to value the child's self-expression, even if it is unformed, incomplete, or different from the parent's. The second step is to create an encouraging environment for the child to experiment in with paints or costumes or musical instruments. And the third, as we have said, is to participate actively and with pleasure in the process of creation the child has chosen. As Picasso says, all children are creative; it is their natural way of being in the world. Often all we have to do is stand out of the way and delight in the uniquely wonderful way our children experience the world.

The conscious parent says yes as often as possible. Some children are convinced that their parents only know the word *NO*. Unconscious parents say no more often than conscious parents do. For them, "no" is a reflex reaction to many harmless and interesting requests their children make of them. Saying yes is a way for parents to honor their children and give them encouragement at the same time. It allows their children to experience the power of making things happen and to glory in their parents' express permission.

PROVIDING STRUCTURE

The conscious parent provides clear boundaries and sets limits that reinforce a child's sense of safety and support. In the six chapters dealing with stages of growth, we will talk specifically about how to do this at every stage. But our general orientation is that all parents have the responsibility to set boundaries for their children. Children need limits. Setting them is an important way that conscious parents meet a child's needs. Appropriate limits do not harm the child or stifle his creativity or restrict his spirit. On the contrary, they make creativity possible. It's a way of providing the safety and support that the child needs to be fully alive and to express his aliveness.

As with so many other aspects of parenting, parents should talk with their children about boundaries. Parents can explain why their limits should be respected and how these limits will help their child achieve her own goals for personal and social success. As often as possible boundaries can be determined cooperatively. Talking about them together doesn't make them less firm. It simply makes it more likely that the child will understand them and follow them.

Before a conscious parent sets up a family rule or a boundary for his child, he asks himself whether this is really for the child's benefit. Does he have a personal fear or prejudice that he is perpetuating in his children? Does this rule make sense given what the present circumstances are, or is he acting from half-realized motivations from his own past?

The conscious parent teaches the child about appropriate personal boundaries by modeling them. All forms of symbiotic behavior involve the transgression of the child's boundaries. Unconscious parents can create serious problems for their children when they ignore appropriate personal boundaries and cross over them. Personal boundaries protect personal safety, and in a less obvious but equally important way they maintain the integrity of personal space, the right to privacy, and a personal sense of identity. If a child doesn't learn what appropriate boundaries are in his relationship with his parents, he won't know where they are in his other relationships.

Obviously, physical and sexual abuse are extreme transgressions of personal boundaries. Less obvious ones that we have already discussed include shaming, manipulation, sarcasm, and demeaning words and actions on the part of parents. Also when a parent treats a child as though he were an adult confidant or adult companion, an important personal boundary is crossed as well.

The only effective way to teach the concept of personal boundaries is for a parent to model them herself as well as explain them. That way her child will integrate the concept. For example, if she wants her child to respect her privacy and the privacy of others, she must respect his. She can't expect to keep him out of her dresser drawers if she has a habit of going through his things.

The conscious parent learns about the stages of growth and development his child will go through before becoming an adult. The conscious parent does what she can to structure the child's environment and create contexts in which he can learn what he needs to learn at each stage of his growth. If the parent is unaware that her child experiences internal impulses to learn certain tasks at particular points in his journey to adulthood, she will be less able to help and support him when he needs it. If she doesn't know what her child is working on at each stage of development, she doesn't know what to expect, and she may be confused about normal behavior that appears contrary or difficult. In Chapters 8 through 13 we will explore in depth how children change as they grow older and how conscious parents can structure opportunities for their children that will help them accomplish the tasks that are appropriate for each stage.

The Circle of Connection: We have made many suggestions in this chapter about how to become more conscious in your interaction with your children. We have talked about so much that conscious parenting may feel out of your reach. If that's the case, this is a good time for a word of reassurance. Becoming more conscious is really a process of becoming more ourselves. We are talking about regaining an original capacity that has been diminished through wounding. When we recover our wholeness by stretching to meet the needs of our children, we will get all of ourselves back. And doing so will feel right and natural.

We're sure that as a parent who is reading this book, you are doing the best you can. We hope that you will treat yourself with gentleness and patience. All of us hold on to incomplete or disruptive strategies as a way of preserving what we're afraid we may lose—even when these strategies injure our children's growth into wholeness. Only through a deeper understanding of our own histories and a deeper respect for the developing selves of our children will we be able to move beyond our own limitations. Every time we have the courage and presence of mind to pause and act with intention in our children's best interests, we take a step toward becoming more conscious people and more conscious parents. In the end what matters is the effort we make to know and be known by our children as we struggle to realize a new vision of parenting that balances the circle of connection that children and parents make together.

7

Growing Yourself Up

When we listen as if we were in a temple and give
attention to one another as if each person were our
teacher, honoring his or her words as valuable and
sacred, all kinds of great possibilities awaken. Even
miracles can happen.
—JACK KORNFIELD, *A Path With Heart*[1]

*M*any of us parents are entrenched in our own view of the world. We don't think of our child-rearing problems as harbingers of healing. Often what we see is disrespectful, uncooperative children who make life difficult for us. But as we've seen, our children can be a light for us if we let them. Even when we are in conflict with them—perhaps *especially* then—children can give us information about ourselves that we can't get any other way. We take a step toward conscious parenting when we understand how our painful moments with our children can become a road map for our own healing journey. Follow the map, and we don't have to walk over the same broken ground over and over again. We can find a new path.

But we must be careful. It's appropriate for our children to show us where we need to heal, but not for us to expect them to become our working partners. They are absorbed in the full-time work of becoming themselves, unfolding their lives according to the inner directives they were born with. We must let them do their work. At the very least, we can adopt the physician's dictum of *primum non nocere* (most important, do no harm). We can keep from interfering with their work while we move forward with our own. It's up to us to take the first steps alone, and then to enlist other adults who can help us.

From our vantage point of working with couples, we believe that the journey is best taken with a marriage partner. Marriage provides the platinum standard for quality healing. No other relationship provides the conditions of commitment and intensity that fire the healing process to the same degree: Two people work to create a conscious marriage by opening themselves to each other. Each learns to treat the wounds of the other tenderly and to make changes that allow the other to heal. They grow strong in the places that are difficult. They are able to stretch beyond their previous limits through the empathic connection that holds them together.

These are the best conditions for healing childhood wounds. But good work can also be done in other adult relationships that are committed and emotionally intimate. Although the healing is not as easily accomplished and perhaps not as complete as it would be between husband and wife, it is enough to make a tremendous difference to the children involved. Children are eager to absorb the positive changes we make, however they are accomplished.

It is important to learn what we can about how healing happens. In our bodies, advances in the technology of medical imaging now make it possible for us to watch damaged tissue repairing itself at a cellular level. But there is much we still don't understand. How do minute amounts of hormones in the brain regulate everything from how much we cry to how much we eat? Why do some people spontaneously recover from cancer and others die?

Emotional healing is also complex and seems even more so because the process is not visible. We bruise our shins and it shows, but a bruise to our self-esteem may be harder to see. We can feel our heart's hurt when we are betrayed or discounted. But there is no way to record this kind of injury precisely, or our recovery from it, although the people around us may observe our hurtful behavior and thus deduce the injury.

But not *seeing* is different from not *knowing*. After years of helping people in families return to wholeness, we *do* know how a broken family becomes whole. There are patterns for healing that cut across individual and family differences. Once you know what the patterns are, you can use this knowledge to do a better job in your own family. The pattern for family healing is this: *Parents take responsibility to repair their own childhood wounds by becoming surrogate parents for each other.* They create a marriage that is characterized by active acceptance and empathic connection. This frees them to respond directly to the needs of their children, who then reflect back to them and to the world the wholeness they experience in the presence of their parents.

Marriage, in our opinion, provides both the core and the context for raising children. The quality of the relationship between husband and wife determines the quality of a child's environment. The parents' level of maturity, their emotional stability, and their relative wholeness allow a child either to flourish or to languish. Her parents either support her well as she progresses through the stages of her development and they meet her needs—or do not support her so well.

The quality of the parents' marriage also directly affects the subjective world that the child carries around inside her. She internalizes or copies what she experiences of her parents—their emotions, behaviors, values, and prejudices—and she manifests these experiences in her own life. Sometimes she internalizes by being *like* the parent, and sometimes she internalizes by rebelling *against* the parent. In either case, it is the parent who has provided the model.

But we all know that marriage does not form the framework of *every* family with children. Sometimes this core is a single parent. For the single parent the pattern of healing is the same as it is for married parents, although the healing relationship is not with a marriage partner. The maturity, stability, and personal wholeness of the single parent provide the context for the child's growth. When there is no marriage partner, the healing of the parent's wounds takes place within whatever personal relationships are available and appropriate. And as the parent's childhood wounds are healing, he becomes free to be fully present to his child, responding more often with clear-sighted intention than with blind emotion. His work on his own unfinished childhood business is rewarded by the wholeness of his child.

Each person puts the pieces together in his or her own way, but the basic pattern of healing holds for everyone. In this chapter we are going to meet two parents who have undertaken to heal themselves and grow themselves up for the sake of their children. The first, Anita, is married. She and her husband, Tim, have walked through the battlefield together, although not always hand in hand. The second parent, Karen, is a woman alone who has invited a variety people to join her on part of her journey to wholeness.

WHAT A MARRIED COUPLE CAN DO: ANITA AND TIM

Anita and her husband Tim were thoughtful, intelligent parents who struggled every day to interact well with their two daughters, aged twelve and three. They were both trained musicians, active in the contemporary music scene. Tim also worked part-time as a housepainter to help make ends meet.

Anita and Tim needed help with parenting. Things had been "normally chaotic" in their family until Amy, their oldest daughter, turned twelve. At that point something snapped. According to Tim, his wife and daughter started behaving like two mismatched roommates who are forced to live together in close quarters. Lots of bickering and lots of tears. Both Anita and Tim were somewhat puzzled (and grateful) that Anita's relationship with Amy's three-year-old sister, Karla, seemed to be fine. When asked about this, Anita was at a loss. On the plus side, her original interview showed a better than average ability to see her own shortcomings and an unusual awareness of how they might be connected to her father and mother.

Anita and Tim had worked hard to integrate their careers and family life, but they were running into trouble. Anita was losing confidence in herself as a parent, and her marriage was suffering as a result. Her descriptions of her parenting and the parenting she received as a child offered many clues about how she had been wounded and why she was in danger of wounding her own children. In a dialogue with Tim she said:

> I feel like I blow it every day, know what I mean? As soon as I lose my temper, I know I blew it. I have a real hard time sitting down with Amy getting her to do her homework. If there's one thing I wish YOU could do, it would be to do homework with the kids, because mine was such a bad experience as a kid, doing homework.
>
> Patience is not a great virtue of mine. I'll say, "Amy, I don't think you should be doing this." She says, "Yeah, right!" That kind of response, like this real snotty kid, and I feel like bashing her head in. Mom has no cool.

Anita was easily able to make the connection between her father's lack of involvement with his children and her own "leave me alone" style of parenting. She described herself as regimented, impatient, and easily moved to anger. When the pressure built too much, she blew sky high. And then regretted it. She said she often felt as if she was going to explode when the kids were around. They seemed to steal her space and suck the life out of her:

So do I react? Yes, huge. And I know that I learned that when I was a kid. No matter how hard I work on it, it's still a huge struggle with me. I am aware of it. I try and change it, and nothing's different. The difference is that Amy talks to me about it. She says she doesn't like it when I blow up. When I was a child, I never expressed anything like this to my parents. I didn't *know* anything; I just was *in* it.

I try and make a decision in the beginning of the day that I'm not going to yell at Amy and nag at her about anything all day. But I never get through a day without nagging or something. The other day, she came home from school; it was Friday. I came home after rehearsal. We were going to take a nap and then go to the park. I wanted it to be *their* time. But it wasn't. Even when I set aside time for them, other stuff seeps through.

At least I say, "Amy, I was out of line. I apologize." I try to be much more affectionate with my kids than my parents ever were. My parents were never affectionate and never said "I love you," or anything like that. I make an effort.

Both Anita and Tim saw clearly that Tim's style of parenting was different from hers. He tended to be more laid back and easygoing. In Anita's opinion this relaxed attitude sometimes slipped into laxness and permissiveness, and they fought about that. But in general she recognized that he was better suited to helping the girls with certain tasks than she was. Her efforts to help Amy with her homework often ended in frustration. She'd told Tim that she wanted him to help, but he still wasn't helping. Continuing her dialogue with Tim, she said, "You are a lot more relaxed. I come home, and Amy's up a half hour later because she's watching *The Nanny*. Then I get bent out of shape. I'll ask you, 'Did Kara brush her teeth?' No, you forgot. I don't forget! I'm as detail-oriented in my parenting as in everything else."

Anita recognized that her short-tempered style of parenting wasn't in her daughters' best interest. She was not blind to her own overreactions. Every morning she vowed to do better, and every evening she went to bed feeling defeated. She was aware of her rigid stance, her nagging, and her rage, but she couldn't seem to change anything. She realized that identifying the problems and saying (even with passionate conviction) that she wanted to solve them wasn't enough. She often made a real effort to be affectionate and to say "I love you," something her own parents couldn't do. But what else could she do?

THE TASK

From our understanding of Imago Relationship Therapy, we knew that Anita had to deal with her own emotional pain before she could become the kind of mother she wanted to be. This was a good time for her to face herself squarely and set to work. Her goal was to reclaim and repair the parts of herself that had been lost during childhood and then reincorporate them back into her personality. She would know she had done that when her defenses relaxed, her responses were appropriate to what was happening with the children, and she didn't feel so driven to repeat the same patterns over and over again. Instead of defining herself in terms of narrow emotional reactions, as she had been doing, she would have to enlarge her capacity to respond directly to her children and others. Her enthusiasm for embracing all aspects of life would have to expand as she came to terms with those repressed aspects of her personality that someone a long time ago had thought were unacceptable.

The way for her to proceed was to identify where she was functioning poorly, learn some new tools for interacting more effectively, and create a healing relationship with her husband that would undo the damage of childhood. Only when she was engaged in this process would she be able to take advantage of parent-education classes and other sources of good ideas about parenting. Before the healing process began, child-rearing information might have been interesting but useless. In our experience when a parent is held prisoner to her own unmet needs, she isn't free to be in empathic attunement with others, even if she wants to be. And she isn't free to change.

ANITA AND TIM TAKE THE FIRST STEPS

Anita went through many steps in this journey, and so did her husband. Fortunately, she had already taken the first one—the step of understanding how wounding is passed down from parents to children. She understood even before she talked to us that the ways she hurt her children were a legacy from her own parents, her father in particular. As we talked about some of the details of her early life, the pattern became crystal clear. Her father had tolerated contact with his children only under controlled conditions. In fact, as she continued to talk with

Tim, she admitted she didn't have a single memory of being able to ask her father directly for anything:

> In my family, my dad wasn't hands-on at all. My memories of him aren't great. He was always angry. When he came home, we hid. He was a scary guy. He didn't participate very much, and I think that my mom burned out trying to raise six kids. In my family the older kids got out as fast as they could. My brothers went into the Army at seventeen or eighteen; my sisters got married after high school just to get out of the house, because it wasn't a real happy, peaceful, loving situation. I think my mom did the best she could under the circumstances. And there *were* boundaries. There wasn't physical abuse or anything, but it was always a real uncomfortable place to be.

The contact she did have with her father was primarily at the dinner table, which was orchestrated like a military exercise: Heads down, silverware quiet against plates, no speaking unless spoken to first. No jostling, no noises, no seconds. Against this background, her own minimizer responses seemed moderate by comparison:

> I am very anal and regimented, and time is time. "It's eight and it's time to get in bed." "Get your homework done; let's take your bath; make sure your teeth are brushed; make sure you're in your pajamas. We have to read the storybook; we have to say your prayers. You know you have to be in bed by eight." "Don't ask me for water. I'm off duty! Leave me alone! It's my time now."

The second step Anita took was also a step of understanding. She began to see that every child does what it can to survive. She had done what *she* had had to do to get by as a child, and she now attempted to allow her daughters to do what *they* had to. Amy's "stubbornness" was really a survival strategy in the face of her mother's impulse to be a drill sergeant: "It's eight, brush your teeth! It's eight-fifteen, get in bed for a story, now! It's eight-thirty—no, I can't get you a drink of water. It's too late!" She realized how often she tapped her watch, hurrying her girls along to the next task. And how often she said no to their requests.

Having this insight helped Anita begin to see her daughter in a different way. Slowly, as we shall see, she came to understand that Amy's "bad" behavior was really her way of trying to cope with conflicts and intrusions she had no other way of handling. For Anita, seeing her daughter differently was like getting a new pair of eyes! She knew Amy's uncooperative behavior provided her with an opportunity to examine her own behavior in the interaction. And she saw that she could teach her daughter some tools for coping with frustration and anger.

Although it took some time, Anita began to see that Amy, with her disregard for neatness, her tardiness, and her resistance to regulation, was doing the best she could to defend herself from her mother's onslaught of orders. And this helped Anita understand that the same pattern of coping must have been operating in her when she was a child. She saw that she may have been a messy child like Amy when she had been little, but she sure wasn't now. If Amy's "negative" traits were formed in response to her mother's authoritarianism, then her mother's "negative" traits must have been forged from the need to protect herself from *her* parents' disapproval.

The first observable action Anita took in her own healing was to short-circuit the "attack-resist" pattern she had set up with her daughter. After she had been in therapy about a month, Anita told this story: One afternoon, Amy came home from school, dropped her coat and her books on the floor and grabbed the TV remote. All of a sudden the house filled with the sounds of the *Maury Povich* show. Anita stormed into the living room, yanked the remote out of her hand, and started yelling complaints: "You're so noisy and so sloppy. I can't stand it. Why can't you pick up your books. Don't you have homework to do?" Amy's face collapsed for a brief second and then became defiant.

Something changed in Anita at that moment. For some reason, she saw herself through her daughter's eyes. What she saw was a red-faced, out-of-control woman yelling at a scared, rebellious little girl. She knew she had the power to change that image and to bring forth another reaction in her daughter. So she stopped yelling and started talking instead. She did something different.

"Cut," she said, putting her hands palms out, in front of her face. "Sorry, let's run this scene again. Sorry, Amy, I don't want to yell at you like that, especially when you just got home from school. How about this instead." And she knelt down and drew her daughter to her for a long hug. "Let's talk about what just happened and why I exploded."

ISSUES IN THE MARRIAGE

The next action Anita took was to talk about this incident with her husband. With her awareness growing, she began to see that she needed to pay more attention to her "hot buttons" with the kids. She knew they could teach her something. She talked with Tim about her obsession with order, her intolerance of "lazy" or unproductive behavior, and what these patterns were saying about her. She asked him what he thought. He said he had tried talking to her about this on many occasions but had given up. Her rigidity was hard for him to take, and he didn't think it was good for the children. He added that he always felt guilty when he wanted to watch a football game on Saturday afternoon. She made him feel that he was being derelict in his duty to do some task only she knew about.

When she talked about this at their next session, she was asked to put into words what negative trait she associated with the things that made her angry—clothes on the floor, TV watching in the afternoon, and unstructured "hanging out." Before she could answer, she started to cry, admitting, "I don't know why I'm crying—I'm sorry. These things seem so trivial."

With a little more coaxing, she said she was thinking of all kinds of things at once. She remembered so many times when she had been hurt by something her parents had done. One time, when she had been about eleven or twelve, she was downtown for her music lesson and decided to visit her father in his office without scheduling it with him ahead of time. She should have known better, but her judgment had been impaired by a wonderful experience she had recently had with a friend's father. When she and her friend had dropped in on *him*, he had greeted them warmly and taken them out for cherry pie with vanilla ice cream. When she appeared at her own father's office door, she knew it had been a mistake. He had not been happy to see her, and he had told her firmly that he had too much work to do to be interrupted. She should take the bus home.

Why was this memory still so painful? Her answer came out all at once: "Because I'm in the way. They don't want my messy, dirty, out-of-control self in their lives." It was hard to hear the pain of these words, but a wonderful thing happened as a result. As Tim was mirroring her, he began to understand for the first time the intense rejection his wife had experienced while she was growing up. He got up out of his chair and put his arms around her as she cried. "I never knew it was that bad," he said quietly. Both of them were struck by the way she was now speaking in the present tense. Clearly the pain of twenty-six years ago was still with her.

This moment was important for another reason. It paved the way for Anita to understand another piece in the pattern of childhood wounding. *An unconscious parent is more likely to have trouble with her child when her child is in the same stage of development as the parent was when the parent was wounded.* It was no accident that the memory Anita related about her experience at her father's office had happened when she was about twelve, her daughter's present age. Her daughter was just beginning to explore farther afield and to test her identity as an independent, secure person in the world of early adolescence. From what Anita related and what we knew about the nosedive their relationship had taken when Amy had turned twelve, it was certain that further exploration of Anita's past would provide evidence of deep wounding when she had been at this age, on the edge of the stage we call Intimacy.

Knowing this helped Tim be more understanding of Anita, and it helped Anita be more understanding of Amy. She could look at the things Amy did and put herself in Amy's place. She now had more insight into her daughter's "survival strategies" and more empathy for herself as a child who had faced sizable emotional obstacles at the same age. In fact, she realized that Amy could be a mirror for the part of her that was missing. Amy could reflect back the part of her that had learned very early not to be relaxed, to work instead of play, and not to question authority.

Tim agreed to make himself available to Anita over the next two weeks as she identified other times when her reactions to Amy were excessive. He seemed relieved that she was ready to see her overreactions herself, and that he didn't have to pretend to ignore them or figure out how to bring them to her attention.

They also scheduled time to talk about how Tim could help her discover moments when she would be willing to practice "letting go." Together they would look for times when Anita could practice resisting the impulse to organize someone else's time or space and just let things happen on their own. Tim suggested a "family movie afternoon" the following Saturday. The four of them could rent a movie, pop popcorn, get into their pajamas, and cuddle up on their big corduroy couch. Anita said she thought she could do that, although she was somewhat reluctant, not completely resisting the temptation to add, "I have so much to do." But she laughed when she said it. The family experience turned out well.

Over the next few weeks, Anita made a conscious effort to invite Tim to let her know *his* thoughts about what he observed about her behavior—both positive and negative. One of his observations was easy for her to accept. He told her he was struck by how often she talked of wanting to learn to spin and work with wool. She would talk about this wistfully, as something out of her reach, but she never did anything about it. He wondered whether she had an urge to be creative in this way but didn't feel that she had either the right or the ability to act on it.

Another of his observations wasn't so easy to take. They were having a talk about money. Anita controlled the family checkbook, "with an iron hand," as her husband put it. On this evening, Tim was in trouble for spending too much money on their younger daughter's third birthday. They had agreed on the purchase of a tricycle, but Tim had spent extra to make the birthday party special. Anita, by her own admission, "pushed him and pushed him" about the cost of little things, like streamers and party favors, an ice cream cake, and tickets to a movie for the children. Things she considered extra, out of range, and even frivolous. Finally, he had called her "tightfisted" and she had called him "irresponsible."

When they recounted these allegations, Anita finally brought herself to accept the possibility that she had a hard time being generous with money and Tim accepted the possibility that he was sometimes careless in his spending. Each of them agreed to tell the other all the positive implications of the trait they most disliked in the other person. They were to think of all the ways that their life together had been made better by his "irresponsibility" and her "tightfistedness."

UNDERSTANDING THEIR IMAGOS

In response Tim said an interesting thing: "It's funny, I would have had no problem answering that question when we were first married. One of the things I loved about Anita was her skill with money." He admitted that it was hard now to feel enthusiasm for a "skill" that had become a straitjacket for him; but after some stumbling he was able to say that Anita's watchful eye had allowed them to save money for the down payment on their home. Her careful way with a dollar had enabled them to have the life in music that they both wanted. He could supplement their income with a part-time job, while she managed their careers and their finances very carefully.

Anita responded by saying how much she loved the tourmaline necklace he'd bought for her thirty-fifth birthday, "even though it was a little lavish." She loved his foolish willingness to buy bottles of "miracle" soap from kids working their way through college or to sponsor walka-thons and Little League teams from the neighborhood. Sometimes she thought he was a patsy, but she also marveled at what a generous, open-hearted man she'd married.

WORKING TO REPAIR THE MARRIAGE

It was comforting to Anita and Tim to realize that their difficulties were falling into predictable patterns for all married couples. Tim had origi-nally been attracted to Anita's tightfisted approach to money matters because this was a part of himself that he repressed, or quelled, because it somehow didn't serve him well in childhood. It was thrilling to meet it in Anita when they were first together. But as time passed, and the romance wore off, he found himself wanting to stifle in Anita what was unacceptable in himself. Tim, of course, was not aware of this. The process of repressing his own natural tendencies and impulses hap-pened over the long years of childhood; it had not been conscious then, and he had not been aware of it until now.

The same was true for Anita's initial attraction to Tim's relaxed atti-tude toward money. Each was originally attracted to what they now wanted to repress in the other. As a way of beginning the process of reintegrating missing parts of themselves, it was vital that Anita and Tim start loving the trait each disliked in the other. Anita had to make an effort to appreciate Tim's easy way with money. Tim, in turn, had to find a way to appreciate Anita's fiscal conservatism. In doing this, they found themselves starting to love in the other what each had not been able to love in themselves. *This is the most effective way to reclaim a lost part of yourself. Love it first in someone else.* Anita would accept the part of her that wanted to loosen the reins, and Tim would embrace the part of himself that was ready to be more goal-oriented and orga-nized.

As we have said, it is sometimes difficult for us to make a distinction between our children and ourselves and between our partners and our-selves. What we hate in others, we hate in ourselves. What we love and accept in others, we can learn to love and accept in ourselves. Other people cannot do this job for us. We will not be able to heal from just the well-intentioned, positive actions of other people toward us. We will reject their overtures and discount their good opinions—*until* we ourselves stop hating the traits we tried to kill in ourselves during child-hood. The only way to break the barrier is to start loving in others the very things we deplore in ourselves.

By the time Anita and Tim had worked on their issues in marriage for several months, Anita had compiled a list of her negative traits, the things she did and didn't do that got in the way of her relationships. From her list, three are of particular interest:

1. Interrupts when other people are talking.
2. Doesn't try to see things from the other person's point of view.
3. Wants Tim to help with the kids more but doesn't know how to communicate her wishes.

The first two, interrupting and not listening, are very common. In fact, they are the most telling evidence of unconscious parenting. Anita and Tim agreed that it was time to address these. She and Tim began using intentional dialogue on purpose every day. She wanted to listen in such a way that she could understand on a deeper level what Tim was saying. She knew that in order to be a more loving, patient partner, she needed to become more aware of his thoughts and feelings than ever before.

Once Anita and Tim were comfortable with dialogue, she began teaching her children how to use it. Obviously, twelve-year-old Amy was better able to absorb and use the ideas than Karla, who was three. But even Karla could understand the basic idea of mirroring. Anita put it very simply for Amy: So you can understand what the other person is saying, do these three things after you listen: (1) Check to make sure you've heard correctly; (2) let the other person know it's okay to feel that way and think that way; and (3) let yourself feel what the other person is feeling.

In addition, Anita and Tim learned how to use another tool to help with the last item on Anita's list: her inability to communicate what she would like from Tim. This tool was the behavior-change request process, which we have discussed in the preceding chapter. The purpose of this process is to help people communicate their needs without criti-cizing, devaluing, or intimidating the other person. Anita learned to use it first with Tim, and then both of them helped her make it part of their interaction with the children. Anita had also identified the frustration she felt about Tim's role in the work of the household. She felt that she worked "time and a half," while he worked less. What did she want from him that would address her frustration? In other words, what three options could she suggest? She replied that during the coming month, she would like Tim to choose one item from the following list: (1) Help Amy every day with her homework; (2) spend at least an hour every day on housework before going to his part-time job; or (3) spend one afternoon a week cleaning the house.

Tim was able to agree that he would be fully responsible for checking with Amy nightly about homework assignments and helping her when needed. In addition, he agreed to an hour a day of housework before he left for his part-time job. And as the result of a separate behavior-change request, Tim agreed to refrain from any "extra" spending for the next month, until Anita could feel comfortable that he was truly considering the financial impact of his actions on their situation. But even more important than what he agreed to do was the way he had received the requests. He had been able to put into his own words what he had heard and understood of his wife's frustration, so that she had felt heard and understood. And he was able to grant her request as a *gift* to her, not as a tit-for-tat favor that needed to be returned.

Later, after these agreements had been in place for a couple of weeks, Tim, using a behavior-change request of his own, was able to express frustration over her breaking a promise to go to a movie with the kids, and she had understood his dismay and had rescheduled a meeting in order to take them to the movies another time. She also understood that complying with his request was a gift of love to him, not a matter of barter or the repayment of a debt.

ANSWERING THE NEEDS OF THE CHILD

The most exciting behavior-change request for Anita and Tim was the first one Anita was able to make of Amy. Once again Amy had cluttered up the living room with her books, blankets, and clothes. Instead of going through the roof, Anita had been able to pause and ask Amy to sit down with her for a moment and talk about her frustration. Anita described her frustration calmly to Amy and asked Amy to repeat what she had said back to her to make sure Amy had understood. She then asked for (and received) permission from Amy to make a behavior-change request. Among the options she proposed was a week during which Amy would keep her school things in her bedroom and put away any blankets and stuffed animals that had made their way into the living room. Amy agreed that at the end of the week they would take a look at how things had gone.

This family was on the road toward more conscious relationships. They now had a way of understanding what had looked to them in the beginning like a chaotic, out-of-control disintegration of relationship. And they had some new tools. Anita and Tim practiced keeping in mind that, as parents working toward consciousness, their role was to provide safety, support, and structure for their children, and that the real progress they were making would occur in small steps. Small, solid steps— that was what they were aiming for. For Anita what was most helpful was being able to parent within a structure she could understand, rather than "being at the mercy of my emotions."

WHAT A SINGLE PARENT CAN DO: KAREN

In the next section, we will show how a single mother of three children, Karen, has followed the same pattern of emotional healing without a permanent marriage partner. Not all single parents have the strong social support that Karen has had. But because Karen learned that her success as a parent depended on taking care of her personal emotional needs, she became highly intentional about cultivating relationships that were sustaining, and she learned how to ask for what she needed from the important adults in her life.

Now in her early fifties, Karen is a single mother whose three children are now adults. Jim is twenty-four, Jared is twenty-five, and her daughter, Patricia, is twenty-eight. Patricia and her husband have a two-year-old daughter of their own. Her sons are unmarried. Karen and the children's father divorced when Jim was four. She has never remarried, although when the children were in high school, their household was joined by Burt, a divorced father, and his son and daughter. This five-year relationship was a committed one that provided a sense of family for the two adults and five children involved. A stabilizing factor for Karen and her children was her ability to earn a good living. She is a corporate accountant.

We asked Karen if she would talk with us about her journey of personal healing and conscious parenting as a single person. We knew that she had made significant changes in her relationship with her children over the course of many years and that her perspective would be valuable. She agreed.

Karen learned the basics of Imago Relationship Therapy ten years ago when she entered therapy, during the time we were writing *Getting the Love You Want*. Her partner, Burt, was an important part of this therapeutic process. Although Karen and Burt ultimately decided not to marry or continue living together, they had been able to perform some of the same healing functions for each other that Anita and Tim and other committed married couples are able to do.

In addition to working with Burt, Karen was able to turn to two of her other close relationships for the support and active cooperation that are required of imago partners. The most important of these was her relationship with Robin, her closest childhood friend. Don, who was a platonic friend she'd met at work more than twenty years earlier, was also an important companion on Karen's journey. Finally, Karen considers the divorce support group she attended just before she met Burt to have been important in helping her get some perspective on both her personal strengths and growth opportunities. Many years later, she still has dinner every month with two of the people from that group.

Karen describes the breakup of her marriage in this way: "Sometimes looking back, I think of myself as shell-shocked. I remember feeling so stressed-out. I was working, of course, and I had these three small children at home. My husband was immature, and in many ways he needed as much attention as the kids. Finally I thought to myself, 'I just can't deal with four children. Three, yes; four, no.'"

WORKING WITH A SUPPORT GROUP

During and after the divorce the members of Karen's support group were a lifeline. They not only helped her cope with fallout from the breakup of the marriage, but helped her see what she needed to do to be a better mother. She remembers one incident that made her think, for the first time, she might need to get some professional help in order to take apart the tangled threads of her feelings and needs and those of her children.

Patty was a very smart toddler. She was first-generation *Sesame Street*. Maybe because of that, she demanded a lot of attention. Her experimenting often got her into trouble. I remember when she poured Clorox into the clean clothes in the dryer. That sort of thing. But there's one time that stands out. I remember going to my divorce group and telling them what a snot she'd been. I'd had a horrible day with her. We had tickets to the *Nut-cracker*, and she got it into her head that she didn't want to go. "No," she said, "I won't go." So I chased her around the house, and of course she outran me. She locked herself in her room, and she wouldn't come out. I missed the performance waiting for her to come out of her room. I wanted to hit her. . . . So I was going on and on about this to the group, and finally, this man in the divorce group asked me a simple question: "What were you like as a little girl?"

Karen had been stunned by the question. What had she been like as a child? She had never thought to ask, especially in the context of the frustration she was experiencing with Patty. She had never thought to make the connection between herself and her daughter, or between her mother and herself, for that matter. She began to think of all the times she had gotten into trouble with *her* mother for the same kind of stunt Patty had just pulled. "I know I was a difficult child for my mother. I remember her saying to me, 'Don't just be difficult. Try a little harder and be IMPOSSIBLE!' " With this incident Karen began to think in terms of intergenerational patterns within families.

The most obvious pattern she could see had to do with anger. She and her mother were what she calls "anger twins." They got mad at their children in the same way. Recalling this, she said:

My mother dealt with anger the same way I dealt with it. What did she do? She hit us kids. What did I do? I hit my kids. I often reacted to my daughter in anger, even though I tried not to. I'd be patient for a while, and then I'd hit. When Patty got a little bit older, around twelve or so, she had real trouble express-ing herself. I think it came from not being able to express herself when she was younger, because I was always trying to control her.

Once Karen understood that her way of overreacting was a legacy from her mother, she could ask herself whether she wanted to pass it on to her own children. Asking the question had focused her attention on the problem in a way that allowed her to moderate her anger, but she was not able to change her behavior completely. She stopped spanking, although her frustration still boiled over in ways she wished it wouldn't. A complete overhaul of her way of handling anger would have to wait until she had done more of the personal healing that would make fundamental change possible. Besides generating the simple question that got her thinking about family patterns, her divorce group made other significant contributions to her journey toward consciousness. According to Karen:

> The facilitator was good. She didn't pretend to be the fount of all wisdom; she helped us be wise for each other. One of the issues that came up was my difficulty settling down to one thing, or one person. After the divorce I went in all different directions. (You would think an accountant would be more steady.) The group could see this in me. I remember when I asked for their help with this issue. I said, "Okay, you guys. I want you to tell me when you see me beginning to make excuses why *this* man isn't going to work out, so I have to jump to the next one. Call me on it." And they did. They helped me see what I did when things got too good or too solid. I would look for excuses to move on. Again, I think it was a family thing—my mother has been married five times.

Although the support group didn't stay together forever, Karen told us that she thinks it's very important for those who are single or divorced to have access to a committed group of people to share feelings and experiences with. We agree. We advise single people to join committed support groups if they can. When the group stays together for a predetermined period of time no matter how tough things get, even when emotions run high and feelings get hurt, then members can become "family" for each other with all the possibilities for empathic sharing and accountability that this implies.

The most successful groups have guidelines to help them navigate intense interactions. Intentional dialogue, which we explored in Chapter 5, provides a structure that support groups can use to facilitate healing work between members, while keeping interactions safe and appropriate. These guidelines allow a group to be more than just a sounding board for its members. The possibility of transformation is present in interactions that involve the deeply respectful skills of listening, mirroring, validating, and empathizing.

When two group members develop strong empathic connections, it is possible for them to become partners in healing. Karen felt such an attachment to an older woman in her group named Dorothy, who reminded Karen of her mother. Dorothy had also been married and divorced several times and was impatient in the same way Karen's mother had been. Without realizing it, she found herself addressing most of her most intense feelings to Dorothy. She remembers a particular way Dorothy helped her get over a problem she'd had for a long time:

> I came from rough beginnings. My mother had six kids. I was raised with one sister and four brothers, and there was a lot of confusion. There were different fathers involved and kids coming and going. My mother had the idea that it was her place— *every* woman's place—to stay at home and make things work. Even when she was between husbands and we were poor, she would take part-time jobs only when things were desperate. I never wanted that life. I did well in school. I wanted to make money, support myself, live in a nice house. My kids have been important to me, but my career has always been important to me, too. When the kids were small, I could have done part-time tax work from my home and been there for them. But I didn't; I wanted to get out of the house and have a real job. Maybe that's why I never expected I would be the same kind of parent my mother had been with me.
>
> My mother was conflicted about my success as a CPA. I overheard her one time talking to her sister about her "big shot daughter who wants to be important." I guess that's one of the reasons I felt guilty about working when the kids were little. This one time I want to tell you about, I went to the group and told them that I had sent my two boys to school when they were sick. I knew better, but I didn't have backup baby-sitting, so I did it anyway and prayed I could get away with it. I always felt like Dorothy was a little critical of me for not dropping everything for my kids. I was saying in group that I felt bad about what I did. She said, "It sounds like you feel guilty for a lot of things," and I started to cry. She asked me if I wanted to talk about all the things I felt guilty for with the kids. I listed them: not staying with their father, not staying home with them, not being a very "cookies-and-milk" kind of mother, loving my work too much, and so on. When I was through, she asked me if I wanted to hear how she had heard all that. I said yes. She said that she felt great tenderness for me. I was trying to do so much, to be such a good person. It sounded to her like I hadn't been appreciated for the parts of me that wanted to be educated and know what it

was like to be successful. She wanted me to know that she saw this in me and that she valued it in me.

Karen told us that she felt something like absolution in that moment. She felt as though she had been forgiven her imperfections and given permission to explore that part of her personality that her mother had turned away.

A COMMITTED RELATIONSHIP

Several years later, Karen was ready to be more systematic about her own personal growth. When she entered therapy, she was ready to build a satisfying relationship with Burt and become a more effective parent for her children. She never expected her relationship with Burt to be permanent, but both of them knew they were "good for each other for the time being" and that they were able to provide stability for the five teenage children they had between them.

The problem they most wanted help with was anger. No surprise. An incident with one of her sons brought this issue to a head. Karen had just gotten a computer-printed notice that Jim was missing classes. She went ballistic: "There was no behavior I saw that indicated he wasn't going to class. He got up in the morning, and he left, just like the other kids. But he wasn't going to algebra or political science or personal finance. He ate lunch, and then he left school."

When Karen got the notice, she grabbed her six-foot-two-inch son by the shirt and yanked him into a chair. What followed was a top-of-the-voice series of accusations: "You never do what you're supposed to. You lied to me. You let me down. I work hard to make life better for you than it was for me. You think you can get a free ride." Burt, who was in the next room, was appalled. This isn't how he would have handled it. He would have minimized whatever anger he felt and treated the skipped classes as boyish stupidity.

It is not unusual for anger to be a dividing issue in close relationships. Often one partner will have trouble containing anger, and the other will have trouble expressing it. In unconscious relationships the tendency is for the self-constrained partner to try to suppress anger in the exploding partner, who, in turn, escalates her intensity in order to get the other person to react.

The work for Karen and Burt involved careful probing of childhood

experiences in order to help them both understand how they had developed these extreme ways of coping with intense negative emotions.
They needed to understand for themselves, and they needed to understand for each other. When partners can experience the wounded child
standing inside the ugly behavior, they can look beyond the ugliness
toward the child inside them who is doing the best he or she can to stay
alive and unharmed.

Karen discovered that her tendency to be quick to anger was rooted
in a fear that her environment would spin dangerously out of control if
things weren't kept calm and orderly. The only way she knew to keep a
lid on things was to jump on them fast and furiously. Ironically, Burt
discovered that his reaction to anger was a response to the same fear.
Loud voices, disagreements, and conflicts were dangerous, because they
upset his personal sense of balance. More than that, in some undefined
way it felt to him as though they upset some precarious *cosmic* balance.

Changing the way people handle frustration and anger is difficult.
As we saw with Anita and Tim, there are three basic experiences a person has to have in order to evolve a durable new response to an old,
unconscious pattern. First, they need to gain an increased understanding of why they do the things they do. Second, they need to experience
the empathic and healing responses of another person in interactions
where the wound is manifested. Third, they need concrete tools to help
them restructure their automatic reactions. As a result of our work together, Karen and Burt increased their understanding by seeing how
messages about anger were passed on by Karen's mother to Karen and
by Burt's parents to him. They were both able to recall specific childhood incidents where their parents had absolutely misunderstood their
needs and caused them pain. And they were able to see that the explosion of anger in Karen's case and the suppression of anger in Burt's case
were ways they had learned to defend themselves from the pain of being
criticized, misunderstood, or ignored.

They also learned to reimage each other as healing partners instead
of polarized individuals competing for the right way to discipline or
guide their children. (Instructions for reimaging your partner are given
in the "Tools" section of this book.) Once they realized that they both
had the same fear that their busy and complex lives might become un-
manageable, much of the healing work dealing with anger involved
each helping the other choreograph a partnership in which their com-
munal family lives could become organized and stay organized. They
knew that life never remains under control in a family with five teenag-

ers, but they became very serious and systematic about providing structure for what could be guided rather than controlled.

Karen recalled to us with amusement one of her contributions in this regard. She instituted the ritual of gathering everybody together every first Sunday of the month in the third-floor bedroom for a meeting in front of the fire: "I had just been exposed to organizational-development principles at work, and I was hot on the idea. I even brought home a flip chart so we could make lists. It started out being a way to organize tasks and schedules, but it soon developed into a way for the kids to voice their complaints. I remember that the girls were able to say to the boys, 'You guys make all this noise, the way you run up and down the stairs! It's like the house is falling apart.' And it was a way for them to give me feedback. One of my kids—I don't remember which one—told me during one of these meetings that I was pretty much a witch on Sundays. All the other kids said, 'Yeah, pretty much.' What was happening was that I was working on Saturdays during that period, because we were opening new factories. On Sundays, I had to do all the housework in a thirty-six-hundred-square-foot house, and I was stressed. I heard them. Burt and the kids started doing more of the work, and I hired a housekeeper."

On a more subtle level, Burt became more intentional about becoming a full partner in the emotional work of parenting. His inclination had been to leave most of that to Karen, but he realized that such an imbalance wasn't good for their relationship or for the children. Specifically, he made two changes. He stepped in more often to support Karen in interactions with the children, and he validated her anger instead of withdrawing and disapproving of it. When her temperature rose, he would say, "I know this makes you mad. I can understand why." And then he would say in his own words what he thought she was feeling: "You come home so tired at the end of the day. Dinner isn't started. The kids are fighting. Jared hasn't done his homework. Patty wants to stay out late on a school night. What a mess. It's too much." And then he would ask, "What can I do to help?"

For her part, Karen tried to honor Burt's natural reticence by recognizing that he didn't have to have the same emotional reactions she had. And she learned from his validation of her how to validate him. She learned to say, "This whole scene makes me want to run away and hide, too. Why don't we pitch in together and try to sort it out. And then we can have some resting time together later tonight."

Karen and Burt also learned to use two new tools: the behavior-change request and the anger-container exercise. First, they learned how to deepen their understanding of each other's needs and to honor those needs by using the behavior-change request. Both of them learned how to make behavior-change requests and to teach their children to do so, too.

One example of making a request stood out in Karen's mind. Karen made it when Patty was sixteen, during an intense discussion about going out with friends on a school night: "Patty, I would like to make a behavior-change request. You can tell how exhausted I am after we go round and round about whether you can spend the night at Amanda's house. You know the rule is that you need to be in your own bed at a reasonable hour on school nights. My request is that you keep this rule for one month. During this time, honor this rule without disputing it. You know that I am as relaxed about your schedule as I can be on the weekends, but during the week, we need *not* to be walking the same old ground." Karen said she never had to decide what to do after the first month, because the problem never came up again. "I think it worked so well because it was reciprocal. Patty had made requests of me, and she saw that I did my best to honor them. She could see that she was paying respect to herself when she participated in such a mutually caring relationship with me."

The second major tool Karen and Burt learned was the anger-container exercise, which we discussed in the previous chapter. They learned to initiate and validate the free-flowing expression of anger when it was naturally ready to burst forth and then to ask, "Is there more?" until everything was out in the open. In this way, they defused the emotional intensity that might otherwise have simmered under the surface. They learned to initiate intentional dialogue, either on the spot or by appointment, to address the frustration that had caused the anger. This was a vital exercise for Karen, since she had a habit of "bursting forth" uncontrollably. But it also helped give Burt a safe way of letting off steam.

WITHIN A COMMITTED FRIENDSHIP

After Karen's youngest son graduated from high school, she and Burt decided to go their separate ways. Although they both felt somewhat dislocated by this decision, it was mutual and amicable. Four years later Karen was having some questions about her relationship with Patty and wanted us to help her clarify why things were starting to go awry. She had experienced several personal breakthroughs during the time she and Burt had been together. Now she was on her own again without a permanent romantic partner, and she had uncovered other issues she wanted to work on. Could she do it without Burt?

Karen felt that the conflict was centered on Patty's marriage. It wasn't that Karen didn't like Patty's husband. As she said, "I like him. In fact, I love him. He's charismatic. He's got followers, people who are in his fan club. He's a good provider. And he's got a personality like mine. He likes to have a lot of space. In fact, Patty and I joke that she married her mother."

The problem was that Patty was thinking of leaving him. She felt that he was too domineering, expecting her to stay home with their baby and support his efforts to move forward in his career.

Karen found herself with very strong opinions about what Patty should do: "She wanted my permission to leave, but I felt she should stay in the marriage and work on the issues."

Karen had come back into therapy because she found herself overly involved with her daughter's dilemma and truly frightened at the prospect that Patty might leave her husband. For some reason, this issue was blurring the boundaries she had worked so hard to establish between herself and her daughter.

After a short time she was able to identify the issues and put into words what she wanted to be able to do differently. First, she wanted to feel less afraid about the prospect of Patty as a single mother with no husband. She wanted to feel that her daughter would be okay if she decided to leave her husband. Second, she wanted to be able to talk to Patty about this issue in a more intentional, matter-of-fact, supportive way than she had so far. Clearly, Patty's situation had triggered symbiotic responses in Karen. She was reliving her own insecurities.

Asked whether there was an adult in her life with whom she shared a committed and personal relationship, she mentioned Robin, her best friend since junior high school. Robin was also divorced, with two high-school age children still living at home. Although Robin was dating the "man of her dreams" at the moment, she still had plenty of time for Karen and deeply cared about Karen's children.

Karen asked Robin if she would be willing to help her do some emotional healing around the issue that had come up with Patty. The process would involve Karen asking for Robin's time for specific therapeutic purposes. It would require that Karen be very clear about what her need was and very specific about how Robin could fill it. Karen conveyed the degree of intentionality and commitment that would be required by both of them, and Robin agreed to help.

Karen told Robin she wanted to spend some time with her to discover more about why she was so afraid for her daughter. She wanted to learn about what had happened *in her own life* that made her heart sink when Patty talked about living on her own. And then she told Robin what she needed her to do: "I want you to invite me to talk about the times when I was a child that I felt afraid. I need you to listen very carefully to what I say. Occasionally, I want you to ask, 'Is there more you want to say about that?' I don't want you to evaluate what I say or give me advice. But I do want you to validate my feelings. I know I'm not totally rational about this. That's how I know there has been some wounding. I want to feel free in your presence to explore the childlike, irrational part of myself and still feel your acceptance. I want you to let me know I'm not crazy."

It turned out that Robin was a good partner for Karen. They met three times for the purpose of uncovering and exploring Karen's fears. At one point during one of the sessions, Karen was crying and she asked Robin to hold her and rock her. At another time, Robin reached out to touch her arm and Karen told her she didn't want to be touched. They trusted each other before these sessions and found that their trust in each other grew stronger as a result of their healing encounters. In the end Robin told Karen she thought she had benefited as much as Karen.

The other piece of work that Karen initiated with Robin was less intense and has been ongoing. Karen knew how to engage in intentional dialogue from her earlier experience. But as her problems with Patty demonstrated, she had drifted away from daily practice of its principles. She told Robin that the main way she could help her was to become her intentional dialogue partner. Karen told her, "The more I practice, the more automatic it becomes. Then, when I'm in an intense situation where I want to run all over the person with my opinions and my feelings, I will be more likely to fall back on the structure of dialogue, because it's familiar, and become supportive rather than directive." Karen and Robin were able to practice intentional dialogue together, and it helped Karen be genuinely helpful to Patty during the time Patty's marriage was shaky. Both Karen and Robin felt that all of their relationships have benefited enormously from making dialogue a way of life.

WITHIN ANOTHER COMMITTED FRIENDSHIP

A year or so ago, Karen had an opportunity to activate another healing relationship. This time Don, her longtime friend, was her partner. She and Don had met at work over two decades earlier, and the bond they felt for each other had survived several moves and job changes.

This time the issue that claimed Karen's attention was money: "I've been thinking a lot about money and what part it's played in my relationship with my kids. I haven't had a chance to talk to Patty about it really. But several months ago, I started talking about it with my boys. What kicked it off was I sent Jim a letter and I enclosed a phone card, a one-eight-hundred collect credit card, so he can call me anytime he wants. He called me and said, 'What's up with this card? Why did you do that? I don't need it. I'm over twenty-one years old, for pete's sake.' "

Karen happened to mention this story to Don over lunch. He responded so sensitively and asked such good questions that Karen asked if he would be willing to help her explore it a little further. They met the following week, and Karen told him she needed him to listen while she tried to answer for herself the question that Jim had asked: "Why did I do that?" Why did she send her children money and buy them things they never expressed a need for—especially since they were now adults?

As their conversation unfolded, Don was able to do more than listen attentively and validate Karen's feelings. He was also able to ask good questions. At one point Karen was talking about how guilty she had felt about the times when the kids had been left in day care while she escaped to the calm and order of her job. Don asked, "If you were feeling guilty, how would that show itself?" At another moment in the conversation, Karen described what it was like for her when she was little and there wasn't enough money for the family to be really comfortable. Karen described it as "a hole in my stomach." Don asked, "When you give your kids money, does that hole fill up?"

Karen has been able to make use of her close relationships to gain insight into her destructive reactions to her children, explore her negative feelings in safety, and rehearse or practice positive behaviors that she wanted to make a permanent part of her relationships. Her journey toward more conscious relationships has helped her see how her childhood environment spurred her on to become personally ambitious, quick to anger, afraid of long-standing intimate commitments, and prone to guilt over not doing enough for her children. It has also helped her find ways to broaden her range of responses so that she has more options in situations that previously called forth rigid, formulaic reactions.

For example, she is now more intentional about balancing her drive to work up to her limits with her need for personal time that is pleasant and "nonproductive." Her anger is still there, but it isn't usually her first response to frustration. She makes an effort to pause, listen, and understand other people rather than automatically blowing her top. She takes the time to talk to herself about her role in her children's lives, acknowledging her positive contributions, and reminding herself that they are adults. When she needs it, she asks for confirmation from friends that she is a good mother. She still hasn't found a permanent life partner, but she feels relaxed about the possibility and at peace with the idea of marrying again, or not marrying again.

She knows that it's not a good idea to ask her friends to be her therapists. And she doesn't feel she has done that. She has been very careful about only asking two of her most committed, long-term friends to play occasional, very specific roles in her journey of healing.

THE HEALING JOURNEY

For all of us, healing happens within the context of significant relationships. Married couples have the convenience of a long-term commitment in which to structure their interactions. Single people have other relationships that meet the criteria of commitment and personal intensity that are necessary for the healing of childhood wounds. The key is to practice in interactions with other adults the qualities we want to manifest in our relationships with our children. And to be with our children the way we want to be in our adult relationships.

Every time we have a conversation with another person or an interaction with another person we are either healing ourselves or wounding ourselves further. When our interactions with others are loving, we bathe ourselves and our various emotional parts in the same healing waters, and we begin to finish the task of growing up.

IV

DISCOVER YOUR CHILD

THE CONSCIOUS PARENT'S PLEDGE

I commit myself to the following, with love, awareness, and compassion:

1

To use intentional dialogue.

2

To provide you with safety, support, and structure.

3

To work on my own issues so I can be a better parent to you.

4

To meet your needs as you evolve through the different stages of childhood.

5

To stay connected with you in positive ways.

6

To have faith in both of us as we grow and learn together.

An Overview

*The process of alternation between union and
separation seems to occur repeatedly throughout the
life of the individual, both in childhood and in
maturity. Indeed, this cycle (or better, spiral) formula
seems to express the basic process of the psychological
development from birth to death.*
—EDWARD EDINGER, *Ego and Archetype*[2]

We have traveled a long way. We have redefined parenthood as a sacred relationship that can preserve the wholeness of the child and heal the childhood wounds of the parent. We have explored our cultural inheritance of unconscious parenting and envisioned a new and more conscious way for parents to be in a relationship with their children. We have seen the power of *dialogue* to infuse this relationship with understanding, validation, and empathy. Now we want to carry these concepts forward and explore the ways in which conscious parents can use them to support the specific developmental impulses that rise to the surface as the child evolves from birth through adolescence. This is the only section of the book that has its own overview, because there are important things to know that apply to all the stages of a child's growth. What can parents do to smooth the way for this miraculous unfolding of nature's plan and, at the same time, complete the work of their own unfinished childhoods?

THE RHYTHMS OF CHILDHOOD

The next six chapters focus our attention on the rhythms of childhood, the tidal motions of the psyche that catalyze the development of the child. There are two rhythms that move through the developing child at the same time: *oscillation* from the center that expands and then returns, and *progression* through stages of growth as the child moves through his preordained evolution toward adulthood. The interplay of these rhythms shapes the spiral pattern of healthy growth

Oscillation begins with attachment, expands into exploration and differentiation and then subsides back into attachment again. The baby internalizes this rhythm during the first years of his life and repeats it naturally as he progresses through the stages of growth. He is born emotionally connected to his mother, and as he feels that this connection is becoming secure, he cautiously moves out (still attached) to explore and connect with his nonmaternal environment, regularly returning to his mother's presence for reassurance.

If this first and most basic rhythm is supported and allowed to follow its natural course without impediment, it will be repeated successfully later when the child falls in love with a romantic partner—or a job, a cause, an idea, or his own child, when he becomes a parent—and then learns to express his unique self within the context of a romantic relationship or other important life experience.

In fact, all of the primary tasks of childhood recur in coordinated rhythms throughout the individual's life. The newborn child has within him all the impulses that will later flower at their appointed time. He falls in love with someone or something. He explores it and crafts a new aspect of his identity within it; he develops new skills; he manifests caring for others. He comes to know the rhythm very well and will repeat this cycle over and over again. The degree of his success depends on how well he has completed his basic evolution during the first eighteen to twenty years of his life.

Perhaps you are aware of this rhythm in your own life. Think for a moment about how it shows up in your experience as a parent. When your child was born, you fell in love with him. With this marvelous and mysterious creature in your life, you began to explore the world of parenting. That may be why you are reading this book. As you cared for your newborn and got used to your new role, you acquired a new layer of identity as a "parent." With increasing experience, you learned to handle yourself more confidently as you expanded your competence. Perhaps you also sought the support and guidance of others who shared your experience, your peers in parenting. And recognizing your participation in the preservation of the race, you became interested in the welfare of others and the quality of life in society. This expansion outward is a natural cycle in our lives.

The child's growth depends also on the other rhythm that propels him forward, even as he comes back around to revisit previous tasks. This rhythm is not just an oscillation but also a progression through distinct developmental impulses. The seeds of them all are present at birth, but each blossoms in its own time in response to an inner impulse and the readiness of the environment. If his parents have nourished the first flower appropriately, the next bud will open. Each time he responds to another developmental impulse that pushes him forward through the developmental stages, he returns to his primary connection with his caretaker for the emotional security to move to the next stage. Each impulse solidifies and then dissolves, one into the other. It is as if the child were being blown unerringly toward the gates of maturity by the wise breath of nature. His life flows from one transformation into another and continues to do so even after he arrives at adulthood.

Each of these stages has it own challenge and its own opportunity. A particular impulse comes into focus around a particular age for the first time. If the impulse is supported and its aim is accomplished successfully, the child is able to integrate the increasing mental, emotional, and physical complexity that is the goal of his personality. Then he is well prepared to begin the next task. He has laid a good foundation for learning the next lesson and for mastering the original impulse at an increased level of complexity when it appears later in a different form.[3]

As we have explained, if he remains secure in his connection to his primary caretaker, he will then become interested in exploring his environment. If this exploration is successful, he will identify with certain objects or persons and integrate them into a personal identity. Having achieved the first layer of selfhood, he will test his ability to have an impact on his world until he feels a sense of competence. He will then go through these first four steps again, this time in the social world outside his family, first with his same-sex peers and later with those of the opposite sex. There is no guarantee, but there is an increased probability that all will be well if each impulse is successfully integrated when it first appears as an internal imperative at a particular stage. The conscious parent helps nature along by maintaining a connection with the child that enables him to integrate each succeeding impulse successfully into his personality.[4]

THE SPIRAL

These two rhythms of oscillation and progression move together in a pattern that is both circular and progressive, suggesting, as Edinger says, a spiral. Think of a spiral staircase: Each step is a progression upward in space and is also a revisiting of a particular point around the circumference of the circle. We spend our lives walking up our own spiral staircases. At each turn, we get the same view we had before at the same spot, but because we are higher up, the view is broader.

At some point, however, we may stumble and fall on a particular step, unless we are supported. Although we may resume our journey, we leave behind a trail that testifies to our injury. Looking back, we can trace the trail to its source and see how our misstep has affected our own successive stages of growth and our ability to help other people, especially our children, negotiate this same step on their own personal journeys.

There are many reasons why we may not be able to plant our feet firmly on a particular step and steady ourselves before we move on. We may be born with something inside us that makes this step more difficult than others; we may have needed extra help and not received it. We may have been pushed off the step by the insensitivity or impatience or blindness of another person.

The beauty of the spiral is that we will always get another chance. Encountering the step again at the same place on a higher level, we can learn to do it better the next time. We can become more surefooted as we get older.

PROGRESSION

These rhythms of childhood exist within the context of the most universal cycle of all—*birth, youth, maturity, old age, death*. Above all else, this is the eternal "truth" of the universe: Conscious energy takes form as matter and is born into the world. This form changes over time, and then it dies. This cycle is as true for horseflies and Siberian tigers as it is for mountain ranges and solar systems.

In some organisms, different stages are easy to tell apart. A butterfly lets you know which stage it's in. It looks completely different at different times in its development. If you didn't know better, you wouldn't think that the small, hard-shelled egg was the same organism as the fat caterpillar, or that *that* was the same as the cocooned pupa, or that the white mummy of the pupa bore any resemblance at all to the iridescent butterfly that dazzles you as it floats away on the summer breeze. Four stages of development; four very different manifestations of the same creature.

We too reflect this universal process of change as we move through our stages. But in this respect we have more in common with mountain ranges than butterflies. We don't announce each new stage with a new body. We evolve gradually, not in jerks and stops. During much of childhood, and especially afterward, we look basically the same—worn down perhaps over the years, like mountains, but generally recognizable.

Not that we don't change. Certainly, our sons and daughters look different in their birth pictures than they do in their wedding pictures. But there is no one moment when the caterpillar takes on the very different body of the pupa. (Although some parents might disagree and pinpoint exactly when their thirteen-year-old metamorphosed into an alien life-form.) The change is gradual and imperceptible in everyday life.

This physical continuum over time can make it harder for parents to be aware of the changes through which their children are going. They look into the same beloved faces every morning and have no way of guessing at the hidden currents that will bring something new to the surface, where it finds expression in behavior the parents don't recognize. They are surprised by their child's new interest, new skill, new attitude. They think they know their children, understand their characters; and so they are thrown off when the turbulent waters bring up something unexpected. "Where did *that* come from?" they ask after one of these surprises.

The real surprise is not that children evolve into adults. The surprise is that this evolution is as predictable as it is and as universal as it is. In the same way that a sunflower seed is programmed to become a sunflower, a human baby is programmed to become a human adult. There is an innate developmental plan that is roughly the same for every baby that will allow it to acquire the physical, mental, and emotional skills it needs. The difference is that a flower needs soil, water, and sunlight to reach its full potential. The human baby needs so much more.

THE DEVELOPING BRAIN

In an earlier chapter we talked about the three structures of the brain: its reptilian base atop the spinal cord, which controls autonomic actions; its mammalian heritage, called the limbic system, from which feelings arise; and the cortex, which manifests thinking, intuition, and all other cognitive processes. In describing the function of the brain, we divided it into two parts called the old brain and the new brain. The old brain includes the reptilian and mammal brain and is the source of unconscious parenting reactions. The cortex, which we called the new brain, houses the potential for conscious parenting. As we focus on interacting with the child at each developmental stage, we will look into the brain and see how it develops, especially during the first three years of life. This will give you some idea of what is happening and how important you, as a parent, are to the process.

The first few months of life can be especially obscure to parents. It's hard to see what's happening inside the infant. You have to be cued to see what's stirring under the surface of your baby's infantile self. Most parents have no idea how much physical and psychological distance their baby is covering in just a few short months.

We are lucky that the objective findings of science can now confirm our suspicions: a great deal is happening inside the baby. Thoughtful parents and child-development experts have always known it. We have marveled at the miracle of transformation that must occur in order for the newborn to become a toddler—and we were right to be in awe!

We now know that the first three years of life are crucially important to the person the baby will become. Neuroscientists have learned a great deal about how the brain forms itself before the baby is born, and how it continues to create itself after the baby is born, in response to the experiences the baby has after conception.[5] It has become clear that the brain is not self-contained and isolated, evolving independent of its context. It can be thought of as a social organ that evolves only through continuous interaction with its environment. Here are some important facts that we now know:

1. A baby is born with about 100 billion nerve cells (neurons), about the same number as the number of stars in the Milky Way.[6] These neurons form themselves into circuits that are laid down in patterns according to instructions from genes. These circuits are not stable and immutable. They can be changed. The genes

provide the framework for the brain, but life experience directs the final construction.

2. After birth the baby's brain explodes with trillions more connections between neurons than the baby can use. The brain is hedging its bets. It's taking no chances on not having a connection that it will turn out to need. The long trek through childhood is one of attrition. The childhood years determine which of these circuits get maintained and strengthened, and which atrophy and die. The brain is in the process of organizing itself into the physical maps that govern such functions as seeing, hearing, speaking, moving. By the age of ten or so, half of these connections will be gone and the child will have about the number of connections he will keep throughout his life. Which ones stay and which go depends on which ones the baby uses in the course of his experiences. Babies in deprived environments develop fewer connections. Babies in appropriately stimulating environments grow brains that are filled with healthy connections and patterns. The brain's *plasticity*—its ability to change its physical and chemical structure responsively as it interacts with the environment—enables it to use the outside world to create itself. The baby's brain becomes increasingly effective at *doing* what the baby's environment demands.

3. The brain's self-creation occurs primarily in the first three years of life. How the brain develops depends on the *kind* and the *quality* of the connections the baby experiences—first with his mother and father and other caretakers, and then with objects in his environment and with other people. How it evolves and what it becomes, as with so much else we've talked about, depends upon the quality of its context. Literally, the brain is created in relationship.

4. Our genes program our brains to be receptive to learning certain critical skills at certain times. There are windows of opportunity when the brain is ready and willing to take on certain tasks. Trying to master those tasks before or after these times may be difficult or impossible. For example, the baby's brain needs the stimulation of the spoken word to activate language cells in the brain, to make the connections that will allow him to understand what you are saying and, at about twelve months, to start saying words. If the baby doesn't hear words, the development of the

appropriate brain cell connections does not occur and language development may be delayed or impaired.

The way the brain develops underscores the importance of attentive, responsive, aware parenting, especially in the early years. This may present another paradox: the very time when the cues from your young child are the hardest to read is the time when parents need to be especially vigilant and responsible in providing appropriate stimulation.

MIRRORING

In the chapters that follow, we will describe conscious parenting at each stage of the child's evolution. You have already learned a great deal about how a conscious parent *is* in the world in general. Irrespective of what is needed to facilitate each stage of the child's development, there is a conscious parenting *stance* that benefits the child no matter which stage she is in or which problems the two of you may be facing.

Perhaps the most important characteristic of this stance is one we have talked about already. *A conscious parent is reflective; she mirrors her child.* No matter how confused you may be or how unable you feel about meeting your child's needs, you can't go wrong if you mirror your baby or young child. Let's talk for a moment about what this means in relation to each developmental impulse.

Mirroring looks different at each stage. In early childhood, mirroring is the single most important thing you can do to nurture and sustain your child's innate program for development. You mirror a baby by laughing when she laughs, gurgling when she gurgles, frowning when she frowns, and so on for all the emotions your baby shows. You mirror an older child with language, which becomes more sophisticated as the child evolves into a verbal being.

Mirroring, which is the first phase of intentional dialogue, is the best way to let your child know "You are okay." This is what every child needs to know in order to master the task at hand and move on to the next one. In conscious parenting, mirroring leads eventually to empathy, which comprises parental attempts to participate in the experience of the child. Mirroring creates a unique bond between child and parent, which, if sustained, facilitates a smooth transition through all the stages and thereby obviates most of the common problems of parenting.

In the first stage of life, the baby and the parent (often the mother, primarily, but increasingly also the father) engage in a circular dance of action and reaction that is called *mutual cueing*. The mother watches her baby and reflects back to her an image of who she is. Think how powerful it is for the mother to send her baby this message, "I see who you are, and I think you're wonderful." The baby becomes the self she sees reflected in the mirroring mother. The parent's mirroring is the catalyst for the child's self-discovery. It helps the baby become able to form a centered self.

The accuracy with which the mother reflects back the essence of the child is critical. The child feels secure when she experiences congruence between her inner experience and the expression on the mother's face. But if the child has an experience that is not reflected back, then she feels a dissonance, a conflict between what she experiences and what is reflected back from the mother. Almost always, *she will believe the mother*, and her own inner self will become diminished. To fill the void of the unreflected self, she will create a false self in order to elicit a positive response from her parent.

The conscious parent mirrors the baby as a way of being with her child, as a form of communion. She doesn't do it to shape or control. And because of the way our brains are designed, the mother receives, reflected back, the caring and affection she gives to her baby. In mirroring her child, she paradoxically begins to validate her own inner experience. She is able to break out of her own self-involvement as she participates fully in the life of another.

Balance: The essence of conscious parenting *at every stage* of childhood is striking a balance between responding in a way that gives the child what she wants and responding in a way that sets limits and establishes boundaries. For the first eighteen months of the child's life, the parent starts way over on the "giving" side of the continuum, but after that he moves toward the center. Increasingly, as the child gets older, the parent provides structure in order to help the child develop a *perspective* on where she fits in with everyone else, a *moral character* that helps her live by the Golden Rule in a social context, and a *self-discipline* that allows her to live a productive and meaningful life. In this sense structure is nurture. The parent is actively loving his child when he helps her develop internalized boundaries. These will serve her well in getting her own needs met while she begins to be aware that there are also other people in the world.

Self-Esteem: When a child learns that she can get her needs met and she learns that it is important to partner with others so their needs can also be met, she is able to move successfully through the gates of childhood. As she negotiates each passage, she grows in self-esteem. Whenever the world reflects back to her that she is okay, she begins to think of herself as okay. She holds within herself the experience of okayness, self-acceptance, and even self-affection. Parents who nurture this sense of being acceptable, adequate, valued, worthy, and treasured plant a seed in their child that flowers for the rest of the child's life. The child will become resilient and able to manage her emotions. The seed grows from the parent's loving, which includes emotional support, and from the parent's insistence on appropriate limits.[6]

A Danger: It is so important to know what "loving" your child means. We know that it means meeting the child's needs. And we have just said that it means providing structure and limits. But there are two important things that loving does *not* mean: it does not mean giving your child everything she wants, and it does not mean acting as though your child were you! We have talked throughout this book about the danger of symbiosis, the danger of fusing with your child. So we can add another layer of meaning to our concept of loving: loving means establishing an appropriate relationship that both honors the innate connection between you and recognizes that you are not your child. You are two separate people.

In the very beginning the mother and her baby are so intimately connected that they appear to be fused, a condition necessary to ensure the baby's survival. A baby has so many needs, and life is so perilous. A mother has to be exquisitely sensitive to the baby in order to do what is necessary for the baby to survive. But the mother must resist the tendency to merge with the child or become isolated from her and must evolve into a parent who is *empathic, not symbiotic.*

It is worthwhile for parents to examine their reasons for becoming parents. Does having a baby fill a void in your life? Does having a baby give you status within your own family or community? Does having a baby mean that you will feel less lonely and empty? Does having a baby mean that you can control *this* relationship even though other relationships have failed?

If a parent can honestly answer "yes" to any of these questions, she needs to be alert to the danger that she may blur the boundary between herself and her child; she may in fact dishonor the sanctity of her own child by becoming symbiotic. Beware!

Empathy, however, is a different matter. This ability to reflect the child's feelings and participate in his experiencing is an essential component of conscious parenting. Empathy fosters attunement,[7] which allows the parent to know what to do to maintain the balance between nurture and structure. A parent who is attuned to his child's needs will know when to meet his child's needs by saying yes and when to meet his child's needs by saying no.

With these general guidelines in mind, we are ready to understand, on a deeper level, how you can help your child grow to become the whole, fully functioning person she was meant to be. In the next six chapters we present a brief description of each of six developmental stages through which a child will travel on her pilgrimage to adulthood. In the description of each stage we will state what the child is trying to do and what the child needs from the parent in order to get it done. We will also discuss how the two types of parenting, overinvolved and underinvolved, manifest themselves at each stage, describing the consequences for the child. Finally, Section VI, "Tools for Conscious Parenting," presents a growth plan that parents can use to restart their own arrested developmental process and continue their healing and growth.

HOW TO READ THE DEVELOPMENTAL CHAPTERS

Here are some suggestions for getting the most out of the chapters that follow:

1. Read all of these chapters at once, no matter how old your child is or how many children you have. This will give you an overview for understanding your child as an evolving being with a history and a future connected to the present. Then read again the chapter that applies to your child now. Having read all of the story, you will have an idea of what to expect as your child grows to the next stage, and you will have the practical information you need to help her. Please understand also that if your children are adults, you can use this information to help heal whatever wounding they experienced while they were growing up. Emotionally, they may still be stuck at the stage in which they were wounded, and you can do a great deal now to meet the needs that were not met then. It is never too late. The exception is your grown-up children who are married. They can more successfully work things out with their spouses.

2. Keep in mind that these stages progress naturally in children, as

long as you provide conscious safety, support, and boundaries. There is nothing you need to do to push your child through these gates. Your job is to help smooth the way once the impulse has arisen. If you don't help, she will probably experience difficulty. The resulting wound could distort the stages that follow and may create problems later in her adult life.

3. Most parents find that one or two stages are harder for them than the others. One woman we know found raising kids to be a snap until they became teenagers. Then she felt she was in foreign territory. If you are having trouble with a particular stage, it is likely that your parents had trouble shepherding you at the same spot. Think of your difficulties as gifts. They let you know what you need to work on in yourself. This is the most important information you can get in your odyssey to become a better parent. Most often, difficulties take the form of your own repetitive, intense emotional response to your child. Your partner's response to your parenting and observations from other adults can also be enlightening. If you find yourself having difficulty, you have probably identified your childhood wound and your growth point. While you initiate your own healing work with your partner or another significant adult, you will have to use the information from the appropriate chapter thoughtfully in order to parent your child successfully through this stage.

4. Remember: You cannot successfully guide your child through a developmental stage that you yourself didn't successfully negotiate unless and until you begin the process of your own healing and growth. As you begin to grow through this stage, your child will begin to grow through it also. The practical information in these chapters will help you become intentional with your child so that you can parent her with conscious intent, but your emotional growth during the process is essential at the same time. Obviously this is good for your child; less obviously, it is also good for you.

5. To heal means to get your needs met. Your healing must come from your partner (and hers from you) or from another significant adult if you are single. Your healing cannot come from your child. Parents who turn to their children to meet their needs wound them in the same way that they themselves were wounded. This is a form of emotional incest. Growth consists in stretching beyond the defenses you erected as a child to protect

yourself from emotional pain to restart your own developmental progress. Your child and your partner will help you with that: they will provide you with opportunities to meet *their* needs and in so doing, you will meet your own. This is the path toward wholeness and to the recovery of your awareness of your connection to the cosmos.

6. So, while you are reading for information about how to become intentional in helping your child develop, understand the sobering truth that you will not be able to implement these new behaviors completely until you attend to your own unfinished childhood business. To do that you must develop a conscious marriage or other conscious relationship with another adult in which you and your partner heal each other's childhood wounds and alter your protective, defensive patterns. (If you wish additional help in sorting out your childhood issues and pinpointing changes you want to make in your parenting now, you might want to order a copy of the *Parents' Manual*. We wrote it for people who want the benefits of attending an Imago Parenting Workshop, but are unable to do so. It may be ordered directly from the Imago Institute. See the back page for ordering information.)

7. From the text and the examples try to identify your parenting style. As we have said, we will be drawing portraits of parenting styles that are quite clearly opposed to each other for the purpose of helping you distinguish between them. It may be that you can't identify with these extremes in your everyday encounters with your children because the characteristics of minimizing or maximizing that *you* are demonstrating are more subtle. For this reason, your style will be easiest to identify in those moments when you feel emotionally charged by something your child is doing. If you become excessively involved and controlling, it means that you use the defense of maximizing when you feel afraid and overwhelmed. If you tend to withdraw, then you use the defense of minimizing when you reach the limits of your knowledge. If you are intense and express your emotions with exaggeration, you are probably a maximizer. If you are constrained and seldom give vent to your feelings, you are probably a minimizer. As you will see, the particular texture of your parenting style is influenced by the severity of your own childhood wound and the stage in which it occurred. A parent wounded

in the attachment stage will become a more rigid minimizer or maximizer than one wounded in a later stage. Remember, also, that you are using these defenses in your relationship with your intimate other. Therefore, your partner can be a resource to help you see what you are doing.

A conscious marriage is the best gift you can give your child, and it is the most efficient path to conscious parenting. You can do the work of creating a conscious marriage, as described in *Getting the Love You Want: A Guide for Couples*, while you are doing the work of raising your child. The two tasks can be addressed at the same time. Since your reactions to your child's needs will mirror your reactions to your spouse's needs, you can, within your marriage, use all the processes described above to heal your own childhood wounds.

8

The Stage of Attachment:

Birth Through 18 Months of Age

*D*uring these first months of her life, the baby begins an amazing journey. Impelled by her own inner wisdom and held tenderly by her parents, she will lay the foundation for her unique and miraculous self. From the very first, she is discernible as a distinct self, able to interact with her caretakers.[1] She shapes them, as well as being shaped by them. Her most important goal is to maintain connection to her parents, through whom she experiences her connection to the universe as a whole. When she is securely connected, at about eighteen months, her energy can then be turned to exploring the world around her.

For the first month or so of the baby's life, nature has planned it so that the baby is dependent and self-invested, but still responsive to her mother and father. Connection to her parents is crucial for her survival, so she comes equipped with capacities that will help her maintain the attachment. She is born with the ability to use her senses—she can see, hear, smell, and respond to touch—even, if at times, she seems to do so from a distance. With every passing day, she gathers the energy she needs to wake up more fully to life. This is the time when parents do almost all the work to take care of their baby's physical needs and strengthen the connection between them, although the baby is helping more than they know through the subtle signals of responsiveness she is sending them. Even at this young age the baby is a social creature, constantly interacting with her world.[2]

Fortunately, parents don't seem to notice this temporary state of self-absorption as they continue to do exactly what the baby needs. They interact with her. Nature has arranged things so that we love our babies without reservation and without thought even when they don't do anything specific to make us feel good. Because of the imperative to do whatever is necessary to ensure the survival of the young, our babies come to us packaged in a way that invites us to protect and nurture them. It's a way of making sure that we spend the time and energy required. Most of us cannot imagine *not* doing it.

Newborn babies give their parents a great gift. It is easy to relate to them in a giving way. At this stage, there is no "I'll do something for you, and you can do something for me." In the beginning, the giving is almost all one-way. This is transforming for the parent! She has the opportunity to live outside her own skin, put aside her own needs, and think entirely of the well-being of another. She must make room in her heart and mind for the birth and the life she has called into being. This is the first of many opportunities that parenting offers to grow beyond self-involvement and self-centeredness.

As the baby grows beyond this initial inward phase, he begins to interact more with his mother and father and a few objects around him. Through this interaction, he is engaged in the continuous process of self-creation. His parents become his cocreators, his partners in brain construction. They surround him with experiences that help him develop his senses, his cognitive abilities, his confidence in his body, and his comfort with all his feelings. At the moment of birth, the newborn bonds to his mother through his sense of smell. At about four months, his brain begins the changes that allow him to develop binocular vision and depth perception. At three months, the baby will become empathic, able to tell if his mother is depressed and will respond with sadness himself as he begins to evolve more complex emotions, such as joy and sadness, envy, pride, and shame. At about the same time, he begins to smile. At six months, he can recognize vowel sounds, and at twelve months, he can begin to talk. Shortly after, he is ready to walk. He learns to do these things because his brain is receptive, eager for the stimulation of raw material. His parents provide the cooing and holding and smiling and playing that allows his brain to do the necessary work.

WHAT THE CHILD NEEDS AT THE ATTACHMENT STAGE

For the first eighteen months after birth, your baby is totally dependent. He is bonding with you and learning that his needs will be met. *During this period, the most important thing you can do is be reliably available and reliably warm.*[3] This means responding to what he needs when he needs it, regardless of whether it is convenient. When you do this, you are ensuring that your baby will survive and that he will maintain that sense of connection with the universe that is the foundation of his future security in the world.

If you find yourself reacting strongly to your child's dependence on you, then you may have been wounded at this stage. You can use this insight to focus your attention on issues that you need to work on in your efforts to become a conscious parent.

In the midst of the unending round of feedings and diapers and baths, the parents hold the baby in their minds as a whole and unique person, whose essence they honor, and whose potential they recognize. In the process they are naturally and gently revealing the world's possibilities to their newborn. As they watch her respond to the treasures they bring her, they do the very important work of coming to understand and accept their baby as a person in her own right.

When parents hold their babies, both physically and symbolically, in this way, they maintain the cosmic connection with which the baby was born. The baby incorporates way down deep, interwoven into her own body, a sense of continuity and a sense of being protected from her greatest fear, the fear of becoming disconnected. The achievement of a secure attachment at this age makes it possible for the child to feel at home in the world, to establish a spiritual yearning for connection with the other people, ideas, and experiences that will arise from her enlarging environment.

Safety and Support: During the attachment stage, it's hard to tell safety and support apart, since keeping the child safe and ensuring her survival is the most basic way to support her continuing development. The child's survival is best ensured by maintaining her connection with you. A rupture of that connection not only feels like death to the young child, it may actually mean death. It takes no imagination to see how estrangement from the parents can pose a threat to a helpless infant or young child. Chronic disconnection is painful, and for the old brain, pain equals death.

There are some basic ways a parent can provide safety and support to a child in the attachment stage:

The parent is consistently available to meet the child's physical needs. Obviously the parent keeps the child warm, dry, fed, and in a safe environment.

The parent is consistently available to meet the child's emotional needs. The parent speaks in a soft, soothing tone of voice, smiling a lot, and communicating that the child is in the presence of a safe, nurturing person and need not be afraid. As much as possible, parents want their baby's environment to be free from loud noises or disconcerting movements or traumas.

As the baby begins to experiment with facial expressions and sounds that will eventually enable her to verbalize her communications, it is important for the parents to validate her nonverbal communications by mirroring them. This means reproducing the sounds and expressions in order to allow the baby to gain confidence in her experimentation. When in doubt about how to mirror, smiling works wonders.

The parent is physically present for as much of this first stage as possible. She carries the baby in a sling as long as possible, has the child sleep in the same bed or at least the same room at night (separation at night can be a major trauma for the child when there are delayed responses to the baby's cries), and takes the baby with her as much as possible when she goes out. The parent is aware that it is important to be available when the baby needs her, and not just when it is convenient for her.[4]

Although it may seem difficult for parents weary of the long hours of responsibility, absences from the baby should be brief. A parent should be with the baby most of the time, and parents should take the baby with them wherever they go whenever possible. There should be few exceptions. If a parent cannot be present for some reason, the baby should have a suitable, familiar, and warm substitute.

The parent is consistently available for breast-feeding, if at all possible. Feedings provide an ideal opportunity for holding. We recommend that babies be breast-fed, and fathers should also receive the experience of holding by supplementing the breast-feeding with an occasional bottle.[5] It is always the right thing to do to feed the baby on demand rather than on schedule. Schedules by design are constructed for the benefit of parents, not babies. And while there is no risk at this age of what our grandparents called "spoiling" the baby by too much attention, there is a fair risk of depriving her by providing too little of the holding she needs when she needs it. A spoiled child is a child deprived of what she needs, not the other way around. Feeding should be done in a warm, relaxed environment where the mother (or father) does not feel rushed. What the baby needs as she is being held is a complete experience with a beginning, a middle, and an end. This can't happen if the parent is hurried or harassed.

The parent is consistently available to comfort the child when the child needs something or is stressed. She mirrors the child's discomfort and acts quickly to remove the cause of the problem. Connecting with the child's distress and not trying to soothe it away is the most effective form of comfort.

Structure: There are three major ways parents can provide structure for their children in the attachment stage. First, they can structure the child's physical environment so that it is safe. That means making sure that all of the actions the parents take to ensure safety and support (cited above) are undertaken within environments that are safe and comfortable for the child.

Second, the parent can begin to teach the very young child which of her actions are unsafe and redirect the child's energy. For example, a father will act quickly to limit his eight-month-old son's access to a sharp knife and will not hesitate to insist that his fourteen-month-old daughter be buckled into a car seat, no matter how plaintive her wailing.

Third, the parent will begin to teach the child that there are other people and other things in her environment that also require care and attention. This teaching is done gently and gradually as the child nears his first birthday. The child has an increasing capacity to understand what it means to cooperate with others, to wait just a little bit while the mother tends to the needs of a sibling, and to not hurt others. A child who is pulling a dog's tail must be told "No." A child who is demanding a cookie while the father is on the phone can be asked to wait a moment until the father is off the phone. The goal is to begin to teach the child what it is like to cooperate by accommodating to the needs of others, occasionally. Thus from the very beginning, the parent lays the foundation for a healthy moral consciousness.

WOUNDING AT THE ATTACHMENT STAGE

What we have just been discussing is what the baby needs. No parent will be able to provide what her baby needs perfectly all the time. The important thing is to do a good job consistently. The wounding we have defined in this book is not the result of a momentary lapse. Few children will be permanently psychologically injured by errors that parents make unless there is a *pattern* to the errors. Unfortunately, patterns do tend to develop in the parenting styles of unconscious mothers and fathers. Types of wounds at the attachment stage include feelings of rejection and fears of abandonment.

Most parents will have trouble with particular aspects of parenting, rather than feeling at ease with the whole process. Specifically, a parent will find it difficult to respond well when his child expresses an impulse that he himself was not allowed to express when he was a child. A parent unattuned to the bonding impulse at the stage of attachment, for example, may respond to his child in one of two ineffective ways. He may fail to respond to the bonding impulse of his baby by minimizing his responses through underinvolvement, or he may maximize, becoming sporadically overinvolved.

If a child learns to feel insecure at the attachment stage, she will either feel rejected by her parent's minimizing behavior and react with avoidance or feel abandoned by her parent's unpredictable maximizing behavior and react with clinging. In adulthood this child will have a problem with contact. She will either be avoidant or excessively clingy.

THE MINIMIZER PARENT AT THE ATTACHMENT STAGE—AVOIDING

Minimizers who were wounded at this stage tend to "underparent." They do not support their child's connectional needs and tend to avoid contact. For example, they are not as apt to pick the baby up and hold her. The minimizing parent's underinvolvement will be expressed as a lack of emotional warmth, a failure of attunement, and this expression may sometimes be abusive and harsh.

Why would a parent act this way? Because he also had an avoidant parent who responded to *him* in the same way. He experienced a ruptured connection with one or both of his parents and the rupture continues to reverberate throughout his life. He erects powerful boundaries between himself and others and feels uncomfortable with emotional contact. Unfortunately, this is exactly what the neediness of his baby arouses—fear of contact.

The parent is afraid, and his inability to conquer his fear activates his baby's fear. The lack of holding and physical interaction will activate the baby's need for survival. She will respond with panic to her parent's unreliable, inconsistent, and cold response. She will experience a rupture in her connection with her avoiding parent and will learn to withdraw upon contact.

She will block her reception of input from the outside world, which is slow to meet her basic survival needs. In order to protect herself she will learn a deep sense of aloneness, masking her yearning for contact and relationship. She is on her way to becoming a minimizer herself.

THE MAXIMIZER PARENT AT THE ATTACHMENT STAGE—CLINGING

The maximizer parent who was wounded in the stage of attachment is unreliably available, but when she is available, she is emotionally warm.[6] Her child sometimes gets what he needs and sometimes not. Sometimes he is the central figure in a carnival of adoration; sometimes he finds himself alone in the desert. The result is a grasping, clinging child who frets when the nurturing is withdrawn because he's not sure it will be there when he needs it. He holds on to his mother for dear life because he knows it's possible to lose her. He develops a symbiotic relationship with her that shuts out the real world. The same defenses that shut the door on the outside world become the building blocks of a distorted inner world that feels real to him. It is this self-created inner world that the child then projects outward as "the way things really are."

Unlike the minimizing parent, who acts as though boundaries are barricades, the maximizing parent acts as if they don't exist. As we have already seen, a lack of boundaries on the part of the parent leads to symbiotic attachment with the child. The child doesn't know whether he will receive safety and support from his mother or not, so he reacts by doing what sometimes works—clinging.

Inconsistent availability is a real problem. The following is a severe analogy and not one we want to use to make parents feel guilty, but think of the way similar responses are consciously used by interrogators to create dependence in the person being interrogated. The interrogator is sometimes warm and friendly and sometimes cold and punishing. The prisoner never knows which to expect, but warmth is present often enough that he will do anything to get it, even though, at some level, he knows it's out of his control. It doesn't take long for these random and extreme emotional responses to cause him to lose his own sense of self and identify with his interrogator.

What would cause a parent to behave in this way? Again, the parent responds as she does because of the way her parents responded to her. She had an unreliable and inconsistent emotionally warm parent who also tried to fill the emptiness in his or her own life by showering her at times with excessive attention. She, in turn, has developed a symbiotic connection with her baby, often becoming overly concerned and smothering him with affection, even when he has clearly had enough and tries to pull away. Unconsciously she is trying to meet her own needs through her child.[7]

We can also make a very good guess that the needs of a maximizing parent for warmth are probably not being met in her marriage. If they were, her childhood wound would be partly or mostly healed, and she would not be manifesting these inner inconsistencies in her interaction with her child.

If she is so excessively affectionate, why does she sometimes withdraw her affection from her baby? Why is a maximizer *inconsistent?* The reason is that she has discovered one of life's great truths: babies are needy. They are demanding. They are insistent. They are urgent. Perhaps, initially, she idealized her son and her role as his mother, and imagined a romantic relationship where she would finally receive the unconditional love she is never sure of. But in the end she cannot handle repeated and incessant demands. It's analogous to the romantic attraction and power struggle that occur in marriage. Inevitably the reality of the baby doesn't match the romantic vision. So sometimes she's warm and loving, and sometimes she's put out, bored, angry, and beleaguered. The messages she sends him alternate: "Don't need." "Meet my needs." "Now go somewhere else to get your needs met." Sometimes, feeling pushed to her limits, she may respond to her child with anger or abuse. And while she wants help from her spouse, she criticizes and instructs him when help is given.

THE WAY OUT

Of course we are speaking in the language of extremes for the purpose of illustration. We want to assure you once again that there is nothing final and nothing is fatal. Parents need to become aware of how they are responding to their children, make an effort to understand what is hidden in themselves, and then take steps to heal the places where they were wounded so they can parent their children consciously. In other words, they need to reparent each other.

It helps to know that when minimizer or maximizer parents practice the corrective responses that make them better parents, they also positively affect their own psychological state. The reliable warmth they learn to express for their children is also a healing gift they give themselves. The old brain cannot distinguish between the mother and the child, so what the mother gives the child is received by the mother's unconscious as if it were sent to the mother. By giving consistent warmth to her child, the minimizing parent will overcome his fear of contact, experience his hidden *need* for contact that was repressed in his childhood, and eventually enjoy the warmth and reliability he gives his child. The maximizing parent will overcome her fear that love will be withdrawn or unavailable, and will be able to establish and maintain the boundaries between herself and her child that allow her to express warmth reliably and with appropriate separation. It's important to know that character structure can be rebuilt and connections can be restored to their proper, natural state.

HOW TWO PARENTS WORKED IT THROUGH

Often we assume that it will be the father who is the minimizer parent and the mother who is the maximizer. But with Pat and Jeff the reverse was true. It's important to remember that *parenting styles are more a matter of how one was parented than gender.* Pat and Jeff were the parents of Neil, who was six months old when they first entered therapy. At that point in their marriage Neil was the focal point of a considerable amount of conflict.

Pat was a stockbroker whose business as a select portfolio manager was really beginning to take off just as her baby arrived. Jeff ran a small design business from their home, which made it easier for him to be available for Neil's care after his birth. Their initial battle had been over breast-feeding. Neil had assumed that Pat would want to be home more regularly in order to accommodate a breast-feeding schedule, and he couldn't understand why she felt she needed to be back at work. He was baffled, asking, "Why don't you want to be home with Neil?" Her response was, "I don't know what drives me more crazy, your demands, the baby, or the ten pounds I can't seem to lose. Don't you understand why I need to work on my business?" Jeff could tell that Neil often wanted to sleep with them, but Pat would complain when he brought Neil into bed. She needed her sleep. Pat wanted to hire a baby-sitter so they could go out more often, but Jeff wanted to "stay at home and be a family together."

Pat complained that Jeff was smothering her with his irrational demands, and Jeff saw Pat as an unfeeling and uncaring mother. As they dug deeper into the underlying patterns of interaction, it became clear that Pat had been using the legitimate needs of her growing business to avoid dealing with Jeff and the baby, who both seemed to her like suffocating burdens. Jeff, on the other hand, overcompensated by clinging to Neil, demanding extra attention for the baby, while in fact wanting more affection for himself. Neither Pat nor Jeff could understand the other's point of view.

When they were helped to look backward at their own childhoods they began to see how their current disagreements over Neil were really reenactments of old, unresolved childhood conflicts. Childhood wounding had created their current difficulties.

Pat's mother, who had been a cook for the local veteran's hospital, had also had the task of raising five children. She had seldom been available for Pat, who had been the fourth child. Even though Pat understood the pressure that her widowed mother had been under, she had never come to terms with her mother's emotional absences. Pat described her mother as aloof, even though she knew that her mother was simply too exhausted to meet the demands of her five children after a full day at work. Although Pat saw herself as vastly different from her mother, she could see how much her avoidance of household interactions was similar to her mother's. It was no accident that Pat had chosen a warm, loving husband who, she thought, would fulfill for her the role of "Mr. Mom," allowing her to retain her emotional distance.

Jeff had been raised by warm and loving parents who, because of their careers in medicine, often had to rely on hired caregivers to meet the emotional needs of their two children. His father's teaching career had, in addition, caused his father to travel a lot, further restricting the amount of time Jeff spent with him. As a result, Jeff harbored a vision of a warm and unified family as something he had missed out on and was determined to re-create in his own home.

WORKING TO REPAIR THE MARRIAGE

In order for Pat to move away from her avoidant stance, she agreed to a trial period in which she regularly initiated more contact with Jeff. Just eye contact and nonsexual touching at first. They were also helped to deepen the change process by changing roles. The plan was for Pat to ask Jeff to hug her. She complained about this suggestion, saying that if she asked him for a hug, he would just want to have sex. He couldn't figure out what was wrong with that. Pat had an answer. "You're just too needy," she said, adding, "If you were less needy, I'd want to have sex more often," implying that she herself was free of needs. When asked what she wanted from Jeff, she replied, "To accept me as I am and stop complaining. To stop smothering me. And to be affectionate without always turning it into foreplay."

They were then taught how to use intentional dialogue. Minimizers have the tendency to avoid dialogue; maximizers have a tendency to do everything they can to maintain a *monologue*. Intentional dialogue helps people meet somewhere in the middle.

After a few weeks Pat and Jeff were smiling and indicated that changing roles had really helped them. "When Jeff asked me to leave him alone, I was devastated, and then I realized that this is what I had been doing to him for years. I found myself following him around trying to apologize until he said I was starting to sound like him." They were making progress.

ANSWERING THE NEEDS OF THE CHILD

Pat took on the assignment to carry Neil around with her whenever she was at home, either in her arms or in his Snugli. She was also encouraged to pick Neil up and comfort him when he cried. In this way she would be overcoming her own fear of contact while at the same time seeing firsthand just how much her son needed her. Pat had not been used to giving Neil his bottle, so she decided to take this responsibility when she was home.

Jeff had been very attentive to Neil, except when his focus shifted to how Pat wasn't meeting his needs. Then he would abandon Neil. Although he seemed almost excessively involved with Neil, it was clear that his own needs came first. He was sublimating these unmet needs by overparenting Neil. Neil was learning not to count on his father.

Jeff's first priority was to become reliable and available to Pat. She needed to know she could rely on him, and he needed to know he could meet that need. It was also important for him to concentrate on being present for Neil when Neil needed him, not just when it suited his convenience.

Of course, Jeff questioned whether he was in fact emotionally inconsistent. He was quite defensive, in fact. As far as he was concerned, if it hadn't been for him their household would have been an iceberg. It took him a while to see that he was often at the mercy of his emotions when he was doling out affection.

Later, Pat encouraged Jeff to go out with friends more often. Not only did this get Jeff out of the house, but it gave Pat more time alone with her baby. During the times she had with her son, she practiced mirroring him and empathizing with his feelings. After several months, this process generated its own momentum. As Pat became more comfortable giving Neil his bath, for example, Jeff became more comfortable scheduling time for himself. As Jeff became more comfortable waiting a minute or two when Neil cried in the night, Pat was more likely to pick the baby up when he didn't go back to sleep right away.

There was much less blaming and a great deal more listening as these two parents practiced intentional dialogue. Pat and Jeff enjoyed each other's company more, and they drew their baby into the warmth of their circle. Neil could expect to begin the stage of exploration from a secure and loving base.[8]

9

The Stage of Exploration:

18 Months Through 3 Years of Age

*I*f your child has successfully maintained connection with you, she becomes interested in exploring and connecting with the world around her, and she brooks no interference with her curiosity. Child-rearing folklore calls this stage "the terrible twos." Sometimes parents view it as the age of aggression. Boundaries begin to be set, both to protect the child from physical harm and to increase the comfort of the parents. What is really happening is the child's "love affair" with the world. The secure child emerges from the parents' cocoon. The parents must practice letting go. But not letting go too much. She still wants you to be around, so that if she needs to, she can come rushing back for safety.

If you find yourself reacting strongly to your child's compulsion to explore, you may have been wounded at the exploration stage. In the course of observing your interactions with your child around this issue, you will discover which parts of you need further healing.

The exploratory impulse of the child at this stage begins the process of differentiation, the first step toward becoming a *self*, distinct from his parents. The ability to take this step depends upon the solidity of the attachment bond. Throughout life, attachment is the essential element of a person's being. No one outgrows the need for belonging, although the need may be expressed in different forms at different times. An evolved form of the attachment bond can be seen later in life, for example, in the desire for spiritual fulfillment, the yearning to feel that you belong to or are at "one" with a larger context. But during this second stage of childhood, this spiritual longing is focused, first and foremost, on attachment to parents. Secure in the presence of his parents, the toddler can wander away to explore the world.[1]

And one of the things he discovers is the power of words. One word in particular. It's a thrill every time he says it: "No!" The vehemence of the child's Everlasting No belies the tentativeness of the step he is taking. He is not as autonomous or independent as he sounds; he is beginning to test his self-ness and finding out what it feels like. In equal and opposite measure, the toddler insists on the parent's presence even as he pushes to be off on his own. In a real sense, he both rejects the parent's commands and demands the parent's presence.

During this time it is important for the young child to experience aloneness (which is different from loneliness), and noninterference from the parent. He requires a kind of *positive solitude*. This is a prerequisite for exploration and creativity. In one of the paradoxes of childhood, he can experience the aloneness he requires only in the context of a secure relationship with the parent. If the parent is available when needed, the young child is able to predict future availability and can therefore be alone in comfort.

The fear of being alone is often written about; the desire to be alone is common; but little has been written about the *ability* to be alone. We remember one mother discussing how a parent can provide a safe haven by letting her children be alone to the extent that they need and want to be. "I remember watching my sister Maureen be a mom. She has a very different parenting style than I do, but I learned something from it. At first, it almost seemed abusive to me. She would just sit in one place and wouldn't intervene with her kids. She wouldn't teach. She didn't direct, or lay the path, or sprinkle the environment with richness. She just sat there. And yet, she was a safe place to come back to, and she did care and does care about her kids incredibly. I remember watching her parent and feeling that those children wanted to be held and touched more than they were. But the truth is, if they had wanted it, she was there."

WHAT THE CHILD NEEDS AT THE EXPLORATION STAGE

What a child most requires at the exploration stage is a parent who provides support and encouragement when he begins to explore his environment. As we have said, there is still a strong attachment need, and the child will express it by wanting his parent to see and approve of all the new discoveries he is making. Any parent of a two-to-three-year-old knows what we mean and is familiar with the incessant demand to "Look at this" or "See." During these conversations the conscious parent provides consistent warmth and positive interest and continues to cultivate the practice of mirroring the child's facial expressions, sounds, and movements.

Sometimes parents are tempted to add a lot of instruction at this point. But a child at this age is not ready to be the perfect pupil. He may be more interested in providing his parents with information and looking for their approval than in receiving a lengthy explanation of how something is done. The parent needs to be patient with the child's Eternal Why in the same way he is patient with the Everlasting No. The "why's" are precious. The child is not only gathering specific information, but he is discovering how to learn.

What the conscious parent supports at this stage is the child's curiosity, allowing him to know it's okay to experience the world firsthand. This is much more important than trying to arrange it so that the child is successful or competent. That comes later. When the parent provides him with support and does not withdraw if the encounter gets frustrating, the child develops a friendship with the world. All that is needed for the development of lifelong curiosity is the parent's physical and emotional availability when the child wishes to return and reattach after his expeditions.

Obviously, in these first stages of exploration, there may be some physical danger involved. More than before, the child needs the safety of clear boundaries. Again, it's a question of balance: keeping his child safe, and at the same time not being overprotective. Within this framework the child can look around at the world at his own pace.

Here is how one mother supported her daughter's self-discovery while keeping her safe:

One of the most joyful experiences for a parent is when a child begins to take its first steps. After weeks of holding on to the coffee table or the edge of the sofa and walking around, holding on for support, Anna one day let go and took a few steps toward me. I looked at her. She looked at me. She was standing unsupported. I waited to see what she would do, holding my breath. She looked down at her feet and back up at me, a slow smile on her face. Then she burst out laughing. This was not the reaction I expected. But at soon as she started to laugh, I did, too. She wobbled and collapsed, laughing and laughing. Pretty soon she stood up again and then plopped down rather dangerously. I had to put pillows around her to give her protection. I'll never forget how proud and happy she was with herself. I was, too.

By providing safety, support, and structure, a conscious parent affirms her child's impulse to explore during this stage.

Safety: *She provides physical and emotional safety at all times.* She provides protection by communicating clear boundaries. While giving him opportunities to explore, she also guides him away from dangerous objects.

Support: *She supports his urge to explore his world.* She says yes as often as possible while preserving structure and values. She is consistently warm and available, taking time to allow the child to satisfy his curiosity and share it. She praises his successes and applauds his discoveries. She creates opportunities for him to discover more than he could on his own and makes a conscious effort for these explorations to be fun and filled with laughter.

She is physically and emotionally available when the child wishes to reattach after exploring his environment. She wants to hear about his exploits. She makes frequent physical contact with him through lots of hugs and praise. She loves him without conditions and without regard to performance.

Structure: *She looks for opportunities to help her child learn about himself and his environment.* When she wishes him to learn more adaptive and efficient behaviors, she uses his behavior to teach or show rather than to discipline or punish. She uses clear instructions, avoiding absolutes and abstractions. In all her interactions she preserves his self-esteem, avoiding shaming and devaluation. She focuses on what he does correctly, rather than on what he does "incorrectly," so that he can internalize and build on success. She rewards him with at least as much emotional intensity as she uses when calling attention to something she wants him to change. When things get tough, she does not withdraw her attention or her affection.

She mirrors his facial expressions, sounds, and movements, including his fears as well as his delights. She offers him opportunities for self-expression and seeks to see things from his point of view.

Parents who are not able to provide safety, support, and structure for their children at the stage of exploration will wound them around issues of smothering and neglect, as we shall see.

THE MINIMIZER PARENT AT THE EXPLORATION STAGE–DISTANCING

A minimizer who was wounded at the exploration stage tends to keep his distance. He is a distancer. He may have done just fine through the attachment stage, so it's not that he's afraid of physical contact. But he looks for opportunities to be alone. As a child he was almost always left to check out the world by himself, since at least one of his parents showed little interest in his discoveries and often left him to his own devices. He came to regard this lack of parental interest as appropriate. Whether he remembers any of this or not, it now seems natural for kids to be left alone to figure things out for themselves, with very little feedback or support.

That's why he welcomes the first signs of separateness as heralding his own freedom. "At last, the kid is pushing me away!" He thinks that the period of attachment and close connectedness is "over." And he is grateful that the age of independence has begun. Of course, as we have already shown, he is mistaking the child's need to explore while still remaining attached to the parent for a need to be completely separate.

He tries to avoid being "stuck" with child care. He is anxious to be free of his child's demands for attention because they overwhelm him. His own life feels swamped and submerged by his children. So he avoids connection, preferring to be in his own separate world.

When his child comes to him with new things to show, he tends to be noncommittal or bored. His attitude implies that the child is intruding on him and, in fact, has no needs. It's the old W. C. Fields approach to child rearing: "Go away, kid—yuh bother me." Of course, these are not the words the minimizer uses, but it's what his attitude conveys. He tends to be annoyed by the child's behavior. He may be overly critical, reacting negatively and punitively to dirty hands, scrapes, bruises, and other minor everyday annoyances. In an attempt to control or restrict contact, he may become overly concerned with setting and adhering to rules.

THE MAXIMIZER PARENT AT THE EXPLORATION
STAGE—PURSUING

A parent who maximizes at the exploration stage has a great deal of trouble letting go during the attachment phase. She is a pursuer, overinvolved in the child's exploits and overly concerned about his welfare. Fearful herself of the outside world, she hovers over her child. The rationale she uses is that she is concerned for the child's safety, but what's really happening is that she is unconsciously identifying with the child as a scared, vulnerable person.

Her behavior stems from her own childhood inability to escape from an overprotective parent when she was just beginning to explore. One of her parents hovered over her fearfully and prevented her from getting away. Internalizing her parent's fears, she learned to stay close to home and to be safe. Safety, consisting of playing at well-understood games in close proximity to her parents became her prime concern. She did not learn to tell the difference between real danger and the behavior that would have allowed her to become a distinct individual. She was not encouraged or supported in her need to try new things. She became overly cautious, learning to respond to her parent's overprotection by being constantly in his or her presence. Her excessive concern for her child's safety reflects the pursuing parent she experienced in her own childhood.

Now, as a parent herself, she follows her child wherever he goes, pursuing him and intervening to make sure he is all right. This not only includes times when the child is engaged in solitary play but also includes his first attempts at interacting with other children. And because this behavior tends to be so noticeable to her child, she may exert the dominant parental influence at this stage. If her partner displays more distancing behavior, which is common, she will increase her level of concern for their child while at the same time noting and resenting her partner's lack of involvement.

The maximizer parent frustrates the child's will to explore. Because of her fears, she restricts her child's curiosity in her effort to teach him to be dependent on her. As a result the child will stop seeking opportunities to break away, and not sure of his parent's assistance in exploring new things, he will become tentative and uncurious, fearing the dangers of the world.

HOW TWO PARENTS WORKED IT THROUGH

John had agreed to come to therapy with his wife, Ann, because they both thought Rebecca, their two-and-a-half year-old daughter, needed help. Rebecca attended a preschool most mornings during the week, and they had already received some concerned notes from the teacher. She was in the habit of hitting other children when they tried to play with her toys and had even bitten another child. One day a book with a torn cover and torn pages was sent home by the teacher to be repaired after Rebecca had deliberately torn it apart. John's question was whether or not Rebecca should see a therapist to help "fix" her behavior. Ann's response was that her daughter didn't receive enough supervision from the teacher—there were too many kids in the class. Maybe they should look for another preschool.

John reported that Rebecca often destroyed books and toys at home. When asked how he handled this, he said he had made it clear that this was not acceptable behavior. He had reprimanded her and put her in her room. There she would cry until he came for her. Then she would try to kick him as he held on to her tightly. He said her behavior made him furious and it was getting worse. It was clear that Rebecca was receiving a great deal of attention from her father, even though the attention was negative.

Ann saw the problem differently. For her the issue was not willful misbehavior but safety. She thought her daughter required more supervision than she was getting. And whenever she talked about this, she started haranguing John for not being an attentive enough father. Rather than shut Rebecca in her room, Ann preferred to follow her around to see that she didn't get into anything.

It took time, but John and Ann finally moved to a point where they could see that the safety issue and how it was being handled triggered responses in each of them that required real work. Rebecca knew what she was doing. She was exploring and testing her own limits and her parents' limits. This was normal behavior for her stage of development. She was innocent in this situation. Her needs were both absolute and appropriate. Her parents, however, were reacting to her behavior out of their own woundedness and not out of any clear perception of what Rebecca was doing or what she needed. Clarifying this distinction was the major work of the first part of their therapy.

John did not know how to support Rebecca at this stage. He was neglecting her just when she needed his support in her first, tentative adventures in the world. John was aloof, not because he didn't want to be with Rebecca, but because he didn't know what to do. His primary observation was that "children sure seem to need a lot of attention at this age."

John was the minimizer in this family. As a child, his own mother had often been unavailable to him. She had been a beautiful, aloof woman to whom John had been quite devoted, but from whom he had received little of the attention that he so badly needed and wanted. He was afraid that if he strayed too far afield, she wouldn't be there for him. He was afraid that she would abandon him. In order to protect himself from this pain, John began to imitate her "independence." His defense against a parent who held herself aloof from him had been to withdraw.

Ann, as you might expect, was the maximizer in the family. She had been smothered as a child. Part of the problem had been a series of minor childhood illnesses that had kept her bedridden and frail for some time as a small girl. Her parents, particularly her mother, had been overly concerned about her and had even held her back a year before she was able to start preschool. Unfortunately, this concern extended far beyond the boundaries of her illnesses. Her mother's constant concern had effectively prevented her from developing an adventurous spirit at the age she when she was ready to explore. At the heart of Ann's behavior was a fear of the unknown. Her excessive concern with Rebecca's safety was an overreaction to the smothering she had received as a child.

WORKING TO REPAIR THE MARRIAGE

John and Ann finally began to understand how their relationship as a couple was reflected in the problems they were having with their daughter. They could see that something was wrong when they nearly came to blows whenever they talked about Rebecca's safety. The real question wasn't whether their daughter was safe or not; it was how each of them experienced safety, or the lack of it, in their own lives.

Ann's chief complaint about John was that he didn't seem to take an interest in Rebecca's welfare or her own. She wanted him to protect her, to be with her, and to show interest in her worries and concern, as she felt she did with him. She would say, "When you come home, I want you to listen to me and help me with my problems. I don't care whether they seem minor to you or not."

When they learned the process of intentional dialogue, they began to share their mutual fears. In a process called the parent-child dialogue, Ann took the role of herself as a child and responded to John as if he were her smothering parent. Her words to him were, "You were always hovering over me. I was so scared of the world. I always thought something was going to happen to me, because you were always warning me to be careful." When asked to tell her "parent" her deepest desire, she said, "Sometimes I like to be by myself. Let me go. Just please let me know that you'll be there when I need you."

John mirrored her back, and Ann broke into tears. She asked him to hold her. When her sobbing stopped, John was coached to say, "I want you to have all that, and I will support you in getting it." Not surprisingly, John admitted he felt both relieved and scared when he said this. He was relieved that Ann wanted to do something on her own, but he was challenged by her need to be supported. His own problems with being underparented made him unsure how to provide the support she needed.

At this point the therapy process shifted to a behavior-change request exercise in which Ann was coached to clarify in very specific ways how her request could be satisfied. When John asked for concrete ways he could support her, she suggested, "Just listen to me for ten minutes while I tell you what I'm interested in without trying to take over and telling me how to do it. And don't tune me out." After John agreed to do this, Ann had a second request: "I want you to encourage me to go bird-watching alone. And please don't ask me about it. I'll let you know if I want to talk about it." Once again John agreed to try this out. He had begun to see the flip side of his problem: Ann had trouble maintaining a distance in her relationships, something with which he had never had any trouble. She needed to be given permission and support in order to be able to distance.

To heal his childhood wound, John had to learn to lean toward Ann rather than away from her, and to work through his resistance rather than let it dominate his behavior. When he felt his reflexive aloofness begin to take control, that was a signal that he had to move toward his wife, extending himself instead of retreating. Eventually, as Ann responded by being there without engulfing him, his old brain would start to get the message and his core wound would begin to heal.

Ann had to learn to take the initiative and work through her defense by moving away from both John and Rebecca. For her old brain to get the message that curiosity is a wonderful quality and not something to be feared, she had to give them both room to explore and create some breathing room for herself at the same time.

The goal of their therapy was to help them explore together, to help them learn a new dance. Now John could share himself and not be neglected, and Ann could be safe when she did things on her own, coming back to John when she wanted to.

ANSWERING THE NEEDS OF THE CHILD

At this point they we were able to see Rebecca in a new way and treat their interactions with her differently. For a long time Ann denied that she was overparenting Rebecca. "She needs me to be there. What if she falls?" Her worries were always over questions of safety. Of course, it's appropriate to be concerned about safety. But in her case, the concern was excessive, more a problem of degree than kind. It was appropriate for her to watch Rebecca in the playground and supervise her on the swings. But not to hover, scaring her with warnings and turning her into a child who was afraid to explore the world.

In general, Ann was encouraged to relax with Rebecca and see what happened. She learned to practice behavior-change requests with Rebecca. She would ask her, for example, to play within a certain area and always check in with her mother if she wanted to go somewhere else. This enabled Ann to let go of her unconscious need to stalk Rebecca at home and on the playground. Ann also learned to practice mirroring Rebecca's joy when she had a new adventure, instead of pointing out the potential danger in it. Whenever Rebecca did fall down and go running to Mommy, Ann learned to comfort her while still allowing her to leave as soon as she was ready to go.

Ann found that her own delight in the projects she shared with Rebecca became a source of great satisfaction to her. Her sense of panic diminished as she realized that Rebecca would always come back. They became a much more openly loving mother and daughter, because Ann was able to recognize and value real affection rather than the automatic responses she had been demanding from her daughter.

For John it was important that the anger and withdrawal cycle he had established with Rebecca be broken. He learned to take his cues from her and let her be the barometer in determining the level of intimacy between them. As a practical way to make this strategy work, John was asked to plan some one-on-one activities with Rebecca. His past practice was to sit and watch television with her when she was in his care alone, letting the TV baby-sit for him. Trips to the playground were suggested as well as projects like finger-painting and playing with Legos, activities they would perform together.

Although it was hard for John to become truly involved at first, the strategy worked. He began to receive the kind of interaction from Rebecca that he had unconsciously feared previously. As they played together, he learned to understand how rewarding and comfortable it could be to be involved with his daughter. He began discussing colors with her, and they found a real enjoyment in a shared love of design. He learned to relax his rigid boundaries without giving up his independence. By walking into his daughter's world instead of running away, he started having fun with her. He relaxed in his enjoyment of her company.

This family still had a long way to go because they had been practicing their defensive behaviors for a very long time. But they were spurred on by their love and concern for their daughter. They didn't want her to have to wrestle with the kinds of fears of smothering and abandonment that had made parenting difficult for them. By consciously sustaining Rebecca during this important stage of exploration, they were healing themselves and creating the conditions that would allow her to become her true self.

10

The Stage of Identity:

3 Through 4 Years of Age

By the time a child is three years old, she has gone through an amazing number of changes transforming herself from baby to toddler. Along the way she has learned to walk and to talk intelligibly and has had her first childhood illnesses. Her parents have had to be on their toes. With such rapid growth, they have sometimes wondered which changes are minor ones, signaling nothing more than a shift in sleeping patterns or eating routines, and which ones signal a distinct shift to a new developmental stage.

The difference between a minor change and a shift to another developmental stage can be dramatic. A new developmental stage is really an entire collection of changes, preceded by an initial period of disequilibrium that is often upsetting to both the child and the parent. The child is getting ready to reorient himself toward the accomplishment of a new set of tasks. His parents may not be sure what's going on. They feel they've just finished getting used to the last major change, and already here is something new. The first question they ask is, "What is he doing?" And then, "What should we do about it?"

What is happening now is that the child is growing up. He has mastered a particular orientation toward his parents and his environment and is ready to begin dealing with who he is in relation to his environment, while remaining connected and curious. His first two questions were, "Who are you?" and "What is this?" Now his question is, "Who am I?" He is walking up the spiral staircase. He started at the bottom with complete attachment to his mother and father. Then he expanded his world to include his environment. Now, following his unconscious innate plan, he moves toward the next level, driven by his impulse to organize his experience into a coherent sense of self.

It is important for parents to know that in his pursuit of something new he doesn't leave the past behind. The experiences he's had in previous stages are part of him forever. The first two stages of growth compose a sequence that the child will repeat throughout his life: a feeling of profound attachment followed by a need to assert his individuality within the context of connection. His ability to apply these lessons to tasks later in life will depend on his success in mastering them now.

If he successfully passes through this sequence as an infant and toddler, sometime between his third and fourth year he will begin to move even closer to becoming a self. First, he will learn through experimentation to establish a personal identity that is acceptable to his parents and comfortable for him.

ESTABLISHING IDENTITY

Before this stage, the child knows he exists because his parents interact with him: they respond to him, and they mirror back *his* responses to them. It's as if they can see something he can't yet feel or see. That "something" is his potential self. Because of his relationship with his parents, he knows he is someone, but he has no secure inner sense of self. While the impulse to become a cohesive self comes with birth, the structure of his inner self is not yet established. Until now, he has relied on the constancy of his parents and their reflection of him to experience who he is.

But now he's ready to do more of the job himself. He is embarking on the journey of becoming his own person distinct from his parents, a separate self he can count on forever. What is becoming clear to him is "I am not you, I am me." While he still needs his parents to be who they are and to be constantly available for him, he is beginning to understand that he is different from them. He can't say it very well in words, but he definitely has his own feelings and thoughts, and he's not shy about expressing them, all the time looking for his parents' approval. Eventually, the child will possess what Erik Erikson identifies as "both a persistent sameness with oneself and a persistent sharing of some kind of essential character with others."[1]

He can engage in the process of becoming his own person because of a remarkable built-in potential he has had since birth. By now, his experiences have enabled him to develop the ability to store the image of his parents in his mind. He no longer needs them to be available in order to feel secure about his survival. They are with him even when they are not physically present, and this knowledge gives him the confidence he needs to venture out into the world. Secure in this internal assurance, he continues to explore his world with a new purpose. He can copy behaviors, imitate the voices of real and fictional characters, and identify with animals as he discovers how it feels to be tough sometimes and vulnerable sometimes.

This process of personal, creative metamorphosis begins between the ages of three and four, as the child begins to operate with a new premise: "I have discovered I can be me and keep my connection with you at the same time."

To some extent he may appear unaware of others as he pursues his own private world. He certainly becomes the focus of his own attention. But, at the same time, he is observing his parents, trying to figure out who they are while trying to figure out who he is. He's interested in the interplay of sameness and uniqueness, how he is like and unlike other people. He measures himself against all important figures in his life in order to find the right combination of characteristics that give expression to his innate sense of his own unique identity. He is ready to develop an authentic self.

WHAT THE CHILD NEEDS AT THE IDENTITY STAGE

The conscious parent understands that his child is "trying on" identities now in the present, *not* forecasting who he will be in the future. If a boy dresses up in the pretty party dress his mother saved from her childhood, that does not mean that he will have problems with sexual identity. Nor does his preoccupation with the toy stethoscope predict that he will be a medical professional. Obviously he won't grow up to be Big Bird or Spiderman, although he may identify with them as characters who have powerful personalities. When a parent mirrors and validates whoever her child is being at the moment, she is not risking future problems. She is preventing them.

If you find that you consistently have intense negative reactions to your child's expression of strong personality traits or difficulty setting and maintaining boundaries, you might want to consider the possibility that you were wounded at the identity stage. If so, you will want to do some healing of your past wounds so that you can consciously parent your child through this stage. For example, you might give yourself permission to enjoy trying on different identities for yourself with your partner's support. Exploring the possibilities of a new job, a new image, a new interest can help you see that such creativity enhances rather than diminishes your functioning in the world.

Ideally, a parent will help her child celebrate his different identities and take delight in all of his various "selves." At this stage, the child is a quick-change artist. He needs to know that he is getting approval from the people he most wants to please. If parents disapprove or ignore him, he flops on opening night. He has no choice but to close the show.

Safety: In all stages of growth, safety means maintaining the health of the connection with the parent. The conscious parent knows that the best way to do this, during the identity stage, is to be a warm and interactive audience for the different guises the child assumes. It may seem, as it does during the exploration stage, that the child is distancing himself from his parents, but he is really experimenting and bringing the results back for approval. His ventures into new and interesting identities cannot be successful without the warm and receptive presence of a parent or other caring adult. The conscious parent will want to listen to himself to make sure that he is not judging or criticizing. He knows that even positive responses can sometimes be manipulative and judgmental. Here's an example: "You look so big and strong, but if you put that shirt on right side out, you'd be even bigger and stronger."

Admittedly, being on call for daily performances may be inconvenient, given a typical parent's busy schedule. But children this age are able to understand busy schedules and are able to wait a little. By now they may have schedules of their own. Planning ahead is one way to make sure the parent will be available. Spontaneous audiences show the child how much his parents value his self-expressions, but planning ahead also gives a child a sense of importance about who he is and what he is doing.

Support: When the parent is consistently appreciative, the child is able to internalize a positive and supportive parental picture that is sustaining even when the parent is not physically present. Using the tools we have discussed in the chapter on conscious dialogue, the parent will mirror back all the child's identifications: "Oh, I see we have a visit from Batman." "What a beautiful princess! Would this beautiful bride like some juice?" The parent is not there just to express support for the child but to participate in the game along with her. Dialogue allows the parent to enter into the game of identities, to express validation and show empathy for the feelings experienced in the enactment. The parent enters the scene and moves the plot along.

Conscious parenting includes the awareness, however, that enthusiastic responses should not overwhelm the child's delight in the experience itself. A warm reception encourages her to continue the play, but the conscious parent does not allow his overenthusiasm to eclipse the child's engagement with her own imagination. And he will not worry about how well something is done. He will focus on what the child does correctly rather than incorrectly. If the child wants to play the role of a doctor, for example, the parent won't be worrying about how well she is putting on the bandages. He lets her put them on any way she wants.

Structure: The parent provides structure by allowing her children to express all of themselves and by teaching appropriate forms of self-expression. "It's okay if you're mad, but it's not okay to bite Stacey." "You wanted that toy didn't you? Sometimes I want something someone else has, but I don't take it from them." "It's hard to wait your turn, but it's important not to crowd in front. Everyone has to learn to wait sometimes." If a nonjudgmental point can be taught during interactions with the child who is trying on a new identity, there is nothing wrong with making it. But, in conscious parenting, teaching opportunities are never turned into occasions to punish. They are limited to neutral information. It's reasonable to point out to a child who is currently a bear—if the bear's growling scares his little sister, for example—that "all bears in this house protect their little sisters from scary noises" and that bears like to eat berries and honey as much as they like to growl.

Conscious parents know that it's important to help the child learn who his parents are while the child is learning who he is. At this stage, the child is equipped only with a survival drive, but *not* with knowledge about how to survive in the world of others. It is important for parents to use this time of emerging self-identity to start imparting a sense of values by showing and talking about how other people are to be treated. They provide a clear picture of what it means to be considerate of others and to remain socially acceptable. Knowing this will help the child internalize a moral perspective without severely restricting his ability to be expressive.

Since children are born *amoral* beings, neither innately moral nor immoral, their character is formed through experience with parents, and then with others. Parents are their first great moral teachers. We know that the child wants to please his parents and be just like them. Conscious parents know that it is critical for them to take a stand on matters of character and values. When they stop to think that what they do and say becomes part of their children, they commit themselves to being good people who know how to set reasonable limits. The child internalizes these limits and finds freedom within their bounds. Where there are no limits, there is no freedom.[2]

A clear structure also provides the boundaries that protect children from the consequences of their playacting. It is all right for the child to set himself up with crayons and paper to draw pictures in Aunt Jane's kitchen, for example, but it is not all right for the "artist" to paint a mural all over the white walls.

THE MINIMIZER PARENT AT THE IDENTITY STAGE—CONTROLLING

Unconscious parents are not able to suspend judgment, and they often react too intensely when the child's behavior triggers either strong disapproval or approval. The minimizer parent who is suffering from a childhood wound experienced at the identity stage feels compelled to control his child's behavior. Whenever his child takes on a personality trait he feels strongly about, even if she is just experimenting, the minimizer parent will step in and express a strong opinion.

The minimizer is the voice of authority. He is opinionated on many subjects and tends to expound on "The world according to me," although he's not very good at seeing how the external world actually perceives him. Often he plays the role of a "good guy" who is longsuffering. He will take a lot of emotional abuse without complaint, because he is "strong." But his behavior is passive-aggressive, uncooperative, and he often has an explosive temper when he feels he has been pushed too far. Using other people—his spouse or a colleague, for example—he will seek sympathetic allies, by stating or implying, "See what I have to put up with." One of his means of controlling those around him is to withdraw, withholding information, feelings, or loving contact. Engaging in intentional dialogue is difficult for him, because he is so intent on monologue.

Not surprisingly, he discourages inventive role playing and permits his child only circumscribed ways in which to expand her identity. He tends to become involved with her only when he is disturbed by the characteristics she is trying on. Otherwise, he ignores her. The minimizer parent practices what we call "split-mirroring." He mirrors only the identifications that meet his approval. If what she is doing is threatening to his worldview, he is critical.

He often argues with his child about her transient identities. This makes her feel that she has done something so shameful that she begins to think there is something wrong with her.[3] So she starts hiding or repressing parts of herself. This results in a split identity. Rejecting her authentic self, she buries it in the underground of her unconscious and presents to others only a substitute self that she thinks will win their approval. Because her minimizer parent is also ashamed of these same parts of *himself*, the same self-hatred is reflected in parent and child. In a sobering twist of fate, they end up sharing the same dark side.

One of the ways a minimizer operates is to allow cultural and societal prejudices to dictate his acceptance or nonacceptance of his child. It's a way out of personal responsibility. He can fall back on received notions—what ought to be done, what is embarrassing, what is unacceptable, what is praiseworthy—rather than taking the trouble to find out what his child really needs from him.

He controls his child through strict boundaries and rules that may be arbitrary or even unknown to her. When the child breaks a "rule," he often punishes her without discussing the situation beforehand. A typical way he avoids conflict is to bring up problems only at the last minute or in a context that makes discussion difficult. His symbiotic attitude is, "You should have known better," thus invading her mind with his own reality.[4]

THE MAXIMIZER PARENT AT THE IDENTITY STAGE—DIFFUSING

When the maximizer parent was a child, she became accustomed to having her experimental identities ignored or deflected. Her assumed traits were not mirrored for her; they were simply tolerated. As a result she developed a fear of asserting herself. She was not able to integrate her transient identifications into a coherent self because her maximizer parent was himself a diffuse personality with no clear sense of self. Following in his footsteps, she turned from a diffuse child into a diffuse adult who is not able to help *her* child mold her many identifications into a clear, secure identity.

Unlike the minimizing/controlling parent, who doles out judgmental attention to his child, the maximizer parent is hesitant about how to respond to her child's role-playing. She is afraid of giving the "wrong" response and not being loved as a consequence. She will ignore her child rather than make a mistake and, as a result, ends up communicating her own confusion. Her child internalizes this confusion and later she experiences it as her own. Sometimes the maximizer's fear allows her child to dominate her. When this happens, they exchange roles: the child becomes the parent, and the parent becomes the child.

Unlike the rigid minimizer, she blows with the wind. She cannot mirror properly because she is unsure of her own identity. She's only too ready to talk about "the world according to everyone else," when what her child needs to find out is who *she* is.

Although the maximizer parent is interested in her child's needs, she does not know what to do to meet them. When she absolutely has to provide structure and discipline to her child, she does so out of frustration and not for clear, constructive reasons.

The child who is most heavily influenced by a minimizer/controlling parent develops a "split self," but the child influenced strongly by a maximizer parent begins to create an "invisible self." When his self-expression is not mirrored or is mirrored in unclear ways, he begins to lose sight of himself, or he may develop an amorphous, unfocused sense of self. He may begin to form a personality with multiple moods, moving between happiness, sadness, and anger with no clear transition or true connection from one mood to another. His sense of identity becomes murky, and without help he will enter adult life with a diffuse sense of self.

HOW TWO PARENTS WORKED IT OUT

As we have said before, in order for parents to support children on their developmental path, parents must proceed with the completion of their own childhoods. Gerald and Beth provide an example of two parents engaged in that process.

Gerald and Beth first entered therapy when they were engaged to be married. He was a physician, well established in the community, clearly a man in command of himself, set in his ways, and rather controlling. He explained that he had to get Beth "organized" because she couldn't do it for herself. She, for her part, seemed willing to let him dominate the relationship. In order to work out the problems they were having before marriage, they had gone through a course of couple's therapy. As a result, Gerald had slowly and hesitantly given up his domineering posture and had learned to let Beth see the "split self" he had kept hidden. Gradually, the rigid control that had been his usual way of being began to define him less and less. As he practiced relaxing control and mirroring Beth's thoughts and feelings, Beth was touched by his willingness to be vulnerable, and she worked hard to mirror him back. They had made a great deal of progress.

When they came back to therapy, their son, Dylan, was four and their new baby, Megan, was six months old. With a new baby in the house Beth was relying on Gerald much more than previously to care for Dylan, and the problems that arose were interesting. As much as Gerald delighted in being with his son, he also felt constantly frustrated. An intelligent man, he knew that four-year-old Dylan was not going to follow orders exactly, and yet he couldn't keep himself from telling Dylan how to behave. He found Dylan's experimentation with new identities distracting. He was far more interested in having his son get down to work learning the alphabet and using the mouse on the home computer. While he never said that he wanted Dylan to become a doctor, he was adamant that it was never too early to teach a child math and the other skills needed to survive in a world of technology.

Gerald tended to ignore Dylan's pretend identifications, becoming frustrated when his son didn't pay attention to more important things. He wanted Dylan to buckle down. "I reach a point," Gerald said, "where I just want to get things back to normal." It was obvious that the identity stage Dylan was going through had touched a pressure point for Gerald. He was unable to see that his son's behavior was *not* a problem and was, in fact, normal for his age.

Beth, on the other hand, had moved from annoyance with her husband's authoritarian high-handedness to true unhappiness. Over the years, their marital arrangement had evolved so that Beth managed the children and the home while Gerald contributed most of the income. She had done most of the hands-on child rearing with Dylan, and she deeply resented what she perceived to be Gerald's interference. She thought that Dylan was moody and withdrawn, and she blamed her husband for that. She wanted Gerald to lay off. He wanted her to quit being so lax and take a stand for once.

It was true that Beth was so exhausted with the new baby that she didn't pay much attention to what Dylan was doing. If he wanted to fly from the sofa as Superman, wear Daddy's tie and hat, and use her makeup to create scary monsters on his face, that was okay with her, as long as he was amusing himself. Essentially, she let him have the run of the house. Gerald complained about the chaos, and when he tried to put things in order, she interfered. She accused him of being insensitive.

Beth's tendency to subordinate herself to her husband's wishes conflicted with her resentment of him. And she was conflicted about what Dylan needed. Sometimes she overprotected him from his father's authoritarian approach, and sometimes she ignored him and his experimental games.

As is true for all couples, Beth and Gerald both had valid points of view. While Gerald's defensive behavior was most obvious and needed to be addressed, Beth also had some problems to address. During most of their marriage, they had gotten along well because they controlled different domains. Gerald's area of control, the family finances and his career, had rarely conflicted with Beth's area of control, the children and the house. Now, however, they were stepping on each other's toes.

It often happens that couples who are in the midst of raising children, even though they feel enriched by the experience of loving their children, return to square one when it comes to the basic issues in their marriage. Fortunately, when both people realize they are in an emotional stalemate, parenting problems can reinitiate the healing process. The fact that caring for a newborn and a four-year-old had pushed Beth to the breaking point turned out to be a catalyst. Realizing she needed professional help, Beth was the one to initiate this second round of therapy. But Gerald readily agreed. In fact, he came in loaded for bear, convinced that both Beth and Dylan needed help, because life at home was "out of control."

It was clear that they needed to start over again on their plan to redistribute the child-care duties now that they had two children. Gerald, the minimizer in the family, had walked into an established routine, and he found that Beth's hands-off style made him very uncomfortable. His well-meaning efforts to aid his wife were eclipsed by his drive to dominate, and his wife perceived him as a disruptive influence rather than a caring father and husband. His need to control was sabotaging his desire to help. This polarized his relationship with Beth. Before they could turn their attention to what Dylan needed, the primary work would have to be done on the roles they were playing in their marriage.

WORKING TO REPAIR THE MARRIAGE

Over the course of their marriage Gerald had reverted to responding to his wife as his parents had responded to him, by exerting more and more control. To help heal his spouse and himself, he was going to have to give Beth the support she and he had not received in childhood. Once again he needed to mirror *her* feelings, ideas, and concerns about their child without exerting his will. By giving this support, he would be moving gradually away from his own deepest defense—the need to control. Gerald had already experienced and still remembered that in the course of mirroring his wife, he would be giving himself the experience he himself needed. He would experience the mirroring of his own denied impulses and, in this way, come to accept the parts of himself that he was denying.

At first Gerald thought that what bothered him most was the condition of the house when he came home. Eventually, he came to see that he was having trouble adjusting to the amount of time Beth was spending with the new baby. "She's breast-feeding when I leave in the morning, and she's breast-feeding when I get home at night." Gerald knew that this was a normal situation with a six-month-old, but he was frustrated at not getting attention himself. During the course of their sessions, Beth agreed to mirror what Gerald was saying and to practice doing this at home, too. She needed to validate his frustration. Almost immediately Gerald became calmer. He could see that he was getting through.

In another session Beth was asked to mirror *all* of Gerald—even the shamed, unexpressed Gerald, the part of him that wanted to be messy and didn't want to be in charge, the part of him that wanted to relax with her, to put his feet up and enjoy his children just as they were. When he complained about her tendency to give up control and defuse important issues, he was really responding to a projection of his own rejected self. Her mirroring helped him receive permission to be more spontaneous and not be so responsible and obsessively organized.

Gradually, Beth was able to talk about her pain at feeling invisible in

Gerald's eyes. It seemed that he noticed her only when he criticized her. The more he attacked, the more passive she became. She needed to learn how to assert herself. She was coached to request a dialogue with Gerald to express her feelings to him. She needed to do this in a non-confrontational manner. The purpose of the dialogue would be to delineate her needs without judgment or demand, expressing exactly what mattered to her most. Then she would ask Gerald to mirror her. By avoiding confrontation, Beth would avoid putting Gerald into a defensive mode, which always activated his need to control. They practiced this dialogue until they were comfortable with it.

One of the things Beth discussed with Gerald was the need to hire a housekeeper to help with the cleaning. He agreed this was a good idea. She also pointed out that if he didn't want Dylan to dress up in his tie and hat, he ought to put them away himself. They laughed at how easily people can lose perspective amid the everyday details.

In some ways, Beth, the maximizer in the family, had the more difficult task. The mother of two young children already has a difficult time establishing boundaries. In a very real sense her boundaries are invaded and redrawn each day. Coupled with her already poorly integrated sense of self, the constant demands of her children and husband left Beth off balance.

In order to strengthen the boundaries between herself and her family, she learned to create an image of herself in a room of her own with a lock on the door. If Gerald or her children wanted to gain admittance, they would have to ask her permission. This concept appealed strongly to Beth. Even if her "monk's cell" were only imaginary, the thought of it gave her moments of delicious tranquillity that otherwise eluded her. At first Gerald thought the idea was ridiculous, but Beth's success gradually won him over. Not only did it encourage her to experience setting her own boundaries, but it also gave her permission to maintain those boundaries, particularly when Gerald assumed she should be available to him.

Beth also needed to help Gerald see that the "no" was *not* a rejection of him but a strengthening of herself. The fact that he had such difficulty "allowing" Beth to practice this exercise helped him see how tightly he was hanging on.

In all marriages the real problems can be traced back to a lack of conscious communication. Even two people who know better and are committed to a conscious marriage can enter a period during which they cease to deal with small problems. These small complaints and resentments don't go away; they collect in tangles that block communication altogether and finally rupture the connection.

That's why we encourage couples to return to the process of intentional dialogue in as many of their interactions as possible. Beth and Gerald needed to recommit themselves to the dialogue process they had learned during their engagement several years earlier. Intentional dialogue tunes up a marriage, and all marriages need to be revitalized from time to time. Gerald and Beth also began to practice the anger-container exercises that had helped them deal with their anger previously. Eventually, Gerald began to recognize and admit to Beth why Dylan's impersonations bothered him so much: they triggered in him the sense of his own childhood feeling of shame at being "out of control."

In addition, Beth and Gerald learned to spend more time alone together. To achieve that, they decided to hire a baby-sitter one afternoon a week so that they could spend the time together. They introduced themselves to the process of re-romanticizing, especially the exercise of "positive flooding." Gerald flooded Beth with positive phrases that dealt with aspects of her that he had been in the habit of criticizing: "You pay so much attention to our children that they will grow up being loved." "You are so creative." "You are so warm and supportive." Beth was so moved by this experience that she melted into tears and Gerald held her. She told him that she had never experienced such a feeling of love and appreciation. It helped them both remember what each had initially valued in the other.

ANSWERING THE NEEDS OF THE CHILD

After they had spent the time working on their own marriage issues, it became easy for Gerald and Beth to understand that they needed to become conscious parents by answering the needs of their children in an intentional way. Dylan was their primary concern. They were already doing quite well with their baby, Megan. But they now felt ready to give Dylan what they were experiencing with each other.

What Dylan needed from Gerald was nonjudgmental mirroring of his various identities. Gerald had to relax and recognize that each identity was a passing attempt by his son to learn something about himself, not an absolute direction that needed to be overruled. Gerald also needed to appreciate the characters he formerly considered to be "unproductive" or "silly." He decided to do the positive-flooding exercise with Dylan and thought of twenty different ways to praise him for his rich imagination. Dylan was surprised, and it was obvious that he loved it. It was hard to tell who benefited more. Gerald found that supporting Dylan in this way helped him get in touch with his own "unproductive," silly self, much to his son's delight.

What Dylan needed from Beth was consistent recognition. She learned to pay attention to his role-playing and to enjoy each role individually, while also exploring for herself how she felt about each character. She also needed to set limits and constructive boundaries for Dylan. The process of establishing boundaries for herself made it easier and more natural to set boundaries for him. She experienced, firsthand, the truth that in the course of meeting the needs of her son, she was meeting some needs in herself.

11

The Stage of Competence:

4 Through 7 Years of Age

Within a few months of her fourth birthday, the child will begin to enter a new stage. She has been exploring and expressing ways in which she and her parents are the same and ways in which they are different. To the extent that she has been successful in integrating her transient identities into a coherent whole, she can now confidently know herself as "I."

With her parents securely internalized in her mind (and therefore constantly available to her even when they are physically absent) and with an intact self, she is ready to see what impact she can make on her world. Her new impulse is to discover her power in relation to other people and in relation to the objects in her expanding world. She wants to see what her newfound self can achieve. Opportunities are all around her. She relishes the process of discovery and is not afraid to try something new. She loves to learn. When she studies and labors and tries over and over again to master her shoelaces, the seeds of competence sprout and flourish. Competence makes her feel qualified. It's her ticket to self-reliance. She practices snapping her fingers, whistling, making her bed, baking cookies, playing the piano, drawing, performing scientific experiments, working with tools. She dares to take risks. She is self-confident enough to know that failure does not lessen her value as a person. With her parents' support, she begins to construct a repertoire of tasks and skills that will enable her to master her world and assume a sense of control over her destiny.

Ever since she was a baby, she's been watching and grasping and pushing and pulling the objects in her world. Now she's ready to find out what makes them work. She picks up hammers, saws, scissors, and whisks. She may practice drawing or painting the same object or person again and again, and she will write letters, words, and numbers over and over as well. Sometimes she becomes frustrated when the execution of a task doesn't go well, and she needs help and encouragement to try again. She will also require encouragement to take a break and try something new before her frustration overwhelms her.

This is the age when she enters the world of real learning in pre-school and kindergarten She's more skillful than she has been in using language to communicate and also to persuade. She lets you know when she is exhilarated because the world is working her way, and she lets you know when she is frustrated because it isn't. Part of what she's finding out is where she stands in relation to other children. She is interested in the power she has relative to her peers, and she enters the world of competition and comparison. Her deeply felt connection to her parents allows her to test her own limits.

Winning is a primary goal. She will wrestle with the dog and with her brother and with her mom and dad, too—and she'll try to win. She will want to run faster than anyone else, and she will want to be wher-ever she is going *first*. She will want to be right, be the tallest, sing the best, and yell the loudest.

She will also continually test to see what belongs to her, activating a drive for possessiveness. Before this stage, things and people were more or less just "there." Now she wants to own them. With an emergent sense of ownership, Daddy becomes "my daddy"; the dog is "my doggy." Mommy, toys, the house *she* lives in—everything is "mine."

The biggest prize, however, is the parent of the opposite sex, and the biggest obstacle to attaining the prize is the parent of the same sex. And so begins the classic struggle that most of us recognize and which Freud called the œdipal conflict. From our perspective, this is the child's fourth love affair, the first being with the parents, the second with the world, the third with her newfound identity, and now the fourth with the opposite sex. Her goal is exclusive possession of the opposite-sex parent's attention. Daddy or Mommy is "mine" and be-longs to no one else. Although this presexual conflict may not always be obvious, it is occurring on some level. It is important to understand that it is vital to healthy adult sexuality, because it is a transition from being ego-centered to being concerned about one's relationship to another.[1]

For this competition to result in the development of healthy adult sexuality, however, it is a contest the child must lose. A victory here would be dangerous. If the child's developmental impulses have been nurtured and supported well at the attachment, exploration, and identification stages, she will be well prepared for this inevitable defeat. She will survive with an appropriate reevaluation of her inner self that will include this defeat as a growth experience. This is an instance where defeat expands the child's horizons.

But the losing must be handled with great care so that the child doesn't feel guilty or ashamed. When her daughter asserts, "Daddy is mine," the mother gently sets boundaries with statements such as, "Daddy is your father, and daddy is my husband. He'll always be your daddy, but he'll always be my husband, too." Mirroring and supporting the child's wish for exclusive attention and making it clear that there are limits to the relationship will help the child eventually surrender, laying the groundwork for healthy relationships with peers in the next stage of development.

THE BASIC STEPS

If these four skills—attachment, exploration, identity, and competence—are properly learned, the child will be ready to meet the world outside the home and will be able to repeat her success when she encounters parallel circumstances. For instance, when she establishes a first friendship or a first love she will parallel the attachment phase. When she moves past the initial infatuation and experiments with the complexities of her own needs and the expectations of a friend or a lover, she will parallel the exploration phase. Successfully working through identity and competence will prepare her to retain her friend or lover while maintaining the appropriate personal and psychological boundaries that belong to a strong concept of self.

Every time the child prepares again to master one of these developmental tasks, she will be in crisis. Once again she is facing an unknown outcome and a possible failure. But if she was able to integrate the impulse successfully before, she has a better chance of being able to do it again now. Competence at age four may be about trying to do Lego blocks or win the full attention of the opposite-sex parent. But the competence impulse also shows up later in academics at school, in making friends, playing at sports, succeeding in marriage, and making a successful career.

If an impulse was not successfully integrated when it first appeared, it is more likely that the child will have trouble with it later. When it comes up again, it will activate a fear of failure, and it will stimulate a defense that is similar to the defense the child used to protect herself the first time. If, for example, the child learned to defend herself by being hypercompetitive at the competence stage, she will tend to be competitive in adult life when her competence is challenged.

A REMINDER OF THE PITFALLS AND OPPORTUNITIES FOR PARENTS

Why would a child not be able to integrate a natural developmental impulse? As we have seen in other parts of our discussion, the answer lies in the parent's interactions with the child around that impulse. That's why we continue to stress how important it is for parents to observe themselves closely as they interact with their children, so that they can seize the opportunities that each conflict offers them to learn more about themselves. The purpose, of course, is not to find additional opportunities for parents to feel bad about themselves, but to gather information they need in order to become better parents. We have pointed out that a connection often exists between the conflict a parent is having with a child and the unconscious self-hatred the parent still carries as a result of not being supported in his or her own developmental journey. Parents cannot successfully help a child through a developmental transition that they did not negotiate successfully in their own childhoods.

For example, a minimizer parent whose competence impulse was not supported when he was little will be impatient with the child who "doesn't do a good enough job" reading at age four. He will also be upset when his junior-high son misses a key fly ball, and again in high school when the boy doesn't achieve a high enough score on his SAT's, and even in adulthood when his son doesn't have the top sales job. The child, having disappointed his father at age four or later when he played sandlot baseball, will keep on trying to get the praise he didn't get earlier. He will work jobs he hates and do things he doesn't want to do in a continuing effort to win his parent's approval.

Parents need to learn cognitively what to do to be good parents, but in order to implement what they learn, they also need to reparent each other. In this sense family members must progress through each developmental stage together if the child is to be parented consciously, without wounding. For this reason, when we work with couples, we focus on how they interact together, helping each partner stretch beyond his or her defenses. By practicing empathy, husbands and wives can overcome their own defenses, and their old brain can reorient itself in a way that helps to eliminate those early wounds. As the parents complete their own childhood tasks and grow toward developmental maturity, their children internalize the growth their parents are experiencing.

WHAT THE CHILD NEEDS AT THE COMPETENCE STAGE

At this stage the child needs the continuation of all the nurturing of the preceding stages, which includes consistent availability and reliable warmth, support for his curiosity, and mirroring and validation for his self-presentations. What needs to be added now is warm and consistent praise for his efforts to master skills and celebration for his new achievements. When the child fails, his frustrations need to be mirrored and his explanations of why things didn't work—why the blocks fell—need to be validated. He must be assured that *trying* itself is sufficient and worthy of praise—*that having the interest, making the effort, showing the curiosity* are all valuable, regardless of outcome. When things don't work out, the conscious parent simply offers information and modeling to increase the chance of success next time. The goal is to reward the child's engagement *with the process itself*, not the successful outcome.

If you find that you are either too overinvolved or too underinvolved in your child's performance, you may be discovering work you need to do in your own life around your own ability to perform. In order to help your child achieve a healthy balance between striving and relaxing, competing and cooperating, you will need to engage with these issues in your own life.

The conscious parent helps her child learn that failure to master a skill can be used as an opportunity to experiment again. A child in the identity stage is vulnerable to feelings of shame[2] about who he is; a child in the competence stage can be wounded by feelings of guilt about not doing well. He's afraid of disapproval for failing. The role of the conscious parent is to offer consistent reassurance when things don't go exactly as planned. And it's important to strike a balance between encouraging the child's naturally competitive instincts and assuring him that losing need not cause damage to his self-esteem.

During this stage a conscious parent provides guidance but doesn't force it. The home is an incubator for trying new crafts and skills, as well as for exploring newly discovered talents. It is a place in which parents can follow the child's inclinations and help the child have fun.

The healthy management of this stage will equip a child with self-confidence. A confident child faces the unknown with the feeling he'll be able to handle the challenges: foreign languages, ice skating, basketball, higher mathematics, driving a car. A secure journey through the stage of competence prepares a child to thrive both academically and socially.

Safety: As always, the conscious parent provides physical and emotional safety. At this stage, physical safety includes teaching the child how to perform tasks using objects and materials that come his way—scissors, for example, or a bike with training wheels. A conscious parent looks for opportunities for his child to use a spoon to stir the dough or pile the rocks to make a fort or use finger paints to decorate the refrigerator.

In conscious parenting the child's need for space and time in which to explore activities is honored. It is ideal if there is one area or room in the house where the child can make a mess now and then. Here he can master the task at his own pace and in his own way.

The conscious parent also keeps the learning process emotionally safe by understanding that negative comparison with others is a form of coercion and emotional abuse. She knows that inflicting emotional pain on the child in order to motivate him does not work.

Support: The conscious parent provides support and lots of praise for the child's experimentation with strength and power. He knows that the most important thing he can do is support the child's impulse to *learn how to learn*. That's much more important than becoming "successful" in the parent's terms. So he remembers to look at his child's efforts from her point of view. Maybe she doesn't want to color inside the lines.

He focuses on what the child does, not on her character or motivation. The attention is on her behavior, not on who she is as a person.

He doesn't use negative labels to describe her character. He doesn't say, "You are so dumb," or "You are always so lazy," or "You are so mean."

Once again, a conscious parent remembers that it is important to practice intentional dialogue in all learning interactions and to avoid temptations to criticize. She mirrors the child when he presents an accomplishment, makes something important happen, achieves some goal, or completes an important task. She validates him by seeing his experience from his point of view and by expressing empathy for both his happiness and his frustration. Instead of mechanically and automatically expressing reassurance and comfort, she mirrors his experience, thus giving the greatest comfort she can give.

Structure: The conscious parent allows the child to question authority at the same time that he is teaching him how to relate to authority and live in the world of cultural norms. He discusses rights and wrongs with his son in an attempt to help him understand his parents' values and to strengthen the child's confidence that he will be able to do the right thing.

He provides clear structure by setting boundaries that the child can internalize. As we have seen earlier, an important boundary at this stage supports the child's competitive impulse to possess the parent of the opposite sex, while at the same time limiting interactions between parent and child to those that are age-appropriate.

The conscious parent provides clear, concrete instructions when teaching the child to do something new. She avoids generalizations and abstractions. She uses both verbal instructions and modeling. She calmly demonstrates that how to do something is tremendously important. She instructs without conveying the message that the child is incompetent. We remember watching a gifted teacher handle a hyperactive first-grader who was creating havoc with a miniature grocery cart he was shoving through a group of classmates. The teacher took the boy aside and said quietly, "Here, Roger, let me show you how you can walk through a room with other people quietly without disturbing them." Then the boy and the teacher pushed the cart carefully, all the way across the room.

Unconscious parenting at this stage will tend to wound the child over issues of competition, personal power, and response to new challenges. Ironically, children wounded during this stage can go on to attain great worldly success in domains where excessive competitiveness, for example, can lead to such success. It is also our opinion that wounds incurred during this stage appear to be less incapacitating than wounds incurred earlier, especially for children who have passed through the earlier stages as fully integrated persons; but they can be disabling enough in their own way.

THE MINIMIZER PARENT AT THE COMPETENCE STAGE—COMPETING

The childhood wound around the issue of competence suffered by the minimizer parent makes her feel deeply insecure about her competence. This is the source of her obsession with competitions—with herself, with her coworkers on the job, with her spouse, and even with her children. Her defense is to "show" her criticizing parent that she can do everything better and faster. Even in areas where competition is not normally an issue—for example, the speed with which she can read a book or the number of books she reads per week or how much busier she is than anyone else—she will manufacture a competition in order to win it. She learned to do this from her own minimizer parent, who criticized her and made her feel incompetent in specific areas.

It's no wonder that she wants her child to win, and she sees it as her job to make him a champion. Youth sport is tailor-made for exploitation by overly competitive parents. Instead of allowing her child to experience athletic competition in a healthy way, the minimizer parent can turn the soccer field or baseball diamond or gym into a proving ground for the child's worth. Academics and music can become equally contentious. After all, for this parent life is a series of contests where, in Vince Lombardi's words, "winning isn't everything; it's the only thing!"

We recently spotted an example of a potential conflict between conscious parenting and athletic achievement in a community newspaper article about a winning girls basketball team. We are offering no opinion about the real father and daughter in this article. No doubt this is an incomplete and slanted view of their actual relationship. But the article itself, whether it is complete or accurate or not, serves the purpose of illustrating our point. We've changed the names, but the article is otherwise as it appeared:

> Most of all she wants to win. But to hear her talk, you'd think she was a boxer, not a basketball player.
> "I want to not just beat my opponent, but dominate my opponent," Megan Jones says. Jones is the 5-foot-4 point guard for

the Lake City High School girls basketball team. The team has attracted the attention of the national sports press.

The head coach for the team is Megan's dad, Ben Jones. Their relationship on the court is strictly business. The two of them are equally competitive.

It used to be when Ben Jones screamed at Megan, she'd cry. She doesn't cry now. She gets mad. That's just fine with both of them.

"I can't worry if my daughter is happy or not," Ben Jones says. "We've got to be playing good basketball."

As represented here, it looks as if there may be a conflict between wanting, perhaps needing, to win games and focusing on what is best for the child. One could wonder whether there may be repercussions when the season is over.

The minimizer parent praises her child only when the child shows interest in what the parent thinks is valuable. Otherwise, she's not interested or she is derisive. Her agenda includes a ready-made value system to which she expects the child to conform, often without explanation or support.

The minimizer parent symbiotically tends to correct or deny her child's perceptions, replacing them with her own: "You don't want to be in the school choir. What about your swimming? That's more important." She lets the child know that some things are worth competing for and some are not. She sets the agenda, often choosing activities in which she herself can compete and win. The message is, "I want you to do this. But you'll never be as good at it as I am (or was)."

Sometimes the minimizer parent criticizes the child for mistakes, because she assumes the child has more competence than he actually does. She thinks he knows more or is more capable than he really is. Sometimes she even assumes more competence than is developmentally possible. She doesn't understand developmental growth and doesn't know that skills and abilities are naturally available to children in stages. She uses criticism, shaming, and comparison to other children to coerce her child into doing what she wants. When things go wrong, she blames him.

The minimizer parent rears her child as though he were in basic training. When military recruits are coerced into abandoning their sense of self for a "higher goal," the expectation is that on the field of battle their anger toward their instructors and officers will become redirected at the enemy. This may be an adequate way to prepare an army for battle, but it's no way to maintain the safety, support, and structure required from a conscious parent.

THE MAXIMIZER PARENT AT THE COMPETENCE STAGE—COMPROMISING

The maximizer parent also is obsessed by competition. But he is driven to avoid it. He has learned to devalue competition. The message he received from his dominant maximizer parent was: "Competition is dangerous. It creates conflict, which is generally bad. And you probably don't have the skills to win anyway. Best to stay out of it altogether." This parent tended to ignore his child's achievements. Now a parent himself, the maximizer has a fear of personal power in himself and others, and he has concluded that humility is more important than pride.

When he becomes a parent, the maximizer has trouble knowing the boundaries between himself and his child. He prefers that she be cautious and safe, rather than take risks. He rewards passive behavior. He teaches her to keep the peace by suppressing conflict rather than by resolving it. He doesn't help her develop the courage that's needed to be a peacemaker; rather, he teaches her to *keep* the peace by suppressing conflict instead of addressing it and resolving it. He generally forces his child to be cooperative, even when doing so denies and represses her healthy competitiveness.

When the child fails, the maximizer tends to offer excessive comfort, making failure a heroic experience. He then steers the child in the direction of another activity. This avoids a win/lose conflict and the issue of competition altogether. It also prevents the child from learning how to try again and again until a skill is mastered. "You are not good at arithmetic, so try to concentrate on reading. You're good at that," he will say. "Besides, I was never any good at math either."

If the child fails, he tends to blame others outside the family. The message is "It's not your fault. The cards were stacked against you. There's no use trying." At first, her maximizer parent makes her excuses for her; later she learns to make them for herself. It's easier than buckling down to learn something she's capable of learning. And because everyone has an innate drive to succeed, even if it gets distorted, the child learns to compete indirectly. She learns how to manipulate rather than face a challenge head-on. In a passive-aggressive way she has learned to win by defeating the efforts of others.

HOW TWO PARENTS WORKED IT OUT

When Stephen and Susan entered therapy, Alex, their older son, was eight and their younger son, Andy, was five. Alex was a highly competitive child with few friends. He was already seeing a therapist because he was having trouble adjusting to school. Andy was just beginning to have problems with his father.

Stephen was adamant about establishing Andy's "self-reliance" and "winning spirit." He worried when Andy hid behind Susan instead of entering into the fray. Susan's opinion was that Stephen acted as though Andy were fifteen rather than five. She was angry and overwhelmed by the "boot camp" atmosphere of their home. She worried that both her boys were being pushed too hard to grow up, and she was tired of the tantrums and standoffs that characterized family life. She admitted that she often intervened between father and sons in order to keep the peace.

The biggest fight was over Andy. Susan described him as musically talented. He had been in a preschool music program and seemed to be a natural musician. He was particularly interested in the piano, but when Susan arranged for him to start piano lessons, Stephen had vetoed the plan. As far as he was concerned, there was plenty of time for him to learn to play the piano later. What was important now was sports. Stephen was leaning toward the local soccer league for five-year-olds, but karate lessons would be okay, too.

One evening Stephen had an awakening. He was trying to teach Andy to dribble a basketball. When Andy didn't get it, Stephen started yelling and escalating his demands. "Come on, try harder!" he yelled, his voice rising in frustration. Suddenly, he stopped cold. He was astounded to realize that he sounded just like his dad. And he remembered a similar situation when his father had pressured him to the breaking point, trying to get him to throw a football.

Stephen sensed that his reaction to Andy was really a reaction to something in his own past, even though he didn't know exactly what. He realized that he wanted to know what was going on, not with Andy, but with himself as a parent. This is what brought him to counseling. Susan didn't need convincing to come in; she was more than ready.

During a simulated parent-child dialogue, Stephen was able to use his revelation with Andy to bring back several memories of his highly demanding, competitive father nagging him to excel, to win, to make him proud. His father had died before Stephen had achieved his business success, but after all these years, that internalized father-voice was still a major element in Stephen's understanding of how the world worked. Although he despised the way his father had dealt with him as a child, he was treating his son the same way. He had to admit that his own dedication to competition, his single-minded workaholism, was out of control, and his family was suffering as a result.

Susan's approach to life was different. She was uncomfortable with competition and striving to win. She didn't enjoy games. She didn't even like cheering from the sidelines. She had been trained by her parents to suppress her competitive impulses, reject her own attempts at self-assertion, and deny her personal power. Being competitive or aggressive was unacceptable. It was important to "be nice." She wanted peace at all costs.

With her boys, she downplayed competition by ignoring it. It was difficult for her to play games with them. She neither noticed nor praised their natural enthusiasm for situations that tested their skills against each other. Her implicit message was "If you don't try, then there is no failure and no conflict."

Susan eventually came to understand that she overprotected her son. In a couple's dialogue Stephen shared his perceptions about the ways Susan babied Andy, including helping him get dressed in the morning and brushing his teeth for him. He told her that it felt to him that every time he brought the subject up, Susan seemed to take satisfaction in his discomfort. At other times, Stephen reported, she became furious when he got uncomfortable with her lengthy evening reading sessions with Andy. Sometimes, no matter how upset Stephen became, she prolonged her time with Andy until he literally fell asleep in her lap. After mirroring Stephen's messages, Susan communicated that it was important for Andy to learn how to read. But she also admitted that she wanted to make Stephen jealous of the time she was spending alone with her son. Her anger was passive-aggressive, rather than direct, in just the way she had learned from her own parents.

One of the potential problems resulting from her excessive attention to Andy and her intervention in his relationship with his father was that Andy might have trouble losing the œdipal battle. She could be sending Andy a message that she and he could ally themselves against Stephen.

At this moment in Andy's development it was unclear which parent's message would prevail. Would he have an excessive need to compete, or would he retreat into indirect and manipulative ways of asserting himself? It was obvious that his parents needed to do some healing work of their own in order to spare him the choice. Their older son was already having trouble dealing with the consequences of their polarization.

WORKING TO REPAIR THE MARRIAGE

The dominant theme of Stephen's healing work was coming to terms with the judgmental voice of his father. Unfortunately, this critical inner voice was matched perfectly by his wife's external criticism of him. Susan needed continual reassurance of Stephen's love. Because she had trouble asking for anything directly, her requests took the form of indirect pleas for more material things. She asked for jewelry, a new car, a private school for the kids, the "right kind of house." Stephen felt many of these requests were beyond his means, and his inability to provide them triggered guilt and fear of failure. Figuring he couldn't win, he did essentially nothing to honor her requests, emotionally or materially. What an elegant vicious cycle this couple was constructing.

As a child, Stephen had needed praise for his real accomplishments. It is not surprising that what he needed now was for Susan to acknowledge the results of his real-world hard work, instead of giving him the message that he wasn't doing enough.

With some coaching, they started making behavior-change requests of each other. This process, which we've discussed in Chapter 6, replaces criticism with requests for changes in behavior that are specific and achievable. So direct an approach was hard for Susan at first, but it was just what she needed to do. After awhile, she reported that she felt good about being able to ask directly for what she needed—more time and attention. She wanted Stephen to pick a time once a month for a romantic rendezvous, which she even offered to plan. Stephen, in his turn, asked her to tell him once a day that she appreciated all the hard work he did for the family. She agreed, but they both knew that in order for Susan to offer appreciation freely, she had to become more secure in his love. They agreed to give each other the gifts they both really wanted. This was a beginning of the healing process.

Another area they decided to work on was Stephen's workaholism. He was a classic Type A personality who worked even when he didn't have to, competing without awareness against others and against the clock. Vacations always included business phone calls and messages over his portable fax machine. Although he could manage the romantic trysts he and Susan were beginning to enjoy, relaxation in general was very difficult for him. Using the dialogue process, Susan stated to Stephen that she understood his need to work and that she wanted him to work as much as he wanted to, but *only* when he wanted to. After mirroring this back to her, Stephen was able to share with her a personal fantasy that offered relief from his workaholism. He dreamed of being alone, away from everyone else, free from responsibilities, in a place where the food was free, and he could eat and sleep whenever he wanted to. This is not an unusual fantasy for someone as driven as Stephen.

Susan validated the spirit of his fantasy by telling him that she understood how someone who worked as hard as he would need private time. She offered to guard his privacy at home and help him plan other times when he could be "off duty." Over the course of several months they began to act this fantasy out. Stephen took time off from work spontaneously in order to surprise Susan for lunch. Occasionally he would take an afternoon off to spend some time alone, then call Susan and invite her to a movie.

As Stephen began to loosen his grip on Susan and the boys, she was gradually able to relax her financial demands on him. Instead of exacting continual proof of his love, she tried to express concern for *him*, telling him more often how proud she was of him.

Although she had trouble understanding it at first, she finally came to see that Stephen's drive to succeed really covered feelings of inadequacy. He worked hard, partly because he was afraid of disapproval. A breakthrough came one Saturday afternoon when he was able to let Susan cut his hair while his boys looked on, laughing and having fun. The way he told the story, his wife was attending to his needs, he didn't have to do anything, and the boys were enjoying the whole process.

But Susan needed some healing as well. She was encouraged to practice direct communication and direct competition. When she got in touch again with the simple pleasure of trying to win at something, she could begin to feel comfortable asserting herself. It took time, but eventually she and Stephen learned to play tennis together. Stephen usually won, but from the beginning he was impressed not only with Susan's game, but also with her attitude. Stephen was able to relax his need to win, and they actually played for pleasure, often making their own "special ground rules" to add to the fun. Enjoying tennis helped Susan learn to support Andy when he played soccer. She could enjoy the game *and* be fully committed to the outcome at the same time. This was a real victory!

ANSWERING THE NEEDS OF THE CHILD

Susan and Stephen had reengaged. And it was their reconnection to each other that began the healing process that benefited their sons. Susan would always be the peacekeeper, but she was willing to accept healthy competition as part of a healthy household. More important, she was able to support Andy instead of hold on to him as he put himself in situations that tested his personal power and his competence.

In the end, Andy played on the soccer team *and* took piano lessons. Both of his parents felt sure that these were his choices. He still practiced reading with his mother, but he also took turns sounding out words with his father. And he was proud of getting himself dressed in the morning, button by button. Finally, as Susan and Stephen recommitted to their partnership in marriage, Andy learned that while Susan would always be his mother, she would also always be Daddy's wife. His œdipal defeat was certain, and the marriage, the family's core, was preserved. The marriage grew in power, and the children were strengthened by knowing their parents were committed to each other and to them.

12

The Stage of Concern:
7 through 12 Years of Age

*N*ow the child is becoming part of a world that places her in uncontrolled environments, and she will live a good deal of her life within new relationships, outside her parent's total control. She is a fluid being, just beginning to become conscious of how she and her new world influence each other. She will change and grow (or fail to grow) as she interacts with these new environments.

From now on, much of the work of growing up will take place out of the parents' sight. This causes many parents great uneasiness. A father may become embarrassed when his three-year-old son has a tantrum in the grocery store, but he knows he can pick him up and carry him out calmly. The storm will pass. A six-year-old who is having trouble reading may worry her mother, but her mother knows she can entice her to sit and experience the magic of books. But now, when the child goes to school and then has lessons and sports and overnights, the mother knows the child isn't going to crawl into her lap for comfort and guidance, or at least not very often.

The child's new environments—with all the problems and challenges they present and all the impulses they call forth—we call *contexts*. The child is able to handle these new contexts, not because her mother or father is always there to help her, but because she has internalized what they have already taught her. Her previous experience has prepared her to cope with what she hasn't yet encountered, so she can continue to learn at increasing levels of sophistication. This process of internalization continues as the child explores new contexts, discovers how to function in them, and, each time, makes lasting changes in herself as she makes adjustments that achieve a congruence between her internal and external worlds.

Inside each child there is an impulse to do what will best help that child become an adult. This inner drive for survival and completion impels every child to become attached, to separate, to explore and differentiate, to develop an identity of his or her own, to achieve competence, to develop social concern for others, and finally to achieve intimacy with another person, so that the transition to adulthood can be completed. It is part of Nature's plan to move the child safely and quickly through these vulnerable young years. In this sense, Nature is not interested in lingering over children. She wants them to mature and get on with it. And she is not interested in grown-ups, which we define as children in adult bodies. Nature is interested in *adults* who have successfully completed the developmental tasks that will equip them to continue the survival of the species.

THE CONTEXT OF THE WORLD OUTSIDE THE FAMILY

In this stage of growth the child's perceptions undergo a fundamental shift. He has been appropriately egocentric, concerned with *his* world, *his* ideas, and *his* feelings. He has been developing a sense of self within the context of his own family, learning to be a fully functional individual in relationship to his parents and his siblings. Now he begins the task of reorienting himself in the social context of the outside world, the world of his peers.

When the child is secure, curious, differentiated, and competent, he is always ready for the next task. Throughout his life, he will be confronted with his insignificance, with his not being on center stage, with the absence of any support for sustaining his grandiosity and specialness. He will repeatedly come face-to-face with his smallness and vulnerability. Like us, his adult parents, he will constantly compensate for his sense of insignificance by trying to again become significant, by belonging to a group and by selecting a primary other person to whom he can be exclusively committed and whom he wants to be exclusively committed to him.

Up until now he has focused on survival, self-development, and achieving personal power. The barrier he encountered to his personal power in the last stage, however, was pivotal. He lost the œdipal battle for the exclusive affection of the opposite-sex parent. This is especially significant for boys, who must move away from the female and begin to identify with being male. But for both boys and girls the resolution of the œdipal battle seems to trigger the internal events that inaugurate the next phase of social concern. The child begins to have room in his world for other people besides himself and his parents. His arms stretch wider than they did before, as he hugs more of the world to him.

In this chapter we will discuss the stage of concern, which prepares children for adolescence and the last passage itself—intimacy. During the stage of concern, from age seven through twelve, the child learns how to form successful friendships with same-sex peers.

ENTERING THE STAGE OF CONCERN

New names crop up at the dinner table, hungry new faces appear in the kitchen. Suddenly Robin and Kara are spending the night. These old clothes are disgusting. She wants a different hairstyle. She wants a different look. Even the "crises" are different. It's not as easy as helping her find a lost toy—her mother must now help her recover her emotional balance when Robin doesn't like her anymore. What her friends think really matters. No amount of comfort or counseling from a parent can replace the simple acceptance by a peer.[1]

It's as if the young child senses that her total security within the family must end. She begins to practice on a larger stage what she has been learning at home. Once again, she acts out her impulses for attachment, exploration, identity, and competence, only this time within peer relationships that are prototypes for future intimate relationships.

At this stage, she must play by some new rules. No preexisting bond exists within these friendships, as it does with her parents. Her friends are free to care or not to care. She cannot assume that they will automatically be there for her, as her parents are. So she must learn what it means to be a friend. For the first time she becomes aware that relationship is a two-way process. Until now her relationship with her parents was one-way for the most part. She was concerned that they be available to her, but she didn't worry too much about their welfare. Now she learns both about love as altruism and love as self-interest. She discovers that she benefits when she watches out for her best friend's welfare, a moral paradox. She can be selfish and selfless at the same time. This is the foundation for later relationships that are based on romantic love.

Intuitively, she understands that her survival depends on how well she learns to make these connections. The questions she asks herself reveal her grasp of this reality: "How do I fit in? Whom do I belong to? Whom do I like? Who belongs to me? How can I get others to like me?" In other words, "How can I secure and maintain connections that will enable me to survive this big world?"

The impulse to explore and differentiate is repeated in her relationships with her friends. But it's different from what it was when she was two years old. Her friends are not objects, and they are not passive. They may resist her curiosity and her desire to know them better. She learns how to gain their allegiance through cooperation and, at the same time, how to be like them and remain herself.

The exploration of intense friendships at this stage fosters concern and caring for others. She is concerned about her own welfare, about being accepted or liked. She engages her parents in lengthy conversations whenever she feels unaccepted or rejected. And a large part of her concern is to care for others. The impulse to care comes as naturally to the child's psyche as the impulse to attach, explore, individuate, and compete. It is becoming natural for her to respond by caring for others. The emergence of caring at this stage becomes the basis for the genuine concern and caring for others that characterizes healthy, well-adjusted people of all ages.

In order to care for others, the child must shift from seeing others as objects to be used selfishly and begin to feel the common bond of humanity she shares with them. This is the beginning of her development of I-Thou relationships, in which others are perceived to be "like me." With this expansion of awareness, the child moves away from the exclusive protection of her parents. She is no longer completely dependent on their response to her. She relies more and more on her friends to let her know that she is okay.

Relationships with others also allow her to continue to develop a personal identity. Her identification with selected peers and significant adults expands her perception of herself. She is more than "daughter." She is also "friend" and therefore, by implication, also "not friend" and even "enemy." She is "student" and "member of a team." She wears all of these hats and more, and she strains to catch her reflection in the eyes of others. Her friends become her mirrors. They acknowledge and validate her. Through the process of comparison and contrast, she is furthering her discovery of who she is.

Exploring friendship prepares her to act on her impulse to develop social competence. She competes with her peers and, in the process, learns to improve her skills and become a member of a team. The very friends she competes hotly against she also defends to the death. Although the context may seem overly competitive, the challenge is always to learn how to share and cooperate, to win and to keep friends.

During this process, when she is about eight or nine years old, she makes a best friend.[2] This first best-friendship tends to be exclusive and obsessive. These two only have eyes for each other. They eat the same foods, dress the same way, and confer with each other before making the next move. They fight over the same toys. They role-play, sharing the same imaginary characters. They begin to share memories that create a shared personal history. They care for each other's welfare as if it were their own. They are practicing falling in love.

WHAT THE CHILD NEEDS AT THE STAGE OF CONCERN

Your child enters this big, new world as a pilgrim, not as a hero. She doesn't yet have the knowledge and skills for the quest. She still needs wisdom and guidance from you. But she also needs the space and time to receive and integrate the input she gets from her peers. You will want to maintain your warm and supportive connection with her and provide a safe haven when she needs to come home and renew her strength.

If you find yourself either withdrawing or jumping in too much as your child searches for ways to give expression to the natural impulse for friendship, you may want to ask yourself whether you could have been wounded at the concern stage when you were dealing with the same issues that are posing difficulties between you and your child now.

At this age your child is taking big risks. She is declaring her devotion to a friend, with all the possibilities of rejection that such declarations imply. She's is not just concerned. She is downright fearful at times: it's natural to shake in your boots when declaring your feelings for the first time. Sometimes, it won't work out right. But even when she succeeds and the invitation is accepted, the ups and downs of these often mercurial friendships can be truly confusing. Sometimes, every-thing is great: the girls are inseparable, and the world is warm and welcoming. Other times, everything is in turmoil: her friend doesn't "like" her anymore, and the world is cold and forbidding.

Safety: Parenting at this stage calls for new ways of interacting. The parent is like a lioness teaching her cubs to hunt. Sometimes she runs the prey down for them, sometimes she nudges them into action, some-times she lets them try and fail, and sometimes she does nothing. Con-scious parents know that parenting well at this stage requires a range of responses. Loving their children always means being emotionally avail-able, but now it also means backing off in order to respect privacy. Parents watch and listen, ready to act intentionally by helping their children learn what they must in order to become successful members of the social group. Intentional dialogue is the best way to discover when to approach and when to make room. It is the core of conscious parenting, because it maintains mutual understanding and individual integrity. Open, consistent communication enables the parent to main-tain a consistent, flexible posture of support and to avoid both the error of intrusiveness and that of neglect. This makes it possible for the child to perform *her* delicate balancing act between involvement with her parents and differentiation from them.

The attentive father used to remind his son that he might need to use the bathroom before he left the house. In the same way, he now reminds his son that he is available and interested if he wants to share his day with him. When his son does talk about the day's events, the father helps him deal with troubling occurrences by helping him name his fears and frustrations, and by involving himself in strategies for working out problems—*if* his participation is welcome. Often adults and children alike don't want problem-solving help; they simply want a sympathetic ear. At this stage, the parent can't solve his child's prob-lems, but dialogue can help the child discover that there are solutions he can find for himself.

Support: One of the most important ways a conscious parent can offer support to his child is by approving of his friends, especially his best friend. This isn't always easy, since it requires consciously suspend-ing judgment. The best way to express approval is to include the child's friend(s) in family activities and to encourage them to spend time alone together. When intense feelings of competition, jealousy, rejection, or passionate involvement arise, the parent can be available for listening with an open heart and mind. When he listens in this way, his child will tell him stories that will give him the opportunity to learn about the person the child is.

Inevitably, these stories will include fights and misunderstandings. Then the parent can provide guidance, if it is welcome. He doesn't immediately start lecturing and instructing; rather, he helps the child articulate his own concerns and needs for the purpose of discovering his own solutions. This is new territory, and the coast is rocky ahead. The child is learning to be the captain of the ship, and his parent often must be content to be a helpful part of the crew.

Structure: Again, a central role for the parent is to provide balance. This time, the parent is helping his child balance her hunger for peer approval with her hunger for autonomy and independence. Often this struggle takes place within the bounds of her new friendships. She has fallen in love with her friends, but their values are slightly different from the ones she grew up with. They don't see anything wrong with shoplifting, for example, as long as they don't take anything "that matters" or anything expensive. At such times a conscious parent will step in and help his child sort out how to resolve the tension between wanting to be an accepted member of the group and following her own inner sense of right and wrong.

Few children have had the benefit of conscious parenting. Often a child's friends may have been wounded in ways that cause them to act out antisocial behavior. The conscious parent will want to have contact with his child's important friends so that he can be available to monitor problems and help sort out which behavior is acceptable and which is not appropriate. The parent may even have to insist on such contact and be able, through intentional dialogue, to discuss with his child a subject as difficult as how to sever contact with friends who refuse to cooperate or who continue to violate established societal norms. The key to this kind of discussion is the preparation and calm that intentional dialogue offers.

At this stage, important boundaries between parent and child continue to be maintained. The child cannot be allowed to become a usurper stepping in between husband and wife. In particular, she should not become confused about her status with the parent of the opposite sex. She's already lost the oedipal battle. It needs to remain lost. Although the child may resist such clear boundaries, maintaining them reduces her anxiety and enables her to venture forth into her close relationships with clear boundaries of her own.

THE MINIMIZER PARENT AT THE CONCERN
STAGE—ACTING AS LONER

The unconscious, minimizer parent who has been wounded in the concern stage takes little interest in her child's shift from home to friends. As a loner herself, she encourages her child to be independent and indifferent to the opinion of others. She doesn't encourage him to make friends and doesn't pay particular attention if he does bring friends home. The message she gives him is "Don't share your feelings with other people. You'll just get hurt. Closeness just brings trouble."

When the minimizer parent was young, her own parents did not support her efforts to become a citizen in a world of her peers. They disapproved of her potential partners as not trustworthy or not good enough. She learned early on to withdraw into the world of her own fantasy. It was easier. In this inner world she could construct relationships that weren't possible in the real world. As a result, this personal world harbored intense feelings, many of them painful, that she hadn't had a chance to explore with others.

She never had a chance to test her feelings in the arena of a real relationship. As an adult she doesn't know about the interplay between dependency and interdependency. All she knows is that she feels different from other people—too intelligent or not intelligent enough, too feminine or not feminine enough. (If the minimizer is a man, he may feel unmasculine, and both sexes are vulnerable to fears of being homosexual.)

On the outside, she may appear quite independent, but she is actually suffering from severe loneliness. She doesn't share her feelings easily and remains private. Although this loneliness may be the basis for creativity in later life and therefore may have positive aspects, most people with this history feel empty and joyless much of the time. It's not hard to see why she might fall prey to some sort of addiction (food, drugs, alcohol, sex, thrills) or workaholism at some point in her life.

A child who is heavily influenced by this minimizing parent will also learn that being alone is normal. At exactly the time when his innate impulse is toward social connection, his normal impulse will be frustrated, and he will retreat into the creation of his own fantasy world.

THE MAXIMIZER PARENT AT THE CONCERN
STAGE—ACTING AS CARETAKER

The unconscious, maximizer parent wounded at the concern stage learned that the emotional rewards he sought were bought at a price.

He was trained to give for the purpose of getting, and to be effusive in his gratitude for what he received. Self-sacrifice was the best way to get his needs met. His feelings and thoughts weren't really very important to his parents. His friends couldn't mirror him, because he submerged his own identity in order to get along. As a result he is a gregarious adult, with many friends and acquaintances, but he never did have a truly close friend and doesn't have one now. He will encourage his child to follow this model.

Since the maximizer's greatest fear is to be excluded or, even worse, ostracized, he trains his child to make friends, keep them at all costs, and nurture them at her own expense. She is encouraged to comply with her friends' wishes and views, giving them presents, seeing things their way. But because these are not friendships based on a mutual sharing and competition—are not in fact a cooperative relationship of equals—she won't develop true closeness. He doesn't allow his daughter to learn self-care, self-containment, and self-worth. His message is "Don't have your own needs. Care exclusively for others, and you won't have to worry about being rejected."

As he models for her the self-sacrifice necessary to gain the approval of others, she begins to feel that her only value exists within her family. This encourages dependency. She begins to lose touch with her natural impulse toward self-motivation and self-direction. Her core identity is threatened because it is effectively denied by her parent.

The maximizer's behavior is insidious because it is so confusing. Obviously, being generous and caring to others is an important value. That's what a good person does. It can be hard for a child to sort out when caring becomes self-denial and when self-denial leads to exhaustion and burnout.

Even harder for the child is to see that this behavior dead-ends in martyrdom. The maximizer does everything for everybody, but nobody cares about him. It's the old lament, "Why doesn't she/he love me? After all I've done for him/her. . . . I don't ask for much in return." If the maximizer were able to ask openly for more, he might begin to feel loved. But he is ashamed of having needs, so he cannot ask. To the child he may look nurturing, but in extreme cases he is guilty of emotional blackmail.

HOW TWO PARENTS WORKED IT OUT

Martin is a microbiologist and a loner. His most intense experiences happen in his lab while he is hunched over his microscope. It's not that he's uncaring; it's just that the people around him, even those with whom he lives, aren't as satisfying and exciting as what he finds in a petri dish. But this wasn't always true. When he first met Monica, he thought she was as exotic as anything he'd ever seen in nature. She was pretty and bright, and magical with other people. Everybody loved her, and she seemed to love everybody. Whenever her campus activities and her social busyness got to be a bit much for him, he would simply pull into his own room, put on a favorite Miles Davis album, and sink into his books.

In his first session in therapy, Martin observed that he had always been solitary. As a child he had collected baseball cards instead of friends. When asked why this happened, he talked about his father, who seemed more like an unknowable force of nature than a loving presence. Martin remembered the negative knee-jerk responses his father had to the few boys Martin had tried to hook up with. He finally concluded that it was easier to go it alone than try to break through his father's disapproval. So he developed elaborate mental scenarios where imaginary baseball teams played against each other on imaginary baseball fields. Later he became interested in electronics and ham radios. Talking on the radio enabled him to have friends with whom he never had to have contact. Inanimate objects brought more satisfaction than other people. He could rely on them to follow his instructions and fight the battles he created in his mind.

Monica was very different. She had been a cheerleader and a member of the student council in high school, and had been joining and leading groups as a way of life ever since. As a medical reporter, she was known as a good interviewer, someone who could draw other people out, a skill that was in evidence early on when she and Martin were just getting to know each other. Once she drew him out of the lab and into a dating relationship, she became indispensable to him. Instead of pretending the outside world didn't exist, he could ride in Monica's wake, living the life she created for the two of them.

But his clumsiness in social situations inevitably led to problems between them even before marriage. Now their daughter, Ashley, was in second grade, and the more she opened up to the world, the more her father retreated into his computer and his research. Her comings and goings, her new dresses, her tryouts for T-ball—all of this was Monica's responsibility, and he felt grateful for that.

When Monica heard her husband describe her mothering as a "merry-go-round," she was hurt. She couldn't see that she had gone overboard as Ashley's social director, expanding the job description to include volunteering at Ashley's school as class parent and becoming chairman of the school fair. The more she busied herself with Ashley's activities, the more tenuous her relationship with Martin became.

These two very different people could see that they were so out of balance they were just about to tip over. Monica wanted Martin to dedicate an afternoon a week for Ashley, but he was resistant: "Why don't you give Ashley an afternoon off?" He felt that what his daughter needed was some unstructured time without prescheduled activities. Monica didn't see it that way. Her defense was an attack on him: "Why can't you do something to help your child have a 'normal' childhood?" He thought Monica was "programming" their daughter and saw Ashley's social life as an extension of his wife's compulsive caretaking.

In many ways Monica was a wonderful mother, encouraging her daughter's friendships and her participation in group activities. In other ways she was forcing Ashley into the role of caretaker by encouraging her to subordinate herself to the desires of the group. She was muddying the distinction between "what I want" and "what the group wants," and teaching her daughter to attend exclusively to the needs of the group without any awareness of her own. Ashley was learning how to do this not only by listening to what her mother said, but by watching what her mother did. It was as if her mother needed to be the center of attention.

What brought them to therapy, however, wasn't these issues. It was Ashley's continual requests for a baby brother or sister. They agreed that it was logical to have another child—they had always intended to have one—but that was about all they could agree on. It was clear to both of them they had some work to do to improve their relationship before they could take on another child.

WORKING TO REPAIR THE MARRIAGE

These two parents could not learn to consistently parent their daughter first, before they gathered the courage to deal with each other. Ashley was trying to keep her balance in the middle of her parents' teetering seesaw. Martin needed Monica to understand that his solitariness was nothing more than a shell covering his pervasive loneliness. Monica needed Martin to help her discover that she could have a satisfying life of her own without "borrowing" her daughter's.

In therapy, as Martin began to talk openly about his lonely childhood and his sense of separateness as an adult, Monica began to understand that although Martin enjoyed time alone, he didn't want to be isolated. He needed help in learning how to connect with the people around him. One of the ways this happened in their sessions together was that Martin began to use his innate power of imagination to craft a new vision for himself. He created a fantasy of a scene he wanted to be able to enact. He imagined a social occasion, in which, accompanied by his wife, he was at ease and enjoying himself. He saw himself on their sofa, relaxed, smiling, listening with real pleasure to the friendly conversation going on around him. After participating in this visualization several times, he asked his wife to help him plan such an occasion in real life. She did. They invited two couples over for dinner the following week, and the evening went well. It turned out to be crucial to Martin that Monica tell him sincerely and often that she wanted to be in his company.

Over the next few months, Martin looked for opportunities to connect on his own with people he knew. It was wonderful to realize that Monica's friends could become his, but he realized he also wanted to be able to establish friendships on his own merit. He felt really good when he took the initiative to contact a college roommate and a lab partner who had started out with him in his first lab. Talking with these people brought him great pleasure. It was fun to laugh and remember their younger selves together. He didn't want to do this every week, but after a while he was able to recognize that Monica's seeking of social contact was less an expression of weakness in herself than a way of meeting a need shared by all people . . . including Martin himself.

None of these changes would have happened without intentional dialogue. Instead of simply being attracted and/or repelled by each other's opposite qualities, Martin and Monica used mirroring, validating, and empathizing to understand each other better. They retraced together the long road each of them had traveled to get to this point and felt the pain of what each had lost along the way. Martin could understand why Monica's fear took the form of excessive social interaction, and Monica could understand why Martin's fear took the form of hiding. Martin had isolated himself to protect himself from social disapproval. Monica had practiced self-denial to protect herself from social disapproval.

The challenge for Monica was learning how to ask for what she needed. She had to give up the vain hope that Martin would be able to anticipate her needs with no help from her. She could see that she had been automatically blaming him for what her life lacked. She felt put-upon by all her obligations: "If he did more, I wouldn't be so burdened." She felt unappreciated: "If he looked up long enough to see me, I would get the love I deserve." As she talked with Martin about what she needed, she asked him to mirror her feelings. In particular she wanted him to hear and to know how exhausted she was and how much she missed a certain lightness of spirit that had been lost in the daily grind of self-sacrifice.

She made a series of behavior-change requests that allowed Martin to participate more in the caregiver chores she had monopolized. He agreed to assume more responsibility for Ashley. With his support, she began to study for her master's degree in journalism, something she had been thinking about for years.

The next year saw them further softening the rigid role boundaries that had kept them apart. Martin and Ashley got closer, as he helped her with her homework, drove her to orchestra practice, and took her with him when he went grocery shopping. Monica fell in love with her graduate study and learned to feel comfortable pursuing her personal goals. They both had to laugh when, one day the next spring, Monica suggested that Martin take more time for himself.

ANSWERING THE NEEDS OF THE CHILD

This process of healing and transformation took approximately a year for Martin and Monica, and not all of it was pleasant or easy. But by recommitting to each other and to healing themselves, they began to relate much more appropriately to Ashley as conscious parents.

Monica began to listen to Ashley when she was having a problem with her friends. She mirrored her daughter's feelings and ideas, rather than insisting that she turn herself inside out to keep the friendship. Intentional dialogue helped Ashley come to decisions on her own rather than simply following her mother's instructions. Monica discovered that her daughter had a lot to say and could teach her some things she had missed in her own growing up. They were both relieved that they could be in each other's presence, enjoying themselves, without a social event to script their interaction. Consciously, Monica started modeling how to let go, how to say no, how to be authentic about her own needs, and how to take care of herself. She figured that this was the greatest gift she could give her daughter, who, like many women, might be tempted to submerge herself in the service of others. In particular, she was pleased to be able to model letting go by allowing Ashley to make, keep, and even lose friendships on her own.

Martin began to look less like a lone wolf as the year went on. Because he was working on his own social relationships, he was sensitive to his daughter's attempts to move successfully in the social world. He used intentional dialogue to validate her feelings when Andrea, her best friend, seemed to abandon her, leaving Ashley devastated and alone. He supported her when she invited a new friend to the park after school, and he listened attentively to her stories about attraction and jealousy in the classroom. One afternoon, when he picked her up after school, he told Ashley sincerely that having close friends is one of life's great pleasures. The great thing was, he meant it. And then he told her she would soon have a new baby sister or brother.

13

The Stage of Intimacy:
12 to 18 Years of Age

We now come to the final passage before adulthood. The adolescent child has come a long way. He is maturing sexually and is feeling drawn to the dance of romantic partners. Although his attraction to girls is center stage, all the preceding impulses are still alive within him. He is still striving for close relationships with same-sex friends and for competence in the world of objects and people. He is still discovering his ever-evolving identity and still exploring a revolving door of contexts in which he practices attachment.

ENTERING THE STAGE OF INTIMACY

The behavior of adolescents is often puzzling, and upsetting. Some catastrophe must have occurred to cause this volcanic behavior, and yet this budding preadult is not open to talking about it. When he's away from the house, the parent may feel some relief, but it's overlaid with a certain amount of worry. The parent isn't sure whether she wants to hear more about what's going on or whether she'd rather not hear at all. But things are changing, and the stage of intimacy seems to change the rules by which parents are supposed to play.

Adolescents are moody and uncommunicative. That's natural. Adults also experience mood swings, although sudden surges of hormones during adolescent years may exaggerate the normal ups and downs into Olympian heights and underworld depths. While hormones certainly play their part, we believe that many of these emotional eruptions are the result of adaptations the adolescent is trying to make to unconscious parents and unconscious parenting. If the connection with parents has been consciously maintained and the child has more or less successfully navigated the social waters of the previous stage, adolescence can be a rewarding time for the family.[1] Think of all the teenager is able to do. He participates in his parents' concerns and interests; he visibly cares for other people; he's capable of learning at a very advanced level; he can talk about what he reads in the newspaper; he shares technicolor dreams of traveling to Africa or bumming around in Mexico or playing for the Celtics. A parent can squint her eyes a little and see this wonderful adult beginning to emerge.

The stage of intimacy lasts a long time in a child's life. It can be broken into three distinct phases, covering the big difference between a thirteen-year-old and an eighteen-year-old. The first stage, early adolescence, includes the onset of puberty, when a physical growth spurt initiates developmental changes. At this point the child enters the whirlwind of sexual feelings, which so powerfully draws the line between childhood and adulthood.

About twelve to eighteen months after puberty begins, midadolescence arrives, and with it comes a preoccupation with the opposite sex that throws the established order out of balance. Well-established peer groupings and intimate friendships are tipped upside down. It takes a while before these new and old elements rebalance themselves in preparation for the third phase. But before the second phase is over, a tension between revolt and conformity begins to build, which often manifests itself as revolt from parental and societal dictates and conformity to peer group standards.

These first and second phases of adolescence provide a setting for rebellion reminiscent of the emergence of the exploratory drive at age two. In fact, for parents who did not deal well with the first exploratory phase, this period is analogous to the "terrible twos."[2] But it's much more trying, especially if the parent wants to maintain a strong grip on the child's thoughts and behavior. Parents need to make peace with the reality that it simply isn't possible to control adolescents—influence yes, control no. Most teenagers have trouble accepting parental wisdom at face value without questioning it. Although the parent may feel insulted and rejected, the fact is that this is the age of reason for children. They are thinking for themselves. They cannot be coerced into arbitrary modes of reasoning simply because their parents wish it. But the use of dialogue, because it fosters cooperation, can result in a continuing partnership.

An important part of the impulse to explore is sexual. Most often it takes the form of breaking through inhibitions and testing one's own limits rather than interest in true intimacy. Intimacy—the romance of sharing an emotional friendship with another person of the opposite sex—may be seen by the child as separate from exploring the sexual drive. The teenager will feel the urgency of his sex drive, but may feel ambivalent about intimacy.

The third phase of late adolescence is a period of preparation when the young person becomes concerned with the tangible tasks of dealing with his future. At this point, the massive reorganization that characterizes adolescence comes to an end. He is busy acquiring the skills he needs to assume the role of an adult. He is learning to accept his limitations, and he is ready to welcome help and guidance from parents and other adults once again. Will he go to college, get a job, get married? How will he prepare for these events? What does he want to do with his life? He is deep in the process of forming his identity in concert with the person he has chosen as an intimate. The emotional and physical aspects of intimacy finally come together in this relationship.[3]

Achieving emotional and sexual intimacy is the daunting task of the adolescent. It includes trying to meet his own needs and the needs of the other. He learns what it means to trust another person enough to reveal himself to his very core. Self-revelation is dangerous. The requirement of personal honesty creates the fear that he might be shown to be the inadequate person he thinks he may be. He is caught in an internal cross fire. On the one hand his old brain warns him to protect himself, while his new brain, armed with all the success he has experienced so far, entreats him to overcome his resistance and share his thoughts and feelings with this other person.

So the internal, unconscious dialogue continues as he courts the girl to whom he might be willing to tell his most intimate secrets and from whom he wishes, but fears, complete honesty. This is the dance of intimacy that beckons him to adulthood. In a way, he has been auditioning for this task all his life, both with his parents and with his buddies.

A passage from James Joyce's literary classic about a young man growing into manhood, *A Portrait of the Artist as a Young Man,*[4] captures the essence of the first tentative steps a boy and a girl take toward each other:

> They seemed to listen, he on the upper step and she on the lower. She came up to his step many times and went down to hers again between their phrases and once or twice stood close beside him for some moments on the upper step, forgetting to go down, and then went down. His heart danced upon her movements like a cork upon a tide. He heard what her eyes said to him from beneath their cowl and knew that in some dim past, whether in life or in reverie, he had heard their tale before.

In this passage the boy and girl begin to move their bodies together in an invisible rhythm of attraction as they dance alone upon the steps. Soon this conversation of the eyes and feet will be followed by the sounds of words, murmurs, and laughter as they discover together which move to make next. In concert, each has begun the tender and perilous adventure of exploring the other's alien world.

By the time children are ready to engage in this dance of intimacy, a major shift has already taken place. They have become entranced with each other, alert to the nuances and subtleties of their interaction together, dulled by or impatient with prolonged conversations with parents. Of course, their parents are still there inside them—all their admonitions, endearments, and lessons internalized as part of their worldview. In spite of casting their eyes toward the horizon, adolescents continue to rely on these internal parents, as well as contact with their real-world parents, to guide them through the last passage before full adulthood.

WHAT THE CHILD NEEDS AT THE STAGE OF INTIMACY

When a child is born into a marriage, it is both the culmination of shared love and the beginning of a new level of intimacy within the marriage. But contained within this expanded intimacy is a paradox: as parents live through this most intimate of experiences—raising the children to whom they have given life—they themselves often drift apart. Over these challenging years, they seal off parts of themselves, so that by the time their children reach adolescence, they may be leading somewhat separate lives. The cohesion they need if they are to supply a ground for the adolescent during this turbulent age may not be available.

Nurturing the capacity for emotional intimacy is a family matter. The child learns how to share his thoughts and feelings by doing it at home. When a child is raised in a family where daily dialogue is a familiar ritual, communication naturally and consistently goes beyond the superficial level. The adolescent from such an environment has a much better chance of becoming intimate with another young adult, while holding on to his own personal boundaries, than does the child whose parents routinely avoid communicating their true feelings. Intimacy involves the exchange of deep feelings and private thoughts. Dialogue provides a safe and structured framework for these exchanges. Such communication does not rise full-blown from the family breakfast table, but must be taught and practiced over time. Not every conversation needs to be intentional dialogue, but when the climate in the home reflects the principles of intentional dialogue, children and adolescents learn to carry this spirit with them into their own relationships.

People who are truly intimate feel safe with one another. They know that intimate moments can arise naturally and spontaneously. They don't always have to be planned for and worked at consciously. In families where sharing is part of daily commerce, where openness between marriage partners and between parents and children is part of the family climate, there exists the condition that teaches children how to trust and how to reap the benefits of intimate exchange.

If you find that you are uncomfortable with your child's sexuality or with your own needs for sexual and intimate contact, you may have been wounded at this stage yourself. You will not be able to guide your child through this stage without confronting your own incompleteness and discomfort in these areas. Beginning to address these areas in your own life will open you up to being a more conscious parent. In a conscious family the adolescent's experience should also be set in the context of a home that stresses consistent values and behaviors. Conscious parents recognize that the most important way to communicate values is by modeling them in their own marriage or relationship. They demonstrate respect for each other and engage in authentic communication with each other. If there are tensions in the marriage, this is a good time to recommit to a conscious marriage and mend any tears in the fabric of intimacy. As we have said before, the best environment for parenting is one in which the parents are working on their own relationship. This is especially true during a child's adolescence. A marriage that is out of joint is a shaky platform from which to guide an adolescent.

Conscious parents hold and exhibit consistent personal moral values as well as strong family values. The unconscious parent who, for example, warns his child about the dangers of drugs with his second or third martini in hand is a joke and will be dismissed as one by his sixteen-year-old. "Do as I say, not as I do," simply doesn't cut it. It's a losing strategy for educating an adolescent about moral values. At this age the preadult is amazingly observant and has a strong distaste for hypocrisy. Children at this stage have too much intelligence to respect parents who haven't straightened themselves out.

Safety: Many cultures permit and even encourage sexual experimentation, but in all cultures, sexual experimentation occurs whether permitted or not. Such experimentation is natural. The role of the conscious parent at the stage of intimacy is not only to provide healthy boundaries, but also to accept and encourage the budding sexuality of their preadult. This helps maintain the connection between parents and children. The parent needs to provide education about the world of sexuality so that the exploration is safe, but the topic itself must become natural and familiar. For preteens and for young teens, the conscious parent is prepared to talk about the subject of sex. Information is safety.

Because sex is a difficult subject for children at all later stages to bring up with their parents, conscious parents are prepared to provide answers rather than wait for questions. The answers must be relevant, straightforward, and true. Conscious parents don't engage in vague generalizations, nor prying questions or authoritarian edicts. It does no good for parents to be more embarrassed than the child.

The child needs to know that his parent is comfortable with his sexuality but will not press him too much. His privacy will be respected. He must feel free to come to his parent(s) when he needs to and confident that he has the information he needs to make the right choices—choices that will help him maintain his own healthy boundaries but also gradually and carefully become intimate with another. Obviously, safe sex is an important topic, for example, as are the many forms sexuality may take.

In addition to developing the ability to discuss sexuality openly, the conscious parent must use great care and skill in creating a safety net for the adolescent. The net must be invisible, but secure. The message needs to be "I'm here if you need me, although I won't intrude on your privacy. I won't abandon you. You can count on me. I trust you to make the right choices and to come to me when you need help." This safety net is based on the understanding that connection with the parent is still of critical importance to the child, even if he looks grown up. Remembering that he is still inexperienced and that the little kid in him is still very present, his parents can offer him a place where he can put down the mantle of adult responsibility for a little while.

Support: Especially in early adolescence, as children are entering puberty, they have a deep concern about how they are changing. Conscious parents assure their child that he is normal. A child may have a concern that he is maturing too fast, way ahead of many of his friends. On the other hand, some friends may be growing up faster, and he feels that he is lagging behind. What is wrong with him? The conscious parent is there consistently with the message that everyone's body changes at its own pace.

Conscious parents encourage dating and group activities for young teens. When it becomes obvious from long, late-evening phone calls and other unmistakable signs that their thirteen-year-old son is circling in on one particular girlfriend, they wisely suggest that she be included in specific family activities—if your child is comfortable with the invitation, that is. Just as the parent accepted and was interested in his son's male friends during the previous stage, he should be interested in his son's new girlfriend. Interested, but not intrusive. The conscious parent lets the child take the lead once the welcome mat is out.

In an open family environment a teenager is often anxious to try on a number of opinions and beliefs, just as he experimented with different identities when he was younger. Now he may deepen his experimentation by trying on alternative lifestyles as he attempts to fill out his identity as an adult. The conscious parent validates his point of view whenever possible. Validation consists of acknowledgment, not necessarily agreement. This gives him a firm base of support and increases his understanding of where his parents stand on some of the larger issues in society.

Structure: Sometimes parents are tempted to greet the returning adolescent with, "Oh, do you still live here?" He is so often out with his friends, working, dating, or at school. The conscious parent must be able to negotiate limits regarding evenings out, schoolwork, use of the car, dating, and the necessity of informing them about changes in plans. Adolescence is a time of great personal growth, but it is not without danger. There are temptations to conform to group behavior, well-considered or not. And mistakes at this age can carry greater consequences than earlier misjudgments. There is no way to deny that teenagers sometimes choose courses of action that have grave social reverberations or that can become life-threatening.

Without a doubt, some of his friends will start flirting with dangerous behaviors. Conscious parents are clear about these dangers, and they talk about the complex issues involved. One possibility that comes up often is that nobody has the right to force another person to act in a certain manner, sexually or otherwise, against his conscience or better judgment. Both boys and girls need to know that "No" is a complete sentence and that they have the right to say it. This applies not only to sex but to many other behaviors that make people uncomfortable—drinking, drugging, violence, stealing, or driving with people who are irresponsible. Consciously helping a child learn to say no is helping him develop respect for himself and a sense of his own inner integrity.

Put simply, the conscious parent pays attention. This is in order to help an adolescent explore his emergent impulse toward intimacy without his incurring emotional wounds and without his being at high risk of promiscuity, drug abuse, or clinical depression. Providing safety in an unsafe world is a major challenge. It requires a balanced approach on the part of the parents. Being rigid is just as damaging as setting no rules at all. If parents are inflexible, the child is compelled to rebel against them or his identity will be consumed by their unreasonable attempts to control him. If parents are wishy-washy, the child is abandoned to the intense pressure of his peers and has no system of checks and balances to help him steer a safe course. Both extremes are dangerous.

When there are clear signals that something is going wrong, and the child is in thrall to self-destructive behaviors—depression, academic problems, alcohol or drug abuse, promiscuous sex, violence, gang-related activities—the wise parent brings in outside support. She is proactive in seeking counseling or other professional help, because she knows that it is hard for parents to deal with serious problems alone. Schools, health-care plans, and community organizations can refer parents to competent professionals. This is the gift a conscious parent gives her troubled child.

THE MINIMIZER PARENT AT THE INTIMACY STAGE—REBELLING

The unconscious minimizer parent who was wounded in his childhood at the intimacy stage tends to be a rebel loner. He is a loner because his parents were underinvolved in his transition to adulthood. He is a rebel because he had little or no instruction about how to negotiate intimate relationships, handle his emergent sexuality, or deal with the complexities of his approach to adulthood. All these matters were overwhelming to the parent, although they were most important to him.

So he withdrew into his isolation, having received the message "Don't grow up. I don't know what to do with you. I don't know how to help you with your feelings and your problems, so you're on your own." Left alone with his hormonally inflamed impulses and the challenging world of preadulthood, and having no clear external boundaries to guide or contain him, he constructed his own inner boundaries to handle his fears. To feel safe with his impulses and the complexity of his external world, he had to construct a rigid self-boundary, which cut him off from his own feelings and the feelings of others.

Disconnected from his emotions, he learned to live by rules, most of which he made up. In a sense, he became a law unto himself. Since his rules were often not consistent with those of other people, he could be a source of fear for his parents and others. They reacted with feelings of helplessness, or with strong countermeasures. Because he didn't know how to negotiate his relationships and was not in touch with the emotions behind his impulses, he tended to act them out with minimal awareness of the boundaries of others or the consequences for himself.

The paradox here is that all his attempts to be independent have little to do with freeing himself from parental rules. He wants and needs structure, and his rebellion against it is an unconscious attempt to make connection. His goal is to get his uninvolved parent involved. To get the parent's attention, he has to provoke him or her into giving him attention and rational information about boundaries. Getting into trouble and ignoring rules are a message back to his parent: "Deal with me."

In this society we tend to romanticize rebels—witness the characters played by James Dean—but in real life they tend to be lonely and prone to depression, which they mask with anger. If the rebel has not been wounded too severely at an earlier stage, he may turn his general distaste for authority into productive directions. He may, for example, become a social reformer. If his wounds are deep, however, he may manifest antisocial or even criminal behavior.

The minimizer parent at this stage is often unavailable for important discussions and often models loner behavior for his child. Lacking adequate information about the complexity of sexual and emotional intimacy, the minimizer will often be more lenient with his child than is prudent. The minimizer parent errs by not providing enough structure. Since he had to negotiate his adolescence on his own, he feels uncomfortable setting boundaries for others. What seems like an "open" attitude, which is supportive on the surface, is really an uninvolved stance born out of ignorance or inability to act. He is not aware that his neglect may constitute abandonment of his child to the dangerous guidance of her peers when it comes to sex, use of drugs and alcohol, and other self-destructive behaviors.

THE MAXIMIZER PARENT AT THE INTIMACY STAGE—CONFORMING

The parent who is a maximizer at this stage was raised by a personally conservative and somewhat rigid dominant parent. She learned to fear intimacy and her budding sexuality. She buried her natural sexual impulses in order to please her parent. Parental approval for not breaking the rules is what passed for intimacy in her family. The message she learned is "Don't do anything I would disapprove of. Be acceptable if you want to be loved." To be different is to be unloved. If she can just follow the rules, everything will be all right. So she becomes a model child—a decision that is more acceptable in our society. As a parent the maximizer substitutes rules for "heart to heart" conversation, thus maintaining the illusion of connection but not the reality. She shares only a minimum of information with her child about sex, and the information she offers is not the beginning of a dialogue on the subject; it's the end. She doesn't feel she needs to offer much rationale for imposing rules: "This is what sex is. Don't do it. You are too young." "Drugs are bad for you. Just say no." Such a unilateral approach isn't sufficient to cover the extraordinary changes her child is experiencing. Rules do not substitute for information. But, like her parents before her, she feels that as long as rules are observed, nothing else is required.

She is overwhelmed by the possibility of sexual intimacy in her own life, so the onset of her child's sexuality is terrifying. She rejects it, and she rejects any of his potential romantic partners that he may introduce to her. She is often so disapproving that he succumbs and chooses only friends of whom she approves.

HOW TWO PARENTS WORKED IT OUT

Tony thought of himself as a daring and creative rebel. When he first began therapy, he accused his wife, Gail, of fencing him in. As a successful landscape architect, he pioneered new ways to use water features and stone in his work. Tony knew that Gail provided him with structure and stability he needed to build a business, but he fretted over the never-ending restrictions of the business world and the social interactions that were required to maintain it.

Gail loved his creativity, his daring to build beautiful spaces that no one else had built before. But she had to admit there was a part of her that wanted to tame him and domesticate his wide-open nature. She cringed when he didn't wear the right clothes at social gatherings. When he shot back that "this is the nineties, and people can dress any way they want," she accused him of being insensitive.

When Josh, their only child, reached puberty, the two of them found themselves in a continual round of conflicts over curfews, Josh's friends, and cars. There was also the issue of sex. Tony's very strong input was "Leave him alone. He'll figure it out." Gail, a worrier by nature, couldn't stop going around and around in circles. "We can't leave him alone. What about AIDS and STDs? What if he gets a girl pregnant?" When Josh finally did bring a girl home, she wasn't the kind of girl Gail had envisioned. She let him know that his girlfriend wasn't intelligent enough or interesting enough for him. She worried about the girl's lack of ambition, her lack of sparkle. Her husband disagreed with her, pointing out, using his old girlfriends as examples, that superficial trappings really don't define the worth of a person. This made matters worse. Gail felt the rejection of her opinions by both her son and her husband.

What finally spurred them to seek help was Gail's suspicion that Josh was experimenting with drugs. Even Tony had to admit that he had noticed Josh was spending a great deal of time alone in his room, being moody, distant, and secretive. He dropped his old friends for a new group whom his parents didn't know much about. And Josh never brought them home. When Gail and Tony first came in, they were scared. They were afraid of alienating Josh further, and at the same time, they wanted to deal with the problem. They were ready to do some work.

After a long discussion, they agreed that they had never been more distant from each other. They had developed separate lives and spent very little time together. Tony avoided Gail because she was always nagging him to do this or that or the other thing. He was tired of hearing about his insensitivity. He felt so tied down. When problems began to crop up with Josh, Tony retreated further and became noticeably depressed. In response, Gail gradually sought a social life outside their marriage.

Finally, Gail admitted that she was attracted to someone else. She had been engaging in a rebellion of her own, and it didn't include Tony. She had met this other man at a party she attended alone. To her delight, she really enjoyed his company. Soon she was spending more and more time with him, and they had begun an affair. She felt guilty about it, but she also felt driven to break away from Tony.

Tony was upset, but he wasn't surprised. He was able to admit his own part in shutting her out of his life. Although he felt betrayed, he was aware that Gail's affair was almost inevitable. It was understandable for her to seek intimacy somewhere else.

WORKING TO REPAIR THE MARRIAGE

The competing styles of Tony and Gail had backfired. At the very time that it was critically important for parents to model intimacy, their relationship had fallen apart. Adolescents cannot be fooled. Josh knew his parents' marriage was in shambles. In order to begin addressing the problems they were having with him, they had to start the process of setting their own relationship in order. The fact that Tony and Gail sought counseling was a good sign that they both wanted to recommit to their marriage. Parenting is a continually evolving process and cannot wait until parents deal with their marital issues, but the process can be greatly helped when parents begin their own healing. A child senses when his parents are trying to repair their relationship, and it comforts him and informs him.

The hardest and most important work for these parents had to be done on their communication with each other. At the time they began counseling, there was almost no communication. We don't want to minimize the problems associated with reestablishing contact in a marriage when the partners have been going their separate ways for some time. Tony and Gail had to learn, painstakingly, to use intentional dialogue in order to see each other as real people and not just as cartoons. Intentional dialogue would lead to a re-romanticizing of their relationship, a triggering anew of the joy and excitement that each of them had once felt in the presence of the other. This process takes a lot of time and patience, and for Tony and Gail the road back was not traveled overnight. But when a marriage connection is not irreparably ruptured—

and an affair is a serious rupture—there is a chance for the partners to recommit to a conscious marriage.

As a start, Tony requested that Gail keep talking to him. He wanted her to rediscover their common fund of experience. They agreed to talk alone together for half-hour sessions at least five times a week. Although this may not seem like much, it is a significant commitment even within a healthy relationship, and it was a major step forward for people who had stopped talking altogether. And as a result of practicing being truly present for these conversations, Tony found that Gail took on a presence and daily reality for him that he had lost. He was able to regain some of the intimacy he had been missing.

Both of them worked hard to be able to express themselves clearly, mirroring and validating each other. One of the first outgrowths of these conversations was the decision to confront Josh and work with him in a counseling setting.

But Tony also wanted Gail to break some rules along with him. One of the biggest sources of pain for him was that she wouldn't break rules for him, but that she had done so for her lover. He wanted his free side to be validated. Because of their very different worldviews this was something they had never been able to do together. It took a lot of negotiation before Gail decided she could risk this kind of behavior. But in the end she agreed to take one unscheduled day off from work, leaving early in the workday by using a trumped-up excuse. She would sneak away with Tony for some unstructured time. She was thrilled by the feelings of freedom this engendered in her. In fact, the first time they did it, they wound up going to a movie and getting a hotel room downtown.

She was able to feel the liberation of these experiences, but she needed to know that Tony was not always going to resist her attempts to civilize him. One of the most important exercises they did in therapy was to exchange roles. He agreed to verbalize the part of a loving and trusting husband who wanted his wife to spend time with him and to remain faithful to their bond. By doing this he could validate for her the restrictions that marriage imposed on both of them. As Tony identified with Gail's need for structure and she identified with his need for freedom, they felt again the excitement they had first experienced in each other's company. They were again able to think through the values they wanted to use to reconstruct the foundations of their marriage.

After several months of revisiting the interests and passions that had brought them together and exploring new terrain they could share, Gail had bought Tony a wedding ring for his fiftieth birthday. She had had no idea about whether he would wear it or not. She saw the ring as an emblem of their recommitment and trust. Tony had always said he wouldn't wear a wedding band, and he never had. Now, when he unwrapped it, he cried. He confessed that he had wanted one but hadn't been able to tell her. He immediately began to wear it all the time.

ANSWERING THE NEEDS OF THE CHILD

Over time, the skills Tony and Gail acquired in intentional dialogue opened up their relationship with their son. As they recommitted themselves to the daily interactions of their marriage, Tony began to see how deficient his hands-off parenting policy had been with Josh. This is not what Josh needed. Although it was tough, Tony had to face his own inadequacy in the face of his son's pressing adolescence. In addition to attending counseling sessions with his son, he decided to actively support the therapist in working out a set of behaviors that Josh could agree to hold to. Instead of making Gail do the follow-up—something she had always been overly zealous about—Tony was the active parent here. Instead of yielding to the strong temptation to run when serious problems arose, he stuck with it and was right there beside Gail when there was talking to be done. He talked frankly with Josh about their expectations of him and swallowed his discomfort when it was time to praise Josh's cooperation and show his own pleasure openly.

It was important for Gail to admit that her own rigid rules for herself had played a role in disrupting her marriage. This made her think about whether she had been too rigid with Josh also. She saw how important it was to talk with him about the expectations she had for him—not just to make pronouncements from on high. She also made a conscious commitment to welcome Josh's girlfriend, Louise, in family dinners. And when Josh and Louise later broke up, she was able to share his disappointment sincerely. In a month or so, when he started to talk about someone new, she was quick to say, "When you're comfortable, why don't you invite her over?" Some of her loosening up also included consciously and visibly trusting Josh to his own decisions. He didn't need her to perch on his shoulder. Josh thrived on this trust and became more open with his mother than he had been for a long time. Gail's comment was, "Boy, it's great to be a mother again. I thought it was all going to be over after junior high." The healing work the parents accomplished with each other was instrumental in the healing of their son. It started them all on their journey to recovering wholeness.

V

CREATION OF A
NEW LEGACY

14

The Possibilities for a Conscious Future

All this can only take place in a living partnership,
that is when I stand in a common situation with the
other and expose myself vitally to his share in the
situation as really his share. It is true that my basic
attitude can remain unanswered, and the dialogue can
die in seed. But if mutuality stirs, then the interhuman
blossoms into genuine dialogue.
—MARTIN BUBER, *Knowledge of Man*

We have charted the terrain of unconscious parenting, indicated its pitfalls, and pointed the way toward conscious parenting and its power to transform us. In this closing chapter, we want to talk about our assumptions of the kind of universe in which conscious parenting is possible and point toward a vision of a conscious future for society. These assumptions, based upon experience and reflection, comment on the nature of the universe, our true nature, and the way things work. Such assumptions are referred to as "metaphysics," a term that refers to the reality behind the "visible" world of our experience. An example of a metaphysical statement from science is that the chair we see is made up of atoms that we cannot see. A religious example posits that the universe is a creation of the divine, and it works the way it does as an expression of divine laws. You may have already detected the spiritual metaphysics behind our view of parenting. We want to say some more about that now and why it is important.

When we are confused about the meaning of our everyday experiences and don't know what to do in a particular moment, a metaphysical view of life can direct us through our confusion and darkness. When we are conscious about our view of the cosmic order, it can help us understand our place in the universe and can guide us into actions that are in harmony with the grand design. And it helps us know when our actions are out of sync with the way the universe works.

Our view of parenting is rooted in our belief that the universe is a creation of God and that conscious parenting as a connectional process is an expression of the laws of the universe. We believe that when we parent our children consciously, in the way we have described, we participate in the cosmic order and contribute to what the universe is trying to do. From this view, parenting is more than just caring for our children as a biological life-form, it is participation in the creation of God and the laws of the universe. Seen in this context, conscious parenting is not only a moral act, it is a moral imperative.

So what kind of universe do we live in? First, based on the observation that our defining characteristic is consciousness, and that we can become self-aware, we believe we live in a Conscious Universe,[1] that the very "stuff" of the universe is Consciousness. Since we are a creation of a Conscious Universe, and since we have the capacity for self-awareness, we, the authors, believe that humankind is a point, the *only one* so far as we know, in which the universe is becoming conscious of itself.[2] As the universe becomes more aware of itself through us, we become more aware of the universe and the intimacy of our connection to all things. We become more aware of how the divine is working through us to achieve its purpose.[3] Therefore, conscious parenting is possible because our very essence is consciousness, and when we parent from the place of consciousness, we participate in the divine plan.

Second, we accept the general view in physics that the universe exploded into being, perhaps 10 to 14 billion years ago, giving birth to all "things"—the galaxies, the stars, and eventually all life-forms, including us. Therefore we, and all things, are made of the same stuff. While scientists are puzzled by the question of how consciousness could arise out of inanimate material, we believe, along with some physicists, that the star dust of which we are made is animated,[4] and in essence, is Consciousness. Our consciousness exists, from our view, not as a quality of our physical reality that arose at some point in our evolution, but as the essence of our physical being.

We believe that Consciousness mutated into energy and matter, giving birth to all things, both animate and inanimate. And, that since all things are made from the same material, the *fundamental principle of the universe is connectivity*. All things are woven into a tapestry of being. Each individual thing is a conscious node in a conscious tapestry, connected to all others.

Third, we believe that Consciousness, which in essence is nonmaterial, yearns to express itself in a multiplicity of forms. The form Consciousness has taken in us is to become human. But Consciousness has also fulfilled its drive to take form in millions of other ways. For instance, when we look at the natural world, we can't help but see how much life loves diversity. There are over 200 ways of being a parrot. There are 250,000 different kinds of beetles. Each one is different from all the others, but remains a beetle nonetheless.

Even identical twins are different people, because their unique experiences shape them in unique ways. And we and our children are far from identical. Through them, we are blessed with a way of seeing the world differently. Through them, we have a chance to notice things that would have been invisible to us and to know things we haven't learned ourselves. Our job as parents is to see this difference and to love it. At the same time, all of us come from the same cosmic act of creation; we share the same atoms; we all follow the same inexorable cycle of being born and dying.

THE ESSENCE OF THE CHILD

Given this perspective, we invite you to think of your child in a radically new way. She is more than she appears to be. She has journeyed through unimaginable eons of time and space to be born to you now. Within her body are the same elements of which the universe is made. She is made from star dust. She arrives whole, in harmony with the elements and the rhythms of the cosmos from which she came. In her original state, she experiences this harmony as a state of relaxed joyfulness; she is connected to all parts of herself, to the social and ecological context, and intuitively aware of her union with the cosmos, and thus with God. In addition, within her brain are the patterns of accumulated wisdom from millions of years of evolution. Most of what she is happened before she was born. Our job as her parent is to help her evolve into her full potential and finish her creation.

IMPLICATIONS FOR PARENTING

For us, as we have said, *connectivity* is the fundamental principle of the universe. It is in connectivity that the spirit of God is manifest. The infant experiences connection, or union, with the universe through his parents. The parents *are* the infant's universe. Her emotional and mental universe will be harmonious or disturbed by the way she is parented. Her relationship with God will be greatly influenced by her relationship to her parents.[5]

Understanding this perspective invites us to change the way we parent. Understanding guides action. If we see parenting as static, rather than dynamic, we miss the possibility of cocreation with God that forms the essence of parenting. When we parent our children consciously, we are participating in one of the great drives of the universe to complete itself and repair itself. For when we become active in a healing relationship with our children, we and our children, the most wounded parts of the universe, have the opportunity to maintain connection and recover our wholeness.

If parents intentionally nurture their connection with their newborn by meeting the child's needs, the child continues to experience harmony with his world and his awareness of his connection to it is unbroken. If the parents are not able to meet their child's needs, he becomes wounded and experiences disharmony or dissonance with his world. Parents don't want to wound their children; they want to meet their needs. But given the fact that our species has not yet evolved to the level where we know how to rear children without wounding them, all of us are born to parents who come to the task damaged, imperfect, and incomplete. They were parented by imperfect people, and they carry within them the wounds that prevent them from responding perfectly to their children. As a result, connection between parent and child is lost.

Collectively, we have developed structures and processes for healing the rupture of connection and the alienation we sometimes feel with loved ones and with the fullness of life. One of the most powerful means of connection is the great religions of the world, which at their essence are about connection to that which is greater than ourselves, as well as our connections to each other. Another is psychotherapy in all its forms, which has played a healing role in many people's lives. But we are suggesting that it is with those closest to us, within our families, that significant transformation can occur. We believe in conscious marriage as a means of profound healing. Now we are adding another—*conscious parenting*—which in the maintenance and restoration of relationship invites you and your child into a connection that, at its deepest level, is spiritual.

EVERYTHING IS CONNECTED

Conscious parenting embraces a relational view of life that focuses on the nature and quality of the connections that form the substance and texture of our lives. When someone asks, "How can I be a better parent?" we know the answer lies deep within the emotional, social, intellectual, and spiritual connections the person is making in his life.

Parenting is not a discrete act, separate from others. Parents and children are not separate from each other. Feelings are not separate from thinking. The body is not separate from the mind. Human beings are not separate from nature. Instead, human beings are open systems that continuously influence each other whether they are in physical contact or not. Reason and emotion are intrinsically connected. Nature and human beings are radically interdependent. The distinction between the secular and the sacred collapses. Everything is connection. Because the tenants of conscious parenting are embedded in this perspective, when we parent consciously, we affirm and participate in the cosmic process.

WHERE WE ARE NOW

To a great extent, we have lost our connection to our true natures and to each other and to the cosmic order. Paradise, which is our natural state, has been lost. This is evident when we take a look at the condition of family life in our country today. According to the 1995 report of the Council on Families in America, "To reverse the current deterioration of child and societal well-being in the United States, we must strengthen the institution of marriage. The weakening of marriage has had devastating consequences for the well-being of children . . . leading to growing family instability and decreasing parental investment in children."[6]

We agree with the council's report that committed marriages provide an environment of strength and stability for sustaining the enormous effort that children require. Parenting is tough; no other human activity demands so much. And it is our contention that it is best done within the context of a marriage where both adults are committed to the health and happiness of each other, as well as their children. That's why we make a passionate plea for recognition of the connection between good marriages and good parenting.

Please understand that we are not saying that all divorces are bad and all marriages are good, or that all children from divorced families are irreparably damaged, or that all the problems children face today stem from the evils of divorce. We are saying that children who grow up with two parents in a stable relationship are better off, in general, than children who do not. Further, we are saying that *people who want to do the best possible job of parenting their children need to be preserving and improving their own marriage relationship while their children are living at home.*

Clearly, for increasing numbers of people, this is not happening. Things are worse for marriage and worse for children than they have ever been in modern times.[7] Although we are aware of the dangers of assigning causal relationships to phenomena that are coincidental, we (and many others) believe the deterioration of marriage and the deterioration of child well-being are connected.

Consider these changes in family life, as outlined by the Council on Families in America, in their 1995 report:

1. Juvenile violent crime has increased sixfold from 1960 to 1992. Seventy percent of juvenile offenders did not live with both parents while growing up.
2. Reports of child neglect and abuse have quintupled since 1976.
3. Psychological problems among children and youth are drastically worse. Eating disorders and depression are soaring. Teen suicide has tripled. Alcohol and drug abuse continues at a very high rate. Recent surveys have found that children from divorced homes have two to three times more behavioral and psychological problems than do children from intact homes.
4. SAT scores have declined nearly 80 points.
5. Poverty has shifted from the elderly to the young. Today, 38 percent of the nation's poor are children. The rate of child poverty, for example, is five times higher for children living with single mothers than for children in intact families.
6. Marriage is in decline. Today 62 percent of all adults are married (compared to 72 percent in 1970). Today over 30 percent of all babies born in this country are born outside marriage (compared

to 5.3 percent in 1960). Today, the probability that a marriage will end in divorce or permanent separation is 60 percent. Today, about half of all children in the United States are likely to experience a parental divorce before they leave home. Today, more than a third of all children live apart from their biological fathers.

Whether we are familiar with these exact statistics or not, there is a feeling of disquiet among people from all walks of life in our country. On some level, we know that all is not well with our nation's children. We can no longer delude ourselves: *our individual and collective futures are at risk when children are not given what they need to grow up centered and confident about the future.* There is no doubt that social reform is needed. But more money and more social service programs alone, no matter how welcome, cannot undo the damage of poor marriage and poor parenting.

It helps to understand that, in part, the behaviors and attitudes we call unconscious parenting spring from our limitations as human beings. Our brains are constructed in a certain way, so we repeat behaviors we are familiar with and act savagely to defend ourselves, even when the "threat" is coming from the two-year-old or the thirteen-year-old we love so much. When we talk about unconscious parenting we are not talking about something that happens *outside* us, to people who are not like us. We are talking about *us*, the condition of nonawareness that describes all of us to some degree. Some people are more self-aware than others, but all of us have moments or periods of unconsciousness when we act as though other people had no real life of their own. It is in this spirit of surrender to the recognition that we are all limited and with a renewed sense of what is possible that we offer these observations.

Given this reality, what must we do to become better stewards of our physical and spiritual gifts in the future?

THE POSSIBILITIES OF FAITH

As we have said above, we have set our concept of parenting into a particular philosophical and spiritual framework. Our lives and our families can recover connection when we act in accordance with the universal laws of the cosmos, in harmony with the life force of which we are a part. To speak in metaphor, we must find our way back to paradise, to the kingdom, by relating to others in ways that incarnate the possibilities of love, faith, and morality. Only then will we restore our rightful connections and reclaim our place in the natural order of things.

Our morality and our spiritual practice must resonate with the cosmic order of life, and they must flow naturally from it. Loving your neighbor isn't just a "good thing to do." Putting aside the newspaper and listening to your child confess her fears isn't just a "good thing to do." Refraining from criticizing your spouse and feeling his pain instead isn't just a "good thing to do." When something is just a good idea, our dedication is conditional. We do it if it's convenient, or it feels good, or it's easy.

We are talking about a way of behaving that is different from this. This way manifests and honors the existential reality of our lives. Our everyday, common acts of love come from an awareness that they are in concert with the higher purposes of the universe. Taken together over a lifetime, these simple acts become the expression of our understanding of our higher purpose.

As we look to the future, we personally find ourselves looking back at our own pasts. One of the things we see is that religion has become more important to us as we have gotten older. We struggle to find new words or to breathe life into old words in order to express clearly what we mean. We honor the role of religion as an expression of cosmic Consciousness. And we speak of the "God essence within" each of us as the incarnation of this Consciousness. Whatever the words, we can see that religious and spiritual practices arise directly from our desire to be more conscious in our lives and to experience profound connection in our relationships.

Religion means to "tie back to" or "return to the source" and is the form in which this impulse is organized into language and ritual. Our roots are potentially meaningful and life sustaining. Religious practice points to the source, to the origins of our existence, and reminds us of who we are. The importance of religion in parenting is that it connects the child to the universe through a particular religious faith.

THE FAMILY AS THE NURTURING PLACE FOR FAITH

We have spoken at length about how family life can nurture the child's physical, mental, and emotional life. Now we want to talk some about the family as the nurturing place for faith. Within our home we have found our faith tradition to be an important part of our parenting process. Among other things, it has helped us strengthen our children's sense of identity as they learned about and from their historical, cultural, and religious roots.

There are many aspects of spiritual practice that are good for children. Rituals, for example, are powerful forces for connection when they have meaning and are enacted with conviction. But here we want to highlight one important impulse that is present in all religious traditions, *the ethic of love*. This is, perhaps, the core teaching of all faiths. What we mean by it is the practice of making the "self" and the "other" coequal by making unconditional love the quality and substance of the space "between." When we achieve that, the "between" becomes the location of the divine.

Our natural inclination is to place ourselves in the center of the universe, much the way the ancient astronomers positioned earth in the center of the universe. We become the global "we." From the center, *we* define what is right or wrong, and good or evil. Those who conform to our world or see the world as we do are *us*. Those who do not are the enemy.

This is the source of enormous personal, social, and global conflict—between marriage partners, between brothers and sisters, between ethnic groups, between nations. It is the tragic condition of the human species. Not only are we as individuals arrested somewhere on the journey to full consciousness and wholeness; the human race is also impeded in its evolution toward consciousness by our collective inability to surrender to the consciousness of our oneness with each other. We are all somewhere far from the promised land, fellow pilgrims searching for our way back to the wholeness created by love.

Our survival is best supported by an ethic of love that espouses the intrinsic value of others and guarantees their welfare. In a paradoxical way, commitment to the welfare of others is the best guarantee of our own. In the sense we mean it, "love" is not an energy or an abstract ideal, but the quality of a right relationship.

A family who participates in a spiritual or religious practice provides an opportunity for children to experience and understand what it means to love other people and other things. Becoming a member of a church, synagogue, mosque, or other group fosters deep bonding in a way that a football game or a trip to an amusement park simply doesn't.

A child whose family is part of a larger spiritual community expands his awareness of our interconnectedness to each other and to the planet.

Spiritual and religious traditions offer children a framework for dealing with human experience, including success and failure. God is always larger than we are. This reality allows children to greet their success with the humble awareness that their achievement was possible only with the support and encouragement of others, and to work out failure in the solace of a safe place to explore the pain and confusion of loss. Spiritual experience helps parents create a steadfast sense of security *for* their children and *within* their children, so that, someday, they will be able to create this sense of security for their children.

The profound love of family—the connection of a father to a mother, of parents to the children, of children to each other—is the truest and most natural place to move into the deeper awareness of love as a manifestation of our innate connection with the divine. In essence, that is what conscious parenting is: love for the child, making love the quality of the relationship, of the "between." The experience of the in-between, as suggested by Martin Buber, is where God is born. All families experience pain. But, when as conscious parents we honor the wisdom of our faith traditions, we transform our relationships and open ourselves to the lessons of vulnerability that only conscious families can teach.

VI

Tools For

Conscious

Parenting

15

Changing Knowledge
into Action

INTRODUCTION

Our purpose in the preceding chapters has been to provide some essential cognitive information about conscious parenting. Cognitive information is an essential first step in the process of becoming more conscious in relationships with other people. When you understand an idea and then put it into practice, it starts to become an integrated, organic part of what you say and do.

Becoming conscious is a process that has no end. It happens gradually as you learn how to be an observer of your own actions, particularly when you notice the discrepancy between your behavior and the outcomes you desire. As you become more self-reflective, the insight and information you receive become the basis for changing the way you respond to other people. Being less self-absorbed and less preoccupied with fears means you are better able to respond to your children as they really are. The process of self-healing brings you many benefits, but this is a primary one.

The exercises in this chapter are designed to assist you in becoming a conscious parent. They follow a sequence. You are invited to gather information about your parenting, how you were parented, and your

293

marriage or intimate relationship. This information will help you develop a growth plan for becoming a conscious parent and a conscious partner. We suggest that you follow the sequence, since each exercise emerges from the one before.

If you are married or part of a committed parenting partnership, we suggest that each of you complete the written exercises alone and then make time to share them, using the dialogue process described later in this chapter. If you are a single parent, we suggest that you complete the exercises and then share the information with a significant adult in your life, inviting that person to help you carry out your growth plan.

USING THIS SECTION OF THE BOOK

This chapter is divided into four parts. Each part contains exercises designed to help you understand more about yourself as a child, as a marriage partner, and as a parent. We have said that information alone is not enough to transform people into conscious parents. So we have designed these exercises to be not only sources of personal information, but also tools to help you begin the process of transformation toward conscious parenting. They will enable you to begin the internal and external changes that will orient you toward a more conscious way of relating to your partner and your children.

To make it easier for you to see this cycle of exercises as a whole, we list the four sections and their accompanying exercises below.

Part I

Getting to Know Yourself as a Parent

EXERCISE 1: Parenting Questionnaire
EXERCISE 2: Identifying Your Parenting Style
EXERCISE 3: Setting Limits
EXERCISE 4: Your Parenting Challenge
EXERCISE 5: Identifying Your Growth Point as a Parent

Part II

Recognizing How You Were Parented

EXERCISE 6: Personal Beliefs
EXERCISE 7: Feelings, Fears, and Defenses

EXERCISE 8: Your Parents' Involvement With You as a Child
EXERCISE 9: How Your Parents Set Limits

Part III

Understanding Your Relationship

EXERCISE 10: Relationship Overview
EXERCISE 11: Beliefs About Yourself in Your Relationship With Your Partner
EXERCISE 12: Identify Your Relationship Fears
EXERCISE 13: Your Core Relationship Issue
EXERCISE 14: Growth Opportunities in Your Relationship
EXERCISE 15: Couples Dialogue
EXERCISE 16: Re-romanticizing or Reimaging Process

Part IV

Plan for Healing and Growth

EXERCISE 17: Using What You Know
EXERCISE 18: Plan for Healing and Growth

Space considerations make it impossible to present here all the exercises we use to help people become more conscious in their parenting. These exercises form the backbone of a more complete process for transformation that is available in a separate publication we have titled *Parents' Manual*. If you find that you and/or your partner want more help in this step-by-step process, we recommend that you obtain a copy of the *Parents' Manual*, which you can order by following the instructions on the order page at the back of the book.

Part I

GETTING TO KNOW YOURSELF AS A PARENT

Below is a questionnaire that is designed to help you clarify what you think and feel about yourself as a parent, about your partner, and about your own parents, and what you would like to change in yourself. It might be helpful to write your answers in a notebook that you can use later as a reference. Complete each sentence with the first thought that comes to your mind.

Exercise 1

Parenting Questionnaire

ME

1. My goal as a parent is _____.
2. My reasons for being a parent are _____.
3. My most frequent feeling as a parent is _____.
4. My deepest need as a parent is _____.
5. When I am my best self as a parent, I am _____.
6. The thing that gives me the most satisfaction as a parent is _____.
7. In general, I think my strengths as a parent are _____.
8. As a parent, I am happiest when my child(ren) _____.
9. My best parenting experience was _____.
10. When I am my worst self as a parent, I am _____.
11. The thing that gives me the least satisfaction as a parent is _____.

12. In general, I think my weaknesses as a parent are _____.
13. My deepest fear as a parent is _____.
14. As a parent, I feel angry or frustrated when my child(ren) _____.
15. My worst parenting experience was _____.
16. I think my relationship to my child(ren) has been _____.
17. When parents express love for a child, they should _____.
18. When parents express disapproval of a child, they should _____.
19. The person I admire most as a parent is _____.

MY PARTNER

20. The best thing about my partner as a parent is _____.
21. The worst thing about my partner as a parent is _____.
22. When my partner and I have parenting conflicts, we _____.
23. This is what I would like us to be able to do better: _____.

MY OWN PARENTS

24. The best thing I learned from my parents about parenting is _____.
25. The least helpful thing I learned from my parents about parenting is

_____.

26. I want to be just like my parent(s) in this regard: _____.
27. I do not want to be like my parent(s) in this regard: _____.
28. I would be a better parent myself if my parent(s) had done this: _____.
29. I would not be as good a parent myself if my parent(s) had not done
this: _____.

CHANGE

30. Five things about myself as a parent I want to change are
    a) _____.
    b) _____.
    c) _____.
    d) _____.
    e) _____.

How to use this information:

So rarely does it occur to us parents to stop and think through our responses to the above questions. Much of what we do, we do by "feel" or by instinct. And, as we have learned, this is one way of describing unconscious parenting. Conscious parenting means becoming aware of what is happening in the moment and making an effort to reveal to ourselves the hidden feelings, assumptions, and half-baked ideas that keep us from being aware of what is happening in the moment. We need to question our own reactions by asking, "What does this mean?" and "Do I want to continue thinking and acting this way?" When the answer is "yes," you can continue on your path with renewed energy and conviction. When the answer is "no," you have identified a growth point for change to which you will want to give further attention.

The growth necessary to become a more conscious parent is often painful. It is difficult to change parts of yourself that have become familiar, even if the change will give you a fuller, more vibrant life. Your defenses have become part of your personality. They have arisen in response to your inner directive to survive. Even though *you* have continued to grow and change, your defenses have not automatically updated themselves or fallen away. And they won't fall away until you intentionally replace them with responses that are more effective. The transition from one protective response to another can be emotionally painful and frightening.

When you gather your courage in your hands and begin to heal your childhood wounds, however, you free yourself from the parts of your personality that no longer serve you and your relationships well. When you give your child what she needs to complete her innate developmental plan and when you give your partner what he needs for his emotional healing, you stretch beyond your character defenses toward the recovery of your own wholeness. Then, your words and deeds make sense in your current reality.

Exercise 2

Identifying Your Parenting Style

A. The chart on p. 300 lists the traits that describe the maximizer and the minimizer. Study the page and assign each trait a score of one to five. Give a 1 to the trait that is least descriptive of you and a 5 to the trait that is most descriptive of you. When you finish, add up the scores and put them at the bottom of each column. Then in a different color pen, score *your perception* of your partner. When you finish, you and your partner may want to discuss your scores using the dialogue process (see chart, page 300).

B. Given what you now know about yourself, your partner, and your parenting behaviors, answer the following questions:

1. Which term below most closely describes your perception of your character structure in relationship with your partner?
   a. Maximizer   b. Minimizer

2. Which term below most closely describes your perception of your partner's character in his or her relationship to you?
   a. Maximizer   b. Minimizer

3. Which term most closely describes your mother's or mothering caretaker's character in her relation to your father?
   a. Maximizer   b. Minimizer

4. Which term most closely describes your father or fathering caretaker in his relationship to your mother?
   a. Maximizer   b. Minimizer

5. Which term most closely describes you in relating to your child(ren) as a parent?
   a. Maximizer   b. Minimizer

6. Which term, in your perception, most closely describes your partner in his or her relationship to your child(ren)?
   a. Maximizer   b. Minimizer

How to use this information:

Knowing how you and your partner tend to express your energy (by exaggerating it or diminishing it) will help you see the complementarity of your relationship. You will see in what ways you are opposite from each other. Since one partner's defense tends to trigger the other's frustration and pain (because it approximates the style of the partner's parents), you may want to consider how you can change. Of course, you and your partner don't just want to trade places. But if you both become

WAYS A MAXIMIZER USES ENERGY Overinvolved	WAYS A MINIMIZER USES ENERGY Underinvolved
Tends to explode feelings outward.	Tends to implode feelings inward.
Tends to exaggerate emotions.	Tends to diminish emotions.
Tends to be dependent on others.	Tends to deny dependency.
Tends to exaggerate needs.	Tends to deny needs.
Tends to be compulsively open and subjective.	Tends to share little of his or her inner world.
Tends to be overly inclusive of others in his or her personal space.	Tends to exclude others from his or her personal space.
Tends toward clinging and excessive generosity.	Tends to withhold feelings, thoughts, and behaviors.
Tends to have unclear self-boundaries.	Tends to have rigid self-boundaries.
Tends to be outer-directed; generally asks for direction from others.	Tends to be inner-directed; takes direction mainly from himself or herself.
Tends to focus on others.	Tends to think mainly about himself or herself.
Tends to act impulsively.	Tends to act and think compulsively.
Tends to act submissively and manipulatively.	Tends to try to dominate others.
Tends to alternate between aggressiveness and passivity.	Tends to be passive-aggressive.
MAXIMIZER SCORE	MINIMIZER SCORE
Your score: The score for your perception of your partner:	Your score: The score for your perception of your partner:

more like each other, you will begin the process of negating unconscious behavior, and that is a significant change.

A child will identify with the parent who is more important to the child, whom *the child* sees as more powerful. This gives you a preview of the character structure your child will tend toward. A conscious parent will want to modify the extremes of the minimizer and maximizer parent and become more flexible, able to express energy as appropriate and necessary in any situation.

Exercise 3

Setting Limits

Setting appropriate limits is one of the most important aspects of conscious parenting. Children learn from their parents how to stay safe, take into account the needs and wishes of other people, and, at the same time, have the freedom to be who they are.

A. In this exercise, select the one answer that best describes the kind of limits you and your partner set.

1. As a parent, I set

    a. Too many limits   d. Inconsistent limits
    b. Just enough limits   e. Harsh limits
    c. Not enough limits   f. No limits

2. As a parent, my partner sets

    a. Too many limits   d. Inconsistent limits
    b. Just enough limits   e. Harsh limits
    c. Not enough limits   f. No limits

B. Which of you has more influence on your child(ren)? _____

C. Which of you do you see your child(ren) trying to be like? _____

How to use this information:

These simple questions can challenge your thinking further and spark discussion between you and your partner. You might ask yourself why you answered as you did about yourself, what the consequences are when you and your partner do not agree, whether you set different limits for each of your children (if you have more than one) and why. What message are your children receiving from the way you help them know about boundaries? If you think it would be a good idea to be setting limits in a different way, is there anything that would prevent you from doing so?

Exercise 4

Your Parenting Challenge

This exercise is designed to assist you in identifying the biggest challenge that you and your partner face in your parenting. Circle all the answers that apply and then underline the two answers that are most challenging. Between those two, double-underline the one that is the most challenging.

1. As a parent, I find my greatest challenges involve

   a. Feeling connected to our child(ren)
   b. Letting our child(ren) explore the world
   c. Letting our child(ren) have privacy
   d. Letting our child(ren) do things by him/herself (themselves)
   e. Setting limits
   f. Being consistent
   g. Handling anger and conflict appropriately
   h. Paying attention when my child(ren) needs (need) me
   i. Mirroring our child(ren)'s communications
   j. Validating our child(ren)'s perceptions and way of thinking
   k. Experiencing empathy with our child(ren)
   l. Dealing with our child(ren)'s incessant needs and wants
   m. Dealing with our child(ren)'s activeness, noise, constant movement
   n. Supporting our child(ren)'s ability and freedom to think
   o. Supporting the expression of all our child(ren)'s feelings
   p. Supporting our child(ren)'s enjoyment of all his/her (their) physical senses
   q. Supporting our child(ren)'s freedom to move his/her (their) muscles and enjoy his/her (their) body
   r. Supporting our child(ren)'s freedom to be who he/she is (they are)

2. In my perception, my partner's greatest challenges include (circle the one that applies most, and underline the one that you believe challenges your partner the most)

   a. Feeling connected to our child(ren)
   b. Letting our child(ren) explore the world

c. Letting our child(ren) have privacy
d. Letting our child(ren) do things by him/herself (themselves)
e. Setting limits
f. Being consistent
g. Handling anger and conflict appropriately
h. Paying attention when my child(ren) needs (need) me
i. Mirroring our child(ren)'s communications
j. Validating our child(ren)'s perceptions and way of thinking
k. Experiencing empathy with our child(ren)
l. Dealing with our child(ren)'s incessant needs and wants
m. Dealing with our child(ren)'s activeness, noise, constant movement
n. Supporting our child(ren)'s ability and freedom to think
o. Supporting the expression of all our child(ren)'s feelings
p. Supporting our child(ren)'s enjoyment of all his/her (their) physical senses
q. Supporting our child(ren)'s freedom to move his/her (their) muscles and enjoy his/her (their) body
r. Supporting our child(ren)'s freedom to be who he/she is (they are)

How to use this information:

These statements represent positive ways parents can support their children through the developmental stages of growth. The ones you marked give you valuable information about yourself. First, they call your attention to what you will have to be especially intentional about doing in order to meet your child's needs. Second, they point to areas of personal growth for you. As we have said, knowing where you are challenged in meeting your children's needs gives you an indication of where you were wounded as a child.

See if you can identify the wound you sustained that makes meeting the challenge so difficult. For example, let's say you circled or under-lined the last item on the list, "supporting their freedom to be who they are." You might want to review your own experience and come up with a memory or explanation that makes sense of your difficulty in meeting this need in your child. Perhaps you remember your father ignoring your artistic efforts and pushing you to play ball instead. Be as specific as you can. Every item you marked will give you clues about changes you might want to make, but the one that is double-underlined is the one you will want to focus your efforts on first. You can begin to do things differently with your children at the same time that you are beginning to heal your own wounds.

In addition, if you have a parenting partner, ask your partner to sit down with you and talk about what you have discovered about yourself and your perceptions of him or her. He or she might want to complete the exercise as a prelude to dialogue. If you can, make specific plans for addressing the challenges that you have discovered separately and together.

Exercise 5

Identifying Your Growth Point as a Parent

The purpose of this exercise is to assist you in identifying your growth points. A growth point is a place in your development where your progress was halted or altered in some way, causing you to develop a defense. Your vulnerability, and its consequent defense, have become part of your personality. They are so much a part of you now that you may think of them as "me." But they are not "you" (i.e., your essential self). They are part of your adaptation to life, and if you wish, they can be changed.

Your partner is as aware of your vulnerability and your defense as you are aware of his or hers. You feel your vulnerability when your partner does something that taps into an unconscious memory of your childhood pain and raises the fear that you may be wounded again. You protect yourself with your defense. And, paradoxically, your defense wounds your partner as his defense wounds you. Your defense works to prevent you from responding to your partner's needs whenever they show up in your relationship. You and your partner can heal each other if you take on the job of becoming each other's surrogate parent.

Your vulnerability and your defense are also operative in your parenting. When your child reaches the developmental stage that you did not negotiate successfully, you will experience frustration, fear, and perhaps a sense of helplessness. Then you will respond to your child's normal developmental need as your parents responded to you. And you will activate your defense. That will frustrate your child, and if this is not changed, you will injure your child in the same way you were injured.

A. In this exercise, you are invited to identify and explore your responses when your child frustrates you. By identifying your frustrations with your child, you will identify your growth point. This will help you to respond to your child with developmentally appropriate behaviors, provide the support your child needs, and assist him through the developmental stage he has reached.

1. To get started with this exercise, take a blank sheet of paper and turn it into the landscape position, so that as it faces you, it is wider than it is long.
2. Label it at the top, "My Growth Point and Plan for Change." Now divide the page into five vertical columns. Label the columns "Frustration," "Feeling," "Reaction," "Thought," and "Hidden Fear."
3. In the Frustration column, list the behaviors (words and actions) that frustrate you with your child.
4. In the Feeling column, identify the feeling you have when you experience that frustration.
5. In the Reaction column, list your emotional and/or behavioral reaction to that frustration.
6. Then, in the Thought column, write down the thought you have: what do you tell yourself?; what is your interpretation of the frustration? Most of us have a hidden fear that we often mask behind our reaction. The reaction, in fact, is an attempt to prevent us from feeling that fear. You may have to do some thinking to identify this fear. When you do, place it in the fifth column entitled Hidden Fear.
7. Next, study your list of your child's frustrating behaviors, and see if you can find a pattern in them. When you discover the pattern or patterns in your child's *behaviors* that frustrate you, write the pattern at the bottom of the list under the Frustration column.
8. In the Feeling column, write at the bottom of the list the most intense feeling you have most often.
9. Then, at the bottom of the Reaction column, write your most intense reactions.
10. And in the column under Thought, write the pattern in your thinking when you are frustrated.

11. Last, look at the column under Hidden Fear, and write the fear you feel most often.

Now think back to your experience as a child, and call to mind the worst frustrations you experienced. How do they compare with your worst frustrations with your child(ren)?

B. In this exercise you are asked to take one of the frustrating behaviors you identified above and elaborate on it. That will help you understand the process more deeply. Since the exercise asks for sentences, you may want to use a separate notebook or piece of paper to record your answers.

1. How long have you been married?
2. What was your age when you married?
3. How many children do you have, and what are their ages?
4. What has been the most difficult age for you with each of your children?
5. Recall a recent situation in which one of your children did something that frustrated or irritated you.

   a. Briefly describe the situation.
   b. What was the child's age?
   c. What did your child do?
   d. How did you feel?
   e. What actions did you take, if any?

6. How does your *partner* typically react to you when this kind of frustrating incident occurs?
7. Can you recall an early frustrating experience from *your childhood* that was similar to this?

   a. If so, briefly describe the situation.
   b. Which parent (caretaker) did it involve?
   c. What did he/she do?
   d. How did you feel?
   e. What did you do in response?

8. Recall a second frustrating incident (with a different child, if applicable).

   a. Briefly describe the situation.
   b. What was the child's age?

    c. What did your child do?

    d. How did you feel?

    e. What actions did you take, if any?

9. How did your partner react to you?

10. Can you recall an early experience from your childhood that was similar to this second incident?

    a. If so, briefly describe the situation.

    b. Which parent (caretaker) did it involve?

    c. What did he/she do?

    d. How did you feel?

    e. What did you do in response?

11. In your perception, what do you do that produces the most intensely negative reactions from your child(ren)?

    a. Briefly describe these actions.

    b. What does your partner do in relation to you when this happens?

12. In your perception, what does your partner do that produces the most intensely negative reactions from your child(ren)?

    a. Briefly describe these actions.

    b. What do you do in relation to your partner when this happens?

13. What does your partner do as a parent that most frustrates you?

    a. Briefly describe the situation.

    b. What do you do when your partner does this?

14. What do you do that, in your perception, produces the most positive response from your child(ren)? (*What is really working?*)

    a. Briefly describe these actions.

    b. What does your partner do when you do this?

15. What does your partner do that, in your perception, produces the most positive reactions from your child(ren)?

    a. Briefly describe these actions.

    b. What do you do when your partner does this?

16. Select the one behavior in the two scenes you described above that frustrates you the most.

17. Now complete these sentences:
    When my child (behavioral pattern) _____, I feel (feeling most often felt) _____ and then I often react by (reaction pattern) _____ and think (your thought pattern) _____ and feel fearful that (pattern of hidden fears) _____. These fears suggest that my wound was _____ and—given that minimizers constrict their energy and are underinvolved in parenting and maximizers explode their energy and are overinvolved—my reactions suggest that I am a (circle one) minimizer/maximizer.

    Compare this with the answers you gave about your frustrations with your parent.

18. Next, using this information, complete these sentences:
    What this suggests is that when my child (behavioral pattern) _____, what he needs is (a positive parenting response) _____, because he feels _____. This requires me to change my thought pattern of _____ and to tell him that I _____.

19. In order to identify your growth point, use the information in the exercise above and in the sentences finished and complete these sentences:
    This suggests that in childhood, when I (behavior pattern) _____, my parents felt (feeling pattern) _____ and reacted by (reaction pattern) _____, because they were afraid that (dominant hidden fear) _____. What I need to do to grow is this: When my child (behavioral pattern) _____, instead of _____, I can instead (positive parenting response) _____. This can help me (positive behavioral pattern) _____ and support my child when my child engages in those behaviors.

How to use this information:

With the information you have gained about your growth needs and the information you have gained from reading this book, make a list of requests you can make of your partner that will help you grow toward more conscious parenting. Then use the behavior-change request process to make your requests. Your partner is your best ally in helping you make the changes you want to make.

Part II

RECOGNIZING HOW YOU WERE PARENTED

How you parent is largely a reflection of how you were parented. All of us tend to internalize our parents and unconsciously set them up in our minds as models for our parenting. They are instrumental in the attitudes we develop and the beliefs we maintain about ourselves in relation to other people. The exercises in this part of the chapter will help you understand what impact the parenting you received as a child has had on your own your parenting.

Exercise 6

Personal Beliefs

The exercise below will assist you in gathering some valuable information about personal beliefs you have developed as a result of your childhood.

1. Draw a line under item L, across both columns on the chart on page 312.
2. Read the positive beliefs from A through L in the left-hand column and the negative beliefs from A through L in the right-hand column.

    a. Circle two from each column that describe your beliefs about yourself.
    b. Underline the one from each list that you think is the *most* descriptive of you.

3. Read the positive beliefs from M through P in the left-hand column and the negative beliefs from M through P in the right-
   hand column.

   a. Circle two from each column that describe your beliefs
      about yourself.

You may want to record your answers in a separate notebook.

How to use this information:

Items A–L on the right refer to beliefs you have developed as a result
of your childhood wound and the likely stage in which you were
wounded. Items A–L on the left gathers information about the stages in
which you were supported as a child.

Items A and B in the *right column* refer to wounds that occurred at
the attachment stage, items B and C refer to the exploration stage, items
D and E to the identity stage, items F and G to the competence stage,
items H and I to the concern stage, and items J and L to the intimacy
stage. The items in the *left column* refer to the same stage as those on
the right, but they indicate, not where you were wounded, but where
you were appropriately parented at that stage.

To complete the exercise, please finish this sentence:

*"I was wounded at the _____ stage and my wound
is _____."*

As you complete this sentence, check with yourself to see how vulnerable you feel when thinking these thoughts.

In both columns, item M refers to the function of thinking, item N
refers to the function of feeling, item O refers to the function of sensing,
and item P refers to the function of movement.

The right-hand column refers to wounds received during childhood
in these four areas of functioning. The left-hand column refers to functions that were supported during childhood. Most of us were asked to
inhibit or repress two of the listed functions, while two were left active.
The suppressed functions are what we refer to as the "lost self." You
have been asked to select two from each column.

Please finish these sentences:

*"Those of my functions that were supported include
_____ and _____. Those that were inhibited or
repressed are _____ and _____."*

The functions that were inhibited or repressed constitute your lost

POSITIVE BELIEFS	NEGATIVE BELIEFS
A. I am able to get most of my needs met.	A. I can't get my needs met.
B. I have a right to exist.	B. I have no right to exist.
C. I can count on others.	C. I can't count on others.
D. I can say "no" and still be loved.	D. I can't say "no" and be loved.
E. I am seen, valued, and accepted.	E. I'll never be seen, valued, and accepted.
F. I can be "me" and be accepted and loved.	F. I can't be me and be accepted and loved.
G. I know how to do things.	G. I don't know how to do things.
H. When I am imperfect, I am still loved.	H. I have to be perfect to be loved.
I. It's okay to have my needs.	I. I have to meet the needs of others.
J. I am lovable just being myself.	J. I am not lovable just being myself.
K. I am free to be myself.	K. I have to be good and be like others to be loved.
L. I am trusted.	L. I am not trusted.
M. I can think clearly, and my thinking is valued.	M. I can't think clearly.
N. I am in touch with all my feelings.	N. I'm not in touch with some, or most of my feelings.
O. I feel comfortable in my body; all my senses are alive.	O. I feel uncomfortable with my body; some of my senses are dulled.
P. I am free to move all my muscles.	P. Some/most of my muscles are constricted.

self. The lost self is hidden from you and from others. For example, you may say, "I am not a feeling person." Others are likely to agree with you. When you complete this sentence, please check with your own experience and the feedback you have received from others to see if they agree with these results.

Exercise 7

Feelings, Fears, and Defenses

This exercise is an elaboration of Exercise 6 and uses the information you have derived from step 2(b) of that exercise. It will help you identify *emotional vulnerability,* which comprises the feelings you have when you are wounded or are afraid of being wounded in your current life and the way you protect yourself when you feel these feelings and fears.

The statements in the *left-hand column* of the chart on page 314 describe common feelings and fears. Circle the two statements that most accurately describe your feelings and fears. Underline the one that is *most* important.

The phrases in the *right-hand column* complete this sentence: "When I feel this, I . . ." They describe common defenses people use in response to the feelings and fears in the left-hand column. Read again the statement you underlined in the left-hand column, and circle the defenses you use (right-hand column) in response to these feelings and fears.

How to use this information:

Items in both columns are related to developmental stages: Items A and B refer to the attachment stage, C and D to the exploration stage, E and F to the identity stage, G and H to the competence stage, I and J to the concern stage, and K and L to the intimacy stage.

When you have made your selections, complete these sentences:

"My major belief is that I _____ (use the underlined negative belief from Exercise 6, 2(b)), which means that my wound is that I feel _____ and I fear (bring down from the left-hand column above) _____. When I defend myself against this fear, I (bring down from the right-hand column above) _____.

One way to deepen your awareness of your wounds, fears, and defenses is to ask your partner how he would rate you in both exercises. He can also complete the exercise for himself, and you can offer to rate him. Share with your partner and invite him into a dialogue.

When you complete your dialogue about how each of you sees himself or herself, then engage in dialogue about how you see each other. This will increase your knowledge of yourselves and each other.

To complete this part of the exercise, finish this sentence:

FEELINGS AND FEARS	DEFENSES. "WHEN I FEEL THIS, I . . ."
A. I feel abandoned and fear being separated.	A. Become clinging, exaggerate my feelings.
B. I feel unwanted and fear being annihilated.	B. Withdraw and isolate and shut down my feelings.
C. I feel neglected and fear being alone.	C. Begin to pursue others and express intense feelings.
D. I feel smothered and fear being absorbed.	D. Create distance from others and diminish my feelings.
E. I feel dominated and fear being used.	E. Become rigid and resistant and withhold my feelings.
F. I feel guilty and not good enough and fear being used.	F. Try harder and become competitive and don't show my feelings.
G. I feel my efforts are devalued, and I fear being seen as helpless.	G. Become manipulative and communicate unclear feelings and messages.
H. I feel invisible and fear being shamed.	H. Become diffuse and sometimes confused and express mixed feelings.
I. I feel my needs are ignored, and I fear I am too needy.	I. Become gregarious, overly concerned about the feelings of others.
J. I feel disapproved of by others and fear being disliked and ostracized.	J. Seek to be alone and don't share my feelings with others.
K. I feel my uniqueness is suppressed, and I fear if I am different I won't be accepted.	K. Conform to what is expected of me and complain a lot.
L. I feel distrusted and fear having to be like others in order to be trusted.	L. Rebel and act out my feelings.

"In my perception, my partner's wound is feeling _____ *, his greatest fear is* _____ *, and he deals with his feelings and fears by* _____ *."*

Exercise 8

Your Parents' Involvement With You as a Child

The questions below will help you to gather information about how you were parented and connect it to your parenting.

A. In the two sentences below, please circle the two answers that best apply to your perception of your parents' relationship to you as a child and underline the one that is most applicable. Put the underlined one in the blank.

1. My mother was most often _____ in her parenting of me.

   a. Self-involved　　　　d. Rejecting
   b. Distracted　　　　　e. Smothering
   c. Nurturing　　　　　f. Attentive

2. My father was most often _____ in his parenting of me.

   a. Self-involved　　　　d. Rejecting
   b. Distracted　　　　　e. Smothering
   c. Nurturing　　　　　f. Attentive

B. Rate your parents' involvement with you when you were a child.
   Use the scale of 1–7 to rate your parent's underinvolvement or overinvolvement.

	Underinvolved			Optimally Involved		Overinvolved	
Mother	1	2	3	4	5	6	7
Father	1	2	3	4	5	6	7
Other	1	2	3	4	5	6	7

C. If, in your perception, you believe that one of your parents was overly involved at some times and underinvolved at others, which was the predominant pattern?

   1. Overinvolved　　　　　2. Underinvolved

D. In your judgment, how often did this parent swing to the other side? Circle one item below.

　　1. Seldom　　　　　2. Occasionally　　　　　3. Frequently

E. In your perception, what do you think was the reason for this inconsistency?

_____

_____

How to use this information:

In Part I of this chapter, you had the opportunity to think about your own style as a parent. Given what you have just indicated about your own parents, you can see how your style has been influenced or formed by one or both of your parents. To help you make the connection, you can answer questions A, B, and C above about yourself and your involvement with your own children. Are you most like your mother or your father? In what ways? What does this tell you about the effect you are likely having on your children?

Exercise 9

How Your Parents Set Limits

In the questions below, choose the one answer that best describes the kind of limits your parents set for you.

A. When I was a child, my mother set

　　1. Too many limits　　　　　　　4. Inconsistent limits
　　2. Just enough limits　　　　　　5. Harsh limits
　　3. Not enough limits　　　　　　6. No limits

B. When I was a child, my father set

　　1. Too many limits　　　　　　　4. Inconsistent limits
　　2. Just enough limits　　　　　　5. Harsh limits
　　3. Not enough limits　　　　　　6. No limits

C. Which parent were you closest to?　　　Mother　　　　Father

D. Which parent had the most influence
    on you?   Mother   Father

E. Which parent are you most like?   Mother   Father

How to use this information:

In your current and future parenting of your children, you will probably find yourself involved with parenting in the same way as your dominant parent. That means that you may be asking your children to inhibit or repress aspects of themselves similar to the ones you were asked to inhibit or repress. Knowing this will help you see what effect your parenting has on your children. You can then ask yourself whether you have reason to change, and if so, in which direction. When you relate your parents' interactions to your interactions with your children, and when you relate the feelings you had as a child to the feelings your child may have, you have an excellent means of gaining a deeper understanding about yourself as a parent.

Part III

UNDERSTANDING YOUR RELATIONSHIP

How you were parented influences both how you parent and how you relate to your partner in an intimate relationship. In this part of the chapter, you will have the opportunity to complete a series of exercises that will give you some information about your relationship with your intimate partner. If you are a single parent, you may want to select a current intimate other or an ex-partner/spouse with whom to do these exercises.

Exercise 10

Relationship Overview

A. On a piece of paper in a notebook, draw a chart like the one that follows, and fill in the columns as indicated. In the first column, list your partner's positive traits; in the second column, list your positive memories of things he/she has done; in the third column, list your positive feelings toward your partner; and in the fourth column, list your most positive thoughts about your partner.

Partner's Positive Traits	Best Memories With My Partner	Positive Feelings Toward My Partner	Positive Thoughts and Beliefs About My Partner

Now rate each item on a scale of 1–5, with one 1 indicating the highest intensity, and 5 indicating the lowest. Then select the items to which you gave a 1, and complete these sentences:

When I think about my partner, I see his most positive trait as _____. *The best memory I have had with him/her was when he/she* _____. *That stirred my most positive feeling of* _____ *and contributed to my belief that my partner is* _____.

B. Make another chart with five columns, and complete it by listing your partner's frustrating behaviors in the first column, your feelings about that in the second column, your reaction to this behavior (what you do) in the third column, your thought or belief about this behavior in the fourth column, and the fear that this behavior arouses in the fifth column.

Frustrating Behaviors	Feelings	Reactions	Thoughts or Beliefs	Fears

Now select the five most frustrating behaviors and rate them on the scale of 1–5 with 1 being the most frustrating, the one you most want him/her to change. Ask your partner to look at the five behaviors you selected and to rate them on a scale of 1–5, with 1 being the most difficult for him to change.

How to use this information:

You will notice that this exercise asks you to recall both positive and negative aspects of your feelings about your partner. It is useful to remember that there are both. When you identify them specifically, you are allowing yourself to see that there are particular things that are positive and particular things that are negative, rather than thinking in vague, general terms that things are all bad or all good. In particular, partners often have trouble talking about the *behaviors* they find frustrating in each other. Identifying them and thinking through to the fears that they generate in you helps you see why they bother you and why they have such power. This exercise is most useful when both partners agree to complete it and then to share the results in dialogue with each other.

Exercise 11

Beliefs About Yourself in Your Relationship With Your Partner

This exercise will help you uncover what you believe about yourself in your relationship with your partner. Until you pause and reflect on your beliefs, you may go no deeper in understanding than vague feelings of satisfaction or dissatisfaction. Circle two items in the chart on page 321 that most closely represent your belief about yourself in your relationship. Then underline the two items that are *closest* to your core belief.

How to understand and use this information:

As is true of other exercises in Parts I and II of this chapter, these belief statements are connected to the developmental stages of growth. Beliefs A and B are connected to injuries received at the attachment stage, C and D to those at the exploration stage, E and F to those at the identity stage, G and H to those at the competence stage, I and J to those at the concern stage, and K and L to those at the intimacy stage.

"IN MY RELATIONSHIP, I BELIEVE THAT . . ."

A. I can get most of my needs met.	A. I can't get my needs met.
B. I am supported in my right to exist.	B. I have no right to exist.
C. I can count on my partner being reliable.	C. I will always be neglected by an unreliable partner.
D. I can say "no" to my partner and still be accepted and loved.	D. My partner always wants to be in control. I can't say "no" to my partner and be assured of acceptance and love.
E. I am visible to my partner and valued and accepted.	E. I'll always be deflected and invaded, but never seen or valued by my partner.
F. I can be who I am in every way and be accepted and loved.	F. I can't be me. My partner will always try to dominate and use me.
G. I can be competent and express my power, and be supported, accepted, and loved by my partner.	G. I don't know what to do. My achievements will always be devalued, and I will have to hide my power and be manipulative.
H. I can be imperfect, make mistakes, and still be loved.	H. I have to be perfect to avoid being disempowered or punished.
I. I can be needy and have my needs valued.	I. I have to meet the needs of my partner and others and ignore my own. Others need me.
J. I am lovable just being myself.	J. I will never be liked and approved by my partner.
K. I can express my uniqueness.	K. I have to be like others and conform to what is expected.
L. I am trusted to express myself and my feelings and say what I want to do.	L. I am not trusted to express myself or my feelings.

If you selected items A, C, E, G, I, or K, you are probably a maximizer. If you checked B, D, F, H, or J, you are probably a minimizer. Does this correspond to what you have learned about yourself in previous exercises?

The items you marked in the *left-hand column* indicate the developmental stages at which you were supported. The items you marked in the *right-hand column* indicate the developmental stages at which you were wounded.

This exercise is one way by which your intimate relationship can provide you with information about your own childhood wounding. This information is useful to you as a parent because it predicts at which stage(s) you are likely to have difficulty helping your own children and at which stage(s) you are not likely to have difficulty.

Exercise 12

Identifying Your Relationship Fears

The next exercises will help you connect your self-experience (your fears, wounds, and defenses) to your relationship with your partner. If you are a single parent, you may want to refer to a current intimate relationship or to your relationship with an ex-partner/spouse. Circle the two answers that most apply to you, and then underline the one that applies most.

My main fear is:

A. Separation, abandonment, and losing myself in my relationship.
B. Not being wanted emotionally and physically and being rejected by my partner.
C. My partner's unreliability—being there and then not being there for me.
D. Being smothered, absorbed, and humiliated by my partner.
E. Feeling invisible, asserting myself, and consequently losing my partner's love.
F. Being shamed for who I am, losing control and losing face in my relationship.
G. Being seen as aggressive, successful, competent, and powerful, and therefore losing my partner's love and acceptance.

H. Being seen as a failure, losing my partner's approval, and having to prove my worth to my partner.
I. Having or expressing my needs and being excluded and rejected by my partner for having them.
J. Being disliked by my partner, who doesn't want to be with me—not being seen as an equal.
K. Being different from others and my partner and not having my partner's approval of my uniqueness.
L. Having my actions controlled by my partner and not being free to express myself as I want to without being criticized.

How to use this information:

As in previous exercises, A and B refer to the attachment stage, C and D to the exploration stage, E and F to the identity stage, G and H to the competence stage, I and J to the concern stage, and K and L to the intimacy stage. By revisiting the results you reached in Exercise 11, you will be able to connect your fears to the wounds you suffered at a particular stage. The second part of Exercise 7 helped you identify the defenses you developed as a result of that wound. By comparing your responses, you can see how your fears about your relationship to your partner are connected to the wounds you received at particular stages of your childhood.

To complete this exercise, finish the following sentence:

"My deepest fear in my relationship is that I _____.*"*

Exercise 13

Your Core Relationship Issue

This exercise will help you identify the core issue in your intimate relationship. Read the following statements, and circle the two that strike you as important. Then underline the one that is *most* descriptive of your perception of your core issue. Read the statements again, this time from the point of view of your partner. Circle the two you think are important to your partner, and underline the one that you perceive to be most important for your partner.

A. My partner's desire for more separateness, his/her detachment.
B. My partner's demands for more togetherness, his/her dependency.

C. My partners neglect of my needs and interests, his/her distancing.
D. My partner's smothering of my freedom and personal autonomy, his/her demands.
E. My partner's rigidity, his/her compulsive need for control.
F. My partner's chaos and passivity and vague sense of self, his/her diffuseness.
G. My partner's compulsive competitiveness, his/her need to win.
H. My partner's manipulative behavior, his/her indirect battle for control.
I. My partner's exclusion of me from his/her thoughts and feelings, his/her aloneness.
J. My partner's invasiveness of my boundaries, his/her compulsive caretaking and need to please everyone.
K. My partner's disrespect for agreed-upon rules and ways of doing things, his/her rebelliousness.
L. My partner's conformity to the expectations of others, his/her need to look good to others.

How to use this information:

You can use the information about your core issue with your partner to identify the basic character structure that defines your parenting style. If you chose A, C, E, G, or I, you are a maximizer. If you chose B, D, F, H, or J, you are a minimizer. You can further refine the identification of your style to a subcategory of each. In the subcategories of the maximizer: A is a clinger; C is a pursuer; E is a compliant diffuser; G is a manipulator; and I is a conformist. In the subcategories of the minimizer: B is an isolator; D is a distancer; F is a controller; H is a competitor; J is a loner; and L is a rebel.

This information can be helpful when you realize that each of us is a composite of opposites, and each of us tends to project our opposite characteristics onto other people and then devalue those characteristics. This has implications for understanding the influence we have on our children. Once we understand that we may be devaluing traits in them for reasons that are specifically tied to our own character structure, we are freed from the misapprehension that these traits absolutely exist (in our children) and are absolutely negative.

This is important because a child will tend to devalue in himself the projected traits that are devalued by his stronger parent, the one who has the most influence on him. The parent thus perpetuates his own character defense in the child, who, when he becomes a parent, will pass it on to his children. The next exercise will help you start the process of change.

Exercise 14

Growth Opportunities in Your Relationship

This exercise will help you develop a preliminary growth plan based on the information you have received so far. In previous exercises, you have consistently chosen certain letters in your answers to a variety of questions. Look over the letters you have selected in preceding exercises, select the same ones below, and read the sentences next to them. For example, if you have selected A, C, E, G, I, K consistently, select those same letters below. These are your primary growth opportunities. Keep in mind that because you are focusing on these particular areas does not mean that the others are not also useful. Read through all of them for any additional growth challenges they offer.

You will be able to further your own growth by

A. Learning to let go and do more things on my own.
B. Claiming my right to be myself, express my feelings, and initiate more contact with my partner.
C. Learning to initiate more separateness, developing outside interests.
D. Initiating more closeness, sharing my feelings.
E. Asserting myself more, setting boundaries for myself, and respecting the boundaries of others.
F. Letting go of control, developing more flexibility and sensitivity.
G. Becoming more direct, expressing my power, and praising my partner's success.
H. Accepting my competence, becoming more cooperative.
I. Expressing my needs to my partner and others, caring for myself, and respecting my partner's privacy.
J. Joining my partner in socializing, and sharing my thoughts and feelings with my partner.
K. Taking more risks, experimenting with being different.
L. Learning to trust others, being responsible to others and to common values.

How to use this information:

After you have identified which growth opportunities apply most directly to you, you are ready to make a decision to engage in the change process on a daily basis for three months. Then you can evaluate whether you need to continue, or whether you need to choose another growth opportunity and experiment with it.

Note: The following two exercises are techniques that should be practiced in all conscious relationships, but that do not have to be done in any particular sequence. They can be practiced at any time.

Exercise 15

Couples Dialogue

Dialogue is the central feature of a conscious marriage. The most important thing you and your partner can do for your relationship and your parenting is to make an agreement to use dialogue in your transactions. In tense emotional situations, use it formally. In all other transactions, the spirit of dialogue should be present, even in casual ones. This will help you break symbiotic habits and come to know and relate to the actual person you are in a relationship with, rather than the imagined one. Refer to Chapter 5, "Intentional Dialogue," for a full discussion of how to engage in intentional dialogue.

Some subjects for dialogue:

1. Your mutual growth points as a parent. What changes you both need to make in order to support your child(ren). How you will support each other in making necessary changes.
2. Your understanding of your respective parents' marriage and how it influenced your relationship. What each of you can do to change that influence and build a conscious marriage related to each other's needs. Identify what you will have to change in your relationship to achieve that.
3. Your understanding of how your respective parents' marriage influenced how each of you parents. What each of you can do to change that influence and become more conscious parents.

Exercise 16

The Re-romanticizing or Reimaging Process

A few months after marriage, and especially after the birth of a first child, romantic attachment tends to fade and is replaced by a power struggle. Using the couples dialogue to recall romantic experiences can often recover the joy of the early days and can sustain the joy if a couple becomes intentional in using dialogue. It is a good idea for couples and their children to pay attention to the positive potential in their relationship as well as to the conflict. Children are able to internalize these joyful moments in memory, making this part of their model for their own future relationships. The following re-romanticizing exercises will assist you in recovering and developing positive memories.

1. Take a blank sheet of paper and turn it to the landscape position. Make three columns and title the first column Past Caring Behaviors, title the second column Present Caring Behaviors, and the third column Future Caring Behaviors.

Past Caring Behaviors	Present Caring Behaviors	Future Caring Behaviors

2. In the first column list all the positive behaviors you experienced from your partner in the past, including the early days of the relationship. In the second column list all the caring behaviors your partner is currently doing. The third column should include all the caring behaviors you wish in the future. You may

want to check Part I, Exercise 1, for any information that should go into these lists.

3. When you complete your list, make an appointment with your partner to share your lists with each other. After you hear your partner's first list, Past Caring Behaviors, ask him which of those behaviors he would like you to reinstate. When you hear his second list, ask him which present caring behaviors he wishes you to continue. When you hear his list of future desires, ask him which is most important and when he would like you to begin. Then ask your partner to go through this same process with you as you share your list.

4. When you finish, place these lists where they can be easily seen. Review them often, and follow through with your agreements. And here is an important idea: The next time your partner is upset with you, give him a caring behavior instead of what you usually do!

Part IV

PLAN FOR HEALING AND GROWTH

This part of the chapter is designed to assist you in developing a personal growth plan. As we said earlier, the first step is increasing your cognitive understanding. Learning more about yourself, your partner, and your children increases your awareness. If you have completed most of the exercises in this chapter, you should have received enough cognitive understanding about who you are, where you came from, and what issues are likely to be points of growth to enable you to make some plans to become a more conscious parent. In the process of becoming more aware, you are preparing yourself to integrate new concepts into your functioning.

Exercise 17

Using What You Know

Below we offer a paragraph that will crystallize the information you already have into a narrative. This narrative will describe your current parenting situation and areas you will be able to work on to assist your children in negotiating their current stages of development. By identifying your reactions and defenses to your children's frustrating behaviors and changing them, you will help them continue their path to adulthood and maintain their wholeness. Whatever part of their wholeness has already been lost, you can help restore. And you can help your children now, rather than waiting until you complete your personal healing.

From reading the book and completing the exercises, I have discovered that my deepest frustration with my child(ren) is when my child(ren) (refer to Exercise 5: Identifying Your Growth Point as a Parent) _____. When my child(ren) does (do) that, I feel _____ and react by _____ and think _____.

This leads me to believe that the stage I failed to complete is the stage of _____. What I failed to achieve is _____. This means that my growth point as a parent is to _____, so that I can help my child _____.

Because I was not assisted through this stage, I developed a fear of _____, which is my wound, and I deal with my fear by _____, which is my defense. This means that I became a minimizer/maximizer whose primary defense is _____. Because of this defense I tend to be overinvolved/underinvolved with my child(ren) and set _____ limits. My biggest challenge around boundaries is to set _____ and _____ limits. Because some of my developmental impulses were not supported, in order to survive in my family I sometimes had to be _____, which I denied to my awareness. At other times I was _____, which I also keep out of my awareness. I understand that I may tend to project my denied-self and disowned-self traits onto others, especially my partner and my child(ren). I am aware that I may tend to inhibit or suppress these functions in my child(ren) and my partner. I understand that while my denied and disowned traits are not visible to me, others see them. My lost-self functions are invisible to others and to myself. The combination of all this is my missing self.

My biggest challenge concerning issues around my missing self is to _____. As a result of my parents' marriage, which was _____ and _____, I learned a model of marriage that is _____ and _____, and a model for parenting that includes _____ and _____. This leads to my belief that in life in general, I (positive behavior) _____ and that I (negative behavior) _____. This, in turn, is a source for my belief that in my marriage/intimate relationship I _____. This belief is the source of my core relationship issue, which is _____. This is because of my feeling of _____ and fear that _____, which I deal with by _____. As a result I am a minimizer/maximizer in my relationship, with the primary defense of _____. From all this, it appears that my biggest challenge in my marriage is _____. And my biggest challenge in parenting is _____.

How to use this information:

It may take some time to complete this exercise. It is a summary of what you can learn from the text and exercises in this book, and it can serve as a guide for any changes you may want to make in parenting your children. Use this exercise as the basis for the next one, which will help you identify concretely how to move immediately toward more conscious parenting.

Exercise 18

Plan for Healing and Growth

Now you are ready to write down what you will need and want to do to become a conscious parent for your children.

1. Take a sheet of paper and, placing it in the landscape position, divide it into four columns. Write "Frustrating Behavior" in the first column, "My Reaction" in the second, "Child's Needs" in the third, and "Constructive Response" in the fourth. Using the results of Exercise 5, fill in the first and second column.

2. In the third column, using what you have learned from reading this book, interpret your child's hidden need in each behavior and write it down. In the fourth column, design for yourself a constructive response to your frustration and record it there.

3. When you finish, draw a line under the last entries. Then study the columns and summarize the main theme. Record this theme under the line. Then complete these sentences:

Given what I now know about what my child is trying to do when he/she (frustration pattern) _____, I know that he/she needs (overall need) _____. So rather than reacting by (reaction pattern) _____, I need to respond by (general response your child needs) _____. This will change me from being a (select one) maximizer/minimizer, which I can consciously do by changing my tendency to (select one) constrict/explode my energy in response to my child.

How to use this information:

You have carefully read the text, worked through the exercises, and reached some conclusions about what your child needs. You now have a sense of what you need to do to meet her needs. Use this exercise as a reminder and guide as you act with intention to respond to your child as she really is, while at the same time continuing the process of your healing. By doing this, you are committing to a more conscious way of living through intention and action for your sake and for your child's sake.

NOTES

Introduction

1. For an excellent book that deals with the impact of one's parents on one's own parenting see Claudette Wassil-Grimm, *How to Avoid Your Parents' Mistakes When You Raise Your Children,* Pocket Books, New York, 1990.

2. We will define consciousness along the way, and particularly in the chapter on conscious parenting. For now, consider consciousness as a personal phenomenon of which we are intimately aware. The explanation of this defining characteristic has stumped all philosophers and scientists in all times. We use it to refer mainly to the fact that human beings can reflect upon themselves and change themselves as a result of the reflection. We also assume that human beings can do this because they are essentially made of consciousness, which we assume to be the defining characteristic of the universe.

3. While the "unconscious" has been posited by scholars for centuries, it was systematically analyzed by Sigmund Freud. While in his early work he described it as a region of the mind, later he changed his view and described it as a quality of mental contents in the mind, contents which has been pushed out of consciousness. See *Freud, Collected Papers,* Volume 4, First American Edition, Basic Books, Inc., New York, 1959, pp. 22–29, 98–136. We use it to refer to automatic behavior that we engage in without self-reflection.

Chapter 1: A World of Connections

1. The term "connection" has appeared in recent years as a defining characteristic of the universe in physics (see Paul Davies, *The Mind of God: The Scientific Basis for a Rational World,* A Touchstone Book/Simon & Schuster, New York, 1992; Danah Zohar, *The Quantum Self: Human Nature and Consciousness Defined by the New Physics,* Quill/William Morrow, New York, 1990; Menas Kafatos and Robert Nadeau, *The Conscious Universe: Part and Whole in Modern Physical Theory,* Springer-Verlag, New York, 1990). For a psychological view of the importance of connection in human relationships, see Heinz Kohut, *The Search of the Self; Selected Writings of Heinz Kohut: 1950–1978,* Volume 1, International Universities Press, New York, 1978; Harry Stack Sullivan, ed. Helen Swick Perry and Mary Ladd Gawel, *The Interpersonal Theory of Psychiatry,* W. W. Norton & Co., New York, 1953. It is essential to an understanding of normal versus disturbed human functioning.

2. Martin Buber, *I and Thou,* 2d ed., Charles Scribner's Sons, New York, 1958. A

Jewish mystical theologian, Buber proposed a radical revision of human reality that placed the space between persons as primary to the places within. For him, reality is the "between." This was a dramatic shift from the focus on the centrality of the person and the intrapsychic, which characterized preceding views in philosophy, psychology, and theology. We believe this emerging paradigm illumines the dynamics of all relationships and is especially useful in understanding intimate partnerships such as marriage and parenting.

3. Paul Davies, op. cit. In this book Davies describes a cosmology that posits that the creation of the universe included the simultaneous creation of space and time. He also posits that at the inflationary stage of the explosion of the universe into being, the material that accounts for the existence of all things in the visible world of experience and the invisible world of the atom came into being. The conclusion is that since everything is made of the same material, everything is by nature so intricately connected that an event occurring anywhere in the universe influences everything else. Therefore, while the visible world of Newtonian physics gives us an impression of things as separate, the invisible world of atoms, of which everything is made, gives us a view of universal connectedness.

4. General systems theory was introduced into family therapy by Murray Bowen, who has long understood the intergenerational impact of families on children. The early concept of repetition of patterns was first introduced into psychological literature by Sigmund Freud in his concept of the "repetition compulsion" (see Sigmund Freud, *Collected Papers*, Vol. 4, Basic Books, New York, 1959, p. 391, and his *New Introductory Lectures*, W. W. Norton & Co., New York, 1933, p. 145).

5. See the report by the Council on Families in America, "Marriage in America: A Report to the Nation, 1995" for a discussion of the impact of failed marriages on the fate of children and its consequences for society. This report is available from the Institute for American Values, 1841 Broadway, Suite 211, New York, NY 10023. Tel. 212-246-3942.

6. Buber, op. cit., p. 25. Buber poetically expresses his conviction that the birth of a child is the beginning of forgetting the world from which they came.

7. We give this term special meaning in this book. In biology, symbiosis refers to a relationship between two organisms that is mutually beneficial for the welfare and survival of both. In psychology, the term also has that meaning when it is used to describe the close relationship of a child to its caretaker parent in infancy (see Margaret Mahler, *On Human Symbiosis and the Vicissitudes of Individuation: Infantile Psychosis*, International Universities Press, New York, 1968). The term also has a negative meaning when it describes the infant's resistance to differentiation or the desire for fusion between adults. Building on this meaning, we define *symbiosis* as "the belief that other people experience the world as we do." It is a common experience of everyday life that shows up in most language of self-reference, such as "it's hot" or "how could you think that?" or "that's wrong." It is the unconscious assumption that we occupy the center of reference for the meaning and value of other people's experience. We are the center, and others are the periphery. We believe this is endemic in our species and is the source of most interpersonal and social problems.

8. Paul McLean, "Man and His Animal Brains," *Modern Medicine*, February 3, 1964.

9. Frank Sulloway, *Born to Rebel: Birth Order, Family Dynamics, and Creative Lives,* Pantheon Books, New York, 1996.

10. Lloyd deMause, ed., *The History of Childhood,* first softcover edition, Jason Aronson Inc., Northvale, NJ, 1995, original edition, 1974, p. 55.

11. Jon Kabat-Zinn, *Wherever You Go, There You Are,* Hyperion, New York, 1994.

12. We take strong exception to the view espoused recently by June Stephenson, Ph.D., in her book *The Two-Parent Family Is Not the Best,* (Diemer, Smith Publishing Co., Inc., Napa, CA, 1991) that the two-parent family is not the best way to raise children. We agree that all families can wound children, but the evidence is impressive that, in general and even when the two-parent family is not ideal, it is the natural and best context for children.

13. The importance of the role of fathers in healthy child rearing is indisputable and is increasingly emphasized in popular and professional literature on parenting. Our view of conscious parenting assumes the inclusion of the father in parenting at every stage, and thus we do not focus on fathering per se as something special. (See *Newsweek,* Special Edition, Spring/Summer 1997, p. 75, and Bryan E. Robinson and Robert L. Barret, *The Developing Father: Emerging Roles in Contemporary Society,* The Guilford Press, New York, 1986.)

14. T. C. Martin and Larry L. Bumpus, "Recent Trends in Marital Disruption," *Demography,* 26 (1989), pp. 37–51.

Chapter 2: The Imago Family

1. This particular version of the story comes from *Anthology of Children's Literature,* Fourth Revised Edition, ed. by Edna Johnson, Evelyn R. Sickels, and Frances Sayers, Houghton Mifflin, Boston, 1970.

2. T. C. Martin and Larry L. Bumpus, "Recent Trends in Marital Disruption," *Demography,* 26 (1989), pp. 37–51.

3. Ken Wilber, ed., *The Holographic Paradigm and Other Paradoxes: Exploring the Leading Edge of Science,* Shambhala, Boston and London, 1985, p. 6.

4. For a highly readable and well-researched view of the healthy family, see Jerry M. Lewis, *How's Your Family? A Guide to Identifying Your Family's Strengths and Weaknesses,* Brunner/Mazel, Publishers, New York, 1979.

5. Devlin, Keith, *Mathematics, the Science of Patterns: The Search for Order in Life, Mind and the Universe,* Scientific American Library, W. H. Freeman & Co., New York, 1997.

6. This reflects a synthesis of the argument of two Greek philosophers, Heraclitus and Parmenides, concerning whether things are in flux or whether things are fixed or permanent. While their views opposed each other, the paradox is that both were right.

7. That one generation influences another and family patterns and problems are passed from parents to children is an ancient insight. Its sources include the Bible as well as modern family systems theory, which has charted the direct line of intergenerational conflict.

8. We tend to agree that we live in a universe that is alive. (See Rupert Sheldrake, *The Rebirth of Nature: The Greening of Science and God,* Park Street Press, Rochester, VT,

1991, 1994, p. 223.) In such a universe, all life-forms, including plants, have awareness and respond to their environment. Their sensitivity depends upon their organization and their survival program. While we do not know if other life-forms have self-awareness, we do know that human beings are not only aware but have the capacity for self-awareness, for self-reflection, and to act on their self-knowledge. However, most human beings are aware only and must make a great effort to become self-reflective and intervene in their behavioral patterns. Even more effort is needed to become aware of the subjectivity of another person, and even more to experience the inner awareness of another, which we call empathy. Our use of the term "conscious" refers to awareness that has become self-aware, aware of the other and of his inner world, and willing to relate to the other on the basis of empathic attunement.

9. Imago Theory refers to a systematic presentation of marital selection, the dynamics of marriage, and a method of therapeutic intervention. (See *Getting the Love You Want: A Guide for Couples* and *Keeping the Love You Find: A Personal Guide* for a complete description.)

10. Imago Theory holds that all persons experienced mild to severe wounds as a result of their interaction with their parents in childhood. The term "wound" refers to the early experience of need deprivation, which is experienced in childhood when needs are not met, or to a fear that they will not be met.

11. There are basically two theories of consciousness. The most prominent theory posits that at some time in the evolution of the organization of the brain, consciousness arose spontaneously. The other theory is that the brain is a conduit of consciousness that exists outside the brain. While the mystery of consciousness eludes science, we lean toward the view emerging in quantum physics that the universe is conscious, and thus consciousness is our natural state. What we refer to as "unconscious," in our view, is a constriction or loss of consciousness due to a rupture caused by emotional pain. It follows that if the wound caused by that pain can be healed, we will experience a restoration of consciousness, which is referred to in many spiritual traditions as expanded consciousness or cosmic awareness. While this has been the provenance of mystics, we believe it is the legacy of every person. For a recent, thorough, and provocative theory of consciousness, see David J. Chalmers, *The Conscious Mind: In Search of a Fundamental Theory*, Oxford University Press, Oxford and New York, 1996.

This view of the relation of consciousness and the unconscious is similar to but different in many respects from the view of Sigmund Freud, the discoverer of the unconscious, who saw consciousness as a narrow point of awareness located in the ego. Originally, he thought of the unconscious as a region of the mind, but later considered it to be contents of the mind that have been pushed out of awareness by repression. (See Sigmund Freud, *Collected Papers*, Volume 4, Basic Books, New York, 1959, pp. 13–30.) We see consciousness as the defining essence of life and the unconscious as a constriction of consciousness, similar to Freud's describing it as a quality of mental contents.

12. The theory of internalization is described by Roy Schafer in *Aspects of Internalization*, International Universities Press, Inc., New York, 1968. This is the most complete description of this process that has yet been published, to our knowledge.

13. This point is well documented in *How's Your Family?* by Jerry M. Lewis, op. cit.

This book deserves a wide reading and will be a helpful supplement to the positions taken here.

14. The stages of development presented here are a synthesis of many developmental models and follow no extant model exactly. Most models (see, for example, Margaret Mahler, et al., *The Psychological Birth of the Human Infant: Symbiosis and Individuation,* Basic Books Inc., New York, 1975) emphasize the first three years of life. Some focus on the first year of life (for example, Daniel Stern, *The First Relationship: Infant and Mother,* Harvard University Press, Cambridge, MA, 1977). Freud and his students outlined the first six years. Freud thought the latency years, which we call Concern, were relatively quiet, but Harry Stack Sullivan (see Harry Stack Sullivan, *The Interpersonal Theory of Psychiatry,* W. W. Norton & Co., Inc., New York, 1953) discovered it was very active emotionally and dynamically. Adolescence has usually been dealt with as a unit. (For a standard and thorough view of adolescence see Joseph L. Stone and Joseph Church, *Childhood and Adolescence: A Psychology of the Growing Person,* Random House, New York, 1957, pp. 263–294.) Our view is that the first six years of life go through a cycle of four impulses—attachment, exploration, identity, and competence—which are repeated in the middle years of childhood and adolescence in the new contexts created by the unique factors of those stages.

Chapter 3: The Unconscious Parent

1. For documentation of the welfare of children in America see the report by the Council on Families in America, "Marriage in America: A Report to the Nation," sponsored by the Institute for American Values, 1841 Broadway, Suite 211, New York, NY 10023.

2. "Marriage in America," ibid. This view is supported by this illuminating and disturbing report in which the authors say, "The most important causal factor of declining child well-being is the remarkable collapse of marriage, leading to growing family instability and decreasing parental investment in children" (p. 5). In their view, and ours, "We as a society are simply failing to teach the next generation about the meaning, purposes, and responsibilities of marriage. If this trend continues, it will constitute nothing less than an act of cultural suicide" (p. 4).

3. See endnotes 8 and 11, Chapter 2, for a discussion of our use of "conscious" and "unconscious."

4. Lloyd deMause, ed., *The History of Childhood,* first softcover edition, Jason Aronson, Inc., Northvale, NJ, 1995, pp. 51–54.

5. Tobias Wolff, "Nightingale," *The New Yorker,* 72 (41):54–57, January 6, 1997.

6. Michael Schwartzman and Judith Sachs, *The Anxious Parent,* Simon & Schuster, New York, 1990. This book is an excellent description of parental anxiety, which is the source of reactive parenting.

7. See endnote 7, in Chapter 1, on our use of *symbiosis.*

8. The concept of projection was first used by Sigmund Freud in a letter to his friend Fleiss in 1895 (Sigmund Freud, "Extracts from the Fleiss Papers," 1895, reprinted in *The Complete Psychological Works of Sigmund Freud,* Hogarth Press, London, 1953–74, Vol. 1, p. 207) and developed in his essay, "The Unconscious" (in the same

source, Vol. 4, pp. 159–215). Essentially, it refers to an unconscious process by which one represses painful mental contents—thoughts, emotions, intentions—and assigns them to others. For an excellent research-oriented book that builds on Freud and develops a broader view of projection, including how parents project onto children see James Halpern, Ph.D., and Ilsa Halpern, *Projections: Our World of Imaginary Relationships,* Seaview/Putnam, New York, 1983, pp. 37–55.

9. Because of the way our brains are constructed, we experience ourselves as the center of our context, much as the ancients viewed the earth to be the center of the universe. This sense of the absoluteness and truth of our experience is historical and universal. However, our ability to imagine other minds who also perceive themselves at the center allows us to conceive of a relative universe in which every perception is contingent upon our position. While we cannot experience ourselves as peripheral, just as we cannot imagine our funeral without including ourselves as the perceiver, the conception and acceptance of relativity helps us live in a world with others. A conscious person lives in the tension of that ambiguity. An unconscious person believes his experience is absolute and tends not to validate the "truth" of the perception of others. This is the source of most interpersonal conflict in marriages, parenting, and in society as a whole.

10. These two parenting styles are adaptations of the survival instinct. In our natural state, and in most life-forms, it is possible to constrict energy or express it. In humans, one or the other of these defenses is selected by the family and gets passed on to their children.

11. An illuminating analysis of characterological styles and their interactions is in Stephen Johnson, *Characterological Transformation: The Hard Work Miracle,* W. W. Norton & Co., New York, 1983, and *Humanizing the Narcissistic Style,* W. W. Norton & Co., New York, 1987.

12. We define *character* as the protective mechanisms one has developed to adapt to one's context. They are built on the core energetic self and determine habitual behavioral responses to any situation, whether relevant to the context or not. Since they are constructions built in childhood, they can be changed.

Chapter 4: The Child as Teacher

1. See endnote 3, Chapter 1.

2. Erich Jantsch, *The Self-Organizing Universe: Scientific and Human Implications of the Energy Paradigm of Evolution,* Pergamon Press, Oxford and New York, 1980.

3. Lloyd deMause, ed., *The History of Childhood,* first softcover edition, Jason Aronson, Inc., Northvale, NJ, 1995. The author provides a comprehensive history of childhood from ancient to modern times, outlining changing views of the child and of parenting. In the first sentence in Chapter 1 he states that the history of childhood is a "nightmare from which we are just awakening," and he goes on to show that the way most children were treated historically would today be considered child abuse. Since the "child is the father of the man," he speculates on the impact of child rearing on the quality of society. He concludes with a description of the improvement of the welfare of children in modern times as a result of changing views of the child.

4. Menas Kafatos and Robert Nadeau, *The Conscious Universe: Part and Whole in Modern Physical Theory,* Springer-Verlag, New York, 1990, pp. 3, 179.

5. Martin Buber, *I and Thou,* 2d ed., Charles Scribner's Sons, New York, 1958.

6. James Halpern, Ph.D., and Ilsa Halpern, *Projections: Our World of Imaginary Relationships,* Seaview/Putnam, New York, 1983, p. 38ff.

7. Ibid, p. 49ff.

8. Jeffrey Seinfeld, *The Bad Object: Handling the Negative Therapeutic Reaction in Psychotherapy,* Jason Aronson, Inc., Northvale, NJ, 1990.

Chapter 5: Intentional Dialogue

1. Frank Conroy, *Stop-Time,* Dell Publishing Co., Inc., New York, 1967, 1971.

2. For an excellent book for learning to communicate with children see Adele Faber and Elaine Mazlish, *How to Talk So Kids Will Listen and Listen So Kids Will Talk,* Avon Books, New York, 1980.

3. While the three-step process of dialogue we use is original in its organization and sequence, the concept of dialogue and its transforming power was developed by Martin Buber in *I and Thou* and *Between Man and Man.* For an excellent development of his thought see Maurice S. Friedman, *Martin Buber: The Life of Dialogue,* Harper Torchbooks/The Cloister Library, Harper & Brothers, New York, 1955. See also Polly Young-Eisendrath, *You're Not What I Expected: Learning to Love the Opposite Sex,* William Morrow & Co., New York, 1993, for an excellent book on dialogue from a Jungian perspective.

4. This point was made by Richard Stuart in *Helping Couples Change: A Social Learning Approach to Marital Therapy,* The Guilford Press, New York, 1980.

5. Sharon Begley, "How to Build a Baby's Brain," *Newsweek,* Special Edition, Spring/Summer 1997, pp. 28–32.

6. Our search for a connectional process began with our work with couples. We sought to find and teach the best communication skills available. We found that instruction in good communication skills has always used a process of reflection that we call mirroring. Other terms are *active listening* or *reflective listening.* The recommended response is generally an accurate paraphrase. In our work, we have found that this skill alone is woefully inadequate. In fact, we have found that it often increases tension in intimate relationships. That consequence led us to search further, and by listening to what intimate partners and children really want, we discovered a phenomenon we call validation—essentially a response after the paraphrase that indicates that the other person's view has a logic, that the other person makes sense. This transaction has power because it differentiates the other person from oneself and makes him visible without judgment. The other person becomes visible, rather than deflected and invalidated, and in that act two people can connect with each other. Theoretically, validation is grounded in the concept of relative perception, which disavows any access by anyone to an absolute position. All of us see "through a glass darkly."

But that was not adequate for full connection. In search for a process that achieved connection and equality at a deeper level, we turned to the empathy studies of Carl Rogers, in *Client-Centered Therapy: Its Current Practice, Implications, and Theory,*

Houghton Mifflin Co., Boston, 1951, and one of his students, Robert Carkhuff, in *Helping and Human Relations: A Primer for Lay and Professional Helpers,* Vol. 1: *Selection and Training,* Holt, Rinehart & Winston, Inc., New York, 1969. We also looked at mirroring by Heinz Kohut, in *The Search of the Self; Selected Writings of Heinz Kohut: 1950–1978* (International Universities Press, New York, 1978), who invented the use of empathy as a therapeutic intervention. Our concept of empathy is built upon these sources. For us, it is the precursor to intimacy in partnership. When we turned our attention to parenting, we found that the same process that works with couples works between parents and children. Dialogue creates a safe structure for the exchange of information, but it is considerably more than that. It furthers the growth of parents toward fuller differentiation, it supports the developmental processes of children, and it creates and sustains deep connection between parent and child. In other words, it is essential in the parenting process if the goal is to support the child's wholeness and sense of universal connection.

7. For an excellent discussion of what happens when empathy is missing in early childhood and its effects on later childhood stages, see John Leopold Weil, *Early Deprivation of Empathic Care,* International Universities Press, Madison, CT, 1992.

Chapter 6: The Conscious Parent

1. Robert Coles, *The Moral Intelligence of Children: How to Raise a Moral Child,* Random House, New York, 1997.

2. The source for the concept of intentionality as a primary feature of consciousness is Rollo May, *Love and Will,* W. W. Norton & Co., Inc., New York, 1969.

3. Menas Kafatos and Robert Nadeau, *The Conscious Universe: Part and Whole in Modern Physical Theory,* Spinger-Verlag, New York, 1990. This provocative book argues that "the discovery that non-locality is a new facet of nature allows us to 'infer,' although certainly not 'prove,' that the universe can be viewed as a conscious system" (p. 3). For a discussion of consciousness see also Robert Ornstein, *The Evolution of Consciousness: Of Darwin, Freud, and Cranial Fire: The Origins of the Way We Think,* Prentice Hall Press, New York, 1991. See also his *Psychology of Consciousness,* W. H. Freeman & Co., San Francisco, 1972.

4. Our continuing reference to oneness with the universe reflects the sentiment of all great religions. It also reflects the sentiment of modern physics. "The wholeness in the universe we have in mind is not an a priori philosophical assumption—it is rather an emergent property of a quantum universe which reveals itself under experimental conditions that clearly indicate that the observer cannot be independent of the observing process *at any level.*" See Kafatos and Nadeau, op. cit., p. 199. For a psychological and research study of "oneness," see Lloyd H. Silverman, Frank M. Lachmann, and Robert H. Milich, *The Search for Oneness,* International Universities Press, Inc., New York, 1982.

5. The behavior-change request process is an adaptation and extension of Richard Stuart's concept of "constructive request making." See Richard Stuart, *Helping Couples Change: A Social Learning Approach to Marital Therapy,* The Guilford Press, New York, 1980, p. 228ff. We initially developed it for couples, but as with other exercises that

work for couples, this is extremely useful for dealing constructively with parent-child interactions. Our adaptation takes into account a dynamic understanding of emotions and the importance of allowing regressive effects to be expressed.

6. This exercise was developed for couples, but it works wonderfully between parents and children. We recommend that parents use it in their own relationship as a model for how their children can handle their anger. When parents model a successful process that resolves feelings or solves problems, the child can internalize and use it in their relationship with their parents and later in their intimate partnerships.

7. Martha G. Welch, *Holding Time: How to Eliminate Conflict Temper Tantrums, and Sibling Rivalry and Raise Happy, Loving, Successful Children*, Simon & Schuster, New York, 1988. Upon seeing this book in the window of a bookstore in New York, we read it and then developed the holding exercise for couples. However, it was developed by Dr. Welch for children, and we include this reference here for parents who want a whole wonderful book on the subject.

8. This comment reflects the Buddhist tradition of nonattachment and acceptance of things in their phenomenal reality without judgment. One is invested not in any particular outcome but in the process.

9. This exercise is generally used in behavior-modification therapy and social learning theory. Creating a positive effect in the parent-child relationship increases safety and promotes bonding.

10. We learned this exercise from John Pierrakos, founder of Core Energetics. We use it with couples and parents who are in therapy and prescribe it for the parent-child relationship. As far as we know, Pierrakos has not committed this exercise to print.

Chapter 7: Growing Yourself Up

1. Jack Kornfield, *A Path With Heart: A Guide Through the Perils and Promises of Spiritual Life*, Bantam Books, New York, 1993.

2. Edward Edinger, *Ego and Archetype: Individuation and the Religious Function of the Psyche*, Putnam, New York, 1972.

3. If you would like to read a systematic and thorough discussion of your child's development, see Richard Lansdown and Marjorie Walker, *Your Child's Development From Birth Through Adolescence: A Complete Guide for Parents*, Alfred A. Knopf, New York, 1991.

4. Melvin Konner, *Childhood*, Little, Brown & Co., Boston, 1991. We recommend this book to the general reader who wants to learn more about how children move through the stages of childhood. It is based on the text of an excellent television series.

5. Ronald Kotulak, *Inside the Brain: Revolutionary Discoveries of How the Mind Works*, Andrews & McNeel, Kansas City, 1996.

6. Sharon Begley, "How to Build a Baby's Brain," *Newsweek*, Special Edition, Spring/Summer 1997, pp. 28–32.

Chapter 8: The Stage of Attachment

1. We take the position that the infant at birth is a distinct being and that psychological birth begins with biological birth. This contrasts with traditional theories devel-

oped by Freud and especially with those of Margaret Mahler, who view the child as symbiotic at birth, completely self-absorbed and nonrelational (Margaret Mahler, *On Human Symbiosis and the Vicissitudes of Individuation: Infantile Psychosis,* International Universities Press, Inc., New York, 1968). We tend in the direction of Daniel Stern, *The First Year of Life: Infant and Mother,* Harvard University Press, Cambridge, MA, 1977, and Karen B. Walant in her wonderful and provocative book *Creating the Capacity for Attachment: Treating Addictions and the Alienated Self,* Jason Aronson, Inc., Northvale, NJ, 1995, and John Bowlby, *A Secure Base: Parent-Child Attachment and Healthy Human Development,* Basic Books, Inc., New York, 1988, who take issue with infantile symbiosis and the primacy of separation. See especially Walant's Chapter 2, "Symbiosis Revisited," pp. 37–71.

2. For a wonderful and complete discussion of the infant's interest in social interaction, see T. Berry Brazelton, M.D., and Bertrand G. Cramer, M.D., *The Earliest Relationship: Parents, Infants and the Drama of Early Attachment,* Addison-Wesley Publishing Co., Inc., New York, 1990. This book is informative for the professional and accessible to the lay reader.

3. John Bowlby, op. cit. See also M. D. Ainsworth, M. C. Blehar, E. Waters, and S. Wall, *Patterns of Attachment: Assessed in the Strange Situation and at Home,* Lawrence Erlbaum, Hillsdale, NJ, 1978. Our ideas regarding attachment are developed from these sources.

4. While this issue is controversial in the age of the two-career family and the debate over substitute care, the issue of the power of "touch," or physical contact, is established in the science of child research. For a thorough discussion of touch see Kathryn E. Bernard and T. Berry Brazelton, M.D., *Touch: The Foundation of Experience,* International Universities Press, Inc., Madison, CT, 1990. The first essay, on the philosophy of touch, is a classic and should be read by all parents. Also see Sarah Van Boven, "Giving Infants a Helping Hand," *Newsweek,* Special Edition, Spring/Summer 1997, p. 45.

5. Daniel Glick, "Rooting for Intelligence," *Newsweek,* Special Edition, Spring/Summer 1997, p. 32. This little sidebar summarizes the value of breast-feeding for bonding but goes on to describe research that suggests that touch and breast-feeding also influence the child's cognitive development and intelligence. There are so many resources that affirm the value of breast-feeding that little more needs to be said.

6. Bowlby op. cit. and Ainsworth et al., op. cit.

7. For an excellent discussion of the phenomenon of the parent attempting to co-opt the child to meet their needs, see Patricia Love and Jo Robinson, *The Emotional Incest Syndrome: What to Do When a Parent's Love Rules Your Life,* Bantam Books, New York, 1990. Dr. Love discusses the phenomenon of "daddy's little girl" and "mommy's little boy" showing the negative emotional impact on a child who is used as a replacement adult by a parent who has an unavailable spouse.

8. Denis M. Donovan and Deborah McIntyre, *Healing the Hurt Child: A Developmental-Contextual Approach,* W. W. Norton & Co., New York, 1990. This book is written for the professional and is thus difficult for the lay reader. For the professional it offers excellent diagnostic and therapeutic guidelines for therapy with children who are severely wounded, as are those who are wounded at the attachment stage.

Chapter 9: The Stage of Exploration

1. In contrast to traditional views that the impulse of the child at this stage is to separate from the mother, our view is that the infant's impulse at this stage is to maintain connection and differentiate but not separate from the caretaker. The older view posits symbiosis as the natural state and separation as the necessary evolution. Any connectional impulses in children and adults is considered regression. And the spiritual longing for oneness is also seen as regression, harking back to Freud's "oceanic experience," as a desire to return to the womb. We do not see the goal of connection or the search for oneness as regressive, but as the essence of a healthy connection to life and the universe. See a thorough discussion of these issues in Karen B. Walant, *Creating the Capacity for Attachment: Treating Addictions and the Alienated Self,* Jason Aronson, Inc., Northvale, NJ, 1995. See also Lloyd H. Silverman, Frank M. Lachmann, and Robert H. Milich, *The Search for Oneness,* International Universities Press, Inc., New York, 1982.

Chapter 10: The Stage of Identity

1. For original formulations of the importance of the development of identity, see Erik Erikson, *Insight and Responsibility: Lectures on the Ethical Implications of Psychoanalytic Insight,* W. W. Norton & Co., Inc., New York, 1964, and his *Childhood and Society,* W. W. Norton & Co., Inc., New York, 1950.

2. For a discussion of moral development in children, see Robert Coles, *The Moral Intelligence of Children: How to Raise a Moral Child,* Random House, New York, 1997. See also William Damon, *The Moral Child: Nurturing Children's Natural Moral Growth,* The Free Press, Macmillian, Inc., New York, 1988. Both of these books posit that the moral development of children is related to the quality of child care by parents and the moral character of parents. See also Nancy Eisenberg, *The Caring Child,* Harvard University Press, Cambridge, MA, 1992, for a discussion of the child who is inclined to be social.

3. Shame is the major wound of this period. For a classic discussion of the role of shame in the development of identity see Helen Merrell Lynd, *On Shame and the Search for Identity,* Science Editions, Inc., New York, 1961.

4. Alice Miller, *Prisoners of Childhood: How Narcissistic Parents Form and Deform the Emotional Lives of Their Gifted Children,* Basic Books, Inc., 1981. Miller describes this dynamic under the heading of narcissism. She is perhaps the most incisive and prolific writer on this subject as it relates to children.

Chapter 11: The Stage of Competence

1. See Erik Erikson, *Childhood and Society,* W. W. Norton & Co., Inc., New York, 1950, pp. 45–87. This is a classic discussion of infantile sexuality that presents and critiques Freud's early formulations. For a critique of the classic theory of infantile sexuality and the oedipus complex, see Alice Miller, *Thou Shalt Not Be Aware: Society's Betrayal of the Child,* trans. by Hildegarde and Hunter Hannum, A Meridan Book, New American Library, New York, 1984, pp. 119–157. In our view, the child competes for

the attention of the opposite sex, but the struggle is not sexual, but for power. It is a competence impulse rather than a sexual impulse.

2. For the best discussion of shame and its relation to the achievement of identity, see Helen Merrell Lynd, *On Shame and the Search for Identity,* Science Editions, Inc., New York, 1961. This resource supports our view that each developmental stage is vulnerable to a specific painful emotion. Specifically, in our view, shame results from wounding during the identity stage only.

Chapter 12: The Stage of Concern

1. Compared to the attention given to the first six years of life, and recently to the first three years, middle childhood has been virtually ignored. Freud viewed the middle years, which he called the latency period, as virtually free of dynamic development. However, Harry Stack Sullivan, in *The Interpersonal Theory of Psychiatry,* ed. Helen Swick Perry and Mary Ladd Gawel, W. W. Norton & Co., Inc., New York, 1953, posited that the middle years were full of dynamic activity that replicated the early years of attachment, now displaced from parents to peers. He introduced the seminal idea of the "chum" of the same sex being the primary focus of activity of this period. For additional information on this period, one has to turn to child psychology texts. One standard text is Joseph L. Stone and Joseph Church, *Childhood and Adolescence: A Psychology of the Growing Person,* Random House, New York, 1957, pp. 202–236.

2. Sullivan, ibid., pp. 245–262. Here Sullivan discusses his concept of "chumship."

Chapter 13: The Stage of Intimacy

1. From our perspective, adolescent "rebellion" is often a reaction to uninvolved parenting rather than restrictive parenting. We believe that adolescent rebellion is much less likely to occur with appropriate, conscious parenting.

2. For a discussion of adolescence as a second individuation process see Peter Blos, "The Second Individuation Process of Adolescence," *The Psychology of Adolescence: Essential Reading,* ed. Aaron H. Esman, M.D., International Universities Press, Inc., New York, 1975. He states that adolescence repeats the dynamics of the first individuation, which came in the exploration stage with the achievement of object constancy and the emergence from the primacy of the attachment impulse. In this second individuation, the child sheds its family dependencies. This book is essential reading for the professional who is interested in adolescence. It covers every conceivable topic of concern, from normal adolescence to pathology.

3. See Joseph L. Stone and Joseph Church, *Childhood and Adolescence: A Psychology of the Growing Person,* Random House, New York, 1957, pp. 264–386, for a systematic discussion of the three stages of adolescence.

4. James Joyce, *A Portrait of the Artist as a Young Man,* Jonathan Cape, London, 1926.

Chapter 14: The Possibilities for a Conscious Future

1. The view of the universe as conscious is not a dictum of quantum physics, or any other science. But some scientists and philosophers of science tend toward infer-

ring from the quantum world that "the universe can be viewed as a conscious system." (Menas Kafatos and Robert Nadeau, *The Conscious Universe: Part and Whole in Modern Physical Theory,* Springer-Verlag, New York, 1990.) Another provocative book, written by Danah Zohar, *The Quantum Self: Human Nature and Consciousness Defined by the New Physics,* Quill/William Morrow, New York, 1990, stops short of the thesis that we live in a conscious universe, but the author posits that consciousness and matter, while wholly different, arise out of a common "mother" in quantum reality. Given that, she offers the observation that our thoughts and relationships mirror the laws and patterns that govern the world of electrons and photons. See also Rupert Sheldrake, *The Rebirth of Nature: The Greening of Science and God,* Park Street Press, Rochester, VT, 1991. Sheldrake, one of the world's foremost biologists, describes an animistic and mystical view of nature that assumes that the "world is alive" and we are a part of that living system rather than a living system living in an essentially "dead" world (p. 223).

2. Paul Davies, *The Mind of God: The Scientific Basis for a Rational World,* A Touchstone Book, Simon & Schuster, New York, 1992, p. 232.

3. For a classic investigation of the development of humankind's mystic relationship to the infinite, see Richard Maurice Bucke, M.D., *Cosmic Consciousness: A Study in the Evolution of the Human Mind,* E. P. Dutton, New York, 1969; first copyright 1901, by Innes and Sons.

4. Ibid.

5. In an article from the Associated Press, May 8, 1997, David Briggs reported a research project conducted at Hope College, Holland, Michigan. He reported that "overall, researchers found a strong relation between how the children perceived their parents and how they perceived God." The most interesting finding was that "those children who perceived their fathers as nurturing were likely to perceive God as nurturing, while it was their perception of others as powerful that best predicted the children's sense of God as powerful." They further found that "when their mothers and fathers were perceived as nurturing and powerful, God generally was perceived as both nurturing and powerful." Researcher Jane R. Dickie concluded that "what parents do matters in terms of what children think of God."

6. The Council on Families in America, "Marriage in America: A Report to the Nation," Institute for American Values, 1995, p. 4.

7. Ibid., p. 6.

BIBLIOGRAPHY

Ainsworth, M. D., Blehar, M. C., Waters, E., and S. Wall. *Patterns of Attachment: Assessed in the Strange Situation and at Home,* Lawrence Erlbaum, Hillsdale, NJ, 1978.

Allport, Susan. *A Natural History of Parenting,* Harmony Books, New York, 1997.

Bernard, Kathryn E., and T. Berry Brazelton, M.D. *Touch: The Foundation of Experience,* International Universities Press, Madison, CT, 1990.

Bowlby, John. *A Secure Base: Parent-Child Attachment and Healthy Human Development,* Basic Books, New York, 1988.

Brazelton, T. Berry, M.D., and Bertrand G. Cramer. *The Earliest Relationship: Parents, Infants and the Drama of Early Attachment,* Addison-Wesley Publishing Co., Reading, MA, 1990.

Buber, Martin. *Between Man and Man,* The Macmillan Company, New York, 1947.

————. *I And Thou* (second edition), Charles Scribner's Sons, New York, 1958.

————. *Knowledge of Man: Selected Essays,* Humanities Press, New Jersey, 1988.

Bucke, Richard Maurice, M.D. *Cosmic Consciousness: A Study in the Evolution of the Human Mind,* E. P. Dutton & Co., New York, 1969.

Carkhuff, Robert R. *Helping and Human Relations: A Primer for Lay and Professional Helpers* (Vol. 1: Selection and Training), Holt, Rinehart & Winston, New York, 1969.

Chalmers, David J. *The Conscious Mind: In Search of a Fundamental Theory,* Oxford University Press, New York, 1996.

Coles, Robert. *The Moral Intelligence of Children: How to Raise a Moral Child,* Random House, New York, 1997.

Conroy, Frank. *Stop-Time,* Dell Publishing Co., New York, 1967, 1971.

Council on Families in America. "Marriage in America: A Report to the Nation," Institute for American Values, New York, 1995.

Damon, William. *The Moral Child: Nurturing Children's Natural Moral Growth,* The Free Press, New York, 1988.

Davies, Paul. *The Mind of God: The Scientific Basis for a Rational World,* Simon & Schuster, New York, 1992.

deMause, Lloyd, editor. *The History of Childhood,* Jason Aronson, Northvale, NJ, 1995.

Devlin, Keith. *Mathematics, the Science of Patterns: The Search for Order in Life, Mind and the Universe,* Scientific American Library, W. H. Freeman & Co., New York, 1997.

Donovan, Denis M., and Deborah McIntyre. *Healing the Hurt Child: A Developmental-Contextual Approach*, W. W. Norton & Co., New York, 1990.

Eisenberg, Nancy. *The Caring Child*, Harvard University Press, Cambridge, MA, 1992.

Erikson, Erik H. *Childhood and Society*, W. W. Norton & Co., New York, 1950.

————. *Insight and Responsibility: Lectures on the Ethical Implications of Psychoanalytic Insight*, W. W. Norton & Co., New York, 1964.

Esman, Aaron H., M.D. *The Psychology of Adolescence*, International Universities Press, New York, 1975.

Faber, Adele, and Elaine Mazlish. *How to Talk So Kids Will Listen and Listen So Kids Will Talk*, Avon Books, New York, 1980.

Freud, Sigmund. *Collected Papers* (Vol. 4), Basic Books, New York, 1959.

————. *New Introductory Lectures*. W. W. Norton & Co., New York, 1933.

Friedman, Maurice S. *Martin Buber: The Life of Dialogue*, Harper & Brothers, New York, 1955.

Gaimm-Wassil, Claudette. *How to Avoid Your Parents' Mistakes When You Raise Your Children*, Pocket Books, New York, 1990.

Halpern, James, and Ilsa Halpern. *Projections: Our World of Imaginary Relationships*, Seaview/Putnam, New York, 1983.

Hendrix, Harville. *Getting the Love You Want: A Guide for Couples*, Henry Holt & Co., New York, 1988.

————. *Keeping the Love You Find: A Personal Guide*, Pocket Books, New York, 1992.

Jantsch, Erich. *The Self-Organizing Universe: Scientific and Human Implications of the Energy Paradigm of Evolution*, Pergamon Press, Oxford and New York, 1980.

Johnson, Edna, Evelyn R. Sickels, Frances Sayers, editors. *Anthology of Children's Literature*, Fourth Revised Edition, Houghton Mifflin, Boston, 1970.

Johnson, Stephen M. *Humanizing the Narcissistic Style*, W. W. Norton & Co., New York, 1987.

Kabat-Zinn, Myla, and Jon Kabat-Zinn. *Everyday Blessings: The Inner Work of Mindful Parenting*, Hyperion, New York, 1997.

Kafatos, Menas, and Robert Nadeau. *The Conscious Universe: Part and Whole in Modern Physical Theory*, Springer-Verlag, New York, 1990.

Kohut, Heinz. *The Search of the Self; Selected Writings of Heinz Kohut: 1950–1978*, Vol. 1., International Universities Press, New York, 1978.

Konner, Melvin. *Childhood*, Little Brown & Co., Boston, 1991.

Kornfield, Jack. *A Path With Heart: A Guide Through the Perils and Promises of Spiritual Life*, Bantam Books, New York, 1993.

Lansdown, Richard, and Marjorie Walker. *Your Child's Development From Birth Through Adolescence*, Alfred A. Knopf, New York, 1991.

Lewis, Jerry M., M.D. *The Birth of the Family: An Empirical Inquiry*, Brunner/Mazel Publishers, New York, 1989.

————. *How's Your Family? A Guide to Identifying Your Family's Strengths and Weaknesses*, Brunner/Mazel Publishers, New York, 1979.

Love, Patricia, and Jo Robinson. *The Emotional Incest Syndrome: What to Do When a Parent's Love Rules Your Life,* Bantam Books, New York, 1990.

Lynd, Helen Merrell. *On Shame and the Search for Identity,* Science Editions, New York, 1961.

Lynn, David B. *The Father: His Role in Child Development,* Brooks/Cole Publishing Co., Monterey, CA, 1974.

Mahler, Margaret S., M.D. *On Human Symbiosis and the Vicissitudes of Individuation: Infantile Psychosis,* International Universities Press, New York, 1968.

Mahler, Margaret S., Fred Pine, and Anni Bergman. *The Psychological Birth of the Human Infant: Symbiosis and Individuation,* Basic Books, New York, 1975.

May, Rollo. *Love and Will,* W. W. Norton & Co., Inc., New York, 1969.

Miller, Alice. *Prisoners of Childhood: How Narcissistic Parents Form and Deform the Emotional Lives of Their Gifted Children,* Basic Books, New York, 1981.

———. *Thou Shalt Not Be Aware: Society's Betrayal of the Child,* trans. Hildegarde and Hunter Hannum, New American Library, New York, 1984.

Newsweek (Special Edition: Your Child, From Birth to Three), Spring/Summer 1997.

Ornstein, Paul H. *The Search for the Self: Selected Writings of Heinz Kohut: 1950–1978,* Vol. 1, International Universities Press, New York, 1978.

Ornstein, Robert. *The Evolution of Consciousness: Of Darwin, Freud, and Cranial Fire: The Origins of the Way We Think,* Prentice Hall Press, New York, 1991.

———. *The Psychology of Consciousness,* W. H. Freeman & Co., San Francisco, 1972.

Robinson, Bryan E., and Robert L. Barret. *The Developing Father: Emerging Roles in Contemporary Society,* Guilford Press, New York, 1986.

Rogers, Carl R. *Client-Centered Therapy: Its Current Practice, Implications, and Theory,* Riverside Press, Cambridge, MA, 1951.

Rowe, Crayton E., Jr., and David S. Mac Isaac. *Empathic Attunement: The "Technique" of Psychoanalytic Self Psychology,* Jason Aronson, Northvale, NJ, 1989.

Schafer, Roy. *Aspects of Internalization,* International Universities Press, New York, 1968.

Schwartzman, Michael, and Judith Sachs. *The Anxious Parent,* Simon & Schuster, New York, 1990.

Seinfeld, Jeffrey. *The Bad Object: Handling the Negative Therapeutic Reaction in Psychotherapy,* Jason Aronson, Northvale, NJ, 1990.

Sheldrake, Rupert. *The Rebirth of Nature: The Greening of Science and God,* Park Street Press, Rochester, VT, 1991.

Silverman, Lloyd H., Frank M. Lachmann, and Robert H. Milich. *The Search for Oneness,* International Universities Press, New York, 1982.

Stephenson, June. *The Two-Parent Family Is Not the Best,* Diemer, Smith Publishing Co., Napa, CA, 1991.

Stern, Daniel. *The First Relationship: Infant and Mother,* Harvard University Press, Cambridge, MA, 1977.

Stone, Joseph L., and Joseph Church. *Childhood and Adolescence: A Psychology of the Growing Person,* Random House, New York, 1957.

Stuart, Richard B. *Helping Couples Change: A Social Learning Approach to Marital Therapy,* Guilford Press, New York, 1980.

Sullivan, Harry Stack. *The Interpersonal Theory of Psychiatry,* Ed. Helen Swick Perry and Mary Ladd Gawel, W. W. Norton & Co., New York, 1953.

Walant, Karen B. *Creating the Capacity for Attachment: Treating Addictions and the Alienated Self,* Jason Aronson, Northvale, NJ, 1995.

Weil, John Leopold, M.D. *Early Deprivation of Empathic Care,* International Universities Press, Madison, CT, 1992.

Welch, Martha G., M.D. *Holding Time: How to Eliminate Conflict, Temper Tantrums, and Sibling Rivalry and Raise Happy, Loving, Successful Children,* Simon & Schuster, New York, 1988.

Wilber, Ken, editor. *The Holographic Paradigm and Other Paradoxes: Exploring the Leading Edge of Science,* Shambhala Publications, Boston, 1985.

Young-Eisendrath, Polly. *You're Not What I Expected: Learning to Love the Opposite Sex,* William Morrow & Co., New York, 1993.

Zohar, Danah. *The Quantum Self: Human Nature and Consciousness Defined by the New Physics,* Quill/William Morrow, New York, 1990.

INDEX

351

THE INSTITUTE FOR IMAGO RELATIONSHIP THERAPY

The Institute for Imago Relationship Therapy was cofounded by Harville Hendrix and Helen Hunt in 1984. Its purpose is to help adults see and use their relationships to significant others, especially their intimate partners and children, as a resource for emotional healing, psychological growth and spiritual evolution. The Institute has certified over 1200 mental health professionals in Imago Relationship Therapy who offer therapy, workshops and professional training, worldwide.

For information on therapy, workshops, products and professional training, phease contact the Institute by letter. The Institute for Imago Relationship Therapy, 335 North Knowles Avenue, Winter Park, Florida 32789, by phone: 1-800-729-1121 or 407-644-3537, by E-mail: IIRT@aol.com or Internet: www/imagotherapy.com.

The **Parents' Manual** mentioned in the text of this book is available through the Institute.